The Sound of Two Hands Clapping

The Education of a Tibetan Buddhist Monk

GEORGES B. J. DREYFUS

University of California Press

BERKELEY   LOS ANGELES   LONDON

University of California Press
Berkeley and Los Angeles, California

University of California Press, Ltd.
London, England

© 2003 by the Regents of the University of California

Library of Congress Cataloging-in-Publication Data

Dreyfus, Georges B. J.
  The sound of two hands clapping : the education of a Tibetan Buddhist
monk / Georges B. J. Dreyfus.
      p.   cm.
  Includes bibliographical references and index.
  ISBN 978-0-520-23260-0
  1. Buddhist monks—Education—China—Tibet. 2. Buddhist
education—China—Tibet. 3. Monastic and religious life
(Buddhism)—China—Tibet. 4. I. Title.

BQ7756 .D74   2003
294.3'75—dc21   2001005494

Manufactured in the United States of America
11   10   09   08
10 9 8 7 6 5 4

The paper used in this publication meets the minimum requirements of
ANSI/NISO Z39.48–1992 (R 1997) (*Permanence of Paper*).

The Sound of Two Hands Clapping

A

Phillip E. Lilienthal

B O O K

The Phillip E. Lilienthal imprint
honors special books
in commemoration of a man whose work
at the University of California Press from 1954 to 1979
was marked by dedication to young authors
and to high standards in the field of Asian studies.
Friends, family, authors, and foundations have together
endowed the Lilienthal Fund, which enables the Press
to publish under this imprint selected books
in a way that reflects the taste and judgment
of a great and beloved editor.

To my parents, my teachers, and all the others who have supported me in the long journey described here

Contents

Illustrations

Note on Translation
and Transliteration

Throughout this text my practice is to transliterate Sanskrit names and to phoneticize Tibetan names when they occur in the body of the text, giving their transliterations in parentheses at their first occurrence. I do the same for the names of the figures that are particularly relevant to my account, to underline their importance. Less significant names are given only phonetically. In transliterating, I follow the system devised by Turrell Wylie (see "A Standard System of Tibetan Transcription," *Harvard Journal of Asiatic Studies* 22 [1959]: 261–67). For pronunciation, I rely on a modified version of the "essay phonetic" system developed by Jeffrey Hopkins (see *Meditation on Emptiness* [London: Wisdom, 1983], 19–21).

Technical expressions used by Indian and Tibetan thinkers are introduced in the text in their English translation. Their original expressions— in Sanskrit or Tibetan, depending on the author—are transliterated in parentheses. Their equivalent in the other source language (either Tibetan or Sanskrit) is also given whenever available.

Since this work is intended for a broad audience, I have quoted English sources whenever they exist, citing the original sources only when translations were not available. In quoting Tibetan sources as part of the body of the argument, I have given the titles in translation. When I simply quote such works in the notes or when they are not intrinsic to the argument, I use the original titles. Similarly, I have used the Anglicized form of Indian words such as *sutra* or *Mahayana* whenever possible, leaving the original Sanskrit for the notes.

Acknowledgments

This work is an attempt to reflect on the fifteen years that I spent among Tibetan monks and the education I received from them. During that time, I learned much from many Tibetan scholars, who generously devoted their time and efforts to teach me. Although I cannot name them all, I am deeply grateful to each one. In particular I would like to mention Geshe Rab-ten, my first teacher; Geshe Lati Rin-po-che, who educated me in the basics of his tradition; and Gen Lob-zang Gya-tso, head of the Tibetan Institute of Dialectics, where I spent many of my most formative years. I would also like to express my deep appreciation to His Holiness the Dalai Lama, who advised and helped me throughout these years. Finally, in Geshe Nyi-ma-gyel-tsen I encountered an incomparable mentor. I am also profoundly indebted to all the Tibetan monks, perhaps less illustrious, who helped me and aided my efforts. They include many of the Nam-gyel monks, the students from the Buddhist School of Dialectics, and many of the monks from the three monastic seats. Some of them supported me materially, giving me food and shelter. Others supported my intellectual efforts, responding to my questions and taking special care to accommodate my needs. I am truly humbled by the help I have received and wonder how I will able to repay their kindness.

In later years, I was also able to expand my knowledge of Tibetan tradition by studying at other schools. My stay at the Sakya College in Rajpur in 1990 was decisive in this respect. The kindness and competence of Migmar Tsering, head of the Sakya College, was crucial to the success of my project. I learned a great deal from him as well as from other Sa-gya scholars such as Ken-po Abe and Ken-po Gya-tso, whose help was invaluable. I am grateful as well to His Holiness Sakya Trizin, head of the Sa-gya order, for encouraging my research. I also greatly benefited from my stay at the Nying-ma monastery of Nam-dröl-ling, where Ken-po Nam-dröl provided me invaluable guidance. He took me under his wing and introduced me to his tradition, acts for which I am deeply grateful. I thank Pe-nor Rin-po-che for encouraging and supporting my study of his tradition.

In addition, this work reflects the education that I received in the Western academic tradition. I am grateful for the opportunity provided by Professor Jeffrey Hopkins and other faculty members at the University of Virginia. They provided substantial help as I continued the learning process that I had started in India. As this learning process has gone on, I have accumulated debts to colleagues who helped me develop the kind of maturity that I hope is reflected in this study.

The pictures reproduced in *The Sound of Two Hands Clapping* come from several sources. Some are the work of talented professional photographers, including Kevin Bubrisky, Fred von Allmen, Devon Cottrell Holmes, and Natasha Judson. All are to be thanked for lending their considerable ability to this enterprise. Still others were taken by unknown people. Such is the case with the pictures of my Geshe examination. At first, the idea of photographing this event did not cross my mind. I was concentrating entirely on passing the exam without making a fool of myself and did not think the use of Western technology would be appropriate. My Tibetan friends thought otherwise. They urged me to take pictures of the entire process and to entrust the camera to several monks, whose productions show great effort and talent. I owe them thanks for their contributions.

Finally, I want to mention the people who have been especially helpful in this project. First and foremost is Gene Smith from the Tibetan Buddhist Resource Center, who provided me with important sources and suggestions. I would also like to acknowledge my colleagues from Williams College who kindly agreed to read this work and provided helpful comments: William Darrow, David Edwards, Nancy Levene, and my fellow scholars at the Oakley Center for the Study of the Humanities. A special mention goes to Thomas Kohut, the dean of Williams College, who agreed to use college funds to cover the editing process and the expenses of reproducing photographs. I am also grateful to Edward Casey, at the State University of New York at Stony Brook; José Cabezón, at the University of California, Santa Barbara; Rebecca French, at the University of Colorado; Matthew Kapstein and his students, at the University of Chicago; Don Lopez, at the University of Michigan; Amélie Rorty, at Brandeis University; and Gareth Sparham, at the University of Michigan. All these friends provided information and insightful comments that greatly improved this project and were crucial in bringing it to fruition. I also want to acknowledge Natasha Judson, for her patience and support, and Paul Hackett at the University of Virginia, who has kept fulfilling my bibliographical needs throughout the years and whose careful reading has greatly enhanced the quality of my work.

r

Introduction

In 1970, at the age of twenty, I left my native Switzerland and traveled to India, where I first encountered the Tibetan community that had been exiled to that country for more than ten years. The worldview I had grown up with, that of a French-speaking would-be intellectual,[1] and the counter-cultural spirit of the times had predisposed me toward leftist politics; but events at the end of the 1960s, particularly the collapse of the student movement and the Soviet invasion of Czechoslovakia, had shaken my confidence in the validity of that option and left me disoriented. Like many of my contemporaries, I was seeking an alternative to wasting my life in ordinary drudgery—what French students used to refer to as "métro, boulot, dodo" (subway, work, sleep). I responded by traveling to Asia, hoping to encounter what seemed lacking in my own culture. On my first trip, I ventured to Turkey; there I met many "fellow travelers" going to India. I decided then that rather than follow the path of studying science that my father had traced for me, I would go to India, a land about which I knew nothing but which exercised an irresistible pull on my imagination. During this time, I also started to become interested in so-called Eastern spiritualities. In particular, I read Yogananda's *Autobiography of a Yogi* (1946), which further strengthened my resolve to go to India, where I could already imagine myself becoming an accomplished yogi.

Against the furious protests of my family, for once united in their thorough opposition to my crazy idea, I made my way to India, traveling overland through Eastern Europe, Turkey, Iran, Afghanistan, and Pakistan by a variety of pleasant and less pleasant means of transportation—train, bus, and my then favorite, hitchhiking. After three months, I reached the Promised Land and quickly made my way to Vārāṇasi (Banaras) by squatting for

1

a whole night in front of the latrines of an overflowing third-class car of the Indian Railways. Vārānasi is the holy city of Hinduism, and I was hoping for some fulfilling encounters. But whereas I had expected a city of enlightened sages, all I encountered was an overwhelming mixture of dirt, misery, swarming beggars, and priestly craftiness. At this low point, when I was contemplating the dreaded return to my sarcastic but relieved family, the gods (I am not sure which ones) finally beckoned to me in the form of a young Frenchman. While we were sipping chai (Indian tea with milk and sugar) on the bank of the Ganga, he said, "I know where you should go . . . Dharamsala. . . . The Tibetans are there . . . they are wonderful, and you can study Buddhism if you wish." Although I had no idea what Buddhism was about (I remember shortly after this encounter asking a Thai monk I had just met whether there was any meditation in Buddhism), I found the idea appealing. My impression was further strengthened by the few Tibetan monks I saw while visiting Sarnath, near Vārānasi, where they were studying at the Higher Institute of Tibetan Studies. I vividly remember getting a glimpse of a group of monks from the institute while visiting the site of the Buddha's first teaching. They suddenly appeared through the bushes on their way to take a bath in the river, and I recall being impressed by the intelligence, kindness, and composure that they conveyed.

A few days later I left Vārānasi for Dharamsala, northwest of Delhi, which had been a hill station under British rule until it was almost totally destroyed by an earthquake in 1905. Because Dharamsala was thinly populated and had a cool climate, it had been chosen in the early 1960s to serve as the headquarters of the Dalai Lama and the Tibetan government in exile. A sizable Tibetan community (around five thousand) had developed there, living in the upper part of the town; there they succeeded in re-creating a Tibetan lifestyle. This is where I first encountered Tibetan Buddhism. I was quickly captivated by its philosophy, which appealed to my outlook—informed, like that of many of my contemporaries, by an existentialism picked up in novels (for me, the works of Malraux and Camus) and in philosophically naive readings of Nietzsche and Heidegger. I soon entered a monastery and began studies that lasted for fifteen years. After following a traditional Tibetan monastic curriculum, I even had the good fortune of becoming the first Westerner to receive the title of Geshe (*dge bshes*, pronounced "ge-shay"), traditionally the highest degree awarded by Tibetan Buddhist monastic universities.

In this book I attempt to share with my readers some of these experiences, to explain the strength of the Tibetan intellectual culture, and to communicate the edification that I received from studying among Tibetan monks. I examine Tibetan monastic education, analyzing its central practices: memorization, the reading of commentaries, and dialectical debate. I contend that understanding this education, which has formed many of the brilliant Tibetan teachers who have captured the modern imagination, is central to comprehending Tibetan Buddhism.

By showing the importance of the life of the mind in this tradition, I present a picture of Buddhism that differs from standard representations. Instead of straining my ears to listen to the mystical sound of one hand clapping,[2] I focus on practices such as debate, where the sound of two hands clapping can literally be heard loud and clear. In this way I make clear the important role played in Buddhism by the tradition's rational and intellectual elements. These elements have often been misrepresented as precursors of scientific inquiry or rejected as clerical corruption of an originally pure message. In *The Sound of Two Hands Clapping*, which examines the role and nature of rationality in Tibetan monastic education, I contend that each of these views seriously distorts the nature of rationality in traditional Buddhist cultures.

My claim is not that Tibetan culture is uniquely spiritual or that monasticism is the only focus of intellectual life. Tibet also enjoys a secular culture with political institutions, literature, music, folklore, and so on. Moreover, there are traditional nonmonastic forms of education, both religious and secular, as we will see later. Nevertheless, it remains true that the sophisticated intellectual culture that developed in the large monastic institutions has been at the center of traditional Tibetan life for centuries. Hence, an examination of the ways in which Tibetan monks are educated can provide an important view of the depth and richness of Tibetan culture. It can also correct the excessive emphasis on the mystical and romantic that at times have been the focus of Western understanding of Tibetan culture.[3]

INSIDE AND OUTSIDE

My approach to monastic education takes a rather unusual path. Whereas most studies examine this phenomenon from the outside, mine includes a large autobiographical element, which derives from my own extended association with Tibetan Buddhism. In many ways I am the "Tibetan Buddhist Monk" referred to in the subtitle, though there is nothing very Tibetan about me. This autobiographical dimension colors my account and thus marks the limits of this book. In studying Tibetan monastic education, I have made no pretense of being objective. I have been privileged to study with Tibetan monks, particularly with the teachers belonging to the older generation. This has been one of the great opportunities of my life, a piece of good fortune made possible by their exile and by the ordeal of the Tibetan people in general. In many ways, I have benefited from their terrible situation, and I am deeply grateful for what I received during those years, which I consider my best and most formative.

Let me emphasize, however, that this account is not an attempt to promote the Tibetan tradition or to justify myself. Nothing could be further from my intention than to present a rosy picture of Tibetan monastic education. I do not believe that my indebtedness to the Tibetan people commits me to present a prettified account. Tibetan Buddhism is an extremely rich tradition that needs no advocates. Hence, this book offers a realistic assessment; I can only hope that my Tibetan readers will not take offense that I portray as accurately as possible the weaknesses as well as the strengths of their tradition.

The use of autobiographical material raises other, more serious problems. Some of the incidents and anecdotes I describe cannot be documented independently of my subjective account. Others could have been documented, but were not. These elements, presented in a factual rhetorical mode, reflect my own interpretations and preoccupations and my attempts at making sense of my past. Hence, they are less pictures of "what really happened" than reconstructions from my present perspective, with all the complex motivations that that approach entails. In certain ways, such complexity is characteristic of the study of human cultures in general, which necessarily has a mythological dimension that includes the author. Here, however, the mythmaking is explicitly about my experience and perspective.

Another consequence of this autobiographical orientation is my narrow focus. Although this book describes Tibetan monastic education as it existed in the twentieth century, its main point of reference is the tradition I saw in the 1970s—a time of transition, when monastic education encountered great difficulties but still could draw on the rich intellectual and religious resources it had in Tibet, resources that the circumstances of exile made readily available. The great teachers of the older generation were free from the political entrapments and the conservative pressures they would have faced in Tibet. Moreover, Tibetan Buddhism was not yet fashionable and relatively few people were competing for their attention. Newcomers could have easy access to these teachers, no longer the powerful and distant figures they had been in Tibet but vulnerable refugees. Hence, in some ways the tradition I encountered appeared in a particularly favorable light. As this book makes clear, my experience would have been quite different had I studied in premodern Tibet, where mentalities and institutions were more rigid and great teachers were relatively unavailable. I also believe that the situation has already changed, with new conditions created by the disappearance of the older generation and the exponential growth of monasteries because of the influx from Tibet that I briefly describe in the conclusion.

The personal orientation of this work is further reflected in the choice of material that I analyze. My readers will notice that my attention is unevenly divided between the four Tibetan Buddhist schools (explained later) and their respective educations. Although I do present the ideas and practices of other schools, I focus mostly on the Ge-luk tradition in which I received my training. In recent years, I have been fortunate to be exposed also to the education offered in other schools, Sa-gya and Nying-ma in particular, thereby gaining a much more balanced view of Tibetan Buddhism. Hence, I can claim that my assessment of the weaknesses and strengths of the Tibetan schools is not partisan. I cannot claim, however, to present all schools with the same richness of material. My experience of Sa-gya or Nying-ma education was limited to a few months' study while I was no longer a monk, whereas I followed the Ge-luk training for fifteen years as a monk. Thus, my account cannot help but be slanted, though I have striven for as much balance as possible. I have also completely omitted any discussion of the Bön school, the only large non-Buddhist tradition in Tibet. But Bön education has been strongly influenced by that of the Buddhist schools, which it therefore largely resembles.

Yet this book is not simply an autobiographical recollection or an emic (i.e., internal) account, but also an etic (external) description of traditional monastic education. It analyzes the elements of that education, describing the way it works and the results it produces. In pursuing this aim, I draw on standard scholarly methods such as interviews and analysis of the published literature. That literature is limited, however, to a few firsthand accounts by Tibetan teachers of their education as well as a few third-person descriptions. Very few studies of Tibetan education attempt to go beyond the surface details to understand the nature of educational practices. That type of analysis is precisely what I provide here, illustrated by autobiographical elements.

In examining Tibetan monastic education, I have also included information on its history that was available to me. Such considerations counteract the tendency to naturalize the present and imagine that what we see now is what has existed for a long time. Tibetan scholastic traditions themselves often make such claims, presenting their educational practices as deriving from the great Indian scholastic centers such as Nalanda. Although the filiation is real, we would be mistaken in assuming a high degree of continuity and failing to notice both the originality of Tibetan practices and the changes that they have undergone. In this work I examine some of these changes; but this book is not a history of Tibetan monastic education and its institutions, though such a study would obviously be welcome. My focus is mostly synchronic, examining traditional education as if it existed in the timeless present of anthropologists. This is obviously a fiction, for monastic education has changed greatly through the centuries, but such an approach is useful in presenting Tibetan monasticism as a living culture in which people are still educated, rather than as a merely historical curiosity.

I have also left out any discussion of monastic education in Tibet since 1959. That region has been dominated by the tragic events that have overtaken the Tibetan people. The senseless repression unleashed by the PRC against Tibetans in general and monks and nuns in particular has affected the situation so profoundly that any discussion of monastic education there would involve an analysis less of the nature of monastic intellectual culture than of the political situation in Tibet, a topic outside of my scope that has been ably examined by other scholars.[4]

Finally, I do not consider the education of nuns. It is said that before the seventeenth century, Tibetan nuns had their own educational institutions that produced sophisticated scholars. There are even reports (mostly oral, I believe) of public debates having taken place between nuns and monks. But the situation of nuns during the last two centuries has been quite different. Until recently, it was difficult for them to gain access to the same education as monks; the Dalai Lama has been pushing to make the kind of monastic education I describe here available to nuns. The problems and difficulties of such a task, the resistance to it from the monastic establishment, and the enthusiasm that it has generated among young nuns as well as its many successes are all elements of an important and new chapter in the history of Tibetan education, which would require a more focused examination than I can provide. Hence, my account is gender-specific. Yet I trust that most of what I am describing here applies to the education of nuns, as it is quickly developing in India.

THE COMPLEXITY OF TRADITION

I have written *The Sound of Two Hands Clapping* not just for those who are involved as scholars or as practitioners in the study of Tibet and its

Buddhism, but also for a wider nonspecialized audience, academic or not, that is interested in religious traditions and the role of intellectual life in them, the nature of education in Buddhism or other religious traditions, or the diversity of Asian cultures. It should also interest those who are intrigued by such intellectual issues as the relation between contemporary theories and traditional views of interpretation, the role of rationality and education in traditional cultures, the kind of practices found in such education, and the kind of intellectuals that it produces.

Too often tradition is understood solely in oppositional terms—as that against which modernity defines itself to assert its unquestionable authority. Tradition is then depicted as static rather than dynamic, as based on custom rather than reflection, and as repetitive rather than creative.[5] This view has been by now criticized by many thinkers, who have exposed at great length its limitations and blindnesses.[6] What may be less often appreciated is that such a critique, as necessary as it may be, still fails to do justice to traditional societies. To expose the dominant modern discourse as hegemonic does not provide an adequate view of tradition, which should be explored on its own terms, insofar as that is possible.

Once we leave the ground of stereotypical oppositions, we realize that far from being simple and mechanical, tradition is complex and multiform. This point is often obscured by reductive assumptions. One of the great temptations in analyzing tradition is to confuse it with traditionalism or fundamentalism, the belief that the validity of tradition requires only the literal repetition of some truth transmitted from the past. Such confusion arises because authority does play a central role in tradition. A tradition, particularly a religious one, is constituted around the transmission of a given truth based on the authority of the past. But that transmission is neither simple nor univocal, as traditionalism would have it, for truth needs to be constantly interpreted. This necessity introduces a tension central to the dynamic of tradition, which must negotiate between authority and the freedom required by interpretation. This intellectual dynamic, as it appears in Tibetan monastic education, will be one of my central concerns.

Those who discuss tradition face other pitfalls as well. First, such discussions tend to reinscribe a kind of great divide between tradition and modernity and to homogenize traditions as sharing some essential features that are no longer found in modern societies. This is not my intention here, as I focus on a particular culture, that of Tibet, and a particular type of traditional education, that received by monk-scholars. I do not aspire to present a general theory of traditional education, defining it once and for all and providing the necessary and sufficient conditions by which we can differentiate it from modern education. On the contrary, I assume that tradition is multiform and escapes essentializing definitions. Hence, the best way to explore it is to provide locally grounded thick descriptions that identify features of traditional educational practices and distinguish them from modern ones.

In this work, *tradition* refers to historically located social practices and cultural forms that existed in Tibet during the first half of the twentieth century, before the PRC's invasion of Tibet, and have continued in the exile community in India where I encountered them between 1970 and 1985. Thus, the distinction drawn here between tradition and modernity is also personal and autobiographical, helping me to understand my own educational experiences as a young European immersed in the Tibetan monastic education.

Second, those who describe traditional Tibetan monastic education and compare it to modern education also are in danger of overemphasizing differences. This tendency is common in academia, where subtle distinctions are often reified into separations that obscure more fundamental commonalities. Dan Sperber puts it well: "[A]nthropologists transform into unfathomable gaps the shallow and irregular boundaries they had found not so difficult to cross, thereby protecting their own sense of identity, and providing their philosophical and lay audience with what they want to hear."[7]

In many ways, this book takes a very different approach, stressing the commonalities between modern and traditional educations as I experienced them. In discussing traditional monastic scholars, for example, I emphasize their similarities to modern ones by describing them (perhaps anachronistically) as intellectuals. But differences are obviously important as well, since they convey, as much as is possible, the idiosyncratic ideas and practices of these figures. In particular, the Tibetan monastic emphasis on reason and arguments must be differentiated from that of modern scholarly approaches; otherwise, it is reduced to an imperfect prefiguration of present scientific norms.

TRADITION AND ITS INTELLECTUALS

Clearly, this work concentrates on the education of the monastic elite, a significant but small minority. In Tibet most monks, even in the great monastic universities, did not participate in the intellectual culture I evoke here. In recent years, modern scholars have reacted against an exclusive focus on the life of the intellectual elite, which they see as leading to the neglect of the culture of the larger lay groups.[8] This reaction, which Bernard Faure aptly describes as "inverted methodological scapegoating,"[9] often targets the emphasis on textuality in studying cultures in general and religions in particular.

The new interest in popular rituals and narratives is a welcome corrective, but it becomes dangerous as a normative restriction. It assumes that traditions can be understood without considering the views and practices of their intellectuals, who can be dismissed as irrelevant and bypassed for a direct contact with "authentically" marginal groups. This approach strikes me as particularly harmful to non-Western traditional cultures, which are thus deprived of their intellectual content and reduced to an atomized network of rituals and narratives displayed and controlled by modern scholars.

In Western academic discourse, traditional religious learning is often seen as something residual, an outdated leftover to be superseded as the world is inevitably secularized and modernized. Edward Shils, one of the scholars who has contributed most to the sociological analysis of intellectuals, describes them as persons "with an unusual sensibility to the sacred, an uncommon reflectiveness about the nature of the universe and the rules which govern their society."[10] He argues, however, that religious activities are increasingly irrelevant to the contemporary world, attracting a diminishing share of the creative capacities of the intellectual elite. Hence, traditional intellectuals represent a static past that has been left behind.[11]

Although this description is not entirely mistaken, it ignores the actual role of traditional intellectuals in the contemporary world; furthermore, it fails to account for their persistence. For better or for worse, traditional modes of behavior and institutions still have their place in our world. Hence, the sweeping dismissal of entire groups and modes of thought is unrealistic. This book attempts to present traditional Tibetan Buddhist intellectuals not as marginal leftovers whose meaningful role lies in the past but as vigorous thinkers in their own right.

One of the great good fortunes of my life is to have learned from these figures, who were educated in an entirely traditional context. Far from being a closed-minded lot, they came across as powerful and inquisitive thinkers, ready to tackle intellectual challenges and discuss issues on their merits. My work is a homage to this generation of scholars, now dying off. Yet it is not simply a nostalgic or hagiographic description by an admiring student. It is also an analysis of the education that produced these powerful minds, a foray into their intellectual culture, and an attempt to re-create its dynamic.

MONASTICISM AND SCHOLASTICISM

Because I focus on the formation of the Tibetan monastic elite, I am not concerned with the whole range of monastic experience but only with its scholarly dimensions. Hence, the key term of this book is *scholasticism* rather than *monasticism*.

Scholasticism is often misunderstood as involving hair-splitting discussions of irrelevant questions.[12] This modern prejudice obscures the nature and importance of scholasticism. Historically, scholastic thinking has been at the center of several traditions, and it continues to prosper today. Many modern thinkers can be considered scholastics, sometimes unbeknownst to themselves.[13] To rehabilitate scholasticism, we need to reconceptualize it as a range of diverse intellectual practices that shape its participants.

Academics typically have studied scholasticism in relation to Western traditions (including Islam), rarely considering it in relation to Buddhism or Confucianism. But in recent years, scholars have expanded this category, which can be fruitful for cross-cultural studies, and have shown that several Asian traditions can be usefully described as scholastic.[14] The question is, what do we learn about scholasticism by including these traditions? By analyzing the nature of the intellectual practices that constitute scholastic experience in the Tibetan tradition, my book attempts to make a substantial contribution to an answer. As a living and thriving tradition, Tibetan scholasticism provides an ideal venue for exploring a range of scholastic methods and their results.

In an important article on the scholastic method, George Makdisi characterizes Christian medieval scholasticism as a mode of presentation and as a way of thinking.[15] Formally, scholasticism consists of intellectual tools such as the lecture *(lectio)*, which provides students with authoritative glosses of the basic texts (mostly the scriptures), and the disputation *(disputatio)*, during which students continue their inquiry into the questions raised during the lecture. Scholasticism also involves a method of argumentation pro and contra *(sic et non)* through which doubts are raised about the contradictions that arise between authoritative texts. Affirmations about the content of the text are matched with objections, leading to a resolution. Finally, scholasticism is also characterized by texts such as Aquinas's *Summa Theologica* that rely on the pro and contra method in offering systematic, detailed, and rigorous explanations of relevant topics (mostly the articles of Christian faith).

As a mode of thinking, scholasticism is concerned with the relation between faith and understanding. As Makdisi puts it: "There is also an inner spirit, the basic characteristic of which is a deep and equal concern for both authority and reason."[16] Because both Islam and Christianity are religions of revelation, they rely on scriptures to provide the unquestionable basis of their tradition. But unconditional acceptance does not necessarily provide unequivocal direction, for the meaning of those scriptures needs to be established, the contradictions between texts resolved, and the fine points clarified. The systematic exploration of the content of faith is the main objective of the scholastic method in medieval Christianity, which assumes that reason and revelation can be harmonized, that "if God gave us reason, then reason and revelation are from the same source, and the two must be in harmony and cannot be in contradiction."[17]

Makdisi's formulation provides a useful starting point. As we will see, Tibetan scholasticism uses some of the same intellectual tools (the lecture and the disputation) as its Western counterpart. Tibetan monastic manuals *(yig cha)* often follow an approach similar to that of the *Summa*, examining each topic by refuting other positions, presenting the right view, and clearing away possible objections. Similarly, the "inner spirit" of the Tibetan Buddhist tradition is in some ways concerned with the relation between faith and understanding. But this formulation is perhaps a bit narrow and fails to include many scholastic practices. For one thing, it is too overtly theological, limiting scholasticism to a religious tradition in which faith is considered as the primary category. Even in medieval Europe, scholasticism was not limited to the study of Christian theology but affected secular branches such as dialectic, rhetoric, grammar, mathematics, and medicine. Moreover, and more relevant to our topic, the notion of faith is not the most felicitous way of approaching Tibetan scholasticism, where faith is considered secondary to the development of wisdom, the primary goal of the tradition.

Thus, rather than discuss scholasticism as revolving around the relation between faith and understanding, revelation and reason, I discuss scholastic practices as being concerned with the relation between authority and interpretation. I believe the most distinctive feature of scholasticism to be its emphasis on interpreting the great texts constitutive of the tradition within the confines of its authority, using the intellectual tools handed down from previous generations. Accordingly, I focus here on the intellectual tools of Tibetan scholars and distinguish three types of practice—or, as I like to put it, intellectual technologies: memory, commentary, and dialectical debate. I ask a series of questions about these technologies: Why do scholastics memorize so much? What is the role of memorization in the curriculum and in the formation of monks? How does commentary function as a focus of authority? What room for interpretive freedom does commentary leave? How does debate participate in this dialectic of freedom and authority? Is the central scholastic activity reading, or is it debating?

An examination of Tibetan scholasticism has also the merit of underscoring that scholasticism is relevant to religious practice, a fact largely overlooked when it is discussed as purely intellectual. I maintain that scholasticism is concerned with important and relevant questions. It participates in the creation of a meaningful universe and provides its practitioners with comprehensive ways to shape their life and character. Thus, this book is relevant both to those who are interested in scholasticism and to students of religious phenomena. By examining education as a form of practice, it explains the ways in which Tibetan scholastic education functions, the educative technologies of its traditions, and its goals. The reader will also gain a greater insight into the ways in which Tibetan scholars practice and understand Buddhism, as well as the intellectual culture that they have developed to sustain their religious commitments.

Understanding the practical relevance of scholasticism is particularly important within the Tibetan context, where the temptation has been to oppose scholarly and hermitic traditions.[18] But it is simplistic to think of scholastic and contemplative cultures in such terms. Though Tibet has a firmly established tradition of hermits engaging single-mindedly in solitary meditation, many of these yogis retreat to their practice after undergoing a scholastic training similar to that of the monks, either within their families, where they are educated by their father or uncle who is himself a trained scholar, or in a monastery.[19] Moreover, scholarly activities and meditative practices do not exclude each other. Most of the important figures of the tradition combine the two approaches, illustrating the ideal of the master endowed with both learning and meditative accomplishments *(mkhas grub gnyis ldan)*, an ideal that Tibetan traditions hold as normative.

It is also true that there is a Tibetan tradition of anti-scholastic thinkers from Kar-ma Pak-shi to Zhab-kar, who stand in opposition to scholars such as Sa-gya Paṇḍita or Dzong-ka-ba. But many of these iconoclastic thinkers began their career with extended scholastic training and hence were not outside of the tradition they sometimes denounced. Typical in this respect is Long-chen Rab-jam-ba, who was a well-trained scholar when he left the monastic milieu to become a hermit. His works, which contain an original blend of philosophical discussions, historical considerations, and inspirational poetry, reflect the role of scholastic education in the formation of the nonmonastic elite and are far from representing a pure hermitic culture existing independently of scholasticism. This is not to say there are no distinctions or tensions between contemplative and scholastic, tantric and nontantric orientations, but to argue, as does Matthew Kapstein, that "neither of these oppositions was absolute, and that in the lives and careers of individual masters differing facets are frequently intermingled."[20]

The Sound of Two Hands Clapping is divided into three parts. The first consists of three chapters that provide context. In chapter 1 I give a brief synopsis of the main elements of Tibetan Buddhism and sketch the history of the tradition. Chapter 2 examines the nature of Tibetan monasticism, focusing on the institutional framework in which scholastic studies take place. Chapter 3 examines monastic discipline by following the course of a typical monastic career and the role played in it by teachers; I also describe my own less typical monastic career.

In the second part, I analyze the intellectual practices that constitute scholasticism. The discussion starts in chapter 4 with memorization and the acquisition of basic literacy, which constitute the heuristic aspect of the process. It continues with an analysis of the two types of complementary interpretive practice that form the core of this work, commentary (chapters 5–9) and debate (chapters 10–12). The constitutive role of commentary is treated in chapter 5, and competing curricular models in chapter 6. Chapter 7 considers the role of oral commentary and its relation to the issue of orality. Chapter 8 discusses the soteriological role of commentary, its relation to meditation, and its participation in the construction of meaning, particularly in relation to the study of the path. Chapter 9 examines commentarial logic, contrasting it with the critical approach embodied in debate, which is taken up next. Debate as a dialectical practice is examined in chapter 10, which explains the rules of debate and how they are learned; the role of debate in the curriculum, particularly in relation to the study of logic, epistemology, and Madhyamaka, is considered in chapter 11; and the use of debate by Tibetan scholastics is the focus of chapter 12, which emphasizes the different approaches in the tradition and the function of debate as a mode of inquiry.

The final two chapters examine the results and limitations of these interpretive practices. In chapter 13, I analyze the use of rationality in Tibetan scholasticism, particularly in its relation to some of the practices associated with folk religion, thereby distinguishing it from modern scientific inquiry. Chapter 14 considers some of the limitations of Tibetan scholastic education, particularly those intrinsic to its structure. It also sets out the external limits imposed by the sociopolitical location of scholastics, sketching how Tibetan scholasticism has been shaped by the pressure of political forces and events. And in the conclusion, I briefly consider the future of scholastic education as modern secular education develops among Tibetans and provide a very provisional evaluation of my own scholastic experience.

Part 1

THE CONTEXT

1 Tibetan Buddhism
A Brief Historical Overview

To contextualize Tibetan scholasticism, I here sketch Tibetan Buddhism, presenting its main elements, describing its lines of evolution, and introducing its main figures. I proceed by heuristically delineating three sets of four: four periods in the history of Tibetan Buddhism, four layers in Tibetan Buddhism, and four schools of Tibetan Buddhism (the Nying-ma, or old school, and the three new schools—the Sa-gya, Ka-gyü, and Ge-luk).[1] In examining the history of these schools, I emphasize the role of historical and political developments in creating sectarian differences in Tibetan Buddhism.

To grasp the whole sweep of the history of Tibetan scholasticism, I define four periods:[2] (1) a first period of assimilation (seventh to ninth century), called the "early propagation of the teaching" *(bstan pa snga dar)*; (2) a period of full assimilation (tenth to mid–thirteenth century), which marks the beginning of the "later propagation of the teaching" *(bstan pa phyi dar)* associated with the age of the "new translations" *(gsar 'gyur)*; (3) a classical period (mid–thirteenth to sixteenth century), when Tibetan intellectuals develop their own interpretive schemes; and (4) a more strictly scholastic period (sixteenth century to the present), when these interpretations are codified into a definitive exegesis enshrined in monastic manuals.

THE FIRST PERIOD: BUDDHISM IN TIBET

The history of Tibetan Buddhism begins with the creation of a powerful Tibetan empire between the seventh and the ninth centuries. Tibet was unified under the rule of the Yar-lung dynasty by the famous emperor Song-tsen-gam-po *(srong btsan sgam po,* 604?–650 C.E.).[3] Before he came to power, the area known historically as Tibet was culturally and politically heterogeneous.[4] By the end of his rule, the process of cultural unification that was to continue for centuries was well under way. Stretching beyond the boundaries of the Tibetan cultural area, the empire was a military power whose imperialistic ambitions extended to the Silk Road, chunks of the Chinese empire, and the entire Himalayan range.[5] But this powerful empire started to collapse in 842, when the emperor Lang-dar-ma *(glang dar ma)* was assassinated. A civil war ensued and the country disintegrated, losing its military power and political unity; Lang-dar-ma was the last emperor.

It was during this time that Tibet acquired many of its cultural and linguistic characteristics. Song-tsen-gam-po is said to have sent his vassal Thon-mi Sam-bhuta to study Sanskrit in India. On the latter's return, a Tibetan alphabet was established on the model of Brahmi and Gupta scripts and the grammar of the language was codified.[6] This system of writing helped create a sense of cultural community. It produced a literate elite, which supported a new intellectual culture that supported the codification of the customs and laws of the various groups inhabiting the country. In addition, during this period Buddhism entered Tibet from India, China, and Central Asia. However, Buddhism became prominent only after the emperor Tri Song-de-tsen *(khri srong sde btsan,* 742–798) adopted the religion and founded Sam-yay *(bsam yas),* Tibet's first major monastic center of learning.[7]

The Buddhism that came to Tibet in the eighth century and has been there since is an extremely elaborate tradition. It may be helpful to view the tradition as consisting of four "layers" that interact and overlap.[8] In the first, the "Hinayana,"[9] the basic teachings of the Buddha are found and monasticism is defined, as in other basic Buddhist traditions such as the Theravada. There we find the usual Buddhist worldview, which has been aptly described as revolving around the three categories of *saṃsāra, karma,* and *mokṣa.*[10] *Saṃsāra,* the life in the cycle of births and deaths, is deeply unsatisfactory, full of suffering caused by actions *(karma)* that have their roots in the passions *(kleśa, nyon mongs).* Yet it is possible to reach liberation *(mokṣa)* and free oneself from suffering by eliminating the passions. This requires the practice of the path to liberation, which consists of practices such as morality, concentration, and insight.

In the Tibetan tradition, these basic Buddhist ideas and practices rarely stand on their own; instead, they are combined with the second layer, the ideas and practices contained in the Mahayana sutras, which propound the ideal of the bodhisattva, the being who seeks to attain the ultimate perfection of buddhahood for the sake of liberating all sentient beings. In order to achieve this lofty goal, the bodhisattva must develop particularly strong compassion and enter into the path described as "the perfection vehicle" *(pāramitāyna, phar phyin gyi theg pa)*, which consists of the gradual and extremely lengthy cultivation of six perfections: giving, ethics, patience, energy, concentration, and wisdom.[11] Together, these two layers form the exoteric part of the canon, which is the focus of most of the scholastic texts we will examine.

The third layer consists of esoteric texts,[12] the ideas and practices found in the tantras, which teach a secret *(guhya, gsang ba)* path, the "Secret Mantra" *(guhyamantra gsang sngags)*, or "Diamond Vehicle" *(rdo rje theg pa, vajrayāna)*, as it is often described in the context of the Supreme Yoga *(rnal 'byor bla med, anuttarayoga)* tantras.[13] Not much can be said here about this aspect of the tradition, which is extraordinarily complex and difficult to explore. The tantras present an entire worldview, with its own philosophy, cosmology, and practices, as well as an impressive amount of ritual lore. Their worldview begins with the idea that reality at its most fundamental is pure. Suffering is a result of fleeting delusions; these do not affect that purity, which remains hidden to ordinary sentient beings. The role of tantric practice is to reveal and actualize reality's pure potential.[14]

One begins this practice through a relation with a tantric teacher, or guru, who plays an especially important role. The guru is seen as a fully enlightened being who introduces his disciple to the pure nature of reality through an act of empowerment *(dbang, abhiseka)*. His quasi-divine status commands from his disciples' particularly intense respect and devotion. Some texts go so far as considering this attitude of intense personal devotion to be at the root of all spiritual accomplishment.[15] The guru also provides the special instructions *(man ngag)* required to carry on the secret practices prescribed by the tantras.

In the Diamond Vehicle, the practice is organized into two distinct stages. The first is that of generation *(bskyed rim, utpattikrama)*, consisting of practices involving identification with a deity, called a *yidam*. During this stage, one visualizes oneself as having the body of the deity. One's environment is seen as the divine mansion represented by the mandala *(dkyil 'khor, maṇḍala)*, and one's speech as the pure speech form of the deity represented by the mantras. The second is the stage of completion *(rdzogs rim, niṣpannakrama)*, consisting of yogic practices aimed at manipulating and controlling subtle physical energies. According to this mystical anatomy, the body is made of channels *(rtsa, nāḍi)* through which circulate different forms of bodily energy, such as winds and vital force, which converge on a few key centers *([rtsa,] khor, cakra)*. These elements can be manipulated to produce special liminal states of awareness that often involve intense nonconceptual feelings of bliss. Under these conditions, the mind is freed from the usual net of conceptuality and is able, when properly trained, to remain in nondual states.[16]

Practiced in this way, the tantric path is restricted to a small elite of super-virtuosi, requiring long periods of retreat and an intense dedication of which very few are capable. However, tantras may be practiced for worldly and instrumental purposes, as individuals develop various miraculous powers or accomplish marvelous feats *(dngos grub, siddhi)*. When these feats are spiritual and pertain to the completion of the path, they are described as supramundane. But they may also be less exalted, simply the result of practitioners' instrumental magical powers. And while these feats are not important for the practice of tantra as a means of reaching liberation, they are extremely important to the ways in which tantra is used and largely explain its success in Tibet.

But Tibetan Buddhism is not limited to these three canonical layers. There is also a wealth of folk practices dealing with possession, exorcism, divination, healing, retrieving of life force, worship of mountain and lake deities, the cult of the house gods, and so forth. These are part of what R. A. Stein describes as the "nameless religion,"[17] a fourth layer that takes a relatively similar form in many traditional Buddhist cultures. Although attaining liberation or buddhahood is the stated central goal of the tradition, Buddhism contains many popular practices that have long coexisted with the normative perspective.[18] In Tibet, the relationship between the two is especially close because of the large role played by tantra in folk religion. Many activities of that layer, including exorcism, the control of elements, and the increase of wealth and power, are either explicitly mentioned by the tantras or are based on tantric visualizations.

THE SECOND PERIOD: THE NEW SCHOOLS AND THE ROLE OF MONASTICISM

Tibet's complex form of Buddhism has developed since the second half of the eighth century. Throughout the centuries, the distinction between its exoteric and esoteric aspects has been a source of tension as well as creativity. The views and practices contained in the sutras and in the tantras seem to clash in many ways. Many sutras present reality as fundamentally unsatisfactory, and the goal of practice is to free oneself or others from its limitations.[19] The tantric view of fundamental purity appears to be strikingly different, as are tantric practices, which seem to subvert exoteric moral standards.

This clash became particularly obvious in the ninth and tenth centuries when the collapse of the empire led to the momentary eclipse of monasticism, which by then was deeply enmeshed in the political life of the kingdom. The lack of a central authority favored the practice of tantras in non-monastic settings. This shift opened the door to a variety of views and practices, alarming those who intended to revive monasticism. The division widened between those who insisted both on monastic discipline and on the study of the exoteric aspect of Buddhism and the tantrikas *(sngags pa)*, who are nonordained (often married) practitioners of the tantras.[20] The monastics argued that Buddhist practice had to conform to canonical exoteric models and criticized the tantrikas, accusing them of subverting Buddhism with immoral practices such as yogic sexual union *(sbyor)* and ritual killing *(sgrol)*. The tantrikas disagreed, rejecting the exoteric monastic path as necessarily inferior to the practice of tantra on which they based their legitimacy.

To resolve this conflict, Ye-shay-ö *(ye-shes-'od)*, the king of Western Tibet and a supporter of redeveloping monasticism, invited Atisha *(atiśa, 982–1054)*, a famous Indian teacher from the monastic university of Vikramashila in Bengal, to reside in Tibet. Atisha greatly inspired Tibetans with his teachings and provided the basis for the solution to the conflict between monastic and tantric practices: he included both in the path of the bodhisattva. The bodhisattva ideal provides an ethical framework for integrating the entire range of religious practices. Monasticism is posited as the best basis *(rten)* for a way of life embodying such an ideal, and tantric practices, when ethically subordinated to the bodhisattva ideal, are the most effective means of attaining its goal. In this way, Atisha was able to propose a vast synthesis of the tradition that included all its teachings (those found in the "Hinayana" sutras, the Mahayana sutras, and the tantras), which he organized as three types of practice intended for three types of person.

This scheme, as proposed in his *Bodhipathapradīpa*,[21] was later developed into the Stages of the Path *(lam rim)* literature, whose most famous example is Dzong-ka-ba's *Great Treatise on the Stages of the Path to Enlightenment*.[22] The model provided a framework capable of organizing the whole range of Buddhist practices. In particular, it enabled the incorporation of tantric practices into the Mahayana tradition. Understood in this way,[23] the path of the tantras becomes an esoteric brand of Mahayana, a particularly effective way of implementing the same ethical goal. Instead of conceiving of buddhahood as reached through a gradual and long accumulation of virtues, tantra holds that it can be attained much more quickly—even in a single lifetime. Tantric practices and ideas are thereby harmonized with exoteric Mahayana. The model described by the Stages of the Path also unifies the goals of "Hinayana" and exoteric Mahayana practices with those of the higher tantric level by describing the former as preparatory practices that develop the virtues necessary to achieve the higher level. Thus the whole range of Buddhist practices can be shown to cohere in a single person's practice.[24]

The revival of monasticism and the development of a synthesis between exoteric and esoteric elements of the tradition are characteristic of the second or later propagation *(phyi dar)* of Buddhism in Tibet, which began at the end of the tenth century and greatly intensified during the eleventh and twelfth centuries. Whereas earlier Buddhism had come to Tibet from different cultures (India, China, Central Asia), during this later period the primary influence was Buddhist India. Material translated from Sanskrit into Tibetan led to the development of the schools that take this later diffusion as their reference point and hence are called "new" *(gsar ma)*. The new schools adopted the model suggested by Atisha, but diverged as they have emphasized different aspects of the tradition.

The Ka-dam *(bka' gdams pa)* school established by Atisha's disciple Drom-dön-ba (1005–1064) stressed monasticism and the practice of the exoteric aspect of Buddhism. Tantric practices existed (mostly belonging to the Yoga tantra category, rather than Supreme Yoga tantra emphasized by the other new schools) but seem to have been kept secret under tight monastic control. Besides monasticism, the Ka-dam school was also associated with the spread of scholarship in general and the study of Buddhist philosophy in particular. At first, the tradition, which was centered on the monastery of Re-ding *(rwa greng)*, was rather hostile to scholasticism and focused mostly on ritual and meditative practices. But inspired by the famous translator Ngok Lo-tsa-wa *(rngog lo tsā ba blo ldan shes rab*, 1059–1109), the Ka-dam later developed into one of the main scholarly traditions. Ngok's tradition centered on the monastery of Sang-pu *(gsang phu ne'u thog*, founded in 1073 by Ngok's uncle, Ngok Lek-bay-shay-rab). It became philosophically oriented and was instrumental in spreading this interest to the other schools, particularly the Sa-gya. The influence of Sang-pu was further enhanced by Cha-ba Chö ki Seng-ge *(phya pa chos kyi seng ge*, 1109–1169), who helped create some of the most characteristic forms of Tibetan scholasticism.

Other traditions developed around nonordained teachers, who exemplified the lifestyle of wandering or home-based tantric yogis. Some of these traditions, however, particularly the Sa-gya *(sa skya)* and the Ka-gyü *(bka' brgyud),* which were at first local groups associated with a teacher and his family lineage, developed monastic institutions with their own extended networks of supporters. In this way, they became more tightly organized schools, able to take part in pan-Tibetan political life.

The Sa-gya school, for example, started from the lineage of the translator Drok-mi (992–1072), who went to India to be educated; when he returned to Tibet he translated several important texts, notably the *Hevajra Tantra.* He led the life of a home-based yogi, setting up an informal circle of disciples in order to support his activities.[25] The institutionalization of his lineage, which was based on the Path and Result *(lam 'bras)* teachings, occurred only gradually. In 1073, the monastery of Sa-gya (lit., "white earth," from the color of a hill behind the monastery) was founded. Though it was to become one of the great centers of Tibetan Buddhism, its beginnings were modest; for long time Sa-gya remained a nonmonastic tantric center. Scholastic studies may have received some impetus under Sö-nam Tse-mo (1142–1182), the second of the five great Sa-gya masters *(gong ma lnga),* but it is only with the fourth hierarch, Sa-gya Paṇḍita *(sa skya paṇḍita,* 1182–1251; hereafter called "Sa-paṇ"), that Sa-gya became an important scholastic center.[26]

Sa-paṇ was extremely influential in the development of a scholastic tradition in Tibet and the transformation of Sa-gya into one of the major scholarly centers. He stressed critical acumen *(shes rab, prajñā)* as central to the Buddhist path and emphasized study as a preparation for meditation. He also played a significant political role, thereby demonstrating the political and religious nature of schools such as Sa-gya and the Ka-gyü. In 1247, the Mongolian Prince Godan selected Sa-paṇ as the temporal authority of Central Tibet over his rivals, the Dri-gung branch of the Ka-gyü. He was succeeded by his nephew Pak-pa Lo-drö (1234–1280), who established the Sa-gya monastic tradition as politically dominant in Tibet for the next century. This supremacy was not uncontested, however, and it became the focus of a struggle between the Sa-gya and other groups, particularly followers of the Ka-gyü traditions.

The emergence of the new schools changed the situation of the nonordained practitioners following the ancient lineages (going back to the teaching's early transmission), who had been less affected than proponents of monasticism by the collapse of the empire. These practitioners were confronted by the claims of the new schools to represent a purer form of Buddhism with closer ties to India, the Holy Land where their religious tradition originated. Their response was to form their own school—the

Nying-ma (*rnying ma,* i.e., "ancient"), now one of the four main schools of contemporary Tibetan Buddhism whose scholarly culture will be examined here—which presented itself as going back to the early development of Buddhism in Tibet as encouraged by the emperor Tri Song-de-tsen.[27] He was said to have invited the Indian yogi Padmasambhava to Tibet to tame the demons who were preventing the construction of Sam-yay and to introduce Buddhist tantras. The Nying-ma tradition used this moment of Tibetan history to define its identity, emphasizing the role and enhancing the stature of its claimed founder, Padmasambhava, as a way to support its claims to legitimacy.[28] The Nying-ma school also developed its own special modes of transmission, relying on the "buried treasures" (*gter ma*), which provided channels for integrating the new material emerging from rival schools.

Although the Nying-ma school has always been quick to assert its religious specificity, it has remained outside most political struggles. Because it was composed mostly of home-based tantric practitioners, it had at first few monastic centers. Later on, it became increasingly monastic and institutionalized. The beginning of this move toward monasticism can be traced back to the foundation of Ka-thok (1159), the first of the six great Nying-ma monasteries. Nevertheless, the monastic element within the Nying-ma tradition remained limited for centuries, until Long-chen Rab-jam-ba (*klong chen rab 'byams pa,* 1308–1363) began a vast synthesis between old tantras and scholasticism to provide the theoretical framework around which the Nying-ma tradition has articulated its views and practices ever since. During the seventeenth century, monasticism became widespread in the Nying-ma tradition, as several other important Nying-ma centers of learning were founded, including Min-dröl-ling and Dzok-chen. Together with Ka-thok, they formed the basis for the further growth of monasticism within the Nying-ma tradition. Monasticization and the development of scholastic learning continued with the nonsectarian movement during the nineteenth century, accelerating with the recent encounter with modernity. This pattern has held particularly true in exile, where the Nying-ma school has tended to stress its conformity to the monastic model, which had first been propounded by the Ka-dam school and then adopted by the other schools.

The development of the new schools was rapid. Started during the second half of the eleventh century, they were well-established by the beginning of the thirteenth century when a new phase of the history of Tibetan Buddhism began. The first two periods—the Tibetan empire (particularly 755–842) and the establishment of the new schools (mid–eleventh to mid–

thirteenth century)—had been times of intense contact with its neighbors, especially India, marked by unprecedented efforts to import a new culture quickly while preserving exacting intellectual standards. It is during those five centuries that lineages were founded and a multitude of texts were translated.

THE THIRD PERIOD: THE SYSTEMATIZATION
OF THE SCHOLASTIC CULTURE

During the third period (mid–thirteenth to sixteenth century), contacts with India diminished and eventually almost entirely stopped because of the Muslim destruction of Buddhist institutions of higher learning in India. This period, which David Ruegg describes as "classical," was a time of systematizing the newly implanted traditions. Tibetan thinkers concentrated their efforts on organizing the material they had received from India. In the process, they also started to develop their own voices and to create the intellectual culture that is the focus of this study.[29]

The first task was to put in order the enormous amount of canonical material transmitted from India through the collaboration of Tibetan translators and Indian scholars. In this process, Rik-bay-ray-dri (*rig pa'i ral gri*, circa 1250–1330) and Bu-dön (*bu ston rin chen grub*, 1290–1364) were the two major figures in the new schools.[30] Through their efforts, the canon was standardized and divided into two parts: the "translated words" of the Buddha (*bka' 'gyur*, which contain the Vinaya, the "Hinayana," and Mahayana sutras and the tantras) and the "translated treatises" (*bstan 'gyur*, i.e., the Indian treatises or *śāstra* translated into Tibetan). This systematization is quite revealing of the Tibetan genius for imposing order on texts that do not seem to have been organized in India.[31]

Another aspect of this third period was the elaboration of a systematic presentation of the whole range of Indian Buddhist material. Instead of just reflecting the thoughts of Indian teachers, Tibetan thinkers started to produce their own syntheses, in the process presenting Buddhism much more systematically than had been done before. Several individuals can be mentioned here, such as Sa-pan, the Third Kar-ma-ba Rang-jung Dor-je (*rang byung rdo rje*, 1284–1339), Bo-dong (*bo dong phyogs las rnam rgyal*, 1376–1451), and Long-chen Rab-jam-ba. For our purposes, the most significant figure is Dzong-ka-ba (*tsong kha pa*, 1357–1419).

Born in Amdo, Dzong-ka-ba moved to Central Tibet at the age of sixteen to be trained in the scholastic tradition, which was by then well-established in that region. He studied with a variety of teachers, including Ren-da-wa (*red mda' ba*, 1349–1412, his main teacher), Sa-tsang Ma-ti Pen-chen, and Lho-drak Drub-chen. During these studies, Dzong-ka-ba focused on mastering the great texts of the tradition, studying each text with the teacher whose specialty it was. He also visited many scholastic centers, where he proved himself a successful debater. In this way he became a well-known figure, producing several brilliant works and attracting many disciples; they included Gyel-tsap (*rgyal tshab*, 1364–1432) and Kay-drup (*mkhas grub*, 1385–1438), who became important intellectual figures in their own right. What attracted them was Dzong-ka-ba's ability to forge a powerful doctrinal synthesis based on his vision of Indian Buddhism. His original interpretation of Madhyamaka philosophy became the foundation of scholastic education that has been largely responsible for the influence of his school. Dzong-ka-ba was as committed to tantric practices as were the thinkers of other Tibetan Buddhist schools, but he differed in his almost exclusive emphasis on scholastic categories as a framework for explaining the whole path. Although Dzong-ka-ba intended to provide a distinctive view, it does not appear that he saw his group—the Ga-den-pas (*dga' ldan pa*, i.e., "those from [the monastery of] Ga-den"), as they were then called—as separate from the broader Sa-gya school to which he and most of his disciples belonged. Even Gyel-tsap, his immediate successor as the Holder of the Throne of Ga-den (*dga' ldan khri pa*, the head of the Ga-den tradition), seems to have understood some of his later works as being in the Sa-gya tradition.[32]

One of the main appeals of Dzong-ka-ba was his insistence on monasticism combined with scholastic training.[33] In stressing the study of the great Indian texts in a monastic context, Dzong-ka-ba was continuing and strengthening a trend that had started earlier with the Ka-dam school. In 1409, Dzong-ka-ba himself established the monastery of Ga-den (*dga' ldan*). The institutionalization of his teachings was furthered by the creation of two other powerful monastic centers. In 1416, Jam-yang Chö-jay founded the monastery of Dre-pung (*'bras spungs*), and in 1419, Jam-chen Chö-jay founded the monastery of Se-ra (*se rwa*). Together with Ga-den, they constituted the three monastic seats (*gdan sa*) whose intellectual culture is at the center of this study. By gradually acquiring preeminence through their strong political ties with the political authorities in Lhasa,[34] these three monastic centers have provided the basis of this school's supremacy.

It is only gradually that the sectarian rift between the new Ga-den group and the other traditions formed. The first signs of the much more severe confrontations that were to follow appeared probably after Gyel-tsap's death, when Kay-drup succeeded him as leader of the Ga-den group. Kay-drup was more preoccupied than Gyel-tsap with questions of ortho-doxy and insisted on sticking to what he saw as the pure interpretation of Dzong-ka-ba's thought. It was also around that time that several Sa-gya thinkers such as Rong-dön and the translator Dak-tsang started to criticize sharply some of Dzong-ka-ba's Madhyamaka interpretations. During the second half of the century, the gap between the two groups further deep-ened. Sa-gya scholars, particularly Śākya Chok-den (*gser mdog paṇ chen śākya mchog ldan*, 1428–1509) and Go-ram-ba (*go ram pa bsod nams seng ge*, 1429–1489), took over earlier critiques, further broadening and inten-sifying them. For example, they vehemently attacked the Ga-den interpre-tation of Dharmakīrti's logic and epistemology, while continuing to em-phasize the degree to which they perceived Dzong-ka-ba's views as being innovations *(rang bzo)* without legitimate bases in the tradition.[35] These hostile critiques in turn strengthened the sense of orthodoxy that was de-veloping among Ga-den-bas, who gradually came to see themselves as forming a separate tradition claiming to possess the right view and hence to represent the apex of Tibetan Buddhism. This claim is reflected in the highly loaded name of *Ge-luk-pas* (the virtuous ones) that they chose for themselves. The sectarian process was further strengthened by the politi-cal climate of the times, particularly the power struggle between the forces of Tsang (the southwestern province whose capital is Shi-ga-tse) and the forces from Central Tibet. It is these events, more than intrinsic doctrinal differences, that led to the rigid division that has characterized Tibetan Buddhism in the last few centuries.

THE FOURTH PERIOD: HIGH SCHOLASTICISM
AND THE RISE OF SECTARIANISM

The growth of sectarianism had already begun with the gradual collapse of political authority after the end of the empire in the ninth century. A po-litical vacuum was created that groups based on kinship and local ties were unable to fill. In this context, Tibetan Buddhist schools rose as candidates for political power because of their leaders' charismatic ability to incarnate "the confluence of divinity, wisdom and power" that had characterized the sacral kingship of the empire.[36] The first group to fill the political vacuum and assume power over Tibet was, as noted above, the Sa-gya school. Its hegemony soon weakened, leading to a struggle for political power between competing politico-religious groups. After the second half of the fifteenth century, the situation deteriorated into a full-fledged civil war between Tsang and Central Tibet, each supported by rival religious schools.

The forces of Central Tibet relied on the rising power of the Ge-luk (as it was by then called) monastic establishment, whereas the forces of Tsang relied on a coalition in which the Kar-ma group of the Ka-gyü played a central role. The intermittent but bitter confrontation between these groups lasted almost two centuries, pitting the two camps against each other in a merciless struggle for power over Tibet. Finally, the forces of Central Tibet won with the support of the Qoshot, a Mongol tribe; in 1642, they established the Ge-luk leader—the Fifth Dalai Lama, Ngak-wang Lo-sang Gya-tso (*ngag dbang blo bzang rgya mtsho*, 1617–1682)—as the supreme authority in Tibet.[37]

The duration of the war between Tsang and Central Tibet, the bitterness that it created, the victory of the Dalai Lama and his coalition, and the imposition of a stable government relying on and supporting the Ge-luk school have been important formative influences on Tibetan Buddhism from this period to the present. Under the protection of the government, the Ge-luk school became by far the most powerful. Its main institutions were established and its monasteries grew exponentially. In particular, the great monastic seats of Dre-pung, Ga-den, and Se-ra, which had close ties with the political establishment, began to accumulate the resources and political pull that would enable them to exercise political influence and intellectual hegemony almost unchallenged.

Political events played a crucial role in the formation of Buddhist schools in Tibet. Whereas Indian schools reflected the lines of doctrinal disputes or distinctions in monastic ordination, the creation of Tibetan schools has often owed more to the chance occurrences of history and to political expediencies than to substantive religious or philosophical differences. All Tibetan schools adhere to the same monastic ordination, the Mūla-sarvāstivāda (see chapter 2). They show slightly greater doctrinal range, but overall their homogeneity is remarkable, especially when compared with the diversity existing in India or China. Most Tibetan thinkers belong to the Madhyamaka school of Buddhist philosophy. Although they disagree on its exact interpretation, a great majority share a substantially similar view.

Under such circumstances, differences are based mostly on personal allegiances and political alliances. Great importance is attached to devotion to one's guru and the related idea of a spiritual lineage as a necessary basis for religious practice. Spiritual lineage is particularly important for transmitting tantric teachings; these are kept secret and entrusted only to a few select disciples, who in turn pass them down. In the beginning, Tibetan schools developed more or less accidentally as such lineages were institutionalized in certain religious, mostly monastic, centers, which consequently grew in wealth, prestige, and political influence. Networks of institutional allegiances, which were first developed out of feelings of personal devotion to a particular person, grew in this fashion into organized constellations of religious and political power. Thus, Tibetan schools became more and more involved in pan-Tibetan political activities.

Inevitably, the relations among Tibetan schools deteriorated. The dominant Ge-luk school established its institutions, philosophy, and religious practices as normative, ignoring the other schools, who resented the political dominance of the Ge-luk as well as its intellectual and religious hegemony. Those following non-Ge-luk traditions were also unhappy at the restrictions imposed on them by a government that claimed to oversee the entire religious life of Tibet but was partial to the Ge-luk school. In this way the gap between the Ge-luk and the other schools broadened into the great divide that still separates the two sides today.

THE REACTION OF THE NON-GE-LUK SCHOOLS: THE NONSECTARIAN MOVEMENT

During the second half of the nineteenth century, the non-Ge-luk schools reversed their scholarly decline and began to establish their scholastic institutions in conjunction with the nonsectarian *(ris med)* or eclectic movement in Eastern Tibet, which had begun earlier in the century around the charismatic personalities of such great teachers as Jam-gön Kong-trul, Jam-yang Kyen-tse-wang-po, and Dza Pa-trül.[38] Disgusted by the rivalries that had torn apart the ruling family of Derge, these teachers promoted an inclusive approach in which all traditions were recognized as valid. Such an attitude was not novel; there had always been some teachers ready to disregard sectarian distinctions. But shaping a revival around such a catholic view was a new phenomenon that transformed Tibetan religious life. The strategy enabled the weaker schools to successfully oppose the dominant Ge-luk tradition by presenting a united front. In short order, the movement revived non-Ge-luk institutions and greatly strengthened their position, particularly in Kham. It left such a strong mark that it must be considered by anyone wishing to understand current Tibetan Buddhism. The movement has largely reshaped the non-Ge-luk Buddhist schools and has further contributed to the contemporary separation of all schools into two clearly distinguishable groups, the Ge-luk and the non-Ge-luk.

Though the nonsectarian movement was mostly focused on religious practices, it also led to the revival of scholarship among the three non-Ge-luk schools, partly in reaction against the intellectual hegemony of the large Ge-luk centers. The central figures in this scholastic revival are Ken-po Zhan-pan (*gzhan phan chos kyi snang ba,* 1871–1927), who wrote the commentaries on the thirteen great Indian texts used by most of the non-Ge-luk institutions, and Mi-pam Gya-tso (*mi pham rgya mtsho,* 1846–1912), who wrote a number of philosophical texts and commentaries that are taken by the Nying-ma-bas as orthodox statements of their views. Such efforts revitalized higher learning among non-Ge-luk schools and led to the development of a type of institution, the commentarial schools *(bshad grwa),* which we will examine in later chapters.

The Ge-luk tradition has been divided in its reactions to this revival. A few Ge-luk lamas, including the Dalai Lama, have been interested in the Great Perfection associated with the nonsectarian movement.[39] The main nonsectarian figures, particularly Pa-trül Rin-bo-che, had some Ge-luk students, and a few texts attest to the genuine dialogue that took place within the movement.[40] Other Ge-luk thinkers, however, have been sharply critical of this interest in nonsectarianism. The most famous was Pa-bong-ka (*pha bong kha,* 1878–1941), who spearheaded a revival movement partly directed against nonsectarian influence on the Ge-luk tradition.[41]

As important as it was, one must be careful not to exaggerate the overall impact of the nonsectarian movement in Tibet and to project back onto traditional Tibet the partial equalization in exile of the power differential between the schools. Before 1950 the Ge-luk political and religious hegemony had not been seriously threatened—particularly in Central Tibet and Amdo, where it was overwhelming. In Kham, the situation was more complex and the nonsectarian movement posed a real challenge, but even there the Ge-luk retained its primacy. Moreover, the influence of its three seats around Lhasa continued to be considerable. Non-Ge-luk monks would often spend a few years in one of these three monasteries for training. Finally, the influence of the nonsectarian movement, as well as Pa-bong-ka's revival movement, on Ge-luk scholastic education was limited.

To observe that the current division of the religious field into two groups, the Ge-luk and the non-Ge-luk schools, each with a specific form of scholastic education examined in this work, is more the result of contingent historical events than the expression of religious or philosophical differences is not to deny that there are real differences between these schools,[42] differences that are reflected in the different styles of their monastic education. But intersectarian differences should not be overemphasized to the neglect of intrasectarian or individual variations. Moreover, the sectarian differences are limited, and Tibetan Buddhist monasticism has a strong tendency toward consonance. When a practice, a doctrine, or an institution becomes successful within a group, other groups emulate this success and develop equivalents. Thus, claims of difference and superiority cannot be taken at face value. More often than not they are rhetorical attempts to legitimize the religious claims of a group or advance some overtly political cause.

2   Tibetan Monasticism

To understand Tibetan scholasticism, it is important to consider its institutional context. Unlike medieval Western scholastics, who were weakly integrated into the church as clerics and thus were obliged to follow few rules,[1] the Tibetan scholars whom we study here are monks. This chapter examines monasticism, which shapes the general tone of Tibetan scholastic practices and to a certain extent determines their purpose.

My own encounter with Tibetan monasticism occurred at the end of the spring of 1971. After being in Dharamsala for a few months, I had decided (for reasons explained in chapter 3) to enter a monastery to devote myself to the study and practice of this tradition. At the intercession of my teacher, I was allowed to stay at Nam-gyel *(rnam rgyal),* the Dalai Lama's own monastery. Soon after, I was ordained as a novice by Lati Rin-po-che, the rather stern monk who would be one of my main teachers.

My stay at the monastery was difficult from the beginning. I was a guest of the Dalai Lama, who had asked the monastery to give me a room. Although Nam-gyel was devoted to his service, its elders could not see any reason why a Westerner without any special qualifications should have the privilege of staying in the Dalai Lama's own monastery.[2] They could not disobey his order, but they rarely missed an opportunity to remind me of my rather precarious status. I remember the first day at the monastery when my Tibetan was so poor that I found it difficult to ask for food. I was too late for the only common meal of the day and went to the kitchen. The steward and the cooks pretended not to understand my rather explicit gestures and gave me nothing. By the next day, I had learned those words of the language!

During my stay at Nam-gyel, I was also surprised by how the monks passed their time. They spent most of it doing rituals, the kind of "mindless" activity that I considered below my newly attained dignity as a Buddhist monk. Moreover, few of the elder monks seemed to be very learned or even interested in study and meditation. The younger monks were involved in studying Buddhism, but it was clear that for them this task was a distant second to ritual, the main task of the monastery.

All this raises obvious questions. How could the elders of Nam-gyel be so unfriendly to this young Westerner, who was so keen to learn their tradition? Were they not bound by the universal brotherhood of Buddhist monks to take him in and give him a special place? Moreover, why were the monks spending so much time in the practice of ritual? Did they not know that Buddhist monks are supposed to study and meditate as prescribed in the canonical discipline? In this chapter I analyze Tibetan monasticism, describing ideal-typically some of its characteristics and discussing its strengths without hiding its drawbacks.[3] I focus on some of the central features of Tibetan monasteries, such as their corporate nature and their role as ritual centers. I also differentiate local monasteries from the large monastic universities where the scholastic culture flourishes.

THE NATURE OF BUDDHIST MONASTICISM AND ITS EVOLUTION

In general, monasticism attempts to create a form of life separate from the world in order that the religious ideals of a tradition can be fully expressed. From the monastic perspective, life in the world prevents the full realization of one's religious vocation. In the Indian context, monastic separation finds its standard expression in the phenomenon of world renunciation *(saṃnyāsa)* Renouncers seeking liberation from the cycle of birth and death enter into a separate mode of life in which they are not bound by social conventions and are free to adopt the discipline that may enable them to transcend the limits of normal existence.[4]

In Buddhism, world renunciation was institutionalized very early on. Buddha's disciples formed communities *(saṃgha)* of like-minded people who left the life of the householder to devote themselves to preserving and practicing his teaching. Leaving the family is described as "going forth" *(rab byung, pravrajyā)*—that is, abandoning the life of the household, which is involved with the world and with sexual reproduction (itself connected with aging and dying), to enter the homeless life, the life of those who have freed themselves from passions such as attachment and aversion, which are the roots of suffering.[5]

One of the central characteristics of such a life is asceticism, the rejection of the confusion of the world for a more disciplined life. In the Buddhist tradition, asceticism is tempered by a certain distrust of its possible excesses. Hence, Buddhist monasticism describes itself as "the middle path." Nevertheless, it is ascetic in that its discipline is aimed at overcoming the limitations of ordinary life. Seeking individual perfection—nirvana (or buddhahood in Mahayana traditions)—it involves a separation from the ways of the world. It is expressed in the commitment that monks assume at their ordinations to observe a large number of precepts: 253 for fully ordained Tibetan monks, who follow the Mūla-sarvāstivāda version of the Vinaya, and 227 for fully ordained Theravada monks.

This separation is marked symbolically and effected practically by ordination, the rite of passage required of those becoming monks or nuns. This ritual marks their abandonment of worldly life and passage into the monastic state, which is devoted to pursuing individual freedom from the passions. While those who enter the community follow the rules concomitant to ordination, they do not surrender their freedom completely. For example, monks or nuns can leave the community at any time, choose another community, or cease to be part of the monastic order, if they so wish. There is no vow of obedience in Buddhist monasticism.

But such individual freedom does not prevent monks or nuns from forming durable alternative religious structures set apart from the rest of society.[6] Buddhist monasticism is not just a collection of virtuosi within a loose framework that enables individuals to seek self-perfection. Rather, it is a social institution oriented toward the soteriological goals of the tradition,[7] which provide its members with a framework that sustains and reinforces the discipline needed to achieve their goal. Hence, Buddhist monasticism is ruled by its own set of laws. The Vinaya (the part of the canon concerned with monastic discipline) is more a legal code than a compendium of spiritual advice. Because it codifies the laws of a community rather than guides individuals, it deals only with external behaviors, not with internal mental states.[8]

This analysis of Buddhist monasticism as an institution directed by an ascetic world-transcendent ideal corresponds to the picture that the Vinaya presents. It captures important elements of Buddhist monasticism as it has existed throughout its history. The typical monastic mentality or ideology is characterized by a certain individualism, a disdain for the life of the laity accompanied by a clear feeling of superiority. The numerous rules that codify monastic life are also central to Buddhist monasticism. Four are fundamental: monks are barred from killing a human being, engaging in sexual intercourse, stealing, and making false claims to spiritual realization. Those who ignore any of these bans incur a defeat *(pham pa, pārājika)* and cease to be monks. Monks also are subject to a host of less important rules, such as the obligation not to eat after noon and prohibitions against killing animals, against staying alone in a room with a person of the other sex, and so on. These rules are meant to underscore the separation between monks or nuns and the life of the world, a separation that is always in danger of being abandoned and hence must be constantly reinforced.[9]

Many of these rules are concerned with maintaining monastic decorum. Monks are respected by the laity as prefiguring and embodying the Buddhist goal, the freedom that comes from detachment. Although monks may not realize it, their behavior is supposed to publicly manifest a commitment to that ideal. For example, monks are prohibited from dancing, singing, moving their arms while walking, making noise while eating, and so on. Such behaviors are not intrinsically blameworthy but they contradict the laity's expectation of detachment. By shunning them, monks avoid even the appearance of impropriety and thus maintain the faith of their followers.[10] Proper decorum is obviously very important for a tradition that depends so closely on the laity's support. Hence, Phra Mahā Samaṇa describes the Vinaya as "the main root of the Buddhasāsana (Buddha's teaching)."[11] In many ways, it was typical that my admiration for the monks, felt in Sarnath, had spurred my interest in Buddhism. There are many examples of such conversions in the history of Buddhism, starting from the canonical period.

Such a life of discipline can be followed by anybody who wants it, but it is chosen only by a minority of strong characters, the virtuosi who lead their life as the heroic enactment of religio-ethical ideals.[12] Buddhist monks and nuns are, according to the Vinaya, such virtuosi. They voluntarily embrace a life of systematic discipline oriented toward perfection, a life that they are free to leave at any time. Such a life implies, as Ilana Friedrich-Silber puts it, a normative "double standard; its rigor is considered neither possible nor necessary for all, either from a virtuoso or a nonvirtuoso point of view."[13] Moreover, because such a life is based on personal achievements, it is to some degree elite. Only those who can follow the systematic and demanding discipline can live this way. Others have to limit themselves to the role of outside supporters.

This emphasis on a world-transcending ideal and an ascetic separation from worldly life does not, however, capture the full reality of Buddhist monasticism. Even ideal-typically, Buddhist monks and nuns are not just renouncers who live the homeless life prescribed by the Vinaya. They also act as priests of a cult, providing ritual services for laypeople in exchange for support. It is difficult to say when this priestly function developed, but clearly it started very early on—perhaps, as Gregory Schopen suggests, even earlier than Ashoka (270–232 B.C.E.)[14]—and developed gradually. This transformation of Buddhist monasticism was greatly encouraged by the institutionalization of the Buddhist tradition during Ashoka's rule.[15] The king's support transformed Buddhism, which had been relatively obscure, into a major tradition that needed to satisfy the religious needs of its followers.

This priestly function is not to be confused with another monastic task, that of allowing laypeople to gain merit *(puṇya, bsod nams)*. The practice of accumulating merit, an integral part of the Buddhist soteriological project, is sometimes misrepresented as not being fully soteriological.[16] In fact, it is based on the realistic recognition that most people need several lifetimes to reach the ultimate goal. From a Buddhist perspective, it makes sense to think about obtaining liberation by gradually developing virtues. According to this view, people's virtuous actions bear fruit as pleasant or spiritually beneficial experiences, whereas unvirtuous actions bring pain and hindrances to spiritual practice. Hence, through the gradual accumulation of virtuous karmas, one can better oneself until one is ready to step beyond the limits of the conditioned world.

This practice is, in principle, the province of the laity, and monastics are supposed to aim for a higher goal.[17] Forbidden to engage in any lucrative activity, they are supposed to depend on the laity, who give them the food they eat. In exchange, they are expected to be of service to laypeople, teaching them and providing them with opportunities to gain merit.[18] Thus the monastic separation from the world of the laity is tempered by a complementarity to that world: allowing laypeople to gain merit is a monastic duty clearly prescribed by the Vinaya.

However, the services provided to the laity are supposed to be limited to those that are directly or indirectly relevant to liberation. The Vinaya explicitly forbids monks and nuns from engaging in other practices, such as astrology, medicine, or ritual offerings for the laity, that are instrumental and hence without soteriological value.[19] Yet over the centuries, such practices have flourished in all the countries where Buddhism has prospered. Even in the Theravada tradition—the most conservative school, which claims to have remained close to the early canon—most monks preside over rituals for the laity. Stanley Tambiah describes the apparent incongruity of monks chanting sacred words that proclaim the transcendence of worldly preoccupations for patrons who attend such rituals to seek blessings, protection from evils and misfortunes, cure of disease, good luck, and even economic prosperity.[20]

Not surprisingly, not all monks or nuns partake equally in this priestly function, which is in tension with the ideals of the tradition. While the majority engage in the rituals that the laity require, thereby helping the order to maintain a large presence, a minority of monks and nuns have focused more exclusively on the activities normatively expected of Buddhist monks, the study and practice of the teaching. In the Theravada tradition, this difference has been institutionalized in the distinction between village and forest monks. The former are the renouncer-priests who perform the Buddhist rituals that laypeople require, and the latter are those rare individuals who try to minimize this priestly role, intensively devoting themselves instead to meditation in isolation.[21]

In Tibet such a difference exists as well, though it is not explicitly institutionalized as in Theravada countries. The enormous majority of Tibetan monks function like village monks, while a small minority devote themselves to meditation in the solitude of hermitages. The scholars whose culture we examine here fall somewhere between these two groups. They view the priestly function with suspicion, for they see it as an obstacle to scholastic pursuits. But because they live in monasteries, they must take part in its numerous rituals.

Monks' and nuns' adoption of a priestly function has had important consequences for Buddhist monasticism. It has changed the nature of the monastic vocation by lessening practitioners' distance from the laity. Canonically, monks and nuns are expected to be virtuosi who follow a difficult path, but in their function as priests they are not; and thus the link between monasticism and virtuosity is weakened. This change in the practice means that almost all monks and nuns see themselves as engaged on an extremely long path lasting many lifetimes. Scholars see study as advancing them on that path, and similarly hermits often undertake meditative retreats hoping thereby less to attain significant insight than to accumulate merit.[22] For many, being a monk or a nun no longer entails a transcendental vocation: it is simply a better way to the same end sought by the laity—accumulating merit.

MASS MONASTICISM

The transformation of the monastic ideal has affected all Buddhist traditions. In the Tibetan context, it merges with a more properly Tibetan phenomenon, which Melvyn Goldstein aptly describes as "mass monasticism": that is, the inclusion of a significant proportion of the male population in the monastic order. Some estimate that before the invasion of Tibet by the PRC in 1950, up to 20 percent of the population may have been ordained.[23] This phenomenon, which probably began during the seventeenth century when the support of the Lhasa authorities enabled the number of monks to substantially increase, appears to be without precedent elsewhere in the Buddhist world. In Theravada countries such as Thailand, monks never represented more than a small fraction of the total population.

The reasons behind Tibetan mass monasticism are complex. Some are ideological, such as the belief that monasticism is the superior way to practice Buddhism. To become a monk is thought to bring great merit to both the ordained person and his family. Because the state has an avowed mission to support Buddhism, it should enable as many people as possible to enter monasteries. But this emphasis on sheer numbers also gives those monasteries a political weight it would be difficult to gain otherwise. The monks—many of them young, vigorous, and quite ready to defend their rights, enforce the wishes of the monasteries, bring recalcitrant laypeople into line, or even defy the authorities—effectively wield considerable clout.

To make monasteries so large, standards of entrance had to be lowered. As Goldstein explains,

> [T]he emphasis on mass monasticism can be seen in the way monasteries made it easy for monks to find a niche for themselves within the monastic community by allowing all kinds of personalities to coexist. The monastery did not place severe restrictions on comportment, nor did it require rigorous educational or spiritual achievement. New monks had no exam to pass in order to remain in the monastery, and monks who had no interest in studying or meditating were as welcome as the dedicated scholar monks. Even illiterate monks were accommodated and could remain part of the monastic community.[24]

Such changes are common when an institution throws open its doors. Standards are lowered, whether consciously as a matter of policy or unconsciously as the members of the institution learn to adapt their expectations.

Tibetans have mixed feelings about this state of affairs. On the one hand, being a monk is seen as a blessing that should not be restricted. On the other hand, the less stringent monastic requirements bring about a lowering of the standards that weakens monastic prestige. A proverb captures this reality: "The great monastic seats are like the ocean." They contain all kinds of fish: scholars, students, meditators, monks involved in trade and politics, monks spending their life comfortably without having to work, and even punk-monks *(ldab ldob)*—gangs who fight each other and play competitive sports. The monasteries use them to maintain order, collect taxes from the recalcitrant, or defend monastic officials on dangerous travels.[25]

The lowering of monastic standards has further eroded the standing of monks as virtuosi. In Tibet before 1959, monks were permitted to spend time as they wished, provided that they did not break any of the four basic rules, followed the particular code of conduct of the monastery, shunned alcohol (at least in the better monasteries), and participated in the rituals. According to Goldstein, the strict keeping of monastic precepts, scholastic studies, and the practice of meditation were seen as "an individual rather than institutional responsibility."[26] Many decisions were left to the individual monk. For example, would he abstain from eating at night as the Vinaya commands, or would he eat dinner, as most Tibetan monks do? Would he abstain from engaging in trade, or would he start a business? Would he study, or would he provide ritual services for the laity? Since they would be the ones reaping the karmic results, individuals should be free to choose. Monastic ritual and the decorum required by each monastery are institutional responsibilities that affect the whole community. Studies, meditation, and keeping the precepts beyond the bare minimum concern only the person who engages in these activities.

But it would be wrong to exaggerate the implications of mass monasticism. Tibet is, or rather was, the country with the largest concentration of monks and nuns devoted to the practice of the monastic ideals of the Vinaya, emphasizing monasticism much as Theravada countries do. The Tibetan and Theravada ordinations are similar, though they reflect different schools (Mūla-sarvāstivāda and Sthaviravāda, respectively).[27] Likewise, the precepts and monastic ceremonies are in most respects identical. As followers of the Vinaya, Tibetan monks and nuns are thus not very different from their Theravada colleagues.

Moreover, contemporary Theravada monasticism has largely been produced by the encounter between the Theravada tradition and modernity over the past two or three hundred years. For example, the strict adherence to the Vinaya, of which the Theravada tradition is so proud nowadays and which it holds to be its defining characteristic, is a relatively recent phenomenon resulting from a complex process that took place mostly during the nineteenth century when the reformist zeal of figures such as Mongkut and Dharmapala received the support of political entities interested in bringing greater uniformity to the order as a way to unify the nation. Medieval Theravada monasticism seems to have been rather different, with greater local diversity and less attention to strict discipline. Some monks led luxurious lives, wore silk robes, ate their meals from beautiful plates,

handled large sums of money, and owned large landholdings (including entire villages).[28] Others lived a more modest life closely connected to their
community, working with villagers, cultivating fruits and vegetables, and
participating in popular rituals. For these monks, the details of the discipline were much less important than their ability to help the villagers.
Monks in parts of Thailand routinely ate after noon, wore pants to work
in the fields, mixed freely with women, and did not repeat the full *Prati-
mokkha,* the summary of the discipline that monks are supposed to recite
every fortnight.[29] This monastic laxity is not unlike that found in Tibet.
Thus, for a meaningful comparison we must contrast Tibetan monasticism,
which has encountered modernity only in the last fifty years, with medieval or early modern Theravada.

In addition, we should not assume that all Tibetan monasteries were
equally lax in their discipline. The great diversity in the discipline's rigor
is typical of a traditional society in which the normalizing power of the
state is limited. Another reason for this diversity is that many aspects of
Tibetan monastic life were, and still are, regulated less by the canonical
Vinaya than by the local monastic constitution *(bca' yig).* Each monastery
has its own constitution—a condensed body of customs, oral lore, and traditional documentation woven together with aspects of the Vinaya. It addresses the governance of the monastery; the duties, responsibilities, and
dress of monastic officers; the order of priority among members; the procedures for making decisions; and the observance of ritual activities. In
some cases, as at Se-ra Jay, the constitution was not written down until recently.[30] In other cases, as at Se-ra (the monastic seat), the constitution was
written down by an outside authority selected on the basis of his knowledge and reputation.[31]

Since important aspects of the discipline are regulated by the particular
code of each individual monastery or monastic unit, the strictness of monastic discipline varies greatly (as one might expect). In general, the large
central monasteries of a tradition tended to be much stricter than the local
smaller monasteries. Among the smaller monasteries, those more centrally
located tended to be stricter than those in outlying regions. In some areas,
monks were routinely offered alcohol by the laity.[32] Similar variations
could be observed within a single monastery. In the three large Ge-luk monastic universities, the discipline differed from regional house *(khang
tshan)* to regional house. Some houses, such as Tre-hor in Se-ra Jay, were
known for their strict discipline and their harsh demands on new monks.
Others with lax regulations were known as havens for punk-monks.

Given that monastic decorum and participation in rituals were the main requirements for membership, most monks *(grwa mang)*[33] in the large monastic universities opted for a relaxed life of leisure. They were often supported by their families (the large monasteries provided food for their members only within the context of a ritual in the assembly hall), and supplemented this stipend by doing rituals for the laity. Lacking intellectual or spiritual ambition, they considered their present life as a meritorious and pleasant preparation for future lives. The life of the scholars *(dpe cha ba)* was quite different, as we will see. They were the few who were ready to endure hardships in order to study. Together with the meditators, they were the virtuosi whom Tibetans most respect, the models and symbols of the values of the tradition.

In exile, monks and nuns have found themselves in very different circumstances, for they have faced the daunting task of reconstituting their monasteries. They have had to build entire monasteries from scratch, and work in the fields, while studying and providing the ritual services required by the laity. Older monks would often humorously comment, "In Tibet, the life of the monks was easy while that of the laity was difficult. In exile, it is the opposite. Laypeople have it easy while monks must work twice as hard." This observation was made without any bitterness, as a matter of fact and an amused reflection on the twists of karma.

Such changes have affected the character of Tibetan monasticism, as the old idea of having as many monks as possible is seen to have drawbacks. As a result, the monastic universities have raised their standards, establishing a mandatory curriculum and obliging the monks who are not interested in scholarship to work for the monastery. Yearly examinations control the studies of the monks who wish to be scholars. Moreover, some of the more obvious abuses, including the punk-monks, have been eliminated. With less scope to engage in the power politics that existed in the old society, monks have sharply reduced their political engagement.

Nevertheless, Tibetan monasticism has kept its mass character. The great monasteries have no limitations on their enrollment and are growing fast. Se-ra, which had about a thousand monks in the 1980s, reached more than four thousand at the turn of the century. Pa-yül monastery, which started in exile in the 1970s with dozens of monks, has grown to two thousand. This increase is due to recent political events in Tibet, particularly the closing down of monasteries and the radical curtailment of their activities by the PRC.[34] Monks escaping from Tibet enter the great monasteries reestablished in India. The exile community, which has prospered but has been powerless to affect the situation in Tibet, cannot turn away this flood of new arrivals, despite the enormous problems that they create as the monasteries must support and integrate their booming populations. This unexpected development has helped sustain the mass character of Tibetan monasticism, though its long-term effects have yet to emerge.

MONASTERIES AS CORPORATE ENTITIES

The discipline is not the only distinguishing feature of Tibetan monasteries. They also have a characteristic institutional structure that differs from the canonical standard. In the Vinaya, monasteries are little more than residences with limited bureaucratic structure and no fixed or mandatory activity, which are open to any properly ordained person according to his or her seniority in the order. To understand the nature and role of Tibetan monasteries, with their diversity of function and size, it may be helpful to think of them both as corporate entities and as ritual communities.

A Tibetan monastery is an association of the individual monks (or nuns) who are a part of the monastery. They own and govern it in accordance with the rules prescribed by the Vinaya and the monastic constitution. That Tibetan monasteries are corporate in nature is in keeping with the canonically recommended monastic individualism. Monks enter the monastery to pursue their own spiritual goals; they belong to the community as individuals who are free to leave at any time. But Tibetan monasteries are often enmeshed in political and economic relations that involve complex bureaucratic structures, mandatory activities, and onerous duties. Such involvement in the life of the world, which the Vinaya had sought to avoid, is an important dimension of monasticism in Tibet, as in many other Buddhist countries. It is to manage this dimension that most monasteries are set up as associations.

Since a monastery is typically an association, mere residence does not qualify an ordained person to be a member. A monk must be formally accepted by the monastic authorities after fulfilling the criteria of admission; these vary from monastery to monastery, but the basic requirement is the ability to read and memorize the monastery's rituals. Once admitted, a member gains certain rights and privileges. For instance, he can share in the wealth of the monastery and participate in making decisions governing the life of the community, provided that he has acquired a certain level of seniority. Together with these rights come certain duties. He must attend the rituals of the monastery and may be appointed by the association to any of the monastic offices, which sometimes involve extremely demanding tasks.

This side of monastic life is often overlooked in the depiction of Tibetan society as feudal, administered by a small autocratic elite of aristocrats and lamas. But monks govern themselves, most of the time through chosen representatives. The abbot or lama who leads the monastery certainly has some power, but he cannot do as he pleases; he has to follow the traditions of the monastery and the wishes of the monks, whose representatives can nullify the leader's actions. Large monasteries in particular were governed by complex bureaucracies appointed by an assembly *(tshogs 'du)* composed of representatives of the constituent elements of the monastery. Gen Lob-zang Gya-tso *(blo bzang rgya tsho;* see figure 1), one of my teachers, used to remark with great pride on the "capitalist" and "democratic" nature of the large Tibetan monasteries, which are powerful self-governing associations with large financial assets.

Monks are very aware of the privileges they enjoy as members of a monastery. Some are financial, though such benefits often do not amount to very much.[35] But however small they are, these privileges always give the monks a proprietary outlook. They feel that they own the monastery; and when the monastic officers do not perform their duties adequately, the monks are ready to criticize them, sometimes quite harshly. The monks also tend to be conservative and stubborn, prone to decry any changes as "inventions" *(rang bzo)* that subvert the traditions of their monastery—remember the resistance of some of the Nam-gyel monks to my residency at the monastery. This conservatism can be very frustrating for outsiders who wish to help or for enlightened leaders who are attempting to promote needed changes. The Dalai Lama has tried to push through many changes, but even in his own monastery he has had limited success; his ability to promote changes in other monasteries is more limited still. Traditionally, he controls some aspects of monastic life, such as the appointment of abbots and the regulation of monastic exams, but outside of these established domains all changes must be agreed to by the monks. In exile, their conservative outlook is little more than an irritating oddity. In Tibet, however, it had disastrous consequences, as when monks put an end to many of the reforms of the Thirteenth Dalai Lama.

Though a few spend more time socializing with friends or relatives than praying, most Tibetan monks work extremely hard. Even in Tibet, many preferred to be active, whether helping some richer monks, engaging in petty commerce, or earning money by performing rituals for the laity. In exile, as already noted, the life of monks and nuns is much more difficult and hard work is a necessity. Monks in the great Ge-luk monastic universities have rebuilt their monasteries, while at the same time pursuing their monastic studies and performing various rituals for laypeople. Besides engaging in daily study, they often work in the fields and spend entire nights outside in all weather, chasing away wild boars or elephants to protect their crops. Despite such travails, these monasteries are thriving. The monks have successfully re-created their scholastic culture and managed in the 1990s to absorb a large population of new arrivals from Tibet.

MONASTERIES AS RITUAL COMMUNITIES

Tibetan monasteries are first and foremost ritual communities, which reflect the priestly role that monks have assumed throughout the history of the tradition. This statement may surprise those who think of Buddhism as a rational philosophy that shuns rituals. Yet that modern view has little to do with the historical reality of any Buddhist tradition. It is because of the emphasis on ritual that the few monks who want to devote themselves to meditation almost invariably leave the monastery to stay in the forest or in a hermitage.[36]

Even in the large monastic universities whose intellectual culture we examine here, life revolves around the practice of rituals; this takes precedence over any other activity, scholastic studies included. To start with, the main requirement to enter the monastery is the memorization of the monastery's ritual material (chos spyod). In fact, admission to the monastery is intimately tied to its practice, giving one the right to go to the assembly hall (tshogs khang) of the monastery to participate in the rituals and to partake in the offerings distributed in them.

Most local monasteries are devoted to satisfying the ritual needs of the laity of the area, and hence their schedule revolves around ritual. The same is true of the central monasteries, the scholarly centers of the tradition. In Dre-pung, for example (see figure 2), during the debating sessions (chos thog; see chapter 11) the day starts with a service in the assembly hall of the monastic seat and then a brief prayer in the debating courtyard. After a debate, there is another service in the temple of the monastery, another prayer in the courtyard, and another debate. There may be another late afternoon service in the monastery or in the regional house, followed by the main ritual of the day: the prayer of the evening debate, which in Dre-pung is called the prayer of worship (sku rim du zhal 'don).[37] This last ritual alone contains more than fifty prayers and can last for more than two hours.

Each monastery is differentiated from others by its own ritual material. The rituals are performed in the assembly hall at the center of the monastery, where all the monks gather; hence, it symbolizes the monastery as a community. Each monastery is very proud of that assembly hall, into which it invests much time, effort, and money (see figure 3). A large assembly hall signifies the strength of the monastery, strength demonstrated by the number of monks taking part in the monastery's rituals, not their learning or discipline. Moreover, the assembly hall is the center for the redistribution of monastic income; there monks are given tea, food, and money by sponsors. Monastic officers also present their accounts there and distribute any profits that have been made. That the ritual activities are performed in this central location underscores their dominant role in the life of the monastery.

Most Tibetan monasteries perform the three monastic rituals prescribed by the Vinaya: the fortnightly confession *(bso sbyong, uposadha)*, the ritual marking the beginning of the rainy season retreat *(dbyar gnas)*, and the ritual marking its closing *(dgag dbye)*. Those that adhere more strictly to the monastic discipline, particularly the Ge-luk monasteries, are mindful of keeping monastic decorum in accordance with the Vinaya. These rituals, which belong to the "Hinayana" part of the canon, constitute only a limited portion of a monastery's practice.

Cyclical rituals are also performed regularly. They are more important than the Vinaya rituals, both absorbing more time and playing a larger role in the life of monasteries. For each monastery, these include the traditional Buddhist holy days, such as the celebration of the Buddha's enlightenment and passing away, and the more specific Tibetan Buddhist holy days, which are often connected with a central figure of the school to which the monastery belongs. For example, Nying-ma monasteries celebrate Padmasambhava's miracles, and Ge-luk monasteries commemorate Dzong-ka-ba's passing away. Another ritual occasion is the Great Prayer *(smon lam chen mo)* celebrated after the Tibetan New Year in Lhasa, a festival discussed later in connection with the Geshe examinations. Moreover, a number of specific rituals must be performed during the year in accordance with the individual traditions of a given monastery. These rituals, often tantric in nature, revolve around a particular deity who is worshiped during highly elaborate ceremonies held over several days. They include the full range of practice associated with a deity, such as the construction and consecration of his or her mandala, self-empowerment, full generation of oneself as the deity, and at times monastic dances.

Each monastery has also its own daily ritual cycle, which may include rituals that are performed by the whole monastery every day. The protectors of the monastery are briefly propitiated daily, as well as monthly more extensively by a group of monks specializing in this task. Some rituals are performed almost daily; for example, the evening debate in the Ge-luk monastic universities involves a long ritual that includes repeated praises to Tārā and a recitation of the Heart Sutra. I will return in chapter 11 to this ritual, which is extremely important for scholastic studies.

The greatest number of rituals are of a third type; they are sought by particular sponsors. These rituals are called "foot firming" (zhabs brtan), and have an instrumental purpose: to cure disease, repel evil spirits, create auspiciousness, bring luck in commerce, and so on. They are requested either by the laity or by the monks, often for the same reasons. Their timing is determined either by a consultation of an astrological calendar, which indicates the particular days when special rituals need to be performed,[38] or by a divination performed by a monk, a tantrika, or a diviner (pra phab mkhan). These rituals can also be requested by corporate entities. The Tibetan government often does so after consulting its oracle, the Tibetan deity Ne-chung, when it wishes to protect the Dalai Lama or the community from some danger. When the PRC invaded Tibet in 1950, for example, the government asked the monasteries to do the rituals to repel the enemy's armies (dmag bzlog).

The foot-firming rituals have become a universal fixture of Tibetan life and are performed with great frequency at the request of those who are ill or facing hardships.[39] If they are to be performed by the entire monastery, all the monks gather for that purpose in the assembly hall. In return, they receive from the sponsors at least tea, and sometimes food and money. These rituals may also be performed (often in the sponsor's home) by a few monks chosen by the monastery. Because foot-firming rituals build a network of supporters who come to rely on a monastery in times of crisis and are therefore willing to be quite generous, they are an important source of income. Individual monks spend much of their time on these rituals, which help support them. In the Ge-luk monastic universities in Tibet, every day that the monastery was in debate session, several ritual assemblies would be held. The refreshments provided during them might be the main or only food that the monks received from the monastery. Many of the scholar-monks consider foot-firming rituals an obstacle to scholarly pursuits—especially the extraordinary ones requested by the government or by rich sponsors, which can last for days. Other monks love these occasions that enable them to improve their diet, make money, and find sponsors. They also enjoy the complexity of the performance and chants. Some monks specialize in them and seek the rituals out, whether for the monastery's sake or their own.

The practice of rituals in Tibetan monastic life illustrates the complex interactions of the layers of Tibetan religious culture. While the Vinaya rituals belong to the "Hinayana" part of the tradition, some of the other rituals belong to the exoteric Mahayana tradition. Most rituals are tantric in origin, but have been domesticated and transformed into monastic rituals. Often, exoteric and esoteric aspects of the tradition are mixed together: a single ritual may involve elements from both. At other times, these two kinds of practice are kept apart. For example, the rituals of the Great Prayer intentionally leave out any tantric element, whereas the rituals of the great tantric deities are exclusively tantric. Such thoroughgoing intermingling characterizes Tibetan Buddhism more generally.

TYPES OF MONASTERIES

Monasteries fall into two general categories: local monasteries, which are often small, and central monasteries, which function as training centers and may number more than ten thousand monks.[40] Some local monasteries are very small, with perhaps as few as the four monks necessary to form a sangha (monastic order); these are often staffed by monks who divide their time between working with their family duties and the performance of rituals. Others are much larger. For example, the Ge-luk monasteries of Kham in Tre-hor, Li-tang, and Ba-tang housed several thousand monks. Most offered little training to their members, preferring to send them for three years to the central monastery with which they were affiliated. Some local monasteries, such as Kum-bum and Ga-den Chö-khor Ling in Amdo, and Dak-po and Ra-tö in Central Tibet, offered some scholastic training and kept their monks longer; but unable to compete with the great scholastic centers mentioned below, they sent their monks to one of the three monastic seats to complete their education.

The central monasteries are by definition training centers for monks from other monasteries, keeping alive the great tradition of learning we are examining here. Each school of Tibetan Buddhism has its own central monasteries, which uphold its traditions scholastically, politically, socially, and economically. Each central monastery is at the heart of an extended network of affiliated local monasteries. This network may be purely regional or may cover all of Tibet, as do the three Ge-luk monastic universities. This network brings the central monastery considerable resources, greatly extending its pool of supporters and sponsors and ensuring that it has considerable influence.

The Nying-ma tradition has six such centers. Two, Min-dröl-ling (*smin grol gling*, founded 1676) and Dor-je Drak (*rdo rje brag*, 1659), are in Central Tibet. The other four monasteries—Ka-thok (*ka thog*, 1159), Dzok-chen (*rdzogs chen*, 1685), Pa-yül (*dpal yul*, 1655), and Zhe-chen (*zhe chen*, 1735)—are in Kham.[41] The oldest of these is Ka-thok, which was founded by Ka-thok-pa Dam-pa De-shek (*ka thok pa dam pa bde gshegs*, 1122–1192) and remained relatively small for several centuries. During the seventeenth century, monastic centers began to develop in the Nying-ma tradition, and four of the other six were founded. One was Pa-yül, whose curriculum and educational practice we will examine in detail; it was founded by Rig-dzin Kun-zang Shay-rab (*rig 'dzin kun bzang shes rab*, 1638–1698). For the last century or so, the most important of these six monasteries has been Dzok-chen, founded by Pema Rig-dzin *(padma rig 'dzin)*.

In the Ge-luk tradition, there are five central monasteries. In Central Tibet were Ga-den *(dga' ldan)*, founded by Dzong-ka-ba in 1409, and Dre-pung (*'bras spungs*, 1416) and Se-ra (*se rwa*, 1419), founded by his two disciples, Jam-yang Chö-jay *('jam dbyangs chos rje)* and Jam-chen Chö-jay *('jam chen chos rje)*. Ta-shi Lhun-po *(bkra shis lhun po)* was founded in 1445 by Ge-dün-drub (*dge 'dun grub*, 1391–1474) in Shi-ga-tse in the Tsang province; Ta-shi Go-mang *(bkra shis sgo mang)* was founded by Jam-yang-shay-ba in 1709 in La-brang *(bla brang)* in Amdo.[42]

We will focus on the first three, for they are the most important—the three monastic seats *(gdan sa gsum)* of the Ge-luk tradition. They were by far the largest monastic centers in Tibet, if not in the world. In 1959, Dre-pung held more than 13,000 monks; Se-ra, 10,000; and Ga-den, 7,000. Even in exile, they are impressively large; Se-ra has close to 4,000 monks, Dre-pung and Ga-den well over 2,000. For the past three centuries, these three seats have dominated the intellectual life of the Ge-luk tradition and indeed of the whole Tibetan world. They played a role not unlike that of the University of Paris in the thirteenth century, when it drew scholars from all over Europe.[43] Likewise, the three seats have gradually eclipsed other centers of learning, attracting scholars from all over Tibet and even beyond (e.g., from Mongolia). Though important and intellectually active, the La-brang seat was no match for them. In fact, it is a branch monastery of Go-mang, one of the monasteries in Dre-pung. The only Ge-luk monastery that attempted to rival the three monastic universities was Ta-shi Lhun-po, the seat of the Pen-chen Lamas, but its influence was never comparable.

Though these central monasteries are the site of the scholastic culture examined here, their activities are not exclusively scholarly. In fact, like other Tibetan monasteries, they are ritual communities whose members are not required to engage in any scholarship. In Tibet, most monks from the three seats did not engage in scholastic studies. For example, in 1959, among the more than ten thousand monks at Se-ra, only two or three thousand (and probably fewer) were students and scholars.[44] These monasteries were quite different from European medieval universities, at which teachers came together to establish and defend their privileges.[45] The very purpose of such institutions was to provide a haven for intellectual life, and their members were therefore expected to be scholars. Tibetan central monasteries are also quite different from madrassas and yeshivas, which are more strictly religious schools that train scholars in their tradition. Life in them revolves around learning; Tibetan central monasteries are first ritual communities.

THE STRUCTURE OF THE THREE SEATS

The complex structure of these central monasteries varies from monastery to monastery. A sketch of the general structure of the three seats will suffice to convey a sense of the complex institutional framework supporting scholastic studies.

First, the three seats each consist of several monasteries, sometimes misdescribed in the secondary literature as *colleges*. This term wrongly suggests that they are merely subdivisions of a larger unit. But in fact these *monasteries*, as they are called in Tibetan *(gwra tshang)*, and not the *seats*, as they are called in Tibetan *(gdan sa)* and here, are the primary units. Each seat has several monasteries. Dre-pung, for instance, has four monasteries: Lo-se-ling *(blo gsal gling)*, Go-mang *(sgo mang)*, Ngak-pa *(sngags pa,* i.e., "tantric monastery"), and De-yang *(bde yangs)*.[46] Se-ra has three, Jay *(byas)*, May *(smad)*, and Ngak-pa *(sngags pa)*;[47] and Ga-den had two, Shar-tse *(shar rtse)* and Jang-tse *(byang rtse)*. Each of these entities has its own assembly hall, administrative and disciplinary structures, economic basis, monastic constitution, scholastic manuals *(yig cha)*, and internal subdivisions into regional houses *(khang tshan)*. Monks owe their primary allegiance to these monasteries, not to the monastic seat. Thus when asked which monastery he is from, a monk would proudly name (for example) Jay rather than Se-ra.[48]

Each monastic seat is administered by a council *(bla spyi)* composed of the representatives of the monasteries and regional houses, the present and former abbots of each monastery (the seat does not have an abbot), and important monastic officials. The council is charged with deciding questions of discipline and arbitrating conflicts between monasteries. Its decisions are implemented by two head disciplinarians *(tshogs chen zhal ngo)* chosen from the different monasteries, whose authority is backed up by formidable resources. Before 1959, they were granted special judicial status by the government to arbitrate a number of disputes. During the two weeks of the Great Prayer, the two head disciplinarians of Dre-pung could render judgment on any matter brought before them. They and the council have no say in the religious activities of each monastery, however.

Each monastery has its own religious, administrative, and disciplinary structure. Its religious activity is directed by the abbot, who heads it. He, the representatives of each of the regional houses of the monastery, and important monastic officials make up the council that administers the monastery. Discipline is enforced by the disciplinarian *(dge skos)*, whose authority is considerable, though less than that of the seat's head disciplinarians. A prayer leader *(dbu mdzad)* leads the monastic assembly in its ritual performances, and the director of studies *(bla ma gzhung len pa)* oversees the scholastic routine—for example, making sure that the proper debate is held and that exams are administered.

At the lowest level are the regional houses *(khang tshan)*, where monks from the different regions reside, grouped much as scholars in European medieval universities had been (there, by nation).[49] Each monastery is composed of several regional houses that group monks according to regional affiliation. For example, in Dre-pung, Go-mang has sixteen regional houses and Lo-se-ling has twenty-three.[50] In Se-ra, Jay has twenty-two houses and May fourteen; Ngak-ba, the third monastery, has no regional house, as its monks belong to the houses of May and Jay.[51]

Like the medieval "nation," which was headed by a procurer appointed by a council of regents, the regional house is ruled by a council, which appoints a house teacher *(khang tshan dge rgan)* to administer the house. He is in charge of the discipline of the house, ensuring that the schedule is respected, young monks memorize their texts, scholars go to debate, and so on. He must also make certain that monks do not keep knives in their rooms, a reminder of the rather heteroclite nature of the monasteries, where the best scholar would live side by side with the worst punk. As with the other monks in charge of monastic discipline, he could not be criticized while in office, even by the house's council. But once he had served his fixed term (often a year), he could be criticized and even penalized by the council for his actions as a house teacher. This system allowed the administrators sufficient authority to govern a large mass of people who were often quite rowdy and difficult to control. And because they would eventually be held accountable for their actions, they had to be mindful not to overstep their authority.[52]

This description of the monastic chain of command does not begin to communicate the bureaucratic complexities involved in running the three seats. Each corporate entity—that is, seat, monastery, and regional house—was managed financially by a complex administration headed by several stewards *(phyag mdzod)*.[53] Even a single regional house, such as Pu-kang in Dre-pung, would have several people in charge of such tasks. Besides the steward, there were three grain keepers *(gru gnyer)* to oversee the lending of grain and three treasurers *(dngul gnyer)* to manage the transactions of the house.[54]

In Tibet, the financial management of large monastic units involved many people, who gained considerable power in the process. Each corporate entity had large estates on which its subjects *(mi ser)* lived.[55] These were the monastery's taxpayers *(khral pa)*, who were bound to the land. The stewards and their administration had to collect the taxes from these numerous tenants. Dre-pung (the seat, not the monasteries) was said to have 185 estates holding 20,000 subjects and 300 pastures containing 16,000 nomads.[56] Each monastery also had estates from which resources could be extracted through a system of taxes paid in goods (grain or butter) rather than in money. These resources enabled the stewards to engage in a variety of profitable operations. Grain would be lent to the peasants and collected back with interest, at annual rates as high as 20 percent.[57] Butter would either be sold at market or bartered for other goods. These commercial practices, which were the main tasks of monastic financial officers in Tibet, have continued in exile in more modest forms. Monasteries often lend money to Tibetans to engage in petty trade, such as selling sweaters. Statues and other religious objects provide the collateral required by the monastic officers, who are often financially astute.

The administration of these monastic entities in Tibet clearly required real political, administrative, and financial skills of the monks who devoted their lives to these tasks. There was a kind of *cursus honorum* for those interested in the politico-administrative side of monastic life. Monks moved from lower to higher positions, eventually reaching the important jobs that were sources of both honor and considerable rewards. Often, but not always, these were monopolized by monks from an aristocratic background, or by those belonging to one of the large households *(shag tshang chen mo)* of the monastery, or by monks who were rich enough to become a monk-sponsor *(chos mdzad)*. These three categories frequently overlapped. Monk-sponsors were often of an aristocratic background and belonged to one of the more powerful monastic households, which were like small dynasties of monastic administrators. The continuity of these households was ensured by care in taking in new monks—either relatives or promising candidates who could be trusted to maintain the household's influence.[58]

The complexity of these monasteries was also marked by the pomp of their ceremonies and the ornate dress that their officials wore. Temples were filled with great riches: statues in precious metals and adorned with jewels, books in gold leaf, and vast amounts of rich silk brocade. Moreover, the temples also served as reserves where gold bars were hoarded (rather surprisingly, given the extreme poverty of many of their monks). Rituals were also quite elaborate and intricate, with sumptuous offerings made by monks specializing in such tasks. Monastic officials emphasized the power of their office by wearing shirts made of brocade and rich woolen robes; they walked slowly, standing tall and balancing their arms with great dignity. The disciplinarians carried a big staff that stressed the severity of their charge, and would pad their shoulders to appear more formidable.

In exile, these organizations have reappeared on a smaller scale. After arriving in India, the Dalai Lama and his government in exile decided to re-create their scholastic institutions. At first, a select number of monks (around a thousand) from the three seats of Ge-luk and from other traditions were sent to Buxadur in Assam, in Northeast India. There, in rather difficult circumstances, they were able to study. The support of the Indian government enabled them to re-create a solid scholarly culture; young monks who had undergone some training in Tibet became scholars well-educated in their tradition. When the three seats were resettled in Karnataka in South India at the beginning of the 1970s, these monks played a crucial role. They first worked with great energy to build houses and bring the land under cultivation. By the mid-1970s, they had rebuilt the scholarly institutions, but without the pomp and power that formerly had surrounded them in Tibet.

The administrative system illustrates the three main characteristics of Tibetan monasteries: as monastic residencies, as ritual communities organized around the performance of a priestly function, and as corporate entities. Tibetan monasteries are autonomous entities administered by their members in mostly democratic ways. All decisions are made by the assemblies to which all the monastic officers are accountable. But these genuine democratic tendencies are limited by several factors: the power of the central government to intervene in certain matters; the predominance of the large monastic households; the special privileges of the monk-sponsors, who are exempted from a number of menial tasks; and the place of reincarnated lamas, who are given special rights and privileges. These restrictions, though very real, are not very different from those found in any complex society.

Tibetan monasteries are far from being the ideal communities of enlightenment seekers that some imagine. Their activities range from the most ethereal intellectual pursuits to the most mundane administrative tasks. They should certainly not be idealized, for they were made possible by a rather rigid and oppressive social structure. Yet to demonize them would be equally mistaken. As this work shows, Tibetan monasteries were and still are also the centers of a vibrant intellectual culture of the highest caliber, involving great minds, an enormous literary production, and rich philosophical elaborations.

Other aspects of monastic life include the role of the teacher and the nature of monastic discipline. An examination of these elements will lay out the social context in which Tibetan scholasticism takes place and will give me the occasion to include some of my own recollections.

3 Becoming a Monk
Teacher and Discipline

I already described my first day at the Nam-gyel monastery and its difficulties. Things became easier as soon as the second day. I was taken under the protective wing of some monks who helped me get settled and explained to me the rudiments of the monastery's routine. I still remember my first contact with the Nam-gyel community as a whole, at lunch on the second day. At the call of a gong, monks gathered in a large room and sat on thin mats spread over a cement floor. Each monk brought his own plates and received the rather plain and not so plentiful food dished out by the cooks. The meal started with prayers of offering to the Buddha, Dharma, and Sangha and ended with the dedication of the merits gained by those who had provided the meal. I recall that while eating I was as intensely scrutinizing my new "comrades" as I was examined by them. I was relieved to see quite a few faces that looked friendly and almost familiar. Some of the elders appeared welcoming, and many of the young monks seemed interested by this young Westerner who was going to live in their midst for a while. With some of them I felt an immediate sense of kinship, which later developed into friendship. As I discovered much later, the young monks looked on my difficulties with some sympathy. They felt that their situation was in some respects not unlike mine. They had received some modern education before entering the Nam-gyel monastery, where they had to obey the sometimes heavy-handed older generation of monks who had no modern education but were quite proud of their status as members of the Dalai Lama's own monastery.[1]

While staying at Nam-gyel, I had my own private room, a privilege usually available to monks who had finished their training but not to rank beginners like me. I also did not attend liturgical services, which I thought irrelevant to my life as a Buddhist monk (except for the twice-monthly confession ritual in which every monk must take part). I would start my day around five by getting up and (when it was not too cold) going out to the water tap to wash my hands and face. I then cleaned up my room, prepared my altar by filling bowls of offering with water, and burned some incense. I would also go to the kitchen to get a thermos of hot water, which I sipped throughout the day. On returning to my room, I prostrated myself in front of the altar and sat on my bed to meditate. Around half past seven the cook brought breakfast (Tibetan tea and a piece of bread).[2] During the day, I studied Tibetan. I attended a private class given by Lati Rin-po-che and reviewed the lessons I received. I also read books about Buddhism and further practiced meditation, particularly at night. I went to bed around ten, after a last prostration in front of my altar.

This life was very pleasant and probably beneficial. It was the life of a monastic dilettante, which left me free to study and meditate as I felt inclined, without having to follow any discipline other than my own. But the life of Tibetan monks is quite different. To make this clear, I must for a time turn from my own experiences to the more typical career of a young Tibetan monk arriving at one of the central monasteries described in the previous chapter, focusing on his relationship with his teachers—a relationship (at times difficult) around which his entire life in the monastery revolves. Tibetan scholastic culture is based on a model of apprenticeship; it supports the whole monastic culture, which relies on daily discipline to promote certain habits. At the end of this chapter, I recount some of my monastic experiences and introduce my main teachers.

ADMISSION TO THE MONASTERY:
THE ROLE OF THE ROOM TEACHER

In Tibet, central monasteries were institutions devoted to training monks from other monasteries. They therefore were staffed mostly by young monks coming from local monasteries. This was particularly true of the three Ge-luk monastic seats; most of their scholars came from Kham, a province quite unlike Central Tibet (a part of the country more familiar |to Westerners). Kham's inhabitants are often depicted as proud, strong, outspoken, and prone to violence. Offenses are not taken lightly, and vendettas used to go on for generations. In some districts, people also engaged routinely in banditry, raiding the cattle of other districts. Kham-pas were courageous fighters and good horsemen. Above all, they loved their guns, though these were often antiquated; they considered them basic to a man's self-respect. In Kon-jo-ra-wa, the home district of my teacher Gen

Lob-zang Gya-tso, in the southeastern part of Kham near the Burmese border, even monks kept guns and were expected to defend the village against bandits. Gen Lob-zang Gya-tso remembers being given a gun by an uncle in his home monastery and his longing for that gun after leaving for Central Tibet.[3] Kham was also a more egalitarian society than Central Tibet; its wealth was relatively evenly distributed. The large estates so important in the economy of the great monasteries of Central Tibet, and such a source of hardship for peasants, did not exist there. Families mostly worked on their own land.

Young boys first would be sent to the local monasteries, where they would learn basic reading skills and memorize rituals. For example, Gen Lob-zang Gya-tso became a monk by entering the small local Ge-luk monastery of Don-drub-ling *(don grub gling)* at the age of eleven. He could have stayed in this monastery, as his family encouraged him to do. But to qualify as a senior monk, he, like other Ge-luk monks from Kham, had to go to one of the three monastic seats near Lhasa. Most of the monks went in their late teens or early twenties, when they would be best able to endure the hardship of the long trip (made on foot). There they would spend three or more difficult years, homesick, until they could return to their home monastery with the honored rank of a senior monk. Most saw this stay as an ordeal, not an opportunity to study.[4]

When the new recruit *(grwa rgyun)* reached Lhasa, he would enter the monastery with which his home monastery or his family was affiliated. The three seats had a network of monasteries that reached throughout Tibet and even into Mongolia. These affiliated monasteries would send their monks to one particular seat; in exchange, the seat would send an abbot if the monastery requested it. Sometimes, the young monk would have a choice. Coming from Kon-jo-ra-wa, Gen Lob-zang Gya-tso could have entered Se-ra Jay or Dre-pung Lo-se-ling. Since he came with another young man, monastic officials decided that their monastic affiliation would be determined by drawing lots.[5] On the other hand, Geshe Rab-ten *(rab brten*; see figure 4), another teacher of mine, went directly to Se-ra Jay, where he belonged by virtue of his having come from Tar-gye monastery in Tre-hor.

Once the young monk reached the monastery, he would be directed to the appropriate regional house *(khang tshan*; see figure 5). Thus Geshe Rab-ten went to the Tre-hor House of Se-ra Jay because he came from that region. Gen Lob-zang Gya-tso went to the Pu-kang House in Dre-pung Lo-se-ling. Had he gone to Se-ra Jay he would have entered the La House, which grouped monks from his area of Kham. These regional houses in

Tibet provided a very important focus of social life. The three monastic seats were large institutions that encompassed a heterogeneous population. Tibetan monks spoke different dialects, and monks from other countries, particularly Mongolians, did not speak Tibetan at all (though they could debate in it). The regional houses helped integrate these different groups, much as the "nations" at the medieval University of Paris described in chapter 2 helped integrate a student population from all over Europe.

When young monks arrived in Lhasa, they would be placed in a regional house with compatriots who spoke their dialect and with whom they could create strong bonds. Only gradually would they learn enough Central Tibetan to communicate with monks from other parts of Tibet and with local people. These linguistic divisions underscore the importance of regionalism in premodern Tibet. Unlike inhabitants of a modern society, who usually place national before regional loyalties, premodern Tibetans thought first of their regional origin. They were from particular regions of Kham or Central Tibet rather than "Tibetan." The system of regional houses served to further strengthen this loyalty, giving it a religious dimension. It also provided new monks with a manageable social context: a group of a few hundred monks within a monastic seat of more than ten thousand (houses as large as two thousand monks, such as Ham-dong in Se-ra Jay, were possible but rare). Finally, they were crucial in the education of monks. At their weekly or monthly formal debates, young monks could watch or debate with seasoned scholars. Often, but not always, monks would choose their teachers from their own house.[6]

Once the young monk is brought to the regional house, he is given a room teacher *(zhag gi dge rgan)*, thereby beginning one of his most important relationships in his life in the monastery. The room teacher, who often is not well educated, lives with the young monks in his charge and directs their daily life. In the Tibetan Vinaya literature, this teacher is described as the "residence guru" *(gnas kyi bla ma)*. A new monk has to remain under his teacher's direction for the entire time he is a novice and for ten years after being fully ordained. Only then can he be independent, provided that he has the education necessary to conduct himself appropriately. In the practice of the three seats, the room teacher introduces the young monk to monastic customs, making sure that he memorizes the required texts, behaves properly, and goes to the required rituals.

In the Tibetan monasteries where each monk is financially self-sufficient and provides for himself, the room teacher is also in charge of the accounts. The young monk gives to his teacher all the money he has when he enters the monastery and what he earns while living in the monastery. The teacher uses this money to supply food, clothing, and so on. He also provides living quarters, often a room shared with others. The room teacher keeps a detailed record of all expenditures; any money remaining when the young monk leaves the monastery or becomes independent is returned to him. The room teacher is also often the person responsible for his student's behavior. He will be punished by the monastic authorities if the young monk gets in trouble. Because his role is limited to these mundane (though extensive) aspects of life, such a teacher is also called "worldly teacher" ('jig rten dge rgan).

The student's relation with his room teacher is thus crucial, largely determining the quality of his life. If it works out well, the young monk can look forward to a relatively happy life in the monastic seat. Things do not always go smoothly, however. A common source of tension is the financial relationship between the two. Teachers or students can become suspicious or greedy and even rob each other. Some teachers use their students to further their own businesses. Gen Lob-zang Gya-tso notes with some bitterness that his teacher cared more for collecting debt than for looking after his education. Instead of studying, he was expected to squeeze money out of very poor families, who had barely enough to eat.[7]

Teachers may strictly hold their students to a rigid discipline, fearing that otherwise they will get in trouble. Some teachers are abusive and beat their protégés. In general, the traditional Tibetan attitude toward corporal punishment is at odds with modern sensibilities. To punish is to brand a person—inflicting some suffering and humiliation—for having crossed the authorized boundaries. In traditional societies, the suffering is often inscribed in brutal and spectacular ways on the body of the guilty party, whereas in the modern West the punishment is more efficiently internalized.[8] While punishment that is physical is not necessarily worse than other forms, it easily leads to abuse. Though such abuses are frowned on, there is no formal mechanism to stop them. Other monks may intercede by reasoning with the room teacher, but he cannot be disciplined for beating his student. During my stays in monasteries, I heard a number of young men screaming. I have also been told many stories of blatant abuses. Yet it is hard to ascertain the extent of such behavior. I rarely noticed physical marks, though I did hear of a few monks who ran away from their teacher.

Before starting his scholastic career, the young monk must be formally admitted to the monastery. That this is done at the behest of the room teacher is another indication of the latter's central role in the newcomer's social integration. The room teacher approaches the house teacher, who takes the young monk for an audience with the abbot. There the young monk prostrates himself three times to the abbot and offers him Tibetan tea (with butter) and a ceremonial scarf. The rules of the monastery specify that the "ceremonial scarf [should be] as clean as possible. The butter to be used in the tea [should be] as delicious as possible and the tea as fine as possible so as to insure that the lord refuge, the precious abbot finds it to his liking."[9] The abbot briefly questions the house teacher and the candidate to verify that the latter has been assigned to the proper regional house, is of sound mind, and is not too arrogant. The postulant can attend monastic rituals provisionally until he has memorized the prescribed texts. Only then is he admitted as a full member of the monastery and allowed to take part in scholastic education. Before that admission, the postulant must make offerings to his house. If he is poor, he will offer just tea. If he is richer, he can make larger gifts and become a monk-sponsor *(chos mdzad)*, a title that relieves him of a number of monastic chores. Reincarnated lamas (discussed below) make even larger offerings, in exchange for which they receive honors proportional to their generosity.[10] This mandatory gift, required for admission to the corporate body and repeated at the end of the studies, is quite like the food given by candidates to European medieval universities to seal their integration into the new community.[11]

THE ROLE OF THE SCHOLASTIC TEACHER

When the postulant is ready to start his scholastic career, he must choose a "text teacher" *(dpe cha'i dge rgan)*, who is in charge of his scholastic and spiritual education. This choice is another major event in the life of a new monk, since it is left to the individuals involved. In the three Ge-luk monastic seats, classes—that is, cohorts—are institutionally structured, as we will see in chapter 11, but the relation between the teacher and the student is not. Each student seeks his own teacher, who agrees to take him as a disciple. A teacher severs this personal relationship, once undertaken, only rarely and under extraordinary circumstances. A student may, and indeed frequently does, study with another teacher, but he must be careful first to consult his text teacher.

In practice, the freedom of choice is limited. Often the room teacher directs his protégé to a teacher with whom he already has a special link. In pre-1959 Tibet, where the institutions were large, regional loyalty often determined the outcome: monks tended to choose their teacher within the network of their regional house. Yet some students based their choices on intellectual inclinations. For example, when Ge-dün Chö-pel came to Go-mang monastery of Dre-pung in 1927, he chose Geshe Shay-rab Gyatso *(shes rab rgya tsho)* as his teacher because of the latter's reputation as having an unconventional and sharp mind.[12] Finally, it must be noted that in Tibet finding a qualified teacher was not easy. Often students who asked for a famous teacher were directed to less qualified disciples.

In exile, the institutions are smaller, the choice of teachers more limited, and the regional loyalties less relevant; monks often choose their teachers purely for their scholarly reputations. At Lo-se-ling, for example, most of the students attended the classes of the most famous teachers, Gen Nyi-ma and Kensur Pe-ma Gyel-tsen. There are also subtle variations among the monasteries. Because Se-ra Jay particularly stresses the personal link between student and teacher, monks there often confine themselves to a single teacher for the entire curriculum. To study with another teacher is considered disrespectful, breaking the close tie between student and teacher. At Lo-se-ling, where flexibility is greater, monks can have several teachers.

In newer institutions, such as the Buddhist School of Dialectic in Dharamsala or the Commentarial School of Nam-dröl-ling in Bylakuppe, the relation between student and teacher is more routinized than in the three monastic seats. A teacher is assigned to a class, and its members must all accept him as their teacher. This change reflects only a partial and limited move toward modernizing studies, however. For even when the teacher is assigned by the school, each student is expected to develop a personal relationship with him. The students who are unable to establish such a tie drop out and find a more appropriate setting for their studies.

Traditional Tibetan education depends heavily on a close and intensely personal link between students and teachers. In this respect, it is more akin to an apprenticeship than to modern schooling. Timothy Mitchell, in describing a similar education in Islamic madrassas, clearly conveys the importance of interpersonal connections:

> Learning occurred as a relationship that, as in every craft, might be found between any individuals at almost any point. Beginners learned from one another, according to their differing aptitudes, as much as from those who were masters; and even masters continued to learn from those who possessed skills, who had mastered other texts. The method was one of argumentation and dispute, not one of lecturing. The individual was to be deferent where appropriate, but never passive.[13]

Reliance on personal relationships, particularly those with the teacher, is probably even stronger among Tibetans. Parents instill respect for teachers in their children from a very young age. As one monk explains, "In Tibet we have always considered it extremely important to obey religious teachers. . . . We had the same reverence for our teachers as for our parents."[14]

Very young children are commonly taken to religious teachers so that they develop the habit of showing respect, often through physical prostrations. Masters are also invited home and children are made to serve them, thereby acquiring the proper respectful attitude. Such early training in obedience and respect is reinforced within the monastery, as new monks establish close relationships with their teachers.

In secular schools as well, education was based on a personal relationship between student and teacher. He (or more rarely she) would be called *Gen-la* (respected teacher) by the students, showing a respect close to that held for one's religious teacher. It is difficult to overemphasize the importance of this relationship in Tibetan culture. Even young Tibetans educated in modern institutions still actively display respect toward their teachers.

THE ROLES OF THE GURU

The guru is another crucial element of Tibetan Buddhism. That this Indian word is translated as *lama (bla ma)* indicates its centrality to the tradition.[15] It is not by accident that L. A. Waddell titled his book *Buddhism of Tibet, or Lamaism*.[16] For him, the term implied a scathing indictment of Tibetan Buddhism, marking a fall from the original purity of its founder's message (much as *papism* was used of Catholicism to signify a degenerate form of the pristine Christian message). Used without an attached value judgment, the term marks the fundamental role of the guru in the Tibetan tradition.

In some ways, all the teachers mentioned here are gurus, insofar as they give spiritual instruction. But Tibetan usage is more selective. The common Tibetan word for "teacher" is *dge rgan* (pronounced "gay-gen"), which is applied to anyone who conveys knowledge or contributes in any way to a person's education. In a more strictly religious context, teachers are called *gurus* or "spiritual friends" *(kalyāṇamitra, dge ba'i bshes gnyen)*. Often the two terms are taken as equivalent. Sometimes (and this is the convention I will follow here) *guru* is reserved for the tantric teacher, who imparts "empowerments" *(dbang)*, "transmissions" *(lung)*, and "special instructions" *(man ngag)*. Such a teacher should be considered an enlightened being who is to be given the greatest respect and even worshiped. The term *spiritual friend* is applied more generally to any teacher with whom one freely and mutually decides to enter into a religious relation.[17] Such a teacher imparts religious instructions of practical relevance, by virtue of his status as a moral and religious exemplar. He is also intensely respected, though he may not be given the quasi-divine status of the tantric guru.

But it would be naive to assume that teachers or gurus are only intellectual and spiritual figures. In Tibetan Buddhism, religious leaders frequently were and still are powerful political figures with their own following and power base. Often these figures of authority, for whom I will reserve
the term *lama*, are reincarnated lamas or *tulkus (sprul sku)*, who play a
central role in the traditional life of Tibetans as the leaders of Tibetan society, heading schools and monasteries. They are called *rin-po-che* (precious
one)[18] and draw the veneration and loyalty of laypeople. Their often substantial holdings are considered to be part of the lama's estate *(bla brang)*.
When a particular lama passes away, his property remains in the estate,
which is inherited by his successor.

Literally, *tulku* means "emanation body" and refers to the embodiment
of buddhas in this world. But when used of lamas, the term is understood
rather loosely. Theoretically, a reincarnated lama is a realized being with the
ability to take birth wherever he or she chooses it. Hence, his new incarnation, unlike that of ordinary beings, can be traced. In practice, however,
Tibetans differentiate among tulkus, who are seen to display a wide range
of qualities. Some are greatly revered, whereas others are viewed more crit-
ically. In any case, the complexity of Tibetans' attitudes toward these figures contrasts sharply with the naive literalism of many Westerners.

Tibetan Buddhism is replete with teachings about devotion to one's
teacher *(bshes gnyen bsten tshul;* lit., "way of relying on one's spiritual
friend"). In the Stages of the Path literature, such devotion is presented as an
indispensable prerequisite for higher tantric practices.[19] The teacher is not
just an ordinary person with some special qualifications but a divinized being, a fully enlightened figure who has assumed an ordinary appearance to
help his student.[20] Some practitioners take their devotion to the guru quite
far. Geshe Rab-ten, my first teacher, was extremely devoted to his teacher.
When Geshe Rab-ten came to Se-ra from his native province of Tre-hor in
Kham, he became the disciple of Geshe Jam-pa Kay-drup *(byams pa mkhas
grub)*. He served his teacher, bringing his meals and cleaning his room. In
the morning, he would rise first and wake his teacher. Geshe Rab-ten also insisted on taking out the chamber pot that his teacher used during the night.
Every morning, he would partake of his teacher's substance as a blessing:

> I would place [the pot] on my head and offer a prayer. Then I would
> pour a little in my hand, drink it and throw the rest away. This is not a
> Tibetan or a monkish custom. I was moved to do so by my deep faith in
> my guru, although there is no necessary relationship between drinking
> urine and receiving his blessing. There is one only if one has heartfelt
> faith in the guru.[21]

Such behavior exemplifies a kind of *bhakti,* a total devotion in which one intensely feels a union with the object of one's love. It also illustrates the guru's divinization. Each aspect of his person, not just his teachings, is held to be sacred. Even his bodily emissions are blessings.

After a few years, Geshe Jam-pa Kay-drup went back to his native Tre-hor. Geshe Rab-ten stayed behind in Se-ra, studying and practicing as ordered by his teacher. He nevertheless longed to see him again. After the departure of another teacher, Geshe Rab-ten decided that he could not stand the separation. He "simply had to be with [his] guru again, at least for a short time." [22] After three months of dangerous travel on horseback, Geshe Rab-ten arrived in Tre-hor. But far from welcoming him, Geshe Jam-pa Kay-drup refused to see him until he had sworn that he would go back as soon as possible to continue his studies in Se-ra. Geshe Rab-ten was devastated, but he had to obey. After a few months, he returned to Central Tibet and never saw his teacher again.

DISCIPLINE

Discipline also plays a central role in the monastic career. This is particularly true for new monks, who have to undergo a trial period (not unlike army boot camp) that can last for several years in the stricter institutions. In Western medieval universities, students were put through brief but elaborate parodic ceremonies of initiation in which newcomers were cleansed of their former uneducated condition. [23] A prolonged period of trial has a quite different purpose and must be understood in relation to the overall ethical goal of monastic education: to develop goodness.

Goodness involves making good decisions, relying not on theoretical reflection but on good character and the ability to discriminate between objects of desire. In most cases, the great challenge is not knowing what the good is but being capable of doing it. Our desires compel us to perform actions that we know to be bad. In order to remedy this weakness, we need to develop the ability to differentiate between mere compulsions and the inclinations we want to encourage because we judge them to be good. Such ability requires training to strengthen the necessary habits.

That training begins in the monastic trial period. The boot camp–like atmosphere encourages young monks to resist everyday compulsions, such as the desire for sense objects. It also gives the trainees the ability to act immediately. Goodness requires that we act for good reasons, which must be internalized. Such internalization is achieved as trainees repeat actions under intense pressure and thereby develop the habit of responding appropriately. Such training also develops the kind of social relationship that supports goodness, creating a community of like-minded people on whom members can rely to further strengthen the required qualities. Finally, it aids agents in seeing how their practice fits into the overall unity of their life. As the philosopher Alasdair MacIntyre explains,

> The agent's life thus should exhibit and exhibit increasingly some degree of overall directedness, a certain narrative unity, so that retrospectively earlier stages in life can be understood as just that, stages on the way to something not yet adequately, but increasingly characterizable. . . . Desire, that is to say, will have been directed towards a further and ultimate object, one in which, were it to be achieved, it could rest satisfied, and one in which, were it not to be achieved, it would be permanently unsatisfied.[24]

In an ethical life, unity is imposed by the goal toward which one's actions are directed.

Like army recruits in boot camp, new monks in strict institutions live under a strenuously enforced discipline. They are often scolded by elders, constantly watched, and frequently subjected to pain. In the Tantric Monastery of Higher (Lhasa), for example, new monks had to sleep in extremely cramped conditions in a single room under the supervision of an older monk for their first three years in the monastery. They were also required for their first nine years to attend all the ritual services of the monastery without exception.[25] In Dak-po, monks were on trial for nine years.[26] During this time, they could sleep no longer than three to four hours a night, again in a single room. Only after this protracted ordeal were the monks fully integrated into the community and given all the rights and privileges of full membership.

In the three seats, newcomers suffered less severe hardships. Still, they were held to a rigorous discipline. They had to spend evenings in their room, reciting the texts they had memorized during the day. They also had to behave with restraint and show special signs of respect toward elders. Geshe Rab-ten used to joke about my lack of external decorum—my propensity to look around, fling my arms about while walking, and the like. Such behavior would have drawn the attention of the monastic authorities in Tibet and been promptly punished. "You are lucky not to be in Tibet," he told me, "for you are the kind of person that would have received constant beatings."

This discipline helped sustain Tibet's monastic communities for centuries. Large and long-lasting communities in which many people act in coordination require special mechanisms of socialization, or what Michel Foucault called technologies of power: that is, micro-practices that aim at forming efficient members of a community and transforming them into "docile bodies."[27] The intense pressure helped mold new monks to internalize the discipline, which could then effectively shape the characters and personalities of the newcomers. As they are formed into members of the community, they develop the kind of restraint and respect for decorum central to Buddhist monasticism.

But the discipline of the three seats applied beyond newcomers; scholars *(dpe cha ba)* followed a strict schedule throughout their scholarly training (as we will see in chapter 11). While most monks *(grwa mang)* led a relatively easy life, that of scholars was rigorous—particularly during debate sessions *(chos thog)*, when the day started around five in the morning and lasted until eleven at night. During the sessions, monks alternated between rituals, studies, and debate, with very little time to rest. In some monasteries, certain classes had to debate for entire nights. For example, during two years in their scholarly training, monks of Se-ra Jay had to stay up on alternate days and debate throughout the night.

The intensity of this discipline was further increased by the physical hardships caused by impoverishment. In Tibet, large monasteries did not provide for their members, except at assemblies at which tea was served.[28] If the sponsor was generous, food would be served as well, but such generosity was uncommon. Hence, monks largely provided for themselves with the help of their families and donors. Nonscholars often supplemented their income by practicing rituals at the home of donors, but scholars devoted themselves single-mindedly to their studies. This system created great difficulties, particularly for young scholars coming from Kham or Amdo.[29] Far from home (many had to travel more than three months to reach Lhasa), they could not ask for their family's support and many lived in appalling poverty. Geshe Rab-ten recalls his living conditions:

> I remained poor until I had become a senior monk. But I continued my studies, and by remembering the purpose of my coming—to cultivate my mind—I did not become discouraged. Through all these years of poverty, I never had anything that was good. Since my shoes always had holes, I often walked barefoot on the cold stone floors. For several years I was so ill that on returning from debate, I sometimes could not climb the stone steps leading to our house, but had to crawl on all fours. . . . I had only ragged cloths that other people had given me, and since I was not concerned with my appearance, instead of sewing the pieces together, I joined them with bits of wire.[30]

Although Geshe Rab-ten's poverty was extreme, many monks report similar experiences. It was quite common for them to run out of food, going hungry for several days until they received some donation that would allow them to buy something to eat. Moreover, there was little variety in the food they ate. Many lived almost exclusively on *tsampa* (roasted barley flour) and butter tea.

I believe that these hardships played an important role in the life of these scholars. They created an atmosphere that led monks to develop new habits and stifle old ones, particularly those antithetical to monasticism. Immersed in a life of singular intensity, scholars ignored the usual desires and redirected their attention to soteriological concerns. Hardships helped in this process, strengthening the scholars' resolution and providing the pressure that effected their transformation. Discarding one's hedonistic desires is never easy, but the task's difficulty is magnified when one is living in comfort, with pleasures readily available. To break away from such desires, it is helpful to enter a new situation from which those pleasures are absent. That is what monasticism is supposed to provide. But mere absence is not enough. The pressure of the milieu and the hardships encountered help break the hold that desires have on one's mind, creating new patterns in which soteriology is central.

Hermits report undergoing a similar experience. Their career often starts with great difficulties: they lack food, fall sick, experience mental problems, and so on. But once they overcome these difficulties, they progress quickly and easily. This pattern, equally clear in the life of many saints, suggests that those initial difficulties are not just obstacles but vital elements of the story. They create the kind of pressure under which inclinations can be reordered. After this transformation, the practice becomes easy, effortless, and intensely fulfilling. So, too, the great hardships and the intense discipline of Tibetan scholars push them toward the change in inclinations necessary to achieve their goal.

This reordering is also greatly enhanced by the narrative unity that scholars find in their existence. As I will show in chapter 8, providing such unity is one of the central tasks of scholastic education, which is often less a direct preparation to meditative practice than an intellectually rigorous framework in which Buddhist practice makes sense. Developing a meaningful narrative structure contributes powerfully to the effectiveness of the discipline. It confirms the value of the tradition and justifies its members in the sacrifices that they have made. It gives them a sense of purpose and achievement, encouraging a decisiveness and resolution that serve them well in their future religious and worldly endeavors.

PERSONAL RECOLLECTIONS: MY FIRST TEACHER

It is this kind of culture that I stumbled on in 1970 when I made my way to Dharamsala as described above. I had heard that Geshe Rab-ten offered classes on Buddhism and I decided to attend them. Geshe Rab-ten must have been close to fifty. He was living on a hill in the mountains in a small and rather uncomfortable hut with a dirt floor and a roof that provided little insulation from the cold. He had few belongings (mostly books) and even fewer amenities. Geshe-la spent his days meditating on his bed, wrapped in a warm monastic coat. He would receive us in the afternoon and teach through his translator, Gonsar Tulku, a charming young reincarnated lama. These two figures offered a striking contrast. Geshe-la was a solid, short, and sturdy man from a peasant family in the province of Tre-hor. He was one of the successful Kham-pa who had come to Central Tibet in their late teens and made a name for themselves as scholars (a familiar pattern) by their own efforts. His translator, who was by then in his early twenties, was tall and thin, with beautiful long hands that gave him an air of refinement and distinction common to members of Tibetan aristocratic families.

Geshe Rab-ten's first few teachings persuaded me to stay in Dharamsala to study this tradition. I had no special revelation, but the teaching of the four noble truths made a lot of sense, answering several of the most important questions I had entertained while growing up in Switzerland. In my early teens I had been intensely preoccupied by death. I would lie in bed, utterly terrorized by the idea that after I died I would forever cease to be. I would then try to reason with myself, pointing out that this condition was not very different from that experienced before my birth. Alternatively, death was not unlike deep sleep, when we lose sense of ourselves. And yet, none of these answers would satisfy and I would anxiously clutch my pillow until sleep put a merciful end to this ordeal. At the same time, I was wondering about the nature of personal identity. I often thought, "Who am I?" "Am I just the chance result of my parents' encounter, or do I have some kind of enduring personal reality?" "What would have happened if my parents had not met each other? Would I exist?"

None of the people around me seemed to have anything to say about these common but fundamental questions. My father, who was a medical doctor, was an intellectual with strong interests in a variety of fields, including physics, biology, history, and anthropology, but he could not offer much philosophical help. The other members of my family, with whom I had less contact, were mostly absorbed by the chores of daily life and seemed to offer even less. The rabbi to whom my father sent me for religious instruction as a token of loyalty to his parents seemed more interested in dogmatically upholding the absolute validity of his tradition than in answering existential questions. School was for the most part a disappointment. Though it was a community of people engaged in intellectual issues—which I now realize is already more than most teenagers find—I felt it offered me little to sustain a life of the mind. The greatest excitement came from my own readings, particularly the existentialist novels of Malraux and Camus, who seemed to deal with the questions that were preoccupying me but gave rather grim answers.

Geshe Rab-ten's Buddhist analysis of life as being unsatisfactory, his depiction of the restless search for an unreachable satisfaction, immediately appealed to my sensibility, as did the Buddhist views that there is no abiding self and that reality is fundamentally dynamic and changing. By pointing out that the problem is with the framing of the question—the assumption that there is a self—Buddhism addressed my questions in a way that immediately inspired me, though I did not understand its intricacies. Finally, the claim that liberation from suffering is possible opened new perspectives, which Geshe Rab-ten's own strength seemed to embody. Here was an intelligent person who offered no quick fix or promise of redemption but rather a long and difficult path of cultivating virtue, a path that seemed to offer the resources to address my questions. Of course, I did not share a number of ideas presupposed by his teachings. The idea of reincarnation seemed to me downright outlandish, a position that had obvious consequences for the possibility of a complete liberation from suffering. Nevertheless, I could sense in Geshe Rab-ten a person who embodied a meaningful path.

I was greatly impressed by Geshe-la's qualities—his personal solidity, the sharpness of his mind, his obvious mastery of his tradition—which were manifest in the crystal-clear teachings he gave.[31] I was also impressed by his confidence in the validity of his tradition, displayed in a readiness to discuss any question. Students could raise many questions, and Geshe-la always had an answer, usually a very good one, which he proposed on its own merits, not relying on the authority of the tradition or himself. Moreover, students, like grown-ups, were given the freedom to think for themselves. When they encountered difficult topics, such as reincarnation and karma, Geshe-la would advocate that they provisionally suspend judgment: "You will be able to form a better judgment later through more study and practice. For now, it does not matter; just go on studying and practicing."

This attitude, which reflected a view that belief was not a precondition of religious engagement but rather derived from a reasoned inquiry into the tradition, contrasted favorably in my mind with the religious traditions I had been exposed to earlier.

At the end of these teachings, Geshe-la left for a pilgrimage. Before leaving, he recommended that we spend the next few months trying to practice the teachings he had given us, particularly concentration on a single point. At first I was very eager to practice this meditation, which consisted of visualizing the deity to whom we had been assigned. The practice of tranquillity *(zhi gnas, śamatha)* can lead to a state of total absorption that can be exhilarating, though this can threaten the development of the more important virtues, such as detachment and compassion. But I soon realized that my expectation of experiencing the joys of concentration was premature, to say the least. My restless mind refused to concentrate, and I was left to shiver in the freezing Dharamsala winter in a house that had been built as a summer residence. I was joined in this endeavor by a young Frenchman who had come to Dharamsala a few weeks before me to be ordained as a monk and who shared in my difficulties.

When Geshe Rab-ten returned at the end of February, we rushed to see him, confessing our defeat. Geshe-la laughed, and said he had not expected us to succeed. Most people require long preparation to meditate, he said. We should learn Tibetan and turn our attention to study. That would enable us to steady our minds and harden our commitment to practice. At that point, I asked Geshe-la if he would ordain me as a monk and allow me to follow my friend, who was about to move into the monastery. I told him that I would like to stay in Dharamsala, instead of going to a Western university. If I stayed, I wanted the best training, and to me that meant becoming a monk, the only choice that allowed a total commitment to the study and practice of Buddhism within a community of like-minded people.

Geshe-la answered that I would need to speak to the Dalai Lama, who would decide whether I could join a monastery, and so I did. My audience with the Dalai Lama was somewhat surprising and upsetting. I was not prepared for a person who was so obviously exceptional. I had expected him to confirm my somewhat cynical view of authorities and celebrities, but his qualities matched in every respect his fame and position. I was impressed by his compassion, which was displayed not just in his kindness but in a quality of attention to others that I had never before encountered. Here was a person who was totally concerned with his interlocutor, who was a complete stranger. I was also struck by his enormous intelligence, his lucidity, and his pragmatic and irreverent readiness to discard elements of his tradition.

The immediate outcome of this first audience was not what I had hoped for. The Dalai Lama was rather evasive and did not allow me to join my friend in his monastery. I was bitterly disappointed, and started to wonder whether I should stay in Dharamsala or try my luck somewhere else. A few days later, however, I received a message through Geshe-la's translator. My wishes would be fulfilled! To this day, I do not know what made the Dalai Lama change his mind. My guess is that Geshe Rab-ten interceded in my favor, but I never dared to ask him. Two days later, I went to the Nam-gyel monastery, where I started my new career.

FIRST MONASTIC EXPERIENCE

Though my time at the Nam-gyel monastery was at first not easy, it turned out to be immensely fruitful. The presence of my friend was helpful. We spoke the same language and could easily bond in the face of the opposition we encountered, but it was hard not to notice that we were not exactly welcome. Our first task was to learn Tibetan, but few scholarly aids existed and several of the books that might have helped were out of print. It was also difficult to find a monk at the monastery who could teach us. Most of them were busy with the ritual routine of the monastery and few had much linguistic talent. We had to learn mostly by trial and error. We would write sentences in Tibetan and ask young monks to correct them. At times, they would look at our sentences with total bafflement, completely unable to figure what we could possibly have meant. At other times, they would approve them. Often this was a good sign. But later I discovered that what they had understood did not necessarily coincide with what I had intended the sentence to mean!

Nevertheless, despite (or perhaps because of) these difficulties, our Tibetan quickly improved and our isolation lessened. Younger monks had been quite friendly all along, and eventually even older monks became more accepting of our presence. Even the manager, who had been our nemesis from the very first day, became almost pleasant. The elders had thought that we were simply nosy Westerners who would leave after satisfying their curiosity. When they realized after a year or so that we were staying and that we were managing to learn their language, their attitude shifted. Though we were not and never would be members of their monastery since we were not interested in the monastery's ritual activities, we were people with whom they had established a strong bond.[32] As a token of their appreciation, the monastery decided to decrease the already small amount that we were paying for food (around fifteen dollars a month). At first the monastery had rather generously decided that they would charge us only for board, not for room. Not understanding the corporate nature of Tibetan monasteries and remaining blind to the unreasonableness of our expectation that a Tibetan refugee community should support privileged members of the Western middle class, we were hurt at having to pay any fee, which seemed to deny our status as Buddhist monks. Mindful of our feelings, the monastery opted for a compromise, which would show their appreciation without making us members of the monastery.

During these fruitful two years spent at Nam-gyel, we studied the basic Buddhist practices contained in the Stages of the Path literature under Lati Rin-po-che and attempted to practice them. Lati Rin-po-che, a highly respected and very learned teacher, was strict and quite conservative. He had been ordered by the Dalai Lama to teach us and he did. But he was skeptical about our prospects, at least for the first year. Indeed, at one point, he seemed to lose all interest in us. We became rather anxious and started to think about other alternatives, but could not find any other teacher. In desperation, we approached the Dalai Lama, fearful of being rebuked for our impatience. His reaction surprised us and exceeded our wildest dreams. The Dalai Lama smiled and asked whether there was any other problem. No, there was no other problem, we replied, but wasn't it bad enough that we had had so few teachings? "Oh, don't worry! This can be fixed very easily," he replied. We left, still unsure of what that meant, and went back to our rooms. A few minutes later we saw Lati Rin-po-che walking rather energetically toward the Dalai Lama's residence. After a few minutes we saw him retracing his steps in a rather somber mood. Soon after, we were called to his room. "Henceforth, you will have classes every day," said Lati Rin-po-che in a glacial tone. At first we felt uncomfortable at his obvious annoyance at having to teach us. Over time, however, he warmed up to us, especially after we were able to follow his teachings without a translator. He became eager to teach us and showed amazing patience at our attempts to understand his excellent and clear teachings.

When we completed our study of the Gradual Path in 1973, we asked the Dalai Lama, who had by now become something of an academic adviser, what we should do. His answer was that we had the choice between two monastic careers: the hermitic or the scholarly. We could go into prolonged retreat and become meditators, or we could enter the lengthy course of a scholarly career, which would give us the solid ethical and mental discipline required for Buddhist practice. His own advice was to follow the second way. As he put it, "You will have gray hair when you are finished, but it's worth it!" We both took that advice, but my friend was not so pleased with it; after trying the scholarly path for a while, he left the monastery to attempt the more arduous task of intensive hermitic practice. I was delighted at the prospect of a rigorous intellectual education, which corresponded to my background and inclination. Accordingly, the Dalai Lama directed me toward the Buddhist School of Dialectics, which was about to open. There, my experience was going to be quite different. My serious training was just beginning.

GETTING (A BIT MORE) SERIOUS

The Buddhist School of Dialectics was intended for young Tibetans who had finished high school and wanted to become monks but were reluctant to enter one of the large monastic educational centers, where the narrowness of the traditional outlook can sometimes be stifling. Up until then, these young people had nowhere to go; most of them soon lost their interest in Buddhism. To remedy this situation, the Dalai Lama opened a school for them and entrusted its direction to Gen Lob-zang Gya-tso. Gen-la, who had first suggested the idea of such a school, was uniquely suited to the task. He was a well-trained scholar but also had some experience with modern education through his work as a teacher of Tibetan language in the Central School for Tibetans in Mussoorie, one of the several high schools run by the Tibetan government in exile. This exposure had given him an understanding of the modern world unusual for a member of a generation that had grown up almost completely outside of any modern influence.

My first meeting with Gen Lob-zang Gya-tso was a pleasant surprise. He was quite different from the conservative Lati Rin-po-che, whose knowledge I greatly appreciated but with whom I could never feel comfortable. Most traditional Tibetans tend to assume that foreigners are rather limited in their abilities, but Gen Lob-zang Gya-tso was unusually broad-minded. He never doubted the abilities of Westerners, and I felt welcomed and accepted as a full member of the community. He also understood quite well that Westerners had special needs and could not be expected to do exactly as Tibetans, though I would have to follow the routine of the school.

In June 1973, the Buddhist School of Dialectics opened its doors and I moved in. The school was located in a small two-story building, near

Nam-gyel monastery. We were eighteen students living in eight rooms, two of which were inhabited by only one person. I was not given one of these private rooms but had to share a larger space with two other monks. Gone was my privacy, the hours of study in the relative quiet of a Tibetan monastic room. Instead of having noise outside my windows, I now had two roommates, who were delightful companions but spent long hours in loud recitations.

My first years at the Buddhist School were extremely fulfilling and pleasant, except for the external difficulties that seemed to multiply. I felt accepted by the students. Because they had been educated in the modern curriculum of the schools of the Tibetan government in exile, they felt comfortable with Westerners. In addition, I was doing quite well academically. I learned to memorize, and my previous exposure to debate gave me an advantage over the other students. I felt valorized and appreciated; but more important, I felt that I was starting to get the kind of training that would enable me to take my Buddhist fate into my own hands, rather than blindly follow the advice of my teachers.

Moreover, the school atmosphere was good-humored and extremely friendly. In general, friendship is a central element, even a virtue, of monastic life. It is visible in the readiness with which monks help each other, particularly in times of sickness. I myself fell very sick (probably with hepatitis) shortly after my return from Switzerland in 1975. I could neither eat nor sleep. I quickly wasted away and soon could not even walk. My two roommates had to do everything for me. They carried me to the bathroom, cooked special food for me, tried to make me eat, and went to fetch medicines. In doing so they were following Gen-la's order, but they did not consider their actions exceptional. Since monks do not have families to take care of them, that task must be performed by the members of the community. Caring for a sick class- or roommate was thus thought to be a routine matter, though demanding at times.

But the intensity of friendship at the school went beyond the kind of solidarity normally expected of monks and even of laypeople in a society in which services are rare and communal aid indispensable. Our community was small and extremely cohesive. Many of the students knew each other prior to entering the school, though those friendships did not interfere with their relations with other students. All the students had an open attitude and nobody felt left out; indeed, most were unusually warmhearted. Tibetans coming from the outside would often comment on how impressed they were by the students' behavior. I am not sure to what this moral excellence was due (certainly not to their being monks, for I have met some pretty nasty characters in Tibetan monasteries), but I always felt privileged to live among such wonderful friends.

The camaraderie was all the stronger because of our poor living conditions. The food was rather scanty and although we were not hungry, we were definitely stretching the limits of a healthy diet for a normal human being, even in a so-called third world country. Gen-la could have gotten more support from the Dalai Lama, who was, and still is, financing the school, but he adamantly refused to do so, claiming that hardship strengthens character and commitment. He himself refused any special treatment or any special financial compensation for his work, and received the same fifteen rupees (then two dollars) per month that every student received to provide for basic needs (such as clothing, washing supplies, etc.) other than food and lodging.

This approach seemed at first to work and the first year was a great success. The difficulties strengthened the bond of solidarity that united the community into which we had freely entered, creating a sense of achievement we could be proud of. We also took hardship with the humor that is often the mark of Tibetan monks. But those hardships started to take their toll. Students fell sick, and after a year one of them died of tuberculosis. Still Gen-la, who for all his fine qualities was extraordinarily opinionated, insisted on maintaining the status quo. Several other students fell sick. I had to leave the school to recover in Switzerland. After a particularly impressive number of students became ill, Gen-la finally gave in and improved the living standard of the school—to the great relief of other students, who did not have the privilege of going back to their country to recover!

These three teachers, Geshe Rab-ten, Lati Rin-po-che, and Gen Lobzang Gya-tso, were my first. Although I did not always study with them, throughout the years I kept in close touch and felt close to them—particularly to Geshe Rab-ten, who often played the role of a stern but loving parent. In later years, when I started to study in the three monastic seats, I encountered other teachers. Following the Dalai Lama's advice, I began visiting the three monastic seats in the winter, usually spending a season in one of them debating the topics I had already studied at the Buddhist School. There I had the privilege of following the classes of several excellent teachers, two of whom will figure prominently in this work: Gen Pema Gyel-tsen, who was a masterful commentator (see chapter 7), and Gen Nyi-ma, a master of logic, epistemology, and Madhyamaka philosophy who figures largely in my discussion of debate. These two famous teachers represent well the great accomplishments of the old generation of Tibetan masters. Together with the three teachers described above and others mentioned later, these great teachers trained me in their tradition. They devoted hundreds of hours to educating me, in utter disregard of their receiving no compensation for their teachings. Moreover, the results of their hard work were impossible to predict. Here was this Westerner, who could leave them any minute to do something entirely unrelated. Would their efforts bear any fruit, or would they go entirely wasted? That my teachers chose to help me despite these considerable uncertainties shows their enormous compassion. It is because of their kindness that I was able to follow the training of Tibetan monks, an experience that I attempt to re-create in the following pages.

Part 2

TIBETAN SCHOLASTIC PRACTICES

4 Literacy and Memorization

In the following discussion, I distinguish three stages or aspects of Tibetan monastic education. It begins with memorization and the acquisition of basic literacy, the heuristic procedures examined in this chapter, followed by two central hermeneutic practices, commentary and debate (each examined later in part 2). By *heuristic*, I mean a technique, itself unproven, that is valuable as an aid for learning or for stimulating and conducting investigations.[1] Gaining basic literacy is one such technique; another, and my main focus here, is committing a large amount of textual material to memory, a practice that Tibetan monks engage in extensively and that helps them store, organize, and retrieve the content of the whole curriculum.

My own encounter with the intense training in memorization on which traditional scholarly training is founded took place at the Buddhist School of Dialectic. When I entered the school in 1973, I was confronted by Gen Lob-zang Gya-tso, who told me that I would have to start memorizing, like everybody else. I was, after all, asking to be trained in the same way as the best Tibetan monks. How could I expect to become a competent scholar if I did not even know the root texts that provide the architecture of the whole curriculum? This demand obviously brought about a large change from the free life that I had enjoyed at the Nam-gyel monastery; it was a rude awakening to the often difficult realities of monastic training. Up until then I had memorized very little, except for the short confession prayer that novices have to recite. Taking the time to memorize texts that I could pull off a shelf and read seemed an obvious waste of time, the type of tedious learning that I had sought to escape by coming to India. Now I would have to memorize. In the process, I would discover that often things turn out differently than what one had expected. But here I am running ahead of myself, for I first need to describe the training in memorization, which provides the basis of traditional scholarly education but has received very little attention in the scholarly literature.[2]

I begin with literacy, examining briefly the wide regional and even local differences in the literacy rate in Tibet, and the formal and informal channels through which literacy has spread. I then provide a short ethnography of Tibetan monastic practices of memorization, describing the methods used by monks and the types of texts memorized. Because Tibetan schools differ little in their approaches to memorization, I focus on the tradition with which I am most familiar, the Ge-luk. I also bring in some of my personal experiences to bring to life this often misunderstood practice.

TIBET AND LITERACY

Generalizing about literacy in pre-1950 Tibet is no easy matter. Robert Ekvall, one of the few scholars to investigate this topic, comments on the difficulty of forming a coherent picture of literacy patterns, which seem to have varied greatly through the region.[3] Few documents are left to help us; we have only individual reports and anecdotal evidence, which are becoming rarer with the passing of time. Such limitations mean that any assessment of the spread of literacy across Tibet, mine included, can be only tentative at best. Nevertheless, I believe that the picture provided here is not untrue to literacy in Tibet as it existed during the first half of the twentieth century, though it contrasts starkly with the dominant view of Tibet as an illiterate culture. For example, the editor of a collection of essays on literacy in traditional societies observes that "under Buddhism it [writing] was mainly an instrument of propaganda and worship; the three hallowed practices of reciting, writing (or printing), and reading the word (CHos) became ends in themselves. Books were carried unopened in procession and used to line the tomb of a grand lama. . . . Tibet demonstrates the epitome of grapholatry."[4] This typically orientalist judgment ignores the considerable intellectual achievements in Tibet to focus on the "odd" aspects of the culture, thereby effectively marginalizing it. It is true that Tibetans use books for ritual display, but this is hardly unique to this tradition.

In fact, basic literacy seems to have been relatively widespread in traditional Tibet. Many people were able to read, though few could write. This state of affairs is something of a surprise; in agricultural and scribal societies such as premodern Tibet, literacy is presumed to be low. Economic transactions are governed less by law than by local custom, and many scholars assume that the dominance of face-to-face exchanges obviates the need for written documents.[5] But others have argued against such assumptions, pointing to fairly widespread literacy in this type of society in certain places and times[6]—as, apparently, in some parts of Tibet.

Variation between regions seems to have been considerable. Central Tibet had a much lower literacy rate than Kham and Amdo or nomadic areas in the Northern Plains. Without undertaking the careful inquiry necessary for a full explanation, we can safely assume that socioeconomic differences were partly responsible. Central Tibet was more centralized; its economic life was dominated by large monastic and aristocratic estates, and its cultural life tended to focus in particular, well-populated locations. By contrast, Eastern Tibet was freer and more egalitarian: the absence of large estates allowed for greater local cultural development, as was true among the nomads.

There were also differences within these regions. The few urban centers, such as Lhasa and Shi-ga-tse, had much higher literacy rates than the countryside and also had schools. Inhabitants of the rural areas of Central Tibet seem to have been largely illiterate. But some variations are hard to correlate with large-scale socioeconomic factors. For example, people read well in some remote areas, such as Kon-jo-ra-wa in Kham, but not in others, such as Dar-gye in Tre-hor.[7] Even on the smallest level large differences existed. Lob-zang Gya-tso reports that the laity in his village had average reading ability, whereas people in the next valley were renowned for their ability to rapidly read the scriptures.[8]

Numbers, even the most approximate, are hard to come by. Relying on the report of De-zhung *(bde gzhung)* Rin-po-che, Ekvall estimates that up to half of the male lay population in premodern Tibet had rudimentary reading skills.[9] I assume that this assessment reflects the situation in Rin-po-che's village, in a region of Kham (Jeykundo), but it may not tell us much about other regions. Still, this number—much higher than one would expect—is supported by evidence from other areas of Kham, such as Ri-wo-che (see below). But what does "rudimentary" mean here? Ekvall describes Tibetans as being able "to read to the extent of being able to identify the letters of the alphabet and to approximate the sound of the combinations. They are thus able to follow the lines of familiar prayers and even haltingly to learn new ones."[10] If half of the male population can painfully read a few prayer texts, should they be called literate? To begin to answer this important question, more information about Tibetan education might be helpful.

In Tibet, reading was often taught separately from writing. This practice seems to have been widespread in many partly literate preindustrial societies.[11] Children would learn to read not by writing letters but by repetition.

They would sit at the teacher's feet, looking at a text or a model piece of writing and listening attentively. The teacher would read a sentence and then repeat it several times, letter by letter. Pupils would then repeat the spelling until they were able to recite the sentence without the teacher's help. After the lesson, they spent long hours on their own, repeating the exercise until they had mastered the spelling and the sentences that had been taught. The teacher then supplied a few new sentences, continuing until the students could start reading on their own.

Reading skills remained basic, with few students going on to further studies. But some developed their skills to be able to read a broad range of materials, including stories, epics, medical texts, popular operas, poetry, songs, and collections of proverbs and tales, thus adding to the spread of literacy.[12] In the Nying-ma tradition, for example, children from Ri-wo-che were encouraged to read Padmasambhava's sagas, such as the *Padma bka' thang,* in order to develop their skills by joining reading practice and the blessing of a sacred text.[13]

Nevertheless, the main motivation for reading in Tibet was religious. Most people would use their skills to read ritual texts or learn them by heart. Tibetan Buddhism strongly emphasizes personal ritual and devotional practices, which permeate all levels of society. Laypeople as well as monks or nuns engage in such practices, which can be quite long, once or twice daily. Thus, the ability to read is central to religious practice, and even the laity had a strong incentive to acquire rudimentary literacy. For some, reading remained limited to these ritual contexts; others, in more favorable conditions, were encouraged to read more extensively.

FORMAL AND INFORMAL EDUCATION IN TIBET

In traditional Tibet, literacy was mostly transmitted informally. Very few schools existed, and they serviced a small group of relatively well-off families that could support their (mostly male) children on their way to higher administrative or medical callings. Moreover, such schools were found only in the few urban centers, such as Lhasa and Shi-ga-tse, in a country where most people were peasants or nomads (or a mixture of both). Lhasa contained several important schools supported by the state and devoted to the different traditional branches of knowledge: administration, medicine, astrology, and literature. Some of these schools, such as the medical monastery of Chak-po-ri *(lcags po ri)* and the Potala School *(rtse slob grwa),* were reserved for monks; others, such as the larger School of Medicine and Astrology *(sman rtsis khang),* were open to laity.

Besides these specialized institutions, there were a few (probably around ten) private schools in Lhasa, such as Nang-ro-sha *(nang rong shag)* and Kang-sar *(khang gsar)*. These schools were small and provided a solid traditional secular education. By "secular," I do not mean that they did not teach or practice Buddhism. Every morning, classes would start with a session of devotional practices that included taking refuge in and praising the patron deities of wisdom and learning, Manjushri and Sarasvati. But the core of the curriculum was devoted to acquiring literacy skills—reading, writing, spelling, grammar, and composition—and not, as in monasteries, to studying Buddhism.[14]

Some have argued that the organization of education in traditional cultures is loose or nonexistent. For example, Timothy Mitchell notes that in Egypt, "Schooling did not exist before the last third of the nineteenth century, and it was not the purpose of any distinct individual or institution to give organised instruction."[15] In Tibet, the few secular schools that existed had well-defined stages of learning. Pupils would first master the intricacies of Tibetan calligraphy before moving on to study the different parts of the Tibetan grammatical system and to acquire spelling skills, an important element of education in a language possessing many homophones. Finally, students would study the different aspects of composition (often in the context of writing letters, which to this day remain extremely formal) and of poetry. All the classes had set readings and standard manuals.[16] Thus, it is clear that the schooling that existed in premodern Tibet was well-organized. Set curricula and clearly delineated levels are also found, as we will see later, in monastic education.

Nonetheless, formal schooling remained extremely limited. Literacy was usually acquired within the household or the monastery. Monks and nuns were often involved in such family matters: the teaching of reading and sometimes writing was among the services that religious were expected to perform. Almost every family had an immediate member or close relative living in a monastic community, often very near their families' home.

Besides monasteries, quasi-monastic lay communities *(ser khyims dgon pa)* added to the store of potential teachers throughout Tibetan society. Their members fulfilled most of the roles of the monks, especially ritual ones, but were not ordained and had families. Often the leader of such a community would informally teach the children of the village. Ken-po Pal-den Shay-rab *(mkhan po dpal ldan shes rab)*, a contemporary Nying-ma scholar from Kham, described to me how his father, head of a quasi-monastic lay community in the area of Ri-wo-che, taught the whole village.[17] Whenever he had time, children would come to his house and receive their lessons. Ken-po started to learn how to read at the age of four. As in many other parts of Kham, his education stressed the acquisition of reading skills. The first year was spent learning individual letters; the second, mastering syllables. The third year was devoted to reading sentences, and the final year concentrated on increasing facility. By the time he was eight, Ken-po was able to read any text loudly and at great speed. He was considered one of the top scripture readers in his village.

Writing was also taught. Because the village was poor, children wrote not on wooden boards *(sbyang shing)* but on slates. As in other parts of Eastern Tibet, Ken-po and his companions were taught how to write in several ways, starting with cursive *(dbu smad)* and finishing with print *(dbu chen)*.[18] This insistence on calligraphy was typical. Even nowadays, Tibetans hold a person's handwriting to extremely exacting standards. Not knowing how to write is not considered a flaw, but writing badly is a mark of carelessness: it signifies that the person lacks quality and counters any claim of being highly literate. A sloppily written letter is a bad letter, whereas a well-written letter is well received, regardless of its content. In Tibet, calligraphy was often the main, if not the only, requirement for obtaining an administrative job.[19] Hence, children learning how to write would, and still do, spend long hours filling wooden boards or slates with lines of letters written in erasable ink or chalk.

After mastering fundamental literacy skills, Ken-po studied spelling *(brda yig)* and grammar *(sum rtags)*. During this time, Ken-po also had to memorize the voluminous liturgy of the community. When Ken-po left his village at age thirteen to continue his studies at the commentarial school *(bshad grwa)* of Ri-wo-che, he had a solid basic education, though his village was quite poor.

Ken-po's education is fairly typical of that received in areas where basic literacy was achieved by many. Higher education was another matter, as only a small minority continued their studies. If they belonged to a wealthy family or were part of a powerful household, they might enter a special school leading to an administrative job, but such opportunities were rare. Sometimes, less favored youngsters would work for a family who promised an education in exchange, but they were often exploited and received little training.[20] The monastic route offered much wider possibilities. Much like the church in medieval Europe, it was the main avenue of social mobility. Many children went to the monastery already knowing how to read; right away, they could start the rigorous training in memorization that constitutes the first stage of monastic education proper. Those who did not know how to read would be taught reading, and sometimes writing, in the monastery when they became monks.

THE PRACTICE OF MEMORIZATION

Most monks, as explained in the previous chapter, start their careers when they are young (between six and twenty).[21] Their first task is to memorize a large number of rituals. Memorization typically proceeds as follows. Every day, the young monk memorizes a fixed and gradually increasing amount of textual material. Usually he starts with a couple of sentences, gradually increasing to one side or both sides of a folio. Some become memory virtuosi, able to memorize five or even ten folios a day.[22] In the evening, the student meets with his teacher, who examines him on the material learned that day and gives him a new piece. The teacher recites the piece, making sure that the student knows exactly how to read the passage. This precision in reading is particularly important for mantras.[23] Though they are in Sanskrit, they are written in the Tibetan alphabet. Hence, they are difficult to read. The teacher's reading is quite important: it is considered a form of transmission *(lung)* and authorizes the student to work on the text. Most Tibetan monks insist on the importance of such transmission (though not all agree, as we will see in chapter 7). Once the teacher is satisfied, the student is ready for the next day's memorization.

After rising and doing the usual chores, such as cleaning his room or that of his teacher, the young monk sits down cross-legged on a bed or on a cushion on the ground and performs a few devotional recitations; in particular he invokes Manjushri, the patron bodhisattva of wisdom. This invocation ends with the syllable *dhīḥ,* the sonic seed of this bodhisattva, which is repeated as many times as possible in a single breath: *dhīḥ, dhīḥ, dhīḥ, dhīḥ,* . . . Such repetition is thought to increase the intellectual faculties and hence to help one memorize. The young monk then proceeds to memorize the passage given to him the night before. He loudly reads it from his text bit by bit, rocking his body back and forth. He starts with the first word or two of the first sentence or line of a stanza (often but not always the text is written as poetry; the verses of seven, nine, or eleven syllables, grouped in four-line stanzas, are easier to retain than prose), reciting that element until he has mastered it. He then moves on incrementally until he has memorized the whole sentence, which he recites, still in a loud voice, several times. The same process is repeated for subsequent sentences; and after memorizing each, he recites the sentences that he has just memorized. Thus, by the end of the session, the whole passage forms a whole that can be integrated with the passages he has already memorized.

The process of memorization is aural. Without relying on visual mnemonic devices, Tibetan monks memorize their texts by vocalizing them. The only support is a tune to which the words are set. In certain monasteries (such as Nam-gyel, where monks are expected to memorize an enormous amount of liturgical material), the text is memorized to the same tune to which it is later chanted. In scholastic monasteries or in smaller monasteries, there is no fixed tune. But in both cases, students concentrate entirely on the text's sonic pattern, ignoring other associations as much as possible.[24]

If the whole day is devoted to memorization, the session is often finished around noon, just before the young monk has lunch (often with his teacher). The afternoon is taken up in various ways, depending on the wishes of the teacher, the age of the student, the day of the month, the type of institution, and so on. Some teachers are quite strict and closely watch their pupils, who have to spend most of the afternoon reciting what they have memorized. Others allow greater freedom. At the Nam-gyel monastery in India, monks memorize new material in the morning and recite earlier lessons through the whole afternoon and evening. Gen Lob-zang Gya-tso had a much easier time: his first teacher was very a kind man who did not keep tight discipline. Gen-la would spend the afternoon playing with other young monks, unless there was some special event (a full-day liturgical service) or a specific task to be done.

The evening is spent practicing the texts previously memorized. The student starts by reciting that morning's passage several times, until his recitation is fluent and almost effortless. He then goes back to the parts of the same text learned on preceding days, ending with the passage learned the same day. He may add other texts learned previously. This exercise, which usually takes one or two hours, is essential to ensure that passages once memorized are not forgotten. At first, the passage newly memorized, which could be recited quite fluently in the morning, comes in the evening with difficulty, if at all. It needs to be fixed again in the memory, a task best done just before the student goes to sleep. After a night of sleep, the text starts to take its fixed form, which has to be constantly strengthened until it becomes ingrained—a process that takes many days of repetition. In this way, the student's hold on previous passages increases, and the new passage is integrated gradually into the memorized text as a whole. It is only when the texts are so well learned that they come to mind automatically that frequent recitation is no longer needed. At that point, reciting them a few times a year can keep them alive in the monk's memory.

In the evening, the young monk being trained in memorization faces the biggest ordeal of the day: the dreaded exam on that day's passage. The student enters the teacher's room and hands over the passage he has been working on. He then sits or squats at the feet of his teacher, who is seated on his bed (the usual position of most Tibetans when they are at home), and repeats the passage by heart. Sometimes the teacher asks him to recite previously learned passages. Any mistake is immediately punished. Some teachers hit their students for any mistake. An error in pronunciation might draw a single stroke, but a failure in memory could lead to a more serious beating. Gen-la was lucky; his teacher, who was also a relative, was kind toward his students. Others are much less pleasant, and there are even some sadists who brutalize their students. Once the exam is over, the cycle starts again with the transmission of a new passage to be memorized the next day.

This process of memorization is practiced not only by monks and nuns, but also by laity. Most laypeople recite religious texts every day and often memorize the briefer ones, using the same technique described here. The memorization of such texts relies only on sound. A friend of mine reported that when he was a child, his parents made him memorize the mandala offering, a text recited in which one offers a symbolic representation of the universe to the deity worshiped or the guru. It describes the objects to be offered: the sun *(nyi ma)*, the moon *(zla ba)*, the precious umbrella *(rin po che gdugs)*. My friend, however, understood these to be the names of people and thought the text referred to Mrs. Sun, Moon, and Rin-po-che being there *('dug)*.

TIBETAN MONASTERIES: ISLANDS OF PEACE, OR OCEANS OF NOISE?

The centrality of sound in Tibetan monastic life, about which I will have more to say, is obvious to anybody who has stayed in any large Tibetan monastery. As I have stressed, a Tibetan monastery is devoted not to meditation but to rituals and sometimes studies. Far from being an island of peace and quiet like a hermitage, it is filled with activities and almost constant noise. It is, in Anne Klein's words, "an arena suffused with sound."[25] The day often starts with a chanted ritual service done on behalf of a sponsor. It continues with the cacophony of memorization, as each monk loudly repeats a different passage to his own rhythm and tune. Later on, further ritual services or sessions of debate may be conducted, while the young monks who have not yet finished their preliminary memorization keep reciting their texts at the top of their lungs. It is only at lunchtime that relative quiet descends on the monastery. After eating, monks relax. Friendly chats take place here and there, but loud discussions are frowned on. There is usually less noise during the first part of the afternoon, when fewer monks memorize and many either read or engage in the different tasks that have been assigned to them. But the noise picks up during the evening, when the main sessions of debate are held. Then the air is filled with the roar from the debating courtyard. When debates end, monks start their recitation sessions, as described above. At this point, hundreds of monks may be reciting as loudly as they can, and the cacophony can reach an almost unimaginable level. Around ten the noise diminishes, and by eleven only scattered recitations can be heard. There are times, however, when some monks decide to spend the whole night reciting. Religious festivals such as the full moon of the fourth Tibetan month, which commemorates the Buddha's enlightenment as well as his passing away, are often chosen for such exercises. At these auspicious times, the practice of virtue is considered much more effective.

Reading or reciting aloud is considered virtuous for several reasons. Vocalizing a text in a rhythmic pattern helps it penetrate one's mind, where it starts to take on a life of its own. One finds oneself spontaneously repeating the words. Such absorption of religious texts is thought to have soteriological value. The virtuous nature of recitation is also tied to a view of the world as alive with a number of invisible entities, a topic to which we will return (see chapter 13). Traditional Tibetans believe that countless gods and spirits live around us in trees, springs, houses, and rocks. Loud recitation attracts these entities, who are then able to hear the Buddhist teaching (an opportunity usually denied by their birth); hence, it is thought to be a highly meritorious form of giving *(sbyin pa, dāna)*. Geshe Rab-ten recalls matter-of-factly,

> There was a cemetery not far from our monastery; it was inhabited by many spirits and other non-human forms of life. It is said in the scriptures that if one recites kind words of Dharma in the direction of such a place, it benefits these creatures. Thus, moved to be of service to them, at night when I was reciting I would sometimes turn towards this cemetery, and in a loud voice chant some fine verses of Dharma.[26]

Tibetans therefore view loud recitation as valuable in and of itself. It helps other sentient beings, particularly if it is aesthetically pleasing.[27]

A small incident illustrates the religious value of recitation and its sometimes unexpected results. During the 1960s, Tri-jang Rin-po-che *(khri 'chang rin po che)* visited the three monastic seats then located at Buxa in

Northeast India. One of the Dalai Lama's tutors, he was an extremely famous teacher and the guru of most of the Ge-luk monks. Students are supposed to please their guru by offering them their services as well as presents, and the best offering is one's virtuous practice. What better way to rejoice Rin-po-che than a highly virtuous action such as a full-night recitation? Or at least so a young monk thought. Thus, he positioned himself near Rin-po-che's room and proceeded to spend the whole night reciting at full volume all the texts he had ever memorized. Rin-po-che's reaction, alas, was not what he had expected. "Who is the idiot who kept me awake the whole night?" was his reported comment. Most Tibetan monks, however, are much less sensitive to disturbances than was Rin-po-che, and they carry on their normal activities, including study or sleep, in the greatest uproar.

Still, one may wonder about the utility of all this noise. Doesn't it interfere with the learning process, much as the faithful disciple's loud recitation prevented Tri-jang Rin-po-che's sleep? The counterintuitive answer is that the noise of monasteries in fact supports and reinforces the learning process—particularly memorization. Monks report that far from being distracted by the sounds of other monks' memorizations, they find them helpful to their own practice. Learning is not just individual but interpersonal as well. When students hear each other, their energy and focus are reinforced. They are supported by the feeling of participating in a common task and pushed to memorize more than they might on their own. At times, a kind of competition develops in which students try to outlast each other, vying to produce the last tune to be heard.

MEMORIZATION AND LITURGICAL DISCIPLINE

Memorization is an important element of the disciplinary practices on which Tibetan monasticism rests. It integrates monks into the monastic community by enabling them to take part in the monastery's collective rituals, which are its central activities. On entering a monastery, the young monk must first memorize its liturgy *(chos spyod)*, which is of two types. The exoteric liturgy contains a few short sutras (such as the Heart Sutra), confessional texts, prayers in the proper sense of the word *(smon lam)*, and devotional practices such as the seven-limb worship. The esoteric liturgy comprises a large number of tantric texts as well as the texts necessary to propitiate the protectors.

The centrality of these liturgical practices varies from monastery to monastery. In those specializing in liturgical services, such as the Tantric

Monasteries and Nam-gyel, ritual is the main activity. The liturgy of these monasteries includes hundreds of folios whose memorization requires several years of extremely demanding effort. The knowledge of new monks is tested: on a number of occasions they must recite the entire liturgy of the monastery in front of their peers. They are also sometimes examined privately by the higher authorities, who may deliberately disrupt the recitation in order to see how deeply ingrained a monk's memorization is. A friend from Nam-gyel recalls that the Dalai Lama suddenly entered the room where he was reciting. Not content with just listening to the recitation, the Dalai Lama proceeded to scratch my friend's back to test if his memorization was unshakable. Despite the considerable emotion provoked by this gesture, my friend did not lose his concentration and was able to continue to recite flawlessly.

In smaller monasteries like Gen Lob-zang Gya-tso's, the requirements are usually less stringent, and the life of a young monk memorizing the liturgy can be quite pleasant, provided that his teacher is not too harsh. By the age of seventeen (he had started at eleven), Gen-la had finished the first part of his task. He had memorized the exoteric part of the liturgy, presumably together with the rituals of propitiation. Having finished the bare minimum of memorization, he was ready to go on to the next step: a three-year visit to one of the three monastic seats.

In the monastic universities, liturgy plays a less important role (relatively speaking). Accordingly, in these institutions less time and effort are spent on memorizing liturgical material. Nevertheless, only after mastering this liturgy are monks admitted as full members of the monastery, able to take part in scholastic activities.[28] Thus, memorization of liturgical texts is a basic practice of Tibetan monasticism. Unlike scholarly training, which is undertaken only by a small minority through many years of intense dedication, memorization is the province of all the monks. It inculcates in them a sense of discipline central to the monastic enterprise as they follow a daily routine under the supervision of an authority. They start the day with an assignment from their teacher and end it with the teacher's examination of that same task. This cannot help but greatly strengthen the sense of obedience that young monks develop toward their teachers—a sense particularly reinforced by the ordeals of the daily examination, and the possible punishments associated with it. But memorization's most important disciplinary role is that it forms monks into efficient members of the ritual community. Rituals can be performed well only when they are properly memorized and recited uniformly by all monks to the same tune and rhythm. This uniformity creates a powerful effect that satisfies performers and supporters alike. The monks can feel confident of the religious power or value of such practices, and sponsors, in turn, feel justified in their support of the monastery.

THE ROLE OF MEMORIZATION IN THE CURRICULUM

Memorization is the first step in any traditional Tibetan monastic career, and initially it is practiced almost to the exclusion of other activities. It continues for those monks who wish to pursue higher monastic studies, for the curriculum is structured around the study of a few basic texts committed to memory. Unlike studies at modern institutions, which are organized according to disciplines, scholastic studies are organized around important writings—the great Indian treatises *(śāstra, bstan bcos)*, the root *(rtsa ba, mūla)* texts, which we will consider in the next few chapters. It is the study of these texts that constitutes the tradition.

These texts are assimilated through commentaries and debates, which themselves are not memorized. Instead, students memorize the root texts, which are written in short, mnemonic verses. The commentaries and debates are retained not verbatim but in relation to the memorized root text. That text provides a nondiscursive template around which ideas that might otherwise seem disconnected can fall into place, enabling students to organize explanations and objections. The memorization of a root text thus contributes not only to the retention of information but also to the accessibility of the information retained. Psychologists distinguish between free recall, in which subjects attempt to recall as many random items as possible, and the cued recall of items organized by rubrics. Their experiments indicate that cued recall is more effective.[29] For the students, the memorization of base texts provides the rubric needed for cued recall, enabling them to recall topics more easily.

Students are also expected to memorize a certain amount of commentarial material. Some memorize entire commentaries, amounting to hundreds or even thousands of pages. These commentaries can provide decisive arguments during a debate. They also supply models for the students, helping them to gradually assimilate the highly technical and precise commentarial style and procedures. Nevertheless, learning root texts by heart is much more important, for sharp students are able to reason persuasively without quoting texts. Similarly, they can rely on their own understanding to comment on texts—but only if they have mastered the root text, which provides the structure according to which knowledge is organized and stored.

This educational process reflects the belief that knowledge needs to be immediately accessible rather than merely available.[30] That is, scholars must have an active command of the texts that structure the curriculum, not simply the ability to retrieve information from them. Knowing where bits of information are stored is not enough: the texts must inform one's thinking and become integrated into one's way of looking at the world. Geshe Rab-ten emphasizes the importance of an active knowledge based on memorization, which he contrasts with the approach he observed among his Western disciples: "Although it was difficult at first, I, like other monks, gradually became accustomed to it [i.e., recitation], so that both memorization and recitation came with ease. In the Western academic tradition, note-taking plays a vital role, and much of one's knowledge tends to be confined between the covers of one's textbooks [or notebooks]. Our corresponding stores of knowledge were held in our mind through memorization."[31] When texts are held in mind, their deeper meaning becomes apparent and the knowledge they convey becomes active and useful. Otherwise, one merely has scattered bits and pieces of information. It is only through memory that these pieces can be combined to provide actual knowledge.

Hence, memorization cannot be divorced from learning. It enables the monks to fully assimilate the content of the texts they study. As William Graham explains, "The very act of learning a text 'by heart' internalizes the text in a way that familiarity with even an often-read book does not. Memorization is a particularly intimate appropriation of a text, and the capacity to quote or recite a text from memory is a spiritual resource that is tapped automatically in an act of reflection, worship, prayer or moral deliberations."[32] In the Tibetan scholastic context, as noted above, quotations can supply effective arguments within a debate; commentaries can be particularly useful to corner an adversary and demonstrate the mistakes in his interpretation. It is also significant that some of the memorized texts have spiritual relevance. But by far the most important role of memorization, especially of the root texts, is to provide the organizational structure of the whole curriculum.

The cultivation of memory is central to Tibetan monasticism in general and scholasticism in particular. As Mary Carruthers has argued in a study of medieval Europe, reliance on memory is characteristic of traditional education; modern societies, in contrast, are primarily documentary. Tibetan monks memorize texts in order to internalize their content, not because of their scarcity. Printing has existed for several centuries and although texts were not always abundant, they were far from rare. Hence, memorization is not just the result of material conditions, or the survival of a practice once dictated by such conditions. The medievalist Jean-Claude Schmitt notes, "Nothing is *outlived* in a culture, everything is lived or not. A belief or a rite is not the combination of residues and of heterogeneous innovations, but experience that has meaning only in its present cohesion."[33]

MEMORIZATION AND ITS MECHANISMS

We understand now the central role of memorization in Tibetan monasticism. We may still wonder, however, about the specific methods employed. Why memorize a text before understanding it, when that approach is so time-consuming (we can memorize much more easily after studying the text)? Why are texts memorized on the basis of their sound patterns alone? This insistence on disregarding context seems counterintuitive, for it appears to make memorization more difficult.

Tibetan teachers are quite well aware that texts whose meaning we understand are easier to memorize than texts we do not comprehend. But what comes easily goes easily; a text memorized in the light of its meaning is quickly forgotten. I myself experienced the difference that understanding the meaning makes to the process. At the beginning of the 1980s, when I was already a seasoned student, I requested a teaching on Nāgārjuna's *Treatise of the Middle Way* from Gen Nyi-ma, one of the greatest authorities on Madhyamaka philosophy in the Ge-luk tradition. Gen-la responded that he would do it once I had memorized the text (about eleven long folios). I immediately started and noticed to my surprise that the memorization proceeded speedily. Because I understood most of the text, I could memorize it quite easily. Soon I was well past the halfway mark, and Gen-la started to teach me the first few chapters of the text. Knowing that we would not go through the whole work, I slowed down my memorization and soon stopped it. I also stopped reciting the text, a fatal mistake. Before we had finished the first few chapters, I had forgotten most of what I had memorized. After a couple of months, the words of the text had become almost as alien to me as they had been before I started to memorize them. A text learned on the basis of its sound patterns alone is not so easily forgotten.

Thus, aural memorization without any reliance on semantic association is a well thought-out way to inscribe texts durably in the mind. The very artificiality of the inscription ensures that the text is retained as exactly as possible. The *Ṛg Veda*, which was preserved for centuries in oral form, provides the most famous example of exact retention. Because the texts memorized by Tibetan monks do have written form, literal preservation is not at issue. What is important is that the monks retain the texts' exact wording. Scholarly texts can serve as objects of precise exegeses and highly technical debates only if their words are known verbatim. Similarly, texts can be used ritually only if participants recite them in precisely the same way. The training in memorization thus aims at the long-lasting and exact reproduction of the words in the context of a scholarly or ritual performance.[34]

One way to understand the means of achieving this exact retention is to consider its opposite, the process of forgetting. Some psychologists argue that forgetting results from an actual decay in the neural connections that support memory. In this model, memorization works because numerous repetitions create strong redundancies—too many connections for physical decay to totally destroy. The psychologist Harry Bahrick calls this forgetting-proof condition *permastore*.[35] With enough practice, learned responses become harder to forget. According to this account, memorizing without understanding is more effective precisely because it is more difficult: it requires more repetitions, which form a large number of neural connections. Material memorized with understanding goes easily because it comes easily: it has been learned before strong redundancies could be created.

Other psychologists offer a more constructivist explanation.[36] For them, forgetting demonstrates not actual decay so much as the interference caused by the constant reorganization of knowledge. These researchers insist that memories do not sit inertly in the mind as books do on library shelves. Memories are instead constantly reconstructed in the light of new circumstances. In addition, this reconstruction seems to affect the various mnemonic subsystems differently. A basic distinction is made in the study of memory between implicit and explicit memory.[37] In the former, the content of the memory is retained independently of how it is learned. For example, when a skilled pianist learns a piece it becomes ingrained; it no longer needs to be recalled but comes out automatically, at least when the pianist is in the proper mood. Similarly, texts are memorized until they become internalized and can be recited automatically, without any conscious effort at recollection. The friend from Nam-gyel I mentioned earlier reports that he and his friends sometimes fell asleep while reciting in front of their teacher. Still asleep, they would be able to continue their recitation for several minutes, stopping only at the intervention of the teacher, who would wake them up. Disoriented, they would have to start the recitation all over again. They were lucky if they could succeed; often such an incident would disturb the mnemonic pattern, making it necessary for them to refresh their memory.[38]

This type of memorization is quite different from that used in explicit memory—that is, the memory of something in relation to how it was learned. This is true in the case both of episodic memory, which enables us to access particular experiences as a whole, and of semantic memory, which relates to concepts and facts and enables us to retain theoretical knowledge. Often the particular associations that accompany the memories have made possible their integration with others that already existed.[39]

These distinctions between different forms of memory are relevant to explaining the method used by Tibetans to train memory. By dissociating texts from meaning before committing them to memory, the monks seek to make memorization a form of implicit memory, ingraining texts in the mind as if they were a motor skill. By contrast, when we memorize a text that we already understand we rely mainly on semantic memory—easier to acquire but less stable. It is open to the retroactive interference of subsequent learnings, especially those having to do with the same subject. Without completely erasing the old memory, new ones take over and modify it in the light of new knowledge. Texts that we memorize without understanding their meaning are not so prone to reconstruction, because of the artificiality of their inscription, which occurs in a mnemonic subsystem not influenced by semantic memory—hence, the practice of memorizing texts without understanding them. What comes with difficulty goes with difficulty.

MEMORIZATION AND ITS RESULTS:
A SHORT AUTOBIOGRAPHICAL INTERLUDE

The role of memorization in Tibetan monastic education is now quite clear, but so far little has been said of the individual experience of practicing memorization so intensely. What do people get out of this focused cultivation of memory? The practical results of memorization are obvious: it makes possible entrance into the liturgical life of the monastery and participation in higher studies. But it has personal consequences as well, shaping the person according to the goals that the tradition values. My own training in memorization can illustrate this dimension.

As mentioned earlier, I was first introduced to the practice of memorization at the Buddhist School of Dialectics.[40] At first I was unhappy at having to memorize, but I quickly discovered—contrary to what I had expected—that this exercise was far from unpleasant or useless. Every morning around eight, after attending the common morning ritual, I would sit down on my bed cross-legged and put my book on my rolled-up bedding or in my lap (see figure 6). At first I felt rather self-conscious. To recite or chant a text loudly seemed foolish, and I was embarrassed by the tune I was using. I tried to emulate the chanting of my friends and they did not seem to mind. I assumed that my mimicry had been successful, but I later discovered that they thought I was using the tune to which Westerners did their memorizations. By then I was established in my memorization, and I did not let this minor embarrassment dampen my spirits. My abilities to memorize improved to the point that I could memorize one side of a folio (at least on good days). That rate was considered average for a native speaker, but was quite respectable for a person who had begun learning Tibetan only two years before. Gen-la, who rarely (to say the least) heaped praises on his students, went so far as to comment favorably on my abilities.

I started by memorizing short prayers, which I was pleased to find that I could do rather quickly. I went on to memorize the more important root texts, starting with the *Ornament of Realization*—a relatively short text (fifteen long folios), but extremely difficult. Because it is basically an extended list, one is left struggling with completely meaningless words, which must be retained as purely sonic patterns. I remember a passage that describes the benefits of some level of realization as "overcoming and so forth by radiance" (*'od kyis mog mog por byed la sogs pa*). At the time these words sounded to me as though they were about meat dumplings (*mo mo*), and I was understandably puzzled by their connection with radiance. As explained above, the advantage of such an incomprehensible text is that once memorized, it is not easily forgotten. Even now, after more than twenty-five years, I remember some passages from it.

During this process, I discovered that after a few minutes of memorization, my usually overactive mind would calm down and become more focused. I would feel happy and soothed, with enhanced concentration. This pleasant mental state was enhanced by the use of a tune, which made the whole exercise quite enjoyable. It created a mental space to which I could retire; there I could observe my mind and how it changed. It was fun to see my mind becoming sharper after a few trying minutes; it would slowly gain focus and strength, before tiredness brought a drop in acuity. Moreover, the increasing ability to memorize had a stimulating effect, making it all into a kind of game. Another source of stimulation was the tunes of the other students around me. I felt energized and focused, and ready to join in—a bit like a musician responding to other musicians.

Memorization greatly helped me gain the focus and mental discipline that I had lacked during my stay at the Nam-gyel monastery. It developed my attention span, for without extended concentration it is impossible to memorize effectively. Moreover, the strict daily routine I followed had an importance hard to overemphasize. Gradually, the mind follows the body and becomes easier to control. Though the natural tendency of the mind to wander never disappears entirely, the commitment to a clearly defined task and the rhythmic effect created by the chanted tune keep it in check.

In this way, my studies steadily improved, not just because of my keen motivation (which was obviously indispensable) but also because of my heightened mental focus and discipline. Whereas previously I was unable to sustain study of even the topics that interested me, I gradually became able to concentrate on any topic. I thus realized that anything can become interesting, provided that one puts one's mind to it. Interest and boredom are largely functions of the quality of one's attention. An attentive mind is not bored, however trivial the task, and a mind trained in memorization can apply the focus thereby acquired for other purposes.

These important benefits are not unlike those provided by meditative training, which is even more effective in giving its practitioner the ability to be attentive and concentrate, as well as the experience of mental calm. The advantage of memorization over meditation is that it is easier. In meditation, one's mind focuses on purely internal objects (when it focuses at all), easily wandering off unnoticed for several minutes. In memorization, the mind is given a clearly defined external task and kept to it by the loud vocalization and the tune that are part of the process. Hence, to memorize is a relatively painless way to acquire the stability and discipline essential to monastic training.

5 The General Structure of the Tibetan Curriculum

However great the importance of memorization training in the life of Tibetan monks, it is only a preparation for the central part of the scholastic education, the interpretation of the great texts. The passage from one to the other is often quite difficult; some monks never manage it and never go beyond memorizing texts. They may be able to retain thousands of pages but cannot understand the content of what they remember, despite their best efforts. These unfortunate monks are sometimes unkindly derided by their more scholarly peers as mere parrots. But even those who manage it successfully find the transition quite traumatic—particularly monks trained in Tibet, where most students began their scholastic careers barely able to read. One can imagine their confusion and bewilderment at confronting the obscure texts of the monastic curriculum that great scholars find difficult to fathom.

In contrast, I had had a standard European high school education before I became a monk. Similarly, my friends at the Buddhist School of Dialectics had gone through the secular training provided for Tibetans in exile in India. Nevertheless, we all lacked a higher education and hence found our first encounter with the great texts rather painful. I remember trying to read commentaries: at first I could make sense of the individual sentences, but I could not follow where they were going. Why did the author make a particular statement at a particular point? I was both confused and frustrated, like an undergraduate first reading a knotty philosopher, such as Aristotle.

Tibetan scholastic education trains its students to develop their interpretive abilities. This capacity is crucial in scholasticism, which was defined in the introduction as aimed at the interpretation of a tradition's great texts within the confines of its authority. Such interpretation is not free: a scholastic tradition tightly prescribes the methods to be followed and trains its followers in them. Truth is reached not through an individual quest but through well-defined and strictly regulated practices.[1] The Tibetan tradition focuses on two principal intellectual practices: the explanation of texts through commentary and the investigation of their meaning through dialectical debate. The bulk of this book concerns these two types of practice.

I begin with the role of commentary, which is explored in the next five chapters. I first discuss the commentarial logic that animates the Tibetan scholastic curriculum, examining the texts used by this tradition that are described as *formative* or, as I prefer, *constitutive*. I then discuss the normative curricular model that provides the general standards of learning within the Tibetan scholarly world, a model quite different from the actual curricula implemented in monasteries. A similar disparity is found in other scholastic traditions, but rarely does the real have a focus so much more limited than the ideal. I conclude this chapter by considering how this commentarial logic is applied to form a commentarial hierarchy, according to which later commentaries are read into basic texts.

AUTHORITY AND THE ROLE OF COMMENTARY

My characterization of scholasticism has emphasized the central role of tradition. Scholasticism, I argued, is first and foremost concerned with the relation between understanding and the authority of tradition. Hence, it often must adjudicate between competing interpretations and resolve perceived contradictions within the tradition. As this interpretive task proceeds, it relies on a view of the past as endowed with a special authority by which it "holds the present in its grasp."[2] That hold cannot be too tight, however, lest tradition become unable to cope with ever-changing circumstances. Scholasticism's adjudications and reconciliations cannot be mechanical; they must leave space for the creativity of supplemental interpretations. Thus, far from precluding new interpretation, the firm reliance on tradition makes it indispensable. This dynamic relation will be at the center of my analysis of Tibetan scholasticism.

The role of commentary clearly illustrates the centrality of tradition and its authority in Tibetan scholasticism. Obviously, commentaries are widely used in other contexts, but in scholasticism they organize knowledge in ways quite different from the disciplinarity to which modern scholars are accustomed. One of the characteristics of scholasticism is its text-centeredness: that is, it structures its knowledge, under the guidance of commentaries, around the appropriation of key texts. Their role is well captured by Moshe Halbertal's distinction between central and formative texts.[3]

A central text is one of the classics of a civilization, such as the works of Homer, Confucius, Shakespeare, and Newton and the Mahabharata. It provides a new paradigm and serves as a milestone for scholars. It may start a new trend or even an entirely new cultural field. In short, a central text is a "great book," embodying a culture's fundamental ideals and seemingly timeless norms of interpretation.[4] For Tibetans, the classical works are the great Indian treatises from the past—mostly from the fourth to eighth centuries, the period often described as the "golden age of Indian civilization." They are the obligatory reference points: the "great texts" *(gzhung chen mo)* that provide the basis and model for the education of Tibetan scholars, setting the standards against which personal achievements are measured.

But a text in a scholastic tradition is often more than classical or central. To use Halbertal's term, it may be formative: that is, "one in which progress in the field is made through interpretation of the text itself. A text-centered culture that has formative texts proceeds in that mode; its achievements are interpretative."[5] Such a text is not merely important to the field (as are classics) but constitutive of it. As we will see, that is how the great Indian texts of the Tibetan curriculum function. For example, for Tibetan scholars Madhyamaka philosophy is unthinkable without Nāgārjuna's *Treatise of the Middle Way* and Candrakīrti's *Introduction to the Middle Way.* They play a role quite different from central texts, whose reading informs but does not form a field. Menachem Fisch perceptively describes the distinction: "Newton's *Principia* obviously figures prominently as a canonical work of Western science, but no one would claim that progress in physics is achieved by discovering new ways of reading Newton."[6]

The centrality to scholasticism of the commentarial mode of knowing follows directly from the constitutive role of the great texts of the tradition. All involved in the field must preserve and refer to them, since studies proceed through their interpretation. Commentaries therefore reflect on the constitutive texts of the tradition, investigate their meaning, and discuss their difficult points.

In contrast, modern scholars usually organize knowledge by anonymous and abstract disciplines. These, as Michel Foucault explains, are structured around "groups of objects, methods, their corpus of propositions considered to be true, the interplay of rules and definitions, of techniques and tools."[7] He points to their distinguishing feature: "In a discipline, unlike in a commentary, what is supposed to be the point of departure is not some meaning which must be rediscovered, nor an identity to be reiterated; it is that which is required for the construction of new statements. For a discipline to exist, there must be the possibility of formulating—and of doing so ad infinitum—fresh propositions."[8] Although Foucault's view lacks nuance (e.g., commentary need not entail self-identical repetition), his opposition between discipline and commentary is very useful.[9] It goes to the heart of one of the most important features of scholastic cultures: topics are tied to the study of a particular text, which sets the limits of and thus constitutes a particular field.

The same commentarial orientation is displayed in other scholastic traditions, such as medieval Christianity and Islam. To study each discipline was to study its authoritative text: in Christianity, these included Aristotle for logic, Justinian for Roman law, and the Bible for theology. As John Baldwin puts it in his history of the scholastic culture of the Middle Ages:

> Since all learning began with past authority, it was essential to read and master the authoritative text. In a technical sense reading meant both reading and explaining an authority publicly before a class of pupils. . . . Although instruction was essentially oral, professors often wished to publish their lecture in writing. . . . Designated as *reportationes*, these writings stood between the precise dictations of a stenographer and the informal notes of a student. A vast amount of these writings have survived in the forms of commentary to the basic texts. . . . Often they [these writings] took the form of glosses in which the basic authority occupied the center of the page and the master's comments filled the margins.[10]

It thus appears that, cross-culturally, scholasticism undertakes intense study of constitutive texts through such intellectual technologies as the lecture and the debate. This focus on the authority of the tradition is not limited to the study of religion, as demonstrated by the curricula of several traditions—particularly the scholasticisms in medieval Europe, in the contemporary Islamic world, and in Tibet.

THE TIBETAN CURRICULUM IN COMPARATIVE PERSPECTIVE

In Tibet, the general normative model of learning is a scheme of five major and five minor branches of learning. Indian in origin, it was gradually developed and implemented in the two periods during which Buddhism was brought to Tibet (between the eighth and ninth and the tenth and fourteenth centuries). This model is the ideal: institutions' actual curricula differ from it to various degrees, as we will see shortly.

The five major branches of learning are internal science (i.e., Buddhism, *nang rig pa, adhyātmavidyā*), logic and epistemology *(gtan tshigs rig pa, hetuvidyā)*, grammar *(sgra rig pa, śabdavidyā)*, medicine *(gso ba'i rig pa, cikitsāvidyā)*, and arts and crafts *(bzo rig pa, karmasthānavidyā)*.[11] As the name of the first suggests, the sciences are divided into the internal and the external. Buddhism is the exemplar of the former, for it is concerned with the realm of the mind and its soteriological transformation. It is considered the foremost of all sciences and is also sometimes described as supramundane. From a modern Western perspective, it belongs with religion and metaphysics. Monastic curricula focus on this branch of learning, sometimes to the complete exclusion of the others. The classification of the second science, logic and epistemology, is not so clear-cut. Some Tibetan scholars, particularly but not only those within the Ge-luk tradition, view it as an auxiliary of the internal science and hence as being at least partly internal; others, particularly but not only Sa-gya, view it as more external, or secular. This ambiguous status is captured in its description as *common* to both internal and external sciences.[12]

The remaining sciences, which are external and secular, were often left out of the monastic curriculum. Grammar and the minor sciences related to it (discussed below) received little attention. In some monasteries, they were studied briefly, whereas in others (including the three seats) they were excluded completely. Medicine was often studied in an apprenticeship outside of the monastery, either with a practicing doctor or in a special institution. In Lhasa, for instance, medicine was taught in two special schools of medicine: the School for Medicine and Astrology *(sman rtsis khang)*, which admitted laypeople, and the Cak-po-ri *(lcags po ri)* Institute, which was reserved for monks who intended to become doctors.

These five major sciences are complemented by five minor ones: poetics *(snyan ngag, kāvya)*, metrics *(sdeb sbyor, chandas)*, lexicography *(mngon brjod, koṣa* or *abhidhāna)*, theater *(zlos gar, nāṭaka)*, and astrology (arithmetic and astronomy but also astrology, *rtsis, gaṇita)*. This list is not exhaustive, as several branches of learning, such as politics and the erotic arts, are not named. Those that are included complement the five major sciences and reflect the centrality of language in this curriculum. Four of the five minor branches are related to grammar—above all, Sanskrit grammar. Although the Tibetan language is unrelated to Sanskrit, it was codified as part of an effort to adopt Indian civilization, particularly Buddhism. Hence, its grammar emulates Sanskrit grammar, which is viewed as normative, and the study of Tibetan grammar culminates in the study of Sanskrit grammar as analyzed in Tibetan sources.

This emphasis on Sanskrit reflects the Indian origins of the curriculum, borrowed from the great centers such as Nalanda and Vikramashila in North India. These may have been the earliest large universities in the world, containing at their height several thousand scholars and students.

Many Tibetans, often undergoing considerable personal hardship, traveled to acquire the knowledge they dispensed. Later on, several Indian scholars came to Tibet, first at the invitation of Tibetans and then, in the twelfth and thirteenth centuries, as refugees from the Muslim invasions that destroyed these centers of learning. Through this process of cultural transfer, Tibetans became deeply imbued with Indian culture, which they saw as providing the content and structure of learning. They extensively studied not only Sanskrit grammar and linguistics but also literature, politics, theater, and the erotic arts.[13]

The dominance of Indian models was greatly strengthened by the influence of Sa-pan, who made them the sole paradigms and normative measures of learning. In his *Entrance to the Gate for the Wise (mkhas pa la 'jug pa'i sgo)*, one of the few Tibetan texts that explicitly deals with scholasticism, he proposed a curriculum based on the Indian paṇḍit model *(pāṇḍityam)*—inclusive learning strongly rooted in the mastery of grammar, linguistics, and poetics. Much like the Western trivium discussed below, this model consists of a threefold discipline: composition *(rtsom)*, exposition *('chad)*, and debate *(rtsod)*. Composition is the study of Indian grammar; it is divided into a linguistic account of language and its elements as well as poetics, which includes a general theory of aesthetics based on emotion *(rasa)*. In exposition or rhetoric, students master the art of explaining a text, particularly the five methods laid out by Vasubandhu in his *Vyākhyāyukti*. Finally, debate focuses on Indian logic: it is the study of the nature of reasoning, with a view to distinguishing the sound from the unsound.[14]

It is useful to compare this normative curriculum to the models found in the Christian and the Islamic worlds. In medieval universities, education was understood to comprise two stages: the more advanced training was preceded by a propaedeutic level consisting of the study of the seven liberal arts—that is, the kind of learning with which a free man *(liber)* should be acquainted. Boys would usually begin studying the liberal arts around the time of puberty, after they had received a grounding in basic literacy. The lower division was the trivium, containing the verbal branches of knowledge (grammar, logic, and rhetoric), and the quadrivium, containing the mathematical branches (arithmetic, geometry, astronomy, and music).[15]

The Islamic curricular model has varied greatly with locality and the specializations of particular teachers. Nevertheless, Islamic education typically starts in a Qur'anic school, where the Qur'an is learned by heart. Around puberty, the student begins his formal education, often entering a madrassa or endowed school. In the Shi'ite world, the curriculum prepares for higher studies with the same subjects as the Western trivium. After mastering these topics and becoming proficient in dialectical debates, the student moves to a higher level; there the main topics are traditional lore *(ḥadīth)*, theology *(kalām)*, Qur'anic exegesis *(tafsīr)*, and law and jurisprudence *(fiqh)*, the last being the most important. The curriculum culminates at a third level, at which the student provides his own synthesis and solutions to the problems (mostly jurisprudential) that he encounters.[16]

A cursory look at these curricular models reveals some striking similarities and differences. The schooling of Christians, Shi'ites, and Tibetan Buddhists focuses on the study of logic, understood as a preparation to philosophy, and of language, the basis of any education. Perhaps the Tibetans put even more emphasis on language than the others do, including not just grammar but also poetics, lexicography, and so on. Rhetoric is also included, at least in Sa-paṇ's paṇḍit model, which strongly resembles the European trivium in its choice of the three central branches of knowledge. Moreover, all three traditions organize knowledge hierarchically, putting religious knowledge in first place, whether it be Buddhism, Christian theology, or Islamic jurisprudence. Yet each also views studying other forms of knowledge as valuable in itself, not just as a preparation to the study of religion.

But the differences among them should not be underestimated. For example, the Tibetan curricular model contains simple calculation, astronomy, and astrology but very little mathematics. This lack is quite remarkable, considering the advanced state of mathematics in India, where the zero and algebra were invented. Even in India, however, the normative form of knowledge was not mathematics but language—particularly grammar, which was considered the most established and basic form of knowledge. The emphasis on language has its roots in the Vedic tradition, but it has also contributed to the development of less obviously religious forms of knowledge, such as linguistics, dialectics, and the philosophy of language.

It is important to remember that in all three traditions, the actual curricula often differed from these normative curricular models. In medieval Europe, the curriculum changed from university to university. Some universities omitted certain fields, particularly those belonging to the quadrivium, and organized their studies according to other schemes; for example, they might divide knowledge into the three philosophies—natural, moral, and metaphysical. Such variation was particularly common during the thirteenth and fourteenth centuries, when the assimilation of Aristotle's newly recovered works led to an eclipse of the rhetorical elements in the liberal arts and a stronger focus on logic and philosophy.[17]

The opposition between rhetoric and philosophy in the Western tradition originated in a debate in the fifth and fourth centuries B.C.E. in Athens among three models: the sophistic model of Gorgias and Protagoras, which was later rejected so strongly that it had little direct influence; the rhetorical model of Isocrates; and the philosophical model advocated by Socrates, Plato, and Aristotle. Isocrates' rhetorical education, with its focus on a general education *(egkuklios paideia)* based on literature as a way to prepare citizens, has tended to dominate. It became the norm for Greek liberal education, was adopted by the Romans (and further developed by Cicero and Quintilian), and became enshrined during late antiquity in the trivium and the quadrivium. At the peak of the scholastic period (in the thirteenth and fourteenth centuries), logic and philosophical inquiry briefly dominated the literary and rhetorical components of a liberal arts education. Yet even during that time, the seven liberal arts structured education at the propaedeutic level. After mastering the liberal arts, the student might go to another faculty (and often to another university, for each had its specialty) to study theology, medicine, or law. And from the fifteenth century on, the rhetorical tradition reasserted its primacy over scholastic logico-philosophical education. "The classical Western tradition," which today is often identified with Plato's and Aristotle's educational ideals, was reserved for only an extremely small minority; not many received a liberal education, and even fewer went on to study philosophy.[18]

In the Tibetan tradition, Sa-pan's pandit model can be seen as an attempt to promote a more literary and rhetorical education. But he was only partially successful in implementing the model of learning he laid out in the *Entrance to the Gate for the Wise*. In nonmonastic circles, Indian literary culture—particularly grammar and poetics—has been the central focus of learning, and lay scholars, mostly from the aristocracy, pay less attention to the inner science of Buddhism and to logic and epistemology. Yet in monastic circles, despite being regarded as normative, Sa-pan's model has had less sway. They have concentrated on the first two branches to the partial neglect of literary studies, which are considered more appropriate to the aesthetic inclinations of the few highly educated laypeople. Thus, the opposition between philosophy and rhetoric in premodern Tibet led not to an internal debate but to the creation of two distinct educational traditions: a lay focus on belles lettres and a monastic emphasis on religious and philosophical subjects.[19]

In not attempting to produce knowledge useful in the "real world," the Tibetan monastic curriculum was quite unlike the other examples of scholasticism considered here. Jacques Verger, for example, argues that scholastic education in medieval Europe was primarily oriented toward utilitarian ends such as preaching or becoming a lawyer or doctor. Similarly, Dale Eickelman describes the Islamic education of the madrassas in Morocco as aimed at training the literate elite to provide legal guidance to the rest of society.[20] The concerns of the texts studied by Tibetan scholars are philosophical or metaphysical, not practical or legal (except for the Vinaya, whose use is limited). The purpose in memorizing texts is not to quote them as authoritative justifications for a judicial or moral decision. They are not even meant to provide advice to the laity, though advisory texts do exist. For example, Sa-pan's *Good Sayings from the Sa-gya [Tradition] (sa skya legs bshad)*, a collection of moral proverbs intended to provide extensive ethical guidance, is studied and often memorized by laypeople who use it in their daily interactions. Though a quote from this text can win an everyday argument or lead to a case being settled to one's advantage, it is not part of the scholastic training.

Technical and abstruse philosophico-religious material is preferred because Tibetan scholastic study is meant for the religious virtuosi who lead a life separate from the mundane concerns of society, though the virtuosi and the laypeople have complementary tasks and positions. In accordance with this pattern of complementary separation, which is basic to Buddhist societies, Tibetan monastic education serves the intellectual needs of virtuosi and deals only indirectly with the topics relevant to the laity's everyday life.

THE COMMENTARIAL HIERARCHY

The philosophico-religious curriculum of Tibetan monastic scholasticism consists of three textual layers. This commentarial hierarchy makes clear both the constitutive nature of the basic scholastic texts and the mechanics of their appropriation.

The first layer contains the authoritative and canonical foundation provided by the great Indian texts *(rgya gzhung)* such as the *Abhisamayālaṃkāra (Ornament of Realization,* henceforth referred to as the *Ornament),* a commentary on the *Perfection of Wisdom* literature attributed to Maitreya; Nāgārjuna's *Treatise of the Middle Way;* and Candrakīrti's *Introduction to the Middle Way.*[21] Each supports an entire field of study. Thus the study of the path is organized around the memorization and study of the *Ornament,* and the study of Madhyamaka philosophy of emptiness revolves around either of the latter two works. These treatises are the root texts *(rtsa ba, mūla)*, written in *kārikā (tshig le'ur byed pa)*, whose memorization was described in chapter 4.

Tibetans did not invent the reliance on root texts; it is part of the methodology used by both Hinduism and late Indian Buddhism. In the Hindu traditions, following Patañjali's grammatical tradition, these aphoristic summaries of a tradition's scriptural basis are called *sutras*. For example, the meaning of the Upaniṣads is summarized by the *Brahmasūtra*, which is in turn the subject of commentaries. In the late Indian Mahayana tradition, the term *sutra* is reserved for the teachings of the Buddha, and these texts are instead called "treatises" *(śāstra, bstan bcos)*. They fulfill the same function as their Hindu counterparts: they summarize, systematize, and explain the meaning of the scriptures. Such works are intended to serve as the basis of further oral and written commentary. They would be read in relation to a *bhāṣya* or a *vṛtti ('grel ba)*, a commentary that in turn could be supplemented by a *vyākhyā* or *ṭīkā ('grel bshad)*, a more detailed gloss.[22] Tibetan curricula are similarly structured. Once the mnemonic verses have been committed to memory, they are studied in the light of further commentaries, which can be of three types: Indian commentaries, Tibetan commentaries, or monastic manuals.

The first type of explanatory text, the Indian commentaries *(bhāṣya* or *vṛtti, 'grel ba)*, explicates a root text. For example, in the field of Madhyamaka, commentaries on Nāgārjuna's *Treatise* include Candrakīrti's *Clear Words;* Buddhapalita's commentary, which bears his own name; Bhavya's *Lamp of Wisdom;* and Śāntarakṣita's *Ornament of the Middle Way,*[23] all of which are considered important by Tibetan scholars. For studying the *Ornament,* there is a standard list of twenty-one Indian commentaries. Sometimes, the texts belonging to this second layer are autocommentaries (i.e., commentaries written by the author of the root text), such as Candrakīrti's own explanation of his *Introduction to the Middle Way.*

Theoretically, the authority of the Indian commentaries is extremely important; practically, they are used in Tibetan education relatively rarely by teachers and students. As translations of the Sanskrit rendered in a highly artificial language (see chapter 7), they are quite difficult to understand; the majority of Tibetan scholars thus tend to prefer Tibetan commentaries, which authoritatively summarize them. Only extremely advanced scholars see the root texts and their Indian commentaries as the real source of their tradition and the central object of intellectual activity.[24]

The second layer consists of those Tibetan commentaries *(bod 'grel)* that were composed later, often between the fourteenth and sixteenth centuries. Because they provide clear glosses on and explanations of the difficult points in the Indian root texts, they can easily be adopted by a school to define doctrinal positions. Each school has its own central commentaries, which are held to be authoritative. For example, Ge-luk-bas use Dzong-ka-ba's texts, particularly his *Clarification of the Thought,* as their main guide in the field of Madhyamaka studies, whereas the Sa-gya-bas focus on Go-ram-ba's commentary.[25] Nying-ma-bas rely on Mi-pam Gya-tso's texts, such as his commentaries on Śāntarakṣita's *Ornament of the Middle Way,* and on the ninth chapter of Śāntideva's *Introduction to the Bodhisattva Way of Life.*[26] Ka-gyü-bas have a still different central text, the commentary on Candrakīrti's *Introduction* by the Eighth Kar-ma-ba Mi-gyö-dor-jay (*mi bskyod rdo rje,* 1504–1557).[27]

In the third level are found the monastic manuals (*yig cha*), which are used quite extensively, as we will see in chapter 6. They present easily digestible summaries of the most important points as well as the material for debate. Manuals fall into two broad categories: summaries, a genre called General Meaning (*spyi don*), and debate manuals, called Decisive Analysis (*mtha' gcod*). The Collected Topics (*bsdus grwa*) examined in the next chapter are a type of debate manual; they are a Ge-luk specialty, though they are certainly not unknown in other traditions.[28]

For each topic studied, the procedure is similar. The process starts with the heuristic memorization of the root text and sometimes of its commentaries. It continues with the interpretation of the root text through commentaries, and culminates in dialectical debates. For example, in the case of the *Ornament,* the first text likely to be examined is Haribhadra's *Clear Meaning,*[29] which provides a brief explanation of the root text. This explanation, which is authoritative but terse and unclear, is in turn supplemented by Tibetan commentaries (second level). Ge-luk monastic universities are likely to rely primarily on Gyel-tsap's *Ornament of the Essence of Commentaries,* which is often complemented by Dzong-ka-ba's *Golden Garland.*[30] These two texts explain the *Ornament* in the light of the other commentaries, particularly the twenty-one Indian commentaries. They also present each topic more systematically. Although these texts are more accessible than *Clear Meaning,* they are not always easy to understand. Hence, they are in turn supplemented by the monastery's manuals, which are more comprehensible and better organized, though less authoritative. There, students find the clearest statement about the subject matter.

As students examine each topic, they rely on this chain of commentaries, which offers an increasingly detailed and clear picture of the contents of the root text. Each level of commentary explicates the terser or less systematic texts of the preceding textual level; ultimately, the elaborate explanations provided by the authoritative Tibetan commentaries and the manuals are read back into the root text, which is assumed to implicitly contain them. By assuming identical content of commentary and commented text, scholars can build a commentarial hierarchy of increasing clarity in which more explicit statements are projected back onto the less clear but more authoritative earlier levels. Thus the views of the more explicit texts, which reflect the views of the school or the monastery, are validated and given full authority, thereby establishing the orthodoxy of the tradition.

Such a structure does not prevent critical interpretation of these texts, as the later discussion of debate will show. Scholars do question the validity of particular glosses offered by the manuals of their monastery or by Tibetan commentaries. Such questions are often freely debated. Nevertheless, the commentarial hierarchy is so central to the construction of knowledge in their tradition that few scholars are willing to discard it. Hence, they tend to gravitate toward its interpretations despite any doubts they may have.

COMMENTARY AND CANON IN THE BUDDHIST WORLD

Other Buddhist traditions also use commentaries, but they focus more on the teachings attributed to the Buddha. For example, Theravadins generally concentrate on the main sutras as contained in the *Majjhima Nikāya* or the *Dīgha Nikāya*, whereas Chinese monks focus their study on a central sutra, such as the *Vajracchedikā*, the *Lotus*, or the *Avataṃsaka*.[31] These traditions do rely on commentaries—for example, Buddhaghosa's *Path of Purification* for the Theravada and the *Awakening of the Faith* for Chinese traditions[32]—but they are not taken to be basic texts.

Tibetans emphasize less the inspirational words of the founder (the sutras) and more the study of their content as summarized by the great Indian treatises. Tibetan curricula consist almost entirely of these treatises, which systematically present Buddhist teachings. These texts are part not of the *bka 'gyur*, the collection of the Buddha's teachings that purports to be the words of the founder, but of the *bstan 'gyur*, the translated treatises.[33] We could almost say that Tibetan scholasticism has opted for a different set of canonical texts.

This curricular choice, though apparently unique in the history of Buddhism, seems less surprising when placed in its historical context, the transmission of Buddhism from India. In its early phase, the Buddhism that developed in Tibet under the patronage of a strong dynasty was drawn from several sources—China and Central Asia as well as India. Under such circumstances, the influence of Indian Buddhism was limited, though obviously strong. At that time the study of sutras dominated, as the respective numbers of sutras and treatises translated during this period make clear. But later, transmission occurred almost exclusively from India in the absence of any strong centralizing authority. Tibetans largely took over these Indian models rather than build on the more synthetic approach employed earlier. Thus scholars adopted the shastric methodology used by late Indian Buddhists, with a resulting focus on the study of treatises rather than the sutras.

By the twelfth century, the formation of scholastic culture reinforced this textual choice; around the turn of the sixteenth century, Tibetan scholasticism started to acquire the configuration since displayed in texts, institutions, and practices. In this process, the sutras continued to lose relevance and receded even further in Tibetan intellectual life. A similar pattern can be seen in the West during the late Middle Ages, when the development of new intellectual tools displaced some of that tradition's more important texts. By the end of the fourteenth century, at most universities even the Bible was not much read in the faculty of theology.[34]

6 Two Curricular Models

My descriptions of the structure of Tibetan scholasticism have not yet provided a full view of Tibetan monastic intellectual culture, for particular monasteries do not strictly follow the general model of the five sciences. This chapter provides a more detailed examination of actual Tibetan monastic curricula. I start with the curriculum of the three Ge-luk seats, focusing on the study of the Vinaya (an area not covered elsewhere in this book), then consider the curriculum of other traditions, particularly the Nying-ma and the Sa-gya. These curricula, I argue, reduce to two basic models: that of the debating institution (rtsod grwa), found in the Ge-luk monastic seats, and that of the commentarial institution (bshad grwa), found in the three non-Ge-luk traditions.[1] Though this discussion is somewhat specialized, it also contains some important observations about the repression of writing in Ge-luk scholasticism (one of its most intriguing features, which I see as indicative of its conservative stance), the role of manuals (yig cha) in Tibetan scholasticism, and the different pegadogies of Ge-luk and non-Ge-luk institutions.

THE CURRICULUM OF DEBATING INSTITUTIONS

As described earlier, each of the three Ge-luk monastic seats has two monasteries devoted to scholastic studies; each of these six monasteries has its own curriculum. Yet those six curricula can be considered variations on the same basic model.[2] It has two aspects: the exoteric study of five great texts (gzhung chen bka' pod lnga), which is the explicit focus of the studies, and the esoteric study of tantric texts, particularly those pertaining to the Guhyasamāja (gsang ba 'dus pa) cycle, which are studied privately or reserved for a later stay at a tantric monastery. This curriculum can be divided into three parts.

Preliminary Studies

Students begin by mastering the techniques and basic concepts necessary to engage in debate. During this period, which usually lasts three years,[3] monks are trained in the art of debate as they study the Collected Topics. They are also introduced to the basic concepts of logic and epistemology that they will use throughout their studies. The texts used are manuals specific to the monastery and contain five parts:

> Collected Topics *(bsdus grwa)* proper (in three parts)
> Types of Mind *(blo rigs)*
> Types of Evidence *(rtags rigs)*

The first three texts of the Collected Topics teach monks the debate's structure, techniques, and terminology. These introductory manuals provide the key to the practice of debate.[4] The first chapter introduces the students to debate by focusing on the logical relations between colors and showing how these relations can be used in simple debates. Later chapters introduce more sophisticated topics, including the basic outline of the Buddhist conceptual universe and its main categories, and examine logical relations such as exclusion and inclusion. But not all of the topics are important for later studies; several are mere brainteasers introduced purely to sharpen the reasoning abilities of the students. In fact, the real topic of the three volumes of the Collected Topics is training in debate.

That training is completed when epistemology and logic are introduced to the students. The Types of Mind presents the main concepts used in Buddhist epistemology, a subject of great importance in the Ge-luk school. From this genre of text, students learn about the nature of knowledge, its types, and its objects. The Types of Evidence delineates the types of reasoning they must use and begins to supply the different logical tools that will be available to them during their studies. For example, students learn how to distinguish probative arguments from statements of consequence, a technique examined in greater detail in the discussion of debate as practice in chapter 10.

This propaedeutic phase of the curriculum is often completed by the study of doxography *(grub mtha', siddhānta)*, which examines Buddhist and non-Buddhist systems of belief. In this way, students acquire a sense of the shape of the tradition as a whole—its main ideas and its most important distinctions. To help them understand the structure of the Buddhist worldview, students have recourse to another genre of text, the Paths and Stages *(sa lam)*. In this stage, they also study the Seventy Topics *(don bdun cu)*, a summary of the seventy topics covered by the *Ornament*. Throughout the first part of the curriculum, no in-depth comprehension is expected of the students, who develop their reasoning abilities and learn the basic philosophical vocabulary needed for the rest of their studies. They also acquire a variety of cognitive maps on which they can locate all the ideas that will confront them in the core of the curriculum, the study of the five treatises.

Central Exoteric Studies

The central part of this monastic training is subdivided into two phases. The first and more important is the study of three texts that summarize the main aspects of nontantric Buddhism as understood by the Ge-luk tradition:

> *Abhisamayālaṃkara (Ornament of Realization)*, attributed to Maitreya
> Dharmakīrti's *Pramāṇavārttika (Commentary on Valid Cognition)*
> Candrakīrti's *Madhyamakāvatāra (Introduction to the Middle Way)*[5]

The *Abhisamayālaṃkara*, which is studied for four to six years, examines the Perfection of Wisdom literature. It provides an understanding of the Buddhist and, more particularly, Mahayana worldview together with a detailed analysis of the path, a topic to which we will return in chapter 8. Every year, one month is devoted to Dharmakīrti's *Commentary*, which outlines in detail Buddhist logic, epistemology, and philosophy of language. This text also provides the philosophical methodology for the whole curriculum, as we will see later. After they have thoroughly absorbed this training, students are ready to examine what is considered the culmination of their education, Madhyamaka philosophy. This philosophy, which provides the doctrinal core of the Ge-luk tradition, is taught with the help of Candrakīrti's *Introduction*, which serves as a guide to Nāgārjuna's seminal *Treatise of the Middle Way*.

The study of these three texts, which may take six to ten years, demands the kind of sustained philosophical thinking particularly valued by the Ge-luk tradition. Sometimes, monks who are keenly intent on leading the hermitic life leave the monastery after finishing this part of their education. Although they could benefit from further study, they are considered ready to start on their meditative careers.

In the second and final phase of studying the exoteric texts, the students already well-trained in philosophy gain more maturity and a richer overview of the tradition. It consists of two treatises:

Vasubandhu's *Abhidharma-kośa (Treasury of Abhidharma)*
Guṇaprabha's *Vinaya-sūtra*[6]

The study of the Abhidharma enriches the understanding of the Buddhist view of the world already conveyed to the students by the *Ornament*. The study of the Vinaya initiates the students in the intricacies of monastic discipline and the collective organization of the order. Because of their importance, both texts receive extended scrutiny (lasting four to eight years). Yet if they are important, why are they taught so late in the curriculum?

One reason is that these texts contribute little to the intellectual qualities most valued by Tibetan scholars—the ability to penetrate difficult theoretical concepts, raise doubts about them, explore their complexity, and come to a nuanced understanding of their implications. Such qualities are developed by the study of the first three texts, which are more philosophical and lend themselves to analysis through the commentarial and dialectical practices that are at the heart of Tibetan scholasticism. Hence, it is important to expose students to those texts when they are young and their minds can be sharpened. Later they will have time to study Abhidharma and Vinaya, which are less demanding but require a more sedate approach.

Moreover, the Vinaya is only partly relevant to Tibetan monastic practice. Although it lays out the monastic discipline, the vows to which monks commit themselves by becoming members of the order, and the principles around which the life of this order is organized, the Tibetan practice of monasticism does not strictly conform to the strictures laid down in the Vinaya. The vows are the same, but they are studied by monks only after ordination, in summaries called "Training for Bhikshus" *(dge slong gyi bslab bya)*. The actual organization of the order in Tibet derives not from the Vinaya but from the monastic constitutions we examined earlier. In addition, the monastic calendar follows the Vinaya's prescriptions only partly, as already noted.

Nevertheless, the postponement of the study of the Vinaya, the canonical discipline incumbent on any monk or nun, is quite surprising, for one would expect monks to know the rules to which they have committed themselves and the procedures they must follow. Monks notice this paradox. A caustic Mongolian Geshe is supposed to have said, "When there are vows, there is no [knowledge of the] Vinaya. When there is [knowledge of the] Vinaya, there is no vow."[7] When monks begin their careers, they are enthusiastic and pure, but do not know the monastic discipline. Instead of studying it immediately, they wait for ten or fifteen years. When they finally turn to Vinaya, they understand what they should have done—but it is too late. By then they have become blasé and have lost their enthusiasm for monastic life.[8]

Such disaffection is a particular worry for monks who have finished the first three texts in an atmosphere of intense discovery and intellectual excitement. They are well acquainted with their tradition and have the intellectual tools needed to gain a deeper, more inward-looking understanding. This change in approach is especially important for the study of the Vinaya, which examines the moral aspects of the tradition—more specifically, monastic morality—not theoretically and philosophically but practically. There is extensive discussion of the moral precepts: their number, their nature, the actions that they exclude, and so on. However, very little philosophical discussion is devoted to the nature of moral concepts.

This approach to morality reflects the belief that it cannot be understood theoretically, since moral rules can never be derived from observation or deduced philosophically. In Buddhist epistemology, morality is described as "thoroughly hidden" (*atyantaparokṣa, shin tu lkog gyur*), a domain of reality that is inaccessible to direct experience or to reason. In Buddhism as in most Indian traditions, good and bad are understood in terms of the consequences of one's karma—that is, in relation to action. An action is bad if, and only if, it leads to negative karmic results.[9] But the only way to understand that an action such as killing will lead in the future to being killed or reborn in painful circumstances is to rely on some authority, whether the instructions of a person or the exegesis of a text.[10] In the Buddhist tradition, such authority is provided by the Buddha and his teachings, particularly the Vinaya, which focuses on monastic rules and by extension provides some guidance to the laity as well.

In this area, monastic studies resemble Islamic studies, which, as noted in the previous chapter, emphasize jurisprudence—particularly in the Sunni branch of Islam, in which philosophy and theology play a limited role. That tradition overwhelmingly privileges religious jurisprudence as the main subject of learning, the central and perhaps only way to gain access to the divine. The yeshivas of Jewish tradition have the same curricular orientation. There, students focus on the two complementary aspects of the study of the Torah: the Midrash, an exegesis of the Torah that seeks to retrieve its content through a creative philological and historiographic interpretation, and the law codes as contained in the Mishnah and its commentaries, the Palestinian and Babylonian Talmuds. Together, these elements form the core of the curriculum in yeshivas, the body of knowledge through which the written scriptures are interpreted and supplemented. These studies are carried on through careful exegesis of the constitutive texts of the tradition. This ongoing conversation takes place in the study hall, the Beit Midrash, where students spend their day in reading and discussion. Moshe and Tova Halbertal describe the process: "The conversational mode of inquiry is created through the institution of the *havruta* (in which students are divided into pairs). The pairs or partners spend twelve hours a day reading together the Talmud and its commentaries, exploring its meaning and debating its complexities."[11] These studies are in part distinguished by being concerned less with philosophy than with exegetical matters or the moral and legal questions treated by the texts they interpret. Students discuss the details of midrashic interpretations or debate the rules contained in the talmudic literature, arguing about the rationale behind the prescriptions. By so doing, they get closer to the divine.

Tibetan scholars take a somewhat similar approach to studying Vinaya and Abhidharma. Rather than emphasizing the sharp dialectical and philosophical focus required in studying the first three texts (a focus discussed below), scholars stress commentarial exegesis, which here provides not just the indispensable basis of debate but the essence of the study. Debate is not a mode of inquiry into these texts but a way to assimilate their content, and it is therefore often replaced by a less formal conversation, not unlike that in which yeshiva students engage. However, the use of this method exclusively for Vinaya and Abhidharma (considered less important than the first three texts) illustrates the difference between Tibetan monastic education, which generally has a philosophical orientation, and that of the yeshiva, which stresses the exegetical and legal. Though rules and regulations can be known only through the enlightened vision of a buddha, their study is not the main way to gain access to such vision. Instead, the study of philosophy, which prefigures meditative practice, is considered *la voie royale*.

Like other parts of the tradition, the Vinaya is studied through commentaries, which in this case are particularly important. There is no other way to learn about monastic morality, for the kind of philosophical analysis suitable for the first three texts cannot be applied to morality. The Vinaya itself is said to have been proclaimed by the Buddha and hence is canonical in the narrow sense of the word. But students focus less on these texts than on their commentaries, particularly Guṇaprabha's *Vinaya-sūtra*. Contrary to what its title suggests, this difficult and long work is a treatise, not a sutra. It is studied by every scholar and memorized by better students. Less enthusiastic students are happy to memorize the verse condensation *(sdom tshig)* of its topics, and the truly reluctant try to get away with committing to memory only the most important parts, which are neither short nor easy to memorize. I must confess that I belonged to this last category.

When I moved to Se-ra to prepare for my final exams, I studied Vinaya with Geshe Lob-zang Tub-ten *(blo bzang thub bstan)*, who was kind enough to teach me. I managed painfully to memorize the key passages of the verse condensation and was able to answer questions concerning the most important points of the Vinaya studies. My overall knowledge of the Vinaya was very limited, as my fellow students knew. Yet they did not hold my ignorance against me. In their eyes, my comprehension of the first three texts was sufficient to establish me as a scholar, and their opinion accurately reflected the consensus of the Ge-luk tradition in exile. Monks nowadays have neither the leisure nor the scholarly gusto for exploring the details of the Vinaya and Abhidharma, as they did in Tibet, where scholars ferociously debated the intricacies of these texts and where knowledge of the Vinaya and the Abhidharma was considered a scholar's crowning achievement.

Another indication of the role played in the curriculum by the Vinaya and the Abhidharma is that the Tibetan commentaries used in studying them, unlike those for the first three texts, are not tradition-specific. All Tibetan Buddhist traditions agree in relying on the commentary by Tso-na-wa *(kun mkhyen tsho na ba)* on Guṇaprabha's *Vinaya-sūtra*.[12] This voluminous text explains the meaning of the root text and presents a masterly overview of all Vinaya practice and literature. It is complemented by the same author's word commentary (i.e., a gloss) of the *Vinaya-sūtra*, as well as by a commentary by Ge-dün-drub.[13] In the Ge-luk tradition, the latter is used extensively, and scholars contrast its sometimes more conservative explanations with Tso-na-wa's broader standpoint. Moreover, though manuals exist (as mentioned earlier), they are very rarely used, since their dialectical and didactic style is taken to be ill-suited to these texts.

Similarly, the study of the Abhidharma is based on a pre-Ge-luk text, the famous Great Chim *(mchims chen)* or Chim-dzö *(mchims mdzod)*, a commentary on Vasubandhu's *Abhidharma-kośa*.[14] One of the earliest of the Tibetan scholastic commentaries, it presents a masterful synthesis of the Abhidharmic systems of the Vaibhāṣika and Sautrāntika schools, as explained by Vasubandhu, and summarizes the Mahayana Abhidharma, as explained by Asaṅga. This large and invaluable summum, which covers the relevant Indian subcommentaries, is studied in conjunction with Vasubandhu's text, which is memorized. Vasubandhu's autocommentary is discussed as well, but in less detail. Often Ge-dün-drub's commentary is also used, for it provides an elegant gloss on Vasubandhu's text as well as a useful summary of the whole system.[15] The Abhidharma can be studied for up to four years, but this is very much a luxury. Compared to the Vinaya, whose study requires a sustained effort, the textual basis of the Abhidharma is easier to master; moreover, most of its topics have been already partly covered in the study of the *Ornament*.

Esoteric (Tantric) Studies

The final portion of these studies concerns the tantras, a part of the Ge-luk tradition not included in the official curriculum of monastic seats.[16] But this omission does not mean that the Ge-luk tradition is not tantric. Tantras play a central role in the Ge-luk tradition, as in any other Tibetan Buddhist tradition. Almost all Ge-luk practitioners commit themselves to tantric practice early in their career,[17] and most of the rituals in Ge-luk monasteries are tantric, as we saw in chapter 2. No traditional Tibetan monastery can be imagined without the practices revolving around protectors, practices that involve tantric elements.

It would be also a mistake to assume that tantra is not part of the overall education of a Ge-luk monk. After finishing their exoteric studies, monks from the great scholastic centers are expected to stay at a separate institution devoted to the study and practice of tantra, often one of the two tantric monasteries of Lhasa.[18] There, they are trained in the different aspects of tantra: the practice of rituals, the construction of ritual implements (including offerings and mandala making), and the study of the philosophy of tantra. The main tantric texts of their tradition revolve around the practice of three meditational deities, Guhyasamāja, Yamāntaka, and Cakrasaṃvara, and they focus on the former. They particularly study its Root Tantra (*gsang 'dus rtsa rgyud*), the Fourfold Commentary (*'grel ba bzhi sgrags*), and Shay-rab Seng-ge's Commentary on the Root Tantra (*gsang 'dus rtsa rgyud kyi ṭika*).[19] In Tibet, monks would stay up to three years at one of the tantric monasteries before passing secret examinations to receive the rank of Geshe Ngak-ram-ba (literally, "tantric scholarly spiritual friend," *sngags rams pa*). In exile, the time required has shrunk to a single year, after which monks are supposed to be experts in a tradition more vast and more complex than the exoteric tradition they study for so much longer. How is it possible that such minimal training can suffice when competence is held to be so important?

The answer to this question is that the role of tantra cannot be deduced from its limited place in the official curriculum of Ge-luk monasteries. Following the model first developed in the Ka-dam school by Atisha's disciples, the Ge-luk tradition insists on keeping tantras as secret as possible. Hence, the study and practice of tantras must be kept private and segregated from the exoteric studies, which are often described as the domain of *mtshan nyid*—which literally means "defining characteristic" and is often translated as *philosophy*. That translation is too restrictive, since the term also applies to nonphilosophical aspects of the tradition, such as the study of Vinaya and Abhidharma. In fact, the study of *mtshan nyid* concerns all the exoteric aspects of the tradition distinguished from *sngags*, the study of tantra that is to be kept secret.

Institutionally, the separation between exoteric and esoteric domains is particularly noticeable in Dre-pung and Se-ra. In Tibet, students entering those two monasteries had to limit their personal devotions to exoteric rituals to ensure that all their efforts went toward their exoteric studies.[20] They were not even allowed to keep tantric recitation texts. It is only when they started to mature into scholars—just before finishing their studies of the *Ornament*, after four to six years of hard work—that this restriction would be lifted. Then, having already gained a solid grounding in the exoteric aspects of the tradition, students were allowed to take empowerments and study tantra on their own, within the context of the private relation they had with their teacher. Moreover, in these institutions, the propitiation of protectors and other tantric practices were often the responsibility of ritual specialists,[21] who were expected to propitiate at length the tantric deities central to the survival of a Tibetan religious community. But all these ritual activities remained out of sight, and most monks, particularly scholars, had little to do with them except privately.

This Ge-luk tendency toward separating the exoteric and esoteric domains should not be overemphasized, however. First, it is hardly unique to the Ge-luk tradition, as we will see when we examine the curricula of the Sa-gya and the Ka-gyü schools. Indeed, it is the Sa-gya that is perhaps most insistent on maintaining the secrecy of tantra (the Nying-ma tradition is not overly preoccupied with this separation). Second, an insistence on separation does not mean that the esoteric practices are not taken seriously. In fact, the difference between, say, Ge-luk and Nying-ma traditions lies less in the actual practices than in how these practices are understood. For the Ge-luk, as for the Sa-gya, tantric practices should ideally be restricted to preserve their esoteric and secret character, whereas the Nying-ma tradition is more concerned with integrating these two domains and understands the restriction on tantras as concerning mainly the more secret practices of the Great Perfection. Third, the Ge-luk tradition is far from consistent in its insistence on secrecy. Empowerments are given quite liberally, and not all monasteries share Dre-pung's and Se-ra's rigorous separation between esoteric and exoteric domains. Ga-den, the seat established by Dzong-ka-ba himself, gave a greater role to tantric practice, particularly in its rituals; it even presented itself as a monastery devoted to the practice of both sutras and tantras *(mdo sngags zung 'brel)*.

ORTHODOXY AND THE REPRESSION OF WRITING

One of the most remarkable features of the Ge-luk curriculum of the three seats (a feature not found in all Ge-luk monastaries) is its discouragement of writing. As we will see later, this tradition relies on debate as the central method of education, a practice that has led to a focus on dialectical questions and the neglect of higher literary skills. José Cabezón remarks that in Ge-luk scholastic education, debate has replaced commentary.[22] Certainly, Ge-luk scholars in the three seats have devoted themselves less to the composition of commentaries than to the practice of debate. As a result, by the middle of the twentieth century few scholars there could write: that skill was reserved for the monks involved in the complex administration of the monasteries (who often were connected to aristocratic families). Geshe Rab-ten used to joke about being one of the "great scholars" in Tibet who could not write his own name!

Such scorn of writing is all the more surprising given the religious tradition's high intellectual achievements and the importance of literature and poetics in Tibetan culture. Tibetans are fond of displaying their verbal skills, and the ability to couch one's ideas in a few terse and expressive verses is considered one of the marks of an educated person. Nevertheless, this skill was mostly lacking in scholars of the three seats. This situation, which monks from these centers now perceive as abnormal, was quickly corrected in exile. Thus Geshe Rab-ten learned grammar and poetry after leaving Tibet, when he was already an established scholar.[23] He became fond of writing poetry and left a few meditative songs, as well as a much less pleasant polemical work of the sort frequently produced by Tibetan scholarship, which is often sectarian.[24] Nowadays, monks from the three monastic universities learn how to write and must pass written exams.

The absence of writing in the curriculum of the three seats in Tibet also flies in the face of the usual connection between literacy and the exercise of power. One would have expected these centers, which have enjoyed hegemony over Tibetan intellectual culture for more than two centuries, to use writing to mark and to spread their ideological influence. But in fact, their hegemony had the opposite effect. Because the Ge-luk centers were so dominant, their scholars could develop a highly idiosyncratic culture in which the mark of scholarly competence was not the possession of the literary skills usual in Tibetan culture but the ability to engage in intricate oral debates.

When monks from the three monasteries are asked about this surprising lack, they respond rather defensively that writing was discouraged to counteract the danger of scholars becoming involved in politics. This answer is not as far-fetched as it may first sound, for distrust of literary skills in the Ge-luk tradition is largely confined to the three monastic universities, whose proximity to Lhasa and the bureaucratic Tibetan government tempted the government to harness their considerable intellectual discipline and moral influence for extramonastic purposes. Hence, institutions that saw political concerns as antithetical to their calling rejected writing to protect themselves. It was during the rule of the Fifth Dalai Lama that the study of the secular branches of learning was disallowed in the three seats. After finishing their studies, scholars would go to the Nying-ma monastery Min-dröl-ling for training in grammar, poetry, and literature.[25] Many scholars chose to omit this part of the traditional curriculum and to focus only on its philosophical and religious aspects.

Other important but more remote Ge-luk centers, such as Ta-shi Lhunpo and La-brang, encouraged literary skills. Thus they (La-brang in particular) are the source of most of the Ge-luk literature written in the past two centuries. The Ge-luk attitude toward writing appears to vary with distance from the political center. By its nature, Ilana Friedrich-Silber points out, monasticism risks co-optation by the state: "Ascetic rationality and efficiency may also become a source of instability and precariousness by encouraging the increasing 'social functionalization' of monasticism, that is, the harnessing of its special efficiency to a variety of social, extramonastic (be they secular or religious) goals. Such a trend, stressed by Weber's study of Christian monasticism, cannot but threaten the insulation and segregation deemed necessary to monasticism's special vocation and purity."[26] In Tibet, the possibility of being sucked into the worldly concerns of politics was quite real for scholars living close to Lhasa, and they refrained from writing as a way to avoid overt political involvement.

Jacques Derrida's searching analysis of language and writing has taught us to see such choices as more than intellectual oddities.[27] The fear of writing often reflects underlying metaphysical assumptions as well as such pervasive cultural attitudes as a distrust of mediation and an inability to come to terms with the intrinsic contingency of language. Paradoxically, this distrust is expressed by a long line of Western thinkers through the very activity that they find so problematic—beginning, Derrida argues, with the writings of Plato. Derrida sketches the history of this dominant tradition, finding two basic variations of the mistrust of writing: a conservative fear of the dangerous proliferation of ideas that writing introduces (as represented by Plato) and a romantic worry that writing necessarily reflects the loss of origin and the fall from immediacy (as represented by Rousseau).

The application of this ingenious diagnosis does not concern only the so-called Western metaphysical tradition. Some Indian and Tibetan attitudes toward writing resemble those exposed by Derrida. The most obvious example of the fear of writing is the Vedic tradition's centuries-long insistence on keeping its text oral. As Donald Lopez argues, the Vedic attitude, like Plato's, is rooted in a conservative preoccupation with thwarting the diffusion of a potentially dangerous intellectual element. In a tradition based on the intrinsic power of the word, writing leads to an uncontrollable proliferation of ideas, which could become dangerous when put in the wrong hands.[28]

The Ge-luk distrust of writing arises primarily from a similar conservatism, rather than a belief in the primacy of oral tradition or a general unease with the mediation of experience. Unlike some Buddhist traditions, Ge-luk puts little emphasis on immediacy, adopting instead a rhetoric of gradual cultivation based on the right view. That right view, according to Ge-luk teachers, is the truth of doctrines, particularly as they are found in the writings of the founder of the tradition, Dzong-ka-ba, and his disciples. Higher spiritual realizations are difficult to attain, they argue; concentrating on basic practices combined with doctrinal studies should convince one of the truth of Dzong-ka-ba's view. Hence, they strongly insist on the doctrinal orthodoxy of the tradition.

This is not to say that preoccupation with immediacy is unknown in this tradition, as the often-recounted story of the temptation of Bo-dong illustrates. Bo-dong is said to have been so gifted that he could have attained the highest realization, buddhahood. Seeing this, a demon gave him a pen. Bo-dong was unable to resist the seduction and spent his time writing instead of meditating. He became one of the most prolific writers of the tradition, with collected works totaling more than 140 volumes, but he is said to have failed to reach spiritual realization. Though his story presents writing as a threat to higher spiritual goals, this suspicion (akin to the romantic fear of loss) has limited force both inside and outside the Ge-luk tradition. For example, the Nying-ma tradition shows a strong inclination toward writing, despite its reliance on various formulations of the rhetoric of immediacy.

The Ge-luk view writing as introducing a commentarial proliferation that may threaten the doctrinal orthodoxy of the tradition. Such a threat has special potency because the founders, Dzong-ka-ba and his disciples, provided clear and detailed doctrinal statements leaving little room for creative writing. The only task left for later scholars is to retrieve the meaning contained in these texts, and the only inquiry allowed is the oral questioning that leads to their appropriation. When his students would ask why he did not write down his ideas, Gen Nyi-ma would reply that there was no need for him to do so. Dzong-ka-ba and his disciples had said it all. What could he add?

Writing is not simply useless but may be actively dangerous. A commentary usually, though not always,[29] attempts to put across some new point or present well-known opinions in a slightly different light. In a tradition that holds that there is nothing new to be said after Dzong-ka-ba, writing threatens the established order by opening the door to the revision of well-established ideas. Ge-luk scholars often express their distrust of contemporary books that claim to raise new doubts about their tradition. Because everything has already been decided, such claims are seen as both pretentious and artificial.

TEXTS AND MANUALS IN GE-LUK EDUCATION

Before we leave the Ge-luk curriculum, a few words must be said about the role of manuals in this tradition. Because some modern scholars have exaggerated their importance, which is certainly considerable, the topic is often contentious.

These manuals are interesting in part because they resemble the texts used in medieval European scholasticism—perhaps best exemplified by Aquinas's *Summa Theologica,* a systematic and rigorous explanation of Christian theology. Each part of his text is divided in topics that are further subdivided into articles. Each article begins with a question followed by contradictory views, both affirmative and negative, each supported by several arguments. It concludes with the solution to the original question and a number of clarifications responding to counterarguments.[30] Several Tibetan monastic manuals follow a similar threefold procedure. First, false opinions are refuted *(gzhan lugs dgag pa)* through a series of debates. Then the text sets forth the correct view *(rang lugs bzhag pa)* on the topic, often by providing definitions and typologies of the subjects examined. It concludes with the repudiation of objections *(rtsod pa spong ba),* as the text raises qualms and responds to them.

But not all manuals follow this model. As noted in chapter 5, there are two general types, one called General Meaning and the other Decisive Analysis. The former, mostly overviews, gathers the relevant material from a variety of texts and provides a few debates. They are very useful to students, for they cull the relevant opinions from numerous commentaries, supply clear summaries that can be used as a basis for further studies, and collect the questions that can be raised in debates. They also provide the views that are proper to the individual monastery and differentiate it from other Ge-luk institutions. The Decisive Analysis focus more exclusively on debate, often following the threefold procedure mentioned above. They offer models of debate and arguments that can be put to practical use.

In Tibet, manuals can also serve as compilations. In European universities, there were a variety of compilations, such as the florilegium, the chrestomathy, and the testimonium, which facilitated scholastic studies by gathering the relevant texts and questions. The most famous was Peter Lombard's *Four Books of Sentences,* which brought together the most important texts and discussed the central questions that they raised. That anthologies have had similar importance in India is illustrated by the large number of texts bearing the title *samuccaya* (compendium). Other texts, such as Śāntarakṣita's *Compendium on Reality*,[31] provided both compilations and commentaries. Tibetan traditions have not taken over this genre of text, preferring to incorporate summaries of the main ideas into their manuals. Early in the history of Tibetan Buddhism, Śāntarakṣita's *Compendium* was used in the study of non-Buddhist philosophies, but it since has been largely ignored, with its most important ideas conveyed in manuals.

Each of the six monasteries that make up the three monastic seats has its own set of monastic manuals. Most monks are quite attached to them, and three—sometimes called the three great manuals *(yig cha chen po gsum)*—stand out. They are the texts composed by Jay-dzün Chö-ki Gyel-tsen *(rje btsun chos kyi rgyal mtshan,* 1469–1544), adopted by Se-ra Jay and Ga-den Jang-tse; Paṇ-chen Sö-nam-drak-ba *(paṇ chen bsod nams grags pa,* 1478–1554), adopted by Dre-pung Lo-se-ling and Ga-den Shar-tse; and Jam-yang-shay-ba *('jam dbyangs bzhad pa,* 1648–1722), adopted by Dre-pung Go-mang and Ta-shi Go-mang in La-brang. They are the main manuals in the Ge-luk tradition nowadays. The distinctions among these three sets of texts, which provide important resources for scholars, are relatively minor. Those authored by Se-ra Jay-dzün-ba and by Paṇ-chen Sö-nam-drak-ba contain similar material, differing only on their standpoints toward that material; the texts by Jam-yang-shay-ba offer slightly different content. That the Ge-luk manuals present very similar views is not surprising given that many questions have already been settled by Dzong-ka-ba and his two main disciples. Some Ge-luk scholars argue that the manuals were written specifically to encourage debate by creating minute differences between monasteries. By now, however, these differences have become so entrenched that monks often retreat from confrontation when they learn that the views they are attacking are found in the opponents' manuals. This view of manuals as quasi-canonical has also spread to non-Ge-luk schools, which now present their own commentaries as being their manuals (I have heard many Nying-ma scholars present Mi-pam's texts as their "manuals"), illustrating once again the degree to which Ge-luk scholasticism has become dominant and provided the norm that other scholastic traditions seek to emulate. Their dominance has enabled Ge-luk centers to create their own world in which scholars focus on minor differences among Ge-luk manuals, while ignoring the views of other schools. The differences between manuals can then serve as justifications of this exclusion: differences are considered, but only acceptable ones.

The Ge-luk ideological unity is not, however, just the result of the genius of the founders of the Ge-luk tradition: it is also the result of a sustained process of normalization of dissenting opinions and absorption by the three seats of smaller institutions. The historical unfoldings of this process are hard to pin down. I already mentioned Kay-drup's role in promoting orthodoxy in this tradition, which likely led to a critique within the tradition of those who were perceived to infringe this orthodoxy. The standardization of the manuals during the sixteenth and seventeenth centuries appears to have continued this process, as the new texts replaced the older manuals *(yig cha rnying pa)* that had been used in these monasteries. The reasons for this replacement are not clear. The new manuals may have been simply better than the older ones, but there are oral reports alluding to differences in the interpretation of Madhayamaka between old and new manuals.[32] However, in the absence of the old manuals it is hard to know how significant these differences were.

The ideological unity of the tradition was further enhanced by the transformation of the smaller monasteries into branches of the three seats. Originally, many of the local monasteries were scholastic centers in their own right, but they were gradually sucked into the orbit of the three seats and lost their scholarly relevance. Typical in this respect is Sang-pu, which used to be, as we will see shortly, a dominant Tibetan scholastic center. With the rise of the three seats, however, it lost its importance and gradually became a branch of Dre-pung. This process further enhanced the role of the manuals of the three seats in determining the range of acceptable opinions among Ge-luk-bas. The manuals of the smaller monasteries lost their importance and often stopped being used.[33] Only Ta-shi Lhun-po seems to have been strong enough to resist this absorption. It has remained as a separate intellectual center, retaining its own sets of manuals and its own scholarly culture. Its influence has been limited, however, and its intellectual culture (including its manuals) has been largely ignored by the mainstream of the Ge-luk tradition in the rest of Tibet.

Some Western scholars have described the Ge-luk tradition as almost solely focused on manuals and as being easily satisfied with secondhand compilations at the expense of the study of the great books, including Dzong-ka-ba's. For example, Guy Newland goes so far as to say that "In the monastic colleges of the Ge-luk school debate manuals have been the primary focus of intellectual life for the last five or six centuries."[34] Other scholars have even questioned whether Ge-luk scholars read the texts of their founder at all.[35] Having studied for many years in the Ge-luk tradition, I feel compelled to comment.

This criticism is not completely baseless. Scholars do tend to focus more on the manuals than on the great texts, as is fairly typical of scholastic traditions in general. In the later Middle Ages, difficult texts similarly were often replaced by secondhand compilations. This shift was driven by the increase in the number of relevant texts, as well as by the increase in the number of students in the university and by the necessity to standardize tools of learning. Young students found it difficult to read the original texts, and it became standard practice to focus on the more accessible summaries and florilegia.[36]

Nevertheless, the tendency of original texts to be displaced by later compilations should not be exaggerated. The historical process that occurred in the West was only partially completed in Tibet. Some commentaries became obsolete, while there has been a tendency to read fewer Indian commentaries. But the important texts, the Indian root texts and their Tibetan commentaries, have not been replaced by manuals. To understand how these texts are used, we must make a number of distinctions.

First, we must distinguish between beginners and more advanced students—not only among Tibetan students but also among Western scholars. Both vary in their ability to deal with difficult texts and in how those abilities are perceived by those with whom they study. It appears that the complaint by Western scholars that Ge-luk scholars are limited to manuals often says more about their frustration with what they are taught by

Tibetan teachers than about the Ge-luk intellectual culture of which they may have little firsthand experience.

Second, the use of manuals reflects the progressive nature of the curriculum, which introduces the most difficult topics gradually. For example, while the doctrine of emptiness is introduced at the beginning of the *Ornament*, it is fully explained much later, when the student has become well-trained. By that time, Madhyamaka has become a relatively easy topic, which in most monasteries is taught in two years. Ge-luk scholars see the incremental increase in difficulty as a great strength of their education. Gen Lob-zang Gya-tso urged me to be patient and wait to understand the hardest topics until my mind was fully ready to deal with them. To study them too early can lead to stress and frustration instead of mental peace. Gen-la often remarked that many scholars tend to be irascible.

In accord with this emphasis on gradualism, manuals are used extensively in the early phases of the curriculum; indeed, students initially rely entirely on the Collected Topics. When the study of the *Ornament* literature begins, they also use original Indian and Tibetan commentaries (such as Gyel-tsap's *Ornament of the Essence of Commentaries* and Dzong-ka-ba's *Golden Garland*).[37] The heavy dependence on manuals during this period, which lasts four to six years, largely reflects the limited abilities of students confronting their first original Indian text and its commentaries. The material is enormously complicated, and the use of manuals enables the students to survey a wide spectrum of topics and opinions. It also reflects the Ge-luk insistence on debate as the central pedagogical methodology, as we will see later. By the time the students advance to Madhyamaka philosophy, some six to eight years after beginning their studies, manuals are less important as they examine Dzong-ka-ba's texts. The last two topics, the Vinaya and Abhidharma, are studied with minimal reliance on manuals, for the dialectical style is inappropriate to topics that require patient exegesis.

Logic and epistemology were studied in Tibet outside the monasteries—monks from the three seats often met at Jang for that purpose (see chapter 11). Obviously manuals, which are monastery-specific, could not be used when scholars from different monasteries learned together. Moreover, most manuals do not fully treat logic and epistemology.[38] Hence, Gyel-tsap's literal explanation of Dharmakīrti's *Commentary* is taken as the most authoritative; those by other disciples of Dzong-ka-ba, such as Kay-drup and Ge-dün-drub, are also used.[39]

The use of manuals also varies with the personal inclinations of teachers, the majority of whom insist strongly on their importance as the expression of the doctrinal correctness of their tradition. Some even conceive their main mission to be the teaching of their monastery's manuals. Jeffrey Hopkins describes one of his teachers, who was so partial to the manuals of his monastery, Go-mang, that he would turn his head away and spit on the floor at the mere mention of the manual of Lo-se-ling, the rival monastery in Dre-pung.[40] Other teachers see the manuals simply as pedagogical tools, their attitude best exemplified by Gen Nyi-ma. He had little patience with students who asked questions about the manuals of his monastery, Lo-se-ling, and would respond with visible disdain, "Manual!" *(yig cha)*, as if that said it all. He would show more interest in a question concerning Dzong-ka-ba's texts or, even better, some Indian treatises.

Thus, the claim that the use of manuals is crucial in the Ge-luk tradition must be examined from a variety of angles. Like many stereotypes, it contains some truth about Ge-luk monastic education, particularly in its early stages. But more seasoned scholars do not neglect the texts of the founders of their tradition. For mature scholars, the Ge-luk tradition is in those works and not the limited secondhand compilations, however useful the latter may be to the student.[41]

THE CURRICULUM OF COMMENTARIAL INSTITUTIONS

The texts studied in non-Ge-luk institutions vary from school to school. The curriculum of Nying-ma institutions often revolves around the study of the "thirteen great texts" *(gzhung chen bco gsum)*, which we will examine shortly, whereas that of Sa-gya consists of the "eighteen texts of great renown" *(grags chen bcu brgyad)*.[42] Sa-gya scholars also mention "six great texts" *(pod chen drug)*.[43] The Ka-gyü curriculum consists of the same five texts found in the Ge-luk tradition, as well as the "eight great texts of the sutra and tantra" *(mdo sngags gzhung chen brgyad)* when tantras are included.

The curriculum in the Nying-ma monastery of Nam-dröl-ling monastery is quite typical of the non-Ge-luk institutions of higher learning.[44] The monastery of Nam-dröl-ling is the exiled version of the Pa-yül *(dpal yul)* monastery, one of the six great monastic centers of the Nying-ma school, founded in 1665 by Rig-dzing Kun-zang Shay-rab *(rig 'dzin kun bzang shes rab)*. The Nam-dröl-ling monastery, containing more than two thousand monks, relocated to Bylakuppe in South India, a few miles from Se-ra. The curriculum examined here is that of the monastery's commentarial school *(bshad grwa)*, the Ngagyur Nyingma Institute (henceforth referred to as Nam-dröl-ling), which has its own administration, kitchen, and temple. It was created by Pe-nor Rin-po-che at the beginning of the 1970s and contains more than four hundred students, making it the largest institution of its type in the exile community.[45] Still, it is smaller than Se-ra, most of whose more than four thousand monks are actively engaged in scholastic studies. In recent years, larger non-Ge-luk institutions have developed in Tibet, such as the monastery founded by Ken-po Jik-may Pun-tsok *(mkhan po 'jigs med phun tshogs)* in Ser-tok (Kham), where thousands of monks and nuns are being trained in the classical scholastic tradition and in the lore of the Great Perfection.[46]

The Nam-dröl-ling curriculum centers on the study of the thirteen great texts. Like the Ge-luk curriculum, it can be divided into three parts: preliminary studies, central exoteric studies (of the thirteen texts themselves), and esoteric (tantric) studies. The first part, which lasts one year, focuses on two texts:

Pe-ma-wang-gyel *(padma dbang rgyal,* fourteenth century), *Treatise Ascertaining the Three Types of Vow*[47]

Śāntideva, *Bodhisattvacaryāvatāra (Introduction to the Bodhisattva Way of Life)*

Along with these texts, which are studied with the help of literal glosses, students are taught grammar, poetry, and the history of Buddhism *(chos 'byung)* in Tibet. Thus, students are introduced not only to Buddhist topics pertaining to the first of the five major sciences (see chapter 5), as in the three Ge-luk monastic seats, but also to the other branches of learning. During this period students learn basic Buddhist ideas and Mahayana practices, as well as the three sets of vows (pratimokṣa, bodhisattva, and tantra) to which Tibetan practitioners usually commit themselves. Tantric concepts such as the difference between sutras and tantras, a topic formally discussed by Ge-luk scholars only after they have completed their exoteric studies, are introduced here.

The main part of the curriculum, centered on the study of the thirteen great texts, is divided into two phases, "lower" and "higher." In the first four years, students are exposed to the classical exoteric tradition, including Madhyamaka philosophy, and the study of Indian treatises. The final two years further develop the students' understanding of Buddhist philosophy. The lower exoteric course covers the first six of the thirteen texts:

Nāgārjuna's *Mūlamadhyamakakārikā (Treatise of the Middle Way)*
Āryadeva's *Catuḥśataka (Four Hundred Stanzas)*
Candrakīrti's *Madhyamakāvatāra (Introduction to the Middle Way)*

Asaṅga's *Abhidharma-samuccaya (Compendium of Abhidharma)*
Vasubandhu's *Abhidharma-kośa (Treasury of Abhidharma)*
Dharmakīrti's *Pramāṇavārttika (Commentary on Valid Cognition)*[48]

These texts are studied with their commentaries, Indian and Tibetan. The curriculum relies throughout on Mi-pam's texts, for they provide the main standpoint of the Nying-ma tradition, much as Go-ram-ba's texts do for the Sa-gya tradition. Ken-po Zhan-pan's literal glosses on the thirteen Indian texts are also used to read the great Indian texts.[49] A distinctive feature of this curriculum is its emphasis on Śāntarakṣita's *Ornament of the Middle Way*, which, though not listed with the thirteen great texts, is studied together with its commentary by Mi-pam.[50] During this phase of the curriculum, a variety of other auxiliary topics (grammar, composition, poetics, history) are also examined.

Also distinctive in Nam-dröl-ling's approach is the limited treatment of logic and epistemology, in contrast not only with the Ge-luk tradition but also with the Sa-gya emphasis on Sa-paṇ's *Treasure on the Science of Valid Cognition*. Those topics are studied only during the fourth year, when Dharmakīrti's texts are briefly considered together with Mi-pam's word commentary. Nam-dröl-ling students readily confess their weakness in logic and epistemology and their embarrassment at the failure of their curriculum to include Sa-paṇ's famous *Treasure*. This text, which Mi-pam has commented on, is omitted, perhaps for parochial reasons: to study a Sa-gya text would be tantamount to admitting that the Pa-yül tradition is somehow lacking. Hence, the text is never officially studied, though it is constantly referred to since it provides the mainstay of non-Ge-luk interpretations of Dharmakīrti.[51] Nonetheless, by the end of this course students can claim a relatively sound command of Buddhist philosophy as well as the general structure of the Buddhist tradition.

The higher exoteric course focuses on the remaining seven texts:

Mahāyānottaratantra (The Superior Continuum)
Abhisamayālaṃkara (Ornament of Realization)
Mahāyāna-sūtrālaṃkara (Ornament of the Mahayana Sūtras)
Madhyānta-vibhaṅga (Differentiation of the Middle and the Extremes)
Dharma-dharmatā-vibhaṅga (Differentiation of Phenomena and [Ultimate] Nature)
Pratimokṣa-sūtra (the only teaching of the Buddha on the list of thirteen)
Guṇaprabha's *Vinaya-sūtra*[52]

This part of the curriculum revolves around the study of the five texts attributed to Maitreya; as we will see in chapter 8, they concern the structure of the Mahayana path. It complements the lower esoteric course and completes the exoteric part of the curriculum. By this time, students should have gained a solid understanding of a variety of points of view in Buddhist philosophy and a good grasp of numerous aspects of the Buddhist path. Now able to articulate a Nying-ma view of the texts they have studied against the dominant Ge-luk view, they are ready to move on to the final part of the curriculum.

That third and final part is the esoteric study of tantras, which relies on the following texts:

the commentary by Yon-den-gya-tso *(yon tan rgya mtsho)* on Jik-may-ling-pa's *('jigs med gling pa,* 1729–1789) *Treasury of Qualities (yon tan mdzod)*

the commentary by Mi-pam on the *Guhyagarbha* tantra

the commentary by Do-grub-chen *(rdo grub chen)* on the *Guhyagarbha* tantra

the *Trilogy of Self-Liberation (rang grol skor gsum)*

the *Trilogy of Resting (ngal gso skor gsum)*, particularly *Resting [in] the Mind as Such (sems nyid ngal gso)*[53]

The Nying-ma tradition focuses on the *Guhyagarbha* tantra, studied during the seventh and eighth years of the curriculum with the help of the first three of the sets of commentaries listed above. It provides the student an understanding of the philosophy and configuration of the tantric path, complemented during the ninth and last year by a brief introduction to the view of the Great Perfection. This central tenet of the Nying-ma tradition is approached by studying Long-chen-rab-jam-ba's two trilogies (the latter two commentaries listed above). Other tantric texts are also examined, particularly Mi-pam's commentary on the *Eight Precepts of Practice (sgrub pa bka' brgyad)* and Jik-may-ling-pa's work on the stage of development of tantric practice. In this way, students begin to grasp the world of tantras, a Nying-ma specialty. But we should notice that even in the Nying-ma tradition, tantric texts are not part of the standard curricular list, an omission that befits their esoteric status. In all Tibetan Buddhist traditions, tantras are the supplement that is supposed to remain secret, and the method of their study varies from school to school. As noted above, in the Ge-luk tradition tantras are studied in separate institutions, the tantric monasteries;

but among the Sa-gya-bas, tantras are usually studied within the confines of a guru-disciple relationship.

In the Kar-ma Ka-gyü tradition, tantras constitute a separate course of study. At least in Rum-tek, the main seat of this tradition in exile, tantras are not included in the nine-year program of the commentarial school. After the study of the five texts is completed, the student enters a supplemental three-year course devoted to obtaining the title of Ngak-ram-ba (*sngags rams pa;* lit., "tantric scholarly spiritual friend," the same title sought by Ge-luk monks in their tantric studies). The Ka-gyü curriculum focuses here on the Hevajra tantra, studied in the light of Rang-jung Dor-jay's *Internal Profundity*.[54] This esoteric study is introduced by Maitreya's *Mahāyānottaratantra*, which provides a bridge between sutras and tantras as the student completes the eight great texts of the sutra and tantra of the Ka-gyü tradition. Unfortunately, this part of the curriculum has yet to be implemented in exile, and students have been studying tantras mostly in private.[55]

TWO PEDAGOGICAL APPROACHES

In comparing the curricular models of the debating and commentarial institutions, we are immediately struck by the difference in the number of texts and the time devoted to their study. Whereas in the Ge-luk curriculum only five texts are studied for fifteen to twenty years, Nam-dröl-ling monks study at least thirteen texts in half that time. The differential is much greater when we include the tantric works (not covered in the Ge-luk curriculum) and additional texts covering auxiliary topics (grammar, poetry, history, etc.). Ge-luk students tend to focus exclusively on the inner science and logic, the first two of the standard five major branches of learning; students in commentarial institutions clearly cover more subjects, as they are introduced to some of the other sciences, particularly grammar and poetics, and receive more extensive practice in writing.

But the commentarial institutions limit their literary focus to an auxiliary role, and all religious traditions keep the emphasis on the study of Buddhism. Thus, for the most part, curricula of commentarial and debating institutions have similar content. Their study of Buddhism and its philosophy can be grouped into five main areas: Madhyamaka philosophy, logic and epistemology, the study of the path, monastic discipline, and tantra. They differ, however, in their approach to those five topics.

For each topic the Ge-luk curriculum tends to focus on a single text, which is then supplemented by further commentaries and manuals. The only exception is the study of the path, which relies on two texts: the *Ornament of Realization* attributed to Maitreya and Vasubandhu's *Treasury of Abhidharma* (which some would not count as a study of the path). But because the textual overlap is only partial—the former covers the Mahayana path, the latter the "Hinayana" path—even here, each topic is in effect examined through a single text. By contrast, the Nam-dröl-ling curriculum includes several of the relevant texts for each main area. For example, when the Mahayana path is considered, students read all five treatises attributed to Maitreya. Similarly, when the Abhidharma is studied, both Vasubandhu's and Asaṅga's texts are examined.

Thus, the main difference between Nying-ma and Ge-luk models clearly lies less in their content than in their educational style. The Ge-luk tradition focuses on a few texts and emphasizes the practice of dialectical debate as the central method of education. This tradition has therefore tended to limit the texts studied and to neglect higher literary skills, especially in the three monastic universities. The Nying-ma tradition, as exemplified by the Nam-dröl-ling curriculum, is more textual. It emphasizes commentary over debate, offering a more rounded education that includes some literary as well as dialectical skills.

A Day in a Commentarial Institution

This commentarial orientation is reflected in the schedule at Nam-dröl-ling, which is typical of such a school:[56]

5:00	Rising time
5:00–7:00	Morning study
7:00–8:30	Breakfast and revision
8:30–11:00	Morning class
11:00–13:00	Lunch and break
13:00–15:00	Afternoon revision class
15:00–15:30	Afternoon tea
15:30–16:30	Evening class
16:30–17:00	Free time
17:00–18:00	Evening debate
18:00–19:30	Dinner
19:30–21:30	Evening study
21:30–22:30	Evening tea
23:00	Bedtime

In even a cursory look at the schedule, we see the importance of commentary in this institution. Debate is practiced for only one hour a day (with a longer formal debate on Sundays). Most of the time is devoted to the practice of commentary, which revolves around the morning class during which students learn new material. This class, which consists mostly of an explanation of a root text with a few debates, is similar to those I attended in Geluk institutions (described in chapter 10).

After lunch, students review the material covered in the morning, check their understanding of the material, and prepare questions. At 15:30 they reconvene with another teacher, either a junior teacher or a senior student, to review the material covered in the morning. This teacher makes sure that students understand the text. Comparatively little attention is paid to exploring the topic in depth. Though questions are raised in preparation for the evening debate, the overwhelming concern is to be able to explain the text and to provide glosses. After dinner, students review their lessons again, in preparation for the dreaded morning examination. Before going to bed, they also review the texts that they have memorized previously.

In the morning, students rise at five o'clock. They wash their hands, faces, teeth, and tongue (with a special scraper also used by Indians); clean their rooms (putting aside the bedding and sweeping the floor); and make offerings on their altar by burning incense and filling seven small bowls with water. Students are then ready to start their day with their personal devotions, memorization, and a final review of the latest lesson before the impending examination.

During breakfast, the names of all students are brought to the abbot, separated by class; a name is drawn out for each class. This student will have to explain and summarize the lesson of the previous day on short notice. At nine o'clock (no more than half an hour later), the gong calls the students to the main class of the day. Before starting on a new lesson, the designated student must comment on the preceding day's text. He starts by explaining its main point and then proceeds to comment on the text, line by line. The student may also provide a summary of the topic, thus providing a useful recapitulation of the lesson. This exercise, which takes from twenty to thirty minutes, can be rather trying. Good students usually do well with practice and are able to refresh the memory of their classmates. Some may even offer their own personal insights, and in capable hands the whole exercise often ends with a discussion on some difficult point. The experience of less adept students or of beginners is frequently not so happy. Left to their own devices, their performance can range from incoherent and clumsy explanations, to bits of explanation painfully sandwiched between long moments of silence, to the inability to articulate a single word.

The Nying-ma Ken-po Pal-den Shay-rab, whose training in basic literacy we examined in chapter 4, recounts a particularly humiliating experience. He had just arrived at Ri-wo-che, one of the more important Nyingma commentarial schools in Eastern Tibet, where he had started his higher education with a complete lack of enthusiasm. He describes himself as having been very young (twelve or thirteen) and extremely arrogant; the son of the leader of the quasi-monastic lay community, he had been the best in his village. He did not feel motivated to study, preferring to spend his time daydreaming or shooting the breeze with friends. He had been in the school for a few months, studying Śāntideva's *Introduction*, when his name was called. In Tibet, students had to explain the lesson of the preceding day immediately. Ken-po-la had not studied, however, and was unable to say anything. Instead of calling on another and allowing him to sit down, the disciplinarian kept him on the spot in a deathly and humiliating silence for close to twenty minutes.

When students are unable to give a convincing performance, they are examined again the next day. I hardly need say that this time Ken-po-la was prepared. He sought help from older students, and because he was bright and already relatively educated, he was able to do quite well. At the end of the examination, the abbot usually starts a new lesson. This day, however, the disciplinarian held up the proceedings: he was not about to let Pal-den Shay-rab get off so easily. He stood up and began a long tirade against Pal-den Shay-rab, accusing him of being proud, lazy, and disruptive. No one finds it pleasant to be singled out in this way in the midst of a crowd, but in Tibetan society, which strongly emphasizes group harmony and cohesion, such treatment is extremely humiliating. For Pal-den Shay-rab, it was worse than being left to stand in deep silence. He was utterly mortified and wondered whether he should leave Ri-wo-che. But he realized that to do so would be to concede defeat. He would have to return empty-handed to his village, which he had left with a great display of confidence in his future scholarly achievements. He therefore decided to stick it out and begin to study seriously. Many years later, he recalled this experience with obvious emotion, understanding that it was a turning point in his life, leading him to transform himself from a mediocre drifter into a committed scholar.

The main events of the day, the morning examination and the teaching, concern commentary, which is both the central method of education and the focus of the community. Here, debate is used to strengthen and support the practice of commentary; in the Ge-luk seats, in contrast, the whole day is organized as a function of debates. Commentary also provides the method to evaluate the progress of students, who are examined not through debate but through their comments on texts.

Commentarial institutions tend to control their students more tightly than do the Ge-luk monastic seats. Students are examined yearly, mostly on their ability to comment in writing on certain passages that they have studied. The tests are similar to those in modern schools: students feverishly prepare and cram before exams, write their exams as fast as they can, and anxiously await the results. A set minimum score must be attained before students move on to the next class; they can be expelled if they repeatedly fail to meet academic standards, but such expulsions are relatively rare. Moreover, an effort is made to care for those students who fail. They might be employed by the institution, or found another job that makes use of their literacy, such as secretary in a monastery.

The final examinations in commentarial institutions take place after the set course of studies is completed. At Nam-dröl-ling, this process is supposed to take twelve years, with three years devoted to doing specialized research on a single topic and to writing a thesis. Unfortunately, the last part of this excellent scheme has yet to be implemented, and thus the course effectively lasts nine years.[57] Students next spend three years teaching in smaller Nying-ma monasteries, where they are in high demand. They then may be called Ken-po *(mkhan po)*, a title usually translated as "abbot," though here it does not imply a monastic charge. This title is not earned simply by examination but is granted by Pe-nor Rin-po-che, Nam-dröl-ling's lama, who judges the moral and scholarly qualities of the candidate. Many express the desire to start intensive meditative practice, but qualified scholars are so scarce that they are often asked to perform the scholarly tasks for which they have been trained.

As this brief description makes clear, the Nying-ma tradition is not exclusively hermitic, rejecting the life of the mind. Far from opposing scholasticism, Nying-ma masters such as Pal-den Shay-rab are profoundly imbued with classical scholarship, while at the same time showing their commitment to the practice of meditation. This combination of learning and practice has been the normative ideal of all the main Tibetan traditions for centuries. Contemporary Nying-ma education displays this dual emphasis not just in exile but also in Tibet, where Nying-ma scholars have attempted to revive their tradition by opening numerous commentarial schools; in Ser-tok, Ken-po Jik-may Pun-tsok is training thousands of monks and nuns. His monastery has become the largest and most vital Buddhist institution in Tibet, following the traditions, texts, and practices of the Nying-ma school.[58]

What distinguishes Nying-ma from Ge-luk masters is their style of scholarship. One of the main Nying-ma complaints against Ge-luk scholars is that they tend to have narrow textual knowledge *(mthong cha chung ba;* lit., "there is little that they see")*. Ge-luk scholars are good debaters, but they have limited their purview of the classical Indian tradition to a few texts, which they interpret selectively. On this account, Ge-luk scholars tend to ignore the interpretations of other Tibetan schools and restrict themselves to a thoroughly ahistorical confrontation between their interpretations and a few Indian texts. Nying-ma scholars pride themselves on their more extensive scholarship, which encompasses numerous texts and takes note of the variety of Tibetan interpretations. While conceding that they are not as proficient at debate as Ge-luk-bas, they argue that their textual understanding is superior, for debate often turns into mere quibbling, favoring cleverness over truth. These claims demonstrate that Nying-ma-bas understand their own tradition as being based on a commentarial style of scholarship, which differs from the Ge-luk dialectical model in emphasizing texts, not in being free from the allegedly polluting influence of clerical scholasticism.

A Brief Historical Retrospective: Dialectic and Rhetoric

The differences between the two Tibetan pedagogical approaches and their institutional forms are clear. What is less clear is the history of these two traditions and how long ago they diverged.

When tracing the development of Tibetan scholasticism, scholars often return to the tradition stemming from Ngok Lo-tsa-wa (1059–1109) and Cha-ba Chö ki Seng-ge (1109–1169), both associated with the monastery of Sang-pu. This monastery, founded in 1073 by Ngok Lek-bay-shay-rab, was at first a minor center of Buddhist practice; it became an important center of study under the guidance of Ngok's nephew, the famous translator Ngok. Though he belonged to the Ka-dam tradition, which at its beginnings looked askance at the study of philosophy, Ngok was deeply interested in scholarly studies. Under his influence, Tibetan Buddhism became more philosophically and scholastically oriented. Ngok wrote summaries of such texts as the *Ornament,* thus starting a new genre—the Summary *(bsdus don)*—that began an indigenous commentarial tradition.

The work of Cha-ba, one of Ngok's followers, made Sang-pu much more important as a center of learning.[59] Under his influence, Sang-pu became the center of an original Tibetan scholastic tradition. He also offered some of the first indigenous explanations of Dharmakīrti's thought, favoring a realist interpretation of this largely nominalist system. In writing the first Summary of Dharmakīrti's thought, Cha-ba initiated a genre of logico-epistemological manuals that has proven immensely successful. Among these manuals figures Sa-paṇ's masterpiece, the *Treasure on the Science of Valid Cognition (tshad ma rigs gter)*, which has been the main text concerning logic and epistemology among non-Ge-luk traditions. The genre also gave rise to the Collected Topics type of literature, which provides the basis for the debate training among Ge-luk-bas.

As elaborated at Sang-pu and in other centers, the purpose of Tibetan scholasticism was to assimilate the Indian Buddhist tradition of higher learning. Hence, its first and greatest efforts were aimed at translating Sanskrit texts. In doing so, it built on the impressive achievements of the early Buddhists in Tibet, who created extensive dictionaries such as the *Two-Volume Lexicon (sgra sbyor bam po gnyis pa)* and translated many texts during a short period (760–840). During the second period of translation (the eleventh to thirteenth centuries), original indigenous commentaries were produced to explain the translated texts.

Because it sought to absorb classical Indian learning, the Tibetan scholasticism of that period used the shastric methodology, taking treatises as the basis for further commentaries. Yet the Tibetan scholasticism of that period was more than just an imitation of the Indian model. For example, its form of debate differed, as we will see later. In addition, new scholarly methods were created to facilitate the study of translated texts, the most salient being the parsing of Indian root texts into "divisions" *(sa bcad)*. When confronted with the unsystematic Indian texts, Tibetan commentaries tried to impose some order by dividing the texts into sections and subsections. This practice has become extremely widespread among Tibetan commentators, who often proceed by dividing and subdividing the text to death. We must also remember that the scholasticism of that period was influenced not just by Indian models but also by other Buddhist traditions, particularly some of the Chinese schools that had affected the earliest development of Buddhism in Tibet.

The complex tradition that developed around Sang-pu was the starting point of Tibetan scholasticism. Later on, however, some thinkers came to disagree with its views and methods. The most important critic was Sa-paṇ, who proposed drawing instead on the paṇḍit model, based on classical Indian learning and focused on a threefold discipline: composition, exposition, and debate. Arguing that monastic education neglected literature and poetry, Sa-paṇ recommended a more rhetorically inclined approach that combined debate with the study of Indian literature. Sa-paṇ also criticized the way that Tibetans conducted debates, urging that in this area, too, they should return to classical Indian procedures.

These two approaches to education—Sa-pan's pandit model and the dialectical model developed at Sang-pu—are paralleled in the Western tradition by rhetoric-based and philosophy-based pedagogies, as noted in the previous chapter. It may thus appear that the opposing models account for the differences between the dialectical and commentarial orientations, with the tradition of the three Ge-luk monastic seats traceable back to Sang-pu and the non-Ge-luk commentarial model to Sa-pan.

Though appearances are not entirely deceiving, the evidence suggests a considerably more complex picture. In the Tibetan world, unlike medieval Europe, dialectic dominated rhetoric, particularly in the monasteries. Even the commentarial institutions, which claim to be inspired by Sa-pan's model, emphasize literature less than he advocated and practice debate much as followers of the Sang-pu tradition do. In fact, Sa-pan did not succeed in displacing the established model of learning. The recommendations of the *Entrance to the Gate for the Wise* were treated by monastic scholars as normative ideals but were never implemented. Hence, the opposition between dialectic and rhetoric, however interesting as a heuristic, was not crucial in shaping the two competing educational styles. Rather than being the source of the commentarial pedagogy examined above, Sa-pan's pandit model constitutes a third curricular approach, whose influence on monastic circles has been limited.

However, Sa-pan did make Tibetan scholasticism more exclusively "Indological." Henceforth, the Indian models of learning dominated Tibetan higher learning to the exclusion of other Buddhist traditions. Those models as set forth by Sa-pan provided the standards according to which learning was to be measured. But they remained ideals that were never fully implemented in Tibetan monasteries, and learning has remained divided between the religio-philosophical orientation of monks and the literary inclinations of the educated laity. To explain the differences between the debating and commentarial institutions, we need to examine how those two traditions crystallized under various forms of pressure, including political forces.

The Fluidity of the Classical Period   In the classical period of Tibetan scholasticism, at least up to the fifteenth century, monks paid little attention to sectarian affiliations. They would go from monastery to monastery to study with teachers of particular specializations regardless of their schools. Doctrinal eclecticism meant that individual thinkers could offer their own personal interpretations without paying a great deal of attention to the orthodoxy of the school with which they were formally affiliated. Differences were seen as reflecting not deep sectarian divisions but individual variations among teachers and lineages. After they had studied a certain number of texts, scholars would tour other centers to be examined on them; successful candidates then graduated. This custom of undergoing a defense during a scholastic tour *(grwa bskor dam bca')*, which was started at Tse-thang *(rtse thang)* at the instigation of the ruler Jang-chub Gyel-tsen (1302–1364), gradually spread to other centers.[60]

Dzong-ka-ba's education exemplifies the eclectic atmosphere of this period.[61] Born in Amdo, Dzong-ka-ba moved to Central Tibet at the age of sixteen to be trained in the scholastic tradition, which was by that time well-established there. He went to Tze-chen to study Madhyamaka, logic, epistemology, and Abhidharma with Ren-da-wa; to De-wa-chen *(bde ba chen)* to study the *Ornament;* and to Zha-lu to study the Heruka tantra. He also toured, and was examined at, the great scholastic centers of Central Tibet, including Nar-thang *(snar thang)*, Sa-gya, and the Ka-gyü establishment of Den-sa-tel *(gdan sa thel)*.[62] Dzong-ka-ba followed the classical commentarial procedure, studying root texts in the light of commentaries and debating. He is said to have taken part at the age of twenty-four in the Spring Session at Nar-thang,[63] but the nature of this session *(chos thog)* is not clear; today's sessions in the three Ge-luk monastic seats consist of debates, but the same may not have been true then. Hagiographies also describe Dzong-ka-ba's successes in his scholastic tours, but even there the details are obscure. Scholastic tours seem to have required that the candidate both give an explanation *(bshad pa)* of the texts on which he was examined and engage in a debate in which he would answer questions about his explanations, as suggested by the name of these tours ("defense [during] a scholastic tour," *grwa bskor dam bca')*.[64] Though it is difficult to know the place of debate in Dzong-ka-ba's daily training, he could not have received as extensive practice as do modern students in the three Ge-luk monastic seats, since he was often on the move and spent long stretches alone. In fact, the education of the founder of the Ge-luk tradition appears in some ways to resemble more closely what is found nowadays in the non-Ge-luk commentarial institutions than in the three Ge-luk seats, where debate has become dominant.

The hagiography of another great figure of the time, Bo-dong, suggests a similar picture. In Bo-dong's education, the study of philosophy did not preclude extensive training in literature. He toured the main scholastic centers at age twenty-three. During his stay at Sang-pu, he encountered the famous Sa-gya teacher Yak-dön (*g.yag ston sangs rgyas dpal*, 1348–1414), who praised him for undergoing such a tour and asked him how many texts he had studied. "Fifteen," answered Bo-dong. "Have you also studied Sa-paṇ's *Treasure?*" asked Yak-dön. When Bo-dong replied that he had, Yak-dön marveled at the accomplishment of such a young mind: "We could almost say that the texts you have studied equal your age." But he also wanted to test the young scholar's comprehension of some of the more controversial points of the *Treasure.* "Does self-cognition have an object?" Yak-dön asked. "Yes, it does," responded our young hero respectfully. Yak-dön was less than pleased by this answer, which contradicts the *Treasure.* But Bo-dong, unimpressed by the authority of a senior scholar, pointedly asked, "How can self-cognition be a valid cognition if it does not have an object?" According to the hagiography, the exchange was considered to be a refutation of Yak-dön, "an unanswerable unwanted consequence" (*zlog med kyi thal ba*). Later on, when examined in front of the great assembly of the scholars of Sang-pu (a formal occasion that usually intimidates even the best thinkers), Bo-dong engaged Yak-dön in another spectacular exchange, during which the latter was obliged to take the position that ordinary objects such as pots are not things (*dngos po*). "If they are not, this precludes their being material," concluded Bo-dong, who was judged victorious by the attending scholars.[65]

This biography, written in praise of Bo-dong, captures some of the tensions that existed in the classical scholastic world of Central Tibet, particularly those between followers of Cha-ba and of Sa-paṇ. Bo-dong's answer was noteworthy because it came from a precocious young man and was seen by some to humiliate a seasoned but controversial defender of Sa-paṇ's views. By vindicating Cha-ba's tradition and its philosophical realism, it gave comfort to those who opposed Yak-dön. The situation at Sang-pu appears to have been quite complex. Followers of Cha-ba and of Sa-paṇ cohabited in the same monastic seat, which was divided into two monasteries. Ka-dam elements presumably favored Cha-ba's views, whereas Sa-gya elements may have favored Sa-paṇ's ideas as expounded by Yak-dön and his student Rong-dön (*rong ston*, 1367–1449). But this division concerned philosophical questions, not pedagogy—there is no sign that one side was pushing debate while the other inclined toward commentary by institutional affiliation.

It is possible that there were differences between scholastic centers. Bo-dong's biography describes his tour in Sang-pu as involving a spirited debate, whereas at Tse-thang and De-wa-chen his explanations of texts were given in much less confrontational settings.[66] Perhaps Tse-thang and

De-wa-chen were more commentarial in their orientation, and Sang-pu more dialectical, but at our current state of knowledge such inferences are highly speculative. In any case, if such distinctions existed, they were seen not as deep oppositions but merely as variations in each center's specialty.

The Crystallization of High Scholasticism   During the second half of the fifteenth century the religious landscape began to change, as political events combined with sectarian disputes to create profound divisions within the scholarly world. Those divisions led to the increasing institutionaliza-tion that characterizes the period of high scholasticism (sixteenth to twenti-eth centuries), a process heightened by the growth of monasteries. It is hard for historians to estimate the size of monasteries, but my impression is that earlier scholastic centers were relatively small (perhaps a few hundred monks), with the possible exception of Sang-pu.[67] Around the turn of the fifteenth century, Dzong-ka-ba began to promote monasticism, which is at the heart of the development of what was then called the Ga-den school. One of Dzong-ka-ba's most important actions was the establishment in 1409 of the Great Prayer *(smon lam chen mo)* festival, which is said to have brought together 8,000 monks.[68] Later that year, Ga-den itself was established, and Dre-pung and Se-ra followed within a decade. These monasteries grew rapidly, with more than 1,000 monks at Dre-pung during the fifteenth cen-tury; its population reached several thousand in the seventeenth century. This trend continued, with government support from the seventeenth cen-tury onward, and by 1959 Dre-pung consisted of more than 13,000 monks. Such growth is at the root of the success of the Ge-luk tradition.

At the same time, monastic structure was becoming more rigid. Rather than wandering freely from center to center, as in the past, scholars became identified with a particular monastery to which they remained tied for their whole lives. The scholastic tour shrank to encompass only other mon-asteries in the same seat or the other classes in the same monastery. As members of large monasteries that dominated the intellectual life of the country, Ge-luk scholars could easily forget that scholarship was not lim-ited to the three seats. This tendency to ignore the other Tibetan schools also had an ideological basis, for the Ge-luk tradition viewed Dzong-ka-ba as the only valid interpreter of Indian Buddhism. The other schools were seen as illegitimate remnants of a tradition now obsolete, and their ideas were dismissed as the views of "previous Tibetans" *(bod snga ra ba)*.

This process was enabled by the advent of xylographic printing, brought during this time from Western China to Tibet. Dzong-ka-ba oversaw the production of the first book printed in Tibet, the *Guhyasamājamūla Tantra*.

After his death, his supporters continued in this vein, printing his works as well as the writings of others.[69] It is difficult to assess the effects of printing and the rapidity of its spread, but the development of scholastic culture was likely aided by this technology; large scholastic centers seem to require some technological support for the mass production of books. In the West, the growth of universities in the thirteenth century took place as the copying of manuscripts was transformed into an industry. Was the growth of large Tibetan scholastic centers made possible by block printing? Probably, but only further research will answer this question; for now, it is clear that the availability of texts favored the institutionalization of learning that took place during the high scholastic period.

This institutionalization manifested itself in the creation of manuals corresponding to the establishment of fixed curricula. In the Ge-luk tradition, manuals first appeared during the fifteenth century in the context of the growth of the three seats. At Se-ra, for example, early during the fifteenth century Gung-ru Gyel-tsen Zang-po and Lo-drö Rin-chen Seng-ge wrote some of the first manuals, which no longer are extant, followed a few decades later by Nyal-tön Pel-jor Lhun-drub, whose texts are still in part available. These early texts were replaced by Jay-dzün Chö-ki Gyel-tsen's more extensive manuals, which became the models for other Ge-luk monasteries. Shortly after, Paṇ-chen Sö-nam-drak-ba wrote his manuals for Lo-se-ling, followed in the seventeenth century by Jam-yang-shay-ba. The Fifth Dalai Lama's prime minister, Sang-gye Gya-tso *(sangs rgyas rgya mtsho),* tried to replace Paṇ-chen's texts with the Fifth's commentaries as the manuals of Lo-se-ling, but he failed, leading to the present situation in which there are three sets of well-established monastic manuals in the Ge-luk tradition of the three seats.

The development of Ge-luk monastic manuals was accompanied by the creation of a new genre of literature, the Collected Topics. The first example of such a text was written at the beginning of the sixteenth century by an abbot from Ra-tö, Jam-yang-chok-hla-ö-ser *('jam dbyangs phyogs lha 'od zer).*[70] Like Cha-ba's Summary, it grouped Dharmakīrti's concepts into eighteen chapters so that they might be more easily grasped by students preparing for further studies. But this text was not just a summary with occasional debates, as Cha-ba's texts and most manuals had been up to that time, but used a debate format. This text became the reference of Ge-luk debaters and was used by all monasteries.[71] It is only much later, mostly during the nineteenth century, that monasteries developed their own Collected Topics, as Pur-bu-jok Jam-ba-gya-tso *(phur bu lcog byams pa rgya mtsho,* 1825–1901) did for Se-ra Jay.

The gradual institutionalization of scholastic learning can also be traced in the development of monastic degrees. From the thirteenth century on, studies in the Ka-dam tradition were organized around four areas—Perfection of Wisdom, Logic and Epistemology, Vinaya, and Abhidharma—leading to the title of Ka-zhi-pa (*bka' bzhi pa,* "the one [having mastered] four texts").[72] For example, Dzong-ka-ba received teachings from such Ka-dam scholars as Ka-zhi-pa Lo-sal *(bka' bzhi pa blo gsal)* and Ka-zhi-pa Yon-ten Gya-tso *(bka' bzhi pa yon tan rgya mtsho).* Around the same time, other titles appeared in the Sa-gya tradition. Gyel-tsap is said to have been one of the earlier scholars to obtain the title of Ka-cu-pa (*bka' bcu pa,* "the one [having mastered] ten texts," or ten difficulties *[dka' bcu pa]).* Similarly, Sang-gye Pel *(sangs rgyas dpal),* a student of Ngor-chen Kun-ga Zang-po's *(ngor chen kun dga' bzang po,* 1382–1477), is said to have been the first to obtain the title of Rab-jam-pa (*rab 'byams pa,* "the one who has studied extensively," i.e., the great scholar), which indicated the mastery of a large number of texts. But rather than reflecting the fulfillment of set institutional requirements, these titles seem to have been given after the scholar had studied the relevant texts in the way he saw fit, often with several teachers in various centers. Moreover, the title was not given by a single institution; it was earned after a scholarly tour of the main centers. Thus Dzong-ka-ba obtained the title of Ka-zhi-pa after visiting several monasteries in Tsang and in Central Tibet.[73] This raises an obvious question about the mechanics of granting these titles. Were they given by any clearly defined authority or were they informally recognized after the completion of a scholastic tour?

The creation of the Ga-den tradition did not immediately change the loose organization of scholasticism, and a variety of titles continued to be used. Paṇ-chen Sö-nam-drak-ba, for example, was referred to as a Rab-jam-pa, while several of Dzong-ka-ba's students were known as Ka-zhi-pa or Ka-cu-pa. At the same time, new titles were created that coexisted with the older ones. Thus the tenth holder of the throne of Ga-den (*chos rje ye shes bzang po,* 1415–1498) brought into the Ga-den tradition the title of Ling-se *(gling bsre,* "the mixing of communities"),[74] which crowned the study of Perfection of Wisdom, Logic and Epistemology, and Madhyamaka.

This looseness started to yield to greater organization during the seventeenth century when the custom of examining scholars during the Great Prayer festival was established. In 1625, the title of Rab-jam-pa was first granted during this festival. This institution was further strengthened in 1648 by the Fifth Dalai Lama, who ordered such an examination to be held yearly. The system of examinations was further codified by the Seventh Dalai Lama, Kel-zang Gya-tso (*skal bzang rgya mtsho,* 1708–1757), who allowed the monks from Ga-den to join the Great Prayer and established a strict hierarchy of titles. The highest title became Geshe Lha-ram-pa *(dge bshes lha rams pa,* "divine scholarly spiritual friend," about which I will have much more to say), while lower titles such as Tsok-ram-pa *(tshogs rams pa),* Ling-se, and Do-ram-pa *(rdo rams pa)* were created, thereby making possible the absorption of older titles such as Rab-jam-pa.[75] This task was completed at the turn of the twentieth century by the Thirteenth Dalai Lama, who in 1923 instituted a mandatory examination at the Nor-bu Lin-ga, his summer palace, to weed out insufficiently qualified candidates.[76]

With the growth of the monasteries, the increase in their scholars' sedentariness, and the gradual institutionalization of scholastic studies, a new scholarly culture emerged in the Ge-luk tradition. This culture was inherited from previous scholastic centers, particularly Sang-pu, but also represented a partly new development marked by the increased place of debate as a privileged pedagogical tool. This orientation is clear in the rapid development of debate manuals in the Ge-luk tradition, starting with the Ra-tö Collected Topics and continuing with the development of extensive Decisive Analyses *(mtha' gcod)* by Jay-dzün Chö-ki Gyel-tsen and Paṇchen Sö-nam-drak-ba.[77]

These developments may have first taken place in Sang-pu and in related monasteries such as Ra-tö, and spread only later to other Ge-luk institutions. From the fifteenth to the seventeenth century, there seems to have been a close link between the three Ge-luk monastic seats and Sang-pu, as illustrated by the fact that several abbots from Sang-pu became abbots of one of the three seats.[78] Signs of this link are found in some of the customs of the three seats, such as the tradition in Ga-den to study logic and epistemology in a special summer session in Sang-pu *(gsang phu gyar chos).* It is also noticeable in the link of the three seats with Ra-tö, and the study of logic and epistemology in Jang, which we will examine later. This link between the nascent Ge-luk scholastic tradition and the Sang-pu tradition accounts to a certain extent for the importance of debate in Ge-luk scholasticism, but it would be a mistake to identify the Ge-luk tradition too closely with Sang-pu, since debates must have been practiced in some of the other scholastic centers. Moreover, it is also clear that the three seats themselves contributed to the promotion of the role of debate.

That debate was not always so important for the Ge-luk is illustrated by the changes in Geshe exams. As we will see in chapter 11, nowadays their primary focus is debate. But in earlier times they included an important commentarial component, as did the examinations undergone during the scholastic tours mentioned above. Candidates would first state their own theses by giving an elaborate commentary on the particular text on which they were examined. Only then would the debate proceed. Today that commentary has become pro forma. Candidates are examined by the abbot, who gives them quotations they must explain in the form of a textual argument *(gzhung sbyor)* in front of the whole assembly.[79] But students are assigned the passages in advance and come prepared; they need simply remember the textual arguments and avoid panic. Reports from some older Ge-luk monks confirm this evolution from commentary toward debate and suggest that some of the changes have occurred even fairly recently. Gen Lob-zang Gya-tso was fond of reporting the complaints that he had heard from older monks before he was forced to leave Tibet. "Nowadays monks focus too much on debate and neglect the exegetical skills essential to the integrity of the tradition," they claimed. Were they remarking on real change, or were they simply displaying the nostalgia of old age?[80]

The Revival of Non-Ge-luk Institutions The gradually increasing rigidity of the high scholastic period and the rise to dominance of the Ge-luk tradition affected the non-Ge-luk schools. Although at first the practices of these schools seem to have been not very different from those of the earlier Ga-den-bas, gradually the two traditions drifted apart. Later the division became more forcefully drawn, particularly by the civil war during the sixteenth century and the Ge-luk victory in the seventeenth century, which led to restrictions on non-Ge-luk schools and the decline of their scholarly institutions. Many of the Ge-luk-bas, who were part of the coalition that supported the Fifth Dalai Lama, were overtly hostile to the other schools, which had resisted the ascension of the forces of Central Tibet, though the Dalai Lama himself apparently displayed more tolerance. He nevertheless agreed to a number of measures aimed at curbing the influence of the groups that had most openly opposed the Ge-luk school. The Jo-nang school was suppressed outright, and survived only in a few remote areas of Tibet. The Kar-ma school was fortunate to escape complete proscription, but its activities were curtailed, the number of its monasteries was limited, and some of its texts were banned.

The Sa-gya tradition was also targeted. The monastery of Na-len-dra, for example, was put under the rule of the Dalai Lama's government and steadily declined,[81] unable to compete with the fast-developing Ge-luk monastic seats. Similarly, severe restrictions were imposed on the monastery of Ta-nak *(rta nag)*. Its most important texts, particularly Go-ram-ba's works, which were so critical of Dzong-ka-ba, and its manuals, written by Ta-nak Ken-po Chö-nam-gyel, were banned. By the end of the nineteenth century, these texts had disappeared from Central Tibet and could be found in only a few monasteries outside of the zone of control of the Lhasa authorities. The fate of these two monasteries illustrates the deterioration during the seventeenth and eighteenth centuries of the non-Ge-luk schools, as they lost the political support and protection that large scholastic centers require to thrive. By the end of the seventeenth century, the Sa-gya tradition could no longer maintain the vitality of its learning centers, and the level of its scholarship fell. In contrast, the Nying-ma school thrived during the seventeenth century, gaining the favor of the Fifth Dalai Lama. It suffered during the eighteenth century, however, when it became the target of Mongol attacks.

Yet higher learning did take place in the non-Ge-luk tradition during this period, though scholars mostly operated outside of institutional channels. Many of the nonmonastic teachers belonging to a line of *tantrikas* received their scholastic education within their families. Others studied with individual teachers. Sometimes students had to move from teacher to teacher, as Dzong-ka-ba had done. The education that did take place through more formal channels does not seem to have amounted to much. Sa-gya scholastic centers such as Sa-gya, Na-len-dra, and Ta-nak had been curtailed; Nying-ma centers such as Min-dröl-ling and Ka-thok had fewer restrictions, but their influence remained limited.

During the second half of the nineteenth century, this decline was reversed with the advent of the nonsectarian movement. While focusing primarily on religious practices, it also led to the revival of scholarship among the three non-Ge-luk schools, partly in reaction against the political and intellectual hegemony of the large Ge-luk monastic centers. One of the dominant figures of this revival was Ken-po Zhan-pan, the author of the commentaries on the thirteen great Indian texts mentioned above. He studied the main Indian commentaries and collected a number of Tibetan lineages of explanation of the great texts. His writings are revered by his followers, who hold them to be as reliable as Indian commentaries. The other major figure of this scholarly revival was Mi-pam Gya-tso, who wrote a number of philosophical texts and commentaries formulating Nying-ma scholastic views. While conforming to the scholarly standards developed by Ge-luk scholars, these texts often defended Nying-ma points of view (particularly against the criticisms of Ge-luk-bas such as Pa-ri Rab-sel). Hence, they tend to follow some of the critics of Dzong-ka-ba, particularly Go-ram-ba.

These changes resulted in the revitalization of non-Ge-luk institutions of higher learning and boosted their scholarly capabilities. Many of the commentarial schools, the main institutional channel through which higher learning is diffused among non-Ge-luk scholars, were created during this period. Particularly significant was Ken-po Zhan-pan's founding at the end of the nineteenth century of a school at Dzok-chen devoted to the study of the thirteen great texts through his own commentaries. From Dzok-chen, this form of training spread to the other monasteries of the Nying-ma and other non-Ge-luk schools, including the Sa-gya, which also enjoyed a scholarly revival because of the efforts of Zhan-pan and his students.

The commentarial schools embodied a competing scholastic model, which could train scholars with a hope of holding their own against the intellectual firepower of the Ge-luk monastic universities. By offering an alternative to Ge-luk scholasticism, which has tended to present itself in Tibet as the inheritor and sole legitimate interpreter of the classical Indian Buddhist tradition, these schools partially reversed the damage inflicted on the non-Ge-luk scholarly tradition. In addition, their creation formalized the adoption of a clearly articulated methodology, the study of commentaries, in opposition to the Ge-luk emphasis on debate. This methodology was presented by Ken-po Zhan-pan and his followers as a return to the classical past, bringing back to life the time in Sam-yay when Śāntarakṣita first introduced monasticism and scholasticism to Tibet. In their eyes, scholars' main concern should be the study of commentaries, not debate. By downplaying the role of debate and stressing the commentarial skills less cultivated by Ge-luk scholars, Ken-po Zhan-pan and his followers further accentuated the differences between these two pedagogical approaches.

Nevertheless, the Ge-luk domination continued to play a central role. Many non-Ge-luk monks spent some time in one of the three monastic seats to receive the dialectical training generally lacking in their own tradition. Moreover, in Amdo, where the nonsectarian movement led to a relation with the Ge-luk establishment much less adversarial than in Kham, several Nying-ma monasteries (including Do Grub-chen's) adopted the Ge-luk exoteric curriculum and simply added to it the study of Nying-ma tantras. Even Jo-nang monasteries felt comfortable adopting Ge-luk manuals—particularly Jam-yang-shay-ba's works, the manuals of La-brang.[82]

7 Scholasticism and Orality
Myth and Reality

I have characterized scholasticism as revolving around the interpretation of constitutive texts in light of commentaries. We now need to examine the nature of interpretation that Tibetan scholastic practices presuppose and the tools that support such practices. In the Western medieval tradition, the core practice was the lecture *(lectio)*, a word that refers both to reading and to the lecture proper.[1] As a lecture, the *lectio* provided students with authoritative glosses of the scriptures, explanations of their meaning, and discussions of important theological questions. Delivered in Latin, it was often structured by a method of arguing pro and contra *(sic et non)* that matched affirmations about the content of the faith with objections. The lecture was supplemented by the disputation *(disputatio)*, during which students debated questions raised by the lecture. But because of its double meaning, *lectio* signals the connection between aural practice and reading, a connection that may surprise those of us accustomed to think of reading as silent and solitary. Earlier readers had quite different assumptions. Reading is not constant, but keeps evolving as the relevant technologies and social practices change.

In this chapter, I explore the connections between commentary, reading, and orality in the Tibetan scholastic tradition, sharply distinguishing the role of oral commentary here—largely a matter of transmission and authority—from primary orality. I also demonstrate that the ends of commentary given by the teacher are more properly pedagogical and hermeneutical, particularly as concerns the art of reading, one of the central intellectual practices of scholasticism.

COMMENTARY AND THE MYSTIQUE OF ORALITY

Twentieth-century researchers produced a considerable literature on orality and literacy. Following the works of Milman Parry and Albert Lord, some scholars have associated orality with being close to the world of experience; they see it as emphatic and participatory, situational and holistic, rather than abstract and analytic, homeostatic, and so on.[2] Summarizing Parry's and Lord's work, Walter Ong elaborated a ninefold list characterizing primary orality, which he defined as the kind of oral communication that exists in simple societies in which face-to-face exchanges predominate. For Ong, primary orality is typical of small-scale communities; it is natural, unproblematic, and closely linked with the world of direct experience.[3] Literacy, in contrast, is artificial and secondary. It requires complex societies, typically urban and bureaucratic, that are characterized by a respect for rationality and impersonal norms.[4]

Though this is clearly not the place for a detailed examination of Ong's theses, we should nevertheless note that the sharp dichotomy between orality and literacy and the idealization of primary oral culture oversimplify and distort, as most cultures fit neither of the two ideal types. As Ruth Finnegan observes, "In practice, a *mixture* of media (oral and written) is far more typical than a reliance on just one, with writing being used for some purposes, oral forms for others (and in recent cases electronic media playing a part too)."[5]

In Tibetan scholasticism, aural practices—vocalizations that also involve written texts—are important. As we saw in chapter 4, memorization of root texts is practiced loudly, and Tibetan monasteries are often noisier than markets. Reading is also often done aloud, particularly in liturgical contexts. Moreover, oral instructions (and commentaries) play a central role in Tibetan education, both inside and outside the scholastic tradition. And a strong link between reading and orality is suggested by the medieval concept of *lectio*, which connects reading and lecturing. These elements all appear to provide evidence of a connection between scholastic practice and orality, indicating that Tibetan monastic culture is still largely an oral culture, as Ong understands it.

Several scholars have made such a connection in relation both to scholasticism in general and to the Tibetan tradition in particular. Anne Klein, for example, argues that several features of Tibetan scholasticism are explained by its proximity to the world of orality.[6] More specifically, she holds that oral commentaries in the Tibetan tradition display some of the features attributed by Ong to orality, in particular its homeostatic tendency to dissolve the distance between past and present. In her otherwise excellent work, she declares that

> This [tendency] is to some extent descriptive of oral philosophical com-
> mentary in Tibet, and even of textual commentary, which often had its
> origins in oral discourse. For example, Gelukba scholars today are ex-
> traordinarily erudite regarding diverse viewpoints within their own or-
> der, but they largely lost the Indian origins and various Tibetan permu-
> tations of many of their tenets. Oral or written, their commentary is
> highly nuanced philosophically, but the relatively small emphasis on
> intellectual history is more akin to oral orientation.[7]

This partial mischaracterization of the Ge-luk tradition can be attributed to her assumption that primary orality explains the role of some of the aural practices. However, I believe that this concept of primary orality is ill-suited to explain scholastic culture and that reliance on Ong to understand the connection between oral commentary and orality is highly problematic.

In general, there are several forms of oral instruction within Tibetan Buddhism, most of them having to do with single-minded practice unconnected with scholastic education. The instructions *(khrid)* or advisory speeches *(gdams ngag* or *man ngag, upadeśa* or *āmnāya)* given by a guru to his disciples concerning liberative practice are often oral, though they need not be (as we will see below). They can play an important role in the tradition, as Matthew Kapstein explains: "*gdams ngag* refers essentially to the immediate and heartfelt practice instructions and admonitions of master to disciple concerning directly liberative insight and practice. *gDams ngag* in this sense is, in the final analysis, a product solely of the interrelationship between master and disciple; it is the non-repeatable discourse event in which the core of the Buddhist enlightenment comes to be manifestly disclosed."[8] This type of pithy instruction comes in several forms. The experiential instruction *(myong khrid)* aims at putting what is taught into immediate practice. In the direct instruction *(dmar khrid)*, the master conveys to the student only the essential points of the teaching, without any concern for comprehensiveness.[9]

More relevant here, because it takes place within the context of scholasticism, is textual instruction *(gzhung khrid* or *dpe khrid)*, an oral commentary given by the teacher on the text being examined at the time. Such an explanation is the main event of the student's day in many institutions (particularly in non-Ge-luk commentarial schools) and is the privileged channel through which the tradition is transmitted. Students value it highly, and to receive these precious teachings they often go to great lengths to find a teacher who accepts them. But does such instruction have any relation to primary orality?

Textual instruction does partake of some of the features generally associated with oral communication, displaying a flexibility and sensitivity to context hard for writing to match. Moreover, the presence of a teacher with charisma and a sense of timing contributes to the effectiveness of his message. But these features obtain in oral communications in any culture, whether predominantly literate or oral, and thus have little to do with primary orality. I also find nothing special in the Tibetan practice of often deriving written commentaries from oral ones: in modern academia, too, lectures frequently become books and vice versa. Rather than proving some assumed primacy of orality in Tibetan culture, the practice shows the interaction between the two forms of communication.

Moreover, there is little reason to hold that some of the distinctive features noticed by Klein of Tibetan scholarship, such as its relatively weak reliance on historical explanations, can be attributed to the oral form of commentary. Among Tibetan scholastic traditions, the Ge-luk school tends to be the most ahistorical. Should we therefore see Ge-luk scholars as more oral than Nying-ma-bas? Or should we seek the reason for their orientation in their ideology, which views Dzong-ka-ba as the only valid interpreter of the Indian Buddhist tradition? Given that starting point, the Ge-luk-bas have no incentive to consider the historical place of other Tibetan interpretations, which can be dismissed as illegitimate remnants of an outmoded past.

Finally, I believe that the Tibetan practice of memorization bears little relation to primary orality. Anything but natural, it is neither intrinsically relational nor naturally integrated into the practitioner's total existential situation; nor does it have the free-floating and adaptive character ascribed by Ong to orality. On the contrary, the monastic practice of memorization is artificial, a contrived cultural artifact in a highly rationalized technology of mnemonic inscription that aims to store texts in memory as exactly as possible.

SILENT OR OUT LOUD READING?

Scholars have often argued that reading in premodern cultures was done out loud and that silent reading is largely a modern phenomenon, the result of the increase in the number of books made possible by the invention of printing and by the personal reading of the Bible spearheaded by the Reformation. According to William Graham, "The evidence is substantial that it is only in relatively recent history, and specifically in the modern West, that the book has become a silent object, the written word a silent sign, and the reader a silent spectator." [10] This alleged difference between reading silently and aloud is then taken to indicate some profound psycho-cultural difference between traditional and modern thinking on the subjects of interiority, subjectivity, and individualism.

One temptation in exploring scholastic reading is to assume that reading is uniform across cultures and that scholastics simply read like we do. Equally strong, however, is the temptation to go to the other extreme and insist on some great divide between cultures. Scholarship about reading has at times succumbed to the latter, arguing that reading out loud radically differentiates traditional from modern intellectuals.

As most people are by now aware, the relation between spoken and silent reading is much more complex than Graham suggests. In the West, silent reading existed well before the Reformation or the invention of printing technology and indeed may have contributed to these events. Even in the High Middle Ages, when reading aloud was most common, three forms of reading existed: silent, murmuring or rumination, and aloud. [11] Reading out loud prevailed because reading was commonly a public performance. In monasteries, where most of it was done, reading often took place during meals; one monk would read to the others while they ate. At other times, monks would read books as a form of meditation.

As scholasticism developed and the large universities were created during the late Middle Ages, the use of books changed and silent reading became more important. Because scholastic culture depended on the reading of many texts, speed was essential. [12] Moreover, the purpose of reading also changed. Whereas monastic readers were mostly concerned with assimilating the book spiritually, scholastic readers were more interested in its concepts. These developments coincided with the translation of many previously lost texts, particularly those by Aristotle, as well as the invention of mass copying, which made books easier to obtain. As a result, a culture of silent reading spread among the educated elites. Among the general population, however, books were still used mainly in public readings and reading out loud remained the rule.

In premodern Tibet as in late medieval Europe, scholars read silently and the less-educated people read aloud. Scholars I interviewed who were educated in Tibet before 1950 reported that they read silently. [13] Reading aloud was used for liturgy or by beginners, not by seasoned scholars. As scholastics, Tibetan intellectuals had to consult a vast literature, and they thus read intensively and swiftly (see figure 7). Tibetan scholars often practice comparative reading, matching the opinions of several texts point by point; this practice, too, requires speed and is incompatible with vocalization. During the fifteen years I spent among Tibetan scholars, I often observed beginners' reading aloud, but I never saw any of my teachers doing so, except for a special purpose. In fact, they read silently even in their daily recitations.

When I asked him whether he read aloud or silently before leaving Tibet, Gen Lob-zang Gya-tso did not understand my question. When he did, he was shocked at the suggestion that he would read aloud, a mode of reading associated in his culture with a beginner's skills. He responded with a typical comment: "These people are so stupid!" I did not ask whom he had in mind, but I can guess. He had immediately realized that behind my question lay an attempt to distinguish between his rudimentary reading and my modern skills, thereby establishing a temporal distance that would demonstrate his implicit inferiority.

These examples show that the form that reading takes is determined more by the ways in which books are used socially than by deep-seated psychocultural differences. Reading out loud dominated in the early Middle Ages not because readers lacked interiority but because the act was usually some kind of public performance. As scholasticism changed the use of reading, it often became silent, as happened in the late Middle Ages in Europe and in premodern Tibet. It thus seems quite clear that the role of aural practices in scholasticism is not to be explained by an appeal to the mystique of orality.[14] Still, we are left to determine what does explain the role of aural practices in Tibetan scholasticism, particularly that of the oral commentary (since practices of memorization were examined in chapter 4).

TRANSMISSION AND AUTHORITY

The role of oral commentary can be better understood by relating it to notions of authority, the continuity of the tradition, and the transmission of the teaching. The oral practices that support the practice of commentary within Tibetan scholasticism are important because they create an aura of authority around the text they explain. In part this authority arises from a felt connection with the originator of the tradition. Donald Lopez alludes to this cultural perception in describing oral commentary as "an isomorphic rendering of the author's intention, as passed down orally from teacher to student, tracked back ultimately to the author himself. That author, in turn, had written his text based on what he had been taught by his teachers, tracked back, of course, to the Buddha."[15]

As I have shown in discussing the repression of writing in the three Ge-luk seats, scholars in the Tibetan tradition fear the contingency of interpretation, a fear also manifest in the great anxiety that accompanies questions of transmission. Direct transmission is the guarantee that their traditions are not contingent but reflect the truth; they are valid because they can be traced back to the Buddha. Hence, Tibetan scholars expend much effort verifying the transmission of their traditions, proving that they come down from the founder in an uninterrupted line of authority.

One of the main objects of the numerous traditional histories of Buddhism *(chos 'byung)* is to trace the continuity of the explanation *(bshad rgyun)* of various texts. Yet the lineages they provide are not in fact continuous: they contain gaping holes and provide conflicting information. At times, the lineage seems to be cobbled together by almost arbitrarily gathering famous teachers; for example, the *Blue Annals* by Gö Lo-tsa-wa *(gos lo tsā ba gzhon nu,* 1392–1481) groups together genuine Abhidharma teachers, such as Vasubandhu, and others only weakly connected to this tradition, such as Dharmakīrti.[16] Traditional historians are aware of these problems, but the importance to Tibetan Buddhism of continuity of explanation drives them to make the strongest link with the past that they can. In order to be legitimate, a teaching has to be traced back to its ultimate origin, insofar as that is possible. By grouping Indian teachers in a lineage, scholars create the impression of continuity, thus reinforcing the authenticity of a teaching and alleviating the anxiety that arises from the temporal and geographical distance that separates the present-day tradition from its origin.

Another means of ensuring the validity of the teaching is the ritual transmission *(lung)* of a text, whereby an audience receives the transmission just by hearing it. A text becomes authoritative in the act of its being recited out loud by an authorized teacher, who has himself received the transmission from his teachers and so on. This ritual transmission underlies once more the place of aural practices in Tibetan scholasticism.

But here again, it is important not to overstate the importance of such aural practice. For one thing, the Tibetan schools do not value ritual transmission equally. The Ge-luk tradition puts little emphasis on it in the context of scholastic studies. When I asked Gen Lob-zang Gya-tso whether his teaching was a transmission, he laughed in my face, dismissing outright such an idea for Indian texts. The transmission has been lost a long time ago, he said, and anyway we don't need it. We just need to study these texts![17] Similarly, Gen Nyi-ma used to say that it was impossible for him to teach the whole canon. All he could do was to teach a few difficult passages well, thereby training the student's critical acumen and providing commentarial models. Accordingly, he rarely finished a given text. He would spend long hours teaching the most difficult points and skip the rest. He saw no place in his teaching for any idea of transmission. Not all Ge-luk teachers agree, however; and, more significantly, most of them that do are not as frank as my two notoriously outspoken teachers. Because the notion of transmission is culturally important and is recognized by Ge-luk teachers in other contexts (such as tantric practice), they may feel slightly embarrassed to admit that their teachings are not properly based on direct transmission and hence do not have the full legitimacy provided by a firm connection with the past.

The role of transmission is more important in the Nying-ma tradition, in which the teaching of the thirteen texts of the curriculum always contains a ritual transmission from the teacher, who transmits the text that he received in an unbroken line from its original author. For the commentaries on the thirteen texts, an unbroken connection does indeed stretch back to their author, Ken-po Zhan-pan. But for the thirteen Indian texts themselves, no unbroken link exists, as Nying-ma teachers are well aware. However, they argue that the transmission of the great Indian texts succeeds in that it can still convey the teacher's blessing. Thus, the point of the transmission is less to restore the full presence of the author than to bring the blessing of the teacher and his lineage, a kind of fortifying influence guaranteeing that the process of interpretation does not go awry.

Textual transmission is not the only connection between authority and oral commentary. The teacher plays a fundamental role as well in mediating between competing interpretations. Basic texts can continue to function as scriptural focal points only if they are open to a wealth of interpretations that enables them to be adapted and applied to an ever-changing reality. But unless commentarial freedom has some limits, anarchy will result. In many ways, the teacher is the person who arbitrates between the tradition's different interpretations. He tells the students which interpretation is correct and how to understand the different choices that are offered. His words provide the final explanations of a text and impart to contingent interpretations an authority that can be close to absolute—especially since disciples who are ready to challenge their teachers are few. Most adopt their teachers' opinions, often to the dot.

But this element of authority introduced by the teacher is not as absolute as it may appear. Students are not obliged to adopt the interpretations of their teachers. Most teachers do not expect doctrinal obedience from their students; and even those who do, such as Geshe Rab-ten, allow their students to leave and study with other teachers. This permissiveness is well illustrated by the story of Dignāga, who first became associated with a teacher expounding the Vatsiputriya view of an ineffable self. One evening Dignāga decided to test his teacher's view by lighting four fires and sitting for hours naked in their midst. When his guru came and asked him what he was doing, Dignāga replied that he was looking without success for the ineffable self. The teacher then told him to find another teacher with whom he would be in greater agreement. Thus, the authority of the guru is not absolute. The function of oral commentary goes beyond the ideological and cultural aspects, as important as they are.

ORAL COMMENTARY AND READING

Oral commentary is a natural outgrowth of the organization and storage of knowledge in the Tibetan tradition. Fields of study are based on root texts, committed to memory, that are cryptically written and require further explanation. The need for explanation is heightened because the texts and their commentaries are written in a language that is accessible only to those with special training.

In most modern languages, written forms have become flexible enough to accommodate the needs of laypeople; but Tibetan texts are rigid and formulaic. The divide between written and oral language is strong. Such a gap is probably the norm in traditional literate societies, but in Tibet it seems unusually wide. The reasons for this gap are complex and need not be rehearsed here; however, one important factor mentioned by Kapstein does deserve attention. Instead of being centered in secular and administrative institutions, as seems to have been the case before the empire's collapse, for most of Tibet's existence literacy developed in monasteries; there the focus was on the Buddhist language (*chos skad;* lit., "dharma language") used to translate and explain Indian texts and concepts. More an artificial code than a living language, this language had little connection with the culture existing in Tibet.[18]

As a result, the Tibetan translations of Indian works are literally accurate but difficult to understand. Most readers, even good scholars, require a commentary originally written in Tibetan—which, though more accessible than that used in canonical translations, nevertheless uses a language that bears little resemblance to the spoken form. The gap is so great that nowadays well-educated young Tibetans who want to learn about Buddhism read books in English rather than in Tibetan. To address this problem, English-educated Tibetan monks, particularly at the Buddhist School of Dialectics, have started to develop a new written language better suited to general use. Yet they have found it easier to use English books as their starting point rather than the original Tibetan, even when the English work is itself a translation of a Tibetan text![19]

Clearly, the teacher must aid the student in understanding these difficult works. Beyond particular techniques, students must also acquire the main hermeneutical skills involved in scholastic training, associated with debate (discussed in later chapters) and commentary.

In an excellent essay, Paul Griffiths argues that reading is the central activity of scholastic traditions that we should emulate.[20] Scholasticism is predicated on a particular attitudinal, cognitive, and moral relationship being established between the reader and the text. The scholastic text is read with reverence, not manipulated as the reader wishes. It is considered by scholars to be a mine, a treasure, an ocean. All these metaphors, which figure in the titles of scholastic texts (especially in the Tibetan tradition), indicate the centrality of commentary as an act of recovery, an opening up of difficult and yet central writings. Such an attitude also favors the mnemonic storing that makes possible the kind of repeated consideration that scholastic texts require. Scholastic commentaries are not quickly consumed, argues Griffiths, but gradually incorporated and internalized. Retained in the treasure chest of one's memory and ruminated over, they gradually yield their secrets. Moreover, he emphasizes that scholastic texts do more than provide intellectual stimulation: they lay the strongest possible moral claims on the reader, who is called to shape his or her life in accordance with or in response to them.

Griffiths's thought-provoking argument is interesting but of questionable historical validity, for the type of reading that he attributes to scholasticism is typical of the prescholastic monastic culture in which monks would meditate on texts. In the universities, scholars tended to read for utilitarian purpose rather than with the reverence Griffiths describes. They often did not read original texts and preferred to read compilations and florigelia. Jacqueline Hamesse explains:

> The continuous and chronological reading of a work that was done slowly, allowing the reader to assimilate the substance if not the totality of the work, is going to give way to a fragmentary and carved up reading. Such a reading will have the advantage of providing a quick grasp of the chosen pieces but will not provoke a deep contact with the text and the assimilation of the doctrine that it contains. Knowledge gives way to utility.[21]

This discrepancy between Griffiths's description of scholastic reading and the actual practice in medieval universities raises skepticism about his proposal to adopt such an ideal in our culture, which is similar to medieval scholasticism, not prescholastic monasticism, in its focus on acquiring useful knowledge rather than cultivating wisdom.[22]

In addition, Griffiths's characterization of reading as the central scholastic practice may be true of some scholastic traditions, but certainly not of all. In Tibet, a distinction must be made between non-Ge-luk commentarial institutions, which privilege commentary and reading, and Ge-luk debating institutions, where reading is in some respects secondary. And even non-Ge-luk institutions display an obvious enthusiasm for debating. The same was also true of European scholasticism during the thirteenth and fourteenth centuries, when debate tended to overshadow reading. Similarly, debate is central to the education provided by yeshivas, where students spend hours in the Beit Midrash noisily hurling arguments at each other. Hence to the scholastic, reading may be less important than debating, as later chapters suggest more forcefully.

Nevertheless, Griffiths's argument has the merit of emphasizing the importance of reading, a practice often taken for granted but involving skills difficult to define. It is precisely here that the role of oral commentary becomes significant. Reading for comprehension requires word recognition, knowledge of grammatical structure, analysis of the literal meaning, and interpretation. The most relevant for our purposes is the last, interpretation, a process in which the reader participates actively (as opposed to passively receiving the message of the text). To understand that process, we may find it helpful not just to examine Tibetan ideas and practices but also to use some of the insights of Western theorists. This recourse to analytical tools that are external to the tradition is somewhat problematic, for it imposes an alien perspective on the tradition. Yet the distorting effects of this imposition can be limited by attending carefully to the tradition's views and practices. I also believe that such recourse is unavoidable if one wants to go beyond mere description in analyzing Tibetan scholastic education, for Tibetans have not developed their own accounts of scholastic education. Some texts prescribe the modalities of interpretation but do not analyze them. While Tibetan scholars occasionally provide piecemeal reflections, they do not go on to develop a body of writings that systematically analyzes their interpretive practices.[23]

There are a variety of theories that seek to account for the nature of textual interpretation.[24] Perhaps the model most appropriate to my partly autobiographical approach to Tibetan scholasticism is that found in the hermeneutical tradition, which explains interpretation in relation to understanding and explanation. *Understanding* concerns the reconstruction of meaning from the point of view of the agent. As applied to a text, it finds its paradigmatic expression in grasping the text's meaning in a moment of insight—for example, suddenly realizing a point in what is often called an "ah-ha experience." Yet such understanding does not come spontaneously; it requires *explanations* through which the text is explicated. The interpreter understands a text only insofar as he or she is able to grasp why the text puts forth certain propositions. In doing so, the interpreter has recourse to a variety of explanatory frameworks that clarify such matters as the context assumed by the text.[25] Thus, the process of interpretation may be understood as involving a dialectic of understanding and explanation: a first, preliminary understanding is later modified by explanations and thereby developed into a more grounded comprehension.[26]

Of these two factors, understanding is perhaps the more difficult to pin down. As Hans-Georg Gadamer argues, understanding a text results not from the application of a preestablished method but from a dialogical exchange between reader and text that proceeds through questioning. I understand the text only inasmuch as I see it as addressing certain questions. Or, as Gadamer puts it, "To understand meaning is to understand it as the answer to a question." But such an understanding is only preliminary. I must also allow the text to question me, making myself vulnerable to its standpoint and remaining open to the possibility that the text has something true to say. Hence, for Gadamer, "the logic of the human sciences is a logic of the question."[27]

Both aspects of the interpretive process, explanation and understanding, are involved in reading difficult texts. I believe that these are what students of Tibetan scholasticism learn from the oral commentaries of their teacher. A few personal and hagiographic recollections will illustrate the role of the teacher in the practice of commentary and the attitude of students toward their teacher.

THE ART OF ORAL COMMENTARY: PERSONAL RECOLLECTIONS

The atmosphere in which the teachings are given by Tibetan teachers is usually quite similar. We would enter the teacher's own room if we were a few, or a special larger room put at our disposal by the monastery. We would then prostrate ourselves three times to the teacher, who would be sitting on a bed. Despite my Western background, I never felt self-conscious about this action, which was such a large part of the culture in which I was living. To fully acknowledge the teacher's superiority seemed entirely appropriate.

Once we had settled down, usually on cushions we had brought with us, the teaching would start with an invocation of the bodhisattva of wisdom, Manjushri, called *gang blo ma*. After this prayer, which is often the first text memorized, the teaching would start. We would be quiet and listen with devoted attention. Most teachers are profoundly liked by their students, though by no means always to the same degree. Some inspire extraordinary devotion. Nevertheless, in the scholarly context students would not necessarily be subservient to them. They would listen carefully, and after the teacher had finished they would raise sharp questions very politely, initially in a barely audible voice. They would speak more loudly only if prompted by the teacher. Often they would start with the kind of slurp that traditional Tibetans consider a mark of politeness. It is so much part of the language that I caught myself several times making the same sound quite naturally.

Among the great teachers of the old generation, unquestionably one of the most skilled at the art of commentary was Gen Pe-ma Gyel-tsen. It should be clear, however, that his considerable pedagogical and commentarial skills can also be found among other Tibetan scholars—particularly those coming from non-Ge-luk traditions, who are often seasoned practitioners of the art of commentary.

I met Gen Pe-ma Gyel-tsen at the beginning of the 1980s in Mundgod in South India, where the Lo-se-ling monastery of Dre-pung had been relocated. He was then in his early seventies, the senior teacher of the Lo-se-ling College, and was deeply loved and respected by almost all the monks.[28] Originally from Kham (the province of Ba), he had come, like many others, to the monastic universities of Central Tibet in his late teens. There he had shown a single-minded commitment to study, an intensity often found among the monks of Eastern Tibet who stay for a long time in Central Tibet. Unlike many of their colleagues who were native to the region, they had no local support and thus often faced great hardships. Because they had few distractions, they focused more intensely on academic endeavors. The Central Tibetans with local support were much less driven, and as a result, they are relatively rare among the great scholars of the Ge-luk tradition. Gen Pe-ma Gyel-tsen was a typical hardworking monk from Eastern Tibet, but his extremely pleasant and smooth personality was unusual among Kham-pa, who are well-known for their outspokenness. Gen Pe-ma Gyel-tsen also had obvious political skills and these, together with his exceptional scholarly achievements, had made him an ideal candidate for the job of abbot of Lo-se-ling monastery. Immediately after fleeing Tibet, Gen Pe-ma Gyel-tsen had taken the lead in reconstituting the three monastic universities in India.

Gen Pe-ma Gyel-tsen was both a master commentator and a great pedagogue. His classes were always very well structured, though he never prepared them. After first reminding the students where the discussion had previously left off, he would summarize the main points of the text, discussing their doctrinal and textual background, and give a word-by-word explanation of the root text, in this case the *Ornament*. He also referred to other commentaries, mostly the manuals of his monastery (in this case Paṇ-chen Sö-nam-drak-ba's *General Summary*), and glossed or paraphrased some of the more difficult passages, particularly the quotations contained in the manual. His explanations were complemented with references to Dzong-ka-ba's *Golden Garland* and Gyel-tsap's *Ornament*. After explaining the text, he compared its views to the views expressed by the authors of other Ge-luk manuals, ignoring the views of non-Ge-luk schools (as Ge-luk scholars tend to do). Finally, he would raise some queries and ask us to answer, pausing as well to answer students' objections and questions. The class always ended with a brief summary of the main points and a prayer of dedication of the merits accumulated during the teaching.[29] The atmosphere of the whole class was delightful, in part because Gen-la was kind toward his students without patronizing them. But more important, he was an extraordinarily skilled teacher, who enjoyed his students and was ready to use his considerable interpersonal skills to facilitate the learning process.

The entire session relied on memorization. Gen Pe-ma Gyel-tsen's explanations assumed that all the students had memorized the root text. In explaining that text word by word, he often entered into long digressions that could last for several classes. At times he referred to other parts of the text, to passages from other texts, and to related or unrelated commentaries, which he quoted from memory. In this way, Gen-la's teachings created a web of oral explanations connecting a number of texts. Such explanations would have been difficult to follow had the listeners not memorized the relevant works. They would have been hard-pressed to instantly find the passages being discussed; even more important, the students would have found those explanations difficult to retain unless they could be organized in relation to the memorized texts.

It should be obvious that my ability to study with such a towering figure is largely a result of the exile. In Tibet, as an abbot or ex-abbot Gen Pe-ma Gyel-tsen would have been inaccessible. He would have been busy leading a powerful institution with substantial political connections. The exile changed all this, taking away the pomp and power and making Gen Pe-ma Gyel-tsen approachable. In many ways, my admiring description of his generation of scholars reflects the exceptional circumstances that separated these great figures from the trappings of monastic power they had held in Tibet. In an environment in which the political implications of monasticism were much more limited, these scholars were free to manifest their simplicity and kindness, qualities that would have been less appropriate in their former roles.

Gen Pe-ma Gyel-tsen presented himself as a staunch defender of the manuals of his monastery. I am not sure whether he genuinely thought that Paṇ-chen Sö-nam-drak-ba's texts corresponded exactly to the truth as he saw it, or he thought that the defense of these texts was his duty as a Lo-se-ling teacher. In either case, his answers never deviated from the views spelled out by Paṇ-chen and his questions always presupposed the standpoint of those manuals. Gen Pe-ma Gyel-tsen's intellectual style is well illustrated by the several books that he has left behind; they are long commentaries on Paṇ-chen Sö-nam-drak-ba's manuals, filled with carefully answered objections and material necessary to make the manuals more complete.[30] These writings show once more the fragility of the distinction between oral and written commentaries. What Gen Pe-ma Gyel-tsen wrote was basically what he had taught during his life. Did his teachings, which had been purely oral, change character once they were written down? Not to any significant extent.

In helping his students to read difficult texts such as the *Ornament,* Gen Pe-ma Gyel-tsen intervened effectively on several levels. He began by providing the technical and linguistic explanations that students require to understand texts written in the heavily technical language of Buddhist philosophy. Gen-la was particularly skillful in providing careful glosses, which constituted the main part of his classes. These comments guided the students through the text and provided models that they could use in future readings. Gen-la was also careful to explain the context of the text, summarizing the preceding lessons, positioning the new passage textually and doctrinally, and connecting the specific passage to other texts. But as a skilled practitioner of hermeneutics, Gen-la would go further, considering the kinds of questions that the text addressed. He thereby provided the kind of understanding that transforms a text from a series of difficult sentences to a related succession of argued points that raise more questions.

8 Commentary and Meditation

The interpretive practices of a tradition are revealed when one examines its message, the audience to which the message is addressed, and how the message is intended to influence its audience. Hence, this study considers both hermeneutical and pragmatic dimensions of Tibetan scholasticism. In this chapter, I examine how commentary functions in the Tibetan tradition. I consider the pragmatic dimensions of commentary, focusing on the ways in which traditions and institutions use texts to form their members and orient them toward their religious goals.

In general, communities can use texts for a variety of purposes, which often revolve around the desire for sociopolitical power. That such is the case with Tibetan monastic education as well should be no surprise. Commentarial and dialectical skills constitute forms of cultural capital deployed in the struggle for power between competing religio-political groups. That aspect of the pragmatics of texts is discussed later; here, I focus on the soteriological dimensions of the use of commentaries in Tibetan scholastic education.

As I have already argued, scholastic practices are often misunderstood as being purely intellectual, and in the Tibetan context they are generally set against the contemplative approach of hermits and yogis. However real such a distinction may be, the divide between Buddhist scholasticism and yogic practice is not absolute: both aim at the same religious goals. Scholastics see their activities not just as a search for knowledge for its own sake but as central to the religious pursuits of the larger tradition of which scholasticism is part. That religious relevance should be understood properly: scholastic studies should be seen not as directly preparing scholars for personal practice but as helping them to construct a cultural universe in which practice makes sense and to develop confidence in the soteriological possibilities of such a universe. In particular, the study of the path plays an important role in constructing a religious worldview and developing virtues such as faith and confidence.

THE THREE ACUMENS

Tibetan scholastics explain the soteriological value of their studies through the classical Indian model of the three types of *prajñā (shes rab)*. This term is usually translated as "wisdom," but in fact that English term is appropriate only to certain forms of *prajñā*—particularly to the third type, the nonconceptual and transcendent wisdom produced through meditation, which is often glossed as *jñāna*, transcendent gnosis.[1] But *prajñā* also refers to less exalted conceptual forms of knowledge, in which case it can be rendered as "critical acumen" or simply "understanding." The first two forms of *prajñā* are the critical acumen arising from studying and from thinking, which Tibetan scholasticism views as preparing for the third, but the range of the tradition's understanding of *prajñā* indicates its overall soteriological orientation. The development of wisdom is understood as a continuous outgrowth of the more ordinary forms of knowledge acquired from one's studies. In this process, the content of the tradition is gradually internalized in three stages.

The first level is the "acumen arising from listening" *(thos pa las byung ba'i shes rab, śrutamayī prajñā):*[2] that is, the kind of superficial understanding one gains from studying. In its most direct sense, the acumen born from studying is the preliminary understanding gleaned from reading a text or listening to somebody's explanations.[3] This superficial grasp helps orient one's investigation but differs from the mature comprehension that inquiry brings. It does not yet enable us to penetrate the text, comprehending its consequences and the questions that it raises.

The second level is the "acumen arising from thinking" *(bsam byung las byung ba'i shes rab, cintāmayī prajñā)*, the more mature comprehension that results from a sustained process of investigating the implications of a text. This is the proximate goal of scholastic training, and it can be understood on at least three levels. First, and most superficially, it implies a greater textual comprehension derived from the sustained practices of commentary and debate; these entail the ability to read a text deeply, to follow its arguments, and to raise doubts. From a soteriological perspective, however, such an understanding is limited; hence, it is sometimes included in the acumen arising from studying.[4] It is not enough to be able to follow the text and raise interesting points. Second, one must be able to take the text into oneself, struggle with the issues personally, and internalize one's comprehension.[5] In this way, on a deeper level, one realizes the religious relevance of the great texts of the tradition—how its ideas can be used to lessen one's defilements and eventually eliminate them. This realization brings about a profound confidence in the validity of the tradition, a confidence whose development is perhaps the main end of scholastic training. Finally, thinking can also lead to an understanding of the view of emptiness, offering insight into the Madhyamaka view and the realization of how that insight can disrupt ordinary ego-centered subjectivity. The development of such an acumen is the third goal of the traditional training. But even these deeper comprehensions are still only conceptual. Nevertheless, each constitutes in its own way a decisive step toward internalizing the content of the tradition; they are therefore depicted by many Tibetan scholars as indispensable preparations for the liberatory insights achieved through concentrated meditation, the tradition's ultimate goal.[6]

The third level is the "acumen arising from meditation" *(sgom byung gi shes rab, bhāvanāmayī prajñā)*, the last phase in the program of soteriological transformation sought by the tradition. To effect such a transformation, the meaning must penetrate the deeper layers of the mind, an internalization that requires the power of meditative concentration. It can lead to a more direct insight into the nature of persons and other phenomena, which gradually frees an individual from the bondage of negative emotions. Vasubandhu summarizes the whole process: "One listens to that which is in accordance with the truth, or hears its meaning. Having listened to it, one gives unmistaken thought to it, and having thought about it, one engages in single-pointed concentration. Hence, the wisdom born from thought arises based on the wisdom born from listening and the wisdom born from meditation arises on the wisdom born from thought."[7] Texts are studied and gradually penetrated in a long process of rumination, followed by a deeper appropriation in which the soteriological implications of the text are understood at a personal level. This process culminates in the full internalization of the content of the tradition through intensive meditation. Scholasticism is less directly concerned with this third stage, which requires the calm and isolation that are difficult to find in scholastic centers. It concentrates primarily on developing the kind of moral and intellectual virtues necessary for successful meditative practices.

Some Abhidharma thinkers compare this process to that of learning how to swim. First one swims by holding tight to a buoy. Gradually, one learns how to rely less on the buoy, until finally one can swim unaided. Similarly, one first learns the content of the tradition by studying its texts. Through a more careful consideration of their meaning, one can internalize that meaning more fully but must still partly rely on the words. It is only when one has developed the insight based on the power of concentrated meditation that one can deal with meanings without explicitly attending to words.[8]

This threefold model plays an important role in Tibetan scholastic traditions. Participants often shape their life in accordance with it, starting with an extensive period of studies and later moving to a hermitage for meditative practice. This pattern is also clear in Dzong-ka-ba's own trajectory, as he summarizes it in his spiritual autobiography: "At first, one should look for extensive listening. In between, one should take all the texts so that they appear as advice [for one's practice]. Finally, one should practice day and night. All this should be dedicated to the growth of the [Buddha's] teaching."[9] In the first stage, students acquire an understanding of the content of the tradition by extensively studying the great scholastic texts and learning how to inquire into their meaning. The second stage involves the appropriation of the soteriological relevance of these texts. Finally, in the third stage, intense practice brings about actual transformation effected by meditation on the internalized content.

A similar model exists in the Western Christian tradition, particularly in the monastic culture of the High Middle Ages. Then, too, the path to wisdom involved three levels of practice. First, texts were read with reverence and often memorized. They were then meditated on to pierce their deeper meaning. This meditation, the equivalent of what I described above as *thinking*, leads to a higher perception (contemplation) that is not unlike what Buddhists call *meditation*.[10] The similarity between these two is obviously only partial, but it suggests substantial convergences between Western monastic culture and Indian monasticism that are quite relevant to our exploration of Tibetan scholasticism.

This threefold model of monastic culture was gradually replaced during the late Middle Ages by a scholastic model based on commentary, debate, and preaching. Rather than focus on cultivating wisdom by ruminating on texts, Christian medieval intellectuals moved toward an ideal of useful knowledge, which could be used in preaching, teaching, and so on. Similarly, Tibetan scholasticism has tended toward a high intellectual culture less directly tied to the process of meditative internalization; the change began in the twelfth century with the development of new intellectual tools, such as the Summaries, and culminated around the turn of the sixteenth century with the consolidation of scholastic institutions in the Ge-luk tradition. But Tibetan scholasticism never severed its connection with the ideal of developing wisdom.

SCHOLASTICISM AND MEDITATION

It is the normative ideal of developing wisdom that the model of the three acumens intends to promote. Monks first undergo an extended scholastic training, which prepares them for the intensive practice of meditation. But not all students are equally concerned about soteriological matters. Some show great devotion early on in their studies and are strongly drawn to the more strictly religious aspects of the teachings. One of my classmates at the Buddhist School represents this type.[11] He was always an enthusiastic participant in devotional practices such as the all-night prostration around the temple. Later, he became a hermit and by now has spent more than ten years in strict meditative retreat. Not everybody is cut out for such a path, and most monks do not see themselves as being capable of such single-minded dedication. I believe that in our class of twenty or so, two became hermits.

Other students, such as myself, see their studies as an occasion for intellectual stimulation as much as a source of religious inspiration. Such an attitude is not rejected by the tradition, which values intellectual activity too highly to belittle anyone who is seriously engaged in scholarship. The tradition sees scholastic studies as a form of merit making and hence as intrinsically valuable. Moreover, the intellectually gifted monks who are committed scholars and less immediately attracted by intensive meditative practice are precious, for it is from among them that the future monastic leaders and teachers are recruited. Meditators are rarely interested in leading others or even teaching. Hence, the more scholastically oriented students are crucial to sustaining the tradition. They will become abbots and teachers, often sacrificing their desire to retire into more intensive meditative practice.

That intensive meditation comes after studies does not mean that the two activities are wholly incompatible. In fact, the monks who become hermits often begin their practice while studying and gradually develop a stronger commitment to intensive meditation. But how many monks meditate in the large Tibetan scholastic centers? Not many, it appeared to me. My impression is confirmed by my interviews of monks trained in Tibet. Though a few, such as Geshe Rab-ten, said that they had engaged in the type of contemplation described in the Stages of the Path literature, most admitted they did not meditate. Some even confessed that they had never followed a teaching on the Stages of the Path during the many years that they spent in the monastery in Tibet. One thus can reasonably claim that most scholars do little or no formal meditation while studying, a claim also backed by my personal experience. I never managed to combine studies and meditation, despite the encouragement of some teachers, and I believe that my failure is typical of all but a few.

Such widespread failure is hardly surprising, for meditation has never been the concern of more than a minority. Some may believe that this lack of interest reflects a degeneration from some purer form of the tradition, but they are wrong. There is in fact no obligation for a Buddhist monk to practice meditation. Being a good monk entails abiding diligently by the numerous rules of the Vinaya, and practicing meditation is not included in those rules. In general, to meditate is not a moral obligation, whereas to follow precepts is.[12] This is not to deny meditation an important role in Buddhism and in monastic practice, but to underscore that its role must be understood properly.

More often than not, meditation's role is normative: it is the means through which the ultimate goals of the tradition can be realized. As such it is highly valued, for without it the whole system of religious practice is in danger of collapsing. That status as a normative practice also implies that it is important to be able to point to some people as practicing meditation. They are the virtuosi who authenticate the ultimate claims of the tradition, but their numbers are small. Meditation is a difficult practice, and not everybody will equally succeed in it or even benefit from it. Moreover, there are many other practices that are important. Why engage in meditation, unless one feels a special call and ability to do so?

A monk at the Nam-gyel monastery expressed a typical view when I asked him why he was not meditating. Visibly becoming defensive, he said, "You Westerners are really quite funny. You all want to become a great meditator and become buddha in this life like Mi-la-re-pa. You think it's easy. You do not realize how difficult this is and how much sacrifice one must be ready to make. In Tibet, there were hundreds of thousands of monks, and one or two managed to achieve realization." Many traditional Buddhists would agree with his reply. This stance is often combined with the cosmological vision of the degenerate nature of the times *(snyigs dus)*, a view pervasive in most Buddhist traditions.[13] Many of my teachers shared this outlook, arguing that our time is too degenerate to allow much spiritual development. One put it this way: "We are not strong enough to reach realization in this lifetime. But we can prepare ourselves so that when Maitreya [the next buddha] comes, we will be in good shape and become one of his chief disciples." The traditional cosmology suggests that the wait will be rather long,[14] and hence there seems to be no compelling reason to rush toward enlightenment.

As some of the monks themselves recognized, this outlook can be taken as authorizing all kinds of accommodations with worldly concerns, and it often is an excuse for laziness. Yet it also reflects a wisdom that Western converts, myself included, are frequently unable to appreciate. Cultivation of virtues is a difficult process undertaken by each individual, requiring time and patience. One should therefore engage in the task in the way that is appropriate to oneself, with no expectation of quick results. The Dalai Lama told me one day, "You will see that you will not be able to achieve too much, but this does not matter as long as the little you do is valuable." I was taken aback by this statement; I was then twenty-two, and the sky seemed the limit. I thought, "Maybe you are talking about yourself or people around you, but don't count on me to wait until Maitreya comes!" I soon learned that the arrogance of the neophyte is indeed no guarantee of success.

To fully understand the role of meditation in monastic education, we must qualify the claim that most Tibetan monks do not meditate, for it presupposes too narrow an understanding of Buddhist meditation. The Buddhist practice should not be reduced to concentration on a single point. The Sanskrit word *bhāvanā*, which is usually the term translated as "meditation," literally means "development" or "cultivation" and thus has a broader application. In Tibetan, it is translated as *sgom pa*, which derives from the word *gom*, "habituation." Thus, if we accept *meditation* as a translation of the Sanskrit and Tibetan words, we see that to meditate entails cultivating positive habits, or virtues. Far from being reduced to a single type of exercise, meditation as traditionally understood appears to include a vast array of practices.

The Tibetan tradition proposes an inclusive twofold typology of meditation. The first type is called "meditation of stabilization" (*'jog sgom;* lit., "meditation [in which one] places [the mind on a single object]"). This exercise, which involves cultivating the ability to remain focused on a single object, corresponds to the cultivation of tranquillity (*zhi gnas, śamatha).* The second type of meditation is called "meditation of investigation" (*dpyad sgom)* and includes all practices in which the mind is not focused on a single point, ranging from the motivational contemplations described in the Stages of the Path to the cultivation of liberative insight (*lhag mthong, vipaśyanā).*[15]

Use of this typology helps clarify the role of meditation in scholastic studies. While most monks do not practice meditation in the first, narrow sense, much of what they do can be seen as falling under the broader sense of the word. Memorization is a heuristic that develops attention and hence can be considered a meditation of stabilization. More important to mental cultivation are investigative meditations, whose practice is crucial to scholastic studies. The goal of studying commentaries and debating their meaning is to internalize the content of the tradition in order to develop virtues. This process is greatly facilitated by debate but also requires personal thought; students must continue the inquiry started in debates, taking their topics to heart. When the topics are internalized, real doubts are generated and insights can be developed that relate more closely to one's personal experiences than those supplied by an external debate in which answers are dictated by the contingencies of the dialectical encounter. Individuals who develop a more heartfelt understanding through reflection can experience real transformation.

When I asked Gen Lob-zang Gya-tso whether he meditated when he studied in Dre-pung before 1959,[16] he responded that he had not practiced any advanced form of meditation, but that he had had several insights that transformed him much as a more formal meditation would do. One day, he was studying a passage of the *Commentary* that presented Dharmakīrti's view of the causal process. The passage (*Commentary*, I:2.ab) explained the material necessity implied by the causal process. An effect is produced by all the different causal factors. Once all its different causes are gathered, the effect is necessarily produced; hence by observing the effect, one can infer the presence of its causes. Thinking about the debates concerning this stanza, Gen-la realized the statement's ethical implications. The necessity implied by the causal process concerns not only the external world but the internal domain as well—the relation between one's intentions in acting and the karmic results that such actions incur. He therefore further realized that he could not continue his preoccupation with external success, but should consider morality to be central to his scholarly pursuits. This realization was of the kind often sought through the practice of motivational meditations in the Stages of the Path; Gen-la attributed it to the profundity of the text that he was studying.

But probably more important was the atmosphere of religious enthusiasm surrounding scholastic practices: studying texts was viewed as leading both to accomplished scholarship and to religious transformation. When Geshe Rab-ten went to the courtyard around four o'clock in the morning before the first morning service to do prostrations, he would find many other monks engaged in similar devotional practice before starting the regular monastic routine. Such shared intensity largely accounts for the religious effectiveness of scholastic studies. As we already saw in examining the role of memory, in Tibetan scholastic centers the learning process is not just individual but interpersonal as well. Monks are led to realizations, insights, and moral transformations by participating in an ongoing intellectual dialogue through which they absorb the content of the tradition.

In exile, the atmosphere needed to support this process still exists but is less intense. People in Tibet were ready to undergo hardships that now seem incredible. Geshe Rab-ten describes how he carried on his early prostrations outside through all weather: "In the biting cold on winter mornings, the skin of my hands and feet would split and bleed. But despite the hardship I was not discouraged." [17] Such resolution was typical; in the monastery, people commonly spent the whole night debating or reciting the texts they had memorized. When students reached the first class on Madhyamaka at Se-ra Jay, they were required to debate through the night on alternate days, a particularly trying exercise in winter when nighttime temperatures fell well below freezing. In exile, similar resistance to fatigue and the enthusiasm that fuels it are rarely seen. Still, on certain nights some monks would debate or recite texts until dawn.

Tibetan scholastic studies clearly are concerned with more than logical consistency, textual studies, and heated dialectical encounters. But to deduce that studies are not just intellectual exercises because they have larger goals would misleadingly suggest an opposition between their intellectual and religious aspects. Nothing could be further from Tibetan scholasticism, which sees intellectual pursuits as embedded within the religious context. Scholastic studies reach their full potential when they involve students in practices of rationality that lead to soteriologically valuable achievements.

The model of the three acumens helps clarify the role of meditation in scholasticism. However, we still need a more precise understanding of the relation between the different components of the scholastic training, particularly how studies lead to the practice of meditation. Studies aim beyond intellectual comprehension to a deeper internalization of the content of the tradition—particularly the study of Madhyamaka, which culminates the scholastic curriculum and can prepare the student for meditating on emptiness. But Tibetan scholars are engaged in studying a variety of other topics. Do these topics also help prepare for meditation? That is the question I explore in the last part of this chapter.

THE STUDY OF THE PATH

In examining the two curricular models, one sees that by far the greatest amount of effort is devoted to the study of the path. In the Ge-luk curriculum, two among the five texts, the *Ornament* and the *Treasury of Abhidharma*, are devoted almost exclusively to this topic, and the other three have some bearing on it. Candrakīrti's *Introduction* is also concerned with the path from the perspective of his interpretation of Madhyamaka philosophy, Guṇaprabha's *Vinaya-sūtra* examines the moral precepts that people must commit themselves to in order to advance on the path, and Dharmakīrti uses logic to prove the validity of the Buddhist path in the second chapter of his *Commentary*.

The length of time devoted to each of these texts also underscores the importance of the topic. The *Ornament* alone is allocated four to six years in the Ge-luk monasteries, where students combine close textual examination with lengthy debates. It is studied with Dzong-ka-ba's *Golden Garland* and Gyel-tsap's *Ornament of the Essence of Commentaries,* as well as with the monastic manuals. And the Abhidharma topics examined in studying the *Ornament* are revisited when students study Vasubandhu's commentary on the Abhidharma for two to four more years. Thus, altogether Ge-luk students may spend the better part of fifteen to twenty years of their demanding course on this topic.

In the Nying-ma curriculum (and that of the other non-Ge-luk schools), less time is devoted to studying the exoteric path, since the overall exoteric curriculum takes no more than six or seven years. Nevertheless, the study of the path is covered in considerable detail. True to its usual methodology, the Nying-ma tradition exposes the students to this topic through the study of many texts. At least three of the five treatises attributed to the celestial Bodhisattva Maitreya are clearly devoted to the study of the path; so are the two Abhidharma commentaries, as well as Śāntideva's *Introduction to the Bodhisattva Way of Life* and Pe-ma-wang-gyel's *Treatise Ascertaining the Three Types of Vow,* which are used as introductory texts.

For experts in a Buddhist tradition, the reason for such extensive coverage in both curricula is self-evident. The path *(lam, mārga)* is the central notion of the tradition. As two Western scholars explain, it "incorporates, underlies, or presupposes everything else in Buddhism, from the simplest act of charity to the most refined meditative experience and the most rigorous philosophical argument. The study of mārga directs attention . . . to a general pattern of discipline encompassing both the whole life of the individual and the corporate life of the whole Buddhist community." [18] A particular formulation of the path is the structure around which a Buddhist tradition organizes its practices, its main doctrinal teachings, and its central narratives.

For those who have little expertise in a Buddhist tradition, this focus on the path may appear alien. But before attempting to replace arcane Buddhological jargon with better-known terms, we can notice that the literature dealing with the path is extremely abundant throughout the Buddhist world. Many classical Indian treatises, such as others attributed to Asaṅga himself, fit in this class. The large literature in Tibetan expounding this topic includes the numerous commentaries on the Perfection of Wisdom literature, the studies of Stages and Paths *(sa lam gyi rnam bzhag)* of the sutra and the tantra, and the texts devoted to the structure of the path in the traditions of the Great Seal and of the Great Perfection. Such texts are also numerous outside of India and Tibet. In Theravada, Buddhaghosa's *Path of Purification* is only the most famous example; similarly, Far Eastern Buddhism contains such important works as the *Mo-ho-chih-kuan* by Chih-i (538–597).[19] When we realize that this classical Buddhist standpoint is a way for Buddhists to understand the practices in which they engage, we begin to understand why students spend so many years in studying the structure and results of the path. I believe, however, that although the various treatments of the path are meant to address the pragmatic emphasis of Buddhist traditions, it is a mistake to assume that teachings on the path are preparations for actual practice.

Robert Sharf has argued in the same vein, criticizing some modern Buddhist scholars and contemporary Buddhist practitioners for erroneously interpreting the literature describing the structure and results of the path in experiential terms. "In fact," he declares, "it is difficult to imagine how somebody could mistake this kind of religious literature for 'expressions' or 'reports' of personal experiences; they are first and foremost scholastic compendiums, compiled by monks of formidable learning who were attempting to systematize and schematize the confused and often conflicting descriptions of practices and stages found scattered throughout the canon."[20] For Sharf, it is a mistake to assume that the literature dealing with the path either directly reflects Buddhist practice or directly prepares for it. This sweeping claim may not hold true for all traditions, but it applies quite aptly to the Tibetan presentations of the path that are central to scholastic education, especially those derived from the works attributed to Maitreya and Asaṅga.

The Study of the Path and Buddhist Practice

Among the canonical works concerning the exoteric path, the one that stands out is the *Ornament*, which is attributed to Maitreya. This work is studied for up to six years in Ge-luk institutions; less time is devoted to it in non-Ge-luk institutions, but it is a central reference of all Tibetan presentations of the path.

The *Ornament* is a commentary on the Perfection of Wisdom Sutra, the main canonical source of the teaching of emptiness. Its primary concern is to delineate the Stages of the Path from the Mahayana standpoint, a subject that Tibetans believe is taught only implicitly in the sutra. Tibetan scholars describe the topic of the *Ornament* as the stages of realization that are the hidden meaning of the sutra *(mdo'i sbas don mngon rtogs kyi rim pa)*. The *Ornament* offers its own summary of its content: "The perfection of wisdom *(prajñā-pāramitā)* has been proclaimed by way of eight themes: (1) the wisdom knowing all modes, (2) the wisdom knowing the paths, (3) the wisdom knowing all [phenomena], (4) the full practice of all aspects, (5) the culminating stages of practice, (6) the gradual practice, (7) the instantaneous practice, [and] (8) the dharma-body."[21] Each of the eight chapters of the *Ornament* addresses one of the eight themes *(dngos po, padārtha)*. They describe the structure of the Mahayana path through the four practices *(sbyor ba bzhi, catvāraḥ prayogāḥ)* or realizations *(mngon rtogs, abhisamaya)*. These four realizations (chapters 4–7) take as their objects the first three themes (chapters 1–3), the three wisdoms of the buddha. The result of this fourfold practice is the dharma-body of the buddha and his special attainments (chapter 8).

I suggested earlier that the importance of the path in Buddhist tradition reflects the tradition's pragmatic orientation. One might therefore infer that since it teaches the Mahayana path, the *Ornament* must bear directly on actual Mahayana meditative practices and that those who study it intensively, as Tibetan scholars do, must be interested in this text for practical reasons. But though these assumptions are tempting, they are unjustified. We cannot simply deduce a text's application from its content; rather, to understand such a text we must consider how it is used by the communities in which it is embedded.

The *Ornament* is used differently in the two main Tibetan scholastic traditions. In the non-Ge-luk commentarial institutions, the *Ornament* is studied for its content—the eight themes, which are explained through seventy topics *(don, artha)*. In this way, students learn about the four realizations, the bodies *(sku, kāya)* of the Buddha, and a number of elements of the Mahayana path, such as the mind of enlightenment *(byang chub kyi sems, bodhicitta)*. Instead of focusing exclusively on the *Ornament*, non-Ge-luk traditions complete this study of the path by examining the other texts attributed to Maitreya, as well as Asaṅga's and Vasubandhu's Abhidharma texts.

Ge-luk monastic universities, in contrast, take the *Ornament* as the central text for the study of the path; they treat it as a kind of Buddhist encyclopedia, read in the light of commentaries by Dzong-ka-ba, Gyel-tsap, and the authors of manuals. Sometimes these commentaries spin out elaborate digressions from a single word of the *Ornament*. Several Ge-luk monasteries, including Se-ra Jay, recognize this tendency to drift away from focused explanation of the text and call these subjects, which are only tangential to the *Ornament*, "special topics" *(zur bkol)*.[22] They are studied in relation to but separately from the *Ornament*. In this way, most of the topics relevant to the Buddhist path, generally or from a specifically Mahayana perspective, are covered in the course of studying this one text. The summarizing commentaries of the manuals, particularly the General Meaning *(spyi don)*, are here helpful in synthesizing treatments of all the relevant topics, introducing students to a variety of perspectives.

Notwithstanding these differences, members of neither Tibetan scholastic tradition find much practical relevance in the *Ornament*, despite some claims to the contrary. Few of the topics directly covered by the *Ornament* or studied in relation to it appear to be related to practice. Among the eight topics, the first three, the three wisdoms of the Buddha, are not meant to be practiced directly. They are taken as the object of the path, which consists of the four practices. Similarly, the last theme, the dharma-body of the Buddha, is the goal of practice but gives no direct guidance on reaching it. To be sure, the *Ornament* presents the four practices or realizations, emphasizing particularly "the practice of all the aspects" *(rnam rdzogs sbyor ba)*, which is treated in the fourth chapter. In fact, that practice is the central topic of the text and may have been an actual practice in which all the aspects of the three wisdoms are brought together, Here, it is called "meditation summarizing the three wisdoms" *(mkhyen gsum bsdus sgom)*. An explanation of this highly technical topic would take us into the stratosphere of Tibetan scholasticism; what matters for our purposes is that this practice seems to be realistic. Rather than involving some extraordinary feat, as do the miraculous qualities of the buddhas and celestial bodhisattvas, it can be implemented by anybody who is interested.

But—and this point is crucial—no teacher I have ever met seems to have practiced this meditation or even to have been clear on how to do so. Non-Ge-luk curricula treat this practice but generally offer no convincing understanding of the topic, even at the textual level. The students I interviewed appear to have gotten very little out of this part of the text. And though Ge-luk scholars probably have a better theoretical understanding of the topic, nobody I encountered could plainly state how to practice this text. Clearly, the work's central themes are not practiced in the Tibetan scholastic traditions.

1. Gen Lob-zang Gya-tso, head of the Buddhist School of Dialectics, 1975. Dharmsala, India. Photo: Georges Dreyfus.

2. Dre-pung, 1993. Tibet. Photo: Natasha Judson.

3. Monks in the assembly hall, 1994. Tshur-pu, Tibet. Photo: Kevin Bubrisky.

4. My first teacher, Geshe Rab-ten, 1973. Switzerland. Photo: Fred von Allmen.

5. The regional house of Pompora at Se-ra May, 1993. Tibet.
Photo: Natasha Judson.

6. The author studying at Nam-gyel, 1972. Dharamsala, India.
Photo: Fred von Allmen.

7. Young monk reading, 1987. Se-ra, Tibet.
Photo: Kevin Bubrisky.

8. The animation of debate, 1987. Se-ra, Tibet.
Photo: Kevin Bubrisky.

9. The good humor of debate during the author's Geshe examinations,
    1985. Ga-den Shar-tse, Mundgod, India. Photo: Anonymous.

10. Collective debate during the author's Geshe examinations, 1985. Ga-den
    Shar-tse, Mundgod, India. Photo: Anonymous.

11. Individual debate in the cold of winter, 1975. Buddhist School of Dialectics, Dharamsala, India. Photo: Anonymous.

12. Evening prayer at Se-ra, 1987. Tibet.
Photo: Kevin Bubrisky.

13. Gen Nyi-ma, India. Photo: Anonymous.

14. Se-ra in exile, 1998. Bylakuppe, India.
Photo: Devon Cottrell Holmes.

Of the auxiliary topics—briefly presented by the text or studied through other texts—some do have direct practical applications. For example, the mind of enlightenment *(byang chub kyi sems, bodhicitta)* is studied in the first chapter. Similarly, the single-pointed concentration that leads to the attainment of tranquillity *(zhi gnas, śamatha)* is studied in great detail. Concentration is studied with considerable care for several months, and in certain monasteries (including Dre-pung Go-mang and Se-ra Jay) it is considered a special topic *(zur bkol)*. Yet even though teachers point out the practical importance of studying these topics, to which much time is devoted, little time is given to those that are of direct relevance to actual meditation. For example, the two methods for generating the mind of enlightenment,[23] which are central to the Stages of the Path *(lam rim,* a type of literature directly relevant to meditative practice), are barely mentioned. The real focus is theoretical. The mind of enlightenment is studied here not as an attitude to be developed but as a function of its role in the overall Mahayana path. Similarly, in the study of concentration, not much attention is paid to the nine stages leading to tranquillity, which are of practical use. And the attainments of the "four absorptions" *(bsam gtan, dhyāna)* and the "four formless concentrations" *(gzugs med, arūpa)*[24]—which have been and are practiced in other Buddhist traditions—are studied but rarely practiced in the Tibetan tradition. When monks become really serious about the practice of concentration and begin extended retreats, they instead focus on the tantric path. At that time, special methods for the attainment of tranquillity are introduced.[25] The texts they have studied seem to have no application.

Worldview and the Study of the Ornament

Once we see how little relation the study of the *Ornament* and other similar texts presenting the path has to actual experience within the Tibetan scholastic traditions, we may wonder why so much time is spent studying them. What meaning do Tibetan scholars find in them?

One answer is suggested by Dzong-ka-ba's own career following the model of the three acumens, as he describes it in his autobiography. The first stage consisted of the extensive exoteric and esoteric studies that he undertook with various teachers. The second stage began with a four-month retreat that he undertook in 1379 in Ngam-ring, where he focused on the teachings of the path, particularly as they are explained in the second chapter of Dharmakīrti's *Commentary on Valid Cognition*.[26] This chapter is unusual in the Dharmakīrtian corpus in that it examines an explicitly religious topic—the validity of the Buddhist path—rather than more philosophical ideas, such as the validity of cognitions and reasonings. While contemplating this chapter, Dzong-ka-ba experienced a breakthrough: his purely discursive grasp of the text deepened into a greater understanding in which the text appeared as "advice [for his practice]," to use his own words (quoted above). In a moment of sudden insight Dzong-ka-ba understood the validity of the Buddhist path. Realizing the strength of Dharmakīrti's reasoning, he "was overwhelmed with a strong faith" and his eyes filled with tears.[27] Dzong-ka-ba was deeply affected by his realization, which left him with strong confidence in the power of reasoning to bring about faith and in the religious value of Dharmakīrti's tradition. After this experience, he continued to study, particularly with Ren-da-wa, and toured several scholastic centers to measure his knowledge through debates. His masterful *Golden Garland,* begun in 1389, summarizes the understanding that he had gained in his studies and reflects this new knowledge.

Dzong-ka-ba then shifted his emphasis to a more strictly meditative practice, the third stage in the process. He engaged in several retreats; one began when he went with eight disciples in the winter of 1392–1393 to Wöl-khar Chö-lung *('ol khar chos lung),* south of Lhasa. He stayed there for the next four years, engaging in preliminary devotional practices such as prostration, which are necessary to the practice of the tantric path. He also completed several tantric retreats and received visions, particularly of Manjushri, his tutelary deity. But even at this stage, Dzong-ka-ba was not convinced that he completely understood the teaching of emptiness. Hence, he went back to studying the great Madhyamaka texts, constantly checking his understanding by asking questions. At first he turned to Lama Uma-pa *(dbu ma pa dpa' bo rdo rje),* who often relayed his questions to Manjushri. Later on, Dzong-ka-ba was able to ask his questions through his own visionary encounters. In 1398 he went back to Wöl-khar, where he spent the next year studying, reflecting, and meditating on the Madhyamaka view, particularly Buddhapalita's commentary. In this way, Dzong-ka-ba achieved at the age of forty-two his final insight into the view of emptiness, thus bringing to an end the long process of developing the three types of acumen through listening, thinking, and meditating—a process that had begun in 1373 when he had come to Central Tibet in search of knowledge.[28] Only then did he start to write works reflecting his own personal understanding, the main source of his fame in the Tibetan world.

When we consider this narrative, particularly its account of the second stage, we realize that the study of and reflection on the great texts is for the most part not experiential. The study of Madhyamaka can be a preparation to meditation, but most of the other topics—particularly the presentation of the path, the curricular area to which the greatest amount of attention is devoted—are not. These "impractical" studies are meant to bring about a strong faith in the validity of the Buddhist tradition, as they did for Dzong-ka-ba in Ngam-ring. The discussion of the path is central to Tibetan traditions because it habituates students to the universe in which these narratives make sense, and thus strengthens their religious commitment.

To be compelling, soteriological practices must be presented within a narrative embodying values central to the tradition. Such narratives in turn require larger cosmological frameworks in which they can unfold. Buddhist practices presuppose a narrative of spiritual liberation and the cosmological framework within which such liberation is possible, the kind of *saṃsāra-karma-mokṣa* worldview mentioned earlier. They make the sacrifices required to maintain a commitment to practice appear to be worthwhile. Some practices are supposed to have immediate effects, but by themselves those effects could not support the kind of intensive commitment required. Most people do not live by quick fixes; instead, they decide on long-term goals and the means to reach them. Hence, they need narratives to direct them and persuade them that they are on the right track. They also need to sense closure in the narrative, to find a point toward which their efforts are aimed and that makes sense of those efforts. To construct such a universe of meaning and to strengthen the faith of participants in such a soteriological possibility are the main goals of the study of the *Ornament* and other related texts in the Tibetan scholastic tradition.

That is how the Perfection of Wisdom literature understands its task. Haribhadra, who wrote the Indian commentary of the *Ornament* on which Tibetan scholars mostly rely, starts his discussion by stressing the role of faith, which he describes as the "main cause" *(rgyu gtso bo)* of spiritual progress. Buddhist practice focuses on the development of detachment and compassion, the central virtues of the tradition. These virtues are gained by a variety of practices, such as meditation, giving, and so on. Hence, for Haribhadra, faith is not the central virtue of the tradition; wisdom and compassion surpass it. But faith is the basis from which the development of these virtues starts. Thus it is the paramount concern at the beginning of the process.

Haribhadra also insists that not everybody generates faith in the same way. In particular he distinguishes two types of trainees. Some are easily convinced of the validity of the tradition and thus find it easy to have faith in the Buddhist path. Hence, they are called "followers of faith" *(dad pa'i rjes 'brang)*. Their faith is less stable, however, since it is based not on evidence and personal appropriation but on external influences. The other type of trainees, the "followers of dharma" *(chos kyi rjes 'brang)* or "followers of reasoning" *(rigs pa'i rjes 'brang),*[29] find it more difficult to generate faith, for they will not commit except on the basis of their own understanding, relying on strong evidence. But once they are convinced, they remain firm in their convictions and are not easily swayed. The *Ornament* fulfills the needs of both types of trainees. It helps the more credulous disciples generate faith by delineating the attainments of the Mahayana path, and it also provides the evidence necessary for the more intellectual disciples to generate faith by relating the developments of the path to the ultimate empty nature of reality.[30]

The construction of a meaningful universe and the path that transcends it must be made to appear self-evident so that students feel confident in their practice. The steps along the path must appear to them as concrete stages whose relation to Buddhist practice they understand. Yet that "concreteness" is itself a reification; the map provided by the *Ornament* literature does not refer to anything that exists independently of textuality. Rather, these mental constructs acquire, through text and teaching, the solidity necessary to inspire and sustain people in their actions. They are best characterized, to use Kenneth Burke's term, as objects of symbolic actions, the representational forces that attempt to influence their audience.[31]

Is this the explanation of the teachers who taught me the *Ornament?* No, or at least not completely. The coalescence of a worldview requires a degree of objectification of which social agents are often not completely aware. In this case, my teachers and their students really believed that the descriptions provided by the text were correct, that such stages and paths existed in ways that to some degree resemble the descriptions provided by the *Ornament* literature. Nevertheless, they were well aware of the limits of these descriptions. They saw clearly that there are, in the Dalai Lama's own words, "no self-evident *(ldog ldog)* paths existing out there." [32] The more thoughtful members of the tradition take descriptions of the path as attempts to refer to complex individual processes. Thus, my teachers would not disagree with my characterization of the path as conveyed by the *Ornament* literature as a form of symbolic action, though they would insist that such action be considered mediately referential.[33] That is, they would insist that this literature refers to some states actually obtainable by practitioners, though not necessarily in the exact ways in which this literature describes them.

Other Tibetan schools put less emphasis on the *Ornament.* Their curricula include other texts attributed to Maitreya; moreover, the tantric path is examined right from the beginning (and studied extensively during the last three years of the nine-year course). But this tantric emphasis does not reflect an experiential orientation. Students at Nam-dröl-ling receive few practical guidelines on how to meditate, for instruction is given mostly in private after students have established a relation with a tantric guru. There is an optional retreat during the winter vacation, though many choose not to attend. In the Ge-luk tradition, monks also go into retreat from time to time, the difference being that the monastery itself offers no retreat facility; monks have to go to hermitages *(ri khrod)*, where practitioners can go on extended retreats.[34]

Thus, the very real differences between the Ge-luk and Nying-ma curricula are concerned less with practice than with rhetorical strategy. The Nying-ma curriculum is distinctive not because it is experiential,[35] but because the universe it constructs is tantric rather than based purely on exoteric teachings (as in the Ge-luk tradition). In such a universe, experience figures as an important and complex rhetorical category essential to the construction of meaning.[36] The Nying-ma model is thus able to integrate scholastically uneducated hermits: their qualities become part of a universe of meaning through which they become intelligible to the tradition at large. In this way, they illustrate and support the tradition's soteriological claims.

As I emphasized earlier, the actual practices of the four Tibetan traditions are quite similar, though not identical. What differs is the rhetoric used to present those practices and the ideological contexts thereby created. In the Ge-luk model, the theoretical universe and the path are exoteric, providing the framework into which the tantric practices fit. Ge-luk texts tend to emphasize the primacy of the exoteric narrative to legitimize their esoteric practices. In the Nying-ma model, the universe to which students are introduced is mostly tantric, and the exoteric teachings support this construction. The actual practices in which students later engage fit easily into the narratives of spiritual progress derived from these tantric models, but members of this tradition sometimes find it harder to justify their practices in reference to the more classical exoteric model.

It is from this perspective that the study of the path within Tibetan traditions must be understood. Topics such as the mind of enlightenment or the attainments pertaining to the form and formless realms are important not because they directly prepare for meditation but because they help elaborate a universe in which Buddhist narratives and the practices that they inspire makes sense. For Tibetans, the *Ornament* and similar texts are not reports on or direct preparations for Buddhist practice, but rhetorical representations of the meaningful universe envisaged by the tradition. As such, they have great soteriological significance, since they develop the faith that participants have in their tradition. That strengthening of faith is one of the central goals of Tibetan scholastic education, particularly of the study of the path.

The construction of a universe of meaning is not unique to Tibetan scholastic traditions or to scholasticism in general. Most religious traditions, however, do not take the doctrinal and intellectualist approach adopted by scholasticism. Rather, they emphasize the role of myths and rituals in constructing a universe available to large groups. While these mythic dimensions obviously exist in scholastic traditions, they play a lesser role than abstract doctrines, which are used to refine and develop the culturally accepted universe of meaning and reinforce the conviction of their participants. This, I suggest, is a distinguishing feature of scholasticism as a religious phenomenon that concerns the intellectual elites.

9   The Supplement

Hermeneutical or Deconstructive?

In the preceding discussion of Tibetan monastic education, I treated the notion of commentary as unproblematic. Hermeneutically, I examined commentary as an incorporative activity. Pragmatically, I depicted the use of commentary as a continuous process in which texts are studied in the light of oral explanation, appropriated through inquiry, and finally internalized through meditative cultivation. But this presentation of commentary as continuous and productive is one-sided, for it ignores the other aspect of commentary—its gaps and aporias. In this chapter I complete the analysis, relying on the poststructuralist critique of commentary to examine the limits of hermeneutical appropriation.

WHAT IS COMMENTARY?

Up to now I have assumed that the meaning of *commentary* is more or less self-evident. That assumption is highly questionable, however, for when Tibetan scholars "comment on a text" they may not simply be glossing it, as is often assumed. We need to explore the ways in which commentary is understood in the Tibetan tradition before we can examine the limits of this commentarial logic. In particular, we need to determine more precisely what commentary is in this tradition.

Although Tibetan scholars use commentary a great deal, they have provided few reflections on its nature beyond a few typologies—and even those do not provide a systematic understanding of commentary in this tradition. Thus it may be helpful to begin by examining some modern definitions of commentary. According to Steven Fraade, "[A]ll commentaries . . . can be said to exhibit the following structural traits: they begin with an extended base-text, of which they designate successive subunits for exegetical attention, to each of which they attach a comment or chain of comments, which nevertheless remain distinct from the base-text, to which the commentary sooner or later returns (that is, advances) to take up the next selected sub-unit in sequence."[1] On this account, a commentary provides an ordered series of glosses on some earlier text. Elaborating on this definition, Paul Griffiths proposes three essential characteristics of every commentary: it is a metawork that bears a direct relation with another well-defined text, it is mostly concerned with the text that it explains, and it does not impose its own order but follows the order of the text it explains.[2]

Both Fraade and Griffiths limit their focus to textual explanations of a particular work, but Tibetan scholars have a broader understanding of commentary. They often mention two types: the word *(tshig 'grel)* and the meaning *(don 'grel)* commentaries. The former, sometimes called doubling commentaries, explain a text passage by passage; these are the textual explanations to which Fraade and Griffiths refer. Mi-pam's explanation of the *Ornament of the Middle Way* and Dzong-ka-ba's *Ocean of Reasoning* are classical Tibetan examples,[3] as are Ken-po Zhan-pan's commentaries on the thirteen great texts of the Nying-ma tradition. But not all commentaries fit in this category. Meaning commentaries summarize the topics covered by a text without giving a passage-by-passage explanation. Examples are Dzong-ka-ba's *Clarification of the Thought* and Go-ram-ba's *General Teaching of the Profound Thought.*[4] This distinction between word and meaning commentaries also applies to Indian texts: Candrakīrti's *Clear Words* is a doubling commentary on Nāgārjuna's *Treatise,* whereas his *Introduction to the Middle Way* offers a general summary of Madhyamaka philosophy.[5]

Yet in classical texts, we find other typologies of commentary that are sometimes hard to systematize, for their categories overlap. For example, the "annotation" *(mchan 'grel)* is often mentioned, but this is hardly a coherent genre. Ken-po Zhan-pan's commentaries, which are called *Annotations,* are mostly word commentaries, whereas the *Annotations to the Great Exposition of Tenets* by the nineteenth-century scholar Ngak-wang-bel-den *(ngag dbang dpal ldan,* b. 1797) is a series of reflections on the meaning of the text by Jam-yang-shay-ba referred to in the title.[6]

In his *History of Buddhism,* Bu-dön lists five types of commentary: (1) The "extensive commentaries" *(rgya cher 'grel)* elaborate both the words and meaning of a text. (2) The "word commentaries" *(tshig 'grel)* explain the lexical components of a text. (3) The "commentaries on difficult points" *(dka' 'grel)* clarify the most central parts of the text. (4) The "summarizing commentaries" *(bsdus don gyi 'grel ba)* synopsize the meaning of the text. (5) The "commentaries on the mere verbal significance of a text" *(ngag don tsam gyi 'grel ba)* condense the text and its meaning in an abbreviated and easy-to-retain form, such as a "verse condensation" *(sdom tshig)*.[7] This typology is certainly helpful in delineating genres of commentary existing in the Tibetan literature. But as is often the case with classical typologies, it only imperfectly captures actual commentarial practices. For example, where in this schema should meaning commentaries fall? Some of them, such as the broad summaries found in the manuals, can be included without question in the fourth category. But would Dzong-ka-ba's *Clarification of the Thought* or his *Essence of Good Sayings* fit with these summarizing commentaries? Perhaps those two texts could be grouped with extensive commentaries, but they provide little lexical explanation.

Explanations of the practice of commentary do exist in the Tibetan tradition. For example, in discussing composition *('chad pa),* one part of his threefold curriculum, Sa-paṇ sets forth the five "methods to comment on" *(bshad thabs)* texts found in Vasubandhu's *Vyākyāyukti:* (1) A commentary should explain the purpose of the text, whether through an homage or through an explicit statement of purpose at the beginning of the text. (2) A commentary should summarize its subject, either concisely or in more detailed topical outlines. (3) It should explain the meaning of the text by glossing each word, explaining relevant grammatical notions, and providing the literary background of the discussion. It should analyze compound words—a function far more important in the Indian tradition than the Tibetan, as such words do not exist in the Tibetan language. (4) A commentary should also pay attention to the connection between words and topics as well as that between the different elements of the text. (5) Finally, it should examine possible objections and articulate answers in a way that reflects the actual practice of debate.[8]

This and other typologies clearly do not limit commentaries to textual explanations. Many commentaries fall into this category, often doing no more than to paraphrase the wording of their primary texts with minor grammatical clarifications. Such commentaries fit Foucault's description of the role of commentary: "to say finally, what has silently been articulated *deep down*. It must—and the paradox is ever-changing yet inescapable—say, for the first time, what has already been said, and repeat tirelessly what was, nevertheless, never said."[9]

But in the Tibetan tradition, not all commentaries double the primary text. Under the guise of eliciting what was articulated deep down, a commentary can also expand on the primary text. A good example is Candrakīrti's *Introduction to the Middle Way,* which extends Nāgārjuna's *Treatise* by integrating the latter's Madhyamaka philosophy with the structure of the Mahayana path. The seventeenth-century Ge-luk commentator Jam-yang-shay-ba explains the word *introduction (avatāra, 'jug pa)* in the title of Candrakīrti's work as meaning "supplementation" *(kha skong)*.[10] This supplementation is seen as reinscribing the original meaning: Candrakīrti thus clarifies and expands what was present all along in Nāgārjuna's text.

Such supplementation might appear to be redundant: what is the use of commentary if everything has already been said by a figure of authority such as Nāgārjuna? The answer rests on the notion of audience—not surprisingly, given the pragmatic nature of Buddhist teachings. Although the founder's original message is clear and complete as far as its original audience is concerned, those who come later will not be able to benefit as fully from his teachings. Each text is addressed to a particular audience, a putative group of trainees for whom it is specially intended *(ched du bya ba'i gdul bya)*. Only that specific audience will fully benefit from that text; another audience will require another commentary appropriate to its background, dispositions, and abilities. Necessary adjustments in the manner of teaching may entail making an obscure text clearer, giving more extensive explanations, developing certain points that are only hinted at in the original, and the like, but expansion is not the only possibility. Some commentaries (such as the *Ornament*) might abbreviate a message that was originally longer and more diffuse.[11] Thus, to comment is to supplement another text by explaining either its wording or its meaning. While such an explanation need not be a doubling commentary, it does assume that the meaning of the text it explains has enough stability to be appropriated. Hence, it does end up repeating "what has silently been articulated *deep down*," to use Foucault's striking phrase. When Candrakīrti in his *Introduction to the Middle Way* comments on Nāgārjuna's *Treatise*, he is assuming that he is explaining what is tacitly present in Nāgārjuna's text. The often-misunderstood poststructuralist attack on commentary takes this assumption as its target, critiquing commentary not just as being a gloss but as assuming that the text can be hermeneutically appropriated.

THE SUPPLEMENT: COMPLEMENT OR DISPLACEMENT?

The poststructuralist critique is perhaps best articulated by Derrida, who argues that the problem with commentary is that in interpreting a text, it assumes that the meaning of the text can be captured. Often this act of interpretation entails the further assumption that the meaning of the text is determined by the conscious, voluntary, and intentional relationship of the author to the work.[12] The latter assumption in turn privileges the dominant but contingent interpretation of the text and strengthens its hold on the minds of interpreters. But, says Derrida, such a restrictive strategy does not exhaust the possibilities of interpretation. We need a different reading of the text, one that does not close and protect the text but keeps it open and reveals the differential logic (the *différance*) at play in it and the wealth of possible meanings that this logic brings about. Commentary is a necessary first step toward serious discussion, but interpretation needs to reveal its limits by bringing out the text's logic in a process that Derrida calls "supplementation":

> [T]he supplement supplements. It adds only to replace. It intervenes or insinuates itself *in-the-place-of;* if it fills, it is as if one fills a void. If it represents and makes an image, it is by the anterior default of a presence. Compensatory and vicarious, the supplement is an adjunct, a subaltern instance which *takes-the-place.* As substitute, it is not simply added to the positivity of a presence, it produces no relief, its place is assigned in the structure by the mark of an emptiness.[13]

Derridean supplementation is quite different from the commentarial logic at work in Candrakīrti's explanation of Nāgārjuna's *Treatise.* Whereas Candrakīrti aims at capturing and reproducing what he assumes to have been there all along, Derrida's interpretation embodies a strategy of suspicion: it seeks to expand the text by a playful dissemination of meaning based on the logic of supplementation at work in the text itself and not determined by the author's intention. For any text, the chain of signifiers through which it can be interpreted is potentially infinite; nor, in principle, is there any one way to differentiate true from false interpretations. Derrida does not mean that every interpretation is as good as another, though he has often, and unfortunately, been so misunderstood. But he emphasizes that there is no way to assign limits to the process of interpretation, no privileged standpoint from which meaning can be determined or closure achieved. Rather than limit ourselves to retrieving the meaning of the text, we should view with suspicion the claims to authority of any interpretation, including those of the text itself, and seek to open the text to alternative readings as much as possible and however much they might seem to conflict with each other.

The word *closure* is essential here. Derived from the Old French, it first appears in Chaucer with the meaning "that which encloses."[14] Spatially, closure defines a given portion of space. Temporally, it is the process of bringing something to a conclusion and thereby making it complete. Hence, it is related to the idea of reaching the limits and delineating the boundaries of an area or a process, enabling one to assign meaning to things or events. In religious practice, closure is the final vantage point from which the members of a community can interpret the world and find meaning in it. It also implies the possibility of finding ultimate harmony, for at that point all strife and conflicts would be overcome.

In the Buddhist tradition, the concept of nirvana or liberation provides the moment of closure to the religious life.[15] It is the state of a person liberated from the causes of suffering—that is, the "negative emotions" *(nyon mongs, kleśa)*—and is the goal toward which practitioners strive. In the Mahayana perspective that informs the Tibetan tradition, the notion of nirvana is understood as the Great or Non-abiding nirvana *(mi gnas pa'i myang 'das):* that is, buddhahood, the state of a person having reached the perfection of knowledge and compassion, which is proposed as the normative goal. It is this sense of closure that differentiates a tradition such as Tibetan scholasticism from modern or postmodern philosophies of interpretation, however similar some of their views may be.

Although this central notion of closure is taken almost as a given by those who belong to the tradition, it is by no means simple or self-evident. Throughout the history of Buddhism, thinkers have struggled with its well-known paradoxes. Closure was described above as the point from which human limitations can be made sense of and, in the Buddhist context, overcome. To enable one to make sense of everything, that point must exist outside of human limitations—but if it exists outside of limitations, it ceases to be understandable. Thus, a peculiar logic of constant deferral is opened up, as we are led to posit a goal that recedes every time we try to approach it. In Buddhist terms, nirvana or buddhahood can provide closure only if it stands outside of the world of conditioned existence. We are then faced with a question: how can humans, who seem to live fully immersed in the conditioned world, comprehend and reach the unconditioned, which is by definition beyond ordinary limitations?

In answering this question at the center of Buddhist philosophy, Buddhist traditions take two basic approaches. The gradualists argue that the unconditioned can be reached by a lengthy cultivation of virtues. The suddenists reject this model, arguing that the unconditioned cannot be realized unless it is already present in us. Cultivation of conditioned states cannot do the job alone; we must already be in touch with a pure dimension that practice reveals. Thus suddenists and gradualists argue not so much about the importance of cultivating virtues as about whether realization of the unconditioned is prior to or the result of such cultivation. Tibetan monastic traditions tend to favor the gradualist paradigm, which is central to our study, though some schools, particularly the Nying-ma, introduce and combine a significant suddenist dimension.[16]

The details of how one attains closure, over which gradualists and suddenists disagree, matter less than closure's paradoxical and ideal nature. It is not a given that awaits our discovery, but something that must be created through discursive (textual) and nondiscursive practices. This belief is held with particular strength by the gradualists, who see the realization of the unconditioned as the end of a process that begins with the study of the great texts of the tradition. But suddenists, too, view the realization of the unconditioned as no simple matter: it requires complex soteriological strategies that are less means to reach the unconditioned than expressions of its presence in the individual.

Each model assumes that closure is possible, however difficult it may be. The religious life, which is based on the appropriation of texts, presupposes the possibility of such closure. In order to fulfill its soteriological mission, the text must yield a moment of insight into its meaning that can later be internalized by meditative practices that lead to the ultimate goal. Thus, closure is both pragmatic and hermeneutical, as we saw in the previous chapter while examining how the study of the path was used to construct a universe of meaning. It is the possibility of such closure that fundamentally distinguishes traditional interpretation from the deconstructive supplementation championed by Derrida, a difference to which we will have to come back. Whereas the latter seeks to reveal the surprising possibilities that have often remained hidden to the author of the text or even contradicts its central message, the former follows a commentarial logic that seeks to preserve the authority of the text by retrieving its meaning.

BUDDHIST HERMENEUTICS

That traditional thinkers believe closure to be possible does not mean that they assume that the meaning of the text is immediate, simple, or even univocal. Tibetan scholars are aware of the complexity of the texts of their tradition, particularly the great Indian texts, which are often described as "having a hundred ways [of being interpreted]" *(lugs brgya ldan)*. Texts have a plurality of meanings, and the exploration of this plurality is the task of a commentary. Nevertheless, "plurality" should not be confused with infinite open-endedness: the meanings are limited and must fall within an acceptable range. To understand this, we need to examine what we may call *Buddhist hermeneutics,* one of the central topics of scholastic studies that can be considered only briefly here.

In general, hermeneutics can be defined as the art of interpretation, analyzed according to a philosophical or methodological system. Buddhist hermeneutics is concerned with the analysis of the interpretation of canonical texts, particularly the sutras. It is of central importance to Mahayana, which is characterized by a wealth of conflicting philosophies, including the Yogācāra and Madhyamaka. Faced with these doctrinal conflicts, the Indian Mahayana tradition developed numerous interpretive strategies that seek to restore some order. These hermeneutical schemes, which reflect the views of the different schools, were given canonical status by being enshrined in Mahayana sutras. Central to most of these schemes is the distinction between the teachings of "interpretable meaning" *(drang don, neyārtha)* and of "definitive meaning" *(nges don, nītārtha).*

The two schools named above each describes the nature of this distinction.[17] In the Yogācāra hermeneutics found in the *Saṃdhinirmocanasūtra,* the distinction centers on the idea of literality. The teachings that are not literally acceptable are interpretable, whereas those that can be taken literally are definitive. This difference can apply to secondary teachings — for example, the Buddha's declaration that by a mere prayer one will be reborn immediately in Sukhāvatī. Such a statement cannot be taken literally and must be understood as referring to the fact that the person who formulates such a prayer will be reborn in Sukhāvatī in some future life.[18] Hence, it is interpretable. The distinction between interpretable and definitive teachings can also apply to more weighty matters, particularly the teachings concerning the ultimate nature of reality. In the Perfection of Wisdom sutra, for example, the Buddha teaches that all phenomena are empty of any essence and hence entityless. Contrary to the more radical Madhyamaka school, the Yogācāra does not accept this statement literally, interpreting it instead as a limited critique of essentialism. On this account, only conceptual constructs (including the sense of duality between subject and object) are entityless; causal phenomena, which are real, have their own individuating essence and hence are not entityless.[19] According to the Yogācāra, the mistake of the Madhyamaka is to take this statement that all phenomena are entityless as being literally true rather than interpretable. Yet even this erroneous literal interpretation is not completely mistaken. It can act as a helpful corrective inasmuch as it de-reifies the unreal conceptual constructs that shape our lives.

The Madhyamaka school disagrees, arguing that the statement of the Perfection of Wisdom requires no interpretation because it is literally true. All phenomena, even the causally effective, are entityless. Moreover, the Madhyamaka denies that the distinction between interpretable and definitive teachings boils down to the literal acceptability of teachings. For the Madhyamaka, those teachings that concern the ultimate are definitive; and because the Perfection of Wisdom concerns the ultimate, it should be taken as it is. Nevertheless, the Yogācāra interpretation has some validity: it is suitable for those who are not ready for the radical Madhyamaka view.

These different views of an important topic are not trivial. The texts of the Perfection of Wisdom have at least two interpretations; though they are contradictory, both are legitimate. Hence, at a certain level there is play in the interpretation. But because its range is tightly limited, we may question whether it qualifies as genuinely polysemic.

MIDRASHIC POLYSEMY AND TIBETAN DIALECTICAL CREATIVITY

In an excellent article, David Stern describes the difference between Jewish midrash (the interpretation of the Torah learned in yeshivas) and postmodern interpretation. Responding to Geoffrey Hartman's argument that midrash resembles postmodernism in its playfulness, Stern shows that the postmodern resistance to closure differs from the midrashic view of polysemy as limited by the divine perspective embodied in the Torah.[20] In the process, he makes the secondary claim that midrashic polysemy is unique to the Jewish tradition. This claim is worth considering in some detail, since Tibetan interpretation may seem similar to midrashic polysemy in that it posits the possibility and necessity of closure while at the same time allowing some room for interpretive freedom.

The freedom of midrashic interpretation is well illustrated by the famous story of Rabbi Eleazar, who calls on heaven in a dispute with other rabbis concerning the laws of purity. Despite several miraculous divine interventions, the majority of the rabbis refuse to accept the divine testimony. They argue that the Torah has been given on Mount Sinai as the full manifestation of the divine accessible to humans. Hence, there is no need to pay any attention to anything else, even a divine intervention. At the end of the story God, who has been listening to this rabbinic debate, laughs and exclaims: "My children have defeated me!"[21] Midrashic interpretations such as those of Rabbi Eleazar and his adversaries are not only contradictory, they are also considered equally valid. They elucidate a divine blueprint contained in the Torah whose fullness cannot be captured by any single correct interpretation. Yet these interpretations must remain within a certain range of meaning predetermined by a tacit knowledge of what is acceptable. All interpretations within those limits can be regarded as equally valid, even if they are contradictory.

In Buddhist hermeneutics, in contrast, competing interpretations are not granted equal validity. Consider the two interpretations discussed above of the Buddha's teaching that all phenomena are entityless. According to either interpretation, there is only one fully correct view; the other is only partially valid. A hierarchy of interpretation places very narrow limits on the text's polysemy. The interpretation that is not fully acceptable is described as being provisional and therefore inferior to the definitive teachings, which alone are fully reliable. Interpretive teachings are also characterized as *intentional* in that their "intended meaning" *(dgongs pa, abhiprāya)* cannot be taken literally but is taught with the intention of leading students toward a more correct view. That view is itself the "basis of intention" *(dgongs gzhi)* of the interpretable teaching. Hence, the multiplicity of meaning in the great texts of the Tibetan tradition is not polysemic in the same way as midrashic interpretations. The room for interpretive play is more limited and there is always a definitive truth that can to some extent be captured.

Several mechanisms contribute to the constriction of textual polysemy in the Tibetan tradition. One of the favorites is the doxographical classification, which claims to organize all the Buddhist views into four schools (Vaibhāṣika, Sautrāntika, Yogācāra, and Madhyamaka). This scheme is not only supposedly inclusive but also provides an immediate way to rank different Buddhist views. The grouping is an attempt by late Indian and Tibetan commentators to bring order to the jungle of conflicting ideas in the commentarial literature. As such, the scheme is a reductive simplification and its applicability is limited, particularly for earlier thinkers.[22]

One of the clearest drawbacks of this classification is that it is severely restrictive, denying the tradition access to the creative polysemy made possible by nonliteral interpretations. Passages that may be troubling to a particular interpretation are brushed aside, described as provisional and reflecting the view of a lower school. As a result, the Tibetan Buddhist tradition has become doctrinally and philosophically more narrow; as José Cabezón explains, it has "creat[ed] a situation in which allegorical or other forms of nonliteral interpretation became more difficult. Scriptures, by their very nature, are supple things; philosophical canons are more rigid.

Scriptures are the objects of interpretation; tenets are the interpretations themselves."[23] The reliance on doxography limits the play of interpretation. The several interpretations that may exist within a single text can be ranked so as not to contradict the assumption that there is only one fully valid interpretation. One cannot imagine the Yogācāra and the Madhyamaka interpretations bringing delight to the Buddha as he exclaims, "My children have defeated me!" Thus, Stern may be right to claim that polysemic interpretation is a unique to rabbinic Judaism; Tibetan hermeneutical literature does not display sufficient interpretive freedom to qualify as a counterexample.

However, its limitations on interpretive freedom do not mean that the Tibetan tradition is closed. Cabezón has argued—rightly, I believe—that debate has tended to replace commentary as a source of creativity, particularly in the Ge-luk tradition.[24] In later chapters, I further argue that in the Tibetan tradition and particularly in the Ge-luk school, the practice of debate embodies a strategy of suspicion that differs from the strategy of retrieval deployed in commentaries. This interpretive strategy follows some of the same principles found in Derrida's deconstructive supplementation. Rather than listen to the text, debate submits it to a relentless process of questioning, in the process creating the kind of freedom without which an intellectual tradition cannot thrive.[25]

This dimension of openness is not unlike the dialectical practice found in yeshivas. There, as Moshe and Tova Halbertal explain, even classes do "not function as the presentation of the truth by the all-knowing scholar imparting knowledge to ignorant or less-knowledgeable receptacles,"[26] but involve chaotic exchanges between teacher and students. This exchange, which is continued by students when they study in pairs, aims at maximizing the diversity of interpretations in ongoing and unique conversations in which unexpected questions may be raised. Such a procedure mirrors the structure of the hagaddic and talmudic texts that support this education. The Halbertals observe of studying the Talmud, "Edited as intergenerational arguments, layer upon layer, most talmudic discussions do not reach a definite legal opinion about previous controversies. Rather they preserve and clarify the wealth and multiplicity of approaches to the problem at hand."[27]

Tibetan commentaries differ from rabbinic interpretations. Even when they are concerned with debates, Tibetan texts rarely display the kind of polysemy that would allow them to entertain conflicting opinions as equally valid; they focus instead on distinguishing right interpretations from wrong. To be sure, the two traditions are concerned with different genres, and narratives lend themselves much more readily to a wealth of interpretations than do abstract doctrines. But that distinction is not decisive: one could imagine analyses of the latter, particularly debate manuals, that proposed alternatives without choosing one as right.[28] Such texts are rarely produced in Tibetan scholasticism, however. Hence, the open-endedness that a lively intellectual tradition requires has to be found elsewhere—in the dialectical debates that give students the freedom to explore alternative interpretations. There, students can seek to multiply the diversity of opinions, like their rabbinical colleagues. A proverb among Tibetan scholars illustrates the spirit that animates debates, a proverb I translate as "Only idiots agree" (*mthun na mkhas pa min;* lit., "if they agree, they are not learned"). It is to the investigation of this practice, which is the most exciting part of Tibetan scholastic education, that we turn next.

10   Debate as Practice

My first encounter with Tibetan debates occurred during my stay at Nam-gyel in the spring of 1972, when monks from the three seats gathered in Dharamsala for a special session of debate. Because my Tibetan was then still rather poor and my knowledge of the tradition even more limited, I understood none of the debates. Nevertheless, I was fascinated by these dialectical encounters, which seemed so lively (see figure 8). I enjoyed their intensity and the dramatic atmosphere that surrounded them, an atmosphere that was greatly enhanced by physical gestures and sometimes play-ful verbal exchanges. I was also struck by the good humor of these spirited clashes. I remember watching the proceedings for hours, trying unsuccess-fully to figure out what was being said. My experience was not unlike that of untrained Tibetans, monks and laity alike, who enjoy debate as a kind of spectacle. They may get a sense—at times misleading—of who is winning and who is losing, but they do not understand the topics debated.

I had a more intimate contact with debate in the late fall of 1972 when I began the preliminary study of debate with Lati Rin-po-che together with my French friend. We started with the rudiments of logic and the proce-dures of debate, which Rin-po-che taught from Pur-bu-jok's Collected Top-ics. At first, he did not insist on our taking part in debate, and we resisted his suggestions that we do so. Right away, we responded differently to what was being taught. I remember trying to help my friend understand, but he had little interest in such intellectual gymnastics. "It's horrible, it's mathe-matics all over again," he would complain. That was the reason I liked it so much: it involved the same kind of logical manipulation as algebra. After a few weeks, my friend dropped out, leaving me to continue alone on a road that would turn into something quite different than what I was expecting.

When Rin-po-che saw that I was becoming engaged by the topic, he decided it was time to see whether there was any hope for me. "Beginning tonight, you will attend the debates of the Nam-gyel monastery. What do you think you are doing? There is no knowing the great texts without debating," he declared, in typical Ge-luk fashion. I was annoyed, for I found the prospect of debating intimidating. How could I, who had but a limited command of Tibetan, stand on my own against all those trained monks speaking in their mother tongue? How could I avoid making a total fool of myself? Nevertheless, Rin-po-che insisted and I had to give in. He was my teacher, and without some compelling reason I could not disobey him. That same evening, I went to the debating courtyard, which is where debates are held in Tibetan monasteries. I felt rather lonely and miserable. The November weather was cold, and it was dark (at Nam-gyel, debates took place around dusk). I was invited to sit down with other students whom by then I knew well.

Obviously, I began with great difficulty. I had trouble understanding some of the students, who quoted passages and hurled what seemed complex arguments at each other at top speed. Such exchanges were difficult for anybody to follow, but for me, whose command of the language was minimal, comprehension was sometimes impossible. I remember a particularly humiliating experience, when I had been debating for a few months. I was able to follow simple debates and I had started to participate, playing a more or less normal role. My opponent that day was a young reincarnated lama, who had a real gift for speed recitation. He started his debate, hurling a few sentences at me rather casually. I had no idea what he was saying; I could not even recognize the language he spoke! I told him I had not understood what he had said and asked him to repeat it. The teacher was right behind me and told him to slow down. The young tulku asked his question again; he must have spoken more slowly, but to me his words seemed as fast and as incomprehensible as the first time. By then I knew I was in trouble. I asked him in a rather shaken voice to try to be really patient. "I am a foreigner, can you speak a bit slowly?" I stammered out, probably sounding like a complete idiot. His third attempt came out as inscrutable as the first. Completely tongue-tied, I could not say anything. The young lama was utterly disgusted and walked away. The teacher was laughing and I was left alone, utterly crushed and dejected in my humiliation. Fortunately, the end of the debates came soon and I quickly retreated, protected by the darkness of the night. Needless to say, my participation was rather limited for the next few days! Yet I persevered and was lucky enough never to experience a similar encounter.

I quickly realized that the debates we were practicing at this stage involved a limited vocabulary and could be understood with relative ease. I also discovered that whatever happens in debate is taken good-naturedly by Tibetan monks, who consider the debating courtyard a separate arena where embarrassments and even humiliations are seen as being part of the learning process. Hence, no stigma is attached to one's mistakes, as bad as they may be, for they are occasions to learn, both intellectually and morally. Similarly, defeat and loss of face in debate are taken in stride. Teachers would even encourage us to lose. "Do not seek easy victory but always prefer a defeat that will advance your learning," was their unanimous advice. Another statement often heard was that the person who loses wins, for he is the one who gains some "better understanding" *(blo rgyas)*.

In what follows I explain Tibetan debate, presenting it as a lively dialectical practice that provides those engaged in it with valuable intellectual resources. My analysis is divided into three parts. In this chapter, I examine the apprenticeship of debaters through the study of the Collected Topics. I analyze the dialectical tools, the rules and procedures of debate, emphasizing its performative aspect. The more advanced practice of debate as a means to deepen one's understanding of Buddhism is the topic of chapter 11, which focuses on the place of debate in the curriculum, particularly in relation to the study of logic and epistemology and of Madhyamka. Finally, chapter 12 offers reflections on debate, comparing diverging approaches within the Ge-luk tradition and emphasizing the critical value of debate as a means of inquiry. Throughout these chapters, I focus primarily on Ge-luk education, the tradition that most upholds the value of debate.

SCHOLARLY CONTEXT

Because debates are so significant within the Tibetan tradition, they have attracted a great deal of attention in the modern scholarly literature. Yet despite their efforts, most modern scholars have failed to do justice to this practice or to adequately capture its most relevant features. Their analyses reflect two dominant views: the humanist or modernist, which rejects debate as a ritualistic vestige of a once meaningful practice, and the logicist, which reduces debate to the embodiment of logical principles.

The modernist view of debate is found in the works of such older scholars as Giuseppe Tucci and R. A. Stein, who have greatly contributed to Tibetan studies. Yet these pioneers were not able to capture the value and importance of Tibetan debates, which they saw as a purely formalistic practice unrelated to any serious intellectual inquiry. Stein, for instance, dismisses Tibetan religious disputation as "no longer anything but an exercise in essentially formalistic logic or rhetoric. Some features, however, show that the institution formerly had the character of a joust or duel in the same way as other ritual contests."[1] For Stein, Tibetans are wrong to see debates as meaningful practices that manifest the vitality of the tradition; their appeal lies wholly in their ritual nature. Debates are important for Tibetans not because they are bona fide intellectual activities but because they are part of Tibetan religious culture. A more extreme position is taken by the anthropologist F. Sierskma, who declares that debates are not a Buddhist practice with strong antecedents in India but a native Tibetan ritual derived from Iranian practices of subduing evil![2] This view of Tibetan debates as meaningless repetitions of a once meaningful practice parallels the Renaissance humanists' rejection of medieval scholasticism as a rigid practice. Their attitude took further hold with the development of modernity. Since then, *scholasticism* has been synonymous with meaningless prattle.

Later researchers, with a fuller understanding of the content of Tibetan debates, have a more sophisticated and knowledgeable view. These nonnative scholars, working with Tibetan scholars, see debates not as sterile intellectual shell games but as lively intellectual practices that embody the creativity of this tradition. In attempting to capture their vitality, these scholars have emphasized the logical aspect of debates. Dealing mostly with the Collected Topics literature, several scholars have used terms borrowed from Aristotelian syllogistic or formal logic to explain their meaning.[3] Consider Margaret Goldberg's catalog of the logical tools used by the Collected Topics: "The theory of logic I encountered deals with inference as a single syllogistic unit. . . . The rules of Detachment (Modus Ponens), its contrapositive (Modus Tollens) are known and used. . . . The Aristotelean techniques of direct proof, reductio ad absurdum (including reductio ad impossibile and consequentia mirabilis) and ecthesis are used routinely."[4] In this logicist view, what is remarkable about the Collected Topics and Tibetan debates is their use of sophisticated logical tools, which the scholars assimilate to notions from Aristotelian or even modern formal logic.

In general, for a scholar to describe the concepts of one culture in terms of another is not in itself objectionable. Nor is an interest in logical matters here problematic. Since Tibetan practices are rational and argumentative in ways that are immediately recognizable to modern observers, they clearly must somehow involve the basic notions and laws of logic. However, Goldberg's particular claims that Tibetan dialecticians know about and use specific logical tools are highly questionable. Tom Tillemans quite rightly objects:

What does she mean by saying that all these things "are known and used"? They are never explicitly formulated, nor, perhaps with the exception of contraposition, are they even discussed clearly. Of course, *we* can, if we wish, use this Aristotelean terminology for comparative purposes, or we can try to transpose/translate *Bsdus grwa* (Collected Topics) into such a logic. We could, with limited utility, do the same thing with regard to the arguments that occur between lawyers, but it would be somewhat silly to say that debaters in courts of law *know and use* Aristotelean logic.[5]

Reliance on etic terms always carries the danger of reading too much into the material one is examining, and Goldberg seems to fall into this trap. The use by Tibetan dialecticians of logical tools seems less like that of modern logicians than like Monsieur Jourdain's use of prose.

This criticism may miss one of the distinctive features of the logic found in the Collected Topics—namely, that in a number of ways absent from its Indian precedent, it prefigures modern formal notions. For example, the Collected Topics uses the pronoun *khyod* much like what modern logicians call a variable. This pronoun, which usually means "you," has a technical sense in the Collected Topics: it refers to whatever phenomenon is being introduced in the logical operations. Similarly, the notion of "subject" *(chos can)* acts for Tibetan dialecticians like a marker of quantification, that is, it indicates the range of a logical function (whether that function applies to all x or to some x).[6] In Indian logic, it is not possible to use logical notions purely formally (i.e., as abstract symbols unassigned to any specific meaning). In the Collected Topics, however, as in formal logic, a meaningless statement that is properly formulated is perfectly admissible, because it can be examined on formal grounds alone. Thus, the logic of the Collected Topics does mark a move toward modern logic's emphasis on form.

Nevertheless, the logicist approach to Tibetan debates is flawed. Even in its more nuanced form, it falls prey to the same tendency toward retrospective distortion that we saw in Goldberg's description. While modern scholars emphasize the features of Tibetan debates that prefigure modern formal logic, those elements are not thought by the tradition to be particularly important.[7] For example, Tibetan scholars recognize the possibility of formulating meaningless and yet valid conclusions, but consider this to be a trivial oddity. Such arguments are intellectual games whose value is limited to training students in verbal manipulation; they are not perceived within the tradition as interesting or significant. Thus, when we take such conclusions and analyze them as if they were formal arguments, we impose a perspective quite foreign to that of the tradition.

Though scholars holding the modernist and logicist views evaluate Tibetan debates quite differently, they share similar assumptions concerning the nature of reasoning. In both approaches, reasoning by definition provides deductive certainty. This assumption goes back to the beginnings of Western modernity. Particularly significant were the separation of rhetoric from logical argumentation by the humanist Ramus (1515–1575) and Descartes's later rejection of dialectic as being unable to lead to knowledge because it is based only on common opinion. Henceforth, most European thinkers have limited logical argumentation to deduction, which is based on and aims at certainty; knowledge is seen as having to conform to scientific models. Arguments that do not conform to such models are assigned to the province of rhetoric, understood as a field of literary study. From this perspective, Tibetan debates either are completely lacking in reasoning or merely prefigure a more advanced way of thinking.

To appreciate the value of Tibetan debates, another perspective is needed. I therefore analyze debates as *dialectical practices* aimed at reaching greater understanding and developing crucial intellectual habits, such as a spirit of inquiry and critical acumen. Following Tillemans's useful suggestion that the logic of Tibetan debates is closer to game logic than to deductive logic,[8] I emphasize the ludic nature of debates, their embodied quality, and their use of intellectual as well as emotional resources.

DEBATE AS DIALECTIC

In describing debates as *dialectical,* I am using a term that has a long history in the Western tradition. In its earlier meaning, dialectic is the conversational art of "seeking and sometimes arriving at the truth by reasoning."[9] It can be traced back to Zeno of Elea, the author of the famous paradox of Achilles and the tortoise. For Zeno, dialectic is an aphoristic method of refuting the hypotheses of opponents by drawing unacceptable consequences from those hypotheses. This dialectic was further extended by such sophists as Protagoras, who developed it into a conversational technique aimed at triumphing in any dispute, regardless of the veracity of one's position. Socrates and Plato opposed this Protagorean view of dialectic, which they call *eristic*—that is, the art of winning through invalid arguments and sophistic tricks. For Socrates, dialectic is not a means to win but a search for truth; its aim is certainty regarding the essence of things, though more often than not, the search ends with the recognition that we do not know.

Aristotle opposes both the Socratic (as expressed by Plato) and sophistic views as extremes.[10] For the Stagirite, dialectic deals with the likely. Certainty is found through demonstration, the scientific and metaphysical method par excellence: it searches for truth from evident first principles and thereby reaches necessary conclusions. Where certainty is not available, dialectic intervenes. Starting from common opinions, it proceeds to show what can be deduced from these views, and then adopts the most likely conclusions. Yet dialectic, unlike sophistic eristic, is a valuable tool in the search for knowledge, for it is rigorous in strictly respecting logical rules.

Aristotelian dialectic proceeds through an exchange of questions and answers between a questioner and a respondent. The task of the former is to "lead the argument so as to make the answerer state the most unacceptable consequences made necessary as a result of his thesis" (*Topics* 159b).[11] The role of the latter is to frustrate this attempt by any lawful means. The proximate goal of the practice is to win the argument by offering valid reasonings that fully respect the canon of logic. Hence, dialectic trains one's ability to reason correctly and contributes to one's philosophical understanding. At the very least, it is an excellent educational exercise.

As we will see, this understanding of dialectic is close to that of Tibetan debaters. For them, as for Aristotle, dialectic is understood as a game. Like a sport, debate has no other immediate goal outside itself, but it can be used for a higher purpose. As the following chapters demonstrate, one can learn a great deal intellectually and morally from debating, though not everybody is able to move to that level. As a game, debate is both agonistic and cooperative, requiring competitiveness and honest participation. It is oriented toward winning—in this case, convincing the opponent. It includes the use of lawful tricks, such as playing on words, dissimulating the conclusions, adding useless propositions to mask the real topic, and using false premises. Some tricks are unlawful; like any other game, dialectic follows rules. There are, for instance, rules concerning the terms of the reasoning. Arguments are also required to satisfy the laws of logic. Premises must be clear and unambiguous, conclusions must be supported by arguments, and there must be an ascertainable link from premises to conclusions; otherwise, the argument falls into one of the various fallacies such as *petitio principii*. Hence, debate differs from most free-flowing discussions, which tend to proceed without much discipline.

But debate also differs from strict logic. One of its most important rules derives from the limitation on the time available to answer. In strict logic, one cannot draw a universal conclusion from particular cases, as numerous as they are. In dialectical practice, a respondent is obliged to concede a universal conclusion based on examples unless he can provide a counterexample. For example, when a respondent is faced with the statement

"It follows that whatever is born must cease," he must either provide a counterexample or accept the statement. To refuse such a conclusion in the absence of counterexamples is to block the progress of the debate, which like any game must be decided in a finite amount of time.

While the procedure followed by debate is predetermined, the outcome is not. Hence, debate cannot be fully described in advance: a good debate is always new, unfolding in unforeseen interactions rather than following a plan. Debaters raise questions that have a life of their own within the debate but are hard to capture outside the dynamic of the encounter. It is because debate cannot be totalized and its outcome cannot be controlled that it provides the creative dimension in the curriculum of Tibetan institutions, particularly in the Ge-luk tradition.

In discussing scholasticism, I have emphasized the tension between the boundedness presupposed by authority and the room required for appropriating knowledge. The dialectic between authority and freedom is central to all scholastic traditions, but the various traditions manage it differently. In rabbinic Judaism, for example, the process of mediation takes place mostly in commentaries through which the scholar, in Gershom Scholem's words, "subordinat[es] himself to the continuity of the tradition of the Divine word and lays open what he receives from it in the context of his own time. In other words: not system but *commentary* is the legitimate form through which truth is approached."[12] Tibetan scholastic traditions rely instead on a dialectic of commentary and debate. The former provides the authoritative dimension by setting forth the orthodox positions that scholars are supposed to hold, and the latter gives them the room for personal inquiry within the confine of the tradition.

During the Middle Ages, this kind of dialectic became a central element of Western scholastic culture, particularly under the form of the *disputatio*. This is the second great intellectual tool that characterizes scholasticism as a mode of presentation. In the West, the *disputatio* evolved from the *lectio* through the intermediary stage of the questions that teachers raised during their classes. These questions resulted from the contradictions perceived among the texts that the tradition had taken as authoritative. By the twelfth century, they began to be collected in texts called *Sententiae*, whose publication made the apparent inconsistencies and contradictions obvious and hence important to resolve. Enter the *disputatio*, in which the teacher proceeds to solve these difficulties and thus harmonize the authoritative texts.

The work of Peter Abelard (1079–1142) was particularly significant in this development. In his *Sic et Non*, Abelard collected a number of conflicting opinions, providing rules for harmonizing these conflicts.[13] Abelard did not, however, provide solutions, a task that would be carried on by the great theologians of the thirteenth century: Albertus Magnus, Thomas Aquinas, and Bonaventure. The process of devising methods to adjudicate these collections of conflicting opinions led to the development of the *quaestio* as an autonomous practice during which a question would be tackled dialectically. This is the basis of the *disputatio,* in which the teacher chooses certain questions and provides his own solutions to conflicts among authoritative sources. Sometimes the teacher would let advanced students debate, dividing them into two groups: the respondents *(respondentes)* and the opponents *(opponentes).* The teacher would then conclude the exercise with his own summary.[14] This practice became further institutionalized during the thirteenth century, when teachers would defend a particular thesis during sessions known as *quaestiones disputatae.* In the *disputatio de quolibet,* a master would debate any question with any person. As John Baldwin puts it, these "were academic free-for-alls which attracted large audiences because of their spontaneity and capriciousness."[15] Offering ample opportunities to vent scholarly rivalries, they were academic tournaments in which scholars could establish or lose their reputations.

THE ROLE OF DEBATE IN INDIA AND IN TIBET

In Tibetan monastic education, debates play a role similar to that described above. In the Ge-luk institutions, debate constitutes the core educative method and provides the scholarly community its focus of activity. In the non-Ge-luk commentarial institutions, debate plays a lesser role, though students devote one or two hours daily to its practice. It is true that non-Ge-luk students are not as skilled in debate as their Ge-luk colleagues, who devote up to ten hours per day to debate (reduced to five in exile). The training of non-Ge-luk students in debate is less far-reaching, as they themselves readily admit. Whereas Ge-luk students often devote several years (as many as four) to acquiring debating skills by studying the Collected Topics, non-Ge-luk scholars do not value such skills as highly. The Sa-gya scholar Lo Ken-chen Sö-nam-hlün-drup *(glo mkhan chen bsod nams lhun grub,* 1456–1532) expresses the non-Ge-luk distrust of the training provided by the Collected Topics when he calls the debates explained in these texts "childish games."[16] Hence, it comes as no surprise that non-Ge-luk students do not have the dialectical fluency and smoothness in debate that Ge-luk debaters acquire through their long and intensive training.

Yet debate is more than a sideshow in commentarial institutions. It excites a great deal of interest among students, and often teachers have to prevent their students from becoming too absorbed in a practice that may distract them from learning the art of commentary. Trained scholars of these schools often display a fondness for debate not unlike that of their Ge-luk colleagues. Ken-po Nam-dröl *(rnam grol)*, with whom I studied at Nam-dröl-ling, took every opportunity to engage in debate with me, even though the text we were studying, a commentary on the *Guhyagarbha* tantra, was less conducive to this exercise than a text on Madhyamaka or epistemology would be. Thus, most Tibetan scholastics, regardless of their sectarian affiliation, are extremely keen on debate, a practice they see as central to Buddhist scholarship. For them, a good scholar is as much a good debater as a good commentator.

The significance of the role debate plays for non-Ge-luk scholars, who greatly enjoy the rough-and-tumble often involved in this practice, pales beside its significance in the Ge-luk tradition, where debate is the scholastic method par excellence. The largest amount of time is devoted to its practice, and examinations are in the form of debate, particularly the final exam for the title of Geshe. Many texts used in scholastic education, notably the monastic manuals, are based on debates. They are written in the form of debate and presuppose an audience focused on this practice. Even commentaries that are not written in debate format often contain debates. Debate is unquestionably central to the Ge-luk tradition, which has excelled in it. A large part of the scholarly reputation of the Ge-luk school rests on the debating abilities of its scholars, for whom Buddhist scholarship is hardly conceivable without this practice.

If we reflect back on Paul Griffiths's claim that reading is the central practice of scholasticism,[17] we remember that it was put in question by the practices of medieval European scholars, who often preferred secondhand compilations to the careful reading of basic texts that he praised. Tibetan scholasticism similarly undercuts Griffiths's claim that the scholastic is *homo lector,* for the Tibetan scholar appears to be first and foremost *homo disputans.* This is particularly true in the Ge-luk tradition, which has dominated Tibetan religious intellectual life for the past three centuries. A great Ge-luk scholar must be a good debater.

The emphasis on debate was inherited from India, where dialectic has played a key role. In fact, a crucial difference between Western and Indian traditions concerns the distinction between logic proper and dialectic. In the Western tradition, logic has tended to be restricted to the study of the logical form of arguments. As Jan Lukasiewicz observes in his book on

Aristotle's syllogistic, "Only syllogistic laws stated in variables belong to logic, and not their application to concrete terms. Logic is devoid of any *hule* (matter) and is concerned only with form." [18] In modern analytical usage, logic concerns not the content of the propositions it posits but their form. It is interested in the deductions that can be drawn from propositions, not in the truth or falsity of those propositions. That concern was already clear in Aristotelian logic, and Rudolf Carnap is quite justified in saying that "All the efforts of the logicians since Aristotle have been directed to the formulation of rules of inference as formal rules, that is to say, as rules which refer only to the form of the sentences." [19] Thus the primary concern of Western logic has always been deductive: only in deduction can absolute (for Aristotle) or formal (for Carnap) necessity be found. This preoccupation also explains why dialectic and logic have been strictly differentiated from Aristotle onward.

The concern of Indian "logicians" is quite different. Their object of study is the difference between correct and incorrect reasonings. Hence, their primary focus is not the formal validity of reasoning but its soundness. In fact, Indian logic is a form of dialectic; or, to put it another way, in the Indian context there is no separation between logic and dialectic. Whereas Western logic since Aristotle has distinguished between logic proper, which concerns rigorous deduction (what Aristotle calls "demonstration") and dialectic, which concerns the topics for which deductive certainty is not possible, in the Indian context these two endeavors were never separated and the main focus has remained the study of sound reasoning.

This concern with soundness translates quite naturally into an emphasis on debate. Indian logic was born out of the codification of debates, which has played an important role in Indian civilization. From very early on, public debates rather than written works were considered the main arena where truth could be decided. This was particularly true in the religious domain, where thinkers holding conflicting opinions would confront each other in public in exchanges arbitrated by political authorities. Such a tradition was later systematized in procedures of debate that often imitated the procedures of courts of law. Several of the terms used by treatises on debate *(tarka-śāstra)*, such as position *(pakṣa, phyogs)* and thesis *(pratijñā, dam bca')*, seem to have been borrowed from treatises concerning law and politics *(artha-śāstra)*.[20]

The centrality of debate greatly influenced Indian Buddhism, which developed its own "logical" (i.e., dialectical) tradition through the works of Dignāga (500 C.E.)[21] and his follower Dharmakīrti (600 C.E.). Around the same time, Indian Buddhism was developing its own institutions of higher learning, such as Nalanda *(nālandā)* in Bihar and Vikramalashila *(vikramalaśīla)* in Bengal.[22] In these institutions, debate was considered an important element in the education of scholars. It is well known that public confrontations between thinkers holding different views, either inside or outside the Buddhist tradition, were important events in the scholarly life of Nalanda and Vikramalashila. Religious history records the confrontations during the sixth century of such Buddhist thinkers as Bhavaviveka and Dharmapāla, as well as the more mythical encounter between Dharmakīrti and the Hindu Śaṅkara. The dialectical skills publicly displayed in these verbal engagements were acquired at institutions of learning, but the exact role of debate in education is hard to determine. Was it similar to that in Tibetan debating institutions, where debate is the main pedagogical method and is practiced several hours per day, or was it, as seems more likely, closer to that in Tibetan commentarial institutions, where debate is secondary to textual interpretation?

Whatever the answers to these questions, it is clear that debate was important in Indian Buddhism and that Tibet inherited this tradition. Tibet further developed the practice, creating in the process a new tradition of debate, which claims to embody the norms and ideals of the Indian tradition but in fact contains some innovations as well. To understand these innovations, which seem to have been started by Cha-ba and the Sang-pu tradition, we need to examine the dialectical tools used in debates.

ARGUMENTS AND CONSEQUENCES

In classical (Indian) Buddhist logic, the main dialectical tools are the statement of proof or, more simply, the probative argument *(sbyor ba, prayoga)*, and the statement of consequence or, more simply, the consequence *(thal 'gyur, prasaṅga)*. Understanding the difference between them is important to understanding how Tibetan debates differ from Indian.

In Indian logic, the favorite tool is the statement of proof, which is sometimes described by modern scholars as a syllogism. Others have argued against the use of this term in Indian logic.[23] The main point here is not that the term *syllogism* is necessarily inappropriate in the Indian context, but that an Indian argument is not identical to an Aristotelian syllogism. To avoid any confusion, I use the translations "proof statement" or "probative argument" (often abbreviated to "argument").

An Indian argument contains four terms: the subject *(dharmin, chos can)*, the predicate *(sādhya-dharma, bsrub bya'i chos)*, the reason *(liṅga, rtags),* and the example *(dṛṣṭānta, dpe).* It can be formulated in several ways. In the elegant and economical formulation favored by Dharmakīrti and his school, it contains two parts: a universal statement of concomitance between reason and predicate and a statement of the agreement between reason and subject. For example:

> Whatever is produced is impermanent, just like a jar.
> As for the sound, it is also produced.

The more usual formulation of the same argument would be

> The subject, the sound, is impermanent because it is produced, just like a jar.

This statement looks very much like an Aristotelian syllogism, until one notices an important difference: the presence of an example. This element underscores that the Indian argument is not a syllogism in the Aristotelian sense of the term. Rather than exhibiting a formal deductive relation, it involves nondeductive elements; chief among these is the example, which is meant to allow the opponent to understand the statement of universal concomitance. This structure follows closely the common practice of supporting one's argument with an example, either positive (to exemplify one's own view) or negative (to undermine the opposite view). For example, while addressing an audience of convinced Democrats I might argue that George W. Bush is an irresponsible politician because he proposes a flawed and demagogical tax break. I will support my argument with an example, just as Ronald Reagan did. The similarity with everyday arguments should not be pushed too far, since Indian arguments aim at producing knowledge in the audience, not just correct opinion. This knowledge is understood in term of certainty *(niścaya, nges pa).* The conclusion reached by an argument is not just probable but certain, though it is not easy to understand how such nondeductive certainty can be attained.[24]

The use of examples shows that arguments are meant to communicate knowledge to a particular audience, not to draw conclusions that hold regardless of the circumstances in which the argument is formulated. My argument is cogent only for an audience favorably inclined toward the Democrats. Made before the local Young Republicans, it is bound to draw jeers. Similarly, the illustrative formulation above provides an example geared to a specific opponent who recognizes that material objects such as jars are impermanent but holds that sound, being a quality of ether, is permanent. Aimed at a person who already understands the impermanence of a sound, such an argument would be pointless, since it would not fulfill any communicative function. An Indian argument is not an axiomatic demonstration but a dialectical tool used conversationally.

A consequence looks superficially similar to a statement of proof. It has three terms: the subject *(chos can)*, the (pseudo-)predicate *(bsal ba;* lit., "that which is to be eliminated"), and the reason *(rtags, liṅga)*. For example:

> It follows that the subject, the sound, is not permanent because it is produced.

This form of arguing should not be confused with the proof statement described above, however. Formally, consequences are set apart from arguments by their use of the format "it follows . . . because" *(thal phyir)* instead of "it is . . . because." Moreover, the consequence contains no example.

As Theodore Stcherbatsky remarked, this formal notation signals important differences in how the consequence functions as a dialectical tool.[25] An argument is used to establish a true thesis (the *probandum,* or that which is proved by the argument) to an audience that has ignored it. It is attempting to make its point persuasively, not prove a statement deductively. Accordingly, a correct argument must satisfy a number of criteria, usually presented as threefold.[26] One requirement, the "forward-pervasion" *(amvayavyāpti, rjes khyab)* or the "counter-pervasion" *(vyatirekavyāpti ldog khyab),* the two being equivalent, is that the argument be connected to the thesis, for an unconnected argument is useless. That link between the reason and the predicate (in our example, being impermanent and being produced) is established by the example and the counterexample. Another requirement, sometimes described as the agreement *(pakṣadharmatā, phyogs chos;* lit., "the property of the position") between the reason and the subject, is that the subject instantiate the reason. This agreement itself also entails that the argument be addressed to a person or a group of people possessing the right epistemic qualifications. They must have understood the agreement between reason and subject but still have doubts concerning the thesis (the sound's impermanence). Only when all these requirements are satisfied is an argument correct.[27]

A consequence differs from a probative argument in that it does not attempt to establish a point but merely draws the consequences of previous statements and brings out the contradictions or falsities that they entail. Hence, it implies no direct commitment on the part of whoever states it, except that the statement follows from previous statements accepted by his opponent. To be correct, a consequence needs to follow from previous statements. It also needs to expose a contradiction or at least a flaw internal to the opponent's positions.[28] For example, the statement "It follows that the subject, a sound, is not produced because it is permanent" is a correct consequence, provided that it is stated to a person who is committed to the position that everything produced must be impermanent and everything permanent must be nonproduced. This person must also hold that sound is permanent but that it is produced. To such a person the above-mentioned statement is correct. The consequence, as given, strictly follows from his commitments and brings out their contradiction.[29]

Both dialectical tools, the argument and the consequence, are known and used by Indian and Tibetan scholars. But whereas Indian logic has tended to favor the former, Tibetan logicians have preferred the latter. To explain this difference, I must say a few words about Indian debate—no easy task. Save for a few stories of spectacular but largely mythical encounters, no descriptions exist of how debates were actually practiced. There are elaborate theoretical discussions, but it is problematic, to say the least, to infer practice from theory. Nevertheless, a consistent picture of debate emerges from the primary and secondary literature on Indian logic.[30]

A debate sets in opposition the proponent (*pūrvavādin, sngar rgol*) and the respondent (*prativādin, phyir rgol*). The first asserts a thesis and offers a proof supporting it. The job of the respondent is to undermine the proponent's statement by showing either that the thesis is faulty or that the supporting argument is mistaken. In addition to the two active participants, there is a witness (*sākṣin, dpang po*), who is in charge of adjudicating the debate impartially. The debate begins with the respondent eliciting the proponent's thesis. If the respondent judges that this thesis is mistaken, he can start to attack it directly. Otherwise, he must inquire into the reason establishing the thesis. The proponent replies by stating the argument, which contains a reason that satisfies the three criteria stated above. He also proceeds to "remove the thorns" (*kaṇṭakoddhāra, tsher ma 'byin*); that is, he shows that his reason is free from any of three specific types of fault.[31] The respondent must then show that this argument is mistaken. That demonstration is the second part of the debate, the statement of refutation (*sun 'byin brjod pa*), as the respondent uses the statement of consequence to show the proponent's mistakes. The proponent responds (*lan 'debs*) in turn by identifying the fallacies committed by the respondent. If the respondent's consequences are correct, he asks the respondent to provide a full-blown argument to positively prove his point.

As this description makes clear, Indian debates proceed mostly through statements of proof. Statements of consequences have only an auxiliary purpose, as they are used to refute particular points. The debate unfolds through the argument, which not only provides the starting point but supports the whole procedure. Moreover, a probative argument concludes the debate: in the final stage, the proponent reverses the roles and asks the respondent to state his own argument.

The Tibetan way of debating instead favors the use of consequences. Statements of proof may be used as starting points, but after that the debate proceeds mostly through consequences. In particular, the defender's arguments are rarely assessed in relation to the formal fallacies (such as the "sixteen points of defeat," *tshar bcad pa'i gnas, nigrahasthāna*) that threaten an argument, as seems to have been the case in India.[32] In Tibetan debates, once the two parties agree on the starting point of the discussion, the debate proceeds through the deduction of consequences with less attention being paid to formal fallacies. There are obviously exceptions and a debate may focus on some feature of an argument; but that focus is a choice made by the participants, not an element in the debate's formal procedure.

The credit for establishing this new format is usually given to Cha-ba and his disciples.[33] Thus, the approach is connected with what I call the *Sang-pu tradition*; it is not surprising that nowadays Tibetan debates are more particularly associated with the Ge-luk school, which has continued the Sang-pu tradition. But this model of debate was not limited to Sang-pu and has spread throughout the Tibetan scholarly world. Although Sa-paṇ tried to undo its influence and set up the Indian model described above, his recommendations had little influence; the practice of debates in the Tibetan tradition continues to follow the procedures developed by Cha-ba and his followers. A few passages in Śākya Chok-den's work suggest a different model of debate, but they seem more normative than descriptive.[34]

The reasons behind the Tibetan departure from the norms established in the Indian texts that Tibetans themselves cherish are far from obvious. One answer may be that chance often influences how traditions form and develop. Consider a related phenomenon, the adoption by Cha-ba and his tradition of a realist interpretation of Dharmakīrti's antirealist philosophy. As I have shown elsewhere,[35] there appears to be no special reason why such a view, which was shared by only a small minority of Indian Buddhist scholars, was adopted. Tibetans encountered this view in India, particularly in Kashmir, where a sustained exchange between Indian Buddhists and Tibetans took place. But once Cha-ba and his disciples embraced this view, it became the established interpretation, and later efforts by Sa-paṇ and his followers to dislodge it met with fierce resistance. It is not unlikely that the form in which debates were established in Tibet reflects a similar historical contingency.

PROCEDURES AND RULES OF DEBATE

Tibetan debates involve two parties: a defender *(dam bca' ba)*, who answers, and a questioner *(rigs lam pa)*. The roles of defender and questioner imply very different commitments, as Daniel Perdue explains: "The defender puts forth assertions for which he is held accountable. The challenger raises qualms to the defender's assertions and is not subject to reprisal for the questions he raises."[36] The responsibility of the defender is to put forth a true thesis and to defend it. Hence, the defender is accountable for the truth of his assertions. The questioner, on the contrary, is responsible only for the questions he puts forth. His questions must be well-articulated, must logically follow from the points already made, and must be relevant to defeating the defender. Their truth content is irrelevant, however, for his task is not to establish a thesis but to oblige the defender to contradict either previous statements or common sense.

The debate starts with a ritual invocation of Manjushri, the celestial bodhisattva patron of wisdom: *Dhīḥ ji ltar chos can* (pronounced "di ji tar chö cen"). This invocation can be translated as "*Dhīḥ* [the seed syllable of Manjushri]; in just the way the subject." Obviously, this statement is rather unclear and hence offers ample scope for various creative interpretations, as is often the case with ritual. Some scholars take the statement to mean "*Dhīḥ*; in just the way [Manjushri investigated] the subject."[37] Others, myself included, read it more simply as "*Dhīḥ*; in just the way the subject [is investigated]." This invocation, however, also plays on the homophonic similarities of the syllable *dhīḥ* and *'di*, that is, "this." Thus, the statement can also be heard as meaning "This is the way the subject is," a statement that can be taken as having deeper implications (an explanation offered by Lati Rin-po-che). The subject, *this*, then refers to conventional objects and the predicate, *is the subject*, to the empty way in which they exist.

After this ritual invocation, the questioner proposes the topic of the debate in the form of a question, which seeks to elicit the defender's thesis. The defender answers, stating his position. The questioner may then immediately begin the debate, or he may first seek auxiliary explanations to clarify the position of his adversary. The point of this crucial preparatory phase *(sbyor ba)* is to establish a starting point for the debate, an area of agreement between the two parties. This may be one of the most delicate phases of an argument, especially if the two parties do not belong to the same tradition or monastery.

Such conflictual situations have long existed in the Buddhist tradition. In ancient India, debates pitched orthodox Hindu thinkers against their heterodox opponents (materialist, Jain, Ājīvika, or Buddhist). These debates, which had political ramifications, were often witnessed by the local authorities, and the stakes could be the conversion of one group to the views of the other. In Tibet, a similar debate is supposed to have taken place at the end of the eighth century when Kamalaśīla is said to have defeated the Chinese Ch'an monk Mo-ho-yen, thereby establishing the primacy of the Indian tradition.[38] More recently, the young Kay-drup is said to have debated and, according to Ge-luk accounts, defeated Rong-dön. Nowadays, such confrontations between scholars from different traditions are rare; they have been replaced among Ge-luk-bas by debates between monasteries. Most debates take place within a single monastery, where the agreement between parties is easier to establish. Even then, however, fashioning that agreement is crucial and requires great skill. The questioner must dissimulate his real point and the defender must try to guess where his opponent wants to lead him.

Once the two parties believe that they agree on the understanding of the terms of the debate, the main part *(dngos gzhi)* can unfold through questions and answers.[39] The questions are meant to draw out the consequences of the defender's statements in order to oblige him to contradict himself or to take a blatantly absurd position. To succeed, the questioner must be able to take apart his opponent's statements to draw out unwanted consequences. His opponent, the defender, must for his part attempt to block these contradictions by making further distinctions. In doing so, he must give one of the *three allowable answers:*[40]

1. I accept *('dod).*
2. The reason is not established *(rtags ma grub).*
3. There is no pervasion [i.e., connection] *(khyab pa ma byung).*

These three answers derive from the link (or lack thereof) of the reason with the subject and the pseudo-predicate. The defender can say "I accept," if he thinks that the consequence supports his position. Or he can say "The reason is not established," when the reason does not correspond to the subject. For example, the consequence "It follows that all dogs are intelligent because they are primates" is faulty because dogs are not primates. Hence, the reason is not established. Or he can say "there is no pervasion" when the reason does not entail the pseudo-predicate as in the consequence "It follows that all dogs are primates because they are mammals." In such a consequence, the reason is established but does not entail the pseudo-predicate. Or, to put it more literally, there is no pervasion.

As Sa-paṇ noticed, these three answers differ from the Indian model. Most clearly a Tibetan invention is the third answer (no pervasion), which does not exist in Dharmakīrti's debating tradition. There, defenders must make explicit whether the reason is contrary *('gal ba)* or just uncertain *(ma nges pa)*, that is, inconclusive. Thus defenders have four answers to choose from and need to make their response more specific.[41] This difference illustrates the originality of Tibetan practices, which go beyond imitating Indian models in responding to the Tibetan context. Moreover, the failure of non-Ge-luk institutions to follow Sa-paṇ's recommendations regarding these answers shows again the domination of the Sang-pu tradition of debate throughout the Tibetan world.

One of the three allowable answers must be given to all well-formed consequences. In order to be well-formed (like the examples above), a statement should contain three terms: a subject, a pseudo-predicate, and a reason. It should also avoid ambiguity. For example, if the questioner asks whether humans have male or female sexual organs, the defender will not be able to answer without disambiguating the subject (human). At that point, the defender must state his objection. In addition, consequences should not lead defenders into paradoxes (so judged by the rules of conversation). For example, consider the following question: "Did you bring back the computer you stole?" Such a statement cannot be answered straightforwardly without implying an admission of guilt. In all these cases, the defender should point to such a faulty formulation by saying, "The subject is faulty" *(chos can skyon can)*. But absent such faults, the defender has no choice. The ability to give one of the three allowable answers while making meaningful statements is a sign of a good defender. In difficult situations, defenders often try to muddle the situation and break the flow of consequences by saying, "What I really mean is . . ." These explanations are not accepted and reflect poorly on the defender. The questioner may reply, "No need to say much; just give one of the three answers." Or he may mock the defender, pretending that his adversary is a great teacher about to give a sermon. In most cases, defenders are brought back, more or less gently, to the three answers.

Another element in debate is that defenders must answer quickly. Whenever a defender delays his answer, the questioner urges him on with rhythmic triple handclaps punctuated by the words "cir, cir, cir" *(phyir;* i.e., *ci'i phyir,* "why"). If this is a formal debate (see chapter 11), the audience joins in, thus increasing the pressure on the defender. If the defender still does not answer, the questioner and the audience may start to tease him: "Are you here or are you absorbed in meditation?" If still nothing is forthcoming, the questioner either provides the required information himself or recasts his point in a simpler form. In this way, the debate is made so clear that the defender must answer. If he still cannot, a member of the audience is likely to step in and answer in his place. Such an outcome is humiliating for the defender, a sign that he is not up to the task.

It is in this framework that the debate unfolds strategically. The questioner tries to force his opponent either to contradict himself or to contradict common sense. To do so, he must be able to break down complex arguments into simple elements that can be expressed in a chain of well-formed consequences that follow each other logically. He must also keep track of the position of his adversary and where he wants to take him. The defender must figure out the questioner's strategy and thwart his efforts, using only the three answers.

Let us take the example of a debate about the definition of impermanence, which is "that which is momentary."[42] The debate starts by delineating the agreement between both parties. The questioner may ask for further clarification, with such questions as "What does *moment* mean in this definition?" "Does it refer to a brief moment or to a longer one?" The defender may answer that the moment implied by *momentary* is brief. The questioner then proceeds to draw consequences, thinking that he has enough to go on. He may start, "It follows that things last only for a short moment since they are momentary." This statement is framed to embody the defender's answer concerning the meaning of momentariness and is considered the *root consequence (rtsa ba'i thal 'gyur)*, which derives from the *root thesis (rtsa ba'i dam bca')* that the defender must be made to contradict.

The questioner proceeds by drawing out unwanted consequences intended to force the defender to give the no-pervasion answer that contradicts his explanation of the meaning of momentariness. For if the meaning of momentariness is to last only for a short moment, then being momentary must entail lasting for a short moment. To deny this and hold that there is no pervasion is thus tantamount to directly contradicting the thesis. Presented with the root consequence that embodies his view of the meaning of momentariness, the defender must try to thwart the questioner's attempts by choosing the answer that he can defend and does not contradict his earlier point. In this example, he has one obvious choice: to assent to the consequence. The other possibility, the rejection of the reason as being not established, is less defe. since it contradicts the fundamental Buddhist view that all things are n. ry. And, as noted, saying that there is no pervasion would contradict . is concerning the meaning of momentariness. Hence, he will assent t. estion, thereby agreeing with a classical interpretation of the Buddhis. ine of impermanence. The questioner's task is then to oblige the defender to back off from his acceptance of the root statement, forcing him to make the no-pervasion answer that contradicts his main thesis. To do so, the questioner will draw unwanted consequences from the defender's position, pushing him to make counterintuitive statements until he reaches the point of absurdity. For example, the questioner will point to a mountain and state: "It follows that this mountain also lasts for a short moment since it is momentary." If the defender still agrees, the questioner may point to the fact that it cannot exist just for a short moment since the mountain has been there for millions of years. He may also try to oblige his opponent to agree with blatantly counterintuitive statements. For example, he can ask: "Have you never seen any object lasting more than a moment? Have you never seen any object older than a moment? Have you never seen any person older than a moment?"[43]

Obliging the defender to make ridiculous statements is one of the ways for the questioner to gain the upper hand, forcing a reductio ad absurdum that can be seen as tantamount to a defeat of the defender. But although this way of ending the debate can be quite fun, it is not favored, for it is difficult to distinguish a blatant absurdity from an apparently counterintuitive but valid point. Hence, debaters prefer to end with their opponents' self-contradiction. In our example, the defender may try to back away from the counterintuitive consequences that the questioner has drawn. He may agree that there are objects older than a moment. At this point, the questioner must take the defender back to his root statement and oblige him to contradict himself. He may state: "It follows that the mountain lasts for more than one moment, since it is older than a moment." The defender will try to resist; for example, he might attempt to make distinctions between "being older than" and "lasting for more than." The questioner must then try to block these attempts. If he succeeds, he will be able to take the defender back to his root statement, which he will restate: "It follows that things last only for a short moment since they are momentary." At that point, the defender has an unenviable choice between two answers: reason not established and no-pervasion. The former implies the rejection of the fundamental Buddhist view that things are momentary. If he chooses this answer, a whole new debate starts. The questioner may try a rhetorical jab: "I thought you were a Buddhist!" But such a move can also backfire. The defender can turn the tables on the questioner, taunting him to establish this fundamental tenet: "I know what great masters such as Dharmakīrti would say. But let us see what you can do!" The questioner will then have to mount a new attack to oblige the defender to retract his rejection of this Buddhist tenet. If the questioner succeeds, the defender will have no other choice than to give the answer that here dooms him: "There is no pervasion." This is the moment of triumph for the questioner, who will express his victory by saying: "The root thesis is finished" *(rtsa ba'i dam bca' tshar)* or, more briefly, "Oh, it's finished!" *(o' tshar)*.[44]

This is the end of this debate, with the clear victory of the questioner. This victory is due to a direct contradiction between two statements and hence is easily detectable. Such clarity of outcome may explain why there is no formal role for a witness in Tibetan debates. Unlike Indian debates, which proceeded according to formal argumentative criteria on which a witness could adjudicate, Tibetan debates proceed through consequences aimed at exposing direct contradictions in the views of the defender. Detecting such contradictions does not require any special skills and hence the presence of a witness is not necessary.

Not all debates end in a defeat for the defender. Sometimes the questioner is unable to force the defender into contradicting himself and the debate ends in a stalemate. At other times, the defender gives an answer that establishes his view as being well-founded. In our example, the defender may succeed in maintaining that not all things are impermanent and hence escape contradicting himself. He might end his successful defense with a little rhetorical dig, marking his understanding that he has contradicted a basic Buddhist tenet for the sake of argument: "Fortunately, Dharmakīrti was smarter than you. If all Buddhists were like you, we would have long ago ceased to be Buddhist!" This is a clear victory for the defender, especially if he succeeds in making some good points in the process. Sometimes the debate ends abruptly when the questioner's debate breaks down *(rtags bsal chad)* and he is left without anything to say. When this happens in an individual debate, the embarrassment is minimal. But in a formal debate *(dam bca')* the experience can be quite humiliating. The questioner may be left standing speechless in the midst of a large audience for a couple of extraordinarily painful minutes, until the abbot or the disciplinarian rescues him by bringing the debate to a merciful end. The defender may then make matters worse with a few unpleasant comments—for example, "You used to brag so much! Where is your debate now?" Most questioners manage to assert, often stammeringly, a few random consequences. However, it is clear to everyone that their debate has broken down and that they are just trying to avoid humiliation.

In the cases of such a victory or of a stalemate, there are no formal criteria according to which the debate can be adjudicated. For example, if the defender is ridiculed, there are no formal ways to determine what is ridiculous and what is not. The same is also true when the questioner's debate simply fades away. In these cases, the outcome cannot be determined formally and hence there is little role for a witness. The outcome is left to the often conflicting opinions of participants and listeners. It is only in the case of a direct contradiction on the defender's part that the outcome can be formally decided, a remarkable feature of Tibetan debates to which we will have to come back in the next chapter.

THE PHYSICALITY OF TIBETAN DEBATES

One of the striking features of Tibetan debates is that they are quite physical. They are marked by emphatic gestures, such as the clapping used by the questioner to punctuate each question (see figure 9). The questioner holds his right hand above his right shoulder—a little over the head—and stretches his left hand forward, its palm turned upward. Then he strikes the palm of the left hand with the palm of his right and immediately crosses his arms before starting the movement all over again for the next question. These gestures are thought to have great symbolic value.[45] The putting forward of the left hand symbolizes closing the doors of the lower states of rebirth. The coming together of the two hands symbolizes the union of the two aspects of the path, wisdom and method (i.e., compassionate actions). Drawing back the right hand marks one's wish to liberate all sentient beings. Debaters are rarely aware of such symbolic meanings, however. For them, the gestures function primarily to stage debates, bringing them a clarity and a decisiveness that can help mobilize the intellectual capacities of the debaters and capture the attention of the audience.

There are also gestures used at more particular occasions. For example, when a respondent gives an answer that the questioner holds to be false, the latter must circle his opponent's head three times with his right hand while screaming in a loud and shrill voice, "These are the three circles" (*'di 'khor gsum*).[46] In more formal settings, the whole crowd joins in with the questioner, thus subjecting the respondent to further psychological pressure. During Geshe exams, when the respondent wears a hat to mark the solemnity of the occasion (see figures 9 and 10), the questioner can grab his opponent's hat and circle the latter's head with it three times to emphasize the mistake.[47]

Debate also involves prescribed modes of behavior. The debate starts, as I mentioned earlier, with a ritual invocation of Manjushri *(dhī ji ltar chos can)* in a loud and high-pitched tone. The debater then puts his questions in a very low voice barely audible to the audience. During this initial phase, he also wears his upper robe *(gzan)* in the usual way (covering the left shoulder and leaving the right bare). His gestures are contained and he often bends forward toward the defender, as a sign of humility and respect. For the parties to successfully engage with differing points of view, they must respect each other. But these gestures are also elements in the skillful strategy that debate requires. A good debater does not show his hand and does not raise expectations. Hence, he should start in a low key, masking his intentions and inducing a false sense of security in his adversary. It is only when the victim is trapped that he reveals his plan and ups the intensity. Then the initial show of respect takes on a retrospective irony, as is appropriate to this ludic and agonistic enterprise. When the questioner feels that the basis for the debate has been laid down and that he has enough material to demonstrate his opponent's mistake, he wraps his upper robe around his waist, a sign of his understanding and control. Instead of bending forward, he stands tall and makes broad and forceful gestures, clapping his hands loudly to stress the power and decisiveness of his arguments. At that point, any pretense to humility is gone, replaced with self-assurance and self-confidence.

This decisiveness also involves some aggression. In its milder manifestations, it takes the form of loud clapping and vigorous verbal exchanges. Sometimes, however, things escalate and one party may start to taunt the other: "Come on, answer; you think you know so much, don't you?" Things can get even more heated, and ridicule may follow. A skilled rhetorician can be devastatingly effective in a large public gathering, hurling a clever name that may stick to a person for the rest of his life. It is hard not to fall apart when one is ridiculed in front of hundreds, perhaps even thousands, of scholars and students. Shoving matches are also common, when several people attempt to put their questions to the defender. Noisy demonstrations of victory and sarcasm to humiliate one's opponents are often observed, particularly when the questioner has obliged the defender to contradict his basic point and expresses his victory by saying, "The root thesis is finished." While saying this, he slaps his hand in a particular way. Instead of hitting one palm against the other, as in the usual accompaniment to every statement, he hits the back of the right hand against the left palm to signify that the defender has contradicted himself. In this psychologically intense moment, the questioner expresses his glee at crushing his adversary. Some take a sadistic pleasure in repeating "The root thesis is finished" several times, with sweeping gestures and humiliating comments. Stein describes a particularly colorful and graphic expression of victory: "The winner of the debate is borne in triumph on his colleagues' shoulders, sometimes, it seems, humiliating the loser (in Sikkim, the loser has been known to get on all fours, with the winner riding on his back and spurring him on with his heels)."[48] I have heard but never observed that on extremely rare occasions, respondents completely fall apart, disintegrating under the onslaught and sobbing out of control. At other times, people get really angry or vicious, creating enmity that can last a lifetime and poison the atmosphere around them. There are even reports of monks coming to blows.

How can Buddhist monks, who are supposed to be peaceful and detached, behave like this? Don't such actions show that the soteriological claims of the tradition are merely pretense? As the earlier discussion of commentary has already shown, answering such questions is not a simple matter. The relation between soteriology and intellectual activities is complex and fraught with tension—but it is clearly not oppositional. Hence, explanations such as Sierskma's thesis of "a conflict between Tibetan tradition and Buddhist religion" will not do.[49]

The Tibetan tradition is quite aware of the dangers of debate but sees them as counterbalanced by its benefits. Because debates are intensely physical, participants can give vent to considerable energy. Their exertions are heightened further by the performance involved in the debate, the theatrics of the respondent's emphatic gestures (some people are very good at making fun of their opponents by their gestures), and occasional pokes and sharp words. Such performances enable debates to be appreciated by laypeople and uninformed monks, who take delight in the spectacle, despite their inability to follow the verbal parrying. Debaters make outrageous comments or look angry while debating, with the understanding that they are putting on a good show. As Sierskma's informant explains, "We look angry when we are debating, but we are not angry. It is our custom. When one is only a beginner, one thinks that the *snga-rgol* (the questioners) are very, very angry and one is very, very ashamed. But when one has become a debater oneself, one knows that they are not angry and that it is a custom."[50] This performative aspect leads to intense emotional involvement—mere intellect is not powerful enough. As one scholar commented, the questions that debates deal with are so technical that it is not always possible to feel excited about their content alone. A little staging is helpful in producing enthusiasm and allowing participants to mobilize intellectual resources that otherwise would not be available. This intense physical and emotional involvement explains why Tibetan scholars love debate so much. They become excited when they talk about it and miss it once their training is finished. Older scholars often advise students to savor their times as debaters: "This is the best time in the life of a scholar. After this, all fades in comparison."

Yet such intensity also can be dangerous. There are clear cases of monks using debate for the sole purpose of settling old scores or advancing their own ambitions. In twelve years of practicing debates, I have sometimes seen abuses committed. I have seen people attempting to wound and humiliate their adversaries or becoming genuinely angry. These cases are rare, however, and most debates reflect an honest interest in intellectual exchange.[51] I have never seen blows exchanged or witnessed any of the other outrageous behaviors reported in the literature.[52] But I have often heard teachers deploring these excesses and urging their students not to forget the real purpose of the exercise. The teachers also regretted the monks' tendency to be too invested in immediate results. "Take the whole thing as an exercise, be open to being shown wrong, and you will learn," was their unanimous advice. Although that advice was not always strictly followed, the overall tone of the debates showed that the attitude it reflected was dominant. As one of my teachers marveled, "Isn't it great to have all these people displaying such engagement and even aggression within such a peaceful atmosphere? Isn't this what the practice of Buddhism is all about?" I am not sure what to make of this last comment, for his description also captures the essence of good sporting competitions. But it does convey the overall atmosphere of debates, which are veritable intellectual sports.

The vigorous cultivation of a sharp mind also has other risks, such as encouraging pride and an inability to use the teaching for anything but self-aggrandizement. Mindful of these dangers, teachers often admonish their students to check and correct their motivations.[53] Nevertheless, they are generally confident that the final result of this practice, the knowledge and insight developed by many students, will offset whatever real dangers and temptations accompany it. The teachers see no reason why something that is intellectually useful cannot be fun. One of their great accomplishments is to give life to a demanding intellectual inquiry into highly technical topics. Debate is for them "a mental sport [that] has the advantage of being most useful and delightful."[54] The enthusiastic responses of those, myself included, who have been privileged to have sufficient exposure to this discipline to understand it seem to support their confidence and testify to their pedagogical successes.

From this brief and necessarily simplified discussion, we can draw several conclusions. First, the character of debate is clearly dialogical. The course of this exchange between two parties is not determined in advance, for it depends on the choices of the participants. Second, debate is a game that is oriented toward winning an argument. The goal of the questioner is to draw the defender into contradicting either himself or common sense. Similarly, the goal of the defender is to ward off unwanted consequences, thereby escaping the questioner's line of argument. Third, like other games, debate is intensely strategic. Each party must try to take his adversary along, either by the power of the arguments used or by lawful tricks. Good debaters keep in mind their target, remembering the starting point and the intermediary arguments. Fourth, debate is complex and instructive. Because it involves making and remembering many choices and distinctions, it requires intense concentration. It is also intellectually challenging, demanding clarity of mind and strong analytical skills. Participants and audience often learn something new from the debate. One of the marks of a good defender is his ability to provide insights into his topic without compromising the strength of his positions. Fifth, debate is performative and fun, because the discussion is enlivened by physical gestures, the intensity and rhetorical skills of the participants, and the influence of the audience. A good debate is akin to a theatrical event. It is full of surprises, with either party apt to outdo the other and escape from seemingly hopeless situations by making new and more subtle distinctions. It is indeed a thrilling intellectual sport, highly appreciated by students, established scholars, and even laypeople. And finally, a Tibetan debate is (at least ideally) impressive for its orderliness and clarity. Questioner and defender have clear roles, and the alternation of questions and answers is easy to follow. This clarity is greatly enhanced by the very strict rules that a debate must follow. For, like any other game, debate follows rules that determine its nature. These rules limit rather narrowly the participants' moves and provide standards for appraising arguments. They also impose order, enabling debate to avoid the confusion that often mars ordinary arguments. But this clarity has its limits, for the practice of debate cannot be fully captured by any formula.

LEARNING DEBATE AND THE COLLECTED TOPICS

Debate is obviously a complex art that involves a variety of skills. Students must be able to string together consequences, perceive contradictions, and so on. They must be able to devise strategies to do in their opponents or to block such efforts against them. They must also be able to keep in mind not only the starting point of the debate but also the chain of reasoning that links the statement they are considering at any point in the debate and the root statement—no small achievement, since the two may be separated by many consequences. This training is acquired during their first years, while studying the Collected Topics. It is only after such training that students are able to examine the great texts of the tradition.

The Collected Topics are monastery-specific debate manuals for beginners. As noted earlier, they are often arranged in five volumes: the Collected Topics *(bsdus grwa)* proper, in three parts; the Types of Mind *(blo rigs)*; and the Types of Evidence *(rtags rigs)*. The Collected Topics proper contains eighteen chapters that detail the basic concepts used by the tradition. The first chapter introduces the practice of debate in relation to an explanation of the colors. Students learn paradigmatic debates in this simple domain, to which other types of material phenomena are gradually added. However, these texts give little sense of real debates. As Perdue explains, "The textual form is a terse notation of the essential points in a possible debate, which is meant not to represent a debate as it would be spoken, but to supply the student with information, to suggest debate, to demonstrate patterns of debate, to clarify points of doctrine, to dispel possible qualms, and so forth."[55] This discrepancy between actual debates and textual material reflects the different conceptions of texts and debates. While texts are seen to be concerned with laying out the material and determining the correct interpretation, debates are conversational encounters. Hence, they are free-flowing and open-ended, providing an important outlet for creativity. To explain the disparity in presentation, we should not look to an intrinsic difference between textuality and orality; we can imagine debate manuals that propose debates and leave issues open.[56] However, that is not how Tibetan manuals proceed. Unlike actual debates, they are fixed and rigid: they almost never leave an issue open, and they decide almost all the questions they raise.

Perhaps not surprisingly, some teachers prefer to teach debate orally, in forms close to what really happens in the courtyard. That was the approach of Gen Lob-zang Gya-tso at the Buddhist School of Dialectic. After the usual invocation to Manjushri, Gen-la would proceed with a debate, reciting each of the statements composing that debate three times. The students would repeat them after him. At the end of the debate, Gen-la would restate the whole thing, followed by the students. He would also teach a few definitions in the same way and add a few explanations. The emphasis was on memorizing the debate paradigms, which could be used in actual debates. After three weeks, we had our first real debate. A couple of other students and I had debated before, so we were not too disoriented; the rest had a harder time. But their having learned a number of paradigms by heart helped a great deal, and the students soon became more proficient. The memorization involved in this exercise was not easy, and its strain was compounded by Gen-la's thick accent, as he came from Eastern Tibet. Most of the Tibetan students were hard-pressed to understand him—imagine my difficulty! Nevertheless, we coped and succeeded in learning debates fairly quickly.

In this training, an often-repeated basic exercise is to examine the distribution (Tibetans speak of the "difference," *khyad par*) of terms. Debate proceeds on what we could describe as a logic of class. Consequences operate by the inclusion of one class by another: the reason is included in the predicate. Hence, establishing the distribution of two terms (or, rather, the two classes determined by two terms) is a useful starting point for someone formulating a consequence. For any two terms, there are four possibilities:

1. Exclusion *('gal ba)*, as dog and primate, or the moon and the sun
2. Equivalence *(don gcig)*, as the morning star and the evening star, or impermanence and thing[57]
3. Inclusion *(mu gsum;* lit., "three extremities"), as the earth and a planet
4. Intersection *(mu bzhi;* lit, "four extremities"), as human and heterosexual being

Two phenomena, or more properly two classes of phenomenon, are said to be exclusive if, and only if, they do not share any common locus; that is, when there is nothing that is both. They are said to be equivalent if, and only if, all their instances are identical. One can be said to include the other when all the instances of the latter are included in the former but only some instances of the former are included in the latter. Finally, two phenomena are said to intersect when they share some instances but each has at least one instance that is not included in the other. Learning how to use these four modes of distribution is one of the first exercises that students practice intensely, and most of the debates at the beginner's level start with an exercise in distribution.

After spending a few weeks to master the basic logical tools of the debate system, students move on to the second chapter of the Collected Topics: the presentation of "established basis" *(gzhi grub gyi rnam bzhag).*

This is an important chapter, for it lays down the main lines of the universe of discourse presupposed in later studies. Existence is defined and its equivalents (such as established basis, phenomenon, etc.) are determined.[58] This general category is further subdivided into impermanent and permanent phenomena, the basic dichotomy around which many Buddhist doctrines are organized. In such a view the real, which is understood as changing and causally efficient, is opposed to the constructed, which is understood as unchanging, causally ineffective, and hence less real. The category of real things is further divided into matter *(gzugs, rūpa)*, cognition *(shes pa, jñāna)*, and associated noncompositional factors *(ldan min 'du byed, viprayuktasaṃskāra)*, which constitute all the impermanent phenomena that are neither mental nor material, such as time. These categories are then further subdivided.

This emphasis on division and typologies is not surprising, given the fundamental role played by lists in the development of Buddhist philosophy.[59] The universe of discourse is organized according to the traditional Abhidharma categories, as understood by Dharmakīrti and appropriated through Tibetan interpretations of his understanding. This organization creates a framework of inquiry for all future studies, as any new topic can first be placed in a preexisting category. For example, when students of Vinaya (one of the last subjects in the whole curriculum) discuss the nature of vows *(sdom pa)*, they argue using the terms learned in this chapter of the Collected Topics. Are vows material, as argued by some Sarvāstivādins, or are they mental, as argued by Asaṅga?[60]

The study of this second chapter of the Collected Topics is also an occasion to get acquainted with deeper and more meaningful topics, as demonstrated by the debate on momentariness sketched above. But that is a secondary purpose; students' understanding will be developed in conjunction with the study of the great Indian texts. From this chapter, they learn primarily how to debate and become comfortable with the manipulation of reasoning within the rules governing the system of debate. My personal recollections can show how the training functions and can illustrate the nature of debate as a dialectical practice as well as a great intellectual sport.

DEBATE AS AN INTELLECTUAL SPORT: A PERSONAL ACCOUNT

I have already mentioned some of the difficulties that I experienced in my apprenticeship of debate begun at Nam-gyel. There, I felt extremely awkward and self-conscious as I made the required gestures. My difficulty was compounded by my left-handedness. The hand gestures of debate described above are intended for right-handed people: the work is done by the right hand, which rotates when the arm is above the head, moves toward the left, and strikes the left palm. For a thoroughly left-handed person such as myself, this was awkward. I remember missing the left hand a number of times, even after I had become a good debater. I asked Lati Rin-po-che if I could strike with my left hand but he dismissed my request as a silly joke, one more bizarre and incomprehensible request that these strange Westerners can make of unsuspecting Tibetan teachers. His reaction was hardly surprising, given that every Tibetan child learns to write with the right hand. I was thus obliged to accommodate myself to these gestures. I remember practicing them intensively in my room until they became automatic.

After a few months, I found that I was almost enjoying the whole exercise. I understood the general principles and strategies of debates. And yet, I was not completely comfortable with the debate format. For example, I was unable to surmount the obstacles that participants would throw in my way. I remember a particular occasion when I was the questioner and my respondent had made a response that he knew to be wrong. The topic was the presentation of distinguishers *(ldog pa ngos 'dzin gyi rnam bzhag)*, a subject that is extremely technical, not to say arcane, but thought important for learning debate.[61] By then my debating skills had improved and people were starting to consider me a reasonable debater (given that we were all beginners). Tibetan visitors would notice me immediately, since they had never seen a Westerner debating. That day, there was a large crowd and I seemed to be in a good position to win the debate. I had my opponent where I wanted, at the point where he had to give in — or so I thought. But in fact he had the alternative of giving the answer that he and everybody else knew to be wrong. He did so and the other debaters, who had by then gathered around us, smiled knowingly, expecting a quick end. My problem was that I had forgotten one point, which is that knowing a position to be wrong does one no good in a debate unless one is able to prove it. When he gave the wrong answer, I was stunned. "Don't you know that this is wrong?" I asked. He smiled and replied, "Prove it!" Unfortunately I was unable to do so. I avoided the humiliation of standing speechless and managed to put forth a few questions that ended in confusion. But it was clear to everyone that I had missed the point. A few weeks later, this episode was brought back to me when I visited Ling Rin-po-che, the senior tutor of the Dalai Lama. He asked me how I was doing and praised me for my debating abilities. His praise was not what it seemed, however, for he quickly added:

"You do not yet know the presentation of distinguishers, do you?" I was brought back to my rightful place, that of a raw beginner who still has everything to learn. In particular, I had yet to master the path of reasoning (*rigs lam*).

That mastery took place later, after I had joined the Buddhist School that opened in June 1973. Following the Dalai Lama's advice (hard to disobey such an adviser!), I joined the first batch of students who had come from the schools administrated by the Tibetan government in exile. By that point I could understand the debating strategies and how to apply them, but my power of debate was still not fully developed. Or, to use the technical term, I had not really "gotten the path of reasoning" (*rigs lam chags*). Fortunately, the studies at the Buddhist School obliged me to study this subject again; the third chapter of the Collected Topics is often thought to mark a decisive step in learning the debate system.

It was while debating the same topic for the second time that I "got the path of reasoning." I remember the afternoon when this became clear to me. I got up and started on the topic of the day, the notion of a distinguisher. At first, my debate progressed slowly and at one point I hit the same roadblock that had thwarted me earlier in the debate with the Namgyel monk. Here again, the respondent was arguing that a distinguisher instantiates itself, though he knew that he was not supposed to say this. Only now I did not get stuck. I suddenly realized how I could prove my opponent wrong and quickly proceeded to crush his position. My thinking was unusually clear and moved swiftly over the topic, well ahead of my opponent's. I felt energized, as if my mind were so sharp that it could defeat any position. I had gotten the path of reasoning. Henceforth, I found debate, which had been quite hard, much more pleasant and sometimes even positively exhilarating.

A few days later we moved to the next topic, the discussion of universals and particulars (*spyi bye brag*), the fourth chapter of the Collected Topics. Unfortunately, I was absent the day Gen Lob-zang Gya-tso started on this new topic. The next day, he repeated the main debate of the chapter that he had taught the previous day. Since I was doing well and had missed the previous class, he thought that I would prove a good guinea pig to demonstrate a possible fault often committed by those studying this topic. He asked me, "What is the distribution between being a particular of a thing and being a material phenomenon?" The correct answer in the Ge-luk system is an intersection, since not all material phenomena are particulars of a thing and not all particulars of a thing are material. But the first answer that comes to mind is an inclusion, since all material phenomena are instances of being a thing. Nevertheless, they are not its particular.[62] Gen-la threw out this question in his usual dismissive style. "Sangye Samdrup [my Tibetan name], he won't know! No way!" I knew that there was a trick here. So instead of jumping at the most obvious answer, I applied the criteria that a phenomenon must satisfy in order to be a particular of another and discovered the answer. "An intersection," I mumbled. Gen-la was taken aback. "Not bad," he grudgingly admitted. This correct answer made me quite proud, though it was less a mark of my intelligence than a sign of the good training I was receiving, the sign that I had gotten the path of reasoning and knew how to use the debate system as a tool of reasoning. I was ready for more important topics.

Getting the path of reasoning was an achievement. Henceforth, it would be my ticket into the debating courtyard. I still remember my first visit in the summer of 1977 to one of the three monastic seats, Se-ra, during one of the Dalai Lama's teachings. By then I was already well-trained, but I had debated only at the Buddhist School of Dialectic, where the limited number of students and the absence of seasoned students limited the level of debate. The three seats were the scholarly centers of the Tibetan world with hundreds of seasoned debaters. To confront them was no small matter. The first evening I was in Se-ra, I went gingerly to the debate, planning to observe and stay out of the way. The disciplinarian showed me the class that corresponded to my level. At first, I was able to remain silent. Later on I became engaged in a discussion with a monk from Se-ra Jay on the ways in which a Madhyamaka reasoning can be established. What had begun as a private discussion quickly mushroomed into a debate, and before I knew it, tens and soon hundreds of monks were listening to our exchange. They had never seen a Westerner debating and were quite curious. I was terrified, but stopping the debate was unthinkable. I kept going and managed to hold my own against my adversary. Although my debate was not profound, it was solid. I managed to score a few points; but most important, I offered the kind of clear debate that comes from getting the path of reasoning. This instantaneously established my reputation in the three monastic seats. I was a foreigner who could put up a mean debate!

When a person who has gotten the path of reasoning debates, the debate flows, each consequence deriving from the previous one. There is no gap in the arguments and hence the informed audience has no problem understanding them. This does not mean that the debates of such a person are profound or interesting. Logical abilities are not enough to make someone a good scholar: such a person requires insight, comprehension, and creativity. Tibetan teachers often contrast dialectical abilities *(rigs lam)* and comprehension *(go ba)*, which is often, but not exclusively, textually based. It is only when dialectical and interpretive abilities are combined that students can develop into the kind of scholar the tradition particularly values.

A scholar who has good comprehension provides rich explanations, which highlight the important points, raise interesting questions, and provide insights into the subject matter. Scholars who have such interpretive skills do not always have strong dialectical abilities. They are at times not very tight in their answers, preferring rich synthesis to analytical rigor. They then become easy targets for other debaters, who may be keener to score a hit than play with interesting ideas. Nevertheless, the abilities of such scholars give them a strong advantage; provided they can discipline themselves they can become great scholars, overtaking those too preoccupied with strictly dialectical abilities.

Lati Rin-po-che was fond of citing the example of Gen Pe-ma Gyel-tsen, whom we encountered in chapter 7 while examining oral commentary. Before he became a Geshe, he was considered a good scholar but a mediocre defender, unable to resist the rigor of debate. Hence, he was not expected to do well during his final Geshe examinations. However, he confounded all predictions by being on top of every debate and undefeatable in his positions. The reason for his success is that he had learned through accepting and even embracing defeat during the preceding years. Instead of trying to win by all means, he had gone to debate and answered as candidly as possible, making himself as vulnerable as possible. One result was that he had been defeated quite often. But another was that he had learned all the tricks and ways in which a position can be undermined. He had also considerably enriched his own comprehension by being open to a great variety of opinions. He was thus completely ready and his brilliant performance got him the first prize for that year.

The training in how to combine dialectical and interpretive abilities does not occur during the study of the Collected Topics, which is merely preparatory. Once students are well-trained in the debate system, they are ready to start using debate as a means of intellectual inquiry to examine the great texts of their tradition. That inquiry is the topic of the next chapter.

11　Debate in the Curriculum

The Collected Topics explain the basic logical procedure and the main philosophical notions as preparation to the use of debate in the study of the five great texts of the Ge-luk curriculum. In this chapter, I show how debate provides the central scholastic methodology in the Ge-luk tradition, examining its relation to pedagogy, logic/epistemology and Madhyamaka, and the plan of a student's day and academic career. In discussing the final point in this training, the Geshe examination, I again draw on my own experience.

TEACHING DEBATE

Ge-luk students first encounter the great Indian texts that support Tibetan monastic intellectual life in their study of the *Ornament,* which initiates them into the art of reading commentaries. At the same time, students also start to use the debate system they have learned previously while studying the Collected Topics. The transition from learning debating skills to using debate as a mode of inquiry into more meaningful topics, which often requires an understanding that comes only after a great deal of reading, is not always easy. Some students need a long time to make the necessary qualitative jump. Some never succeed and remain forever at the level of the Collected Topics.

The process of studying starts with the heuristic memorization of the root text; it continues with the reading of commentaries in the light of oral teachings during which the master explains the meaning of a passage in the root text and the different commentaries relevant to the passage. But teaching concerns not just commentary but also how to debate the deeper questions raised by the text. After explaining the text, the teacher starts to debate, focusing on a concept or a word in the text and raising relevant questions.

For an example, take the cognitive nature of compassion, a topic that comes up during study of the *Ornament*. The teacher may start by asking, "What is the definition of compassion?" Students usually answer by giving the definition contained in the manuals: "Compassion is [defined as] the mental factor that wishes in reference to all sentient beings to protect [them] from all suffering."[1] The teacher continues by asking whether compassion is part of the path or not. If students answer that it is, as they are likely to do, he will then ask whether compassion is a knowing mental state. Students are again likely to answer affirmatively, because "being an enhanced knowing mental state" *(mkhyen pa)* is the definition of the path. Hence compassion must be an enhanced knowing mental state if it is part of the path. The question is then likely to be "What does compassion know?" Here, the response is likely to be less straightforward, for the inquiry has reached an uncertain area of the tradition.

Some students may try to be tricky, arguing that compassion does not know anything despite being an enhanced knowing mental state. The teacher is then likely to state ironically, "You mean that it is an enhanced form of knowing that does not know anything, right?" Or he may ask, "How can compassion be a form of knowing if it does not have any object?" When the students get stuck, the teacher goes back to the basic question and asks for other answers. Some students may try to argue that compassion knows sentient beings' freedom from suffering. But the teacher will then ask: "Is this freedom from suffering already existing or is it future?" The first answer is not defensible, since compassion is the commiseration with beings who are presently suffering. If students answer that this freedom exists only in the future, the teacher will then ask whether compassion takes as its object the future happiness of sentient beings. What about their present suffering? Such a question reveals that compassion is focused not on the future but on the present, which is taken as profoundly lacking. Thus, future freedom from suffering cannot be the object of compassion.

Another possible answer is that compassion takes as its object sentient beings' present suffering. This answer is by far the most plausible but is likely to elicit the following question: "What is the difference between understanding the suffering of sentient beings, which is the cause of compassion, and feeling compassion itself?" In order to develop compassion, one needs to realize the suffering of sentient beings, but that realization does not necessarily make one compassionate. To generate compassion one must be concerned for their suffering and feel it as intolerable. Thus, to merely understand the suffering of others is not enough: if compassion is cognitive, it must know more.

We could argue that compassion is knowledge of our connection with others. But this answer is not easily defended, for compassion also includes consideration of others' suffering. The response that compassion takes as its object both our relation with others and their suffering, though in some ways more accurate, runs into other problems. It implies that a single mental state can take two objects; but within the understanding of mind presupposed here, that is impossible if these objects are differently valued. That is, a single mental state cannot at the same time hold one object negatively (the suffering of others) while another object positively (one's relation with others). Therefore, compassion cannot simultaneously have as its object the suffering of others and one's connection to others.

This example shows how debate works within an overall conceptual system whose foundations were laid during the study of the Collected Topics. The understanding of mind that is presupposed in this debate comes from the preliminary studies, particularly of the Types of Mind; there mind is explained as a succession of phenomenologically available but fleeting mental states, each directed toward particular objects. Hence, since compassion is mental, it must be a discrete mental state oriented toward a particular object. Whatever topic is debated, students assume that states of mind are momentary and intentional. Reliance on such foundations enables knowledge to build gradually and cumulatively, as is necessary to the development of critical skills. Debate presupposes a context without which the critique cannot proceed.

At this point, the teacher may stop and urge his students to explore the question further in their debates. Teachers debate in class to demonstrate how to use the practice to inquire into the relevant topics. The debates they propose are exemplary and students are encouraged to find their own. In debating, teachers often raise questions without answering them. By not proposing their own solutions, they push their students to debate on their own. A good teacher encourages students' efforts and piques their intellectual curiosity so that they become engaged by the search rather than being satisfied merely to repeat handed-down truths.

As one can see from this example, debate plays a central role in the Tibetan scholastic pedagogy. A significant proportion of the class is spent on debate, with the specific amount determined by individual teachers. Some, such as Gen Pe-ma Gyel-tsen, spend more time commenting on text; others emphasize debate. Gen Nyi-ma was in a class of his own, as far as debate is concerned: his entire class was spent debating. Gen-la would start the debate and students would answer. The class would stop as soon as they could no longer sustain the debate. "We will start again when you are able to say something intelligent," he would say. Gen-la also encouraged students to disagree with him and to start to debate him. As we will see, not all teachers followed that practice; many argued that it is inappropriate for students to debate their teachers.

ANALYSIS AND CRITICAL THINKING

One of the striking features of debate is its analytical emphasis. Concepts are dismantled into elementary parts, whose implications are examined. The analytic procedure is particularly important for the questioner, who must be able to take apart the concepts used by the defender to involve him in contradictions that will overturn his answers. To succeed, the questioner must avoid being taken in by the concepts of the defender, ignoring their apparent self-evidence and focusing on their questionability. Such an approach does not come easily, and debate aims at cultivating it until it becomes second nature. In this way, students learn not to accept ideas on the basis of their superficial plausibility and appeal but instead to check their implications. Thus, debate is a training in critical skills.

The debates that arise from this analytical and critical approach can vary in their interest for both participants and observers. Sometimes participants engage in a meaningful inquiry, while at other times the debate remains superficial. Or it may focus on the ambiguities of the Tibetan language or some elementary questions of logic examined in the Collected Topics. Such an approach is perfectly admissible. As Lati Rin-po-che used to say, one cannot always be profound. But it would be ridiculous to think that dialectical tricks are the main staple of monastic debates. Debates are used and valued because they train students and help them understand the content of tradition. To be sure, "interesting" is a highly contextual notion—not all topics found intriguing by a debater would interest a modern academic scholar. But it is also true that a number of discussions, such as the one we examined, can interest those outside the tradition.

An intellectual skill that receives relatively little emphasis in debate is the ability to synthesize concepts and offer broad and interesting presentations of a topic. However, that skill does play a role, for a defender needs to be able to synthesize to make his point. Good respondents are able to combine strong answers with a profound understanding of a topic. Their answers provide broad-ranging and rich pictures, while maintaining overall analytical rigor. It is nevertheless true that debate tends to favor analytical rigor over richness in understanding. Moreover, the answers required in a debate are brief and the time allotted always short. Often, a defender will be limited to one of the three answers, and thereby locked into a difficult choice. Thus, a person who has a superficial understanding of the topic but is good at warding off unwanted consequences can do quite well, whereas a person with good insight but poor logical skills will quickly be destroyed.

I have often been amazed how individual the styles of debate are. Every scholar has his distinctive approach and intellectual signature. Some focus almost exclusively on winning arguments and exposing contradictions. Such people can make good debaters, though they tend to favor allowable tricks at the expense of more meaningful inquiry; their answers are consistent but uninteresting. Others, on the contrary, are so preoccupied with finding meaningful patterns that they forget that consistency is key in debating; hence, their positions quickly dissolve into incoherence. But because they take risks, they can learn more than the first group and strengthen their positions.

As may have become clear by now, there is little of the fuzzy about the logic used in Tibetan debates, which scrupulously follow the laws of logic. Contradiction is central to the whole system of debate. The law of the excluded middle is seen to support the entire inquiry, though traditions disagree about its status. Whereas non-Ge-luk thinkers limit its application to the conventional realm, Ge-luk scholars are ready to extend it to the domain of ultimate reality as well. Moreover, this approach is far from holistic. Debate proceeds by asking more and more narrowly analytical questions, and one cannot escape by claiming some special insight or pretending that this mode of inquiry is antithetical to spiritual development. Monks who made such claims would be mercilessly ridiculed and dismissed as hopeless flakes, lacking the capacity for rigorous thinking that the tradition values. There is also little of the immediacy of mystical intuition often associated with so-called Eastern religions, for debate emphasizes the critical approach that is the basis of any sustained intellectual inquiry.

THE STUDY OF LOGIC AND EPISTEMOLOGY

We are starting to understand the kind of intellectual skills that debate involves and the role they play in Tibetan scholasticism. We need now to see how these skills connect to the curriculum. In examining commentary, we began to review the subjects of the monastic curriculum, particularly the path. Also central are logic and epistemology, which are studied through Dharmakīrti's works, particularly his *Commentary on Valid Cognition*.[2] Since the time of Sa-paṇ, this work has been considered one of the most important texts in the Tibetan scholastic tradition. It not only covers important areas such as logic, philosophy of language, and epistemology; it also provides the philosophical methodology for scholastic studies generally, as well as a large part of the philosophical vocabulary and the tools (arguments and consequences) used in debate.

In Tibet, prior to 1959, Dharmakīrti's *Commentary* was studied in special sessions held outside the three monastic seats. Every year, students would interrupt their regular studies and examine this text for a one- or two-month stretch. These special sessions were held at Jang near Lhasa during the winter *('jang dgun chos)*, or at Sang-pu during the summer *(gsang phu dbyar chos)*.[3] The history of this custom is yet to be documented, but it seems to be related to the connection between the three monastic seats and the Sang-pu tradition. As a survival of this link and an acknowledgment of the monastery's role, the monastic seats held special sessions on Dharmakīrti's tradition. The Shar-tse monastery of Ga-den held its special session at Sang-pu itself, whereas Dre-pung and Se-ra held their sessions at Jang under the direction of the monastery of Ra-tö *(rwa stod)*.[4] The session at Sang-pu was gradually overshadowed by Jang, as a proverb suggests: "At Jang, one becomes learned; at Sang-pu, one begs for food."[5]

The importance of this session at Jang increased during the twentieth century. In earlier times, it was attended mostly by the monks of Dre-pung, particularly those of the Lo-se-ling monastery with which Ra-tö is affiliated. Later, as participation from Se-ra increased, the session at Jang became the occasion for an intense competition between the two largest monasteries, Dre-pung Lo-se-ling and Se-ra Jay. Participation from Ga-den monks became more substantial later (around the 1930s or 1940s).[6]

Monks of the three seats often speak very nostalgically about the Jang session. As is often the case, it is hard to separate the mythological from the real in their recollections, but the session at Jang does seem to have been remarkable. There monks often debated through an entire day with only short interruptions. The conditions were quite difficult (see figure 11). Each monastery or regional house provided limited accommodation for its monks, who had to bring their own food. My teachers often described how they lived for more than a month on supplies, mostly roasted barley wheat, that they had carried on their backs from Lhasa.[7] Moreover, conditions at Jang were extremely harsh in the winter. A reincarnated lama, Ratö Khyongla, recalls:

> Many of the nights were windy and cold, and our feet on the bare
> stones froze. It was now December and those evenings were something
> of an ordeal. We wore no underpants, and so the lower parts of the
> body became numb. And when my teacher and I would at last be back
> in our room, we would brew ourselves some hot buttered tea and light
> a fire in our fireplace to thaw out.[8]

Elders remember that their hands would often crack and bleed from the cold during the evening debates.

Despite or, perhaps, because of these hardships, the atmosphere seemed to have been remarkably intense and monks greatly benefited from the sessions. Geshe Rab-ten recounts, "During these winter sessions, I became so involved in the subject of debate that I did not notice that other monks took breaks, throughout the day, to go to the assembly hall for prayers and tea. So I ended up spending the whole day on the debating ground."[9] After a full day of debate and prayers, monks would meet for the major event of the day: the debate between the monasteries. Two defenders would be examined intensely for at least three hours by the best scholars of the rival monastery, who would submit them to a dialectical barrage in front of several thousand attentive listeners. Sometimes, veritable traps were laid out by their rivals. During this contest, reputations of scholars would be established or lost. The two monks being examined would sit on a lofty throne (more than six feet high) and respond to the debates from the monks of the rival monastery. Monks from all the six monasteries would sit around the throne, leaving a strip a few feet wide in front for the debaters to stand. The most exciting events were the confrontations between Lo-se-ling and Jay.

Gen Nyi-ma recalled how he and several other scholars from Lo-se-ling plotted against Gen Thab-key *(thabs mkhas)*, one of Se-ra Jay's most famous scholars, who later became its abbot. They set him up by sending one of their stupidest students to begin the debate. The first question was "What are the definitions of impermanence and permanence?"—a question studied early in the first year of training. Gen Thab-key was taken aback. "Are you serious?" he asked. He expected the debate to start with an elaborate textual examination, as was the custom, and then proceed toward the most difficult topics, but instead he was asked what seemed a raw beginner's question. Monks from Lo-se-ling assured him that they were dead serious and started to taunt him: "Let's see what you know!" Instead of keeping his composure, an absolute must in a debate of such intensity held in front of a large assembly of experts, he felt insulted and became impatient. That was exactly what Gen Nyi-ma and his acolytes had hoped for. Just when Gen Thab-key was threatening to leave unless he was given an adequate debate, Gen Nyi-ma and his friends got up and started to unveil their line of attack, an attempt to blur the line separating permanence from impermanence. Gen Thab-key, who by that point was unsettled, was unable to sustain the dialectical onslaught. Each of the criteria he proposed to demarcate the two classes of phenomena was taken apart. The Lo-se-ling monks were delighted, for their success confirmed their known ability for close reasoning and fine analytical distinctions. Needless to say, the monks from Se-ra Jay had another opinion about the whole exercise, for they felt that one of their best minds had been shortchanged by a cheap trick (a not altogether unreasonable view).

In exile, Dharmakīrti's tradition is also studied during special sessions. Up until the middle of the 1980s, these sessions were held independently by each monastery. Most but not all monasteries chose the winter as a reminder of the ways in which studies were conducted in Tibet. At the Buddhist School of Dialectics the sessions were held in the summer, because the school was in recess during the winter. But since the mid-eighties, the practice of a special common session devoted to the study of Dharmakīrti's tradition has been revived. The winter session of Jang is now held every winter at one of the three seats in South India. There, the monks of the three monasteries and of the new institutions such as the Buddhist School debate. In this regard as in others examined here, the attempt to re-create traditional Tibetan monastic education in exile appears to be quite successful. The common session is having an impact even on the non-Ge-luk institutions, which feel that they have to participate in an event that is gaining new fame in the exile community.

An elaborate discussion of Dharmakīrti's thought would take us far from our study. Two aspects of his system are relevant here: logic and epistemology.[10] We have already examined the nature of "Indian logic," which is more dialectical than logical in the strict sense of the word. But Dharmakīrti's main concern is not logic, even in this extended sense. For him, logic is only one element in a broader inquiry into the nature of knowledge. In the Indian context, this question is formulated, What is the nature of *pramāṇa (tshad ma)* and what are its types? Whereas his Hindu opponents tend to present a realist theory,[11] which liberally allows a diversity of *pramāṇa*, Dharmakīrti offers a more restrictive view in line with his nominalism. Dharmakīrti limits the number of valid cognitions to two: perception *(pratyakṣa, mngon sum)*, which is the foundation of our knowledge, and inference *(anumāna, rjes dpag)*, which is based on but not reducible to perception. It is in the context of inference that logic is discussed, for inference rests on reasoning and the epistemologist must be able to separate the correct from the incorrect.

The scope of the discussion of *pramāṇa* is not limited to the analysis of knowledge, however; it constitutes a distinctive philosophical method used in investigating other fields of study. At the heart of this method is the assumption that all pronouncements about the world must rest on the attested forms of knowledge, perception and inference. A claim can be validated by experience. If it is not, then it must be supported by inference, which must rest on some argument. When Buddhist epistemologists claim that all things are impermanent, they cannot simply invoke the Buddha's religious authority. Since such a claim is not given in experience, it must be supported by reasoning. The discussion then proceeds by assessing the correctness of the argument, following the rules of Indian logic. Such a method puts a heavy emphasis on rationality—the assessment of evidence in accordance with the laws of logic.

The study of logic and epistemology can also be a stepping-stone to the understanding of Madhyamaka philosophy. In the Ge-luk tradition, Dharmakīrti's texts are used to lay out an ideal terrain for the practice of debates that lead students to the Madhyamaka insights into the limits of theoretical rationality, especially in its foundationalist mode. The Madhyamaka view, particularly as expounded by Candrakīrti, is considered radical and difficult to grasp. Because the practice of debate in Dharmakīrti's system offers the most systematic philosophical presentation of foundationalism in Buddhist philosophy, it is ideal for leading students from unquestioning assent to essentialization to skeptical questioning. Once the student understands Dharmakīrti's system, which is based on the difference between a reality definable in terms of essence and a projected essenceless conceptual realm, he is shown how this distinction leads to unsolvable difficulties. Numerous debates analyzing Dharmakīrti's system on its own terms gradually convince students that what is wrong with Dharmakīrti's system comes not from the intellectual limitations of its author but from his systematic approach and the essentialist assumptions that it entails. Precisely because of its philosophical rigor, Dharmakīrti's system exemplifies the type of problems encountered by any highly systematic and foundationalist thought.

Because of its philosophical importance and the occasion that it provides for debate, the thinking of Dharmakīrti has a strong place within the Ge-luk tradition, which prides itself on its command of the *Commentary* and its skillful use of this study in education. This area of study is also the favorite topic of many scholars; Gen Nyi-ma—like his teacher, Gen Tom-pön—was considered a master in it. I myself greatly enjoyed this kind of close philosophical analysis, in which topics can be tackled using reasoning and ordinary experience without presupposing knowledge of some extraordinary realm—as does study of the path, which is accessible only through textual studies.

MADHYAMAKA PHILOSOPHY

After several years of studying the *Ornament* literature and Dharmakīrti's *Commentary,* students move on to the study of Madhyamaka philosophy, whose understanding is considered by all four Tibetan traditions to be the central goal of monastic education. As should be clear by now, Tibetan tradition is relatively homogenous.[12] Whereas Indian Buddhists differ on important philosophical questions, all Tibetan schools tend to take Madhyamaka as formulated by its founder Nāgārjuna as the apex of Buddhist philosophy. Yet they favor different interpretations of Nāgārjuna.

Ge-luk scholars are adamant in their choice of Candrakīrti (sixth century) as the best interpreter of Nāgārjuna. They hold his views, which they describe as Prāsaṅgika,[13] to be the most authoritative as well as radical interpretation of Nāgārjuna's *Treatise.* Accordingly, Ge-luk Madhyamaka focuses on Candrakīrti's *Introduction,* which guides the study of Nāgārjuna's *Treatise.* These texts are read in the light of Dzong-ka-ba's commentaries, particularly his *Clarification of the Thought,* and the monastery's manuals (though the degree to which those are used in this field varies greatly, according to the teacher's inclinations or his students' abilities). Together these texts provide an interpretation of Madhyamaka that the Ge-luk tradition considers its crowning achievement.

Though non-Ge-luk schools put less emphasis on Candrakīrti, the difference is mostly of degree and does not constitute a different philosophical orientation. The Nying-ma tradition, for instance, stresses the value of Śāntarakṣita's *Ornament of the Middle Way,* a text classified as Svātantrika, which is studied in the light of Mi-pam's commentary. Śāntarakṣita's approach uses Yogācāra themes and is more germane to the Great Perfection, which the tradition holds to be the highest view. In general, non-Ge-luk thinkers such as Go-ram-ba and Mi-pam argue that the Svātantrika and Prāsaṅgika interpretations differ not in the view of emptiness but in the dialectical tools required for understanding emptiness. But even then, they grant some preeminence to the Prāsaṅgika explanation, which is seen as the most direct expression of Nāgārjuna's view.[14]

The use of debate as a method of inquiry is particularly appropriate to the Madhyamaka approach, as a very brief review of some of the main points of this philosophy will show. I must make clear, however, that in the following discussion of emptiness I greatly simplify, choosing a particular interpretation to explain Ge-luk practices.[15] In fact, I use the views of the Sa-gya thinker Śākya Chok-den, one of Dzong-ka-ba's most vocal critics—a choice that inevitably raises some questions. Nevertheless, I believe that the views of the Sa-gya and Ge-luk are ultimately compatible; thus, in using the former's view to explain the latter's practice I am taking a convenient expository shortcut that does not significantly affect the main issues. Indeed, my approach follows the famous statement made by the Fifth Dalai Lama's teacher, Pan-chen Lob-zang Chö-gi gyel tsen (*pan chen blo bzang chos kyi rgyal mtshan*, 1467?–1662): "From the point of view of individually ascribed names, there are numerous traditions. Nevertheless, when scrutinized by a yogi learned in scripture and logic and experienced [in meditation], their definitive meanings are all seen to come to the same intended point."[16] My own inclination and experiences have led me to accept Pan-chen Lob-zang Chö-gyen's statement, and in doing so I follow the opinion of several contemporary scholars, both inside and outside of the Ge-luk tradition. To be sure, many disagree; to engage with their opinion here would require an extended discussion that would take us far from the subject at hand. Readers may take this inclusive approach as reflecting my own view and experience, and I believe that the discussion in the next chapter of Dzong-ka-ba's view and Gen Nyi-ma's explanations will go some way toward justifying my position.

One of the standard ways to present Madhyamaka is through the framework of the two truths. As Nāgārjuna explains, "The Buddha's Teaching of the Dharma is based on the two truths: a truth of worldly convention and an ultimate truth."[17] This schema is basic to the structure of the views and practices of Tibetan scholastic traditions. It supports a gradualist model, according to which the resources of the conventional realm are used to penetrate the ultimate realm, emptiness. However, the twofold distinction is deceptive: the juxtaposition of the two truths suggests that they are two types of comparable objects that a smooth progression from one to the other is possible, masking their discontinuity. But because the two truths are not two types of objects to be put on the same level, it is necessary to take different approaches to understand them.[18]

Conventional truth is the domain of common practice; it concerns objects we know by differentiating them from other objects. For example, we distinguish a pot from other objects, such as a table, the maker of the pot, and the self who sees the pot. In discerning these conventional objects, we proceed through dichotomies such as self and other, agent and object, pot and nonpot, and the like. In this way, we divide the universe of knowledge and reify these differences, as if these objects had their own essence and existed independently of each other. These dualities enable us to classify these objects and appropriate them, but they distort reality, for the objects do not in fact exist in the ways that we hold onto them. This distortion in turn leads to suffering created by our grasping at objects, which gives rise to attachment, aversion, and so on.

To free our minds, we need to undo the dualistic tendency to grasp objects by reifying differences. To succeed in this effort, we need to realize that things do not exist in the way we grasp them: that they are empty from existing through their own essence. However, this emptiness is not another type of object, a kind of supertruth, which could be approached by differentiating it from other objects. It is also not simply a rejection of the conventional, which would amount to a negative reification—what Derrida calls "nothing more than the clamorous proclamation of the antithesis."[19] To understand emptiness requires that one free oneself from any reification, negative as well as positive. Doing so necessitates a particular approach, which Śākya Chok-den explains as follows.

First, establish the moral foundation of the practice by following precepts and keeping commitments. Second, refute the first extreme (existence) and realize that there is no self in persons and in phenomena. Third, eliminate the second extreme (nonexistence) and thus reach the understanding of the ultimate, emptiness. At that point, the mind is not locked on any alternative. Free from any subjective and objective determination, it realizes that all phenomena are beyond determination. This three-step approach is not just a convenient way to arrange Madhyamaka practice but follows a conceptual necessity that goes to the heart of Madhyamaka. For when one negates the first extreme, one realizes that the subject—for example, the person—does not exist ultimately. At that point, one grasps at the negation itself and one's mind is not yet free from elaboration. It is necessary to undo this negation and realize that the subject does not not-exist either, thereby comprehending that the person is beyond the extremes of being and nonbeing. This is Nāgārjuna's Middle Way, according to Śākya Chok-den and many non-Ge-luk thinkers.[20]

Yet freedom from fabrication is not just the mechanical result of negation. In general, negating nonexistence is tantamount to asserting existence, but when it follows the negation of existence it functions differently. It deprives the mind of any object to hold onto and leads it to relinquish its habit of conceptualizing reality in dualistic terms.[21] This therapeutic overcoming of a logic based on the assumption that things can be grasped as entities, in turn, has consequences for conventional reality. Because objects are beyond determination, they are not completely nonexistent. Hence, they can be said to exist provisionally or conventionally. Emptiness does not cancel out the conventional domain but relativizes it. Thus, rather than considering conventional distinctions unimportant, people who have realized emptiness cease to absolutize them, seeing them as fluid, fragile, illusionlike, and interrelated. These individuals are then freed from the compulsion to reify objects as having their own intrinsic reality and can relate to conventional reality appropriately—that is, as being merely conventional.

Because emptiness requires the overcoming of any reification and thus of any differentiation, it cannot be understood conceptually in the same way as other points of Buddhist doctrine such as impermanence. Applying a concept will not do, for emptiness is not a thing or an object that can be captured by distinguishing it from other things. Hence, it cannot be said (i.e., directly signified); it can only be skillfully shown (i.e., indirectly indicated). This is the famous *upāya* teaching that emphasizes the importance of the conventional realm as providing the resources or skills that are indispensable for reaching the ultimate but that must be transcended as well. Nāgārjuna explains, "The pacification of all objections and the pacification of illusion: No Dharma was taught by the Buddha at any time, in any place, to any person."[22] The ineffability of emptiness should not be understood as implying some essential nature too deep or too mysterious to be described. Emptiness is ineffable not because it is some kind of mystical truth but because it cannot be conceptually captured: from the point of view of ultimate analysis, there is no thing to be captured.

DECONSTRUCTION, MADHYAMAKA, AND DEBATE

To grasp such an unusual insight, the traditional philosophical method will not do. A new approach is needed that enables one to understand emptiness while at the same time undoing any characterization used in the process. This self-subverting approach can be usefully characterized, I believe, as *deconstructive*. Bringing this often-misused term into a discussion of Buddhist philosophy necessarily creates some problems, including an unfortunate impression of trendiness and perhaps a false suggestion of equivalence.[23] It should be clear that I do not mean here to conflate Madhyamaka and the deconstruction characteristic of postmodernism[24]—two styles of thought that differ greatly in their views of interpretation, as I have already noted (see chapter 9). Moreover, I do not mean to say that Nāgārjuna and Derrida are doing even remotely similar things or that the former was, like the latter, "a deconstructionist" attempting to subvert his tradition. For postmodernists, deconstruction entails a radical loss of confidence in the possibility of any closure, as announced by Nietzsche's prophetic proclamation that "God is dead."[25] It also implies a rejection of traditional views of knowledge, particularly the idea that the mind needs a formation *(Bildung)* that will allow the person to realize the goal of a tradition.[26]

These views differ profoundly from Madhyamaka, which sees its analysis as confirming the value of its narratives and fulfilling their promises of liberation from one's own and others' suffering. They also conflict with the ways in which Tibetan thinkers conceive scholastic education. As I argued earlier, scholasticism is a way of creating a universe of meaning. In the Tibetan tradition, the cornerstone of that universe is emptiness. Thus, far from implying the sense of disorientation sought by postmodern thinkers, emptiness is taken to confirm the soteriological validity of the grand narratives of the tradition. This validity is embodied in the traditional education, which attempts to form monks by exposing them to this way of viewing reality, according to which they will thereafter shape their life. In fact, from a Madhyamaka perspective, postmodernism can be read as representing a nihilistic discarding of conventional distinctions and thus a stance to be avoided.[27]

Because Madhyamaka involves a radical negation of all the apparently available alternatives, it is always in danger of falling into nihilism—and that accusation has been made repeatedly against the school. Once one enters into the process of negation, it is easy to be carried away and feel that one has gone beyond the conventional, that one is freed from its moral and practical constraints. A systematic engagement in shooting down all possible answers may leave one feeling disoriented and without anything at all. Such risks are well known to Madhyamaka, which has taken great pains to distance itself from nihilism. The very name of this philosophy is meant to underscore that it is the Middle Way between eternalism (i.e., reification) and nihilism. Emptiness is not nothingness. It entails not the demise of the conventional world but the assertion that it is just that—conventional.[28] As many Tibetan scholars emphasize, the negation of alternatives provides an insight into emptiness only if it leads to the understanding that emptiness is fully compatible with the interdependence of conventional phenomena. Hence, the insight into emptiness does not destroy morality but shows its fragility. Good and bad are not in⸱ ⸱sically distinct. Their boundary is delicate, constantly shifting, and easy to miss. A good person will therefore be attentive, knowing that he or she needs to follow the basic precepts of the tradition while remaining alert to their limitations.

It is also here that the study of the path, which we examined in earlier chapters, becomes relevant. By providing a narrative structure in which the insight into emptiness becomes meaningful, it ensures that the practitioner affected by the shake-up of categories involved in Madhyamaka does not fall into nihilism. In general, Tibetan traditions are aware that individuals respond differently to the teaching of emptiness. It is said that when realizing emptiness, brighter students feel exhilarated, as if they had been freed from the heavy burden of an essentialized self, whereas slower students sometimes feel frightened by this loss of self. Jay Shay-rab Seng-ge was so frightened by Dzong-ka-ba's teaching of emptiness that he clutched his monastic shirt, as if to hold on to his nonexistent self, yet he did not feel as if he had lost all moral bearings in a meaningless universe. Because he lived in a Buddhist universe in which the insight into emptiness made sense, She-rab Seng-ge saw it as a way to reach closure and was able to assimilate its undermining of the most basic categories.

Despite these fundamental differences, there are intriguing similarities in Nāgārjuna's Madhyamaka and Derrida's deconstruction. Both philosophical approaches recognize at the same time the essenceless and hence enigmatic nature of existence and the indeterminate and provisional character of interpretation. More specifically, the two thinkers approach this insight similarly—namely, by relentlessly undermining their own interpretations. Thus Derrida claims that "the enterprise of deconstruction always in a certain sense falls prey to its own work."[29] In Nāgārjuna, this translates into the insight that "[t]he Victorious Ones have said that emptiness is the relinquishing of all views. For whomever emptiness is a view, that one will accomplish nothing."[30] Based on this family resemblance, I characterize the Madhyamaka philosophy that underlies the Tibetan practice of debate as deconstructive;[31] moreover, I believe that the very strategy of debate favors the self-undermining approach that we associate with deconstruction.

Because debates proceed mostly by unearthing contradictions and allow minimal production of constructive syntheses, they are particularly fit to embody the radical Madhyamaka approach. Members of the tradition seem to agree. The Dalai Lama asked me one day, "Have you ever noticed that every opinion one can put forth in debate can always be undermined, however right it may be?" Ling Rin-po-che expressed a similar insight when I visited him during my first year as a debater. After underscoring that I still had a lot to learn, he stated the goal I should aim for: "The mark of a good debater is that he is able to establish that what is is not and that what is not is." This statement could be taken as advocating sophistry, but in fact it alludes to the self-undermining approach. No opinion can be fully maintained given the essencelessness of phenomena and the provisional nature of conventional distinctions. The skilled debater recognizes this, keeps in mind the limits of concepts and the paradoxes that they entail, and uses his knowledge to confuse his adversaries.

This deconstructive emphasis is also clear in the criteria used to judge the outcome of a Tibetan debate. As we noticed in the previous chapter, the only time a debate can be formally adjudicated is when the defender's thesis is directly contradicted. In the other cases, the outcome may be clear but there are no logical criteria for determining the decision. This privileging of direct contradictions differs from the Indian practices, in which the outcome was often decided by reference to formal fallacies. I believe that this emphasis on direct contradiction is not unrelated to the deconstructive philosophical strategy that Tibetan debates tend to promote.

It must be emphasized, however, that Tibetan debates are not necessarily deconstructive. For example, the debate on the cognitive nature of compassion described above can be but need not be seen deconstructively. That is, one can, but need not, take the debate to proceed by explicitly identifying binary oppositions to undermine all alternatives. As I will show in the next chapter, debate in the Ge-luk tradition can be a self-undermining process that relentlessly pushes the investigation forward, preventing the mind from indulging in its tendency to seize on a final answer. From this perspective, any stance can and should be undermined, not just because doing so displays one's cleverness but because it is necessarily based on dichotomies whose absoluteness is illusory. This self-undermining approach explains why teachers often refuse to answer their students' demands for positive answers. Such an answer would discourage the student from investigating the question himself; but more important, any answer claims an ultimate status that is, in the final analysis, incompatible with realizing the limits of any characterization implied by the view of emptiness.

One often hears the complaint, inside and outside the Tibetan tradition, that debate is superficial, unduly privileging cleverness over truth, and that a skillful debater can prove anything.[32] Already in the fifth century B.C.E., Gorgias had argued that dialectic brings victory not to the one who is right but to the one who can defeat his opponent, often by using tricks. To prevent that dangerous outcome, Socrates and Plato offered a model of dialectic as a separate and special quest for certainty through which contradictions can be unearthed not just to confound one's opponent but to move him to a higher level of understanding. Aristotle rejected both views as extreme, arguing that although dialectic cannot reach certainty, it can lead to greater understanding. He believed that humans are naturally disposed to grasp the truth. Hence, given the choice between true and false alternatives, most will chose the former.[33]

Although I am not sure that Tibetan debaters would share Aristotle's optimism, they agree that debate is useful in the search for greater understanding. It is not a way to reach infallible truths but a means to train the mind so that it becomes able to explore the complexities of human thinking. And while Tibetan debaters also agree with Gorgias that dialectic makes us discover the uncertainties in what we thought to be well-established truths, they are unlike him in finding these pervasive uncertainties no cause for relativism but rather something akin to a Socratic lesson in the fragility of human understanding. Since things are without essence, distinctions are conventional and contingent. Hence, we should keep in mind that our interpretations are provisional and in need of constant critique. This is the Madhyamaka, which Tibetan debates at their best can teach.

Given this connection, it is tempting to assert a historical connection between the form of Tibetan debates and the Madhyamaka agenda that they serve. Didn't Cha-ba and his tradition choose to emphasize consequences because they thought that doing so would best serve their understanding of Madhyamaka? This is a complex question that can be answered only through further study of Cha-ba and his tradition. It is worth noting, however, that Cha-ba was not a follower of Candrakīrti's more radical Prāsaṅgika, which stresses the importance of consequences as a dialectical tool. On the contrary, he was a follower of the Svātantrika, according to which Mādhyamikas should not limit themselves to consequences but should offer autonomous arguments that establish the emptiness of phenomena. It is thus far from clear that Cha-ba's choice of dialectical tools was dictated by his Madhyamaka commitments.[34]

Finally, we must observe that the emphasis on debate is not without its problems, for it encourages students to put more effort into performing spectacular debates than into pondering texts. The temptation is strong to neglect the important textual groundwork that is the basis of the Tibetan practice of debate and focus more strictly on the dialectical fireworks. If I reflect on my past inclinations, I can see that I was guilty of overemphasizing debate. Spending little time discussing textual interpretations, I would rush to focus on more strictly philosophical topics, which could be discussed on their own merit. Although this practice is valuable and represents an original aspect of Tibetan scholastic culture, by allowing students to get away with reading less it threatens the intellectual integrity of the tradition. This became particularly clear to me when I began to study with non-Ge-luk teachers, who would confront me with important texts on which I had little to say, despite my excellent training in critical thinking.[35]

THE SCHEDULE OF DEBATING INSTITUTIONS

The importance of debate in the Ge-luk tradition should by now be quite clear. Our investigation is far from complete, however, for we have yet to examine its practical modalities—the schedule that structures such a practice and the ways it was organized. In discussing the schedule of the three Ge-luk seats, we need to recognize the differences between premodern Tibet and exile. The fundamental distinction drawn in Tibet between debate sessions *(chos thog)* and debate breaks *(chos mtshams)* is less marked in exile. In Tibet, there were eight debate sessions in the year, which alternated with eight breaks.[36] During the sessions, students debated; during the breaks, they memorized and studied commentaries with their teachers. Five sessions would last one month, and three a fortnight, while seven of the eight breaks lasted from five to fifteen days; the great break during summer retreat lasted a month and a half. The rest of the time was apportioned to a variety of celebrations, such as the New Year and the Great Prayer festival. Each of the debate sessions had prescribed topics that students had to cover.[37]

An exact pre-1959 schedule is hard to reconstruct, for few Tibetan monks then had watches. Hence, accounts tend to be vague. Moreover, the precise times of activities may have also been influenced by various circumstances (the season, festivities, etc.). Nevertheless, Geshe Rab-ten offers the following schedule for debate sessions in the Jay monastery of Se-ra:[38]

5:30–7:00	General assembly
7:00–10:00	Morning debate
10:00–11:00	Monastery assembly
1:00–13:00	Noon debate
13:00–13:30	Lunch
14:00–16:00	Afternoon debate
16:00–17:00	Evening assembly
17:00–19:00	Evening prayer and short debate
19:00–20:00	Teaching
20:30–21:30	Night debate
22:00–23:00	Recitation

Though the schedule in other monasteries was probably slightly different, its rhythm was similar, as debate alternated with ritual. Monks would start the day with the morning prayer in the great assembly hall *(tshogs chen)* of the monastic seat (here Se-ra), where they would pray and receive tea (hence the name of this prayer, *mang cha:* i.e., "common tea"). Rich sponsors might provide food and money. After that, they alternated debates and more prayer sessions. At noon, they would go to the assembly hall of the monastery (here Jay). There they were given tea—and perhaps food and money, if the donor was generous. If there was a sponsor, an assembly would be held in the evening. Otherwise, monks had to provide for their own evening tea and food (if they ate).[39] After the evening assembly, the evening prayer took place (see figure 12). This ritual usually lasted at least two hours, as long as or even longer than the evening debates. The night then went on with debate, classes, and recitations.[40]

There is no point in detailing Tibetan monastic rituals, a subject that would take us too far afield.[41] Yet a few words on Tibetan rituals, particularly on the Mahayana and tantric practices that are central to Tibetan monasticism, are in order here. Not all rituals follow the same pattern. For example, the monastic rituals prescribed by the Vinaya are not forms of worship but communal functions during which monks assemble, such as the fortnightly public confession when monks confess their faults and proclaim their purity. Most of the Tibetan rituals, however, follow a different pattern: the worship of one (or several) divine being(s) treated as an honored guest to whom offerings are made. Its origins lie in the most typical form of worship in India, the *pūjā* (*mchod pa;* i.e., "offering"). In this practice, which goes back to the Vedic literature and has been adopted by Buddhists, Hindus, and Jains alike, one makes various offerings to a divine being. After purifying oneself and one's surrounding, one invites the divine being, who is installed as a guest. Offerings are made, often starting with water for drinking and washing, continuing with garments and perfume, and culminating with praise, homage, food, and the lighting of a lamp (not necessarily in that order). In the Buddhist tradition, the divine beings that are worshiped are not the gods of the Hindu pantheon—since they are thought to be like us, trapped in the cycle of birth and death—but buddhas and bodhisattvas, who are represented according to exoteric or esoteric canons.[42]

The tradition's own explanation of worship relies on the idea of merit *(bsod nams, puṇya)*, an idea that covers a considerable range of intertwined meanings. Worshiping a deity is a meritorious action and as such is thought to bring a variety of future favorable results, including pleasures and occasions for spiritual practice. It is also believed to be effective in this very life-time, particularly in removing obstacles, curing disease, and so on. But wor-shiping is also seen to contribute more directly to an individual's spiritual growth; in particular, it develops the virtues without which understanding cannot mature into wisdom. For example, to worship Manjushri, the bod-hisattva of wisdom, is thought to be effective in increasing one's intellec-tual abilities by creating merits. That is why monks start their sessions of memorization with an invocation to Manjushri, which they end by repeating the syllable *dhīh* (see chapter 4). Similarly, worship is thought to ensure that intellectual learning bears spiritual fruits. Worship thus expresses the faith that animates scholastic studies, even as it strengthens faith though the accumulation of merits. The development of this faith is one of the main objectives of monastic education, particularly of the study of the path. Finally, at the highest level, worship is seen as a form of giv-ing, the first perfection that the bodhisattva must develop. All these differ-ent ways in which worship is thought to be effective are included in the idea of *bsod nams,* as is the bodhisattva's practice of the perfection of giving. It is part of the collection of merits or virtues *(bsod nams kyi tshogs),* which together with the collection of wisdom *(shes rab kyi tshogs)* will bring the bodhisattva to the ultimate perfection.

Among the various rituals performed in the monastic seats, undoubt-edly the most important is the evening prayer, which takes place before the evening debate. While other rituals are held to satisfy donors and receive tea, the evening prayer is concerned more specifically with the participants' spiritual welfare. Hence, it is taken more seriously and is performed with greater intensity. The prayers recited on this occasion are many and vary from monastery to monastery. For example, the Lo-se-ling evening ritual includes more than thirty and changes according to the time of the lunar month.[43] But two elements are constant: the invocation to Tārā and the rec-itation of the Heart Sutra. Together, they embody and lead to the cultiva-tion of two of the key virtues of scholastic training, faith and wisdom.

Tārā is the deity who protects her followers and rescues them from a va-riety of dangers. She was Atisha's favorite deity and has been central to the Tibetan pantheon since then; monastics and laity alike invoke her protec-tion. Because her blessing is also considered particularly potent, it is sought by scholars to ensure that studies become spiritually fertile.[44] The Heart Sutra, a shorter version of the Perfection of Wisdom, encapsulates the teach-ing of emptiness.[45] It thereby helps students develop their comprehension of this philosophy and thus represents wisdom. The sutra is recited several times, often to excruciatingly slow tunes *(dbyangs)* that are monastery-specific. In Tibet, Se-ra Jay took great pride in its special way of chanting the sutra, which could last nearly two hours.[46] Some monks use this opportunity to reflect on the meaning of the sutra and contemplate the teaching of emptiness. But its effectiveness lies primarily in its ritual power, not its content. This text is thought to be particularly effective in warding against obstacles and is used for exorcism.[47] Hence, the recitation of the sutra ends with the ritual repelling *(bzlog pa)* of evil forces, punctuated by a collective triple hand clapping.

Ritual, which is a vital part of scholastic education, plays a strikingly important role in the schedule. It consumed at least as much time as debate, as illustrated by the monastic formula "half worship, half study." And debate was practiced a remarkable eight to ten hours a day. These debate periods left little time for studying, which took place mostly during the breaks scheduled through the year. Monks spent most of the day in the debating courtyard, and the brief time in their room was devoted to preparing a debate. It was a grueling experience. Monks would go to bed around eleven o'clock at the earliest, and many stayed up longer, remaining in the debating courtyard or reciting texts they had memorized. In Se-ra Jay, some monks had to debate through the night on alternate nights for a full year. Monks would also get up quite early. Geshe Rab-ten remembers rising around four (as did other scholars) to practice prostration before going to the morning assembly. This schedule would continue throughout the session, broken only by a weekly rest day aimed at collecting the necessities of life (hence its name: *shing slong,* "begging for wood").

During the breaks, the schedule was much looser. In Dre-pung, monks often spent the break in caves above the monastery, where they would memorize and study texts. Gen Gya-tso describes the delight of reciting texts in the midst of flowers high above the monastery. They would start early and continue memorizing for the entire morning, with a break for tea at eight. After lunch, monks would spend a couple of hours relaxing. Then they would resume their memorization until ten or eleven at night.[48] In Se-ra, most monks stayed in the monastery, memorizing and studying texts, or went to some hermitage in the vicinity if they could; in Ga-den, they often tried to find sponsors willing to gain merit by offering them hospitality and supporting their memorization. Breaks also afforded students more time to take teachings and to reflect on the texts in a more leisurely way as they prepared for the intense session of debate.

In exile, the schedule still alternates between debate sessions and breaks, but the distinction between the two is not as sharp as it used to be. A typical debate session now has the following schedule.

5:30	Rising time
5:30–7:00	Morning assembly
8:30–10:30	Morning debate
11:00–13:00	Lunch and break
13:00–17:00	Afternoon class and individual study
17:00–17:30	Dinner
18:00–21:30	Evening prayer and debate
22:00	Bedtime

This schedule is more consistent, with few changes throughout the year. There is a weekly holiday during which students can attend to the necessities of life. During break sessions, the schedule varies little. Mornings are devoted entirely to memorization, but even during these sessions (unlike in pre-1959 Tibet) monks keep debating at night. The schedule is also now much less intense than it had been; debate is practiced for a mere four or five hours a day (about half as long as in Tibet), and monks have ample free time. There is also more emphasis on a continuous study of texts. Students can devote the whole afternoon to reading and studying with their teachers.

EXAMINATIONS AND THE ORGANIZATION OF DEBATE

The practical organization of debate in exile has undergone changes, though its overall structure has remained the same. Debate is still carried on in the courtyard, where monks confront each other in two ways:

In the *individual debate* (*rtsod zla;* lit., "debate with a partner"), monks pair with each other, one standing and playing the role of the questioner, and the other sitting down and playing the role of the defender. Before ending the encounter, they may switch roles. If the debate goes well, it can last for a while and attract other monks who have finished their individual debates. As the debate continues (sometimes for hours), the surrounding circle grows. Some observers may jump in on one side or the other. This is a time of high excitement for the debating pair who find themselves enveloped by tens and sometimes hundreds of monks listening attentively.

In the *formal debate* (*dam bca';* lit., "defense"), the entire group focuses on a single debate. One or two students sit as defenders while the others sit in rows facing the empty space in front of the answerer(s). A student stands, moves into this empty space, and starts the debate, knowing that the whole group will support him. If he gets stuck, those in the audience can jump in and help him. Thus, in a formal debate, all who are present can question one or two defenders, who must stand alone. As we will see, this exercise is quite difficult when a large crowd is involved, as during the Geshe exam. On such occasions, the candidate's ability as a defender is tested to its limit.

Monks move through such practices in an organized and systematic fashion. They follow a prescribed curriculum in a set order, the studies being organized by classes, or cohorts. When a student starts his studies, he enters into a class of students, who study a set number of topics per year. They start together with the Collected Topics and move on to the study of the five texts, each topic being studied at the prescribed time by all the members of the class. Each year, the class moves ahead with all of its members. In Se-ra Jay, there are fifteen classes:

Classes 1–3	Collected Topics (beginning, intermediate, and advanced; i.e., *bsdus chung, bsdus 'bring,* and *bsdus chen*)
Classes 4–8	The *Ornament*[49]
Classes 9–10	Madhyamaka (beginning and advanced)
Classes 11–12	Vinaya (beginning and advanced)
Class 13	Abhidharma
Class 14	Ka-ram (review of both Vinaya and Abhidharma)
Class 15	Lha-ram (review of the whole curriculum in preparation for the Geshe exam)

Each class chooses a reciting leader *(skyor dpon)*, who is responsible for organizing collective debates and memorizing the prescribed texts at ritual occasions.[50] This reciting leader also ensures that students debate the designated subject at the proper time. Because students of the same class debate with each other every day, they spend a great deal of time with members of their cohort. For example, every day of the debate session (discussed above), monks debate collectively with their classmates, as each class engages in one formal debate. Larger collective debates involving the whole monastery or even the whole seat are done only on formal occasions, usually at examination time. When students debate individually, often young monks will seek older students to test their skills. It is considered poor form for a senior to refuse to answer a younger monk.

A given class does not share the same teacher, for each student may choose his own. This diversity is a good thing for the class, as different teachers express conflicting views, which give rise to further debate. It also drives home the point that the teachers' opinions cannot be taken as authoritative. In a debate, saying "This is so because my teacher said so" is considered tantamount to admitting that one lacks any ability to think for oneself. Reasonings or texts, not people, are held to be definitive.

Tibetan scholars permit the quotation of texts in debate, if a questioner is unable to make his point purely on the strength of his arguments. He may say, for instance, that compassion is the loving attitude that wishes sentient beings to be free from suffering because this is stated by such-and-such an authoritative thinker (usually the author of the manual of the monastery, or Dzong-ka-ba and his disciples). Such an argument is allowed and used quite frequently in debates, even though it blatantly violates a basic rule of Buddhist logic: a citation cannot be used to prove a fact that can be established otherwise.

For Dharmakīrti, statements can be taken as reliable indicators of the intentions of their speakers but cannot provide proof in an argument.[51] For example, a statement about impermanence cannot be used to establish that notion as correct. There is, however, a special class of thoroughly hidden (*atyantaparokṣa, shin tu lkog gyur*) phenomena that cannot be established by experience or reasoning. They can be approached only by relying on an authoritative statement. It is only in relation to these phenomena that a quote can serve as a reason, though for Dharmakīrti it is difficult to judge the degree to which even this kind of quote provides actual knowledge.

Although Tibetan scholars accept the use of quotes in debate on all topics, they disagree on the value of such a move. This disagreement parallels their different understandings of the role of debate, a topic treated in chapter 12. Some scholars see debate mostly as a pedagogical tool useful for internalizing the content of the great texts. For them, the use of a quote is perfectly legitimate in that it helps students commit the tradition to memory. Others see debate as a means of intellectual inquiry in its own right. Hence, they prefer an argument to a quote, as the use of the quote reveals the weakness of the debater's position. Moreover, using a quote in a debate is not as strong a move as one may think, for it is often possible for the defender to interpret away the quote by providing a convenient gloss.

In pre-1959 Tibet, scholastic studies were optional and reserved for those who were really committed.[52] Beginners could expect to start with several hundred students in their cohort. By the end, ten or fifteen would be left. Every year, many students would leave, either going back to their native province or settling for the more leisurely life of a nonscholar monk. On the other hand, monks who were interested in studying could expect to be able to continue if they were reasonably diligent—particularly since most examinations precluded the possibility of failure. A student might never reach a given examination, but once he did he was assured of a positive outcome, regardless of his performance.

There was no system of yearly examinations and the assessment of knowledge was not very effective. Students would be promoted regardless of their scholarly progress. Only at certain crucial junctures would they be examined. These examinations differed among the monasteries, according to the customs of each institution. The student's first examination demonstrated that his memorization of his monastery's prescribed ritual texts had qualified him to start his scholastic study. The next trial came several years later, at the end of the studies of the Collected Topics, when he would sit in a formal debate in front of his regional house. But as was often the case in examinations, there was no question of failing. Not every student would be examined; and when a candidate did poorly, more seasoned scholars would answer for him, suggesting that the main point was not to demonstrate possession of knowledge but to signify a ritual passage from one stage of study to the next.

When the student was well into the study of the *Ornament,* he would again be examined in ways that varied among different monasteries. At Se-ra Jay, for instance, students were tested on their memorization and examined through debates while studying the *Ornament* in the second class devoted to this text.[53] The better students would then be given the opportunity to take part in a special ceremonial debate in front of the whole monastery called the Small Reasoning *(rigs chung).* During this debate, for which they prepared with great care, students would be paired, one debating and the other answering. The debate was preceded by preliminary examinations in the form of formal debates in the different regional houses. Other monasteries, including Go-mang and Lo-se-ling, emphasized the Small Reasoning less and debate between classes more. The main exam concerning the *Ornament* would consist of debates between the classes studying this text. On this formal occasion, the debate would be started by the recitation leader, who oversaw the whole procedure. But here again, not every student was examined. Many would sit through these proceedings without saying very much, leaving the task of dealing with the other class to their more active colleagues.[54]

In exile, the trend has been toward a more rationalized system in which the progress of individuals can be more tightly monitored. Unlike in premodern Tibet, where even in the great monastic seats only a minority of monks would study, in exile most now study. Accordingly, students are tested yearly on their memorization and their debates. A written examination, which is taking on increasing importance, has also been instituted. Students can be and are failed, although that outcome is still relatively rare. A similar system also exists at the Buddhist School of Dialectic and other smaller institutions, where students are examined on a regular basis. Even Tibetan monks find it difficult to escape the iron cage of modernity!

FINAL EXAMINATIONS AND THE TITLE OF GESHE

Examinations concern not only the passage from one class to another but also the conclusion of the studies, the examinations for the title of Geshe.

With the completion of Madhyamaka, after roughly ten years, students enter a new phase. They are considered intellectually mature and able to start on the arduous hermitic life, if they so wish. However, most go on to the last two topics, the study of the Abhidharma and Vinaya. In Tibet, scholars would spend up to ten years examining these texts in great detail. The length of time reflected not just the large amount of textual material but also, and more significantly, the desire to keep these advanced scholars in residence, so that they themselves become teachers and share their knowledge before leaving the monastery. In this way, the cross-generational exchange is maximized, ensuring a strong transmission of acquired knowledge and a better socialization of the new students.[55] In exile, Vinaya and the Abhidharma are examined less enthusiastically and much more briefly (for four years).

Only after they have completed these studies are students allowed to stand for the different levels of the title of Geshe (*dge bshes,* pronounced "ge-shay"; i.e., *dge ba'i bshes gnyen, kalyāṇamitra*), bringing to an end the exoteric part of the training. It is the highest degree awarded by Tibetan Buddhist monastic institutions. This title, which means "scholarly spiritual friend," has considerable prestige among Tibetans. Although nowadays it appears mostly within the Ge-luk tradition, its use was once widespread. Many of the most saintly figures of the Ga-dam traditions were described as Geshes. Yet Geshes are not always presented in a favorable light: they are often depicted as arrogant, convinced that they know more than anyone else, and—unlike the morally pure nonscholastic practitioners—overly interested in worldly concerns. One of the most sinister characters in Mi-la-re-pa's biography is Geshe Darlo, who attempted to poison Mila out of jealousy.[56]

In the Ge-luk tradition, this title designates those scholars who have finished their exoteric studies and passed their final exams. It is important to realize, however, that it is no guarantee of the scholarly excellence of its bearer, for there are several categories of this title. At the Lo-se-ling monastery of Dre-pung, for example, there are four types of Geshe:

Do-ram (*rdo rams*, "scholar [examined on the monastery's] stone [platform]")

Ling-se (*gling bsre*, or *seb*, "[scholar examined by] mixing of communities")

Tsok-ram (*tshogs ram*, "scholar of the assembly")

Lha-ram (*lha rams*, "divine scholar")[57]

These titles are ranked according to the kind of examination that candidates undergo. To receive the two lower titles, candidates are examined only within the precincts of their monastery (in this case, Lo-se-ling).[58] Candidates to the third, Tsok-ram, are examined by the assembly of both monasteries (here Lo-se-ling and Go-mang). The highest title is awarded only to those who are examined by the three monastic seats during the Great Prayer festival. They are supposed to be the best products of scholastic education, though even their knowledge is uneven. In Tibet, where candidates were carefully selected and had to wait for a long time (five to ten years after finishing the curriculum) before taking their exams, to obtain this title was often a sign of scholastic excellence. But many first-class scholars chose to receive instead one of the three inferior titles so that they would be free to leave the monastery. In exile, where access to the highest title has at times been easier, the lower echelons of Geshe are mostly given to less-accomplished scholars. And even the Lha-ram title is not always a sign of scholarly quality. Many candidates obtain the degree by sheer determination; much as in Western graduate studies, earning the loftiest degree (whether that be Ph.D. or Geshe) is the sure sign less of a brilliant mind than of scholarly perseverance.

The process of becoming a Geshe also involves the offering of a feast (*gtong sgo*) to one's regional house and one's monastery. This gift, which is quite similar to the profuse wining and dining of colleagues required of successful candidates in medieval universities, is not a small affair. It involves giving tea, money, and food to hundreds and sometimes thousands of monks. Reincarnated lamas are expected to go all out and make lavish offerings, but even simple monks are expected to be generous. In Tibet, where they could often rely on a network of relatives and neighbors who would gladly contribute to such a momentous event, such generosity was not very difficult. In India, where relatives are often without much resources, it is harder.

The Dalai Lama has tried to discourage this custom, but without much success. When he gave me permission to become Geshe, he insisted that I use my money more usefully. Armed with his recommendation, I was able to go against tradition, paying for the printing of a book rather than a feast.[59] Lati Rin-po-che almost had a fit when I announced that I was not going to offer a feast, but he could do nothing since I was fulfilling the Dalai Lama's own wish. Many monks taunted me, telling me half-jokingly that they had high expectations: "With a rich Westerner, gold is going to rain down!" In the end, however, they had to recognize that the printing and wide distribution of a book, which is still being used, was more useful than a wasteful feast in a scholarly institution that had only a limited range of books available. They also knew that they could not follow my example, though many wished they could.

Traditionally, access to the Lha-ram title is granted by the abbot of each monastery. The procedure of the Jay monastery of Se-ra is typical. Students who have completed the curriculum in the Abhidharma class[60] enter the Ka-ram *(bka' ram)* class where they are to review both Abhidharma and Vinaya. The abbot then selects those who will go on to the Lha-ram class to review all five treatises, with special emphasis on Vinaya and Abhidharma. In an institution such as Se-ra, which has at the most a couple of thousand scholars who all know of each other, reputations are well-established and the abbot has a good idea of the scholarly capacity of the more advanced students. Hence, he can choose those who can be admitted to the highest scholastic honor without formal examination. As one might imagine, this abbatial privilege gives rise to many complaints, as some of those who are passed over blame their failure on some bias. Thus, it would be a mistake to think of the power of the abbot as unquestioned.

Monks are independent-minded and they take no vow of obedience. Young monks must obey their room teachers; but once a monk is considered mature, only his guru has any authority over him. He must show the abbot the respect due to a social superior, but the abbot's authority is not religious and hence is limited. This is particularly true in exile, where the respect for elders and authorities has greatly diminished. In Tibet, monks displayed an extraordinary degree of respect. If an ordinary monk from the monastic seat encountered the abbot, for example, he was required to bow down very low and turn away while burying his face in his upper robe. In the Tantric Monastery of Higher Lhasa, monks were not even allowed to cross paths with the abbot. Khyongla recounts that once he was in a street in Lhasa when suddenly the abbot appeared. Khyongla had to flee but was hobbled by an uncomfortable pair of shoes; his only escape was to hide in the courtyard of an adjacent house and wait for the abbot to leave before hurrying back to the monastery.[61]

In Tibet, the Lha-ram class had enormous prestige, a special discipline, and a few (mostly symbolic) privileges. Monks were not obliged to participate in the monastery's ritual but could get tea and offerings even while remaining in their rooms studying. But the discipline was extremely strict. While other classes met only during debate sessions, they would gather every day in a place set apart. Those arriving late to a class in session would be punished. The monks would discuss the meaning of different texts. One member of the class would memorize a passage in a commentary, often amounting to ten or twenty folios. He would recite it by heart and would discuss it with his peers. Students would spend between five and ten years in this class before being allowed to stand for the final exam.[62] Nowadays, the procedures and discipline of the Lha-ram class do not differ from those of the other classes.

In Tibet, candidates for the Lha-ram title had to undergo a rigorous process that involved three steps.[63] First, they had to pass a preliminary exam *(rgyugs sprod)* at the Nor-bu Ling-ka *(nor bu gling ga)*, the Dalai Lama's summer palace. There, the candidates were examined in front of the Dalai Lama's spiritual assistant *(mtshan zhabs)* and sometimes the Dalai Lama himself. Candidates would be given questions to debate with other candidates, each one taking his turn to answer and debate on each of the five texts.[64] Though in the next two examinations one can disgrace oneself but cannot fail, failure was possible in this first examination. The Thirteenth Dalai Lama sent a few candidates back, humiliating both the candidates and the abbot who had admitted them to the Lha-ram rank.

In India, access to the Lha-ram title has sometimes been easier. In the mid-1980s, when I went through the whole process, any student who had gone through all the classes could lay claim to the title. At the end of the decade, the Dalai Lama attempted to raise the standards by reestablishing the examination held by a central authority, but this proved difficult to organize. In 1995, it was decided that all Lha-ram candidates would take a series of written examinations over seven years, administered by the Ge-luk Society. This change has considerably lengthened the process and created some resentment; it is possible that further changes will follow.

The second step, both in Tibet and in exile, is the monastery's formal debate *(gwra tshang gi dam bca')*, during which candidates are examined by their own monastery. They start by visiting all the classes of the monastery, from the beginners studying the Collected Topics to the most advanced Lha-ram class. They then defend their view in front of the whole monastery in a formal debate. One cannot fail but one can be humiliated in this difficult trial, which requires the candidate to spend up to ten hours answering questions on any topic related to the curriculum. This examination also involves a strong psychological element, since the defender stands against the entire audience (numbering several hundred to several thousand), which is expected to support and help the questioner. When the defender hesitates in answering, the audience joins the questioner in pressuring him by loudly intoning "cir, cir , cir." If the answer is still not forthcoming, the questioner may start to make fun of the defender with the vocal support of the audience. Conversely, if the questioner falters, members of the audience may jump in and pick up the debate. At times, several questioners bombard the defender with a variety of questions. Sometimes they may join in unison as they forcefully press their points. When the defender loses, the whole audience joins the questioner in loudly slapping their hands and pointedly proclaiming, "Oh, it's finished."

Withstanding such intense psychological pressure is not easy. Being jeered or ridiculed by thousands is a disconcerting experience. Some candidates fall apart, becoming rattled, angry, or unable to answer. Most candidates, however, are able to withstand the pressure because of the long training they have undergone. It is crucial to remain calm and good-humored, while keeping an eye out for sharp rejoinders that can turn the presence of a large crowd to one's advantage. I remember an incident that took place while I was answering in Se-ra Jay. The abbot, Geshe Lob-zang Thub-ten, who was my teacher, made a joke at my expense, implying that my answers were weak. The whole assembly burst into laughter. I was not fazed and without blinking I replied, "Some may laugh, but I challenge them to back up their laughter!" The audience exploded. I had won the exchange.[65]

After the candidate has performed in front of the whole monastery, he is qualified to stand for the third and final stage of the examination: the formal debate of the Great Prayer *(smon lam chen mo'i dam bca')*. This festival, which takes place a few days after the Tibetan New Year (February or March, according to the Western calendar), is meant as a way to bring about the coming of the future buddha, Maitreya.[66] It was instituted by Dzong-ka-ba in 1409, a key event in the life of the Ge-luk tradition. The yearly re-creation of this event is the main festival for the three monastic seats; its importance goes well beyond the boundaries of the tradition, as thousands of pilgrims came to Lhasa to attend this festival.

In Tibet, the great festival took place in the Central Temple *(Jo khang)* in Lhasa. This temple has long been the spiritual center of the Tibetan world. It contains the most venerated statue in Tibet—the Jo-wo *(jo bo)*, an Indian statue, which was brought to Tibet by the Chinese wife of Emperor Song-tsen-gam-po. The temple, too, is said to date back to the emperor himself. Hence, it is a symbol of the Tibetan community, linked closely to its sense of identity. Standing for examination in this symbolic center of the Tibetan world in front of twenty thousand monks would have to be a decisive experience in a person's life.

In the morning, candidates for the Lha-ram title are examined on the *Ornament* and Madhyamaka philosophy. At noon, they are tested on logic and epistemology. These two sessions are too short to allow serious debate. The real exam occurs at the end of the afternoon, when the last two topics, Abhidharma and Vinaya, are debated in front of several thousand monks. In Tibet, the study of Vinaya and Abhidharma was taken very seriously. Older Geshes would examine the candidates, putting forth special "stirred-up debates" *(rtags gsal dkrub ma)* in which all the categories contained in a passage of the Abhidharma or the Vinaya are combined (hence the debate's name). The candidate is then asked to enumerate them and find how many are contained in others, how many are exclusive, and so on.[67] At these debates, which were real Tibetan *casse-têtes,* surprises occurred and reputations were done or undone. At the end of the festival, each candidate received the title of "divine scholarly spiritual friend," the crowning achievement of often more than twenty years of arduous scholarly training, together with a ranking among the candidates (bestowed by the Tibetan government) based on their performance.

In exile, the Great Prayer festival has lost its relation to the symbolic center of the Tibetan universe. Often the three seats, which have been relocated far apart in South India, cannot get together and the festival is held in two separate locations.[68] Candidates then travel from one place to the other and are examined twice. During the festival, there is little time to debate except during the evening. In exile, the Vinaya and the Abhidharma are not studied in much depth and nobody has the time to get into stirred-up debates. Thus, the evening examination during the festival is not very difficult, unlike the monastery's formal debate. It remains a great honor to stand for the highest scholastic title of the Ge-luk tradition. It is the end result of a process that still has much integrity and that provides much prestige to its holders.

Many Tibetans still believe that once one has mastered the difficult monastic training, everything else can be learned easily. From a modern viewpoint that has abandoned any idea of unified knowledge, such a belief appears naive. In its own context, however, it was not unjustified, for monastic studies trained the mind well, making it a disciplined tool ready to tackle any subject. Moreover, in a world as limited as traditional Tibet, monastic learning represented a large proportion of what there was to know. Buddhism, with its complex philosophy, was also by far the most sophisticated area of Tibetan culture. Hence, those trained in it could indeed learn most other topics with relative ease. For traditional Tibetans, it seemed plausible that a person could know almost everything that is to be known. Several great scholars were thought to match this ideal and were called by such titles as the "all-knowing one" *(thams cad mkhyen pa)*, hyperbole that refers nevertheless to a real possibility in the Tibetan world.

Given the centrality of their form of learning and the impressive achievements of monastic scholars, it is not surprising that in Tibet monastic scholars had an enormous prestige—or to use Pierre Bourdieu's term, a large amount of symbolic capital. They commanded the kind of language, the set of manners, and the orientations and dispositions that would make them successful in their society.[69] Being a Geshe was recognized as a great achievement, and families would often go into debt to help their offspring make the required offerings. Parents frequently expressed their pride, stating that raising a child who had accomplished such a feat was worth more than anything else in their own lives. This cultural capital was the result not of the social origin of the scholars but of their own achievements. Many scholars came from humble backgrounds and had little or no schooling at home. Thus the achievements of monastic scholars were made possible not by their social background but by their insertions into a powerful monastic network. For the most part, monastic scholars did not participate in the reproduction of the privileges of their own family, but they contributed to the prestige of their institutions. Education in traditional Tibet was a means of social reproduction, not so much of a class structure as of a social organization dominated by monastic institutions.

Nowadays the role of monastic intellectuals is different. Since 1950, modern education has spread among Tibetans. In exile, refugees have had spectacular educational successes, breaking the quasi-monopoly that monastic scholars held in Tibet. Nevertheless, Geshes retain a large degree of prestige. They still often staff the modern schools administrated by the government in exile, where they teach traditional subjects—Tibetan language and the rudiments of Buddhist philosophy.

LEARNING HOW TO LOSE AND HOW TO WIN

It is clear that the process that leads to becoming Geshe Lha-ram-pa is changing, as is the regard in which Tibetan society holds monastic scholars. Still, the process remains arduous. Candidates have to sustain for hours the on-slaught of their fellow scholars, who try to undo them in front of and with the active help of a large assembly of hundreds and sometimes thousands of highly knowledgeable onlookers. People who have not gone through this training often wonder how these monks can sustain such pressure.

The answer is that learning how to answer in a formal debate is a skill that one learns gradually throughout the training. Right from the begin-ning, debates are divided into individual encounters and formal debates, during which one learns the difficult points, the moves, and the tricks used by seasoned scholars. But another part of the answer is that there is a moral dimension to this process. I can illustrate this point by referring to my own limited experience.

I remember particularly clearly the first occasion I took the role of de-fender in a formal debate held at the Buddhist School of Dialectic in 1975. I already had a fair amount of practice in the short formal debates that are held every day, but this was the first time I was standing as the defender in an extended formal debate, which started around six o'clock in the evening and should have gone on until around one o'clock the next morning. Two students would answer and the rest would debate them. I was still a begin-ner, but I was considered one of the better students of the school. I was ob-viously quite satisfied with what I considered to be my achievements. I was paired with another monk who was supposed to answer as well but was of little assistance. At first, things went well and I stood my ground. But as the evening wore on, I began having serious difficulties. The topic was re-lated to the notion of nirvana, the state reached by an Arhat in which all negative emotions are eliminated. The question was, Whose negative emo-tions are eliminated? Those of the Arhat? This is not possible, since he or she has no such emotion left. Those of the person prior to becoming Arhat? This is not possible either, since these emotions are already gone and hence do not need to be abandoned. One could answer that it is the negative emo-tions in general that are eliminated, but this reply raises delicate problems as well. For if the Arhat abandons the negative emotions in general, then it follows that those do not exist after he or she abandons them. But what about the negative emotions of other people?

This debate was more a pretext for dialectical fireworks than a serious theoretical inquiry. But in a dialectical joust, one cannot shut down the de-bate. One must answer. That is what I could not do that evening in 1975, and I became trapped in my own answers. I tried several of the answers I just laid out but none of them worked. My smug self-assurance started to disappear and I became badly rattled. This made things only worse, as one can imagine, and I started to lose my sense of the overall question. Instead of trying new answers, I became fixated on the two or three answers I could come up with, my mind racing to try to find the gap that would allow me to escape. But far from finding an escape, I became more trapped. I would try one answer, and a few minutes later receive a loud and humiliating "Oh, it's finished." I would then try another one, only to receive the same verbal slap. I would then go back to my first answer, thereby digging deeper into the hole in which I found myself. My friends found the whole thing hilarious. By then, several of them had risen to push their case with great excitement. They knew they were winning and took delight in playing with me like cats with a mouse. Their delight was greatly increased by my reputation as supposedly one of the better students. Here was a great time to hit back. "Hey Sang-gye Sam-drup [my Tibetan name], where are you? We thought you were so good! Come on, this is a simple question!" I was in a state of collapse, utterly humiliated and barely able to mumble. And then came the supreme humiliation: my friends gave me the answer, which involved a dialectical trick.[70] But I was so crushed that I could barely repeat the words. I just looked at the group standing in front of me with glassy eyes and considerable resentment. The teacher decided that things had gone far enough. It was time to stop the massacre and the session stopped, a couple of hours earlier than usual.

I felt terrible about the whole incident. The beginning of the next day was difficult. People were friendly and did not bring up the incident, but I felt so humiliated that their smiles seemed to me to have obvious sarcastic overtones. Finally, at the end of the morning, I brought myself to talk about the debate with my friends. They had a very different assessment of the whole incident. For them, I had lost a debate and had been proved wrong. And that was it! Everybody can be defeated, and we had better be ready to face this possibility. This realistic assessment was tremendously helpful and changed my feelings about the debate. I realized that one of the main sources of trouble had been my own mental rigidity, which was rooted in the fear of losing and the desire to win. Instead of focusing on the topic, my mind became entangled in its own creations. The trick in answering is to be open, unconcerned by the final outcome, and just focused on the topic— and ready to be proven wrong at any step. Once one gives up the fear of losing and is ready to admit one's mistakes, one can take the whole exercise for what it is, a useful game in the search for greater understanding.

This realization never left me. I had several occasions to answer in formal debates but I never again found myself in the hopeless situation I had gotten into during that evening. Obviously, before starting to answer in front of a large crowd, one feels a certain apprehension, a kind of stage fright. But this apprehension is helpful in focusing the mind and very different from the fear of losing. Whereas stage fright is brought about by a focus on the performance, the fear of losing is a result of excessive self-concern. To be sure, everybody who enters a debate wants to win, since that is the proximate goal of the practice. But many other goals are much more important. When one realizes that a debate is fun and useful in the learning of the tradition, one forgets one's concerns for oneself and becomes captivated by the flow of the game.[71] One also develops the ability to consider arguments on their own merits without much concern for personal feelings. In particular one develops a thick skin, making it possible to consider alternatives in as detached a way as possible. Such detachment does not preclude stubbornness, however. A proverb says, "Do not debate a Geshe! Do not bang your head against a pillar!"

This quality of openness should not be confused with true humility. It is more a readiness to accept mistakes than a realization of one's narrow limits. In fact, new Geshes are well-known for their tendencies toward arrogance. In their training they acquire a sense of mastery of a very complex tradition. They often compare their sense of competence to the exhilaration conveyed by a panoramic view from the top of a mountain. But monastics themselves clearly recognize that this sense of surveying the tradition is misleading. It can become an obstacle, feeding a deep-seated pride that takes the scholar away from the ethical and religious goals of the tradition. Ge-luk scholars must be reminded that scholarly mastery is only the proximate goal of the education and is partly illusory. The real task, the eradication of selfishness, is yet to be accomplished. Toward the end of my training Geshe Nyi-ma told me, "When I became a Geshe, I thought I knew a lot. It is only since then, by repeated confrontations with the great texts of the tradition, that I have learned how little I know."

Nevertheless, an attitude of openness helped me greatly during the final part of my studies, the Geshe examinations. I was allowed to stand for the highest examination much earlier than my seniority would have allowed me. In 1982, I was nearing the end of the study of Madhyamaka, when I realized that the most important part of the studies was over. The question of what to do next would arise sooner rather than later. I started then to toy with the idea of becoming a Geshe, a thought that had not entered my mind previously. When I started my scholastic studies in 1973, Lati Rin-po-che had urged me to be ambitious in my long-term aims and become a Geshe. I do not know how serious he was, but I did not give the prospect much thought. It was hard to imagine receiving such a prestigious title when one barely knows how to speak the language! Meanwhile, I just enjoyed my studies without thinking too far ahead.

Nevertheless, by 1982 it was difficult to avoid the issue of what to do after the end of the studies. I could have gone on for several years, learning the intricacies of the Abhidharma and the Vinaya, but I knew that the training had already produced the benefits that I could expect. I also felt that I needed some kind of formal recognition that would bring closure to the years I had devoted to this pursuit. Thus, the idea of becoming a Geshe began to seem like a fitting means of indicating to myself and others the completion of the valuable training I had undergone. I asked the Dalai Lama whether it would be a good idea to become a Geshe and how I should approach this new phase. I expected him to approve my project, and he did so—but in a way that surprised me.

I had expected to be told that I could just enter one of the monastic seats and go through the normal examination procedures in one of the monasteries in an accelerated way, as lamas and monk-sponsors are allowed to do.[72] Instead, the Dalai Lama told me I should stand as an independent candidate. He would talk to the abbots and let me know about the practical details. A few weeks later, the abbots of the six monasteries met in Dharamsala with the Dalai Lama. Later on, Lati Rin-po-che, who was the abbot of Ga-den Shar-tse, organized another meeting to which I was called. Rather nervously, I entered the room where the abbots of the six monasteries were sitting. I prostrated myself and made my request formally, as Lati Rin-po-che had told me to do. I was then informed by the abbots that my request had been granted. I would have to stand as an independent candidate, and that implied being examined in each of the six monasteries. I would not need to visit all the classes, as Geshes usually do, but I would need to stand in a formal debate in each of the six monasteries for a minimum of one day. Could I do this? The prospect of facing hundreds of scholars on my own did give me pause. I briefly contemplated withdrawing but decided against it.

My first trials took place at the end of 1984 at Se-ra, where I had spent the last two years preparing for the final examinations, studying Vinaya and Abhidharma. The first debate took place in the May monastery. I remember being utterly terrified by the idea of facing a large group of outstanding debaters. These people were the best in debate, well above the students of the Buddhist School of Dialectics, where I had done most of my studies. I was starting to realize what I had gotten myself into, but it was too late to go back. My comrades of debate at Se-ra made the exercise more difficult by putting on considerable psychological pressure. For weeks I would hear such comments as "You want to jump ahead of us? That's fine, but we will see what you can do in the courtyard. It is only by testing gold than one can know its true value!" This teasing was quite good-humored, but had an edge. They were a little envious, and they were going to make sure that things would not be easy for me.

The evening before the first debate, I could not sleep at all. I tossed about in my bed, visualizing the events of the next day. Finally, in the early hours of the morning I decided I would be better off studying than vainly trying to sleep. I got up and read until it was time to go to the May temple, where I would be examined. In the morning, I entered the temple accompanied by the disciplinarian. I prostrated myself in front of the main statues, under which I then took my seat, facing the rest of the monks, who were sitting in rows on my side. The empty alley in front of me would be the place where the questioners would come to put forth their challenges. The proceedings started with a short collective invocation and continued with my own chanted invocation. After that, the debate started. The first few answers were difficult. It was hard to get over my apprehension. I quickly realized, however, that my anxiety was unfounded. I was able to identify almost every topic debated, and after the debate had been engaged I was able to answer. Never in these encounters did I lose it completely, as I had done at the Buddhist School of Dialectics.

The next exams followed the same pattern. I repeated the whole exercise in each of the six monasteries, where I stood for a period of six to ten hours, depending on the customs of the monastery and the time available. A few episodes stand out in my mind, particularly those that turned out well for me. In the Jay monastery, my costudents from the Madhyamaka class had prepared specially for this occasion. I had studied with them for many years and they were not going to let the occasion slip by. But fortunately, the topic they had chosen, the Prāsaṅgika view of epistemology, was one of my favorites. The confrontation lasted for about three hours, but I stood completely vindicated. I remember taunting them: "Come on, you are not going to let me go so easily!" Even the efforts of one of my teachers in Sera, Gen Lob-zang, could not breach my defenses, and he was reduced to shaking his finger, saying, "Don't lie, don't lie."

In another encounter, at Lo-se-ling monastery, the topic was the epistemological status of karma. How can one know the law of karma? This is a particularly difficult topic in Buddhist epistemology, which rejects scriptures as an independent source of knowledge. Knowledge comes either from reasoning or from experience. Yet the moral domain is not accessible to either of these two forms of knowledge. How can one know the causal connection between an action, a karma, and its results in future lives? The answer is far from obvious. To solve this problem, Tibetan scholars posit a special kind of inference called "inference from belief" *(yid ches rje dpag)*, relying on trusted instructions.[73] In this debate, the question was, What is the purview of this form of reasoning? Is it the general law of karma, or just its details that are to be established? I took the second position. The debate became extremely heated. Several monks had risen in excitement and were standing in front of me. The abbot, who had previously been sitting behind me on a high throne, was standing on his throne, seemingly enraged by my answers. At some point, it became clear that I had made my point. I would not lose. Still, the abbot would not give up and started up the same debate. At that moment, I decided to stop the whole exercise by a sharp rejoinder: "What's the point of going in a circle? If you want to do this, do it around the temple; at least that will be virtuous!" The room exploded and the debate was over.

I was taken by surprise in a few debates, but I was ready for that. At one point, a friend from Se-ra Jay started a debate on the four applications of mindfulness *(dran par nyer bzhag, smṛtyupasthāna)* according to the Abhidharma. The debate looked completely innocuous, but since it came from a seasoned debater, I knew I was missing something, and soon enough, I found myself cornered. Instead of digging myself into an entrenched position, however, I readily conceded defeat, thus defusing the possibility of being entrapped in a hopeless situation. Obviously, such admissions cannot be too frequent, or there will be no contest and the whole exercise becomes pointless. This is when other monks step in and answer instead of the defender. Although the defender is not failed, everybody understands that he is not up to snuff. As the first Westerner to stand for Geshe, I was particularly keen to avoid such a humiliation. I may not have been the best, but I wanted to prove that I deserved the honor that was bestowed on me. Fortunately, by that time I was sufficiently trained as a scholar to stand my ground on most questions. Thus, I did not need to be afraid to concede defeat and could be flexible enough to be able to yield whenever the situation seemed hopeless.

Throughout this endeavor, the monks were extremely supportive. They appreciated my starting from scratch and my willingness to learn from them. They were also delighted to see a Westerner, the first one, standing for such a high honor. Many compared me with the outstanding Mongolian scholars who had come to Tibet before 1959. Although I did not think that I could sustain the comparison with those great scholars, I was deeply honored by the whole experience, which was an exhilarating conclusion to what I still consider to have been the most fruitful period of my life.

12   Is Debate a Mode
of Inquiry?

Scholasticism is rarely understood as involving a critical dimension. In this
chapter, I consider Tibetan debate from this angle and ask, Is debate merely
an exercise to validate a pregiven truth, or does it represent a genuine avenue of inquiry? I examine the different answers existing within the Ge-luk
tradition: whereas some view debate as a pedagogical tool helping students
to internalize a party line, others regard it as a practice of inquiry that pro-
motes critical thinking, a quality not usually associated with scholasticism.
My interactions with my teachers help illustrate these two views.

DEBATE AND INQUIRY

The importance of the critical element at work in debate is not always
obvious. Like any other ludic activity, debate needs to be learned. Because
it takes a long time to internalize the rules and procedures of debate, the
learning process at first seems limiting and constraining. The beginner typically feels restricted in his expression because he has difficulty expressing
his ideas in the form of consequences or acceptable answers. This experience is reflected in the secondary literature, where debate is often depicted
as a mechanical exercise without creativity. Stephen Batchelor describes his
own experience:

> I had naively started this course in logic and debate through heeding
> the claims of lamas that reason alone could prove the truth of many
> Buddhist axioms: the infallibility of the Buddha, rebirth, emptiness,
> etc. What I realized in the end was that, despite all the claims, reason
> was subordinate to faith. In other words: *you set out to prove what you
> have already decided to believe.* As a Westerner I assumed, wrongly it
> turned out, that the Tibetans saw logic as I had been taught to see it: as

a Socratic enquiry where you subject propositions to ruthless analysis in order to discover whether they are true or false. The Tibetan Buddhist approach (like that of the medieval schoolmen in Europe with regard to Christianity) is to analyze a point of Buddhist doctrine in order to prove that it is true (or to analyze a point of non-Buddhism inferior to Buddhist doctrine to prove that it is false).[1]

The view of debate as merely validating a pregiven religious conviction corresponds to the opinion of those members of the tradition who consider debate a useful but limited pedagogical exercise (notably, as we will see shortly, it was the view of Geshe Rab-ten, Batchelor's teacher). It also corresponds to the perceptions of the beginner who is learning the debate system. Yet some of the more advanced members of the tradition describe their experience in strikingly different terms. These scholars, who have mastered the system, speak of an exhilarating sense of openness that debate makes possible for them as they use it as a mode of inquiry in studying the tradition's great texts. Who is right? That is one of the questions I address in this chapter.

To understand the place of debate in Tibetan scholasticism, we need to consider the role of questioning in the interpretive process. Following Gadamer, we noted in chapter 7 the central role of questioning in the process of understanding a text. Understanding, it was there observed, is not the result of the application of any predetermined procedure. Or, as Gadamer himself puts it, "There is no such thing as a method of learning to ask questions, of learning to see what is questionable."[2] Tibetan scholars would certainly agree with this statement: there is no rule whose application will lead to a good question. They would also add, however, that one can be trained to learn how to ask questions, in an education that fosters the habit to see what is questionable in the propositions one encounters. This is what debate provides—and as an admirer of the Socratic dialogues, Gadamer would probably not disagree.

When I started to study the great texts, my teachers would often ask me whether I had questions. I often did, for these texts were difficult and at many points obviously needed clarification. But these immediate questions were not what my teachers had in mind. They wanted to know whether I was able to go beyond what the text was saying, whether I was able to question the concepts within the text rather than accept them as self-evident. At that stage, I had little practice in using debate as a mode of inquiry and, hence, I was rarely able to push the inquiry to the level they were seeking. Once my immediate questions were answered I would be satisfied, feeling that everything had been clarified. But this satisfaction was the sign of my lack of understanding. As one of my teachers put it, "You do not really understand, for it is only when one has doubts that one understands!" Another teacher was even blunter: "Only buddhas and idiots have no questions. Which one are you?" I was none too pleased! I thought that my ability to comprehend the text and repeat its points demonstrated my understanding, but I was quite mistaken. I grasped only the surface meaning of the text; unable to take apart its concepts, I could not avoid being taken in by them. To develop this kind of critical thinking I would need to learn debate.

But Tibetan debates do more than provide a training in questioning, important as that function is. They also highlight the nature of interpretation and the scope of questioning within Tibetan scholastic traditions. For Gadamer, questioning is first a task of "reconstruct[ing] the question to which the traditionary text is the answer."[3] But questioning is not merely a reconstructive endeavor that reinforces the authority of the text. Gadamer is quite aware of the limits of such reconstruction; he argues that "[a]s the art of asking questions, dialectic proves its value because only the person who knows how to ask questions is able to persist in his questioning, which involves being able to preserve his orientation toward openness. The art of questioning is the art of questioning ever further—i.e., the art of thinking. It is called dialectic because it is the art of conducting a real dialogue."[4] Yet he fails to clearly distinguish between reconstructive questioning, which constitutes a strategy of retrieval that grants the text authority, and a more radical questioning of the horizon of the text. The former hermeneutics—which according to one critic "is animated by a faith, a willingness to listen, and it is characterized by a respect for the symbol as a revelation of the sacred"[5]—is important but insufficient. An interpreter who remains bound by the respect for the text can never reach an in-depth understanding.[6] To comprehend a text one must introduce a hermeneutics of suspicion that enables one to read it against itself.[7]

It is this kind of questioning that can be at work in Tibetan debates at their best. There students are confronted with other views. Seeing that the other students understand the same topics differently, they come to realize the limitations of their own comprehension. Their interpretation is no more self-evident than the others', but just one possible understanding among many. But as important as it is, the mere noticing of differences does not foster the critical spirit required for debate. To simply realize that disagreements exist without attempting to resolve them is a form of mental laziness, as students fail to push the inquiry to its full extent. They must go further, confronting these different points of view and learning how to undermine each by finding its weak spot. In doing so, they acquire the habit of looking at these other views with suspicion, seeking the proverbial chink in the others' armor rather than listening to them with respect.

To be sure, such a strategy of suspicion plays only a limited role, for the tradition aims at the closure necessary to create a religiously meaningful universe. Hence, suspicion is ultimately subordinated to a strategy of retrieval. Moreover, it operates within the parameters of the tradition rather than attempting to use modern theoretical tools. The Ge-luk tradition in particular extols the correctness of its views and strongly insists that its members' inquiry remain confined to orthodox terms. Nevertheless, even in this tradition, the interpretive process is not internalization alone but contains an element of suspicion. Thus, we should not lose sight of the degree to which debating may represent an avenue for free inquiry in scholastic traditions.

Similarly, medieval European practices did not merely validate pre-established points of view, as is often assumed. Medieval debates were exercises in intellectual inquiry and presupposed a large degree of freedom. Such freedom explains why the Catholic Church was so careful to monitor these debates and tried to regulate the questions that could be debated. Thus in 1277 Etienne Tempier, bishop of Paris, convened a committee of theologians that issued a list of 213 forbidden propositions. Students were prohibited from taking either side of these questions under threat of excommunication. The forbidden topics ranged from the serious to the downright silly. Here are a few examples:

> That Aristotle was right when he wrote that the world is eternal.
>
> That if the heavenly spheres stood still fire would not burn flax, because God would not exist.
>
> That the teaching of theology is based on fables.[8]

This famous edict came after the church's long struggle to limit the diffusion of Aristotle's works, which had been received from the Arabs and translated into Latin during the twelfth century. During the first half of the thirteenth century, ecclesiastical authorities had tried to prevent their use altogether. After losing that battle, they opted instead for the strategy of control, targeting in particular the famous "Latin Averroists," such as Siger of Brabant and Boethius of Dacia, who followed the great Arab commentator Averroës (Ibn Rushd, 1126–1198) in insisting on a literal interpretation of Aristotle.[9] Once restrictions were imposed, the thought of the Stagirite could be domesticated and made compatible with Christian dogma on such difficult questions as the eternity of the world, divine omnipotence, the unity of the intellect, and human happiness.

The breadth and diversity of the questions addressed by Tempier's condemnation suggest that medieval debates, at least at times, presupposed a great deal of freedom of inquiry—in certain ways more than in modern universities, where the range of allowable questions is often tightly restricted through a variety of covert disciplinary mechanisms including funding, peer reviews, and tenure denial. The variety of topics over which medieval debates ranged attests to the space open to critical inquiry. But the threat that this critical openness posed to the church's authority had to be controlled, leading to the crackdown on all signs of heterodoxy. Hence, the medieval university, particularly the University of Paris during the thirteenth century, is often described as "a golden cage." [10]

In Tibetan Buddhism, too, a critical dimension often runs against limitations imposed by the tradition. It is particularly prominent among Ge-luk scholars, who are devoted to debate. It would be wrong, however, to assume that the tradition is unified in this respect. In fact, there are significant differences in the pedagogical approaches *(khrid lugs)* of Ge-luk scholars concerning debate. These differences have received little attention in the secondary literature because the members of the tradition themselves do not discuss them. Moreover, because they arise not from organized groups with opposing ideas but from the orientations of individual teachers, they are hard to pin down.

To illustrate these differences, I focus on two figures, Geshe Rab-ten and Gen Nyi-ma. Whereas the former sees debate only as a tool aimed at internalizing the tradition, the latter also values debate as a mode of inquiry into the tradition. These individuals do not represent two well-established traditions but rather offer two approaches from a vast array of possible views, often finely nuanced. In addition, they substantially agree on the pedagogical value of debate. For both, it is an ideal method for students to learn the content of the tradition's great texts. Those who must debate a topic are forced to assimilate the texts that present that topic. Students without the words and the concepts at their fingertips find it difficult to stand up and debate, especially in a formal debate that may attract a large audience. Hence, Ge-luk scholars agree that debate is an excellent way—probably the best—to remember a topic.[11] But whereas for Geshe Rab-ten the value of debate is limited to this mnemonic and instrumental dimension, for Gen Nyi-ma it is a practice of inquiry with intrinsic worth.

These two approaches reflect different views of the role of the life of the mind in religious practice, a difference already observed in chapter 8 in the brief discussion of Haribadhra's description of the two types of trainees: the followers of faith, who approach the teaching by believing what they are taught, and the followers of reasoning, who rely primarily on the understanding gained through personal investigation. That fundamental difference in religious temperaments is relevant to the role of debate as well.

DEBATE AS A PEDAGOGICAL TOOL

In my mind, my first teacher, Geshe Rab-ten, exemplifies the follower of faith. He was himself an excellent scholar with a great ability to synthesize complex teachings, a skill that served him well with Western audiences. His teachings were impressive in their clarity, offering a solid and well-grounded picture that combined learning and personal experience. He was also well known as a good debater. Nevertheless, for him, the value of debate was limited and secondary to more strictly religious matters. The important task of a Buddhist monk was not intellectual inquiry but practice based on an intense devotion to one's teacher and the tradition he embodies. Students should study the great texts and debate as a way to internalize the tradition, but should not forget that debate is just a means to learn the truth contained in the great texts—the truth explained by the founders of the tradition and handed down through a lineage of teachers. Once students have debated a topic, they have learned what they need to know, the correct view, and are ready to move on to more explicitly religious practices, such as meditation. Geshe Rab-ten himself had meditated during his studies and he encouraged his students to do the same.[12] In later years he would scold me for not meditating: "If those like you who know something do not meditate, who will do it?"

This emphasis on the direct religious value of scholastic studies was due not just to Geshe-la's personal inclinations but also to the training he had received from his main teacher, Geshe Jam-pa Kay-drup. Geshe Rab-ten explains that

> Geshe Jampa Khedrub had a very special way of teaching. For about three days he would instruct us in logic (i.e., philosophy); then he would leave this for a day, and relate some accounts from the *Jātaka* scriptures describing previous lives of Lord Buddha. Or he might tell us the life stories of sages and realized meditators who had great spiritual attainments. It was so peaceful, so beneficial to be in his presence that I never got bored or tired.[13]

This approach is fairly typical of a lineage of Ge-luk teachers who conceive of scholasticism as the handmaid of religious life. Often they are associated with Pa-bong-ka, who spearheaded a movement of Ge-luk revival at the beginning of the twentieth century in opposition to the nonsectarian movement in Eastern Tibet. In the perspective shared by many of Pa-bong-ka's disciples, debate is a way to take in a completely predetermined truth. The teachings of the founders of the tradition contain that truth, which is further clarified and explicated by the words of the teacher. Hence, the task of the student is not to inquire but to internalize the truth handed down by the teacher.

Geshe Rab-ten was representative of this tradition, viewing debate as useful but limited. It is, as I have emphasized, a kind of game in which answers and questions must be formulated rapidly. Such a procedure is quite different from the in-depth thinking required to develop conviction in the tradition and insight into emptiness. Moreover, debate encourages pride: students have the impression that they know the central teachings of the tradition and are thus lured into a false sense of mastery. Geshe Rab-ten often commented on the superficiality of the knowledge one acquires in debate: "People think they understand emptiness, but their view has nothing to do with emptiness. It is only directed at words and does not produce the disruption of ordinary subjectivity required to free the mind." For Geshe-la, students who were serious in their practice should first learn the content of the tradition, including Madhyamaka, through commentary from their teacher. They should also debate as a way to internalize these teachings. But only when they go beyond this external *(kha phyir ltas)* approach and turn their minds to the practice of meditation can they hope to achieve any valuable insight.

This attitude toward debate was also reflected in his stance toward his students. Whereas some teachers see the student-teacher relationship as providing a context for inquiry, Geshe Rab-ten saw it as a context for the transmission of the truth, all of whose details were decided by the tradition. Hence, he expected his students to adopt his interpretations and considered any serious attempt to question them a sign of lack of respect. Students were free to raise doubts, but only as a way to get clear on the meaning of the teaching. Any disagreements with him signified not a legitimate difference but his students' immaturity of thought.

I still remember a particularly difficult exchange I had with him. He was teaching his own commentary to one of Dzong-ka-ba's most important texts, *The Essence of Good Sayings*, which examines Buddhist hermeneutics. I did not quite agree with his interpretation and started to mount some objections in an appropriately polite way. Geshe Rab-ten looked at me icily. "Am I not your teacher?" he asked in a calm voice that did not allow any answer. I was completely taken aback, since I was by then used to other more critical approaches. Fortunately, I had the good sense not to argue. I just apologized and we stopped the class for the day. It should be clear that Geshe Rab-ten's reaction was caused not by any insecurity about his own scholarship but by his strict view of the way he wanted his students to relate to him. He expected to see in them some of the devotion that he had shown toward his own teachers.

DEBATE AS A MODE OF INQUIRY

Some teachers, those who exemplify the followers of reasoning, disagree with Geshe Rab-ten's view. They consider debate to be a mode of inquiry, an investigation whose result is not entirely predetermined. To be sure, unlike modern intellectuals they do not conceive of this search as being free, at least in principle, to discard any previously held view.[14] Like other members of the tradition, they hold that truth is found in the tradition and hence is largely pregiven. Yet "largely" leaves a sizable gap. Although truth is conveyed through the tradition, it cannot be found fully in any of its teachings, for any statement has at best a partial hold on truth. Hence, there is room for Socratic free inquiry. As we will see later, this open-endedness is partial and often actively limited by the tradition. But it is important to recognize that it is real.

Their emphasis on inquiry affects the pedagogical style of these teachers, who use debate extensively in their teachings. Classes become less a setting in which final answers are provided than a place in which to learn how to inquire. Teachers who emphasize this aspect of the tradition often deflect their students' demand for solutions to difficult questions. "That is a difficult point *(dka' gnad)* and cannot be easily resolved," they are likely to say. Some teachers will refuse to give any positive answer, even after their students have debated the topic for weeks. They see their task as laying out the difficult points without necessarily resolving them. Resolution is left to individual students, who must come to their own understanding—often after years of careful reflection and inquiry. Their motto is "Do not underinvestigate and overdecide" *(dpyad pa ma nyung mtha' gcod ma mang)*. Inquiring into complexities in the light of the tradition's view, but without coming to any hasty decision, is what higher scholastic learning is all about.

This conception of debate as a mode of inquiry is also reflected in these teachers' view of the student-teacher relationship and the role of the student therein. For example, Gen Pe-ma Gyel-tsen, whom we encountered while examining Tibetan commentarial practices, did not mind students' objections and would answer them appropriately. Others would actively delight in objections, which they took as providing an opportunity to get back into the practice of debates, the great love of most Ge-luk teachers. I still remember a 1973 incident involving the abbot of the Nam-gyel monastery. He was an excellent scholar whose strong personality left an indelible impression on his often-terrorized disciples. Even after thirty years, I can visualize quite clearly his reaction when a hapless student was brave enough to raise an objection during his teachings. The abbot was genuinely pleased by the question, which was a sign of the student's commitment, but his delight was also not unlike that of a cat playing with a mouse. He started by clarifying the student's objection, in the process explaining it to the other students. He then forced the student to defend the positions implied by the objection and began to debate the poor student, who by then must have been cursing himself for speaking up. Needless to say, the student was destroyed in short order. Other students, myself included, were completely silent, trying to pretend they were not there and only too happy not to be targeted themselves.

The great master in the art of using debate in his teachings was Gen Nyi-ma (see figure 13). He believed debate to be at the center of his teachings, and classes often consisted of debates between him and students.[15] I devote a few words to this figure, whom I consider my main source of inspiration and who best exemplifies the role of critical thinking in religious tradition. In writing about him, I obviously do not claim to objectively assess his achievements but intend through hagiography to illustrate the limited but real presence of a Socratic element in Tibetan monastic education. He also enables me to present a picture of the strength and vigor of a traditional intellectual. For although Gen Nyi-ma was exceptional in his sharpness, insight, and learning, he was by no means unique. Comparable teachers included Gen Pe-ma Gyel-tsen, whom I have already described as a master in the art of commentary. Several friends who studied with non-Ge-luk teachers mentioned De-zhung *(sde gzhung)* Rin-po-che, Ken-po Rin-chen *(rin chen)*, Ken-po Sang-gye Ten-zin *(sangs rgyas bstan 'dzin)*, and others.[16] Thus, it is important to realize that although Gen Nyi-ma had his own style, which I valued particularly, and an exceptional mind, he was also a product of the traditional education described here. He embodies the strength of the premodern intellectual who feels completely secure in his way of looking at the world. This assurance gave him a readiness to tackle intellectual challenges on their own merits. His openness to inquiry was itself an expression of his certainty in the value of his tradition.

AN UNUSUAL FIGURE

Gen Nyi-ma was from Ba, the same remote province where Gen Pe-ma Gyel-tsen was born.[17] Both men, who were friends, illustrated the intensity and dedication of scholars from Eastern Tibet. They were of the same age (born in the 1910s) and arrived around the same time at Dre-pung Lo-se-ling; there they studied with several teachers, including Gen Tom-pön, with whom Gen Nyi-ma developed a special connection. Both men were intensely respected, first as scholar-students and later as teachers. After becoming Geshes in their forties (in the early 1950s),[18] they spent the rest of their lives teaching, first in Tibet and after 1959 in exile. The similarities, however, stop here, for these two men were very different in character, career, and pedagogical style.

Whereas Gen Pe-ma Gyel-tsen was smooth and skillful in his relations with others, Gen Nyi-ma was rough and at first difficult to approach. My first encounter with him was in the early 1970s; I was then staying in the Nam-gyel monastery, where I had just started to learn debate. I met the person whom I would later call just *Gen-la* (revered teacher) one day in the debating courtyard of the Nam-gyel monastery, where he was staying in order to teach the Dalai Lama a Madhyamaka text. The courtyard was empty and he was talking with a monk official from the entourage of the Dalai Lama. He saw me and asked me whether I could speak Tibetan. When I answered positively (in the heavily understated way prescribed by Tibetan social conventions), he asked what I was studying. When I told him that I was just starting to learn debate, he immediately proceeded to debate me about the usual questions used to introduce Madhyamaka: "What is a window?" "Is the glass the window?" "Is the frame the window?" I tried to answer but quickly got stuck. Gen-la ended the debate, which was turning into a rout. He smiled and sought to assuage my feelings by praising me. "How intelligent you are! You know so many languages. I know only Tibetan," he said, turning to the monk official who gave a servile slurp as an answer. His words of praise hardly had the effect he might have wished for, however. I was seriously annoyed.

Gen-la's appearance also reflected his approach to life, which he devoted entirely to intellectual and religious pursuits rather than to superficial external refinements. He often showed little concern for personal grooming and paid little attention to his robes. Often his students had to clean him up. His eyes were his most striking feature, however. Because his eyelids could not stay open on their own, he had to hold a finger to the side of his right eye. This, combined with his shortsighted peering, gave him a wrathful appearance that was, to say the least, not very attractive. The unpleasant impression would be heightened when Gen-la read: as he kept his two eyelids open with his two hands, his big red eyes would bulge out. Students would often comment that it had taken them several weeks to get used to Gen-la's appearance and to be able to look at him.[19] But his influence on his students and their admiration for him were so strong that after some time students would completely forget their first impression. Some students would even go as far as to unconsciously mimic Gen-la, putting their hands by their eyes.

Gen Nyi-ma's career was also quite different from Gen Pe-ma Gyeltsen's successful tenure as abbot of Lo-se-ling. Gen-la knew himself to be politically inept and had never been interested in holding any monastic office. He had been appointed as abbot of Sha-kor *(shag skor)*, one of the monasteries that had originally made up Dre-pung but was later absorbed by Lo-se-ling. Hence, this appointment was purely honorary and involved no charge or duty whatsoever. One of his students described Gen-la's title quite aptly as making him "an abbot without any monks [under him]" *(grwa pa med pa'i mkhan po)*!

Gen Nyi-ma's approach was influenced by his main teacher, Gen Tom-pön, who was from De-ma in Kham. He was a renowned teacher, famous for his knowledge of Madhyamaka and for his outspokenness. He took part in a strident polemic among Ge-luk thinkers in the 1930s concerning a religious practice called "cutting" *(gcod)*.[20] The partisans of this practice, led by Geshe Dön-den *(don ldan)*, included a number of Pa-bong-ka's disciples. They argued that the three monastic seats should accept it as a normal part of their routine. Gen Tom-pön vigorously opposed them, believing that as monastic universities the seats should focus on the great texts of the tradition and not involve their monks in other practices.[21] There would be time, after they had trained their minds, to engage in systematic meditative practices. Gen Tom-pön is thought to have won the argument, but in doing so he antagonized many Ge-luk scholars, particularly Pa-bong-ka and his followers. As a result Gen Tom-pön was exiled to Beijing, where he became abbot of the imperial monastery. There he participated in the translation from Chinese of the *Mahavibhaśa-śāstra*, one of the main Abhidharmic commentaries that had not been available in Tibetan.

A SOCRATIC APPROACH IN THE GE-LUK TRADITION

What was most remarkable about Gen Nyi-ma was his approach. For him, the goal of studying the great texts was not just to learn a set of well-established positions. Truth cannot be imparted dogmatically but needs to be appropriated by each person individually. It cannot be captured immediately and certainly not in simple statements, but must be understood through a process of inquiry that involves a certain open-endedness.

This critical approach was reflected in Gen Nyi-ma's idiosyncratic pedagogy. I have already mentioned his disdain for monastic manuals *(yig cha)* and his preference for the great Indian texts of the tradition. But Gen-la was particularly passionate about questioning. Putting little stock in questions relating to manuals, he highly valued any inquiry concerning more fundamental texts. But his favorite questions were those, even the seemingly most stupid, that were based on personal reflection. For example, one day a student asked, "I understand the impermanence of my body; but what about the large stone in front of this house?" Gen-la was delighted. This is what he would call "a real doubt," in distinction to the kind of contrived questions raised by clever but superficial students.

In accordance with his predilection for questioning and contrary to most teachers, Gen-la rarely commented on a text or explained a point but proceeded almost entirely through debates. He would pick up a term in the text and would start to explore its meaning; as he sat, he snapped his debates to students who were in charge of answering. The class would continue only as long as his students were able to answer. Most of the time, Gen-la was able to shoot down any answer put forth by his students. This was no small achievement, for his teachings often attracted seasoned scholars. Sometimes, however, students were able to answer Gen-la quite well and even put him in jeopardy. On those rare occasions students would stop, slightly embarrassed, as soon as it had become clear that they had established their points. They would then defer to Gen-la's summary of the argument, but it was clear to everybody, Gen-la included, that they had won the argument.

Following Gen-la's classes was a treat for good scholars but quite difficult for those with minds less well prepared. Gen-la considered himself a poor teacher. He was fond of quoting a student who had told him, "Gen-la, when I come to see you I think I have some understanding of the topic. After your class, I am completely confused and have lost the little I knew!" Gen-la viewed his classes not as channels for imparting some truth but as means to further the inquiry. Hence, his teachings were thrilling for those who could follow them, for they had the impression—quite rightly—of being taken on a search for greater understanding by one of the best minds of their time. But the classes could be very difficult for those who had not yet gained the knowledge and experience required by his probing questions.

Scholars with ties to Dre-pung Lo-se-ling were unanimous in recognizing both Gen Pe-ma Gyel-tsen and Gen Nyi-ma as great scholars, but they disagreed on which they preferred. Some teachers particularly valued Gen Pe-ma Gyel-tsen's commentarial skills; I remember Lati Rin-po-che expressing enormous admiration for his textual learning. Others esteemed Gen Nyi-ma's dialectical skills more. At one point, the Dalai Lama asked me whom I considered the best teacher. Coming from a great teacher, this question put me in an embarrassing position. Who am I to tell the Dalai Lama who is better? I nevertheless found a tactful but truthful answer: "I do not really know, but as far as I am concerned nobody is above Gen Nyi-ma." The Dalai Lama seemed to agree with me; he himself had studied Madhyamaka philosophy with Gen-la and was impressed by his insight.

The value put on critical inquiry by a figure such as Gen Nyi-ma might seem surprising, especially given the role of faith in scholasticism, as explained in chapter 8. Inquiry presupposes doubts and thus is apparently antithetical to the certainty that faith implies. How can Gen Nyi-ma be constantly raising doubts while at the same time entertaining a strong conviction in the validity of his tradition? An adequate answer to this question would require us to examine the nature of faith in general and its place in the Buddhist tradition, large topics that are well beyond the purview of this work. For the time being, I will simply emphasize that faith and doubt are not polar opposites but are involved in a complex relation. The opposite of doubt is belief: either I believe a proposition I am entertaining or I doubt it (provided I do not reject it entirely). Faith, however, is different. Perhaps a convenient way to articulate the relation of these three elements is to say that at its best, faith is the result of the dialectic of belief and doubt.[22] Faith presupposes conviction in the validity of the tradition, but it is not limited to belief. In particular, it cannot be reduced to an endless literal repetition of the truths handed down by the tradition. Rather it is conviction that the validity of the tradition requires and bears further exploration.

Tibetan scholastic training starts with some belief in the validity of the tradition, some commitment to the inquiry; otherwise, students would not put up with the considerable hardships that this training sometimes entails. It continues with interpretive practices—commentary and debate—that seek to deepen this confidence. To that end, students question the tradition in order to reach their own conclusions. In doing so, they suspend judgment concerning the questions they investigate until they develop a firm conviction. They may reach opposing conclusions, and they may not follow the tradition on certain points. But as long as they are convinced of the validity of the tradition, they remain within its orbit and can gradually deepen their understanding.

Inasmuch as it is genuine, this process is not risk-free. In raising doubts, the scholar opens himself to the possibility of coming to an understanding not consonant with the tradition. Often such multiplicity does not matter very much, for traditions are rich enough to accommodate a variety of views. But if his understanding diverges too far from the dominant interpretations, the scholar may have to renounce his allegiance and leave the tradition, as Ge-dün Chö-pel did (see chapter 14). Fearing this outcome, scholastic authorities rein in scholars when they are seen to be on a collision course with the tradition's orthodoxy. Unlike modern academic scholarship, scholastic investigation finds it difficult to seriously question its bases: its field of inquiry has boundaries.

Gen-la understood and valued intellectual complexities, realizing that the Indian sources of the tradition have a diversity of views not easily exhausted by any party line.[23] He also emphasized the deconstructive dimension of inquiry—the central insight of the Madhyamaka tradition, that reality is essenceless and hence no distinction can be completely consistently maintained. Yet he was quite aware of the potential risks of his approach. No relativist or nihilist, he held that the ability of the mind to undermine concepts must be at some point restricted. One day, he told me: "The inquiry has by itself no limit. One must decide for oneself what the limits are. For me, the limits are determined by Dzong-ka-ba and his direct disciples." This statement was obviously an invitation—but it was also an admission that "reasonable people" (here teacher and student) could disagree, since there is no intrinsic essential property that can separate conflicting approaches. The point is not that no distinction can be made, but that such distinctions are fragile and that to remain within the circle of acceptable views one must recognize that fragility. I remember answering by mumbling something about the importance of the great Indian texts.

As soon as I started to study with Gen Nyi-ma in 1977, I knew that I had found what I had hoped for. His emphasis on taking the study of the great texts as support for inquiry appealed to me enormously. Gradually I became quite close to Gen-la and felt that I shared with him a profound bond that was obvious to other monks. Some followers of other teachers were even slightly offended by my obvious preference for Gen-la. I had had so many teachers; why did I need to be so partial to one? But though I always remained appreciative of other teachers, Gen-la was clearly the major influence in my life. Gen-la appreciated my interest in his approach, but he also knew I was a part of a world that had only minimally impinged on his own and hence in some sense was quite different from his Tibetan disciples.

I still remember with profound emotion our last meeting, when both the bond that we felt for each other and our differences were clear. I had finished my Geshe exam and I was about to start my Ph.D. at an American university. Gen-la was by then in his mid-seventies, already a ripe age for a traditional Tibetan. It was evening, the weather was mild, and we were seated outside, Gen-la on a chair and me at his feet on a cushion that his attendant had laid out. We knew that this would be our final meeting and that we would not see each other again. I do not remember what we talked about but I recall that Gen-la did not attempt to give me advice. Unlike other teachers, who would often impart advice (some of which was excellent), Gen-la felt that he had nothing to add. His advice was his teachings, the principle and the practice of inquiry. It was up to me now to use what he had tried to impart.

The reasons for my preference for Gen Nyi-ma are not difficult to find; they have to do with my own background. Because I had been raised in an intellectual family, I found myself at ease with an approach based on realizing the complexities of the tradition. My response had little to do with my being a Westerner, however. Other Western students found his approach to Buddhism much less appealing. Some thought that it was a distraction from more essentially religious concerns such as meditation.[24] Others became profoundly uncomfortable: they wanted certainties and were not ready to question fundamental concepts. One could even say that many Western Buddhists seem particularly lacking in their abilities to reflect on and problematize the basic concepts of their newly adopted tradition. Terms such as *wisdom, path,* and *enlightenment* are used as if their referents were perfectly self-evident. I particularly remember a Western friend of mine who would often question me about points of Buddhist doctrine. At first, I would answer him by laying out the different opinions and the subjects of debate, but he would respond impatiently, "I am not asking for a list of possible opinions, I am asking for an answer." I would then have to choose, more or less arbitrarily, what seemed to be the most appropriate answer and give it to him as *the* answer, keeping to myself the realization that this was just one interpretation among many. The ability to tolerate complexities is certainly not a Western birthright.

MADHYAMAKA WITHIN THE GE-LUK TRADITION

The existence of a diversity of approaches within the Ge-luk tradition is not in itself surprising, given the large number of its members; indeed, uniformity would be astonishing. As the Tibetan proverb says, "Each area has its guru and each guru has its own dharma." This diversity has been greatly limited by the sociopolitical considerations briefly touched on in chapter 1. Such limits are particularly evident in the Ge-luk school, which adopted the teachings of Dzong-ka-ba as they had been interpreted by his disciples— Gyel-tsap, Kay-drup, and the authors of the monastic manuals. Their views have come to define a strict orthodoxy within the tradition that is all the more severe in that their works spell out positions quite explicitly. Hence, there is a remarkable doctrinal agreement within the Ge-luk school and philosophical differences are rather small.

This doctrinal unanimity does not prevent diversity. Debate trains the mind to make subtle distinctions, enabling scholars to find room for expressing different views within the constraints of orthodoxy. Moreover, Ge-luk scholars often disagree on how Dzong-ka-ba's ideas are to be implemented. This is particularly true in the realm of Madhyamaka, an abstruse subject that lends itself to subtle differences, slippages, and unnoticed confusions. In what follows I discuss Madhyamaka philosophy, particularly in relation to Gen Nyi-ma's approach, to show how despite significant differences, Dzong-ka-ba's interpretation of Madhyamaka embodies the deconstructive approach described in chapter 11. I will also justify my claim that at its best, debate represents a deconstructive strategy.

We will begin with a claim encountered in the last chapter: that Madhyamaka is not amenable to the descriptive method of classical philosophy. Because ultimate reality is beyond description and thus cannot be grasped, a deconstructive approach is necessary. But throughout the history of Madhyamaka, scholars have disagreed over the extent to which Madhyamaka should be limited to this deconstructive approach and should exclude systematic thinking.

In India, Bhavya and Candrakīrti argued about the best way to understand emptiness. Believing that one can approach though not capture emptiness through the classical tools of Indian logic, Bhavya supported the use of arguments (*prayoga, sbyor ba*) to establish emptiness provisionally. In his view, Madhyamaka is ultimately deconstructive yet offers ample room for systematic philosophical discussion. Candrakīrti rejected this approach even provisionally, finding it antithetical to the Madhyamaka deconstructive standpoint. Classical logical tools are inappropriate to the task of awakening students to the Madhyamaka insight.[25] Usual philosophical categories such as ontology and epistemology are part of the problem, not the solution.

Related disagreements exist in Tibet, though they do not map onto the so-called Svātantrika-Prāsaṅgika distinction, a very muddled subject that I plan to explore in a separate work.[26] Particularly relevant here is the view of Dzong-ka-ba and his tradition, which differs from Indian Madhyamaka in several respects. One of Dzong-ka-ba's innovations is in applying to Prāsaṅgika a systematic and consistent framework based on a realist interpretation of Buddhist epistemology.[27] In his approach, the ineffability of the ultimate is weakened and the gap between the two truths bridged. Emptiness is described philosophically, though not with full semantic adequacy, and integrated into a larger philosophical structure. In this way, Dzong-ka-ba removes the paradoxical element from Madhyamaka and creates an impressive clarity, which other interpretations often lack (though his approach has its own internal tensions).

In the context of Madhyamaka, Dzong-ka-ba's realism manifests itself in an insistence on the laws of logic in the context of the ultimate. That is, he insists not only that thinking must follow the laws of logic while investigating the ultimate, a point on which there is little disagreement, but also that its conclusions must conform to the laws of logic. This issue is central to the Madhyamaka approach. Consider, for example, the famous fourfold schema: things are not existent, or nonexistent, or both existent and nonexistent, or neither existent nor nonexistent.[28] This formulation seems at first highly paradoxical—a flagrant contradiction of the law of the excluded middle, which states that for any x, if x is not a, then it is non-a. How then can something be neither existent nor nonexistent?

At this point, Dzong-ka-ba and such critics as Śākya Chok-den part company. The latter holds that the very purpose of the tetralemmic formulation is to undo the mind's habit of holding onto objects and to establish a new, self-undermining way of thinking. Madhyamaka reasoning follows the laws of logic not to produce some coherent philosophical conclusion but to oblige the mind to abandon its compulsion to reify. This therapeutic release is a first step toward a cure. The adequate answer to the question "How can something be neither existent nor nonexistent?" is not a positive assertion but a letting go of the habit of thinking in terms of a something. There is no thing that can be neither existent nor nonexistent, and understanding this truth is precisely the point of the whole enterprise.[29]

As a realist, Dzong-ka-ba disagrees with this formulation, which he holds to be inconsistent. It can only lead to confusion, a belief one is thinking something when in fact one has descended into an incoherence hidden by protective but meaningless verbal quibbles. For Dzong-ka-ba, tetralemmic negations cannot be taken literally: they are to be interpreted as being modified by a modal operator, so that what is being negated is not the object itself but the tropic component.[30] This is the putative "object of negation" *(dgag bya)*, which is designated by a variety of terms, including "ultimate existence" *(don dam par yod pa)*, "real existence" *(bden par grub pa)*, and "intrinsic existence" *(rang bzhin gis grub pa)*, and is the target of Madhyamaka reasonings. The statement that things do not exist is then understood to mean that they do not exist ultimately *(don dam par)* or inherently *(rang bzhin gyis)*. Reality can thus be understood through conceptual schemes that follow the classical canons of rationality.

Yet Dzong-ka-ba goes further. Earlier Madhyamaka thinkers such as Bhavya had used modal operators to limit the paradoxical nature of Madhyamaka, but their domestication of Madhyamaka deconstruction had not gone very far, for they never attempted to bridge the radical gap between the two truths—as does Dzong-ka-ba in a move that seems to be entirely original within the history of Madhyamaka. The "identification of the object of negation" *(dgag bya ngos 'dzin)*,[31] which is at the core of his Madhyamaka interpretation, is described as the prerequisite for understanding emptiness. The putative object of negation is the tropic component, determined by a modal operator such as *intrinsic existence*. Thus Madhyamaka deconstruction does not concern existence proper. Things do not exist ultimately, as Nāgārjuna's deconstructive reasonings demonstrate, but they do exist conventionally (and therefore can be said to exist). Madhyamaka reasonings do not affect the existence of phenomena, including emptiness, that can be understood according to the canons of rationality presupposed by a moderate realist interpretation of Buddhist epistemology. Essencelessness can then be integrated within a global account in which reality can be described coherently, without any conflict between the two truths. This account also strengthens the validity of the conventional realm, which gains a kind of existence (albeit only conventional).

The crucial identification of the object of negation is not as straightforward as the brief sketch above might suggest. Though it is necessary to understand emptiness, Dzong-ka-ba also recognizes that such an identification is problematic until one has realized emptiness. It presupposes the separation of two approaches to conceptualizing things: the conventional mode, in which things exist as objects of mostly linguistically embedded practices, and the ultimate mode, in which things exist intrinsically (and therefore can be the object of negation). Yet to distinguish these two modes, one must have already realized emptiness and become able to see the second mode as deceptive and the first one as valid; until then, they remain confused. Thus, Dzong-ka-ba's approach seems to be beset by a circularity of which the tradition is well aware. The generally agreed-on solution is to take the identification of the object of negation prior to realizing emptiness as being only provisional—that is, something one can understand only approximately. In terms of Ge-luk epistemology, only after realizing emptiness can an individual understand fully the difference between the conventionally existing object and its nonexistent reified essence; until then, the object of negation is identified not by valid cognition but by correct assumption *(yid dpyod)*. Such a solution introduces further difficulties. At the very least, it constitutes a sleight of hand that hides the radical difference between the two truths. Emptiness can be called "describable" in the Madhyamaka system only by making its description a unique sort; no other phenomena are described provisionally, contingent on the realization of emptiness.

Given this difficulty in Dzong-ka-ba, the range of approaches among Ge-luk thinkers is not surprising. In particular, they differ on the role of the identification of the object of negation, though all understand that such an identification is necessary and can only be provisional. Teachers in Pa-bong-ka's lineage, such as Geshe Rab-ten, stress meditative experience. The task of identifying the object of negation is not discursive but experiential, as one observes how the mind grasps objects (particularly oneself) as having intrinsic existence. This mindful process can be greatly helped by introspective exercises during which one imagines oneself to be under great emotional duress, a situation in which the self-grasping tendency becomes obvious and easier to identify. The putative object of negation—the object grasped by ignorance—is thereby identified provisionally by the meditator and can be taken as the target of deconstructive Madhyamaka reasonings, which monks have learned during their studies.

This approach, which is advocated by Pa-bong-ka in his text on the Gradual Path, insists on the importance of meditation and limits the role of conceptual inquiry. In discussing Candrakīrti's refutation of the self, Pa-bong-ka makes clear the limited role that he sees for debate: "You could use these words in debate and they would serve to silence your opponent, but you have not identified the object of refutation until you have determined it through experience. . . . You must recognize the object of refutation through vivid, naked, personal mental experiences brought on by an analytic process."[32] The preliminary experiential determination of the object of negation is necessary to avoid the danger of erroneously negating the conventional existence of things.

By ensuring that conventional existence is not affected by the deconstructive strategy, this approach risks completely separating emptiness and conventional existence. The Madhyamaka reasonings are then taken to apply only to a constructed and hence irrelevant object of negation. Ge-luk teachers are quite aware of the danger of creating an artificial *(blos byas)* emptiness that has no relation with reality.[33] Geshe Rab-ten often warned students against this error; he used to speak ironically of the difficulty of Madhyamaka, a philosophy in which one is never sure whether one's method is a part of the solution or a part of the problem.

GEN NYI-MA'S APPROACH TO MADHYAMAKA

Although Gen Nyi-ma never explicitly rejected the emphasis on introspection, several of his more outspoken students did. One of his more advanced students explained to me privately that reliance on the experiential identification of the putative object of negation presupposes an immediacy that is not available, given that such an identification can be made only after one has realized emptiness. I was rather taken aback by this statement, for at that time I (like many teachers) accepted Pa-bong-ka's approach as authoritative. I later came to recognize its problems.

Gen Nyi-ma was considered by other Ge-luk scholars to be a Madhyamaka expert, and his approach differed from most others in several ways. Textually, Gen-la focused on Nāgārjuna's *Treatise* instead of Candrakīrti's *Introduction*. In fact, Gen Nyi-ma's Madhyamaka teachings were often little more than dialectical demonstrations of Nāgārjuna's approach in the *Treatise*. Pedagogically, Gen-la differed in that he did not provide a complete gloss of the text but just focused on important passages. Once the key passages had been analyzed in depth, students were supposed to be able to tackle the rest of the text on their own. Needless to say, an authoritative transmission *(lung)* was out of the question. Philosophically, Gen-la took an unusual approach to the identification of the object of negation. Instead of proceeding introspectively, Gen-la would insist on a more classical deconstructive approach. A few words about his strategy will demonstrate the degree to which Madhyamaka in all versions, including Dzong-ka-ba's, is deconstructive and how debate embodies this philosophy.

For Gen-la, the preliminary to any further inquiry was a relentless taking apart of things. Such an undermining of concepts implies not that they had no bearing at all on reality but that things do not have any essence that can be pinned down. Hence, they do not exist ultimately or intrinsically. Yet phenomena do exist, because they function when one uses them linguistically. As Dzong-ka-ba claimed, their essencelessness does not contradict their existence..

Such an approach stays quite close to classical Madhyamaka formulations while drawing on Dzong-ka-ba's object of negation. But unlike some other Ge-luk thinkers, Gen-la did not insulate conventional existence from

Madhyamaka reasonings. The object of negation is taken not as an observable entity, a kind of fixed target, but as the guardrail that prevents the undermining of essentialization from degenerating into nihilism, which is nothing but an essentialization of negation. The student is thus taken along the Middle Way, between the extremes of reification (eternalism) and negation (nihilism). This middle ground cannot be seized once and for all, however; it needs to be approached by a constant self-corrective oscillation, which undermines positive as well as negative answers. In this way, the mind, prevented from locking itself into any one stance, is pushed into a new dimension of openness.

Gen-la would start the process by pointing to some common object. When I studied with him, the example was a buffalo. Gen-la asked, "What is the buffalo?" "Are the legs the buffalo?" "Is the head the buffalo?" "Are the horns the buffalo?" As readers may remember, Gen-la had tried the same kind of annoying interrogation on me when I had first met him. But now I was prepared to cope with the questions and I understood the point of the exercise: the undoing of any attempt to pin down the concept by which the object could be identified. No part of the buffalo can be taken as corresponding to the concept of the animal. Even the sum total of the parts is not the buffalo, for the animal is never perceived in its totality: to identify it, one need not identify all its components.

After shooting down all positive answers, Gen-la would insist that the failure to define the buffalo does not mean that it does not exist. The buffalo exists; otherwise, how could one be injured by its horns? Nobody has ever been injured by the horns of a rabbit! Hence, the negative nihilist extreme will not do. To understand the buffalo, Gen-la would introduce the notion of conventional existence. The buffalo exists conventionally, not ultimately. That is, the buffalo exists as the object of effective linguistically embedded practices, which are sufficient to guarantee its existence. We can point to the buffalo and effectively use the concept of the buffalo, but we cannot go beyond this practice. In particular, we cannot grasp the buffalo as if it were more than an object of linguistic designation. Whenever we try to do so, we lose contact with our practices and become trapped by our illusory constructions. And yet, we constantly make the attempt.

This explanation of the notion of conventional existence was important and unusual for Gen-la. Only rarely did he offer students a positive explanation to give them some insight into the notion of conventional existence. Those who understood would be able to follow later teachings without getting lost, entering a deconstructive movement guided by the view that things can exist as objects of conventional practices although they do not exist ultimately. This guidance was not the final answer, but it enabled students to avoid the two pitfalls of the Madhyamaka: the reification of concepts or their total rejection. Gen-la thus led his students on the Middle Way, accepting no view as absolute and keeping the pragmatic dimension of the inquiry in sight.

Once Gen-la had introduced students to the notion of conventional existence and drawn their attention to the putative object of negation, his explanations would stop and he would revert to his favorite strategy, debate. He taught the first chapter of Nāgārjuna's text by debating students along the lines of inquiry set by the work. Rather than explain each stanza, he would ask such questions as "When an effect is produced, is it produced from an existing cause or from a nonexisting cause?" As students tried to answer, each of their responses would be shot down. An effect cannot be produced from causes existing at the time of its production, for causes and effects cannot coexist; yet an effect cannot be produced by completely nonexistent causes. How then is an effect produced?

In Gen-la's teaching, no answer—especially the presumably correct one—was allowed to stand as final. Some students might confidently reply, "An effect is produced by causes only conventionally, and hence the question is inapplicable." This answer is theoretically right, especially in the Ge-luk perspective, which strongly emphasizes the validity of the conventional. But Gen-la would continue the inquiry: "How can we then know that a phenomenon causes another one? Is any kind of inquiry into what is a cause impossible?" It is this method of questioning—the insistence on pushing students forward in their inquiry and the refusal to settle on any answer as "correct"—that is, I believe, usefully characterized as *deconstructive*.

Such a method is based on a readiness to keep the inquiry going and a refusal to limit the scope of investigation by appealing to a party line. It recognizes that one of the great dangers in Dzong-ka-ba's approach is that students tend to fall back on ready-made answers that allow them to close their minds. Instead of questioning concepts, students get stuck in answers such as "Things are not produced ultimately but only conventionally." Although such answers are orthodox from a Ge-luk doctrinal standpoint, they can lull students into a false sense of understanding. Good teachers are keenly aware of this pitfall but deal with it differently. Geshe Rab-ten would urge his students to internalize the search, moving from text and doctrine to meditative experience. Gen Nyi-ma would use debate as a way to undermine students' attempts to stop the investigation and fasten on any one answer, especially the traditional one. In this way, he was illustrating the full potential of the practice as a mode of inquiry, not just a useful pedagogical tool.

It is not inappropriate to speak of a wisdom acquired through the practice of debate. Because it is developed by thinking, it corresponds to the second among the three acumens (the other two being the wisdoms developed from hearing and from meditating; see chapter 8). It merely prefigures the ultimate wisdom, which brings about a lasting transformation after one has directly experienced the nature of reality. The understanding developed through debate involves the more limited conceptual ability to recognize the values and limits of ideas. When one realizes that any idea can be shot down, the temptation is to adopt either a relativist stance toward all ideas, viewing them as equally ungrounded, or to reject the realm of thought entirely, viewing it as hopelessly confused. Both positions are immature, for they fail to take into consideration our ongoing involvement in thoughts and ideas—we cannot ignore them. Thus, we need to deal with them, though we need to be cognizant of their limitations. Debate develops the ability to explore ideas and take a stance while keeping in mind the fragility and uncertainty of those ideas. This wisdom, which Gen Nyi-ma incarnated to the highest degree, is not opposed to a life of the mind.[34] Only long intellectual training can lead us to realize that the questions raised by debate are worth thinking about not because they bring final clarity but because they oblige us to grow by relinquishing our tendency to cling to ideas.

A TRADITIONAL INTELLECTUAL

While the thought of Gen Nyi-ma was in many ways close to certain contemporary philosophical approaches,[35] he was also in many ways quite different from modern intellectuals. As a conclusion to this hagiographic chapter whose tone is meant to convey a disciple's attitude toward his teacher, I will touch on those differences.

Gen-la saw no discrepancy between his hypercritical intellectual approach and a worldview that assumes a number of things that seem impossible to modern minds. Like other Tibetans, Gen-la experienced the world as alive, peopled by a variety of entities whose existence was as self-evident as that of humans and animals. Anne Klein recalls that when a group of Tibetan monks came to perform sacred dances at Rice University, a professor asked the monks who normally watched such performances in Tibet. The response was immediate: "Do you mean the human or the nonhuman audiences?"[36] Gen Nyi-ma shared that traditional worldview.

One of my friends at the Buddhist School of Dialectics would sometimes enter into a possessed state. His voice would change and he would start to scold his fellow students, accusing them of being slack in their studies, insufficiently respectful of their precepts, and so on. One day, Gen Nyi-ma happened to be at the school when my friend entered such a state, and he was called in. Gen-la was well acquainted with this type of phenomenon and knew immediately what to do: he tied all the fingers of my friend's hand and started to squeeze his head. The goal was to literally squeeze out the spirit who had taken hold of my friend (I guess spirits cannot leave through the feet) and force it to promise not to come back. Gen-la succeeded and the cure seemed to work; for the several years I stayed at the school, my friend was not possessed again.

I never asked Gen Nyi-ma whether he believed that the world was round or, as stated in the Abhidharma, flat.[37] He never talked about the subject, and my sense is that he was perhaps amenable to the scientific view. Several of my teachers were certainly not so flexible. I remember a particularly painful exchange with Lati Rin-po-che on this topic. Rin-po-che was teaching me Abhidharma in preparation for my Geshe exam. He thought it was about time to set me straight and started a debate on the shape of the earth, presenting the kind of arguments I had given my father as a child (e.g., "If the earth is round, why do those that are under not fall?"). I was horrified and humiliated (it felt like being back in kindergarten), but Rin-po-che would not desist and continued his debate. His persistence in turn annoyed me more. Finally I just could not take it anymore and I stopped the proceedings, declaring them a complete waste of time. Needless to say, Rin-po-che was shocked by this total breach of the teacher-student relationship. A student may be free to disagree but certainly is not the person in charge of deciding what should be discussed. Gen Nyi-ma would probably have been less adamant on the subject; he understood that I was coming from a different world. Perhaps his small but real exposure to modern Chinese culture as a child and as a member of the Dalai Lama's party during a visit to China in 1955 had prepared him for one of the possibilities opened by science. But such encounters never undermined his confidence in his worldview.

As a consequence of his worldview, Gen-la felt completely at ease in tantric practice. He had spent some time in the Tantric Monastery of Lower Lhasa *(rgyud smad)* and was an expert in both the theory and practice of tantra. As the anecdote about dispelling the possessing spirit illustrates, Gen-la was an accomplished ritualist. Nothing about him of the Protestant Buddhist uncomfortable with rituals! Though himself an intellectual, he never saw any conflict between reason and the aspects of religious practice with which modern intellectuals are often uncomfortable. He was also an accomplished tantric teacher. He would conduct his tantric classes much like classes on exoteric topics—that is, mostly through debates. Only the topic differed. Gen-la would apply the same critical and caustic spirit to a discussion of the number of deities contained in the mandala of Yamāntaka, one of the main meditative deities in the Ge-luk tradition, as to an analysis of the fine points of Nāgārjuna's philosophy.

Philosophically, Gen-la was a traditional Buddhist thinker, and as such he held the classical Indian view of cyclic existence. The existence of past and future lives was, for him, as obvious as their nonexistence is for most Westerners. There was nothing symbolic about this belief in rebirth, which he could support with several arguments (mostly based on the processual and dynamic nature of the mind). He was also convinced, on similar grounds, that human limitations can be transcended, that we can free ourselves from suffering and even reach complete omniscience.

His beliefs should not be oversimplified, however. In fact, they were anything but simple. Gen-la held many of the ideas that dominated twentieth-century philosophy concerning the limitations imposed on us by language and conceptual schemes. He understood that our experience of the world is not immediate and that language has a vital role in constructing that experience; but he held that such limitations are not intrinsic to the human mind, which can reach an undistorted view of reality. Klein explains this key distinction well: "Thus, although Buddhist and contemporary Western intellectual traditions share a general emphasis on the constructed nature of experience as well as an acute awareness of the limitations intrinsic to language and other conventions, they seem to reach diametrically opposite conclusions regarding the possibility of an unmediated, complete, universally available and objective perception, at least within their different understandings of the term."[38] As Klein herself notes, to attain a nonconceptual and nondistorted view of reality is a complex matter, not an attempt to hark back to some prelapsarian purity lost through excessive intellectualization. Yet despite showing some striking affinities with (post)modern ideas, a traditional Buddhist thinker takes a very different stance in trying to attain that view.

Part 3

REFLECTIONS

13   Rationality and Spirit Cult

In the preceding chapters, we examined in detail the educational practices of Tibetan monasticism. It is now time to stand back and reflect on the significance of those practices, focusing on two areas. This chapter considers the conception of rationality that Tibetan scholasticism presupposes, particularly in its relation to some of the practices associated with folk religion. Because scholastic rationality is a large topic, I cannot avoid overgeneralizations in this brief heuristic exploration, which I hope will highlight some of the differences between traditional and modern conceptions of rationality. This important topic is one of the most misunderstood aspects of Buddhism, which is too often misrepresented as scientific. The following chapter more narrowly examines the limits of the system of inquiry described here and the relation of inquiry and orthodoxy.

A DIFFERENT RATIONALITY?

My general focus on dialectical practices underlines the importance of rationality in traditional Tibetan education. But this emphasis must be put in perspective if we are to avoid the danger of misunderstanding the role of reason within Tibetan monastic education, as Tibetan scholars are made to look too much like modern intellectuals.

In certain respects this comparison is not unjustified, as traditional and modern intellectuals engage in similar activities supported by similar kinds of reasoning. A figure such as Gen Nyi-ma seems close to us intellectually, with an interpretation of Madhyamaka that resembles some contemporary philosophical views. Some readers may suspect that I have overemphasized the similarities and neglected the differences, and there is truth to that accusation. However, it is important for me to communicate the closeness that I felt with my teachers and the commonality I experienced with the Tibetan monks with whom I lived.

As we analyze some of the particular features of the model of rational inquiry presupposed by Tibetan scholastic traditions, it may be useful to briefly consider what is meant by *rationality*. For one thing, such a term is loaded: its application is often more normative than descriptive. To call any action, belief, or desire rational implies that we ought to have chosen it. Yet there is no consensus on what the term means. Different actions and beliefs are taken to be rational, and it is not clear whether what is rational is required or merely allowed. Nor does understanding the term descriptively reduce the disagreement. Rationality is sometimes attributed to actions and their relation to the goals that they seek to achieve.[1] At other times, rationality is discussed abstractly, apart from any action. Theoretical rationality is the object of reflection by intellectuals who seek consistency in the ideals of their tradition. As Max Weber observes, it rests on the "metaphysical needs of the human mind as it is driven to reflect on ethical and religious questions, driven not by material need but by an inner compulsion to understand the world as a meaningful cosmos and take a position toward it."[2] This is the aspect of rationality that most concerns us here.

It is no easier to establish minimal standards for theoretical rationality than for rationality in general. Some argue that following the laws of logic is its necessary and sufficient condition. More important, however, are the use of reasoning and the assessment of evidence. This understanding of theoretical rationality as the ability to evaluate reasoning and to support one's point by providing evidence is directly relevant to Tibetan practices. Although no Tibetan word translates exactly as "reason" or "rationality," the closest equivalent is *rigs pa*. This term—derived from the word *rigs*, "to fit," "to be appropriate"—means "reasoning." In the Tibetan scholastic tradition, a reasonable person bases his or her judgments on the assessment of the reasoning that supports it. This view of rationality is also central to the Western tradition. Plato characterizes reason as the capacity to understand on the basis of evidence. To grasp by reason is to be able to give reasons, to give an account that supports one's standpoint.[3]

The ability to give and evaluate arguments in accordance with the laws of logic is at the heart of Tibetan scholasticism. While the Tibetan reliance on logic, particularly in debate, is shared with Western classical and modern thinkers, important differences remain between modern and traditional views of rationality. In this chapter I sketch out some of these differences, focusing on how rationality functions within Tibetan scholastic culture. I examine the relation between scholastic rationality and rituals, particularly those that bear on folk practices. I focus on the practice of protectors, showing the role that rationality plays in a dispute that arose over this practice in recent years.

The differences between Tibetan monastic and modern educations have little to do with any East-West divide and much to do with scholastic traditions. For example, the dialectical emphasis of Ge-luk education strongly resembles that of the medieval European universities. Similarly, the spirit cult I describe here has parallels in other traditional cultures, though its details may be specific to Tibet.

RATIONALITY AND POPULAR PRACTICES

Besides the elite practices examined here, Tibetans both before and after exile engaged in a variety of folk practices such as exorcism, divination, healing, retrieving of life force, worship of mountain and lake deities, cults of house gods, and the like.[4] Although not directly part of the scholastic curriculum, some of these practices figure in various ways in the scholastic experience. They provide an important background for Tibetan scholasticism and affect the ways in which Tibetan scholars see the world, which do not always faithfully mirror the normative Buddhist views they encounter in their formal education. For example, Buddhism teaches that people are selfless combinations of aggregates *(phung po, skandha)* driven by the forces of karma. But scholars' understanding of the concept of person cannot be reduced to this philosophical view. For them, people also possess a spirit force *(bla)* that keeps them alive, a force located in an individual's body as well as in trees and places that have particular significance for that person.[5] If it wanders away after being frightened or is removed forcibly by one of the many invisible entities that inhabit the Tibetan universe, the person will fall sick and eventually die unless a ritual of spirit force retrieving *(bla bkug)* or spirit force repurchasing *(bla bslu)* is performed.[6]

The concept of spirit force is a significant feature of the Tibetan cultural understanding of the person, for it underpins the nature of the traditional Tibetan universe. Perhaps the most salient characteristic of this universe is that it is alive with a multitude of invisible but real entities, including ghosts, local spirits, mountain and lake gods, snake spirits, and so on. As Locho Rim-bo-che declares, "In Tibet we accept many things that cannot be seen by the eye; the West does not accept many unseen things. This is the kind of difference there is."[7] Traditional Tibetans have a deeply ingrained feeling that natural entities such as trees, ponds, lakes, and mountains are endowed with life forces, a profound belief that they hold to be self-evident. One day a friend from the Buddhist School of Dialectics confided in me: "We see the universe quite differently. For me, things are not just dead bodies moving mechanically. The universe is alive with forces which I cannot comprehend but which I can tap into, especially in my dreams. When I am waiting for something to happen I pray to the protectors before going to sleep. Usually I awaken the next day having had an omen, which turns out to be accurate most of the time." This friend, a monk born in the 1950s in Tibet but educated in India in both modern and traditional ways, was careful in his statement and slightly coy about it, knowing that as a Westerner I would probably be skeptical. Nevertheless, he did not show the kind of doubt that would accompany a description of traditional cosmology, which he knows has been rendered obsolete by science. The experience of the world as being alive is of another order. It is not empirical and hence is beyond the reach of any factual refutation.[8]

Living in such a universe is not always pleasant. One has to make sure that one is not infringing on any of the disquieting figures that people the landscape. Fortunately, there are also positive forces, the gods belonging to the white side *(bkar phyogs kyi lha)*, who offer protection from these dangers. These include the gods of the traditional Indian Buddhist universe, such as Brahma *(tshang pa)*, as well as the more properly Tibetan regional mountain and lake gods, who help the people who are devoted to them. This devotion is shown during annual festivals and in daily rituals. Prayers are made, incense is burned, and prayer flags are offered regularly. Local gods also help defend against such dangers as war, the arrival of bandits, and the like. To Tibetans, one of the most disturbing aspects of the Chinese invasion is the inability of their gods to protect them. Even now, many believe that the gods of Tibet *(bod kyi lha)* had the power to crush Chinese armies but chose not to exercise it.[9]

All of these gods are mundane *('jig rten pa'i lha)*. Despite their powers, they remain prisoners of the realm of cyclic existence. They thus differ profoundly from the tantric deities, who are enlightened and hence beyond the limitations of the world. This distinction between mundane and supramundane deities *('jig rten las 'das pa'i lha)* is very important in Tibetan culture, but also quite problematic. As Buddhists, Tibetans are supposed to take refuge only in the Triple Gem—namely, Buddha (the teacher, compared to a wise doctor), the Dharma (his teaching, compared to medicine), and the Sangha (the community of realized practitioners).[10] They therefore cannot entrust their spiritual welfare to these worldly deities, though they may propitiate them, asking for help and protection.

THE ROLE OF PROTECTIVE DEITIES

The key distinction between mundane and supramundane deities affects a set of practices that are particularly important to Tibetan Buddhists, the propitiation of the dharma protectors *(chos skyong, dharmapāla)*. Protectors are gods from whom Buddhist practitioners can request protection and help. Some are supramundane, such as Six-Armed Mahākāla *(dgon po phyag drug)* and the Great Goddess *(dpal-ldan lha mo,* pronounced "belden-lha-mo"; the Tibetan equivalent of *Mahā-devī)*. Because they are beyond the concerns of this world, their worship creates no difficulties. But because their distance from the world also makes their protection weak, people often rely on the more problematic but more potent and closer mundane protectors. These violent spirits have taken an oath, often under the constraint of a great tantric adept such as Padmasambhava, to protect the Buddhist teaching.[11] Despite this commitment, they are not completely tamed and are prone to quasi-human emotions such as anger, jealousy, and so forth. Hence, they are partial and can be enlisted in morally unseemly actions such as helping practitioners to secure worldly advantages or even killing an adversary. Because the practices of these deities are in tension with normative Buddhist ideals, they can only be propitiated, not worshiped. Hence, they are never explicitly studied by scholars, though they play an important role in monastic life.

To these deities (mundane and supramundane) the monks, individually or collectively, turn for help and support. When Gen Lob-zang Gya-tso enters the Pu-kang regional house of Dre-pung Lo-se-ling, his first act is to prostrate himself to the Great Goddess, the protector of the house. She is there for him in time of crisis. When the house asks him to work as a grain collector, it is the Great Goddess who appears in his dream and persuades him to accept this particularly distasteful task.[12] This reliance on protectors makes perfect sense, given the traditional conception of the universe as alive with invisible entities. In such a universe, protection from the unseen is important.

Protectors also figure prominently in the life of monasteries, where they serve as focal points of collective identity. Each school, monastery, regional house, local group, or family has its own protectors, often a combination of mundane and supramundane deities. For example, the monastic seat of Dre-pung has as its own protectors the Great Goddess and Pe-har, the deity appointed by Pamasaṃbhava as the main guardian of Buddhism in Tibet. But each monastery in Dre-pung also has its own protector. Go-mang relies mostly on Lion-Faced Dakini *(mkha' 'gro seng ge'i gdong pa can)* and Six-Armed Mahākāla, whereas Lo-se-ling relies on several Female Protectors of the Doctrine *(bstan ma)*.[13] The importance of this relationship becomes clear if one remembers that the deities who are protectors are defined as such because they protect the person or the group, often by violent means, from enemies. These "enemies of Buddhism" *(bstan dgra)* are the "Other" in opposition to which the person and the group define their identity. Because the protectors are in charge of enforcing this distinction, they are closely related to the monks' sense of identity and affiliation, and it comes as no surprise that they figure prominently in the ritual life of Tibetan monasteries. Most collective prayers include some rituals concerning them. For example, every service in the temple of the monastic seat of Dre-pung includes an offering to the Great Goddess.[14] But most of the rituals devoted to these deities are not performed in public but in the House of the Protectors *(dgon khang)*, a separate temple devoted to them. There, the deity is propitiated daily by the monk appointed as guardian of the House. Moreover, special rituals are held there monthly by a group of monks specially appointed to this task. Without such regular rituals, no monastic life is conceivable in the Tibetan tradition.

Many Tibetans feel the tension between the reliance on these deities and the normative ideals of the tradition. Monastic intellectuals are particularly sensitive to this tension, since their life is deeply penetrated by the great tradition they study at such length, and thus controversies concerning these deities sometimes arise. Such disputes follow the methods and canons of rationality used in other scholastic endeavors, methods and canons that are readily understandable from a modern perspective. The content of these disputes, however, is more difficult for non-Tibetans to grasp and indicates the distance between these practices and modern views.

Typical in this respect is the controversy I have described elsewhere as the "Shuk-den Affair," which concerned the protector Gyel-chen Dor-je Shuk-den *(rgyal chen rdo rje shugs ldan)*.[15] It started in the mid-1970s, when the Dalai Lama issued cautionary statements against the practice of this deity; he was reacting to the publication of a 1973 work promoting Shuk-den by a learned Ge-luk scholar, Dze-may Rin-po-che *(dze smad rin po che, 1927–1996)*.[16] In the *Yellow Book*, Dze-may Rin-po-che argues that Ge-luk lamas should absolutely not practice the teachings from other schools, or else they would incur Shuk-den's wrath and die prematurely. He supports this assertion with a number of cases, emphasizing that the dire warnings are not empty threats but are based on "facts." Typical is the fate of the Fifth Pan-chen Lama, Lob-zang Pal-den *(blo bzang dpal ldan chos kyi grags pa,* 1853–1882), who is described as incurring Shuk-den's anger because he adopted Nying-ma practices. Despite the repeated warnings of the protector, Lob-zang Pal-den refused to mend his ways. After a ritual self-defense that backfired, he died at the age of twenty-nine.[17] Many similar incidents are described by Dze-may.

The Dalai Lama reacted strongly to this *Yellow Book,* interpreting it as an attack on his views and practices—particularly on his association with the Nying-ma tradition, which he considers a vital part of the ritual system that supports the institution of Dalai Lama.[18] It is this association that the most conservative elements of the Ge-luk tradition object to. They see in Shuk-den the spirit in charge of defending the integrity of the Ge-luk tradition by "taking care" of those, such as the Dalai Lama, who are tempted to adopt practices from other schools. The dispute was all the more divisive because the main proponent of the Shuk-den cult was Tri-jang Rin-po-che, one of the foremost contemporary Ge-luk masters and the Dalai Lama's own teacher.

This controversy, which has profoundly divided the Ge-luk tradition, has continued to grow. While the details of its developments do not concern us here, I was directly affected by the tragic entanglement of two of my teachers. In 1978, Gen Lob-zang Gya-tso published a small pamphlet against Shuk-den in support of the Dalai Lama's stance. Particularly controversial was a verse alluding to a "knotless heretic teacher" *(ral pa med pa'i mu thegs ston pa)*—that is, a heretic disguised as a Buddhist monk. People took this as aimed at Tri-jang Rin-po-che and his advocacy of Shuk-den. Attacking such a towering figure was no small matter, and it provoked almost indescribable outrage among his numerous followers. Geshe Rab-ten, one of Tri-jang Rin-po-che's main disciples, responded in defense of his teacher with a vicious polemic against Gen Lob-zang Gya-tso.

At the time, I was studying at the Buddhist School, and most of the students, myself included, were appalled by these events. Our only desire was to be left alone to study Buddhist philosophy. The last thing we wanted was to be involved in a bitter dispute between two such giants as the Dalai Lama and his teacher, Tri-jang Rin-po-che. Nevertheless, the school, whose head was Gen Lob-zang Gya-tso, was engulfed in the controversy and was the target of the hostility of most Ge-luk monks, who were devoted to Tri-jang Rin-po-che. All the students were demoralized, feeling ourselves caught in events wholly beyond our control. We feared above all for our teacher's life. Yet nothing happened, and gradually—over a period of years—the heavy atmosphere of gloom and dread lifted; the school once again became a vigorous, lively institution.

The situation was particularly difficult for me: my two teachers were going at each other, and I was in the middle. Fortunately, Tibetans are very good at managing ambiguities and maintaining appearances, so I was allowed some breathing space. Both teachers tried to downplay their hostility when they talked to me. Geshe Rab-ten even pretended that he really liked Gen Lob-zang Gya-tso and that the whole episode was just an exercise in skillful means (i.e., using unseemly means for a good end). This polite fiction was highly implausible, given the extraordinarily polemical tone of his pamphlet, but it enabled everybody to maintain a polite facade. Tibetan friends also warned me to stay out of the dispute and not to say anything in public. This was wise advice, for Tibetans I had never met would come to me to ask me what I thought of the disagreement between Gen Lob-zang Gya-tso and Geshe Rab-ten. I would respond by feigning surprise. "A dispute? I am not aware of any disagreement between them." Everybody understood this answer as a refusal to get involved and respected my wish to be left out of the argument.

Greatly aiding my commitment to remain uninvolved was my failure to share my Tibetan friends' interest in protectors. For traditional Tibetans, these entities are unquestionably real and their propitiation is an integral part of the culture. For me, such practice was profoundly alien and of little interest (beyond piquing my intellectual curiosity). Moreover, because the propitiation of protectors is closely linked to group identity and to the ways in which the group distinguishes and defends itself from others, Tibetans are often unwilling to introduce outsiders to its secrets. Temples are always open to anybody, but the House of Protectors is often less accessible and can even at times be closed to non-Tibetans. Hence, my friends and teachers were not overly keen to involve me in this matter.

Nevertheless, as Geshe Rab-ten's close student, I was sometimes asked to attend Shuk-den rituals. I would just chant the ritual text, which by the mid-1970s I could read quite well. But I had no idea what the ritual was about or that Shuk-den was controversial. After this perfunctory participation had continued for a few months, Geshe Rab-ten decided that it was time to give me a chance for fuller involvement, but he first wanted to sound me out. "What do you think about protectors?" he asked one day in 1976. "I do not know. They may exist but they are not very meaningful to me," I replied. "Like spirits?" "Yes, pretty much." After that, I was never again asked to attend any protector ritual. At the time, I did not understand the significance of this exchange, since I was unaware of the controversy surrounding Shuk-den, which had started a few months earlier. I also did not understand the implications of my answer. It was only a year later, when the Dalai Lama began to make his opposition to this deity more public, that I realized what had happened. In retrospect, I consider my response to have been lucky, as it allowed me to sidestep a bitter conflict between people I respected profoundly. But I also understand that Geshe Rab-ten was showing me favor in asking to participate, giving a sign that he accepted me as his close disciple. I could not, however, reciprocate his goodwill. I also realize that I paid a price for my choice, for I increasingly drifted away from Geshe-la. Cultural differences have ways to assert themselves and drive individuals apart, despite our best efforts.

This dispute did not lead to immediate bloodshed, contrary to what I feared. Despite being hurt by the polemical attack, Tri-jang Rin-po-che made it clear that violence was out of the question. Gradually, tempers cooled down and the incident was forgotten—or so it seemed. In 1996, the Dalai Lama issued a stronger statement against Shuk-den, and a year later Gen Lob-zang Gya-tso and two of his students were brutally murdered in Dharamsala. Nobody has been apprehended but the Indian police have issued indictments against some known followers of Shuk-den, who escaped into Tibet.

EMBEDDED AND DISEMBEDDED RATIONALITIES

The tragic conflict is remarkable in several respects. It shows the importance to Tibetan scholastic intellectuals of the propitiation of protectors, despite their understanding of the tension between such a practice and normative Buddhist ideals. It also makes clear the depth of passion attending the controversy over Shuk-den, which leads monks to murder other monks merely because of the opinions they express. But this dispute reveals not just a breakdown of rationality but also the place of rationality in the Tibetan scholastic milieu. Modern sensibilities (modern Tibetans are as puzzled as Westerners) find the involvement of scholastic intellectuals and their arguments in such a matter quite surprising. For one thing, the arguments used in such a dispute appear less than compelling: to take one example, the reasons adduced by *The Yellow Book* in advocating Shuk-den are not exactly ironclad. Indeed, many Tibetan scholars would agree, seeing *The Yellow Book*'s arguments as at best providing indications of the practice one should follow, and at worst cynically manipulating unrelated tragic events.

Another difference is more striking: that Tibetan scholars feel that arguments are appropriate at all in discussing what we would consider magical and hence outside of the purview of rationality altogether. Unlike modern intellectuals, Tibetan scholastics are never tempted to reject magical elements and often engage in these practices, though they may view them as limited in their effects and not relevant to the soteriological goals of the tradition.[19] In this regard they are also unlike modern Buddhists, who are profoundly uncomfortable with the magical practices that exist in Asian Buddhist traditions. This is not to say that modern people never engage in magic or that such a dispute can never involve logical arguments. We may reason about the practice of protectors in general, debating whether it is justified, in accord with Buddhist prescriptions, and so on, but not about the respective merits of deities that belong to a domain of reality that seems to us not to call for rational evaluation. And yet the dispute over Shuk-den involves precisely such a discussion.

Although the Dalai Lama and Gen Lob-zang Gya-tso raised some issues concerning relying on protectors generally, and at times used the rhetoric of reform, their real target was a specific protector, Shuk-den. The Dalai Lama and Gen Lob-zang Gya-tso are as committed as other traditional Tibetans to the propitiation of protectors. The Dalai Lama, for example, despite understanding the possible excesses of reliance on protectors, never travels without a *thanka* (painted scroll) of the Great Goddess. And the worldly god Ne-chung *(gnas chung)*, who is the state oracle, is often consulted for important political decisions. Thus, the Dalai Lama's stance is not inspired by Buddhist modernism,[20] which detaches rationality from the practices in which it was traditionally embedded.

In the Tibetan cultural universe, a dispute over propitiating a specific protector is perfectly understandable, though deplorable. It concerns a deity whose followers—through dreams, visions, and states of possession—experience him as real. In that context, using reasoning to discuss the merits of such a deity makes perfect sense, whereas this application of rationality seems incongruous to modern thinkers. This gap underlines the degree to which Tibetan scholastic rationality remains embedded in the order of the world and hence is significantly different from modern rationality.[21] It also demonstrates the inappropriateness of describing Buddhism as "scientific." The dispute over Shuk-den concerns a practice that has been and still is central to the religious life of most Tibetan Buddhists, high and low. Within a traditional Tibetan context, such a dispute makes sense and can be justified, but it can hardly be said to be scientific!

I already noted the embeddedness of rationality in discussing some of the differences between traditional and (post)modern views of the possibility of meaning. As I have emphasized throughout this book, scholasticism intends to create a universe of religious meaning, and hence is based on the possibility of closure—a possibility that is deeply problematized by the advent of modernity, the disenchantment with the world that it brings forth, and the sense of nihilism and moral anomie that it induces. Although not always immune to these dangers, Tibetan thinkers are much less prone to them. They see themselves not as separated from the world but as participants with a definite place in the order of things. Moreover, they recognize the possibility of closure through the study of the path, a central notion of the tradition. By articulating a narrative of spiritual progress, the study of the path ensures that the students' glimpses of emptiness as they study and reflect on Madhyamaka are seen as important events in a meaningful process of liberation rather than as disruptions. In this way, students' confidence in the tradition is reinforced and the truth of its universe of meaning is confirmed.

This embedded and confident rationality also results from the constitutive role of the great texts of the tradition, which do not just inform but form fields of study. Because scholasticism proceeds by examining and, in the final analysis, appropriating constitutive texts, the understanding that is derived from their studies remains embedded within the tradition. Scholastic reason can be used to critique certain aspects of the tradition but finds it difficult to question the tradition as a whole, for it necessarily remains within the parameters determined by the basic texts.

Such a procedure is strikingly different from modern scientific rationality, which is based on a readiness to cast aside previous theories in the light of new facts. Such readiness should of course not be exaggerated, as Thomas Kuhn has made clear in drawing a distinction between normal and revolutionary sciences;[22] a good deal of science involves working within an established paradigm. Nevertheless, the scientific enterprise in principle is prepared to let go of past theories, to reject the familiar disciplinary matrix and shape a new one. The same is not true of scholasticism, which is inconceivable without the constitutive texts around which it revolves. Unlike great scientific texts, these are not held provisionally as a basis for problem solving. Although their exact interpretation may be up for grabs, there is nothing tentative in how scholasticism regards its great texts. They are the authority within their own domain and the given basis of the tradition, which evolves as scholars constantly reappropriate their content. As we have seen in previous chapters, this means not that such a tradition is uncritical but that its critical spirit remains within the orbit of the tradition delimited by the scholastic curriculum.[23]

14   The Limits of the Inquiry

One of the important focuses of this study has been the value of debate as a mode of inquiry. Debate, I have argued, is not just an invaluable pedagogical tool; it is also a way of reaching greater understanding. I further asserted that this inquiry required a certain degree of freedom. But this claim needs closer examination, for it seems to be contradicted by the homogeneity and orthodoxy that are well-known features of Tibetan traditions in general and the Ge-luk school in particular.

There is striking unanimity among the Tibetan scholastic groups concerning the main doctrinal questions. Although monks debate forcefully in the courtyard on any question relevant to the curriculum, controversies are rare outside this well-circumscribed area of inquiry. Most contemporary Ge-luk scholars hold the exact positions laid out in the manuals of their particular monastery. It was typical that Gen Pe-ma Gyel-tsen considered his mission in life to be explaining Sö-nam-drak-ba's texts, the manuals of the Lo-se-ling monastery. This quasi-unanimity among the members of the schools seems to argue against the claim that debate is a mode of inquiry in which students have latitude to explore contradictory standpoints. Is the freedom necessary to inquiry and experienced by participants in debate largely illusory?

In what follows, I argue that in the Tibetan tradition the freedom to inquire is real but limited. Some of those restrictions are internal, arising from the conceptual system in which debate takes place. Others are external, deriving from the sociopolitical context of Tibetan scholasticism. But more important, it is incorrect to see inquiry and orthodoxy as polar opposites: in a tradition that invests the past with great authority, they are both necessary and in a productive tension. The very authority of the tradition requires that participants be able to find meaningful ways to use the resources offered by the past; otherwise, tradition degenerates into mere traditionalism. But inquiry within it cannot go too far; otherwise, participants will feel that the authority of the past is being undermined.

THE SYSTEMATIC NATURE OF GE-LUK LEARNING

One of the important features of Tibetan scholastic education emphasized here is the progressivity of its learning and the cumulative character of its knowledge. Tibetan students are led gradually to the harder topics through a curriculum designed to enable students eventually to understand the topics that at first appeared formidable. This is particularly true of the teaching of emptiness, which at first appears incomprehensible but becomes clear further along the path. This progressivity, which members of the tradition stress, is made possible by the systematic organization of knowledge. That claim may be surprising, as Madhyamaka—a philosophy with a central role in the Tibetan tradition—is often viewed as antisystematic. But most Tibetan scholars do not understand Madhyamaka to exclude a certain amount of systemization.

In the Ge-luk tradition, as we have seen, the curriculum starts with the study of the Collected Topics, which provides a core conceptual system (though qualifications are later introduced). Typologies play a crucial role in constructing this system. I have already noted the importance of lists in Buddhist scholasticism, conceptually as well as historically. For example, existence is divided between impermanent and permanent phenomena. The latter category is further subdivided in three subcategories (matter, mind, and a nonassociated compositional factor). Definitions are also a key element. Thus existence is defined as "that which is observed by a valid cognition," and impermanence is defined as "that which is momentary."[1] For any given topic, students learn by heart both the definitions of the main notions and the relevant typologies. They thereby acquire a sense of the overall conceptual landscape in which future investigations will take place, as well as basic knowledge.

The wide use of definitions provides a prescriptive dimension, giving students the rules governing the concepts they use. It enables them to decide the extension and boundaries of any given concept, which is in turn systematically related to other concepts. But does this use of definition contradict the antiessentialism that is at the heart of Madhyamaka philosophy? Does the systemization of knowledge in Tibetan scholasticism impose tight restrictions on the freedom of inquiry in debate? If students must adopt a system bound by definitions, how much room is left for free inquiry? The answers to these questions are complex.

The Role of Definitions

There is undeniably an opposition in the Tibetan scholastic tradition between its antiessentialism and its knowledge system. Better scholars are aware of this tension, though they often do not realize the extent to which their views are permeated and largely governed by the overarching system that guides their studies. But the contradiction diminishes when one realizes that Tibetan scholastics employ a different notion of *definition* than do philosophers in the Western tradition.

In the Western tradition, a strong essentialism initially tended to dominate. In his early dialogues, Plato proposed a theory of knowledge based on definitions, which provided an account *(logos)* of the essence of disputed phenomena. In his view, definition is the cornerstone of knowledge; by stating a definition, the seeker of truth can solve all problems and secure authentic knowledge. Similarly, Aristotle saw definition as necessarily the basis of scientific or systematic knowledge.[2] This account proceeds by defining a phenomenon (e.g., human being) through its genus (e.g., animal) and differentia (e.g., rational), thereby indicating the essence of a human being: a rational animal. This essentialist notion of definition has remained strong throughout the history of the tradition.

In the Middle Ages, an opposing view emerged; it holds that definitions should be thought of not as real but as nominal.[3] They concern not the real world but only the terms we use to describe it. In this view, defended by Hobbes and Pascal, definitions have no informative content; they introduce terms and merely prescribe how these terms are to be used. In the twentieth century, Bertrand Russell and W. V. Quine have similarly taken the mathematical stipulative definition as paradigmatic.

The Indian and Tibetan traditions understand *definition* quite differently. What we call in English "definitions" are in the Indian and Tibetan contexts statements providing a defining characteristic *(lakṣaṇa, mtshan nyid)*. *Lakṣaṇa* comes from the Sanskrit root *lakṣ*, meaning "to mark, indicate, define."[4] It is glossed by the Sanskrit grammarians as *cihna*, "[physical] sign, mark, scar." Louis Renou, quoting Patañjali, defines this term as "that through which something is characterized *(lakṣyate)*." It has also the meaning "rule."[5] Indian and Tibetan thinkers see a defining characteristic not as the essence of the defined object but as an epistemically salient uncommon property *(asādhāraṇadharma, thun mong ma yin pa'i chos)* that unambiguously identifies the phenomenon. Hence, definition is intended to enable an object to be properly identified within a certain context, not to provide a final statement on it. In their pragmatism, Indian definitions differ from either real or nominal definitions in Western philosophy. They are more akin to the context-bound definitions used in everyday speech.

This contextual and low-key approach explains why Indian philosophers have never devoted much thought to definition, a notion they borrowed from the Sanskrit grammatical tradition.[6] Their pragmatism is all the more noticeable in a school like the Nyāya. Even though it holds an extreme realist view and hence is essentialist in its view of universals,[7] the Nyāya does not define a phenomenon by referring to the universal that constitutes its essence. Instead, a definition only provides an epistemically salient feature; for example, the cow is defined by having a dewlap, a rather superficial feature. Indian Buddhist thinkers similarly use definitions to single out an object among other objects so that it can be properly identified.[8] Even Candrakīrti, the most radical proponent of the deconstructive Madhyamaka approach, employs definitions to explain the objects of the conventional realm.[9] Definitions are of practical importance but not central to the knowledge at which the tradition aims, and using them does not imply an essentialist view of knowledge.

Seen in this light, the reliance on definitions in the Tibetan tradition in general and the Ge-luk school in particular appears less contradictory, for it is not tied to an essentialism incongruous with the overall antisubstantialist stance of the Buddhist tradition. Yet it is surprising in another way. On the view just sketched above, one would expect definitions to be of relatively low interest. They are, after all, supposed to be provisional statements that are not meant to bear too much scrutiny. However, definitions are often a major preoccupation, both in manuals and in actual debates, where the participants tend to pay attention to finding minor discrepancies and exceptions to proposed definitions. Criticizing debates that focus excessively on the precise wording of definitions, the Ge-luk thinker Jang-gya (1717–1786) complained that

> present-day logicians, not valuing the great texts highly, take refuge in mere deceptive entanglements when disputing with others. They take a garland of foam—dry consequences that do away with the essential meaning—as the best of essences. Such people see only a portion [of the meaning of the great texts]; the actual thought is beyond their ken. Therefore, for them the scriptures have become like diamond words [i.e., impossible to penetrate].[10]

He believed that studies should focus not on finding minor exceptions to definitions but rather on the meaning of the great Indian texts. The definitions provided by manuals offer valuable guidance to those trying to understand the texts, but they should not be taken as the final and exhaustive statements on a given question. The distinctions they convey pertain to the conventional domain, a domain that by its nature can be analyzed only superficially, not in terms of essence. Hence, there is little point to finding minor exceptions; the appropriate way to deal with a definition is as something contextual and provisional.

Underlying Jang-gya's criticism is his perception that the pragmatic understanding of definition has given way to a practice that treats definitions as essential, despite claims to the contrary by members of the tradition. Upholding definitions or undermining them has come to be considered the heart of dialectic. This trend that he censured in the eighteenth century has only grown worse. Many learned teachers believe learning definitions and being able to defend them to be major goals of the studies. For them, the aim of debate is to understand and assimilate these definitions, which are beyond doubt. Definitions are crucial to students' internalization of the truth of the tradition received from the teachers, in that they state positions that students can memorize and hold onto easily. But in the process, definitions lose their pragmatic and provisional character and become absolute statements bearing quintessential knowledge.

In some ways, the manner in which debates in the Ge-luk tradition are practiced may encourage the tendency to essentialize definition. Because the procedures of debate privilege finding contradictions over the meaningfulness of statements, students have an incentive to focus on definitions. Early in their training, the Collected Topics proceed mostly by definitions and typologies. By learning these definitions, students are able to gradually build a precise understanding of the more complicated notions. They also learn how to debate by investigating definitions and attempting to falsify them with counterexamples. There is nothing problematic in this practice per se, provided that one recognizes it for what it is—a preliminary exercise that prepares students for a more mature understanding developed through the study of the great texts. Yet in the contemporary Ge-luk tradition, the provisional nature of manuals is often forgotten, and rather than being comprehended the great texts are sometimes merely debated on the basis of the definitions provided by the manuals. Thus, the use of definitions in the Ge-luk tradition is a complex matter. Although reliance on definitions need not entail an essentialist commitment, the quasi-canonization of manuals and the definitions they contain in contemporary Ge-luk practices manifest an essentialist tendency that is frequently overlooked.

As Jang-gya's complaint makes clear, some Ge-luk scholars are quite aware of these dangers. They perceive a discrepancy between classical Indian texts and contemporary practices. Some members of the tradition are greatly concerned about the tendency of the excessive emphasis on debate to push textual studies to the side. Others have noticed the essentialism underlying the increasing focus on definitions. Gen Nyi-ma, for example, relied little on definitions. Every time one came up, he would point out the difficulties it entailed and its tension with the other elements of the system. He took great delight in asking his students searching questions whose sole aim was to point to the very minor clarifications that can ever be achieved by the use of definitions. He would also point to the limits of definitions as context-dependent, showing that we cannot define everything and must appeal to undefined terms.

Systematization and Freedom

The importance of the conceptual system that supports the Ge-luk curriculum and the tensions created by the use of this system may once again suggest that the freedom of inquiry necessary for debate is not real. Students appear to be led right from the beginning through a system that ensures that they will hold the right positions when the training is complete. To some extent, that observation is quite accurate, partly because of the systematic nature of knowledge building in the Ge-luk tradition. Students rely on definitions for much of their studies. They are trained to take these definitions as targets of debate, and they develop the habit of viewing the definitions of their manuals as authoritative statements. They see their task as understanding and defending these positions rather than inquiring into the meaning of the great texts. Given the propensity of most people in most cultures to conform, a propensity heightened in Tibetan culture, the end result—that is, the enormous degree of conformity found among Tibetan scholars—can hardly come as a surprise.

Nevertheless, explanations that rely on culture and students' training do not fully account for the prevalence of orthodoxy in the Tibetan scholastic tradition. To be sure, the conceptual or systematic limitations put on inquiry are real enough, and knowledge in the Ge-luk tradition does rest on a conceptual system in which the use of definitions seriously restricts the range of what can be said. But systems are not as hermetically sealed as their proponents may wish. A skilled debater discovers that even in the tightest conceptual system, there is room for maneuver. Hence, freedom may be found even in a system that at first sight seems to offer little hope of avoiding foregone conclusions.

This freedom is a consequence of knowledge's deconstructibility, which debate illustrates. Debate leads students to realize that whatever is said can be undermined, however self-evident it may at first seem. They come to see that they can get out of almost any situation. Such an escape may involve artificial or counterintuitive dialectical tricks,[11] and at certain points one will have to acknowledge defeat. As I emphasized, that is one of the students' most important lessons. But such defeats arise not so much from the inherent weakness of one's position as from the realization that the dialectical tricks needed to escape the trap are too artificial or too costly. More often than not, the good debater finds it possible to defend unusual positions within the limits of the conceptual system in which knowledge is organized.

Moreover, those limits are not absolute in a tradition in which scriptural authority is not absolute, as the parable of the goldsmith makes clear: "O Bhikshus, just as a goldsmith gets his gold, first testing by melting, cutting and rubbing, sages accept my teaching after full examination, and not just out of devotion [to me]."[12] This eloquently illustrates the normative status of the Buddha's teachings and its relation to the critical spirit that Buddhists claim as central to their tradition. Of course, people do not necessarily turn to Buddhism in that spirit, and dogmatism is by no means alien to it.[13] Yet the commitment to a critical perspective has normative importance. There is no credo to which Buddhist monks must subscribe under the threat of exclusion, and no institutional mechanism holding monks to orthodoxy. There is no religious authority that can step in and ban heterodox opinions, as Bishop Tempier did in Paris in 1277 (see chapter 12). When asked to appoint his successor, the Buddha is said to have refused and told the monks that henceforth their refuge would be his teachings, the Dharma and the Vinaya.[14] Historical or not, this story reflects the Buddhist view that people should be left to inquire and decide for themselves. Monks, too, are left free to inquire and meditate under the guidance of their teachers. Monks can be expelled if they create dissension within the order by propounding heterodox views, but no action can be taken against them purely because of those views. Hence, a full explanation of the place of orthodoxy in Tibetan scholasticism must take into account sociopolitical factors.

EXTERNAL CONSTRAINTS ON INQUIRY

The Case of Ge-dün Chö-pel

The sociopolitical influences on Tibetan scholasticism are well illustrated by the story of Ge-dün Chö-pel (1904–1951), a gifted scholar from the province of Amdo in Northeastern Tibet. Already when he was a young monk studying at La-brang, Ge-dün Chö-pel is said to have been a legend. His brilliance made him the leader of a lively bunch of scholar-students. He was also a talented painter, a skill he used throughout his monastic career to support himself. His inquisitive mind was not satisfied with the set curriculum, however, and he started to explore other alternatives. He developed an interest in mechanical toys that did not endear him to the disciplinarians of the monastery, who viewed this extracurricular activity with suspicion. He also created a sensation by giving answers that contradicted Buddhist orthodoxy in a public debate. He argued for the Jain view that plants are sentient and won the argument over seasoned scholars.[15] In a further display of nonconformism, he and his friend scandalized the assembly by ridiculing the manuals of the monastery during a public examination.

After that, Ge-dün Chö-pel left in 1927 for Go-mang monastery of Drepung; there he studied with Geshe Shay-rab Gya-tso, one of the great Ge-luk scholars of the day. Under the direction of Geshe Shay-rab, who was also a nonconformist and a rather self-assertive scholar,[16] Ge-dün Chö-pel quickly became one of the best debaters in the monastery. He was particularly feared by the members of the class just above him, for he was unbeatable in the encounters between classes. These sessions, which are less momentous in India where classes are small, were important events in the life of the three Ge-luk monastic seats. Cohorts were pitched against each other, as each class debated the one immediately above and below. Ge-dün Chö-pel became famous for defeating a number of seasoned scholars. But this fame, which would have contented most scholars, could not satisfy him. He became bolder and started to openly disagree with the Ge-luk orthodoxy. In quick order, he drew the disapproval of more conservative monks, who were outraged by his views and his brash manners. In a famous encounter with Mi-nyag Kyor-pön *(mi nyag skyor dpon)*, one of the most senior Lo-se-ling scholars, he astonished the whole assembly. Thinking that he had cornered Ge-dün Chö-pel during a public debate, Mi-nyag Kyor-pön told him: "I will give you my water bottle if you can answer this question!" Ge-dün Chö-pel took it and answered without any hesitation.[17] The assembly burst in laughter, while Mi-nyag Kyor-pön stood speechless.

Not all monks disliked Ge-dün Chö-pel; the more open-minded considered him to be one of them. Scholars around Gen Tom-pön (Gen Nyi-ma's teacher) sympathized with his iconoclastic approach. Tsuk-gang Gen Lama, a famous teacher from Lo-se-ling who was Gen Tom-pön's senior student,[18] was known to be particularly friendly to Ge-dün Chö-pel. The majority, however, did not like him and considered him a troublemaker—not an altogether unreasonable assessment in a society where the government was in control of scholastic studies and could intervene harshly. Their worries were all the more well-founded given that Ge-dün Chö-pel was critical of Jam-yang-shay-ba's and even of Dzong-ka-ba's interpretations of Madhyamaka.[19] This breach of orthodoxy shocked and outraged many, and on one occasion Ge-dün Chö-pel was beaten up by some angry Go-mang monks.[20] Disgusted by these reactions and realizing the limits of inquiry possible in a monastery, he started to drift away from the monastery. After a meeting with the Indian scholar Rahul Sankritayana, he decided to go to India to explore new areas. There he ceased to be a monk and became interested in a variety of subjects, ranging from history, nationalism, and anticolonial politics to erotic poetry. But it is mostly his involvement with left-wing circles that led him into trouble when he came back to Tibet after the Second World War. He was imprisoned for three years, and died shortly after his release in 1950 from the combined effects of the detention and his alcoholism. Since then, his stature has continued to grow within the Tibetan community, where he is considered a modernist hero, a symbol of the political and technological path that Tibet should have taken.

Ge-dün Chö-pel's intellectual career illustrates the resources of the scholastic tradition in general and of the practice of debate in particular. In many respects he was a product of the education of the Ge-luk monastic universities. His ability to question, investigate, and open new avenues in the Tibetan intellectual landscape reflects the strengths of that traditional education. Freedom of inquiry is possible in such a system, which allows scholars to come to positions that conflict with the tradition. In doing so, they do not discard the tradition but take its ideas seriously, using its own resources to test them. Tibetan scholastic traditions have the intellectual resources to support an inquiry that can ultimately overturn it.

But it is also characteristic that Ge-dün Chö-pel's story ends in failure. Although the Tibetan scholastic tradition values the freedom to question, it views with great suspicion any innovation or departure from accepted norms. Most people within it are happy enough to be well trained and to hold the positions that they are expected to hold. In fact, the dominant characteristic of this tradition is its unshakable conservatism, which makes it reject any person who deviates from the accepted path. To innovate, Ge-dün Chö-pel had to leave the monastery and seek inspiration from the world outside.

We may wonder why this conservative tendency persists in Tibet. Is it the expression of national character? Though mountain people typically are rather conservative and limited in their outlook, such generalizations about cultural traits are not very useful. Indeed, many of the opposite generalizations also hold true among Tibetans: they are also very practical, pragmatic, and ready to make accommodations. For a better explanation, we should look to the social and political context in which monastic education takes place.

Dealing with Dissent

As the story of Ge-dün Chö-pel illustrates, monastic communities have ways of dealing with dissenters and ensuring that they will not threaten institutional stability. Pressure often is the first line of defense against the disrupting effects of dissent. Strong minds are warned by their friends that they should not be too outspoken. A friend of mine reported that when he started to teach his students some views that were in disagreement with the monastery's manuals, friends started to express concern and worry about his future prospects. The next stage is likely to be less amicable—an informal campaign aimed at discrediting and ridiculing the person. If he still persists in his ways, he may be verbally attacked during public debates for holding heterodox views. My friend, for example, was the target of a number of unpleasant exchanges that always came back to a single point: his failure to uphold the monastic manuals in his teachings. Other scholars would make sure that the community saw the defeat of any of his students in a public debate as tied to his views. My friend quickly understood and decided to leave the monastery.

In some cases, monastic authorities can bring sanctions against a dissenting scholar, but they can be officially imposed only if the person has breached one of the important rules of the monastic discipline. In such rare cases, the person can be made to prostrate himself in front of the whole assembly, can be beaten, or can even be expelled. Much more common is public humiliation, like that experienced by Pal-den Drak-ba from Lo-se-ling monastery during his Geshe examinations. Such an examination is a formal occasion at which opinions matter a great deal, unlike the less formal occasions that allow students freedom to explore heterodox views. During examinations, students are expected to defend not only Dzong-ka-ba's positions but even those of the manuals of their monastery. If a student fails to do so, other monks will chide him for "letting go of his manuals" *(yig cha lhod pa)* and "kicking the bowl [from which he is fed]" *(phor ba la gdun kya zhu)*. The latter expression, alluding to the food received by monks during rituals held by the monastery, implies that those who do not uphold the views of the monastery on formal occasions show a lack of gratitude. To which Geshe Pal-den Drak-ba would, in private, reply: "As if the monastery was feeding us just to repeat the views of its manuals like parrots!"

When he was answering in front of his monastery, Geshe Pal-den Drak-ba made a point contradicting the views on the nature of nirvana set forth by Paṇ-chen Sö-nam-drak-ba, the author of Lo-se-ling's manuals. Monks became very excited by Geshe-la's defiance and a spirited debate followed. But Geshe-la was too good and the attackers were routed. Once Geshe-la's point was vindicated, there was nothing that the scholars of Lo-se-ling could do. The disciplinarian of the monastery, however, did not let the occasion slip by. On the next day, after the examinations were over, during the morning prayer he publicly admonished "those who were so proud that they did not feel bound to uphold the views of the monastery." In a society like the Tibetan community, where face and shame are so important, such an admonition is extremely humiliating. People feel branded and their relation with other monks is significantly affected. For this reason, monastic constitutions advise disciplinarians to proceed gently and avoid directly singling out an individual if it can be avoided. For example, Se-ra Jay's monastic constitution declares, "[T]his college (i.e., monastery) is an honorable and compassionate college. Hence, one is not allowed to point a finger from the very beginning."[21] The disciplinarian should instead proceed indirectly, at first alluding to the monk held responsible and singling him out only if he persists in his mistaken ways. In scolding Pal-den Drak-ba, Lo-se-ling's disciplinarian did not feel bound by such restraint; moreover, he took action beyond the scope of his powers. He was in charge of the discipline, not of upholding the orthodoxy of monks, a matter that concerns only the monks themselves and their teachers. But by abusing his power, he succeeded in pushing Geshe-la's answers into the realm of the unacceptable. The message was not lost on the other monks: public humiliation would be the price of dissent. It is this kind of pressure that usually keeps monks in line. Few people are willing to go against social pressure and risk being sanctioned by authorities.

Thus, we can see that the limitations on intellectual freedom that exist in Tibetan scholasticism are as much external as internal. The conceptual systems used by Tibetan Buddhist schools, particularly the Ge-luk, impose some internal restrictions on the freedom of inquiry, but those limitations can be overcome by well-trained minds. Moreover, monks can always appeal to the freedom of inquiry that the tradition normatively accepts. The more tangible limitations come from the social context in which monastic studies take place and the kind of pressure exercised by the institutions to which the monks belong.

The Role of the State in Scholastic Education

Another type of constraint on freedom of inquiry in Tibetan scholasticism derives from the involvement of political interests in monasticism. Throughout their history, monastic institutions in Tibet, as in other Buddhist societies, have depended on political power. What is more peculiarly Tibetan is the close alliance between authorities and monastic groups that has resulted from the failure of stable secular groups to gain and hold power. This close alliance has been most obvious in the past three centuries, during which the Dalai Lama and his government have asserted their power by relying on a coalition of political forces and monastic groups, mostly from the Ge-luk school.

Throughout this period, the central Lhasa government has closely regulated monastic institutions in Central Tibet. The government has overseen monastic examinations, ranks, and titles. In particular, the government has kept a tight rein on the examinations for the title of Lha-ram Geshe, which is, as we saw in chapter 11, supposed to be given to *la crème de la crème* of Ge-luk scholasticism. In Tibet, the government ran the first and the last of the three examination that the candidates had to undergo, the first one being at Nor-bu-ling-ka and the final examination in Jo-khang during the Great Prayer festival. It also kept an eye on the examinations held by the monasteries and on the integrity of the whole curriculum. It ranked candidates according to their performance and gave official prizes to the better ones.[22] Finally, the government was in charge of appointing the abbots of the monasteries of the three seats. Its control over non-Geluk schools greatly varied according to local conditions, but its authority over Ge-luk scholasticism was quite real, at least in Central Tibet.

The government in exile has no real power beyond what Tibetan communities recognize. Nevertheless, the authorities in Dharamsala have continued the same policy of supervising religious institutions through the Office for Religious Affairs. The Ge-luk institutions are the most obedient to Dharamsala's directives, while the other schools' relationships with the office vary greatly depending on the institution and particular circumstances. Yet it is clear that even now political institutions exercise some degree of control over scholastic institutions and thereby restrict freedom of inquiry.

The political authorities intervene when dissenters refuse to leave the monastery or contest the decision of monastic authorities. In Tibet, such interventions were rare. Ge-luk monastic universities were powerful institutions with internal resources that included tax collectors, administrators, and armed monks. They thus had the means to settle most disputes. But sometimes the government had to intervene in doctrinal matters, as during the dispute about the practice of cutting *(gcod)* discussed in chapter 12. The government settled the case in favor of Gen Tom-pön, but exiled him to pacify the other faction.[23] In that instance, the intervention of the government was decisive and final. In general, however, the government was very careful in its relations with the main Ge-luk monasteries, which it could not afford to alienate. Without the support of the three monastic universities, it could not effectively wield power. For example, if the six abbots of the three monastic universities were opposed, no decision could be taken at the Assembly of Notables.[24]

The marked orthodoxy among Tibetan scholars reflects these sociopolitical realities. Because they know that dissent will lead to a rebuke by the monastic authorities, backed by the government, scholars are unwilling to openly express opinions that may draw attention. In one of his tantric teachings, Gen Nyi-ma began expressing doubt about a practice relating to one of the main meditational deities of the tradition. But Gen-la quickly halted, saying, "I think I'd better stop here, otherwise I will be scolded once more." I have no idea what he meant by "once more" and did not dare ask, but clearly Gen-la had previously been reprimanded by some higher authority.[25] It is also clear that the knowledge of such incidents influences scholars and leads to a careful self-censorship. Authorities do not need to intervene often as long as monks remain aware that such intervention is a real possibility.

Orthodoxy, Texts, and Debates

The political constraints on intellectual freedom in monastic education are also functions of the nature of Tibetan schools and the allegiance that they have instilled in their members. As we saw in chapter 1, Tibetan schools are not based only on the religious commitments implied by their affiliation with a particular spiritual lineage. They are in part political entities whose activities go well beyond the building of local networks and alliances. The Sa-gya, Ka-gyü, and Ge-luk schools were political groups supported by extended networks of patronage vying for temporal power at a pan-Tibetan level.

The political character of Tibetan Buddhist schools became stronger during the protracted civil war between Central Tibet and Tsang during the sixteenth century. In that politically charged atmosphere, small doctrinal differences became markers of sectarian divides. Despite their marginal relevance to the political situation, the topics of the scholastic curriculum took on symbolic political value: knowledge of them provided a form of cultural capital that could be used to assert the supremacy of one's school. Holding the orthodox position became an expression of one's loyalty, and any deviation from the line adopted by the school came to be seen as political treason. In the Ge-luk tradition, failure to agree with the positions both of Dzong-ka-ba and of the monastic manuals is considered a sign of ingratitude if not outright betrayal, as expressed by the graphic condemnation of "kicking the bowl [from which one is fed]."

The stress on doctrinal correctness influences the intellectual freedom of monastic intellectuals. Because they are trained in an atmosphere in which having the right view is emblematic of valuing one's tradition, these scholars know that any doubt they express publicly about the orthodoxy of their school or even of their monastery's manuals will be taken as attacking the overall value of these institutions and their legitimacy. It also explains why Tibetan scholars distinguish so sharply their treatment of debates and of texts. Whereas in the former students are free to explore all kinds of ideas (except on more formal occasions), the latter are tightly restricted to presenting the "correct" interpretation. A book is not just a pedagogical exercise but publicly expresses the author's degree of commitment to a tradition. Scholars can become enraged when books are published that differ even slightly from the doctrinal lines of the institutions to which they belong. The best example is Ge-dün Chö-pel's book, which scandalized his Ge-luk contemporaries by questioning Dzong-ka-ba's Madhyamaka interpretation.[26]

Even less audacious publications can create a great deal of controversy. On one occasion Geshe Pal-den Drak-ba got into trouble for questioning the way in which the fortnightly confession service *(bso sbyong, upoṣadha)* was held. He pointed out that the method of calculating the date in the Vinaya does not match Tibetan practices. His observation drew the ire of several Ge-luk scholars, who were outraged at the idea that the monastic practices of the whole tradition could be put into doubt. Although this point may seem innocuous, in the context of the Vinaya it is crucial, for a confession service held at the wrong time may not be valid. Such an error in turn would invalidate the whole Tibetan monastic practice, for the confession service is one of the three most important Vinaya rituals; it is said that without it, no monastic practice is possible.[27] Geshe Pal-den Drak-ba became the focus of aggressive polemics that seemed based less on rational arguments than on ad hominem attacks and appeals to the sanctity of the tradition. How could he doubt the practice that a whole stream of great minds had approved?

The number of scholars involved grew. Gen Nyi-ma defended Geshe Pal-den Drak-ba, arguing that he was raising a valid point that had to be investigated, not just dismissed because the weight of the tradition was against it. One day he scolded several of his students who had derided Geshe Pal-den Drak-ba for getting bigger than his boots: "The guy is talking about the meaning of important texts, not just about customs, you idiots!" Nevertheless, the majority was clearly against Geshe Pal-den Drak-ba and he was advised by several friends to let the topic die down. This is what he did, once more illustrating the power of the tradition to keep its members in line. If he had not, the Tibetan government in exile would have intervened. A commission of scholars might have been created to study the question, and their final decision would almost certainly have come down on the side of the monasteries, which are still important supports for the government.

As I emphasized in chapter 10, the difference in freedom between debate and texts cannot be explained by the orality of the former. Texts could be open-ended, offering alternative views within an acceptable range; but Tibetan scholastic texts, like their medieval Christian counterparts, instead determine an orthodoxy. Thus, the distinction between debate and text reflects the role of orthodoxy in this tradition, which developed in response to specific influences. The overall history of Tibetan scholasticism was a major element. In particular, such thinkers as Bo-dong, Long-chen-ba, and Dzong-ka-ba, who belong to the period described in chapter 1 as classical and produced their own syntheses of the Indian material assimilated during the preceding period, had to put forth their own interpretations that differentiate what they considered correct from false views. These determinations in turn promoted orthodoxy among their followers, who gradually came to magnify the importance of minor distinctions. The increasing rigidity of these positions was greatly favored by the sociopolitical factors sketched earlier that led to the present division among Tibetan schools.

SECTARIAN DIFFERENCES AND
THE RHETORICS OF TRADITIONS

The role of orthodoxy is particularly strong in the Ge-luk tradition, which uses doctrinal correctness as its main rhetorical strategy. Unlike members of several other Buddhist traditions, Ge-luk thinkers put little emphasis on the immediacy of experience, insisting instead on the truth of doctrines. For example, Tu-gen Lob-zang Chö-gyi-nyi-ma (*thu'u bkwan blo bzang chos kyi nyi ma,* 1737–1802) claims superiority for his tradition on the grounds that it faultlessly presents the correct view, practice, and meditation. He unabashedly declares, "Since there is no other Tibetan tenet system whose view, practice, and meditation are as faultless as the Ge-den [i.e., the Ge-luk school], the Ge-luk [school] is superior to all the other tenet systems from these three points of view."[28] Tu-gen then proceeds to explain this threefold superiority. Dzong-ka-ba's presentation of Madhyamaka is the only one to fully capture the meaning of Nāgārjuna's philosophy and to provide the right view. Similarly, Dzong-ka-ba's explanations of the three types of vows (pertaining to the pratmoksha, bodhisattva, and tantra) are the only ones respecting the integrity of each class of vows, which are not conflated, as they are in the presentations of other traditions, but instead are separated, as they are in the original texts that explain them. Finally, he extolls the Ge-luk discussion of meditative practices over those of other Tibetan schools, which are seen as incomplete or even dangerous. Hence, viewed from either a theoretical or a practical point of view, the Ge-luk tradition is clearly superior.

Such powerful sectarian rhetoric is all the more striking in a figure belonging to the liberal wing of his school. Unlike his teacher, Sum-pa Ken-po Ye-shay-bel-jor, who dismissed the revealed treasures (*gter ma*) of the Nying-ma as pure fabrications, Tu-gen supported their validity, arguing that their rejection would lead to the rejection of the entire Mahayana and tantric corpus.[29] But despite his respect for other schools, Tu-gen never doubted the superiority of his own, a superiority that he located in Dzong-ka-ba's works.

One of the strategies pursued by this rhetoric is to marginalize other traditions and exclude them from consideration, leaving Dzong-ka-ba as the sole inheritor of Indian Buddhism. Characteristically, Ge-luk teachers do not mention the views of other Tibetan thinkers during their classes, commenting only on Dzong-ka-ba's interpretation of Indian texts. For example, when they explain Nāgārjuna's *Treatise,* they use Dzong-ka-ba's commentaries to relate it to the root text. In this way, Nāgārjuna's text is filtered wholly through Dzong-ka-ba's interpretations. By the time that senior scholars come across the writings of other Tibetan traditions, it is too late for them to be influenced: their worldview is already formed, and they have built their entire intellectual career on the validity of the Ge-luk tradition. Critiques of Dzong-ka-ba are mentioned solely to illustrate their authors' lack of comprehension.

The intellectual rigor of the tradition is seriously damaged by its failure to consider the objections of other Tibetan thinkers. Ignoring non-Ge-luk ideas is clearly a political move: other Tibetan interpretations are disallowed because they do not accept Dzong-ka-ba's definitive interpretations. As a result, Ge-luk teachers ignore important Tibetan works in favor of more orthodox accounts. For example, Ge-luk scholars almost never read Sa-paṇ's *Treasure*, which is probably the best explanation of Dharmakīrti's thought written in Tibetan. They also take no notice of Gyel-tsap's commentary on Sa-paṇ's text, even though it expresses views similar to those found in authoritative Ge-luk texts.[30] Gyel-tsap's commentary is not even included in his Collected Works. Although the reasons for this exclusion have yet to be established, one cannot help but feel that the wish to push non-Ge-luk traditions into oblivion played a part.

This strategy of marginalization is made possible by the dominance enjoyed by the Ge-luk school and its institutions of higher learning. From the seventeenth century on, non-Ge-luk institution could never hope to match the three Ge-luk monastic universities in power, wealth, number of scholars, and prestige. Even in exile, where the advantage of government support is limited, Ge-luk institutions still eclipse other schools. They set the standards of scholarly excellence and the topics of learning. In this context, their ignorance of the views of other schools is not merely an omission. It reflects a strategy of marginalization intended to deprive other schools of any scholarly legitimacy.

Non-Ge-luk scholars proceed quite differently. Because they are skeptical of Dzong-ka-ba's ideas, which they consider to be innovations and therefore suspect in a culture that derives its legitimacy from the past, non-Ge-luk scholars tend to bring out the differences among Tibetan interpretations. In doing so, they too have political motives: they know that they are working from a position of inferiority. Their institutions are not as powerful as the Ge-luk ones and their scholars are usually not as well-trained as Ge-luk Geshes. It also true that non-Ge-luk scholars tend to hold tightly to their own great commentaries—Mi-pam's texts for the Nying-ma, Mi-gyö-dor-jay's for the Ka-gyü, and Go-ram-ba's for the Sa-gya. Nevertheless, their acknowledgment of differences is a positive move and supports their claims to present a less one-sided view of Tibetan Buddhism than do the Ge-luk.

The Ge-luk marginalization of other schools shows the limitations placed by this tradition on the freedom of inquiry in debate. Monks may be free to raise objections in debate even against Dzong-ka-ba's views; but absent alternative interpretations, their objections do not seriously threaten the dominant orthodoxy. Thus the availability of alternative views, not the ability to raise objections, is most crucial to the freedom to inquire. This point has been made forcefully by Thomas Kuhn in his study of change in science. Against Karl Popper's view of falsification as the dominant logic of the scientific enterprise, Kuhn objects that it is not enough to falsify a scientific theory. One must also have an alternative theory that accounts for the same range of phenomena. Without that alternative, mere criticisms cannot overthrow an established paradigm.[31]

I believe that Kuhn's point can help us understand the configuration of Tibetan scholasticism. Through its strategy of marginalization, the Ge-luk tradition can maintain its hegemony while allowing its scholars a certain degree of freedom. As long as these scholars are not presented with legitimate alternatives to the views of the tradition, the qualms that they raise in debate represent little danger to the Ge-luk hegemony. Because of their unwavering commitment to Dzong-ka-ba as the sole legitimate interpreter of the Indian tradition, all doubts voiced stay at the level of intellectual exercises, fully contained within the tradition's paradigm.

That paradigm enjoys added protection from the commentarial logic central to the scholastic tradition, which bases knowledge on the appropriation of authoritative texts. In this approach, to overthrow an established interpretation one needs commentaries that support the alternative interpretation. By disallowing the commentaries of other traditions, the Ge-luk tradition renders its interpretation of the tradition immune to any serious challenge. The same is true of other Tibetan traditions as well, though to a lesser degree. Here the far-reaching consequences of the commentarial hierarchy laid out in chapter 5, with its three textual layers, become clear. As long as the great Indian texts are approached through the interpretations by Tibetan commentaries, and as long as these interpretations are mediated through monastic manuals and other interpretations disallowed, each school's orthodox views are safe. It is not so much that, in Stephen Batchelor's words, *"you set out to prove what you have already decided to believe,"*[32] but that in the absence of alternatives, you end up believing what you are supposed to, despite your best efforts to question. This pattern may hold not just for Tibetan traditions but for scholasticism in general, which tends to keep inquiry within the parameters of the tradition. The dialectic of authority and understanding, which I have argued animates such a mode of thinking, is not a free-for-all but a controlled process; suspicion remains subordinated to the retrieval of the tradition without foreclosing the possibility of inquiry, disagreements, and innovations.

Conclusion Past and Future Uncertainties

In this work, I have focused on the traditional aspects of Tibetan monastic education, bringing to life the Tibetan scholastic experience as it existed both before 1959 and afterward in exile. In doing so, I have argued that scholasticism is characterized by three types of practice. First, scholasticism, which is memorial rather than documentary, gives memorization an important role. Second, scholasticism relies on commentary through which the tradition is transmitted, interpreted, and enshrined. Third, scholasticism in Tibet involves debate, which provides room for inquiry in a tradition in which truth is not discovered but rather is transmitted.

Throughout this study, I have delineated the particular features of Tibetan scholasticism, focusing on the ways in which commentary and debate support the dialectic of authority and freedom that I see as a central dynamic of scholastic traditions. I have described the constitutive role of the great Tibetan texts, the root texts (often memorized) that delineate the outlines of the tradition. I have emphasized their centrality in constructing a universe of meaning and in strengthening one's confidence in the validity of the tradition, one of the main functions of scholasticism. I have also shown that the closure presupposed by tradition distinguishes rational scholastic practices from the practices of modern scholars. It would be a mistake, however, to assume that the boundedness of scholasticism necessarily implies a dogmatic and uncritical spirit. To flourish, scholasticism needs freedom to interpret its own constitutive texts. In the Tibetan tradition, debate provides this freedom of inquiry, which allows scholars to examine rigorously the content of the tradition, though that examination is limited in its scope. Questions may be raised, but they may not undermine the foundations of the tradition, particularly its constitutive texts. In Tibetan scholasticism, when such limits are transgressed, authorities (secular or monastic) step in to restore what they perceive to be the integrity of the tradition, thus illustrating the reality and limits of this tradition's freedom of inquiry.

SCHOLASTICISM AND ITS ACCOMMODATION TO MODERNITY

One of the striking features of Tibetan scholasticism that I have yet to touch on is the degree to which even today its practices have remained unaffected by modernity. This is particularly true of the Ge-luk tradition, which still offers an education that revolves around commentary and debate, very much as it was in Tibet before 1959. Traditional education persists because of a deliberate effort on the part of the exiled community to re-create its culture in exile, despite the hardships and difficulties. These considerable efforts have been largely successful. The exiled versions of the great Tibetan monastic centers are flourishing (see figure 14), and so is the scholastic education they provide. These reconstructed institutions offer a good window into Tibetan scholasticism as it existed in Tibet before 1950. But the preoccupation of exiled communities with maintaining their heritage, though it provides a raison d'être, also nurtures a fixation on the past that makes future evolution difficult. The Tibetan scholastic culture has carried this tendency to an extreme, making little effort to adapt itself to a changing world. Yet modernity cannot be kept at bay forever.

When I left Tibetan monasticism in 1985 after completing my Geshe degree, the process of accommodation to modernity seemed to be finally under way. Encouraged by a generous sponsor, Luca Corona (then a young Western monk), the Se-ra Jay monastery had decided to create a curriculum that would include modern education. Up until then, before joining the traditional training described here young monks were taught how to read and write in Tibetan, but little else. The new plan at Se-ra Jay was to train them in modern subjects (Tibetan, English, mathematics, history, geography, and civics) up to the high school level. Only then would they be allowed to begin the traditional scholastic training.

Despite its drawbacks (the largest being the creation of two separate academic systems), the plan seemed to offer a serious prospect of better integrating Tibetan monastic education into the modern world. From its inception, however, it encountered vigorous opposition from the more conservative elements. I remember discussing the plan, in which I was marginally involved, with Lati Rin-po-che, who was then the abbot of Ga-den Shar-tse. He was, and still is, completely opposed to the innovation, which he thought would undermine traditional training by providing a new outlet to monks, who would leave the monastery. As a result, Shar-tse and other monasteries have not implemented the plan, and the old limits on the education of monks continue. More "enlightened" elements of the tradition have supported the plan, however. In particular, the Dalai Lama is strongly in favor of it, as are the more open elements of Se-ra Jay. As a result, the plan has been implemented in Se-ra Jay, where the school has successfully trained a number of students in modern subjects.

The process of accommodation to modernity also affects the curriculum itself. In recent years, younger monks who have been raised in India have expressed some dissatisfaction with the education provided by monastic institutions. One of their main complaints is the duration of the studies—particularly in the three seats, where completing one's studies still takes at least fifteen years. In 1995, another seven years were added when the written examinations held by the Ge-luk Society were made compulsory for the title of Lha-ram. This is simply too long for many younger monks. Unlike their elders, these monks do not perceive their studies as a lifelong enterprise leading to a towering achievement, the title of Geshe. Rather, they see it as a form of education that leads to a monastic career, much as secular education in the modern world permits laypeople to make their way in their chosen profession.

The pressure for reform is increasing as the global economy creates new possibilities. Globalization has reached the Tibetan monastic community, providing new resources for its institutions and enabling monasteries to absorb the considerable number of new arrivals from Tibet. But it has also tempted many well-trained monks to leave the monastery for new pursuits in industrialized countries (in the West, but also Taiwan, Singapore, and Malaysia). After completing their exams, monks may choose to enter into retreat, remain in the monastery as teachers, or become an abbot in a smaller monastery, as their elders did in Tibet. But they can also opt for one of the newly created Buddhist centers, which are in great need of teachers. Younger monks, who are interested by the material and intellectual resources of the modern world, find the prospect of teaching there very exciting; but to be accepted as teachers, they need the proper accreditation, the title of Geshe. Although they appreciate the rigor of this training, they also find it too long, particularly when the time for the new mandatory written exam is included.

Another complaint concerns the nature of the studies themselves. Some of the younger monks resent the centrality of debate to the curriculum. Though this practice may be intellectually challenging, it does not have any direct application to the real world. Some younger monks are interested in more useful training—for example, in preaching, which would help them function as Dharma teachers in the newly created Buddhist centers. Others argue for more radical changes. They want to transform the monastery into a modern university where many subjects are taught and students are free to choose their subjects, like the Central Institute for Higher Tibetan Studies in Sarnath, near Vārānasi, where students may study a variety of topics ranging from traditional Buddhist learning to Hindi and English. Their elders strenuously disagree with this model, for the alteration would eliminate the central element of Tibetan monastic education, the dialectic of commentary and debate, and would greatly diminish the strength of its focus.

In the meantime, however, accommodation with the modern world, a topic that was center stage in the mid-1980s, has been superseded by the more urgent problem created by the influx of monks from Tibet that began in the early 1980s. At first it was slow, and new arrivals from Tibet *(gsar 'byor ba)* were a small minority. In the 1990s, the process accelerated and the trickle became a flood. This influx of newcomers has radically transformed the monastic institutions in exile, increasing their size dramatically. At the beginning of the 1970s, Se-ra was given land to accommodate a population of 300. When it restarted its scholastic program, the monastery grew by drawing new recruits from the exiled population. By 1985, Se-ra had about 1,000 monks. Aided by new arrivals, the monastery has grown to more than 4,000.

The first and most obvious problem has been to accommodate and feed these new arrivals, requiring new efforts on the part of the monks who had worked so hard to re-create their institutions. Social integration is another difficulty, as many of the new arrivals have received little training in Tibet. Even the few who are educated (the monks coming from Amdo appear to be much better educated than those coming from Kham) find themselves literally in a foreign land, where the exile community has lived for the past forty years. As a result, the tension between the two groups is considerable, particularly between the youthful newcomers and the young generation of monks raised in India.

The massive flow of the new arrivals from Tibet has changed the intergenerational dynamics of the monasteries. The old-new balance has been replaced by a triangular relation: the old generation of monks who were educated in Tibet and in Buxa prior to their resettlement in South India, the generation of monks raised in exile and educated in South India, and the new arrivals from Tibet. The relationship among these three groups is complex and well beyond the purview of this work.[1] It is clear, however, that this triangular relation has greatly complicated the process of accommodation to modernity. Often the elders, who were raised in a society largely governed by regional affiliations, have much more in common with the new arrivals than with the generation of monks raised in India. Hence, they have tended to side with the new arrivals against the Indian-educated generation. This realignment has both exacerbated the rift between older and younger generations and shifted the orientation of the monastery away from accommodating to the modern world toward integrating newcomers who follow traditional models. For example, the regional houses, which in exile had lost most of their historical role, have become much more important. They function as they did in Tibet, that is, as centers of social integration along regional lines for monks newly arriving at one of the three seats. These changes have further complicated the future of Tibetan scholastic education, which appears more uncertain than ever. Will the tradition evolve to provide an education that its members find relevant to the modern world? Or will it remain limited to traditional forms, as it has been up until now? Only time will provide answers to these large questions.

SCHOLASTICISM: A PERSONAL ASSESSMENT

This book has been not just a description of Tibetan scholasticism but also a personal inventory. In going to India I stumbled on a rich tradition in which I had the good fortune of being trained for the next fifteen years. Throughout the preceding pages I have analyzed the experiences of members of the Tibetan scholastic traditions, and I have tried to be as careful as possible in distinguishing their experiences from my own. Yet in many ways, our experiences were similar. The training aimed at developing conviction in the tradition and understanding of Madhyamaka philosophy. It also aimed at promoting such qualities as focus and discipline, readiness to inquire, and the ability to interpret. In certain respects, I believe that my training was successful.

Such an assessment raises some obvious questions. Autobiographical evaluations are uncertain. My present positive evaluation of my monastic training could change, though this seems unlikely. There is also the danger of self-delusion, the tendency to see one's story in a favorable light. Finally there is the temptation to self-aggrandize, presenting minor incidents as personal achievements.[2] Inasmuch as this work is about myself, it runs those risks. My hope is that I have made plain how far I was from exemplary and that readers will understand that the merit, if there is any, belongs less to me than to my extraordinarily generous teachers, who tried to educate me without expecting much in return. The only hope they had was to share their conviction in the validity of their tradition. But did they succeed?

This question is important for our inquiry, since it goes to the heart of scholastic training, which aims at developing in its members conviction in the tradition. I have tried to problematize the notion of faith, showing that the commitment to a religious tradition is far from self-evident, since such a tradition neither entails the literal acceptance of all its doctrines nor excludes a certain amount of disagreement. Religious traditions require interpretation, and scholastic training largely consists of learning that art. But interpretation implies the possibility of legitimate divergences in how the most important ideas and practices are formulated. For most Tibetan monks, who fully believe in the traditional Buddhist worldview, these differences remain limited. For a Westerner such as myself, conviction in the validity of the tradition has different implications. It can be expressed in ways that may diverge from orthodox formulations, though one hopes they remain inspired by the tradition.

Similarly, in carrying on the work started in the monastery, I have had to find my own path. Traditionally, Geshes have used their knowledge by becoming hermits dedicated to meditation or by leading monastic communities. As a foreigner, I did not have such obvious channels of expression. After finishing my training, I was faced with the question of what to do next. I could have remained among Tibetan monks, teaching students and continuing to learn more about the Ge-luk tradition, particularly its tantric aspects. But I was not enthusiastic about this prospect. The idea of teaching in a monastery seemed a poor way to use my training, an imitation of what Tibetans could do better. Studying tantra in the traditional way also had little appeal. I have always been most taken by the philosophical aspects of the tradition and I was doubtful whether traditional esoteric studies would offer the kind of stimulation I had received in the monastery. I could have associated myself with one of the many Buddhist centers in the West, but I felt it would be difficult to find the kind of environment I was looking for.

While I was in this state of indecision, Jeffrey Hopkins offered me the possibility of entering the Ph.D. program at the University of Virginia. This looked like a promising means of furthering my intellectual development and providing myself with tools to understand better what I had learned in the monastery. The intellectual traditions I encountered at the university were obviously very different from what I had been immersed in for many years. But I believe that I was well prepared for the encounter. The years of study of commentary and debate had trained my interpretive abilities, so that the transition posed few intellectual difficulties. The main one was learning how to write in an academic environment, given that writing plays a minor role in most Tibetan scholastic tradition, particularly in the Ge-luk training I had been exposed to.

My greatest disappointment in coming to an American university was the lack of debate. I remember at first trying to debate in classes with other students or with the professor, but such attempts usually ended badly. In one class, I was told that debating was not what "gentlemen" should engage in. In another, the professor was only too delighted to debate me in his area of specialization, where he obviously had the upper hand, but this made the other students uncomfortable. "How can you be so harsh toward a student?" they asked him. "Oh, don't worry. He is well trained. He can take it," was the reply. As I have tried to make clear, the monastery allows for freer encounters. There nobody is offended at being defeated in debate or even made fun of. I find this culture of disagreement too often missing in American higher education, where students and faculties are at times overly sensitive and preoccupied with their reputations.

On the more positive side, the academic training considerably widened my intellectual horizon and gave me a variety of theoretical tools to pursue my interests. It also gave me a better appreciation of the variety of Buddhist traditions. In particular, it led me to broaden my understanding of the Tibetan tradition by including the views of such schools as the Sa-gya and the Nying-ma, which I had not encountered in my Ge-luk education. Discovering these views was an enriching experience, which I could have had while living in the Tibetan community but did not.[3] Nor was I encouraged to do so. In retrospect, this is where I find the education I received most lacking.

This broader understanding also marks where I have come to differ the most from the views of my teachers. They had trained me to become a good Buddhist monk belonging to the Ge-luk tradition. Although they perhaps succeeded in making me a Buddhist, they certainly did not make me an active proponent of the Ge-luk tradition.[4] I had understood that being trained by Tibetan scholars meant embracing a tradition, but I never defined this tradition as Ge-luk. Rather I saw myself as a Buddhist who happened to be associated with a particular Tibetan tradition. Some of my teachers saw things differently. They had hoped that I would propagate their tradition in the West, and I can only regret that I have disappointed them. For others, this hope was perhaps less important, though I often wonder what Gen Nyi-ma would have said about my interest in the views of other schools. What would he have said if I had presented him with the Madhyamaka views of

Śākya Chok-den I have used here? Would he have risen to the occasion and engaged in the debate warranted by the difficulty of this topic, as I would hope and want to believe? Or would he have shown annoyance at my interest in interpretations that he found lacking? I will never know.

What I do know is how beneficial I have found my engagement with the views of other schools. It has given me a better understanding of the texts I had studied in the monastery. I realized then that I had often been unable to understand their main insights, as I was lost in the textual and dialectical details. Confronting different interpretations gave me the opportunity to gain a better view of some of these essential points. In this way, I was able to continue the process of internalization that I had started in the monastery but had not been able to push very far. There, I was able to put together a debate, but I had difficulty finding the concepts relevant to my own experience. In short, I had developed the first of the three types of acumen—the understanding that "arises from listening," or extensive study of the texts constitutive of the tradition—but had not been able to move to the second level and see how the texts could "appear as advice [for my practice]," to use Dzong-ka-ba's words (see chapter 8).

Gen Nyi-ma often chided me for my clever but superficial understanding. "You are good with words but you are unable to see what they mean!" "Words, only words!" he would say, often when I had given the right answer. Such statements would annoy me no end, and I would press Gen-la to show me what he meant. But his point was that there is a limit to what words can say, and that there is more to the development of insight than the right answer. Though I could understand everything that he said and I could even raise the right question, I could go no further, and there was no way for him to tell me how to do it. It is only later that I began to understand what Gen-la had in mind. At some point, one must forget one's book learning and tackle subjects on one's own terms. This approach may be disorienting for the person used to scholastic intricacies, for it involves a certain degree of simplification. Confronting the views of other schools greatly helped me in starting the process.

It is important to keep in mind that this "forgetting" does not reject but enhances thinking. For example, in the search for the view of emptiness, the other main goal of the scholastic training, deeper understanding is reached by the gradual cultivation and internalization of the Madhyamaka mode of inquiry through thinking and meditation. In this way, ordinary subjectivity, particularly our obsession with our own self-importance, is disrupted and we gain the ability to deal with things, ourselves included, without grasping onto them. This understanding is quite different from the purely intellectual approach developed by debate. Gen-la was quite aware of the distinction. At one point he ironically commented, "We are getting pretty good at debating on Madhyamaka but this is not the real understanding of emptiness, for it is bound by conceptual elaborations *(prapañca, spros pa)*. We could even defeat a person who had realized emptiness! Such a person would be able to see through conceptual elaborations but could not answer our questions."

Gen-la's comment puts scholastic studies in their proper perspective. They are means to develop an insight into the nature of reality but are unable in and of themselves to bring to full maturity the process that they start. After I finished my training, a monk, who had been in meditative retreat for years, asked me a question that clearly indicated the limits of the scholastic approach: "When will you become serious and engage in a long-term retreat?" Yet scholasticism also has definite strengths, for it fortifies concentration, develops confidence and resolution, and trains the mind in the art of inquiry, an ability without which deeper understanding is impossible. Thus, far from being an obstacle to higher religious pursuits, scholasticism is an important step toward appropriating the tradition. However, such an appropriation is constituted less by standard doctrinal formulations than by an inquisitive mind that can see through the limitations of its constructions and yet remain within the orbit of the tradition.

Notes

1. I grew up in La Chaux-de-Fonds, a small industrial town in the French-speaking part of Switzerland.

2. The "sound of one hand clapping" alludes to the now-famous Zen koan, based on an exchange between Mokurai, master at the Kennin temple, and his young protégé Toyo, who wanted to practice Zen. Mokurai told him, "You can hear the sound of two hands when they clap together. Now show me the sound of one hand" (P. Reps, *Zen Flesh, Zen Bones: A Collection of Zen and Pre-Zen Writings* [1957; reprint, New York: Anchor, 1989], 25). For a critique of the Western appropriation of Zen, see B. Faure, *The Rhetoric of Immediacy: A Cultural Critique of Chan/Zen Buddhism* (Princeton: Princeton University Press, 1991), and R. Sharf, "The Zen of Japanese Nationalism," in *Curators of the Buddha: The Study of Buddhism under Colonialism*, ed. D. Lopez (Chicago: University of Chicago Press, 1995), 107–60.

3. On the romanticization of Tibet, see D. Lopez, *Prisoners of Shangri-La: Tibetan Buddhism and the West* (Chicago: University of Chicago Press, 1997).

4. See in particular R. Schwartz, *Circle of Protest: Political Ritual in the Tibetan Uprising* (New York: Columbia University Press, 1994).

5. For example, E. Durkheim declares: "In the lower societies, since social organization is very simple, morality takes on the same [unchanging] character; consequently it is neither necessary nor even possible that the nature of discipline be very elaborated (lit., *éclairé*, i.e., enlightened). This same simplicity of moral behavior makes it easy to transform such behavior into habits, mechanically carried out; under such conditions, such automaticism poses no difficulties" (*Moral Education: A Study in the Theory and Application of the Sociology of Education*, trans. E. K. Wilson and H. Schnurer, ed. E. K. Wilson [New York: Free Press, 1961], 1:52). M. Weber expresses a similar view while discussing the four types of social action. What he calls "traditional behaviour" (the other three types being instrumental, value-rational, and affective) is "a matter of almost automatic reaction to habitual stimuli which guide behaviour

in a course which has been repeatedly followed" (*Economy and Society: An Outline of Interpretive Sociology*, trans. E. Fischoff et al., ed. G. Roth and C. Wittich [Berkeley: University of California Press, 1978], 25).

6. For criticism of viewing tradition as simply oppositional, see in particular E. Said, *Orientalism* (New York: Pantheon, 1978), and J. Fabian, *Time and the Other: How Anthropology Makes Its Object* (New York: Columbia University Press, 1983).

7. D. Sperber, *On Anthropological Knowledge* (Cambridge: Cambridge University Press, 1985), 63.

8. See, for example, G. Schopen's excellent "Archeology and Protestant Pre-suppositions in the Study of Indian Buddhism," in *Bones, Stones, and Buddhist Monks: Collected Papers on the Archaeology, Epigraphy, and Texts of Monastic Buddhism in India* (Honolulu: University of Hawaii Press, 1997), 1–22.

9. Faure, *The Rhetoric of Immediacy*, 91.

10. E. Shils, *The Intellectuals and the Powers* (Chicago: University of Chicago Press, 1972), 3.

11. A similar description of traditional intellectuals is given by M. Fischer in *Iran: From Religious Disputation to Revolution* (Cambridge, Mass.: Harvard University Press, 1980), 41, 59.

12. On scholasticism as mere hair-splitting, see A. Gramsci, *Selections from the Prison Notebooks*, ed. and trans. Quintin Hoare and Geoffrey Nowell Smith (New York: International, 1971), 200, and B. Russell, *A History of Western Philosophy* (New York: Simon and Schuster, 1945), 435; both quoted in J. Cabezón, introduction to *Scholasticism: Cross-Cultural and Comparative Perspectives*, ed. J. Cabezón (Albany: State University of New York Press, 1998), 3.

13. Heidegger, with his way of doing metaphysics, comes to mind as an unwitting scholastic, but he is certainly not the only one.

14. See, for instance, Cabezón, *Scholasticism*.

15. G. Makdisi, "The Scholastic Method in Medieval Education," *Speculum* 49 (1974): 640–61.

16. Makdisi, "The Scholastic Method," 642.

17. Makdisi, "The Scholastic Method," 654.

18. For analyses that rely on such oppositions, see, for example, G. Samuel, *Civilized Shamans: Buddhism in Tibetan Societies* (Washington, D.C.: Smithsonian Institution Press, 1993). Although Samuel's work contains a great deal of useful information (an extensive bibliography; the refusal to reduce Tibet to the central area controlled by the Tibet government; a helpful inclusion of marginal groups such as nomads, the Golok from Eastern Tibet, practitioners of popular religion; etc.), his description of the Tibetan tradition as constituted by the opposition between clerical and shamanic elements makes a mockery of any scholarly use of the term *shamanism*. Granted, such a term is difficult to define; but Samuel's exuberant inclusion of all practices involving an altered state of consciousness, including all meditative practices, is in a class of its own. Some practitioners of folk religion can be described as *shamans* in the narrow (and more or less proper) sense of the word, but not all tantrikas, meditators,

or hermits fit this category. Moreover, Samuel's identification of the Nying-ma with shamanic and the Ge-luk with clerical Buddhism seriously misrepresents them, ignoring the considerable tantric Ge-luk tradition and the importance of scholasticism in the Nying-ma tradition. A contemporary master such as Dudjom Rin-po-che *('dud 'joms rin po che)* was not just a yogi but also a scholar with an extensive textual knowledge of his tradition, a combination that made him a central figure. Hence, the complex relation between scholars and yogis cannot be captured by a simple intersectarian distinction, for it is largely intrasectarian. As I will show in subsequent chapters, the most significant difference between Ge-luk and Nying-ma traditions is not that the former is scholastic and the latter is shamanic, but that they have different scholastic styles and orientations.

19. It is also true that there are hermits who bypass scholastic channels, as illustrated by the story of Milarepa, the prototype of the Tibetan yogi. See L. Lhalungpa, trans., *The Life of Milarepa* (1977; reprint, Boston: Shambhala, 1985). Nevertheless, though some of these yogis may have remained personally unaffected by the scholastic tradition, their appropriation by their own tradition as living embodiments of its central teaching connects them to scholastic culture.

20. M. Kapstein, *The Tibetan Assimilation of Buddhism: Conversion, Contestation, and Memory* (Oxford: Oxford University Press, 2000), 86. My brief mention of an anti-scholastic tradition is based on Kapstein's excellent discussion (97–106).

CHAPTER 1. TIBETAN BUDDHISM:
A BRIEF HISTORICAL OVERVIEW

1. The division into only four schools is a convenient fiction; it reflects neither historical developments nor the present situation, as it excludes, for example, the still existing Jo-nang school.

2. This heuristic scheme is inspired by but differs from that of D. S. Ruegg, "On the Reception and Early History of the dbu ma (Madhyamaka) in Tibet," in *Tibetan Studies in Honour of Hugh Richardson: Proceedings of the International Seminar on Tibetan Studies, Oxford, 1979,* ed. M. Aris and A. Suu Kyi (Warminster, Wilts.: Aris and Phillips, 1980), 277–79. As with any periodicization, its divisions can be contested. For example, should the fourth period start in the sixteenth century, when the consolidation of previous interpretations occurs, or in the seventeenth century, when the political institutions corresponding to such a consolidation are established?

3. D. Snellgrove and H. Richardson, *A Cultural History of Tibet* (Boston: Shambhala, 1986), 25.

4. See E. Haarh, *The Yar luṅ Dynasty: A Study with Particular Regard to the Contribution by Myths and Legends to the History of Ancient Tibet and the Origin and Nature of Its Kings* (Copenhagen: Gad, 1968).

5. See C. Beckwith, *The Tibetan Empire in Central Asia: A History of the Struggle for Great Power among Tibetans, Turks, Arabs, and Chinese during the Early Middle Ages* (Princeton: Princeton University Press, 1987), 14.

6. T. Shakabpa, *Tibet: A Political History* (1967; reprint, New York: Potala, 1984), 12, 25.

7. Snellgrove and Richardson, *A Cultural History of Tibet*, 92.

8. That is, the layers are not self-enclosed fields of practices but mutually interpenetrating, as suggested by S. Mumford's helpful view of Tibetan Buddhism as heteroglossic. See his unjustly neglected *Himalayan Dialogue: Tibetan Lamas and Gurung Shamans in Nepal* (Madison: University of Wisconsin Press, 1989), 23–30.

9. I use this obviously loaded term, which implies that such views and practices are inferior, when speaking from the Tibetan perspective. When I discuss the same views and practices from a modern scholarly perspective, I use the term *basic Buddhism*.

10. S. Collins, *Selfless Persons: Imagery and Thought in Theravada Buddhism* (Cambridge: Cambridge University Press, 1982), 29.

11. Indian traditions have taken great delight in emphasizing the inconceivable vastness of the universe, measuring time and space through mind-boggling numbers. The time necessary to becoming a buddha is extremely long—at least three immeasurable aeons *(asaṃkheyakalpa, bskal pa grangs med)*, each aeon composed of twenty intermediary aeons *(antarakalpa, bar bskal)*. See J. Nattier, *Once Upon a Future Time: Studies in a Buddhist Prophecy of Decline* (Berkeley: Asian Humanities Press, 1991), 10–19, and Kongtrul Lodrö Tayé, *Myriad Worlds: Buddhist Cosmology in Abhidharma, Kālacakra, and Dzog-chen.* trans. and ed. International Translation Committee (Ithaca: Snow Lion, 1995), 140–45.

12. By using the terms *esoteric* ("internal," "secret") and *exoteric* ("external," "public") in their strict senses, I do not intend to associate tantra with pop-spiritual culture. It is in the latter sense that F. Crews defines *occultism* as "the belief that nature possesses secret properties contradicting the presumed laws of science" and *esotericism* as "the broader project that weds occultism to self-transformation" ("The Consolation of Theosophy," review of *Madame Blavatsky's Baboon: A History of the Mystics, Mediums, and Misfits Who Brought Spiritualism to America,* by P. Washington, *New York Review of Books,* September 19, 1996, p. 26).

13. For an introduction to tantra, see J. Gyatso, *Apparitions of the Self: The Secret Autobiographies of a Tibetan Visionary: A Translation and Study of Jigme Lingpa's "Dancing Moon in the Water" and "Dākki's Grand Secret-Talk"* (Princeton: Princeton University Press, 1998), 85–197. For a discussion of the four types of tantra, see D. Snellgrove, *Indo-Tibetan Buddhism: Indian Buddhists and Their Tibetan Successors* (Boston: Shambhala, 1987), 1:147–52; J. Hopkins, trans. and ed., *Tantra in Tibet: The Great Exposition of Secret Mantra* (London: Allen and Unwin, 1977); and F. D. Lessing and A. Wayman, trans., *Introduction to the Buddhist Tantric Systems,* 2nd ed. (Delhi: Motilal Banarsi-

dass, 1980). For a discussion of the so-called lower tantras, see J. Hopkins, *Deity Yoga: In Action and Performance Tantra* (1981; reprint, Ithaca: Snow Lion, 1987), and S. Beyer, *Magic and Ritual in Tibet: The Cult of Tārā* (1973; reprint, Delhi: Motilal Banarsidass, 1988).

14. Do Grub-chen *(rdo grub chen 'jigs med bstan pa'i nyi ma)*, dPal gsang ba'i snying po'i rgyud kyi spyi don nyung ngu'i ngag gis rnam par 'byed pa rin chen mdzod kyi lde mig, in *The Collected Works (gsung 'bum) of Rdo Grub-chen Jigs-med-bstan-pa'i-nyi-ma* (Gantok, Sikkim: Dodrub Chen Rimpoche, 1974), 3:1–237.

15. See, for example, Dzong-ka-ba, *The Great Treatise on the Stages of the Path to Enlightenment*, trans. Lamrim Chenmo Translation Committee (Ithaca: Snow Lion, 2000), 69.

16. The exact nature of the nonduality realized in tantric practice is the subject of considerable debate among Tibetan thinkers. The Ge-luk tradition assimilates tantric nonduality to the emptiness or essencelessness of phenomena, as taught by the Perfection of Wisdom sutras *(prajñāpāramitāsūtra)*. Other schools understand tantric nonduality not just as emptiness but as including the pure and luminous nature of phenomena, particularly that of the mind. See D. Cozort, *Highest Yoga Tantra: An Introduction to the Esoteric Buddhism of Tibet* (Ithaca: Snow Lion, 1986), and T. Thondup, *Buddha Mind: An Anthology of Longchen Rabjam's Writings on Dzogpa Chenpo*, ed. H. Talbott (Ithaca: Snow Lion, 1989).

17. R. A. Stein, *Tibetan Civilization*, trans. J. E. Stapleton Driver (Stanford: Stanford University Press, 1972), 191. These popular practices are similar to those described by J. Z. Smith as *locative*, since they concern the places of people in the world *(Map Is Not Territory: Studies in the History of Religion* [1978; reprint, Chicago: University of Chicago Press, 1993], 101). Such practices do not seek to extricate people from the world, but rather help them restore and maintain the constantly threatened balance within society and between the levels of the cosmos. They are also often limited to local concerns. Hence, they are usefully described as *local supernaturalism;* see S. Collins, *Nirvana and Other Buddhist Felicities: Utopias of the Pali Imaginaire* (Cambridge: Cambridge University Press, 1998), 28.

18. This coexistence is well captured by R. Gombrich's description of Buddhism as an accretive symbiosis between soteriological and communal practices; see *Precept and Practice: Traditional Buddhism in the Rural Highlands of Ceylon* (Oxford: Clarendon Press, 1971).

19. I am here greatly simplifying, since some of the Mahayana sutras, particularly those of the third turning of the wheel, present a view that is not unlike that of the tantras. See Snellgrove, *Indo-Tibetan Buddhism*, 94–109.

20. I call these tantrikas *nonordained* rather than *lay* because they too are virtuosi. Hence, they are not part of the laity but form a different class of religious specialist whose status is similar to that of monks and nuns. For a description of the conflicts between proponents of exoteric and esoteric traditions during the tenth century, see S. Karmay's two classic articles: "King

Tsa/Dza and Vajrayāna," in *Tantric and Taoist Studies in Honour of R. A. Stein*, ed. M. Strickmann (Brussels: Institut Belge des Hautes Études Chinoises, 1981), 192–211, and "The Ordinance of lHa-ma Ye-shes-'od," in Aris and Suu Kyi, *Tibetan Studies*, 145–49.

21. Atiśa, *Byang chub lam gyi sgron me dan de'i bka' 'grel* (Dharamsala: Council of Religious Affairs, 1969); for a rendering in English, see Geshe Sonam Rinchen and Ruth Sonam, *Atisha's Lamp for the Path to Enlightenment* (Ithaca: Snow Lion, 1997). Atisha's description of the three types of persons differs from that found in the later Stages of the Path. For Atisha, the inferior person is non-religious, whereas in the Stages of the Path he or she is the person seeking a good rebirth by accumulating merits. The middling individual follows the "Hinayana" ideal of self-liberation. The superior one is engaged on the path of the bodhisattva, seeking buddhahood through either the exoteric or esoteric paths.

22. Dzong-ka-ba, *The Great Treatise*. The Stages of the Path literature tends to be favored by the Ge-luk school. Other schools use a similar genre of texts, the Stages of the Teaching *(bstan rim)*, whose most famous examples are *Revealing the Thought of the Muni* by Sa-paṇ and *Jewel Ornament of Liberation* by Gam-popa *(sgam po pa)*. For *Revealing the Thought of the Muni*, see *Thub pa'i dgongs gsal*, in *Complete Works of the Great Masters of the Sa sKya Sect* (Tokyo: Tokyo Bunko, 1968), 5: 1.1–50.1; a partial translation is available in Sakya Pandita, *Illuminations: A Guide to Essential Buddhist Practices*, trans. Geshe Wangyal and B. Cutillo (Novato, Calif.: Lotsawa, 1988). For the latter, see H. Guenther, trans., *Jewel Ornament of Liberation* (London: Rider, 1959); the Tibetan title is *dam chos yid bzhin nor bu thar pa rin po che'i rgyan zhes bya ba theg pa chen po'i lam rim gyi bshad pa*. For a discussion of the differences between Stages of the Path and Stages of the Teaching, see D. Jackson, "The *bsTan rim* ('Stages of the Doctrine') and Similar Graded Expositions of the Bodhisattva's Path," in *Tibetan Literature: Studies in Genre*, ed. J. Cabezón and R. Jackson (Ithaca: Snow Lion, 1996), 229–43.

23. It should be emphasized that this Tibetan way of understanding tantra is a later sanitized attempt to integrate tantra into the normative Buddhist framework; tantra may have been practiced quite differently during an earlier period in India.

24. The importance of the Stages of the Path is well captured by Dzong-ka-ba's enumeration of the four special qualities of this type of literature, which contains the greatness of enabling one to know that all teachings are free of contradiction, the greatness of enabling one to understand that all the scriptures are instructions for practice, the greatness of enabling one easily to find the Conqueror's (i.e., the Buddha's) intent, and the greatness of enabling one to refrain automatically from great wrongdoing (*The Great Treatise on the Stages of the Path*, 46–53).

25. Snellgrove, *Indo-Tibetan Buddhism*, 490–91.

26. For a history of the Sa-gya school, see C. Trichen, *The History of the Sakya Tradition: A Feast for the Minds of the Fortunate*, trans. Ven. Phende Rinpoche, Jamyang Khandro, and J. Stott (Bristol: Ganesha Press, 1983), and

C. Stearns's *Luminous Lives: The Story of the Early Masters of the Lambras Tradition in Tibet* (Boston: Wisdom, 2001).

27. For scholarly descriptions of the development of the Nying-ma school, see S. Karmay, *The Great Perfection: A Philosophical and Meditative Teaching of Tibetan Buddhism* (Leiden: Brill, 1988); D. Germano, "Architecture and Absence in the Secret Tantric History of the Great Perfection," *Journal of the International Association of Buddhist Studies* 17 (1994): 203–336; and Dudjom Rinpoche, Jikdrel Yeshe Dorje, *The Nyingma School of Tibetan Buddhism: Its Fundamentals and History* (Boston: Wisdom, 1991).

28. Scholars disagree about Padmasambhava's actual historical role, which remains difficult to determine. See M. Kapstein, *The Tibetan Assimilation of Buddhism: Conversion, Contestation, and Memory* (Oxford: Oxford University Press, 2000), 155–60; Karmay, *The Great Perfection*, 6; and two works by A. M. Blondeau, "Le lHa-'dre Bka'-thang," in *Études tibétaines, dédiées à la mémoire de Marcelle Lalou* (Paris: Maisonneuve, 1971), 29–126, and "Analyses of the Biographies of Padmasambhava according to Tibetan Tradition: Classification of Sources," in Aris and Suu Kyi, *Tibetan Studies*, 45–52.

29. In fact, the work of organizing and commenting on the material received from India started earlier with figures such as Rong-zom Paṇḍita (eleventh century); such observations underscore that the periodization relied on here is little more than a device to introduce the reader to the historical development of Tibetan traditions. See Ruegg, "On the Reception and Early History of the dbu ma (Madhyamaka) in Tibet," on this period as "classical."

30. The Nying-ma school accepts the new canon as established during the thirteenth century by Bu-dön-rin-chen-drup, as well as the early translations made from the time of Vairocana (late eighth century) to that of Paṇḍita Smṛti-jñānakīrti—especially the translations of the old tantras, which are collected in the "Collected Tantras of the Ancient School" *(rnying ma rgyud 'bum)*. The other schools accept only the later translations, from Rin-chen-zang-bo onward.

31. The tantric material does not seem to have been systematically collected, and even the Mahayana sutras were not organized canonically. For an analysis of the Tibetan canon, see P. Harrison, "A Brief History of the Tibetan bKa' 'gyur," in Cabezón and Jackson, *Tibetan Literature*, 39–56.

32. This is particularly true of Gyel-tsap's *Tshad ma rigs pa'i gter gyi rnam bshad legs par bshad pa'i snying po* (bkra shis 'khyil, n.d.), which was composed in the later part of his life. This text is a commentary on Sa-paṇ's *Rigs gter* and presents itself as following Ren-da-wa's views (which perhaps explains why it was not included in Gyel-tsap's Collected Works).

The Holder of the Throne of Ga-den has by now become the nominal leader of the Ge-luk tradition, its effective leader being the Dalai Lama. Originally, however, the Ga-den tradition was not directed by reincarnated lamas. The Holder of the Throne of Ga-den was, and still is, chosen among senior scholars. Gradually, however, his power was eclipsed by that of reincarnated lamas, who became the tradition's de facto leaders.

33. This emphasis is presumably the basis for the frequent and misleading

representation of Dzong-ka-ba as "a reformer." There is little evidence that he saw himself as reforming Tibetan Buddhism or its monastic tradition, though he did stress the centrality of the latter.

34. These political ties were already forming in the time of Dzong-ka-ba, who had sustained relations with the Pa-mo-dru-ba (*phag-mo-gru-pa*) family, which had dominated Tibet politically since 1358.

35. See G. Dreyfus, *Recognizing Reality: Dharmakīrti's Philosophy and Its Tibetan Interpreters* (Albany: State University of New York Press, 1997).

36. Kapstein, *The Tibetan Assimilation of Buddhism*, 17.

37. Shakabpa, *Tibet*, 110.

38. On Jam-gön Kong-trul (*'jam mgon kong sprul blo gros mtha' yas*, 1813 – 1899), Jam-yang Kyen-tse-wang-po (*'jam dbyangs mkhyen brtse'i dbang po*, 1820 – 1892), and Dza Pa-trül (*dpal sprul*, 1808 – 1887), see E. G. Smith, *Among Tibetan Texts: History and Literature of the Himalayan Plateau* (Boston: Wisdom, 2001), 235 – 71.

39. In particular, Den-dar-hla-ram-ba (*bstan dar lha rams pa*, 1759 – 1840) and the Fifth Pen-chen Lama, Lob-zang Pal-den (*blo bzang dpal ldan chos kyi grags pa*, 1853 – 1882), were interested in the Great Perfection. The Thirteenth Dalai Lama also seems to have some interest in this tradition.

40. For example, Kun-zang Sö-nam (*kun bzang bsod nams*) wrote a commentary on Śāntideva's *Bodhicaryāvatāra* inspired by the teachings of the nonsectarian movement; but in it, the ninth chapter sets out the view of Madhyamaka in accordance with Dzong-ka-ba's interpretation. See *sPyod 'jug gi 'grel bshad rgyal sras yon tan bum bzang* (Qinghai: Krungo'i Bod kyi Shes Rig dPe bsKrun Khang, 1991).

41. See G. Dreyfus, "The Shuk-den Affair: History and Nature of a Quarrel," *Journal of the International Association of Buddhist Studies* 21 (1999): 227–70 .

42. For example, the view of extrinsic emptiness (*gzhan stong*) held by the Jo-nang-bas has been considered heterodox by many Tibetan scholars. See D. S. Ruegg, "The Jo nan pas: A School of Buddhist Ontologists according to the *Grub mtha' śel gyi me long*," *Journal of the American Oriental Society* 83 (1963): 73 – 91, and S. Hookham, *The Buddha Within: Tathagatagarbha Doctrine according to the Shentong Interpretation of the Ratnagotravibhaga* (Albany: State University of New York Press, 1991).

CHAPTER 2. TIBETAN MONASTICISM

1. For a description of the important privileges and the few duties of clerics, see J. Verger, *Les gens de savoir dans l'Europe de la fin du Moyen Age* (Paris: Presses Universitaires de France, 1997), 209.

2. Nam-gyel was created by the Fifth Dalai Lama to fulfill the ritual role that is a vital part of the institution of the Dalai Lama. That Tibetans refer to Westerners as "foreigners" (*phyi rgyal*) expresses quite well their distance from and suspicion toward the West, felt until recently (when attitudes have changed

dramatically). Although this term theoretically applies to any non-Tibetan, in fact it is not used of Indians, Chinese, and other people from Asia.

3. Adequate analyses of Tibetan monasticism are surprisingly few. There are a number of personal accounts, mostly by Tibetans, and a few descriptions by outside observers, but there is no study, for example, of the rich Tibetan Vinaya (*'dul ba)* literature. The most significant exception is Melwyn Goldstein's analysis of Tibetan monasticism, particularly noteworthy for his important but limited concept of *mass monasticism,* to which we will return. See, for example, M. Goldstein and P. Tsarong, "Tibetan Buddhist Monasticism: Social, Psychological, and Cultural Implications," *Tibet Journal* 10, no. 1 (1985): 14–31.

4. Louis Dumont has insisted on the centrality of world renunciation in Indian religions; see "World Renunciation in Indian Religions," in *Homo Hierarchicus: The Caste System and Its Implications,* trans. M. Sainsbury, L. Dumont, and B. Gulati, rev. ed. (Chicago: University of Chicago Press, 1980), 267–86. But for my taste, his understanding of renunciation is still too close to Weber's characterization of inner- and otherworldly asceticisms in the *Protestant Ethic,* which was meant to capture the important distinctions between the world-transcendent ideal of Buddhist monasticism and the practical activism of Protestant asceticism. Though Weber may be right to emphasize the practical effects of religious ideas and the differences between styles of asceticism, he goes too far in presenting otherworldliness as entailing an almost complete lack of interest in the world and what happens in it. His description does not hold for Buddhist monks, who are and always have been closely connected to the laity's concerns. In his terms, Buddhist monasticism is world-transcendent but not otherworldly.

5. See S. Collins, *Selfless Persons: Imagery and Thought in Theravada Buddhism* (Cambridge: Cambridge University Press, 1982), 169.

6. See I. Friedrich-Silber, *Virtuosity, Charisma, and Social Order: A Comparative Sociological Study of Monasticism in Theravada Buddhism and Medieval Catholicism* (Cambridge: Cambridge University Press, 1995), 40.

7. The term *soteriology* derives from the Greek word *sōtērion:* i.e., "salvation" or, in the Buddhist context, liberation. It is the systematic and reflective ordering of life and death that brings about a transcendental vision in which it becomes (at least imaginatively) possible to escape suffering and attain the final happiness of salvation. Soteriological practices contrast with locative ones, which concern the places of people in the world.

8. For an excellent introduction to the Theravada Vinaya, see M. Wijayaratna, *Buddhist Monastic Life: According to the Texts of the Theravada Tradition* (Cambridge: Cambridge University Press, 1990). For a translation, see I. B. Horner, *The Book of Discipline,* vols. 1, 2, and 5 (London: Pali Text Society, 1938–52). For a list of Tibetan Vinaya literature, see C. Prebish, *A Survey of Vinaya Literature* (Taipei: Jin Luen, 1994), 84–113.

9. Wijayaratna, *Buddhist Monastic Life,* 90; see also Friedrich-Silber, *Virtuosity, Charisma, and Social Order,* 193. For the list of rules according to the Theravada Vinaya, see P. M. Samaṇa, *The Entrance to the Vinaya* (Bangkok:

King Mahā Makuta Academy, 1969), 1:27–225. The list in the Tibetan Vinaya is similar; its few minor differences remain to be explored by scholars.

10. Wijayaratna, *Buddhist Monastic Life*, 130.

11. Samaṇa, *The Entrance to the Vinaya*, ii.

12. M. Weber, *Sociology of Religion*, trans. E. Fischoff (Boston: Beacon, 1963), 162.

13. Friedrich-Silber, *Virtuosity, Charisma, and Social Order*, 191. In this paragraph, I rely on her account of the five core characteristics of virtuosity.

14. G. Schopen, *Bones, Stones, and Buddhist Monks: Collected Papers on the Archaeology, Epigraphy, and Texts of Monastic Buddhism in India* (Honolulu: University of Hawaii Press, 1997).

15. S. J. Tambiah describes the development of the priestly function in this way: "I would argue that when Buddhism became institutionalized religion, the Buddhist monk had to make a passage that was the reverse of the one made by the *brahman* (who while remaining in the caste system appropriated some *sannyasin* [renouncer] values). The monk, while standing for a way of life set apart from that of the householder, nevertheless had to have regular ritual and material transactions with the laity" (*Buddhism and the Spirit Cults in North-East Thailand* [1970; reprint, Cambridge: Cambridge University Press, 1987], 65–66).

16. For example, M. Spiro separates kammaic or folk Buddhism, which is not seriously soteriological but merely interested in merit making and good rebirth, from Nibbanic or true original Buddhism, in which morality is superseded by wisdom (*Buddhism and Society: A Great Tradition and Its Burmese Vicissitudes* [New York: Harper and Row, 1970]). Other scholars, such as R. Gombrich in his *Precept and Practice: Traditional Buddhism in the Rural Highlands of Ceylon* (Oxford: Clarendon Press, 1971), argue for the continuity of the village and elite forms of practice. The Tibetan view—as expressed, for example, in the Stages of the Path literature—is closer to Gombrich's.

17. Tambiah, *Buddhism and the Spirit Cults*, 53.

18. As Friedrich-Silber remarks, the pattern of relation between monastics and the laity is not just segregative but also aggregative. That is, monastics are clearly marked apart from the laity and lead a separate life, but the two groups are connected and interact through a constant exchange of services (*Virtuosity, Charisma, and Social Order*, 70).

19. Wijayaratna, *Buddhist Monastic Life* , 57.

20. Tambiah, *Buddhism and the Spirit Cults*, 195–222.

21. See K. Tiyavanich, *Forest Recollections: Wandering Monks in Twentieth-Century Thailand* (Honolulu: University of Hawaii Press, 1997). Forest monks find the priestly role difficult to avoid, however; their purity makes them highly attractive to the laity, who believe that they have special potency.

22. G. Bond has made a similar point about the Theravada tradition, in which he differentiates three models of practice: a canonical model, in which liberation is within reach; a traditional model, in which the idea of reaching nirvana over many (often thousands) of lifetimes dominates; and a modern model,

in which enlightenment is seen again as being more widely accessible, available to laypeople as well as monks. See *The Buddhist Revival in Sri Lanka: Religious Tradition, Reinterpretation, and Response* (Columbia: University of South Carolina Press, 1988), 22–40.

23. M. Goldstein gives the following numbers: "97 528 monks in Central Tibet and Kham in 1694, 319 270 monks in 1733. Assuming a population in these areas in 1733 of about 2.5 million, about 13 percent of the total population and about 26 percent of the males were monks" (*A History of Modern Tibet, 1913–1951: The Demise of the Lamaist State* [Berkeley: University of California Press, 1989], 21). Monks vastly outnumbered nuns, who made up only 2 to 4 percent of the population of religious practitioners. These figures are not as surprising as they may at first appear. Many of these monastics resided only occasionally at the monastery. Moreover, a similar number of priests, monastics, and clerics were found in medieval Europe. In the town of Reims, 15 percent of the male population were clerics, and a large number were monks and priests (J. Verger, *Les gens de savoir dans l'Europe de la fin du Moyen Age*, 209).

24. M. Goldstein, "The Revival of Monastic Life in Drepung," in *Buddhism in Contemporary Tibet: Religious Revival end Cultural Identity*, ed. M. Goldstein and M. Kapstein (Berkeley: University of California Press, 1998), 18–19.

25. M. Goldstein, "A Study of the *ldab ldob*," *Central Asiatic Journal* 9 (1964): 123–41. Though punk-monks existed in Tibet, they are not allowed in exile.

26. Goldstein, "The Revival of Monastic Life," 22. The situation was further complicated by the existence (fortunately rare) of a monk-tax: in a few places, families were obliged to provide someone to enter the monastery. They could, however, look for a substitute for a family member.

27. Mūla-sarvāstivāda and Sthaviravāda are two among the many schools that emerged in the fourth century B.C.E. when the Buddhist community began to split. They are distinguished not by their views but by the canon they follow, particularly the Vinaya. These differences are quite small and sometimes due to geographical reasons. Thus, the creation of such schools is largely unrelated to the emergence of the Mahayana, which started as a religious movement within some of these schools. See A. K. Warder, *Indian Buddhism* (Delhi: Motilal Banarsidass, 1970), 288–319, and P. Williams, *Mahāyāna Buddhism: The Doctrinal Foundations* (London: Routledge, 1989), 20–36.

28. See M. Carruthers, "They Will be Lords upon the Island: Buddhism in Sri Lanka," in *The World of Buddhism: Buddhist Monks and Nuns in Society and Culture*, ed. H. Bechert and R. Gombrich (London: Thames and Hudson, 1984), 133–46.

29. Tiyavanich, *Forest Recollections*, 163–71.

30. For the constitution of Se-ra Jay, see J. Cabezón, "The Regulations of a Monastery," in *Religions of Tibet in Practice*, ed. D. Lopez (Princeton: Princeton University Press, 1997), 335–51. For the full Tibetan version, see *Byang chub lam rim chen mo dang 'brel ba'i ser byes mkhas snyan grwa tshang bca' khrims chen mo* (Bylakuppe: Sera Jhe Printing Press, 1991).

31. For the constitution of Se-ra, see T. Ellingson, "Tibetan Monastic Constitutions: The bCa Yig," in Reflections on Tibetan Culture: Essays in Memory of Turrell V. Wylie, ed. L. Epstein and R. Sherburne (Lewiston, N.Y.: Mellen Press, 1990), 204–30.

32. L. Gyatso, Memoirs of a Tibetan Lama, trans. and ed. G. Sparham (Ithaca: Snow Lion, 1998), 54.

33. In Tibetan, a "monk" is generally called grwa pa: i.e., student or scholar. This does not mean, however, that most monks are scholars. The term covers fully ordained monks as well as male and female novices (dge tshul dang dge tshul ma).

34. For a description and analysis of events in Tibet in the late twentieth century, see R. Schwartz, Circle of Protest: Political Ritual in the Tibetan Uprising (New York: Columbia University Press, 1994).

35. The wealth of the monasteries varies greatly. Moreover, even a rich monastery may distribute little of that wealth to its members; such was the case with the three Ge-luk monastic seats.

36. There are exceptions to the overriding emphasis on ritual; in a few monasteries, meditation is a normal part of the daily routine. Monks conduct their individual practices in separate houses and gather for collective rituals. S. Ortner describes such monasteries among Sherpas (Life and Death on Mt. Everest: Sherpas and Himalayan Mountaineering [Princeton: Princeton University Press, 1999], 101), but they also existed in Tibet.

37. G. Lodrö, 'Bras spungs chos 'byung, in Geschichte der Kloster-Universität Drepung (Wiesbaden: Steiner, 1974), 205–8.

38. Astrology plays an important role in the life of Tibetan scholars; for a general description, see P. Cornu, Tibetan Astrology, trans. H. Gregor (Boston: Shambhala, 1997).

39. J. Cabezón has suggested that the term zhabs brtan, understood as a prayer for the guru's long life, did not exist before the eighteenth century ("Firm Feet and Long Lives: The Zhabs brtan Literature of Tibet," in Tibetan Literature: Studies in Genre, ed. J. Cabezón and R. Jackson [Ithaca: Snow Lion, 1996], 350). Probably the extension of this term to the ritual services requested by the laity came even later.

40. A third type of institution, the hermitage (ri khrod), is called dgon pa in Tibetan; P. Kvaerne describes it as a third type of monastery ("Continuity and Change in Tibetan Monasticism," in Korean and Asian Religious Tradition, ed. C.-S. Yu [Toronto: Korean and Related Studies Press, 1977], 83–98). I would argue, however, that hermitages should be distinguished from monasteries. They are not corporate entities but are owned by a person or a limited group. Moreover, they are devoted to a particular purpose beyond providing a residence. Finally, rituals are rarely performed in them. In fact, they are often a refuge for monks who want to escape the tasks and duties of regular monastic life to practice solitary meditation. Thus hermitages are not called grwa tshang, the term more properly translated as "monastery."

41. T. Thondup, *Buddhist Civilization in Tibet* (Cambridge, Mass.: Maha Siddha Nyingmapa Center, 1982), 23.

42. Some Ge-luk monasteries besides the five monastic centers mentioned in the text offered scholastic training: in Kham, Den-chö Kor-ling *(ldan chos 'khor gling)*, founded during the fifteenth century by Nga-re Do-gyel *(ngag re rdo rgyal)*, a disciple of Jam-yang Chö-jay; and in Kong-po, Cab-ngak Ri-wo Gen-den *(chab ngag ri bo dge ldan)* and Ta-shi Rab-ten *(bkra shis rab brtan)* (see T. Tulku, *A Brief History of Tibetan Academic Degrees in Buddhist Philosophy* [Copenhagen: Nordic Institute of Asian Studies, 2000], 10). The history of the gradual eclipse of these local centers, some of which had been great centers of learning, and their increasing dependence on the three seats remain to be explored.

The central monasteries of the Kar-ma branch of the Kagyü are Tsur-pu near Lhasa *(tshur phu,* founded in 1185 by the First Karmapa) and Pel-pung *(dpal spung)* and Sur-mang in Kham. In the Sa-gya tradition, some of the main centers were Sa-gya itself, founded in 1073 by Gon-chok-gyel-po *(dkon mchog rgyal po)* in Tsiang; E-vam Chö-de *('ewam chos ldan)*, founded by Ngor-chen Kun-ga Zang-po *(ngor chen kun dga' bzang po,* 1382–1456) in Tsiang; and Dzong-sar Ta-shi Lha-tse *(rdzongs gsar bkra shis lha rtse)* in Eastern Tibet (Thondup, *Buddhist Civilization in Tibet,* 34).

43. J. Le Goff, *Les intellectuels au Moyen Age* (1957; reprint, Paris: Seuil, 1985), 24–30.

44. With monastaries, numbers are difficult to estimate; there are no formal statistics available, and informants disagree. M. Goldstein puts at two hundred the number of scholars at Go-mang, a monastery that was in crisis in the 1960s, when the number of scholars had dropped to an all-time low ("The Revival of Monastic Life," 32). Most of my informants gave higher numbers for other monasteries but all agree on the low proportion of scholars. In exile higher percentages, but not all the monks from the three seats, focus on studies.

45. This description is true at least of the University of Paris, which provided the model for higher education in the West. At other universities, such as Bologna, students gathered to study together, occasionally hiring teachers; but their influence was limited (J. Verger, "Patterns," in *Universities in the Middle Ages,* ed. H. de Ridder-Symoens, vol. 1 of *A History of the University in Europe* [Cambridge: Cambridge University Press, 1992], 35–55).

46. The history of the creation of these monasteries is complex. Dre-pung, founded in 1416, was divided into several monasteries in 1449. At one point, there were seven: Lo-se-ling, Go-mang, De-yang, Sha-kor *(shag skor)*, Gye-pa *(rgyas pa)*, Dul-ba *('dul ba)*, and Ngak-pa. Several of the smaller monasteries—Sha-kor, Gye-pa, and Dul-ba—were later incorporated into Lo-se-ling, which nonetheless continued to name abbots of these vanished monasteries. Hence, there were abbots of Sha-kor and Gye-pa, but no monasteries. Of these small monasteries, only De-yang survived to 1959, but it has not reestablished itself in exile (Lodrö, *'Bras spungs chos 'byung,* 145).

47. Ngak-pa, as its name indicates, is in charge of the tantric rituals of the monastic seat. Ga-den does not have a Ngak-pa monastery, because Shar-tse and Jang-tse consider themselves to be monasteries in which both sutra and tantra are practiced. Ga-den is particularly famous for its practice of Kalacakra.

48. Se-ra was founded in 1419 by Jam-chen Chö-jay with the support of the donor Ne-wu-dong Mi-wang Drak-pa Gyel-tsen (sne'u gdong mi dbang grags pa rgyal mtshan). Two years later, the assembly hall of the May monastery was built at the instigation of Jang-chub Bum-pa (byang chub 'bum pa). The quick growth of the monastery under Gung-ru Gyel-tsen Zang-po (gung ru rgyal mtshan bzang po, 1383–1450) led to the creation of three other monasteries: Tö-pa (stod pa), Gya (rgya), and Drom-teng ('brom steng). Gya and Drom-teng were later incorporated into Tö-pa; a third monastery, Jay (byes), was created in 1481 by Nyal-tön Pel-jor Lhun-drub (gnyal ston dpal 'byor lhun grub, 1427–1514) with the support of several sponsors. In establishing Jay, Pel-jor Lhun-drub revived some of the texts and practices of an earlier teacher, Lo-drö Rin-chen Seng-ge (blo gros rin chen seng ge, a disciple of Dzong-ka-ba), particularly the worship of Tam-drin yang sang, a Nying-ma deity who was chosen as the deity (yi dam) of the monastery. Hence, the monastery is often described as being "externally Ge-luk and internally Nying-ma" (phyi dge lugs nang rnying ma). It grew quickly and soon absorbed Tö-pa, though two regional houses (spo bo and gung ru) of Tö-pa retained the right to have their own abbots. At the beginning of the eighteenth century, the two monasteries left in Se-ra (May and Jay) were complemented by a third monastery, Ngak-pa, created at the demand of Lhab-zang Khan (lha bzang). See Ye-shay Wang-chuk (ye shes dbang phyug), Sera smad thos bsam nor gling grwa tshang gi chos 'byung lo rgyus nor bu'i phreng ba (Bylakuppe, India: Se-ra May Printing Press, 1985), 31–32, and C. T. Zongtse, mKhas mang rgya mtsho'i bsti gnas dbus 'gyur gdan sa chen po gsum gyi ya gyal se ra theg chen gling gi chos 'byung rab gsal nor bu'i me long (Delhi: International Academy of Indian Culture, 1995), 234–39.

49. For example, the University of Paris had four nations: the French, the Picard, the Norman, and the English (Le Goff, Les intellectuels au Moyen Age, 82).

50. Lodrö, 'Bras spungs chos 'byung, 189–92.

51. Lodrö, 'Bras spungs chos 'byung, 420; Ye-shay Wang-chuk, Sera smad chos 'byung, 32. In Ga-den, Jang-tse has twelve houses and Shar-tse eleven (Lodrö, 426).

52. For a lively description of the duties of house teacher, see Gyatso, Memoirs of a Tibetan Lama, 159–97.

53. These managers were not always called phyag mdzod; for example, at the Lo-se-ling monastery some were known as cha bu. Still, their functions were similar. In exile, the structure is simpler: the monastery is administered by four stewards, who are appointed by the monks for a period of three years.

54. Gyatso, Memoirs of a Tibetan Lama, 204. It is quite remarkable that there is still no systematic study of the administrative and financial structures and practices of monastaries, institutions so central to traditional Tibetan culture.

55. M. Goldstein, whose work provides a good view of some of the major socioeconomic problems of pre-1950 Tibetan society, calls these subjects "serfs," a term I find loaded and inappropriate. Some of the people he so labels were quite wealthy and enjoyed substantial rights. Nevertheless, it is true that they were bound to the land and that they lived under significant constraints. See his "Serfdom and Mobility: An Examination of the Institution of Human Lease in Tibetan Society," *Journal of Asian Studies* 30 (1971): 521–34, and "Reexamining Choice, Dependency, and Command in the Tibetan Social System," *Tibet Journal* 11, no. 4 (1986): 79–112. For a critique of Goldstein's terminology, see B. Aziz, *Tibetan Frontier Families: Reflections of Three Generations from D'ing-Ri* (New Delhi: Vikas, 1978), and E. Neumaier-Dargyay, *Tibetan Village Communities: Structure and Change* (Warminster, Wilts.: Aris and Phillips, 1982).

56. Goldstein, *A History of Modern Tibet*, 34.

57. Gyatso, *Memoirs of a Tibetan Lama*, 207.

58. In exile the situation is quite different; because monasteries have lost their political and financial clout, their administration is much simpler and less attractive.

CHAPTER 3. BECOMING A MONK: TEACHER AND DISCIPLINE

1. This description of Nam-gyel no longer applies. It is now a thriving community, directed by the same monks who had felt disempowered when young.

2. Tibetan tea is made with salt and butter. Contrary to popular belief, it can be quite tasty, especially if the butter is fresh. It has the texture of a soup and is particularly welcome in cold weather.

3. Gen Lob-zang Gya-tso, interview with author, Dharamsala, fall 1995.

4. For lively descriptions of experiences at the monastic seat, see Geshe Rabten, *The Life and Teaching of Geshé Rabten: A Tibetan Lama's Search for Truth*, trans. and ed. B. A. Wallace (London: Allen and Unwin, 1980), 3–119, and L. Gyatso, *Memoirs of a Tibetan Lama*, trans. and ed. G. Sparham (Ithaca: Snow Lion, 1998).

5. Gyatso, *Memoirs of a Tibetan Lama*, 55.

6. Regional houses have played a different role in the three seats in exile. At first, their connection to regional loyalties declined: young monks educated in exile were admitted to a particular house not because they were from the same region but because they knew monks in that house. For these young monks, the more significant unit was the household *(shag tsang)*, in which they pooled together resources. But the massive influx of new arrivals from Tibet in the 1990s has changed the regional houses yet again. Unlike their already-present colleagues, these monks have fled a particular region with which they strongly identify and rarely have any social connections in India. Hence, the regional house is the center of their social life, much as it had been in Tibet. Moreover,

the regional houses in exile have become large enough (the Tre-hor House of Jay has close to a thousand monks) to function as a focus of scholarly life.

7. Gyatso, *Memoirs of a Tibetan Lama*, 77.

8. On the modern internalization of punishment, see M. Foucault, *Discipline and Punish: The Birth of the Prison*, trans. A. Sheridan (1977; reprint, New York: Vintage, 1979).

9. J. Cabezón, "The Regulations of a Monastery," in *Religions of Tibet in Practice*, ed. D. Lopez (Princeton: Princeton University Press, 1997), 349.

10. Lamas in the three seats were ranked, mostly as a function of the size of their estates rather than of their spiritual achievements. There were three types of reincarnated lamas. Tulkus of the Great Assembly *(tshogs chen sprul sku)*, who were recognized by the Tibetan government, had to make offerings to the whole seat, not just to their own monastery. Monastery Tulkus *(gwra tshang sprul sku)* were appointed by the monastery to which they made offerings. Small Tulkus *(sprul sku chung ga)* were considered to be ordinary monks and had to do the same chores. Although they were excused from working and were seated in the front rows of monks during rituals, lamas of the first two types were treated like other monks in regard to their scholarship; they were assumed to have no special knowledge and had to prove themselves. Though they had the right to stand earlier for their Geshe examinations than other monks, their performance was judged by the same standards. See D. Bärlocher, *Testimonies of Tibetan Tulkus: A Research among Reincarnate Buddhist Masters in Exile*, 2 vols. (Rikon/Zurich: Tibet-Institute, 1982).

11. J. Le Goff, *Les intellectuels au Moyen Age* (1957; reprint, Paris: Seuil, 1985), 89.

12. H. Stoddard, *Le mendiant de l'Amdo* (Paris: Société d'Ethnographie, 1985), 144. The case of Ge-dün Chö-pel is examined in greater detail in chapter 14.

13. T. Mitchell, *Colonising Egypt* (1988; reprint, Berkeley: University of California Press, 1991), 84.

14. Rato Khyongla Nawang Losang, *My Life and Lives: The Story of a Tibetan Incarnation*, ed. J. Campbell (New York: Dutton, 1977), 125.

15. For a genealogy of the term *lamaism*, see D. Lopez, *Prisoners of Shangri-La: Tibetan Buddhism and the West* (Chicago: University of Chicago Press, 1997), 15–45.

16. See L. A. Waddell, *The Buddhism of Tibet: or Lamaism, with Its Mystic Cults, Symbolism, and Mythology, and in Its Relation to Indian Buddhism* (London: W. H. Allen, 1895).

17. A student must actively decide to take a teacher as his own, and similarly the teacher must decide to accept that individual as his student; simply hearing or giving a teaching does not suffice. Once it has been established, Tibetans consider this connection to be one of the most important social relations, a bond on par with that with one's parents and hence unbreakable. Tibetans view lack of gratitude toward a parent or a teacher as one of the worst moral faults.

18. The title *rin-po-che* is honorific and can be applied by extension to important religious figures, even if they are not reincarnated lamas. Thus an abbot will be called *Ken Rin-po-che* (precious abbot).

19. See, for example, Dzong-ka-ba, *The Great Treatise on the Stages of the Path to Enlightenment*, trans. Lamrim Chenmo Translation Committee (Ithaca: Snow Lion, 2000), 69–92.

20. Some Tibetan teachers take this description of the guru fairly literally. Others realize that this tantric notion of the student-teacher relation on which the Stages of the Path insists is atypical in the Buddhist tradition; that relation is usually viewed in less personal and less absolute terms. The teacher is generally depicted as an indispensable mediator, not as quasi-divine.

21. Rabten, *The Life and Teaching*, 94. As described here, the practice was undertaken in relation to another teacher, Geshe Tu-tob *(mthu stobs)*.

22. Rabten, *The Life and Teaching*, 57. The intense longing to be with the object of devotion is also typical of bhakti.

23. Le Goff, *Les intellectuels au Moyen Age*, 89.

24. A. MacIntyre, "The Recovery of Moral Agency," in *The Best Christian Writing, 2000*, ed. J. Wilson (San Francisco: HarperCollins, 2000), 123.

25. Rato Khyongla, *My Life and Lives*, 144–53. Such lengthy restrictions on new arrivals did not apply to more senior monks. Geshes coming from the three seats would submit to this strict discipline for only a few days, after which they would be admitted as elders.

26. Dagpo Rimpotché, *Le lama venu du Tibet* (Paris: Grasset, 1998), 79.

27. See M. Weber, "The Meaning of Discipline," in *From Max Weber: Essays in Sociology*, ed. H. H. Gerth and C. W. Wright (Oxford: Oxford University Press, 1946, 1954), 253; Foucault, *Discipline and Punish*, 170.

28. The description of Ge-luk monks as "state-supported" is misleading, since that support consisted of daily tea (sometimes with food) and the rare distribution of money during rituals. In Tibet large monasteries had considerable resources but felt it necessary to hoard rather than distribute them. Hence, monasteries would pile gold in their temples while some of their own monks went hungry. Though I have not heard of monks directly dying of hunger, many became sick because of poor nutrition. In local monasteries, monks' circumstances were not so dire. They often lived with their own families, and those residing at the monastery would receive regular support. Such support from nearby families was not available for monks who had left their native province to be trained in a central monastery.

29. The families and provincial donors of younger scholars from Kham or Amdo were often too far from Lhasa to be of help. Only the more advanced scholars could establish relations with important local donors within the great aristocratic or merchant families of Lhasa. It was not rare for such families to support several scholars—for example, giving them the money for the feast offered during the Geshe exams (see chapter 11).

30. Rabten, *The Life and Teaching*, 45.

31. To get an idea of Geshe Rab-ten's style and approach, see Geshe Rabten,

Treasury of Dharma: A Tibetan Buddhist Meditation Course, ed. B. Grabia (London: Tharpa, 1988).

32. Whenever I meet the Nam-gyel monks whom I knew in those days I feel an immediate connection with them. I am now grateful for the possibilities that the monastery offered and I understand the unwelcoming reactions of the elders. The monks seem to see me with pleasure and to take a certain degree of proprietary pride in my modest achievements.

CHAPTER 4. LITERACY AND MEMORIZATION

1. M. Carruthers, *The Book of Memory: A Study of Memory in Medieval Culture* (Cambridge: Cambridge University Press, 1990), 20.

2. One noticeable exception to this scholarly neglect is S. J. Tambiah's analysis of Thai practices of memorization; see "Literacy in a Buddhist Village in North-East Thailand," in *Literacy in Traditional Societies,* ed. J. Goody (1968; reprint, Cambridge: Cambridge University Press, 1975), 85–131.

3. R. B. Ekvall, *Religious Observances in Tibet: Patterns and Function* (Chicago: University of Chicago Press, 1964), 124.

4. J. Goody, introduction to Goody, *Literacy in Traditional Societies,* 16.

5. See J. Goody, *The Logic of Writing and the Organization of Society* (Cambridge: Cambridge University Press, 1986).

6. Similar arguments have been made regarding higher-than-expected literacy in medieval Europe by J. Verger, *Les gens de savoir dans l'Europe de la fin du Moyen Age* (Paris: Presses Universitaires de France, 1997), 44, and in India and China by K. Gough, "Implications of Literacy in Traditional China and India," in Goody, *Literacy in Traditional Societies,* 70–84.

7. These observations are based purely on anecdotal evidence and hence are tentative. A joke about the monks of Dar-gye monastery seems to confirm the poor level of education in that area. A monk is looking at a letter and pretending to read it. "Hey," says his friend, "don't you realize that the letter is upside down?" The other quickly recovers: "Yes, but this is the best way to appreciate the quality of its calligraphy."

8. Gen Lob-zang Gya-tso, interview with author, Dharamsala, fall 1995.

9. Ekvall, *Religious Observances in Tibet,* 124.

10. Ekvall, *Religious Observances in Tibet,* 124.

11. Tambiah reports that in northeast Thailand, too, reading and writing were taught separately ("Literacy in a Buddhist Village," 93). R. S. Schofield gives a similar picture of eighteenth-century England; see "The Measurement of Literacy in Pre-Industrial England," in Goody, *Literacy in Traditional Societies,* 316.

12. Tambiah argues for similar patterns of reading in pre-1930 Thailand ("Literacy in a Buddhist Village," 120).

13. Ken-po Pal-den Shay-rab, interview with author, Charlottesville, Va., fall 1991; these techniques are discussed in greater detail later in this chapter.

14. Ta-shi Dor-je *(bkra shis rdo rje),* "bod kyi slob gra'i skor" (About Tibetan schools), *gTam Tshogs* 1 (1991): 24–43.

15. T. Mitchell, *Colonising Egypt* (1988; reprint, Berkeley: University of California Press, 1991), 87.

16. Dor-je, "bod kyi slob gra'i skor," 36–37.

17. Ken-po Pal-den Shay-rab, interview with author.

18. Dor-je mentions four writings ("bod kyi slob gra'i skor," 36–37). In Central Tibet, the use of cursive was less common, and children would instead focus on printing.

19. M. Goldstein, W. Siebenschuh, and T. Tsering, *Struggle for Modern Tibet: The Autobiography of Tashi Tsering* (Armonk, N.Y.: M. E. Sharpe, 1997), 32–33.

20. Tashi Tsering was among those sent to a family with the false promise of education (Goldstein, Siebenschuh, and Tsering, *Struggle for Modern Tibet,* 18–20).

21. A few individuals become monks at an advanced age (after forty or fifty). Such people, who are called *rgan chos* (i.e., "[those who practice] dharma in their old age"), are considered second-class monks and are not expected to memorize very much; often they are accepted in monasteries only if they can provide for themselves.

22. Traditional Tibetan books are not bound; the loose pages contain five to seven long lines, printed from wood blocks. Dzong-ka-ba is said to have been able to memorize up to seventeen folios a day. See Cha-har dGe-bshes bLo-bzang Tshul-khrims, *rJe thams cad mkhyen pa tsong kha pa chen po'i rnam thar go sla bar brjod pa bde legs kun kyi byung gnas,* in *The Collected Works (gsung 'bum) of Cha-har Dge-bshes Blo-bzang-tshul-khrims,* vol. 2 (Kha) (New Delhi: Chatrin Jangsar Tenzin, 1971), 104.

23. A basic premise in Indian and Tibetan cultures is that a mantra is fully effective if, and only if, it is pronounced exactly right. This requirement, which goes back to Vedic culture, is viewed by Tibetans with some flexibility and even humor. They know that they do not read mantras in the same way that Indians do. Nevertheless, they have kept the old injunction requiring precise pronunciation. On the general theory of mantra, see H. Alper, ed., *Mantra* (Albany: State University of New York Press, 1989).

24. To be sure, the memorizers look at a page, thereby introducing a visual dimension. Changes in the appearance of that page (e.g., in a different edition) can disturb the process, a sign that visual patterns contribute to memorization. But a completely memorized text becomes fully sonic. Sometimes the memorizer relies solely on the spoken words of the teacher, a practice that eliminates any visual dimension. It is less common, however, for it is time-consuming.

25. A. Klein, comp., trans., and ed., *Path to the Middle: Oral Madhyamika Philosophy in Tibet* (Albany: State University of New York Press, 1994), 6.

26. Geshe Rabten, *The Life and Teaching of Geshé Rabten: A Tibetan Lama's*

Search for Truth, trans. and ed. B. A. Wallace (London: Allen and Unwin, 1980), 81.

27. The example of the Indian master Sthiramati (fifth century C.E.) is often cited to demonstrate the value of recitation. He was a dove when he listened with reverence to Vasubandhu's melodious recitation. As a result he was reborn as a human being and shortly after his birth he started to inquire about Vasubandhu's whereabouts. See J. Tarantha, *Tāranātha's History of Buddhism in India,* trans. Lama Chimpa and A. Chattopadhyaya, ed. D. Chattopadhyaya (1970; reprint, Calcutta: Bagchi, 1980), 179–80.

28. J. Cabezón, "The Regulations of a Monastery," in *Religions of Tibet in Practice,* ed. D. Lopez (Princeton: Princeton University Press, 1997), 351.

29. R. G. Crowder, *Principles of Learning and Memory* (Hillsdale, N.J.: Erlbaum, 1976), 9.

30. For a distinction between accessibility and availability, see Crowder, *Principles of Learning and Memory,* 11.

31. Rabten, *The Life and Teaching,* 53. A Sanskrit proverb puts it this way: "As for knowledge that is in books, it is like money placed in another's hand: When the time has come to use it, there is no knowledge, there is no money" (quoted in W. A. Graham, *Beyond the Written Word: Oral Aspects of Scripture in the History of Religion* [Cambridge: Cambridge University Press, 1987], 74).

32. Graham, *Beyond the Written Word,* 160.

33. J.-C. Schmitt, "Religion populaire et culture folklorique," *Annales: Economies, sociétés, civilisations* 31 (1976): 946; quoted in B. Faure, *The Rhetoric of Immediacy: A Cultural Critique of Chan/Zen Buddhism* (Princeton: Princeton University Press, 1991), 89.

34. The exact reproduction of commentaries is less important. Often they are memorized less precisely and more superficially than other texts. Monks with great mnemonic abilities can remember them, but frequently their wording is not exact. Similarly, quotations in traditional commentaries are commonly imprecise; though the meaning is preserved the words vary slightly from the original, probably a sign that they are quoted from memory.

35. H. P. Bahrick, "Semantic Memory Content in Permastore: Fifty Years of Memory for Spanish Learned in School," *Journal of Experimental Psychology* 113 (1984): 1–29.

36. For a constructivist explanation of memory, see U. Neisser, "Interpreting Harry Bahrick's Discovery: What Confers Immunity against Forgetting?" *Journal of Experimental Psychology: General* 113 (1984): 32–35.

37. On the distinction between implicit and explicit memory, see A. D. Baddeley, *Human Memory: Theory and Practice* (Boston: Allyn and Bacon, 1990).

38. When they are unable to recite a text, monks say that "a text does not go" (*'gro gyi mi 'dug*), much as a musician might speak of a piece of music.

39. On memory generally, see E. Tulving and W. Donaldson, eds., *Organization of Memory* (New York: Academic Press, 1972); see especially E. Tulving, "Episodic and Semantic Memory" (381–403).

40. Though I began the practice at the Buddhist School, most of my train-

ing took place at the Tibetan monastery of Rikon in Switzerland, where I went at the end of the summer of 1973 (three months after starting school). When I returned to India a year later, I quickly fell sick and had to leave again. Only from early 1977 was I was able to stay in India continuously. By then, I had already completed the most important memorizations.

CHAPTER 5. THE GENERAL STRUCTURE
OF THE TIBETAN CURRICULUM

1. See R. Panikkar, "Common Patterns of Eastern and Western Scholasticism," *Diogenes* 83 (1973): 103–13; cited in M. Schwartz, "Scholasticism as a Comparative Category and the Study of Judaism," in *Scholasticism: Cross-Cultural and Comparative Perspectives*, ed. J. Cabezón (Albany: State University of New York Press, 1998), 95.

2. B. Stock, *Listening for the Text: On the Uses of the Past* (Baltimore: Johns Hopkins University Press, 1990), 162. Stock sees three elements as necessary to tradition: "pastness, authoritative presence, and the means of transmission."

3. See M. Halbertal, *People of the Book: Canon, Meaning, and Authority* (Cambridge, Mass.: Harvard University Press, 1997).

4. H. G. Gadamer puts it this way in *Truth and Method* (trans. and ed. G. Barden and J. Cumming, rev. J. Weinsheimer and D. G. Marshall, 2nd rev. ed. [New York: Crossroad, 1989], 288):

> The "classical" is something raised above the vicissitudes of changing times and changing tastes. It is immediately accessible, not through that shock of recognition, as it were, that sometimes characterizes a work of art for its contemporaries and in which the beholder experiences a fulfilled apprehension of meaning that surpasses all conscious expectations. Rather when we call something classical, there is a consciousness of something enduring, of significance, that cannot be lost and that is independent of all the circumstances of time—a timeless present that is contemporaneous with every other present.

In providing this phenomenological description of the attitude of participants in a tradition toward certain texts, Gadamer neither analyzes the cultural reality of these texts nor accounts for the contingent nature of tradition. Textual choices come and go; what is considered classical by one age may be forgotten by the next.

5. Halbertal, *People of the Book*, 94.

6. M. Fisch, *Rational Rabbis: Science and Talmudic Culture* (Bloomington: Indiana University Press, 1997), 168.

7. M. Foucault, "The Discourse on Language," in *The Archaeology of Knowledge*, trans. A. M. Sheridan Smith (1972; reprint, New York: Harper and Row, 1976), 222.

8. Foucault, "The Discourse on Language," 223.

9. To be sure, the opposition between commentary and discipline is not absolute. Modern disciplines such as anthropology and philosophy, while not organized around commentarial practices, involve commentary. Conversely, the

systematic aspects of traditional branches of knowledge are sometimes systematic in ways that resemble modern disciplines.

10. J. W. Baldwin, *The Scholastic Culture of the Middle Ages, 1000–1300* (Lexington, Mass.: Heath, 1971), 60.

11. In discussing the Tibetan branches of learning, I follow D. S. Ruegg's excellent monograph *Ordre spirituel et ordre temporel dans la pensée bouddhique de l'Inde et du Tibet* (Paris: Collège de France, 1995), 93–147, and Dudjom Rinpoche, Jikdrel Yeshe Dorje, *The Nyingma School of Tibetan Buddhism: Its Fundamentals and History* (Boston: Wisdom, 1991), 97–109. For a Tibetan source, see Kong-trul, *Theg pa sgo kun las bstus pas gsung rab rin po che'i mdzod bslab pa gsum legs par ston pa'i bstan bcos shes bya kun khyab* (Beijing: Mi Rigs dPe sKrun Khang, 1985), 2:204–358.

12. For a discussion of the ambiguous status of logic and epistemology, see G. Dreyfus, *Recognizing Reality: Dharmakīrti's Philosophy and Its Tibetan Interpreters* (Albany: State University of New York Press, 1997), 438–41.

13. Ruegg mentions several forms of Indian literature studied in Tibet during this period: the *Jātaka* (stories of the past lives of the Buddha); the *Stotra* or encomia; the *Subhāṣita* or didactic maxims; the epics, such as the *Rāmāyana*; and the legends and tales, such as the "Tales of the Vetāla" (*Ordre spirituel*, 111–16).

14. See D. Jackson, *The Entrance Gate for the Wise* (Vienna: Arbeitskreis für Tibetische und Buddhistische Studien, Universität Wien, 1987), 195. I briefly examine the five methods of exposition in chapter 9 and discuss Sa-paṇ's view of debate in chapter 10. For a discussion of Sa-paṇ's role in the "Indianization" of Tibetan learning, see M. Kapstein, "The Indian Literary Identity in Tibet," in *Literary Cultures in History: Reconstructions from South Asia*, ed. S. Pollock (Berkeley: University of California Press, forthcoming).

15. In this brief description of medieval education, I am following G. Leff, "The *Trivium* and the Three Philosophies," in *Universities in the Middle Ages*, ed. H. de Ridder-Symoens, vol. 1 of *A History of the University in Europe* (Cambridge: Cambridge University Press, 1992), 307–408.

16. See R. Mottahedeh, "Traditional Shi'ite Education in Qom," in *Philosophers on Education*, ed. A. Rorty (London: Routledge, 1998), 451–57.

17. J. Verger, *Culture, enseignement et société en Occident aux XIIe et XIIIe siècles* (Rennes: Presses Universitaires de Rennes, 1999), 159.

18. For a discussion of the rhetorical and philosophical models of education, see B. A. Kimball, *Orators and Philosophers: A History of the Idea of Liberal Education* (New York: Teachers College, Columbia University, 1986), and M. L. Clarke, *Higher Education in the Ancient World* (London: Routledge, 1971). For a discussion of *paideia*, see H. I. Marrou, *A History of Education in Antiquity*, trans. G. Lamb (New York: Sheed and Ward, 1956). For the relevance of these models to contemporary American higher education, see F. Oakley, *Community of Learning: The American College and the Liberal Arts Tradition* (New York: Oxford University Press, 1992).

19. For a discussion of the belletristic tradition in Tibet, see Kapstein, "The Indian Literary Identity in Tibet." In drawing a sharp opposition between lay

literary and monastic philosophico-religious orientations, I obviously over-simplify; Tibet has seen a number of literarily inclined monks and religiously learned laypeople. And the monastic neglect of literature was far from universal. Some monasteries, such as Ta-shi Lhun-po and La-brang, devoted more attention to such subjects than did the three seats around Lhasa. Nevertheless, the two milieus usually differed in their scholarly orientations as described. In exile, this generalization no longer holds true; many monks have made considerable efforts to learn about and promote Tibetan literature.

20. J. Verger, *Les gens de savoir dans l'Europe de la fin du Moyen Age* (Paris: Presses Universitaires de France, 1997), 39; D. F. Eickelman, *Knowledge and Power in Morocco: The Education of a Twentieth-Century Notable* (Princeton: Princeton University Press, 1985).

21. Maitreya, *Abhisamayālaṃkāranāmaprajñāpāramitopadeśaśāstraka-rikā* (*shes rab pha rol tu phyin pa'i man ngag gi bstan bcos mgnon par rtogs pa'i rgyan zhes bya ba tshig le'ur byas pa*, D: 3786, P: 5184); Nāgārjuna, *Prajñā-nāma-mūlamadhyamakakārikā* (*dbu ma rtsa ba'i tshig le'ur byas pa shes rab*, D: 3824, P: 5224); Candrakīrti, *Madhyamakāvatāra* (*dbu ma la 'jug pa*, D: 3861, P: 5262).

22. L. Gomez, "Buddhist Literature: Exegesis and Hermeneutics," in *Encyclopedia of Religion* (New York: Macmillan, 1987), 2:529–40, esp. 532. A brief examination of the Tibetan catalogs of the *bstan gyur* suggests that the Tibetan translation of the Sanskrit terms is far from systematic: *bshad pa* appears as the translation of *vyākhyā* as well as *bhāṣya* (see P: 5555, 5565).

23. Candrakīrti, *Mūlamadhyamakavṛttiprasannapadā* (*dbu ma'i rtsa ba'i 'grel pa tshig gsal ba*, D: 3860); Buddhapālita, *Buddhapālitamūlamadhya-makavṛtti* (*dbu ma'i rtsa ba'i 'grel pa shes rab buddha pā li ta*, D: 3842); Bhavya, *Prajñāpradīpamūlamadhyamakavṛtti* (*dbu ma'i rtsa ba'i 'grel pa shes rab sgron ma*, D: 3853); Śāntarakṣita, *Madhayamakālaṃkārakārikā* (*dbu ma rgyan gyi tshig le'ur byas pa*, D: 3884).

24. The distinction between these commentaries and root texts is not rigid. For example, Candrakīrti's *Introduction* is a commentary on Nāgārjuna's *Treatise* and fits into this second category of Indian commentaries. Yet it is often used as a root text, particularly in the Ge-luk institutions; indeed, there it often replaces Nāgārjuna's *Treatise* as the central text of Madhyamaka studies. In Tibetan education, these Indian commentaries (when used at all) play a role similar to that of the root texts. Hence, I group them with the root texts in the first textual layer of authoritative Indian works.

25. Dzong-ka-ba, *dBu ma la 'jug pa'i rgya cher bshad pa dgongs pa rab gsal* (Varanasi: Pleasure of Elegant Sayings Press, 1973); Go-ram-ba, *rGyal ba thams cad kyi thugs kyi dgongs pa zab mo 'i de kho na nyid spyi'i ngag gis ston pa nges don rab gsal*, in *Complete Works of the Great Masters of the Sa sKya Sect* (Tokyo: Tokyo Bunko, 1968), 14: 1.1.1–167.3.3 (*Ca*, 1.a–209.a).

26. Mi-pam, *dBu ma rgyan gyi rnam bshad 'jam dbyangs bla ma bgyes pa'i zhal lung* (New Delhi: Karmapa Chodhey, 1976); Śāntideva, *Bodhicary-āvatāra* (*byang chub sems dpa'i spyod pa la 'jug pa*, D: 3871, P: 5272); trans. by S. Batchelor as *A Guide to the Bodhisattva's Way of Life* (Dharamsala: Li-

brary of Tibetan Works and Archives, 1979). Mi-pam's commentary is *Shes rab le'u'i tshig don ga sla bar rnam par bshad pa nor bu ke ta ka* (Varanasi: n.p., n.d.).

27. Mi-gyö-dor-jay's texts are also used for the study of the *Prajñā-pāramitā* literature, the Vinaya and the Abhidharma, thus providing the core of the Ka-gyü curriculum, which is completed by the masterful synthesis of Buddhist logic and epistemology by the Seventh Kar-ma-ba Chö-drak-gya-tso (*chos grags rgya mtsho*, 1454–1506).

28. Here again, I am drawing boundaries that are in fact not entirely rigid. Main Tibetan commentaries are sometimes called *manuals*. For example, members of the Sa-gya tradition often describe Go-ram-ba's commentary on Madhyamaka as their manual. This shift in terminology corresponds to the increasing importance of manuals (particularly in the Ge-luk tradition), a topic to which I will return. But it should be clear that not all manuals are debate manuals, as some scholars imply; e.g., see G. Newland, "Debate Manuals *(yig cha)* in dGe-lugs Colleges," in *Tibetan Literature: Studies in Genre*, ed. J. Cabezón and R. Jackson (Ithaca: Snow Lion, 1996), 202.

29. Haribhadra, *Abhisamayālaṃkāranāmaprajñāpāramitopadeśaśāstra-vṛtti (shes rab pha rol tu phyin pa'i man ngag gi bstan bcos mgnon par rtogs pa'i rgyan zhes bya ba 'grel ba*, D: 3793, P: 5191).

30. Gyel-tsap, *rNam bshad snying po rgyan* (Varanasi: Pleasure of Elegant Sayings Press, 1980); Dzong-ka-ba, *bsTan bcos mngon rtogs rgyan 'grel pa dang bcas pa'i rgya cher bshad pa legs bshad gser gyi phreng ba* (Kokonor: Tsho sngon mi rigs dpe skrun khang, 1986).

31. Bhikkhu Ñyāṇamoli, trans., *The Middle Length Discourses of the Buddha: A New Translation of the Majjhima Nikaya*, ed. and rev. Bhikkhu Bodhi (Boston: Wisdom, 1995); M. Walshe, trans., *Thus I Have Heard: The Long Discourses of the Buddha* (London: Wisdom, 1987); E. Conze, trans., *Vajracchedikā Prajñāpāramitā* (Rome: I.S.M.E.O., 1957); L. Hurwitz, trans., *Scripture of the Lotus Blossom of the Fine Dharma* (New York: Columbia University Press, 1976); T. Cleary, trans., *The Flower Ornament Scripture: A Translation of the Avatamsaka Sutra*, vol. 1 (Boulder: Shambhala, 1984). On the different canons, see W. E. Clark, "Some Problems in the Criticism of the Sources of Early Buddhism," *Harvard Theological Review* 18, no. 2 (1930): 121–47. For the Pāli canon, see K. R. Norman, *Pāli Literature: Including the Canonical Literature in Prakrit and Sanskrit of All the Hinayana Schools of Buddhism*(Wiesbaden: Harrassowitz, 1983), and S. Collins, "On the Very Idea of a Pāli Canon," *Journal of the Pali Text Society* 15 (1990): 89–126. On the Chinese canon, see K. S. Chen, *Buddhism in China: A Historical Survey* (Princeton: Princeton University Press, 1964), 365–86.

32. Buddhaghosa, *The Path of Purification of Bhadantācariya Buddhaghosa: Visuddhimagga*, trans. Bhikkhu Ñyāṇamoli, 2 vols. (1956; reprint, Berkeley: Shambhala, 1976); Y. Hakeda, trans., *The Awakening of Faith, Attributed to Asvaghosha* (New York: Columbia University Press, 1967).

33. See P. Harrison, "A Brief History of the Tibetan bKa' 'gyur," in Cabezón and Jackson, *Tibetan Literature*, 39–56.

34. J. Hamesse, "Le Modèle Scholastique de la lecture," in *Histoire de la lecture dans le monde occidental*, supervised by G. Cavallo and R. Chartier (Paris: Seuil, 1997), 136.

CHAPTER 6. TWO CURRICULAR MODELS

1. The reduction of Tibetan curricula to two models is obviously a simplification. While it reflects the polarization of Tibetan Buddhism in the last century or so, it does not capture the diversity of curricula that have existed through the centuries. As we will see in this chapter, Sa-paṇ offers another more literary model, which has been widely followed among the educated laity but was not taken on in the monasteries. Similarly, there also seems to have been an encyclopedic model of learning that is reflected in Kong-trul's *Theg pa sgo kun las bstus pas gsung rab rin po che'i mdzod bslab pa gsum legs par ston pa'i bstan bcos shes bya kun khyab*, 3 vols. (Beijing: Mi Rigs dPe sKrun Khang, 1985), but the degree to which this model was ever implemented is not clear.

2. There are few sources on the curriculum of the three monastic universities. Clearly relevant works include Geshe Sopa, *Lectures on Tibetan Religious Culture* (Dharamsala: Library of Tibetan Works and Archives, 1983), 41–43, and Geshe Rabten, *The Life and Teaching of Geshé Rabten: A Tibetan Lama's Search for Truth*, trans. and ed. B. A. Wallace (London: Allen and Unwin, 1980), 47–49. See also T. Tarab's helpful *Brief History of Tibetan Academic Degrees in Buddhist Philosophy* (Copenhagen: Nordic Institute of Asian Studies, 2000).

3. Monks who have already received some training are often allowed to cover these preliminary classes in one year.

4. Hence, the Collected Topics are often called the Magical Key to the Path of Reasoning *(rigs lam 'phrul gyi lde mig)*. See, for example, the Se-ra Jay Collected Topics: Pur-bu-jok Jam-ba-gya-tso, *Tshad ma'i gzhung don 'byed pa'i bsdus grwa rnam par bshad pa rigs lam 'phrul gyi lde mig las rigs lam chung ba rtags rigs kyi skor* (Palampur, India: Library of Bkra Bshis Rjongs, n.d.). This text is often known as *Yongs 'dzin bsdus grwa (The Collected Topics of the Tutor)*, because its author was the tutor of the Thirteenth Dalai Lama.

5. Maitreya, *Abhisamayālaṃkāra-nāma-prajñāpāramitopadeśa-śāstrakarikā (shes rab pha rol tu phyin pa'i man ngag gi bstan bcos mngon par rtogs pa'i rgyan zhes bya ba tshig le'ur byas pa*, D: 3786, P: 5184); Dharmakīrti, *Pramāṇa-vārttika-kārikā (tshad ma rnam 'grel gyi tshig le'ur byas pa*, D: 4210, P: 5709); Candrakīrti, *Madhyamakāvatāra (dbu ma la 'jug pa*, D: 3861, P: 5262).

6. Vasubandhu, *Abhidharmakośakārikā (chos mngon pa'i mdzod*, D: 4089, P: 5590); Guṇaprabha, *Vinaya-sūtra ('dul ba'i mdo tsa ba*, D: 4117, P: 5619).

7. "sdom pa yod dus 'dul ba med / 'dul ba yod dus sdom pa med." Because they do not belong fully to Tibetan society, Mongolians have the reputation of

being unusually outspoken and candid; comments critical of the establishment are often attributed to them.

8. A Tibetan proverb captures this loss of monastic zeal: "New monks drink filtered water. Elder monks delight in gulping down alcohol." The monastic code prescribes that monks strain water before drinking it, to avoid killing small insects; the jaded monks may be tempted to ignore not only this minor rule but even the absolute ban on alcohol.

9. Such an emphasis on the results of actions may sound like utilitarianism, but it is not—at least, not the usual form of utilitarianism. Here the consequences are believed to extend over several lifetimes, making any utilitarian calculus impossible. Moreover, such consequences are not accessible to reason or experience but have to be understood by relying on the tradition. See G. Dreyfus, "Meditation as Ethical Activity," *Journal of Buddhist Ethics* 2 (1995): 28–54, and C. Hallisey, "Ethical Particularism in Theravaada Tradition," *Journal of Buddhist Ethics* 3 (1996): 32–43; both articles are available online at *Journal of Buddhist Ethics,* http://jbe.la.psu.edu (accessed February 2002).

10. This point about the role of authoritative statement is made well by J. N. Mohanty, *Reason and Tradition in Indian Thought* (Oxford: Clarendon Press, 1992), 256.

11. M. Halbertal and T. H. Halbertal, "The Yeshiva," in *Philosophers on Education,* ed. A. Rorty (London: Routledge, 1998), 458. For a spirited discussion of the logic behind education in yeshivas, see M. Halbertal, *People of the Book: Canon, Meaning, and Authority* (Cambridge, Mass.: Harvard University Press, 1997, and M. Fisch, *Rational Rabbis: Science and Talmudic Culture* (Bloomington: Indiana University Press, 1997).

12. Tsho-na-pa-shes-rab-bzang-po, *'Dul ba mdo rtsa ba'i rnam bshad nyi ma 'od zer legs bshad lung gi rgya mtsho* (n.d.).

13. Tsho-na-pa-shes-rab-bzang-po, *'Dul ṭik nyi ma'i 'od zer legs bshad lung gi rgya mtsho* (Beijing: Tibetan Culture Institute, 1993); Ge-dün-drub, *Dam pa'i chos 'dul ba mtha' dag gi snying po'i don legs par bshad rin po che'i phreng ba,* in *Collected Works,* vol. 2 (Kha).

14. *Chos mngon pa mdzod kyi tshig le'ur byas pa'i 'grel pa mngon pa'i rgyan* (Zi-ling: Krun-go'i Bod kyi shes rig dpe skrun khang, 1989). The authorship of this work is not well-established. The book is attributed to a member of the Chim clan. Though there are several possible candidates, the most likely is Chim Jam-be-yang (*mchims 'jam-pa'i* [or *'jam dpal*] *dbyangs,* early fourteenth century). See Ngak-wang-chö-drak, *Mkhan chen ngag dbang chos grags kyi pod chen drug gi 'grel pa phyogs sgrigs* (Rimbick Bazar, Dist. Darjeeling: Sakya Choepheling Monastery, 2000), 44.a.

15. Ge-dün-drub, *mDzod ṭik thar lam gsal byed* (Varanasi: Ge-luk Press, 1973).

16. Dre-pung and Se-ra, at least, which claim to be monastic establishments devoted to the sutra *(mdo lugs kyi grwa tshang),* do not include these esoteric studies in their official curricula; in contrast, Ga-den describes itself as a mo-

nastic establishment in which sutra and tantra are united *(mdo sngags zung 'brel gyi grwa tshang)*.

17. In Tibet, an excellent scholar was quite famous for refusing any tantric involvement. Accordingly, he was nicknamed "Geshe Vaibhāṣika" *(dge bshes bye brag smra ba*, the Vaibhāṣika being one of the two "Hinayana" schools among the four named in traditional Tibetan doxographies). That his refusal was seen as so remarkable illustrates the degree to which tantric practice is normative within the Ge-luk tradition.

18. The two institutions of Lhasa, the Lower Tantric Monastery *(rgyud smad grwa tshang)* and the Higher Tantric Monastery *(rgyud stod gwra tshang)*, have now relocated in India. In the La-brang monastery of Amdo, monks who have studied in the Monastery of Philosophy *(mtshan nyid gwra tshang)* become Geshes on passing their *bka' rams* examinations. They are then required to spend three years in one of the five tantric monasteries: the Lower Tantric Monastery *(rgyud smad gra tshang)*, the Higher Tantric Monastery *(rgyud stod gra tshang)*, the Hevajra Monastery *(kye rdor gra tshang)*, the Kalācakra Monastery *(dus 'khor grwa tshang)*, or the Medical Monastery *(sman pa gwra tshang)*. Similarly, one of the four monasteries in Ta-shi Lhun-po is tantric.

19. Sopa, *Lectures on Tibetan Religious Culture,* 64–65.

20. Ge-dün Chö-pel (about whom I will have much more to say in chapter 14) recited the *Recitation of the Names of Manjushri ('Jam dpal mtshan brjod)* while he was in Dre-pung. Although this text is cataloged as a tantric text, it is counted as exoteric since it does not teach a full-blown tantric practice; see Dor-jay Gyel *(rdo-rje rgyal)*, *'Dzam gling rig pa'i dpa' bo dge' dun chos phel gyi byung ba brjod pa bden gtam rna ba'i bcud len* (Kansu: Kansu People's Press, 1997), 27. The situation has changed in exile, where there is no longer any restriction on tantric practice.

21. Monasteries may have a special Yi-dam. Se-ra Jay, for instance, is devoted to Haya griva *(rta mgrin yang gsang)*. In Tibet, this deity, which is Nying-ma in origin, had a special chapel in the temple of the monastery where its statue was intensely worshiped. The statue was thought to have special curative properties and sick monks would circumambulate this chapel.

22. J. Cabezón, *Buddhism and Language: A Study of Indo-Tibetan Scholasticism* (Albany: State University of New York Press, 1994), 84.

23. Rabten, *The Life and Thought,* 113.

24. See Geshe Rabten, *Song of the Profound View,* trans. S. Batchelor (London: Wisdom, 1989).

25. Dungkar Lobsang Thinley, "Development of the Monastic Education in Tibet," *Tibet Journal* 18, no. 4 (1993): 11.

26. I. Friedrich-Silber, *Virtuosity, Charisma, and Social Order: A Comparative Sociological Study of Monasticism in Theravada Buddhism and Medieval Catholicism* (Cambridge: Cambridge University Press, 1995), 42.

27. See J. Derrida, *Of Grammatology,* trans. G. C. Spivak (Baltimore: Johns Hopkins University Press, 1976).

28. D. Lopez, "Authority and Orality in the Mahayana," *Numen* 42 (1995):

21–47, esp. 38. Obviously, there are other reasons for working to keep the Vedas oral, such as the pragmatic consideration that priests must memorize formulas to use them. But the strong injunction against writing and the depiction of writing as polluting reflect deep anxiety.

29. Unlike modern scholarship, the texts of traditional cultures commonly repeat verbatim and without attribution passages by previous writers. Tibetan commentaries are no exception, as they seek not to be entirely original but to transmit a tradition. Moreover, in a culture in which written or printed books can be scarce, restating a point may be useful. Nevertheless, the difference between traditional and modern practices should not be pushed too far: a commentary is supposed to offer something new. Tibetan scholars often make sarcastic comments about the works that do nothing more than repeat the opinions of others. At the same time, the modern way of doing research makes them uncomfortable, for it seems to require an originality that they do not necessarily want to encourage. For a discussion of plagiarism in medieval Europe, see M. Carruthers, *The Book of Memory: A Study of Memory in Medieval Culture* (Cambridge: Cambridge University Press, 1990), 220.

30. See G. Makdisi, "The Scholastic Method in Medieval Education," *Speculum* 49 (1974): 642–43.

31. Śāntarakṣita, *Tattvasaṃgraha* (*de kho na nyid bsdus pa*, D: 4266, P: 5764).

32. For example, it is sometimes said that Lo-drö Rin-chen Seng-ge and Gung-ru Gyel-tsen Zang-po were favorably inclined toward the view of extrinsic emptiness. Given Dzong-ka-ba's unambiguous opposition to such a view, such an inclination appears unlikely; these reports may misrepresent the views of the old manuals.

33. Long-döl *(klong rdol)* mentions several of these manuals in his list of the collected works of Ka-dam and Ge-luk masters *(bka' gdams pa dang dge lugs bla ma rags rim gyi gsung 'bum mtshan tho)*. See L. Chandra, *Materials for a History of Tibetan Literature* (Kyoto: Rinsen, 1981), 798–807.

34. G. Newland, "Debate Manuals *(yig cha)* in dGe-lugs Colleges," in *Tibetan Literature: Studies in Genre*, ed. J. Cabezón and R. Jackson (Ithaca: Snow Lion, 1996), 203.

35. E.g., see A. Wayman, "Alex Wayman Replies to Geshe Sopa," *Journal of the International Association of Buddhist Studies* 3 (1980): 93–97.

36. J. Hamesse, "Le Modèle Scholastique de la lecture," in *Histoire de la lecture dans le monde occidental*, supervised by G. Cavallo and R. Chartier (Paris: Seuil, 1997), 136.

37. Gyel-tsap, *rNam bshad snying po rgyan* (Varanasi: Pleasure of Elegant Sayings Press, 1980); Dzong-ka-ba, *bsTan bcos mngon rtogs rgyan 'grel pa dang bcas pa'i rgya cher bshad pa legs bshad gser gyi phreng ba* (Kokonor: mTsho sngon mi rigs dpe skrun khang, 1986). The use of Dzong-ka-ba's *Golden Garland* has been controversial in the Ge-luk tradition; many Ge-luk scholars prefer to rely on Gyel-tsap's work or on manuals. Thinkers outside of the Ge-luk tradition mockingly question this refusal to use a book by the founder of

the tradition. But the Ge-luk scholars point out that the *Golden Garland* was written when Dzong-ka-ba was only thirty-one, and hence cannot be taken as reflecting mature Ge-luk views.

38. Among the three main sets of manuals, only Pan-chen Sö-nam-drak-ba's contain a full treatment of Dharmakīrti. Those by Jay-dzün-chö-gi-gyel-tsen and Jam-yang-shay-ba offer only partial discussions of logic and epistemology.

39. Gyel-tsap, *rNam 'grel thar lam gsal byed* (Varanasi: Pleasure of Elegant Sayings Press, 1974–1975); Kay-drup, *Tshad ma sde bdun gyi rgyan yid kyi mun sel* and *rGyas pa'i bstan bcos tshad ma rnam 'grel gyi rgya cher bshad pa rigs pa'i rgya mtsho*, in vol. 10 of *Collected Works* (1897; reprint, New Delhi: Guru Deva, 1982); Ge-dün-drub, *Tshad ma'i bstan bcos chen po rigs pa'i rgyan* (Mundgod: Lo-ling Press, 1985).

40. J. Hopkins, "Tibetan Monastic Colleges: Rationality versus the Demands of Allegiance," in *Mythos Tibet: Wahrnehmunger, Projektionen, Phantasien,* ed. T. Dodin (Cologne: DuMont, 1997).

41. It is difficult to determine how extensively Ge-luk scholars read the Indian exoteric texts, outside of the five basic treatises. Here again, several considerations have to be factored in. First, the availability of texts in Tibet seems to have been limited. Most monastic libraries concentrated not on providing texts for scholars but on hoarding the books and locking them away. Hence, works besides the manuals and the writings of Dzong-ka-ba and his disciples were difficult to access (and even those may not have been always easy to obtain). Second, scholars read outside of the usual texts according to their own individual inclinations, which could vary widely. To judge from my teachers' readings, seasoned scholars read most of the works of the great Indian thinkers—Nāgārjuna, Āryadeva, Asaṅga, Vasubandhu, Dharmakīrti, Śāntarakṣita, etc. Some of the most important sutras, such as the Perfection of Wisdom, were also read. Some scholars also read pre–Dzong-ka-ba works, such as Bu-tön's, and works critical of Dzong-ka-ba, particularly Go-ram-ba's and Mi-pam's (and in exile Śākya Chok-den's, which were not available in Tibet). Among the writings of these authors, however, scholars usually preferred the commentaries on Indian texts to purely Tibetan works. For example, Sa-paṇ's *Treasure* and its numerous commentaries were largely ignored by Ge-luk scholars, as were the works of Ngok, Cha-ba, Bo-dong, etc. But there seems to have been a limited tradition of "bibliographical connoisseurship," as evinced in *dPe rgyun dkon pa tho yig* by A-khu Shay-rab Gya-tso (1803–1875) (M. Kapstein, *The Tibetan Assimilation of Buddhism: Conversion, Contestation, and Memory* [New York: Oxford University Press, 2000], 238 n. 77).

42. Thirteen of Sa-gya's eighteen texts are listed in the chapter text; the other five are Śāntideva's *Bodhiscaryāvatāra* (*byang chub sems dpa'i spyod pa la 'jug pa,* D: 3871, P: 5272), which is studied with but not counted among the thirteen; Dharmakīrti, *Pramāṇaviniścaya* (*tshad ma rnam par nges pa,* D: 4211, P: 5710); Dignāga, *Pramāṇasamuccaya* (*tshad ma kun btus,* D: 4203, P: 5700); and Sa-gya Paṇḍita, *sDom gsum rab byed* and *Tshad ma rigs gter,* in

The Complete Works of the Great Masters of the Sa sKya Sect (Tokyo: Tokyo Bunko, 1968), 5: 297.1.1–323.2.6, 155.1.1–167.1.6.

43. See, for example, Ngak-wang-chö-drak, *Bod kyi mkhas pa snga phyi dag gi grub mtha' shan 'byed mtha' dpyod dang bcas pa'i 'bel ba'i gtam* (Thimphu, Bhutan: Kunzang Tobgey, 1984). The six texts are the five texts of the Ge-luk curriculum and Sa-gya Paṇḍita's *sDom gsum rab dbye (Differentiation of the Three Vows)*.

44. Although the scholastic institutions of Nying-ma, Sa-gya, and Ka-gyü differ slightly, all follow the same commentarial model of education. These institutions were all shaped by the scholarly revival initiated by Ken-po Zhan-pan toward the end of the nineteenth century as part of the nonsectarian movement.

45. Another active commentarial school is the Sa-gya College in Rajpur, which has more than one hundred students.

46. See D. Germano, "Re-membering the Dismembered Body of Tibet," in *Buddhism in Contemporary Tibet: Religious Revival and Cultural Identity*, ed. M. Goldstein and M. Kapstein (Berkeley: University of California Press, 1998), 53–94. The situation unfortunately changed in 2001 when restrictions were imposed by provincial authorities. Thus, the future of this institution is seriously in question.

47. Pe-ma-wang-gyel, *Rang bzhin rdzogs pa chen po'i lam gyi cha lag sdoms pa gsum rnam par nges pa zhes bya ba'i bstan bcos* (Delhi: n.p., 1969).

48. Āryadeva, *Catuḥśataka śāstra (bstan bcos bzhi brgya pa*, D: 3846, P: 5346)*; Asaṅga, *Abhidharma samuccaya (chos mngon pa kun las bstus pa*, D: 4049, P: 5550)*.

49. Zhan-pan Chö-kyi-nang-ba, *gZhung chen bcu gsum gyi mchan 'grel* (Dehra Dun: Kocchen Tulku, 1978). Zhan-pan's works are also used by Sa-gya scholars but are shunned by most Ka-gyü-bas, for he is an outspoken opponent of the teaching of extrinsic emptiness *(gzhan stong)* supported by many Ka-gyü scholars. The Sa-gya tradition also draws on the works of such authors as Ngak-chö *(ngag dbang chos grags*, 1572–1641) and Tuk-je-bel-zang *(thugs rje dpal bzang*, a direct disciple of Go-ram-ba who wrote complements, or *kha skong*, to his teacher's commentaries); they are used less frequently than the Ge-luk manuals that they somewhat resemble.

50. Śāntarakṣita, *Madhyamakālaṃkāravṛtti (dbu ma'i rgyan gyi 'grel pa*, D: 3885, P: 5286), and Mi-pam, *dBu ma rgyan gyi rnam bshad 'jam dbyangs bla ma bgyes pa'i zhal lung* (New Delhi: Karmapa Chodhey, 1976). Also studied is Mi-pam's own *mKhas'jug (Entrance Gate for the Wise)*, a text that complements the Abhidharma treatises and is quite different from the text with the same title composed by Sa-pan.

51. Sa-pan's work provides the interpretation adopted by all non-Ge-luk schools since at least the sixteenth or seventeenth century. See G. Dreyfus, *Recognizing Reality: Dharmakīrti's Philosophy and Its Tibetan Interpreters* (Albany: State University of New York Press, 1997).

52. Maitreya, *Mahāyānottaratantraśāstra (theg pa chen po'i rgyd bla ma bstan bcos*, D: 4024, P: 5525); Maitreya, *Mahayana sūtrālaṃkāra kārikā (theg pa chen po'i mdo sde'i rgyan gyi tshig le'ur byas pa*, D: 4020, P: 5521); Maitreya,

Madhyāntavibhaṅga (dbus dang mtha' rnam par 'yed pa, D: 4021, P: 5522); Maitreya, *Dharmadharmatāvibhaṅga (chos dang chos nyid rnam par 'byed pa,* D: 4023, P: 5523).

53. Yon-den-gya-tso, *Yon tan rin po che'i mdzod kyi 'grel pa zab don snang byed nyi ma'i 'od zer* (Gangtok, Sikkim: n.p., 1969); Mi-pam, *gSang 'grel phyogs bcu'i mun sel gyi spyi don 'od gsal snying po;* Do-grub-chen, *dPal gsang ba'i snying po'i rgyud kyi spyi don nyung ngu'i ngag gis rnam par 'byed par rin chen mdzod kyi lde mig,* in *Collected Works,* vol. 3 (Gangtok: Dodrup Chen Rinpoche, 1974); Long-chen-rab-jam-ba, *Rang grol skor gsum* (Gangtok: Sonam Kazi, 1969); Ngagyur Nyingmay Sungrab, vol. 4; Long-chen-rab-jam-ba, *Ngal gso skor gsum* (Gangtok: Dodrup Chen Rinpoche, 1973).

54. Rang-jung Dor-je, *Zab mo nang don* (Zi-ling: Kokonor Tibetan Medical School, 1999), with a commentary by Kong-trul Lo-drö Ta-yé.

55. Pon-lob Rin-po-che, author interview, Woodstock, N.Y., spring 2000.

56. From *Ngagyur Nyingma Institute* (Bylakuppe: Ngagyur Nyingma Institute, 1995). This schedule is only for weekdays. Saturday is free from 10:30 to 21:30, and Sunday is free until 19:30, when collective debates are held for the evening. The schedule of the Sa-gya College is similar. See Lama Pema Wangdak, "The Sakya College—Preserving the Sakya Lineage of Tibetan Buddhism" at http://www.geocities.com/Tokyo/Pagoda/4595/COL LEGE .html (accessed November 2001).

57. Similarly, Rum-tek is supposed to have a twelve-year program, but the last three years have yet to be implemented. The Sa-gya College has a nine-year course.

58. See Germano, "Re-membering the Dismembered Body of Tibet." The Nyingma style of scholarship is well represented by Dudjom Rinpoche's *The Nyingma School of Tibetan Buddhism: Its Fundamentals and History,* trans. Gyurme Dorje, ed. Matthew Kapstein (London: Wisdom, 1991).

59. L. van der Kuijp describes Cha-ba as a nonsectarian thinker primarily associated with the Ka-dam-pa; see "Phya-pa Chos-kyi-seng-ge's Impact on Tibetan Epistemological Theory," *Journal of Indian Philosophy* 5 (1978): 355–69, esp. 357.

60. C. T. Zongtse, *mKhas mang rgya mtsho'i bsti gnas dbus 'gyur gdan sa chen po gsum gyi ya gyal se ra theg chen gling gi chos 'byung rab gsal nor bu'i me long* (Delhi: International Academy of Indian Culture, 1995), 331.

61. See Kay-drup, *rJe btsun tsong kha pa chen po'i ngo mtshar rmad du byung ba'i rnam par thar pa'i 'jug ngogs,* in Dzong-ka-ba, *Collected Works (gsung 'bum) of Rje Tsong-kha-pa Blo-bzang-grags-pa* (Dharamsala: Tibetan Cultural Printing, n.d.), 1: fols. 1.a–71.b.

62. R. A. F. Thurman, ed., *Life and Teachings of Tsong-khapa,* trans. Sherpa Tulku et al. (Dharamsala: Library of Tibetan Works and Archives, 1982), 8; Paṇ-chen Sö-nam-drak-ba, *bKa' gdams gsar snying gi chos 'byung yid kyi mdzes rgyan* (Delhi: Gonpo Tseten, 1977), 24.b.4.

63. Lob-zang Trin-ley *(blo bzang 'phrin las),* '*Jam mgon chos kyi rgyal po tsong kha pa chen po'i rnam thar* (Kokonor: Kokonor People's Press, 1996), 148.

64. Cha har dGe bshes bLo bzang Tshul khrims describes these tours: "Hav-

ing asked the permission of the teachers of the monastery, one sits in the midst of the assembly led by these teachers. One then answers, distinguishing through debate the meaning [in the questions] asked by the scholars of this monastery" *('dus sde'i bla ma dag la zhu nas bla ma rnams kyis gtsos pa'i 'dus sde tshogs pa'i nang du bsdad nas dgon pa de'i mkhas pa rnams rim bzhin rigs lam gtong la gang dris pa'i don phye ste lan 'debs pa yin la)* (Lob-zang Trin-ley, *rNam thar*, 96).

65. Jik-may Wang-po *('jigs med dbang po)*, *Bo dong paṇ chen kyi rnam thar* (Xhinhua: Old Tibetan Texts Press, 1991), 68–78. Bo-dong's biography was written at the prompting of Stag-lung-thang-pa Chen-po Ngag-dbang-grags-pa (1418–1496).

66. Jik-may Wang-po, *Bo dong paṇ chen kyi rnam thar*, 66, 79.

67. For similar impressions of monastery size, see Jik-may Wang-po, *Bo dong paṇ chen kyi rnam thar*, 68–78.

68. Sö-nam-drak-ba, *bKa' gdams gsar snying gi chos 'byung*, 29.b.4.

69. See D. Jackson, "The Earliest Printings of Tsong Khapa's Works: The Old dGa'-ldan Editions," in *Reflections on Tibetan Culture: Essays in Memory of Turrell V. Wylie*, ed. L. Epstein and R. Sherburne (Lewiston, N.Y.: Mellen Press, 1990), 107–16.

70. Jam-yang-chok-hla-ö-ser, *Tshad ma rnam 'grel gyi bsdus gzhung zhes bya'i sgo 'byed rgol ngan glang po 'joms pa gdong nga'i gad rgyangs rgyu rig lde mig* (Dharamsala: Library of Tibetan Works and Archives, 1980).

71. Geshe G. Lodrö, *'Bras spungs chos 'byung*, in *Geschichte der Kloster-Universität Drepung* (Wiesbaden: Steiner, 1974), 232. Later some monasteries developed their own Collected Topics. While Lo-se-ling, Shar-tse, and Se-ra May kept Jam-yang-chok-hla-ö-ser's original text, Go-mang adopted Jam-yang-shay-ba's text and Se-ra Jay and Ga-den took over Shang-tse Pur-bu-jok's *Yongs 'dzin bsdus grwa*. In addition, a text written by Btsan-po Don-grub-rgya-mtsho (1613–1665) is used in Ku-bum and other monasteries in Amdo. These alternative Collected Topics deviate from the original only in minor details.

72. Sö-nam-drak-ba, *bKa' gdams gsar snying gi chos 'byung*, 24.b.2–4; see also Tarab, *A Brief History of Tibetan Academic Degrees*, 11. As Tarab points out, there is disagreement over the "four texts" intended; the *Bod rgya tshig mdzod chen mo* mentions Madhyamaka instead of Prāmaṇa.

73. Tarab mentions nine centers: Sa-kya, Sang-den *(bzang ldan)*, Ngam-ring *(ngam rings)*, Ga-rong *(ga rong)*, Bo-dong, and E *('e)* in Tsang; Sang-pu, Gung-tang *(gung thang)*, and Tse-tang in Central Tibet (*A Brief History of Tibetan Academic Degrees*, 13). Sö-nam-drak-ba names the same three in Central Tibet but only Nar-tang in Tsang (*bKa' gdams gsar snying gi chos 'byung*, 23.b.1).

74. The title of Ling-se seems to have been created in Sang-pu, where it was bestowed after a formal debate that brought together both parts of the monastery, the Upper Community *(gling stod)* and the Lower Community *(gling smad)* (Zongtse, *Se ra theg chen gling gi chos 'byung*, 339).

75. Zongtse, *Se ra theg chen gling gi chos 'byung*, 347; Tarab, *A Brief His-*

tory of Tibetan Academic Degrees, 20–22. The *rams* in *lha rams, tshogs rams,* etc., appears to be meant as a reference to the title of Rab-jam (great scholar).

76. Zongtse, *Se ra theg chen gling gi chos 'byung,* 349.

77. The history of debate manuals is difficult to reconstruct. The complexity of Jam-yang-chok-hla-ö-ser's Collected Topics suggests that it builds on earlier debate manuals, now lost. Cha-ba is often credited with creating the ancestor of this genre; but because his Summaries are no longer extant, this claim is difficult to verify. His only writing to survive is his discussion of Madhyamaka, which shows a preoccupation with debate but is not couched as a debate; see H. Tauscher, ed., *Phya pa Chos kyi Senge ge: dBu ma Shar gSum gyi stong thun* (Vienna: Arbeitskreis für Tibetische und Buddhistische Studien, Universität Wien, 1999). The use of that format to present scholastic topics thus probably was begun by his followers, but few texts from that period have survived. But the use of the debate format was well-established in the fourteenth century, as evinced by a recently discovered work by Lama Dam-pa Sö-nam Gyeltsen (*bla ma dam pa bsod nams rgyal mtshan,* 1312–1375), *Tshad ma rnams grel gyi 'grel pa legs par bshad pa'i snying po,* in *Collected Works,* vol. 14 (Dha) (Rajpur: Sakya College, 1999), 1–672.

78. See S. Onoda, *Monastic Debate in Tibet: A Study on the History and Structures of Bsdus grwa Logic* (Vienna: Arbeitskreis für Tibetische und Buddhistische Studien, Universität Wien, 1992), 13–36.

79. Textual arguments are explications, not arguments aimed at persuading another person to agree with one's point of view.

80. We should also note that the debate depicted in Bo-dong's biography, a relatively unstructured back-and-forth exchange, does not seem to follow the rigid format that became standard in Ge-luk debates; defender and questioner now have predetermined roles, with the former limited to a set number of answers (see chapter 10).

81. D. Jackson, *The Early Abbots of 'Phan po Na-lendra: The Vicissitudes of a Great Tibetan Monastery in the Fifteenth Century* (Vienna: Arbeitskreis für Tibetische und Buddhistische Studien, Universität Wien, 1989), 29.

82. See M. Kapstein, "From Kun-mKhyen Dol-po-pa to 'Ba'-mda' dgelegs," in *Tibetan Studies,* ed. H. Krasser, M. Much, E. Steinkellner, and H. Tauscher (Vienna: Österreichische Akademie der Wissenschaften, 1997), 1:457–76.

CHAPTER 7. SCHOLASTICISM
AND ORALITY: MYTH AND REALITY

1. J. Hamesse, "Le modèle scholastique de la lecture," in *Histoire de la lecture dans le monde occidental,* supervised by G. Cavallo and R. Chartier (Paris: Seuil, 1997), 127–28.

2. See especially M. Parry, *The Making of Homeric Verse: The Collected Papers of Milman Parry,* ed. A. Parry (Oxford: Clarendon Press, 1971), and A. Lord, *The Singer of Tales* (Cambridge, Mass.: Harvard University Press, 1960).

For an overview of literature on orality and literacy, see B. V. Street, *Literacy in Theory and Practice* (Cambridge: Cambridge University Press, 1984).

3. Thus W. J. Ong declares, "The oral, as we noted, never exists in a simply verbal context, as a written word does. Spoken words are always modifications of a total, existential situation, which always engage the body. Bodily activity beyond mere vocalization is not adventitious or contrived in oral communication, but is natural and even inevitable" (*Orality and Literacy: The Technologizing of the Word* [1982; reprint, London: Routledge, 1988], 67–68).

4. M. McLuhan makes a similar point: "Until WRITING was invented, we lived in an acoustic space, where all backward people still live: boundless, directionless, horizonless. The clash of the mind, the world of emotion, primordial intuition, mafia-ridden. . . . A goose quill put an end to talk, abolished mystery. . . . It was the basic metaphor with which the cycle of CIVILIZATION began, the step from the dark into the light of the mind" (*Counter Blast* [London: Rapp and Whiting, 1970], 13–14).

5. R. Finnegan, *Literacy and Orality: Studies in the Technology of Communication* (Oxford: Blackwell, 1988), 141; emphasis hers.

6. For example:

> Ong observes that peoples from primary oral cultures are likely to externalize their psychological imbalances whereas literate cultures create persons who, regarding their own interior consciousness as private, like the pages of a text read silently and in solitude, experience themselves as "holding" individual characteristics unseen by others. Traditional Tibet was *not* a primary oral culture; yet its oral orientation was sufficiently strong that if Ong is right about how such an orientation can shape interiority, the visualizations and associated textual practices just described would resonate differently for traditional Tibetans than for modern Westerners.

A. Klein, comp., trans., and ed., *Path to the Middle: Oral Madhyamika Philosophy in Tibet* (Albany: State University of New York Press, 1994), 25.

7. Klein, *Path to the Middle*, 5.

8. M. Kapstein, "*gDams Ngag:* Technologies of the Self," in *Tibetan Literature: Studies in Genre*, ed. J. Cabezón and R. Jackson (Ithaca: Snow Lion, 1996), 275.

9. Klein, *Path to the Middle*, 4, 6, 21.

10. W. A. Graham, *Beyond the Written Word: Oral Aspects of Scripture in the History of Religion* (Cambridge: Cambridge University Press, 1987), 45.

11. A. Petruci, "Lire au Moyen Age," *Mélanges de l'École Française de Rome* 96 (1984): 604–16.

12. See P. Saenger, "Silent Reading: Its Impact on Late Medieval Script and Society," *Viator* 13 (1982): 367–414. M. Carruthers seems more skeptical about the oral character of reading in late antiquity and the early medieval period (*The Book of Memory: A Study of Memory in Medieval Culture* [Cambridge: Cambridge University Press, 1990], 170–72).

13. Gen Lob-zang Gya-tso and Geshe Gon-chok Tse-ring *(dkon mchog tshe ring)*, interviews with author, Dharamsala, fall 1995.

14. It is only fair to point out that Ong himself did not connect the notion

of primary orality with Tibetan monastic education. That highly intellectual culture falls outside the purview of his theory, regardless of its merits.

15. D. Lopez, "Foreigner at the Feet of the Lama," in *Curators of the Buddha: The Study of Buddhism under Colonialism*, ed. D. Lopez (Chicago: University of Chicago Press, 1995), 271.

16. G. Roerich, trans. and ed., *The Blue Annals*, 2nd ed. (Delhi: Motilal Banarsidass, 1979), 346.

17. In his *Memoirs*, Gen Lob-zang Gya-tso expresses a similar view: "The simple transmission of a text through having heard it read aloud was not considered particularly helpful or important either" (*Memoirs of a Tibetan Lama*, trans. and ed. G. Sparham [Ithaca: Snow Lion, 1998], 86).

18. See M. Kapstein, *The Tibetan Assimilation of Buddhism: Conversion, Contestation, and Memory* (Oxford: Oxford University Press, 2000), 11.

19. It is said that some Germans find it is easier to read Kant's *Critique of Pure Reason* in its English translation than in their own language.

20. P. Griffiths, "Scholasticism: The Possible Recovery of an Intellectual Tradition," in *Scholasticism: Cross-Cultural and Comparative Perspectives*, ed. J. Cabezón (Albany: State University of New York Press, 1998), 201–36.

21. Hamesse, "Le Modèle Scholastique de la lecture," 129–30.

22. In his later work, P. Griffiths appropriately describes the reading he is recommending as being religious rather than scholastic; see *Religious Reading: The Place of Reading in the Practice of Religion* (New York: Oxford University Press, 1999).

23. Similarly, memorization, to my knowledge, has never been systematically analyzed by traditional Tibetan scholars. This silence is quite unlike what we find among European medieval scholastics, who produced several treatises explaining the techniques of memorization (see Carruthers, *The Book of Memory*).

24. For example, for U. Eco, "texts are lazy machineries that ask someone to do their job" (*The Role of the Reader: Explorations in the Semiotics of Texts* [1979; reprint, Bloomington: Indiana University Press, 1984], 214). They require us to make the inferences that supply the information necessary to understand the sentence. This is what Eco calls framing, i.e., providing a typical scenario that corresponds to the expectations we have about objects and actions. This notion of frame somewhat resembles both Wittgenstein's "forms of life"—namely, typical sets of action that we recognize and engage in unproblematically and routinely—and Bakhtin's idea of speech genre (see M. M. Bakhtin, *Speech Genres and Other Late Essays*, ed. C. Emerson and M. Holquist, trans. V. W. McGee [Austin: University of Texas, 1986], 88).

25. I am here following J. Habermas, *Moral Consciousness and Communicative Action*, trans. C. Lenhardt and S. W. Nicholsen (Cambridge, Mass.: MIT Press, 1990), 30, and P. Ricoeur, *Hermeneutics and the Human Sciences: Essays on Language, Action, and Interpretation*, trans. and ed. J. B. Thompson (Cambridge: Cambridge University Press, 1981), 145–64. The distinction between understanding and explanation is often drawn differently; as in Gadamer's

hermeneutics, explanation is frequently limited to an exploration of the causes of a phenomenon and the interpretive process reduced to understanding. Though this is highly debatable, Gadamer's insights remain valuable and can be integrated into a broader theory of interpretation, as Ricoeur has done.

26. P. Ricoeur, *Interpretation Theory: Discourse and the Surplus of Meaning* (Fort Worth: Texas Christian University Press, 1976), 79. Ricoeur argues,

> Then the term interpretation may be applied, not to a particular case of understanding, that of the written expressions of life, but to the whole process that encompasses explanation and understanding. Interpretation as a dialectic of explanation and understanding or comprehension may then be traced back to the initial stages of interpretative behaviour already at work in conversation. And while it is true that only writing and literary composition provide a full development of this dialectic, interpretation must not be referred to as a province of understanding. It is not defined by a kind of object—"inscribed" signs in the most general sense of the term—but by a kind of process: the dynamic interpretative reading. (74)

27. H. G. Gadamer, *Truth and Method*, trans. and ed. G. Barden and J. Cumming, rev. Weinsheimer and D. G. Marshall, 2nd rev. ed. (New York: Crossroad, 1989), 375, 370. Along with Martin Heidegger's *Being and Time* (1927), R. G. Collingwood's *Autobiography* (1939) is one of the main sources for Gadamer's view on the centrality of the question.

28. This is quite rare, for politics is as bitter in monasteries as it is in most human communities and very few escape public envy or criticism. A few teachers such as Gen Pe-ma Gyel-tsen are highly respected, and hence are rarely criticized.

29. Gen Pe-ma Gyel-tsen's procedure follows almost exactly the ideal Tibetan pedagogical model as described by Geshe G. Lodrö; see *'Bras spungs chos 'byung*, in *Geschichte der Kloster-Universität Drepung* (Wiesbaden: Steiner, 1974), 257.

30. Because most of Paṇ-chen's textbooks are not very extensive, the monks from Lo-se-ling and Ga-den Shar-tse, whose curriculum relies on those works, are assailed by their Ge-luk colleagues as having a limited textual knowledge *(mthong cha chung ba)*—the same accusation hurled by non-Ge-luk scholars against their Ge-luk counterparts. Gen-la's books are intended to remedy this state of affairs.

CHAPTER 8. COMMENTARY AND MEDITATION

1. In equating the third type of *prajñā* with transcendental gnosis I am greatly simplifying. In some accounts, the third type of *prajñā* precedes the rise of gnosis; others point to a difference between *prajñā*, which is the product of gradual cultivation, and gnosis, which appears more directly. For the latter view, see J. W. Pettit, *Mipham's Beacon of Certainty: Illuminating the View of Dzogehen, the Great Perfection* (Boston: Wisdom, 1999), 89.

2. The term *listening* reflects the emphasis on the oral transmission of texts. Written texts come to life when they are mediated by qualified teachers, who

bring out their full soteriological value. However, the understanding that comes from silently studying and reading texts is also included in this category.

3. Ge-luk scholars often use the concept of "correct assumption" *(yid dpyod)* to explain this preliminary understanding, contrasting it with "valid cognition" *(tshad ma, pramāṇa),* which is identified with the acumen arising from thinking. A correct assumption is the equivalent of Plato's *doxa,* or mere opinion; it is opposed to knowledge, which is grounded in reality and entails the certainty that assumption lacks. For a discussion of this notion, see G. Dreyfus, *Recognizing Reality: Dharmakīrti's Philosophy and Its Tibetan Interpreters* (Albany: State University of New York Press, 1997), 389–91.

4. As in Dzong-ka-ba's spiritual autobiography, *rTogs brjod mdun legs ma (Rang gi rtogs pa mdo tsam du bshad pa,* in *The Collected Works* [Delhi: Guru Deva, 1975], 2:3202–80), considered later in this chapter.

5. My use of the external/internal dichotomy to describe the scholastic process is meant to reflect the tradition's own view. Studying is depicted as outward-looking *(kha phyi ltas),* whereas contemplating and meditating are inward-looking *(kha nang ltas).* This does not mean that the two exist apart, but it does signal the hierarchical way in which they are regarded.

6. See, for example, Dzong-ka-ba, *The Great Treatise on the Stages of the Path to Enlightenment,* trans. Lamrim Chenmo Translation Committee (Ithaca: Snow Lion, 2000), 109–16.

7. Vasubandhu, *Abhidharmakośabhasyam of Vasubandhu,* ed. P. Pradhan (Patna: Jayaswal Institute, 1975), 341–42; quoted in J. Cabezón, *Buddhism and Language: A Study of Indo-Tibetan Scholasticism* (Albany: State University of New York Press, 1994), 48.

8. This explanation reflects the Vaibhāṣika point of view and provides a useful starting point in the understanding of the three types of wisdom. However, it is criticized by Vasubandhu on technical grounds that need not concern us here. See Cabezón, *Buddhism and Language,* 49–50.

9.

dang por rgya cher thos pa mang du btsal
bar du gzhung lugs thams cad gdams par shar
tha mar nyin mtshan kun tu nyams su blangs
kun kyang bstan pa rgyas pa'i ched du bsngos

Dzong-ka-ba, *rTogs mrjod mdun legs ma,* 302.

10. J. Hamesse, "Le Modèle Scholastique de la lecture," in *Histoire de la lecture dans le monde occidental,* supervised by G. Cavallo and R. Chartier (Paris: Seuil, 1997), 135.

11. As always among Tibetans, he never advertised the fact that he meditated; but he could not hide from his roommates, who used to talk about his interest. Because he was careful to conceal it, his involvement was judged to be genuine and respected. Had he been open about his practice, as Westerners often are, he would not have received the same respect and might have been ridiculed for his spiritual pride.

12. Many Western Buddhists seem to reverse the ranking of these directives. They fault themselves for not meditating, but see little wrong in violating the precepts (see the interviews in *Tricycle* 6, no. 1 [1996]).

13. The belief in the degeneracy of the present is widespread throughout the Mahayana world, as J. Nattier shows in *Once Upon a Future Time: Studies in a Buddhist Prophecy of Decline* (Berkeley: Asian Humanities Press, 1991). It also plays an important role in the Theravada tradition; see G. Bond, *The Buddhist Revival in Sri Lanka: Religious Tradition, Reinterpretation, and Response* (Columbia: University of South Carolina Press, 1988), 22–33.

14. We are now at a time when the human lifespan is 100 years; this span will start to decrease until it reaches the minimum of 10 years. Lifespans will have to return to their maximum of 80,000 years before Maitreya appears (Nattier, *Once Upon a Future Time*, 14).

15. Dzong-ka-ba, *The Great Treatise on the Stages of the Path*, 109–16.

16. Gen Lob-zang Gya-tso, interview by author, Dharamsala, fall 1995. See also L. Gyatso, *Memoirs of a Tibetan Lama*, trans. and ed. G. Sparham (Ithaca: Snow Lion, 1998), 115.

17. Geshe Rabten, *The Life and Teaching of Geshé Rabten*, trans. and ed. B. A. Wallace (London: Allen and Unwin, 1980), 35.

18. R. E. Buswell and R. M. Gimello, introduction to *Paths to Liberation: The Mārga and Its Transformations in Buddhist Thought*, ed. R. E. Buswell and R. M. Gimello (Honolulu: University of Hawaii Press, 1992), 6.

19. See J. McRae, "Encounter Dialogue and the Transformation of the Spiritual Path in Chinese Ch'an," in Buswell and Gimello, *Paths to Liberation*, 339–70.

20. R. Sharf, "Buddhist Modernism and the Rhetoric of Meditative Experience," *Numen* 42 (1995): 238.

21.

shes pha rol phyin pa ni
dngos po brgyad kyis yang dag bshad
rnam kun mkyen nyid lam shes nyid
de nas tham cad shes pa nyid
nam kun mngon rdzogs rtogs pa dang
rtse mor phyin dang mthar gyis pa
skad cig gcig mngon rdzogs byang chub
chos kyi sku dang de rnams brgyad

prajñāpāramitāṣṭābhiḥ padārthaiḥ samudīritā
sarvākārajñatā (1) mārgajñatā (2) sarvajñatā (3) tataḥ

sarvākārābhisaṃbodho (4) mūrdhaprāpto (5) 'nunpūrvikaḥ (6)
ekakṣaṇābhisambodho (7) dharmakāyaś (8) ca te ṣṭadhā

E. Obermiller and T. Stcherbatsky, *Abhisamayālaṃkāra-nāma-prajñāpāramitopadeśa-śāstra, The Work of Bodhisattva Maitreya*, new ed. (Osnabrück: Biblio, 1970), stanzas I:3–4, P: 5184, *Ka*, 1.a–15.b, 1. This work has been translated into English by E. Conze as *Abhisamayālaṃkāra* (Rome: Ismeo, 1954). E. Obermiller's study of the content of this work remains unmatched; see "The

Doctrine of the *prajñāpāramitā* as Exposed in the *Abhisamayālaṃkāra* of Maitreya," *Acta Orientalia* 11 (1933): 1–100. My translation is based on this last work.

22. Some monasteries consider topics deemed central—such as tranquillity, or the distinction between interpretable and definitive teachings—to be "separate." They have special texts devoted to them, and in the case of Se-ra Jay they are also studied apart.

23. The tradition of the Gradual Path often speaks of two methods to develop the mind of enlightenment: in the first, the seven causes and one effect, we consider the debt we owe all sentient beings for having been our mothers and having shown us countless other kindnesses. The second focuses on the equality of self and others and proposes an exchange of one's attitudes toward oneself and others. See Geshe Rabten, *The Essential Nectar: Meditations on the Buddhist Path*, ed. M. Willson (London: Wisdom, 1984), 305–66.

24. The Ge-luk views on the four absorptions and the four formless concentrations have been well presented in L. Zahler, ed., *Meditative States in Tibetan Buddhism: The Concentrations and Formless Absorptions* (London: Wisdom, 1983), and Geshe G. Lodrö, *Walking through Walls: A Presentation of Tibetan Meditation*, trans. and ed. J. Hopkins (Ithaca: Snow Lion, 1992). For a detailed Theravada treatment of the topic, see Buddhaghosa, *The Path of Purification of Bhadantācariya Buddhaghosa: Visuddhimagga*, trans. B. Ñyāṇamoli (reprint; Berkeley: Shambhala, 1976), 1:84–478. For an easier exposition, see A. Solé-Leris, *Tranquillity and Insight: An Introduction to the Oldest Form of Buddhist Meditation* (Boston: Shambhala, 1986), 56–73.

25. See D. Cozort, *Highest Yoga Tantra: An Introduction to the Esoteric Buddhism of Tibet* (Ithaca: Snow Lion, 1986), 55–56.

26. In both traditional and modern scholarship, there is a controversy concerning the order of chapters in Dharmakīrti's *Commentary on Valid Cognition*. Jina (tenth–eleventh century C.E.) is among those who accused Dharmakīrti's direct disciple Devendrabuddhi of having inverted the order of the chapters. For Jina, the "Establishing [Buddha] as Valid" (*pramāṇasiddhi, tshad mar grub pa*, traditionally the second chapter) should be first and the "Inference for Oneself" (*svārthānumāna, rang don rjes dpag*, traditionally the first) should be third. Here I follow the traditional order. See T. Stcherbatsky, *Buddhist Logic* (1930; reprint, New York: Dover, 1962), 1:44; E. Frauwallner, "Die Reihenfolge und Entstehung der Werke Dharmakīrti's," in *Asiatica: Festschrift Friedrich Weller*, ed. J. Schubert (Leipzig: Harrassowitz, 1954), 142–54; and E. Steinkellner, *Verse-Index of Dharmakīrti's Works* (Vienna: Arbeitskreis für Tibetische and Buddhistische Studien, Universität Wien, 1977).

27. Lob-zang Trin-ley, '*Jam mgon chos kyi rgyal po tsong kha pa chen po'i rnam thar* (Kokonor: Kokonor People's Press, 1996), 145.

28. Traditional biographers count Dzong-ka-ba's final retreat not as part of his studies but as a period of meditation (Lob-zang Trin-ley, *rNam thar*, 247). Hence, they stop in 1398, when Dzong-ka-ba is forty-one (forty-two by the Tibetan calculation). But it is clear that even at this stage Dzong-ka-ba was en-

gaged in studying and thinking about particular texts; hence his final stay in Wöl-khar can be counted as belonging to his scholarly career.

29. Dzong-ka-ba, *bsTan bcos mngon rtogs rgyan 'grel pa dang bcas pa'i rgya cher bshad pa Legs bshad gser gyi phreng ba* (Kokonor: Tsho sngon mi rigs dpe skrun khang, 1986), 39–40. This point is made by many other thinkers; for example, Jang-gya-röl-bay-dor-jay *(lcang skya rol ba'i rdo rje*, 1717–1786) states: "[E]ven though certainty brought forth by pure reason is not born in the fideists, though a faith involving conviction may well be born in them, it is hard [for them] to get beyond a conditional [sort of faith]. If certainty is born on the basis of a genuine reason, it won't be turned back by conditions; a firm disposition is established" (quoted in M. Kapstein, *The Tibetan Assimilation of Buddhism: Conversion, Contestation, and Memory* [Oxford: Oxford University Press, 2000], 240).

30. See H. Amano, "A Study of the Abhisamayālaṃkāra-nāma-prajñāpāra-mitopadeśa-śāstra-vivṛtti," *Bulletin of the Faculty of Shimane University* 23, no. 1 (1989): 1–7, esp. 2.

31. K. Burke, *A Rhetoric of Motives* (New York: Prentice-Hall, 1950), 22–23.

32. I heard these words used by the Dalai Lama several times during my stays in Dharamsala between 1970 and 1983.

33. R. Sharf explains some of the difficulties in relating scriptural descriptions to actual experiences; see "Buddhist Modernism and the Rhetoric of Meditative Experience," *Numen* 42 (1995): 228–83. Discrepancies exist both within a single tradition and between competing traditions. For example, the descriptions of the attainments of absorptions given by Asaṅga, whose views are adopted by Tibetans, and those given by Buddhaghosa differ greatly. One wonders sometimes whether they are speaking about the same topic! There are also long-running controversies within Buddhist schools concerning the identification of actual realizations.

34. There were several such hermitages around the three Ge-luk seats—Pabong-ka, Gon-sar, etc.—which were also used by those engaged in memorizing texts. Periods of intensive memorization were considered retreats as well.

35. Among the texts of the curriculum, only Śāntideva's *Bodhiscaryāvatāra* is studied for its direct relevance to meditation.

36. For a thoughtful essay on the place of experience in Tibetan tantric tradition, see J. Gyatso, "Healing Burns with Fire: The Facilitations of Experience in Tibetan Buddhism," *Journal of the American Academy of Religion* 67 (1998): 113–47.

CHAPTER 9. THE SUPPLEMENT:
HERMENEUTICAL OR DECONSTRUCTIVE?

1. S. Fraade, *From Tradition to Commentary: Torah and Its Interpretation in the Midrash Sifre to Deuteronomy* (Albany: State University of New York Press, 1991), 1–2; quoted in P. Griffiths, *Religious Reading: The Place of Reading in the Practice of Religion* (New York: Oxford University Press, 1999), 83.

2. Griffiths, *Religious Reading*, 81.

3. Mi-pam, *dBu ma rgyan gyi rnam bshad 'jam dbyangs bla ma dgyes pa'i zhal lung* (New Delhi: Karmapa Chodhey, 1976); Dzong-ka-ba, *dBu ma rtsa ba'i tshig le'ur byas pa shes rab ces bya ba'i rnam bshad rigs pa'i rgya mtsho* (Varanasi: Pleasure of Elegant Sayings Press, 1973).

4. Dzong-ka-ba, *dBu ma la 'jug pa'i rgya cher bshad pa dgongs pa rab gsal* (Varanasi: Pleasure of Elegant Sayings Press, 1973); Go-ram-ba, *rGyal ba thams cad kyi thugs kyi dgongs pa zab mo'i de kho na nyid spyi'i ngag gis ston pa nges don rab gsal*, in *Complete Works of the Great Masters of the Sa sKya Sect* (Tokyo: Tokyo Bunko, 1968), 14: 1.1.1–167.3.3 (*Ca*, 1.a–209.a).

5. Candrakīrti, *Mūlamadhyamakavṛttiprasannapadā* (*dbu ma'i rtsa ba'i 'grel pa tshig gsal ba*, D: 3860), and *Madhyamakāvatāra* (*dbu ma la 'jug pa*, D: 3861, P: 5262).

6. Ngak-wang-bel-den, *Grub mtha' chen mo'i mchan 'grel dka' gnad mdud grol blo gsal gces nor* (Varanasi: Pleasure of Elegant Sayings Press, 1964).

7. J. Wilson, "Tibetan Commentaries on Indian *Śāstras*," in *Tibetan Literature: Studies in Genre*, ed. J. Cabezón and R. Jackson (Ithaca: Snow Lion, 1996), 125–37.

8. D. Jackson, *The Entrance Gate for the Wise* (Vienna: Arbeitskreis für Tibetische und Buddhistische Studien, Universität Wien, 1987), 195.

9. M. Foucault, "The Discourse on Language," in *The Archaeology of Knowledge*, trans. A. M. Sheridan Smith (1972; reprint, New York: Harper and Row, 1976), 221; emphasis his.

10. J. Hopkins, *Meditation on Emptiness* (London: Wisdom, 1983), 404.

11. See J. Cabezón, *Buddhism and Language: A Study of Indo-Tibetan Scholasticism* (Albany: State University of New York Press, 1994), 82.

12. J. Derrida, *Of Grammatology*, trans. G. C. Spivak (Baltimore: Johns Hopkins University Press, 1976), 158. For a clarification of what is at stake in the critique of commentary, see J. Derrida, *Limited Inc* (Evanston, Ill.: Northwestern University Press, 1988), 143–50.

13. Derrida, *Of Grammatology*, 145; emphases his. For another treatment of supplement, see J. Derrida, *La voix et le phénomène* (Paris: Presses Universitaires de France, 1967), 98.

14. I am here following S. Critchley's helpful but obviously greatly simplified explanations in *The Ethics of Deconstruction: Derrida and Levinas* (Oxford: Blackwell, 1992), 61–63.

15. For a study of nirvana as an element of narrative closure, see S. Collins, *Nirvana and Other Buddhist Felicities: Utopias of the Pali Imaginaire* (Cambridge: Cambridge University Press, 1998).

16. For a discussion of the synthesis of suddenism and gradualism in the Nying-ma tradition, see M. Kapstein, *The Tibetan Assimilation of Buddhism: Conversion, Contestation, and Memory* (Oxford: Oxford University Press, 2000), 176.

17. See D. Lopez, ed., *Buddhist Hermeneutics* (Honolulu: University of Hawaii Press, 1988). I am giving here a simplified account based on a particu-

lar interpretation of the distinction between Yogācāra and Madhyamaka. Other interpretations in Tibet emphasize the compatibility of these two schools; yet even these restrict the range of possible polysemy and offer their own doxographical hierarchies. For example, Döl-bo-pa argues that the supreme school is the Great Madhyamaka, which is superior to Candrakīrti's Madhyamaka and the Mind-Only view. See C. Stearns, *The Buddha from Dolpo: A Study of the Life and Thought of the Tibetan Master Dolpopa Sherab Gyaltsen* (Albany: State University of New York Press, 1999), 86–97.

18. Jang-gya Röl-bay-dor-jay, *Grub mtha'i rnam par bzhag pa gsal bar bshad pa thub bstan lhun po'i mdzes rgyan* (Varanasi: Pleasure of Elegant Sayings Press, 1970), 151.

19. Jang-gya, *Grub mtha'i rnam par bzhag pa*, 152. For a discussion of Geluk views concerning this topic, see J. Hopkins, *Emptiness in the Mind-Only School of Buddhism: Dynamic Responses to Dzong-Ka-Ba's "The Essence of Eloquence,"* vol. 1 (Berkeley: University of California Press, 1999), and R. A. F. Thurman, trans., *Tsong Khapa's Speech of Gold in the Essence of True Eloquence: Reason and Enlightenment in the Central Philosophy of Tibet*, trans. R. Thurman (Princeton: Princeton University Press, 1984).

20. D. Stern, "Midrash and Indeterminacy," *Critical Inquiry* 15 (1988): 132–61. G. Hartman's original statement is found in *Criticism in the Wilderness: The Study of Literature Today* (New Haven: Yale University Press, 1980); see also his "Midrash as Law and Literature," *Journal of Religion* 74 (1994): 338–55.

21. Stern, "Midrash and Indeterminacy," 152.

22. For an analysis of the Tibetan doxographical literature, see three works by K. Mimaki: *Le Chapitre du Blo gsal grub mtha' sur les Sautrāntika (Présentation et édition)* (Kyoto: Zinbun Kagaku Kenkyusyo, 1979), *Le Chapitre du Blo gsal grub mtha' sur les Sautrāntika (Un essai de traduction)* (Kyoto: Zinbun Kagaku Kenkyusyo, 1980), and *Blo gsal grub mtha'* (Kyoto: Zinbun Kagaku Kenkyusyo, 1982). For a Ge-luk view of the topic, see Geshe L. Sopa and J. Hopkins, trans., *Cutting through Appearances: The Practice and Theory of Tibetan Buddhism* (Ithaca: Snow Lion, 1989).

23. J. Cabezón, "The Canonization of Philosophy and the Rhetoric of Siddhānta," in *Buddha Nature: A Festschrift in Honor of Minoru Kiyota*, ed. P. J. Griffiths and J. P. Keenan (San Francisco: Buddhist Books International, 1991), 18.

24. Cabezón, *Buddhism and Language*, 83–85.

25. Derrida himself has emphasized the limits of polysemy, which is superior to a linear and monosemic reading but is still limited in its assumption that a totalizing interpretation is possible. For Derrida, interpretation should aim not for the truth of multiple interpretations but for the productivity of dissemination, which seeks to disrupt any appropriation by emphasizing the turbulence and instability of the meaning of the text. See J. Derrida, *Positions: Entretiens avec Henri Ronse, Julia Kristeva, Jean-Louis Houdebine, Guy Scarpetta* (Paris: Éditions de Minuit, 1972), 62.

26. M. Halbertal and T. H. Halbertal, "The Yeshiva," in *Philosophers on Education*, ed. A. Rorty (London: Routledge, 1998), 459.

27. M. Halbertal and T. H. Halbertal, "The Yeshiva," 460.

28. Such texts are being written nowadays, but in a tradition in which orthodoxy dominates and novelty is viewed with great suspicion, these texts have a limited impact. See, for example, Ge-she Pal-den Drak-ba, *Legs bshad dad pa'i mdzes rgyan* (Mundgod: Loling Library, 1979).

CHAPTER 10. DEBATE AS PRACTICE

1. R. A. Stein, *Tibetan Civilization*, trans. J. E. Stapleton Driver (Stanford: Stanford University Press, 1972), 161.

2. F. Sierskma, "*rTsod pa:* The Monachal Disputation in Tibet," *Indo-Iranian Journal* 8 (1964): 130–52.

3. Most of the recent literature on the Collected Topics can be included in this group. See M. Goldberg, "Entity and Antinomy in Tibetan Logic," parts 1 and 2, *Journal of Indian Philosophy* 13 (1985): 153–99, 273–304; D. Perdue, *Debate in Tibetan Buddhism* (Ithaca: Snow Lion, 1992).

4. Goldberg, "Entity and Antinomy in Tibetan Logic," part 1, 157; quoted in T. Tillemans, "Formal and Semantic Aspects of Tibetan Buddhist Debate Logic," in *Scripture, Logic, Language: Essays on Dharmakirti and His Tibetan Successors*, ed. T. Tillemans (Boston: Wisdom, 1999), 139.

5. Tillemans, "Tibetan Buddhist Debate Logic," 140; emphasis his.

6. See Tillemans, "Tibetan Buddhist Debate Logic," 121–25, and S. Onoda, *Monastic Debate in Tibet: A Study on the History and Structures of Bsdus grwa Logic* (Vienna: Arbeitskreis für Tibetische und Buddhistische Studien, Universität Wien, 1992), 49–59.

7. In Tibet, the monastery of Ra-tö (now affiliated with Lo-se-ling) specialized in the study of the formal elements of debate, which were mostly ignored by the scholars from the larger centers.

8. Tillemans, "Tibetan Buddhist Debate Logic," 117–49.

9. R. Hall, "Dialectic," in *The Encyclopedia of Philosophy* (New York: Macmillan, 1967), 1–2:385.

10. In this discussion I leave aside the difficult relation between dialectic and rhetoric, particularly as it figures in Aristotle's work. For a treatment of that question, see J. Brunschwig, "Aristotle's Rhetoric as a 'Counter-part' to Dialectic," in *Essays on Aristotle's Rhetoric*, ed. A. Rorty (Berkeley: University of California Press, 1996), 34–55. I also sidestep the question of the nature of rhetoric. Does it concern "the art of symbolic inducement," that is, "the ways in which men influence each other's thinking and behaviour through the strategic use of symbols," as argued by D. Ehninger in his "On Systems of Rhetoric" (in *Contemporary Rhetoric: A Reader's Coursebook*, ed. D. Ehninger [Glenview, Ill.: Scott, Foresman, 1972], 3)? Or should rhetoric be limited to "the art of persuading through discourse," as O. Reboul argues in his *Introduction à la rhétorique: Theorie et pratique* (Paris: Presses Universitaires de France, 1991,

4)? Similarly, C. Perelman, one of the leading modern analysts of rhetoric, defines it, following Aristotle, as including the "discursive techniques for obtaining the mind's adherence" (C. Perelman and L. Olbrechts-Tyteca, *Traité de l' argumentation: La nouvelle rhétorique,* 2nd ed. [1970; reprint, Brussels: Université de Bruxelles, 1983], 5).

11. Aristotle, *Topics,* trans. R. Smith (Oxford: Clarendon Press, 1997), 28.

12. G. Scholem, "Tradition and Commentary as Religious Categories in Judaism," in *Arguments and Doctrines: A Reader of Jewish Thinking in the Aftermath of the Holocaust,* comp. A. Cohen (New York: Harper and Row, 1970), 307; emphasis his.

13. J. Verger, *Culture, enseignement et société en Occident aux XIIe et XIIIe siècles* (Rennes: Presses Universitaires de Rennes, 1999), 25–42.

14. Verger, *Culture, enseignement et société en Occident,* 164.

15. J. Baldwin, *Scholastic Culture of the Middle Ages, 1000–1300* (Lexington, Mass.: Heath, 1971), 61. For a more detailed study of medieval debate, see P. Glorieux, "L'enseignement au Moyen Age; Techniques et méthodes en usage à la faculté de Paris au XIIIe siècle," *Archives d'histoire doctrinale et littéraire du Moyen Age* 35 (1968): 65–186.

16. Lo Ken-chen, *sDe bdun mdo dang bcas pa'i dgongs 'grel tshad ma rigs gter gyi 'grel ba'i rnam bshad rigs lam gsal ba'i nyi ma* (reprint of Derge edition; Manduwalla, India: Ngorpa Center, 1985), fol. 129.2.

17. P. Griffiths, "Scholasticism: The Possible Recovery of an Intellectual Tradition," in *Scholasticism: Cross-Cultural and Comparative Perspectives,* ed. J. Cabezón (Albany: State University of New York Press, 1998), 201–36. See also chapter 7.

18. J. Lukasiewicz, *Aristotle's Syllogistic from the Standpoint of Modern Formal Logic,* 2nd ed. (Oxford: Clarendon Press, 1957), 14. Also see J. M. Bochenski, *History of Formal Logic,* trans. and ed. I. Thomas (Notre Dame, Ind.: University of Notre Dame Press, 1961), 3.

19. R. Carnap, *The Logical Syntax of Language,* trans. A. Smeaton (1937; reprint, London: Routledge and K. Paul, 1959), 258.

20. E. A. Solomon, *Indian Dialectics: Methods of Philosophical Discussion* (Ahmedabad: B.J. Institute of Learning and Research, 1976), 89.

21. As is usual for figures in ancient India, it is impossible to establish Dignāga's exact dates. S. C. Vidyabhusana gives 450–520 C.E. (*A History of Indian Logic: Ancient, Mediaeval, and Modern Schools* [1921; reprint, Delhi: Motilal Banarsidass, 1978], 270), but M. Hattori puts Dignāga later, 480–540 (*Dignāga, On Perception; Being the Pratyakṣapariccheda of Dignāga's "Pramāṇasamuccaya" from the Sanskrit Fragments and the Tibetan Versions,* trans. and ed. M. Hattori [Cambridge, Mass.: Harvard University Press, 1968], 4).

22. Vidyabhusana places the emergence of Nalanda as a major center of higher learning earlier, around 450 C.E. (*History of Indian Logic,* 515).

23. T. Tillemans, "Sur le Parārthanumāna en Logique Bouddhique," *Asiatiche Studien* 28, no. 2 (1984): 73–99.

24. An interesting comparison could be made with Aristotle's enthymeme,

which is presented as a kind of syllogism. But because its conclusion is not obtained deductively, its degree of certainty is in question. See M. F. Burneyat, "Enthymeme: Aristotle on the Rationality of Rhetoric," in Rorty, *Essays on Aristotle's Rhetoric,* 86–115.

25. T. Stcherbatsky, *Buddhist Logic* (1930; reprint, New York: Dover, 1962), 1:38.

26. *tshul gsum.* See Y. Kajiyama, *Introduction to Buddhist Philosophy* (Kyoto: Kyoto University Press, 1966), 65–72.

27. Particular arguments are assessed in direct relation to their specified audiences; when an argument is stated generally, it can be correct only if it has some potential audience. For example, the argument "A sound is impermanent because it is produced, just like a jar" is in general correct, because one can imagine a person to whom it could be meaningfully addressed. On the other hand, the argument "A sound is not produced because it is produced, just like a jar" is not correct, for there is no possible audience to whom it could be addressed.

28. In practice, a consequence may expose a contradiction only indirectly. It may also lead to a contradiction with some well-established fact.

29. A consequence does not need to be a reductio ad absurdum; in our example, the following statement would also be correct: "It follows that the subject, a sound, is not permanent because it is produced." To the person imagined, such a statement is a correct consequence, for it amounts to the same consequence as the previous statement and fulfills the same function.

30. In this discussion, I am paraphrasing D. Jackson's excellent *Entrance Gate for the Wise* (Vienna: Arbeitskreis für Tibetische und Buddhistische Studien, Universität Wien, 1987), 196–200.

31. A reason *(rtags, hetu)* is "unestablished" *(ma bsgrub, asiddha)* if the reason is not established on the predicate, as in the argument "The sound is permanent because it is uncompounded." It is "uncertain" *(ma nges pa, anaikāntika)* if the reason does not prove the predicate, as in the argument "The sound is permanent because it exists." It is "contradictory" *('gal ba, viruddha)* if the reason contradicts the predicate, as in the argument "The sound is permanent because it is produced." Reasons that are free from any of these three types of mistake are valid. See T. Tillemans, ed., *Scripture, Logic, Language: Essays on Dharmakīrti and His Tibetan Successors* (Boston: Wisdom, 1999), and K. Rogers, "Tibetan Logic" (M.A. thesis, University of Virginia, 1980).

32. Vidyabhusana, *A History of Indian Logic,* 84–90.

33. See L. van der Kuijp, "Phya-pa Chos-kyi-seng-ge's Impact on Tibetan Epistemology," *Journal of Indian Philosophy* 5 (1978): 355–69.

34. Śākya Chok-den, *Tshad ma rigs gter gyi dgongs rgyan rigs pa'i 'khor los lugs ngan pham byed,* in *The Complete Works (gsung 'bum) of Gser mdog Paṇ chen Śākya mchog ldan* (Thimphu, Bhutan: Kunzang Tobgey, 1975), 9:302–6, 339–42. Present practices in the Sa-gya and Nying-ma traditions are of little help in settling these questions, for they were established relatively recently, during the nonsectarian movement, in imitation of and as a response to Ge-luk practices.

35. See G. Dreyfus, *Recognizing Reality: Dharmakīrti's Philosophy and Its Tibetan Interpreters* (Albany: State University of New York Press, 1997), 189–202.

36. Perdue, *Debate in Tibetan Buddhism*, 28.

37. So Perdue puts it: "Dhīḥ! The subject, in just the way [Mañjuśrī debated]" (*Debate in Tibetan Buddhism*, 103).

38. See D. S. Ruegg, *Buddha-nature, Mind, and the Problem of Gradualism in a Comparative Perspective: On the Transmission and Reception of Buddhism in India and Tibet* (London: School of Oriental and African Studies, University of London, 1989).

39. Sa-paṇ differentiates three phases in the debate: a preparation *(sbyor ba)* in which the two proponents seek a common basis, the main part *(dngos gzhi)* of the debate, and the conclusion *(mjug)* during which the witness summarizes the argument and establishes the winner (C. Beckwith, "The Medieval Scholastic Method in Tibet and in the West," in *Reflections on Tibetan Culture: Essays in Memory of Turrell V. Wylie*, ed. L. Epstein and R. Sherburne [Lewiston, N.Y.: Mellen Press, 1990], 307–13). In actual Tibetan debates, the third element is absent since there is no witness.

40. The three answers concern complete statements containing three terms (subject, pseudo-predicate, and reason). In the Ge-luk tradition, an incomplete consequence is allowable. Consider this statement: "It follows that the subject, a mountain, lasts only for a short instant." Such a statement has only two parts, but is nonetheless considered well-formed since it allows a straightforward answer. An incomplete statement can be answered in two ways: either by accepting (*'dod;* lit., "[I] accept") or by refusing (*ci'i phyir;* lit., "why") it. In our example, these answers mean: I accept that the mountain lasts only for a short instant; or, I do not accept that the mountain lasts only for a short instant. If the latter answer is given, the questioner can immediately state the incomplete consequence: "It follows that the subject, the mountain, does not last only for a short instant." The only possible answer to such a consequence is positive; any other is considered a breach of rules of rational discourse. Because other traditions have reconstituted their practice of debate by imitating Ge-luk practices, they follow this usage. Śākya Chok-den seems to disagree with this practice, however, arguing that only three-part consequences should be used.

41. Jackson, *Entrance Gate for the Wise*, 361.

42. Perdue, *Debate in Tibetan Buddhism*, 275.

43. The defender is in a difficult position in this debate. Non-Ge-luk scholars would answer such a claim, which is often presented by Ge-luk scholars as a refutation of their views, by making a quasi-Humean distinction between the domain of reality, where duration does not exist, and the conceptual domain, where duration is necessary. In reality, there is no duration—only a succession of similar moments that create the false but useful impression that things last. True to their moderate realism, the Ge-luk tradition understands momentariness in a more commonsensical way. For them, a phenomenon is momentary not because it lasts only a moment but because it is composed of temporal parts

and hence is in constant transformation. On these differences in the understanding of the concepts of impermanence and momentariness, see Dreyfus, *Recognizing Reality,* 63–65, 106–16.

44. The exact meaning of the statement *o' tshar* is not easy to establish. I have translated it as "Oh, it's finished," where *o'* is taken as an interjection. It could also be taken as directed at the opponent: "Oh, you are finished." Some scholars think that the actual words are *ngo mtshar* (amazing) or even *ngo tsha* (shame), but that interpretation makes less sense in the longer expression *rtsa ba'i dam bca' tshar* ("amazing for your root thesis," or "shame on your root thesis").

45. For a description of the symbolism of monastic gestures, see Geshe Rabten, *The Life and Teaching of Geshé Rabten: A Tibetan Lama's Search for Truth,* trans. and ed. B. A. Wallace (London: Allen and Unwin, 1980), 12–24.

46. The "three circles" refer to three conditions that the consequence must satisfy to checkmate the respondent. In the example "It follows that the subject the sound is not produced since it is permanent," such a consequence is appropriate only to a person who fulfills three conditions: he admits that the sound is permanent, holds that whatever is permanent is not produced, and holds that the sound is produced. Such a person has completed the three circles and hence cannot give a correct answer without contradicting himself. In practice, the expression is used to signal any mistake in the respondent's answer and not just the ones that satisfy these three criteria.

47. Rules govern how the respondent wears his hat. When the topic is introduced, the respondent takes his hat off out of respect for the debater, holding it until the basis for the debate has been laid out. He then puts the hat on again, a sign that he has mastered the topic and is ready to answer. Should he lose, however, the respondent has to take his hat off, admitting his defeat. If he does not do so, the questioner may grab the hat himself.

48. Stein, *Tibetan Civilization,* 161.

49. Sierskma, "*rTsod pa*," 141.

50. Sierskma, "*rTsod pa*," 140. Unfortunately, Sierskma does not take his informants' comments seriously; he elaborates his own far-fetched theory of debate as a non-Buddhist element in Tibetan culture, ignoring the rich Indian dialectical tradition.

51. One hesitates to call the motives of debaters "pure." Monks, like most people, act for complex reasons. Serious intellectual and religious interests do not exclude personal dislikes and ambitions. Knowing this, teachers do not object to ambition as long as it does not become a student's main preoccupation.

52. Sierskma, "*rTsod pa*," 139–41.

53. Motivation is obviously important, but it is also highly individual and volatile. Some students remain driven throughout their studies by personal ambitions. This was particularly common in Tibet, where a title of Geshe could lead to considerable power. Others lose such worldly ambitions during their studies, while still others acquire them at the monastery. Lati Rin-po-che used to comment on how the exile changed the perspective of many. Some who were good scholars lost interest in studying, perhaps realizing that their ambitions

had become unattainable or perhaps becoming interested in the new possibilities of the modern world. Conversely, others became much better scholars in exile, realizing the fragilities of worldly goods. In any case, we must recognize both the importance and the complexity of motivation.

54. Sierskma, "*rTsod pa,*" 140. Sierskma is here quoting an informant, not expressing his own opinion.

55. Perdue, *Debate in Tibetan Buddhism,* 99–100.

56. See, for example, Geshe Pal-den Drak-ba, *Legs bshad 'dad pa'i mdzes rgyan* (Mundgod: Loling Library, 1979).

57. Equivalence is broader than synonymity. *Impermanence* and *thing* are said to be equivalent, though they are not synonymous.

58. In Buddhist epistemology, the concept of existence is usually explained in relation to that of valid cognition (or means of valid cognition, *pramāṇa, tshad ma*), the central notion in Indian and Tibetan epistemological traditions. Things exist if, and only if, they are the object of a valid cognition *(prameya, tshad ma'i gzhal bya).* See Dreyfus, *Recognizing Reality,* 73–82.

59. See R. Gethin, "The Mātikās: Memorization, Mindfulness, and the List," in *In the Mirror of Memory: Reflections on Mindfulness and Remembrance in Indian and Tibetan Buddhism,* ed. J. Gyatso (Albany: State University of New York Press, 1992), 149–72.

60. Ngari Panchen Pema Wangyi Gyalpo, *Perfect Conduct: Ascertaining the Three Vows,* trans. Khenpo Gyurme Samdrub and Sangye Khandro (Boston: Wisdom, 1996), 17–18.

61. A distinguisher *(ldog pa, vyāvṛtti)* is the property possessed by a phenomenon of not being what it is not. For example, a jar is distinct from everything else. This is its distinguisher, according to the Collected Topics. Since such a property is a distinction made by thought, it is conceptual and hence unreal; but its unreality does not prevent it from being instantiated by a real thing, the object that it distinguishes. Distinguishers have further interesting logical properties that make them particularly important for those learning debate. Since a distinguisher is the property that distinguishes an object from everything else, it is itself distinct from that object. Hence, a distinguisher does not instantiate itself. Non-Ge-luk scholars have another view of a distinguisher; they describe it as an unreal conceptual projection that is not instantiated by a thing but is falsely projected on it. Thus for them the whole discussion of a distinguisher being permanent but its instance being impermanent does not arise. For a more detailed treatment of this topic, see Dreyfus, *Recognizing Reality,* 154–88.

62. Those interested in further explanation should see Dreyfus, *Recognizing Reality,* 165–68.

CHAPTER 11. DEBATE IN THE CURRICULUM

1. "sems can thams cad la dmigs nas rnam pa sdug bsngal mtha' dag las skyob par 'dod pa'i sems byung"; Paṇ-chen Sö-nam-drak-ba, *dBu ma spyi don zab*

don gsal ba'i sgron me, in *The Collected Works (gsung 'bum) of Paṇ-chen Bsod-nams-grags-pa*, vol. 9 (Jha) (Mundgod: Drepung Loseling Library, 1985), 10.a.

2. Dharmakīrti, *Pramāṇavārttikakārikā*, ed. Y. Miyasaka (*Sanskrit-Tibetan*, Acta Indologica 2, 1971–72). This work is a defense and vindication of Dignāga's (fifth-century) *Pramāṇasamuccaya (tshad ma kun btus*, D: 4203, P: 5700).

3. An exception was Ta-shi Lhun-po, where Dharmakīrti's works were at the center of the studies. After the students had gone through the Collected Topics, which could take up to four years, they spent up to six years studying Dharmakīrti before turning to any other texts. The *Ornament*, for example, would be examined only after ten years of study. The curriculum of Ta-shi Lhun-po has changed in recent years, both in India and in Tibet, but education in this monastery is difficult to assess. Unlike the three monastic seats, it has not succeeded in reproducing its education in exile; and in Tibet, the political troubles and the restrictions imposed by the PRC authorities on monastic practices have restricted its practices.

4. In India the Jang session is now controlled by the three monasteries, not by Ra-tö.

5. "'jang la mkhas pa sbyang gsang phu la do blang"; H. Stoddard, *Le mendiant de l'Amdo* (Paris: Société d'Ethnographie, 1985), 151.

6. My reconstruction is extremely tentative, based on the many oral reports I heard over the years; it is difficult to establish a precise chronology.

7. Jang is less than an hour away from Lhasa by car, but before 1950 Tibet had no roads. All goods had to be transported on animal or human backs.

8. Rato Khyongla Nawang Losang, *My Life and Lives: The Story of a Tibetan Incarnation*, ed. J. Campbell (New York: Dutton, 1977), 70–71.

9. Geshe Rabten, *The Life and Teaching of Geshé Rabten: A Tibetan Lama's Search for Truth*, trans. and ed. B. A. Wallace (London: Allen and Unwin, 1980), 101.

10. For a study of Dharmakīrti's logic, see Y. Kajiyama, *Introduction to Buddhist Philosophy* (Kyoto: Kyoto University, 1966). For his epistemology, see G. Dreyfus, *Recognizing Reality: Dharmakīrti's Philosophy and Its Tibetan Interpreters* (Albany: State University of New York Press, 1997). Here I leave aside the second chapter of Dharmakīrti's *Commentary*, "Establishing [Buddha] as Valid" (*pramāṇasiddhi, tshad mar grub pa*), which was discussed in chapter 8.

11. In this context, a *realist* theory holds that language captures properties that exist independently of our conceptual schemes and even, sometimes, of their instantiations.

12. The major exception to this quasi-unanimity is the view of extrinsic emptiness, which is particularly nonconformist in its Jo-nang version. See S. Hookham, *The Buddha Within: Tathagatagarbha Doctrine according to the Shentong Interpretation of the Ratnagotravibhaga* (Albany: State University of New York Press, 1991), and C. Stearns, *The Buddha from Dolpo: A Study of the Life and Thought of the Tibetan Master Dolpopa Sherab Gyaltsen* (Albany: State University of New York Press, 1999).

13. My use of *Prāsaṅgika*, the Sanskrit form of a term invented by Tibetans, is meant to reflect the Tibetan usage.

14. See Go-ram-ba, *rGyal ba thams cad kyi thugs kyi dgongs pa zab mo dbu ma'i de kho na nyid spyi'i ngag gis ston pa nges don rab gsal*, in *Complete Works of the Great Masters of the Sa sKya Sect* (Tokyo: Tokyo Bunko, 1968), 14: 1.1.1–167.3.3 (*Ca*, 1.a–334.a); Mi-pam, *dBu ma rgyan gyi rnam bshad 'jam dbyangs bla ma bgyes pa'i zhal lung* (New Delhi: Karmapa Chodhey, 1976), and *Shes rab tshig don go sla bar rnam par bshad pa nor bu ke ta ka*, in *Collected Works*, vol. 13 (Gangtok: Sonam Kazi, 1979).

15. On the different views of emptiness, see D. S. Ruegg, "A Kar ma bKa' brgyud Work on Lineages and Traditions of the Indo-Tibetan dBu ma (Madhyamaka)," in *Orientalia Iosephi Tucci Memoriae Dictata*, ed. G. Gnoli and L. Lanciotti, vol. 56, no. 3 (Rome: I.S.M.E.O. 1988).

16. "so sor ming 'dogs mang na yang / nges don lung rigs la mkhas shing / nyams myong can gyi rnal 'byor pas / dpyad na dgongs pa gcig tu 'bab"; *dGe ldan bka' brgyud rin po che'i phyag chen rtsa ba rgyal bzhung lam*, in H. H. the Dalai-Lama and A. Berzin, *The Gelug/Kagyü Tradition of Mahamudra* (Ithaca: Snow Lion, 1997), 353.

17. Nāgārjuna, *Prajñā-nāma-mūlamadhyamakakārikā* (*dbu ma rtsa ba'i tshig le'ur byas pa shes rab*, D: 3824, P: 5224), hereafter *Treatise*, XXIV:8; trans. by J. Garfield as *The Fundamental Wisdom of the Middle Way: Nāgārjuna's Mūlamadhyamakakārikā* (New York: Oxford University Press, 1995), 296.

18. The Ge-luk tradition insists that ultimate truth is an object in that it can be known, but that insistence should not mask the fact that emptiness is not an object in the usual sense of the word. For a Ge-luk view of the topic, see G. Newland, *The Two Truths in the Madhyamika Philosophy of the Ge-luk-ba Order of Tibetan Buddhism* (Ithaca: Snow Lion, 1992). Keep in mind that my brief summary of the doctrine of the two truths reflects a point of view that at least superficially conflicts with that of the Ge-luk tradition.

19. J. Derrida, *Spurs: Nietzsche's Styles*, trans. B. Harlow (Chicago: University of Chicago Press, 1979), 95.

20. Śākya Chok-den, *Theg pa chen po dbu ma rnam par nges pa'i mdzod lung dang rigs pa'i rgya mtsho*, in *The Complete Works (gsung 'bum) of Gser mdog Paṇ chen Śākya mchog ldan* (Thimphu, Bhutan: Kunzang Tobgey, 1975), 14:593–94.

21. D. S. Ruegg has insightfully distinguished three types of negation, following J. Lyons's distinction among assertions as propositional, tropic, and performative. Negations can similarly be threefold, depending on the element on which they bear. The fourfold conception of negation as understood by such non-Ge-luk thinkers as Śākya Chok-den can be seen as bearing not just on the propositional content but also on the performative element. See Ruegg, "Does the Mādhyamika Have a Thesis and Philosophical Position?" in *Buddhist Logic and Epistemology*, ed. B. K. Matilal and R. Devans (Dordrecht: Reidel, 1969), 229–37, esp. 235.

22. Nāgārjuna, *Treatise*, XXV:24; trans. Garfield, *The Fundamental Wisdom of the Middle Way*, 334.

23. See, for example, R. Magliola, *Derrida on the Mend* (West Lafayette, Ind.: Purdue University Press, 1984), and R. Jackson's response, "Matching Concepts: Deconstructive and Foundationalist Tendencies in Buddhist Thought," *Journal of the American Academy of Religion* 57 (1989): 561–89, as well as D. Lopez, *Elaborations on Emptiness: Uses of the Heart Sūtra* (Princeton: Princeton University Press, 1996), 187–216.

24. Postmodernism, for J.-F. Lyotard, is characterized by the loss of belief in the grand narratives—of progress, liberation, etc.—that have served to legitimize modern societies; see *La condition postmoderne: Rapport sur le savoir* (Paris: Éditions de Minuit, 1979).

25. F. Nietzsche, *Thus Spoke Zarathustra: A Book for Everyone and No One*, trans. W. Kaufmann (Harmondsworth: Penguin, 1985), 12.

26. Lyotard, *La condition postmoderne*, 14.

27. The question of nihilism is obviously much more complex than I make it here. While for Mādhyamikas, thinkers such as Nietzsche represent nihilism, such thinkers would argue that Madhyamaka itself stands for this view by affirming the possibility of transcending ordinary existence. And for Nietzsche, the Madhyamaka position is the one closest to his own stance. See F. Nietzsche, *The Will to Power*, trans. W. Kaufmann and R. J. Hollingdale, ed. W. Kaufmann (New York: Vintage, 1968), 16, 43; and *The Anti-Christ*, in *Twilight of the Idols; and, The Anti-Christ*, trans. R. J. Hollingdale (Harmondsworth: Penguin, 1984), 129.

28. Here again I am greatly simplifying, for in calling the world conventional I am giving a very approximate translation of *samvṛti (kun rdzob)*, a word that means not just "conventional" but also "interdependent" and "distorted." See C. W. Huntington, "The System of the Two Truths in the *Prasannapadā* and the *Madhyamakāvatāra*," *Journal of Indian Philosophy* 11 (1983): 77–107.

29. J. Derrida, *Of Grammatology*, trans. G. C. Spivak (Baltimore: Johns Hopkins University Press, 1976), 24. On comparing such disparate thinkers, see A. P. Tuck's entertaining *Comparative Philosophy and the Philosophy of Scholarship: On the Western Interpretation of Nagarjuna* (New York: Oxford University Press, 1990), and G. J. Larson and E. Deutsch, eds., *Interpreting across Boundaries: New Essays in Comparative Philosophy* (Princeton: Princeton University Press, 1988).

30. Nāgārjuna, *Treatise*, XIII:8; trans. Garfield, *The Fundamental Wisdom of the Middle Way*, 212.

31. D. S. Ruegg puts it very well: "What the Mādhyamika achieves by means of his *prasaṅga*-type reasoning is, then, the *dissolving*, or *deconstruction*, of all propositional theses positing hypostatized self-existent entities *(bhāva)*, rather than a *refutation* in the strict sense which would involve the setting up, within the frame of binary alternatives, of a counter-thesis and the

holding of a counter-position presupposing some kind of self-existent entity" (*Three Studies in the History of Indian and Tibetan Madhyamaka Philosophy* [Vienna: Arbeitskreis für Tibetische und Buddhistische Studien, Universität Wien, 2000], 151; emphases his).

32. For such a complaint within the Tibetan tradition, see M. Kapstein, *The Tibetan Assimilation of Buddhism: Conversion, Contestation, and Memory* (New York: Oxford University Press, 2000), 119.

33. See R. Wardy, "Mighty Is the Truth, and It Shall Prevail?" in *Essays on Aristotle's Rhetoric*, ed. A. Rorty (Berkeley: University of California Press, 1996), 56–87.

34. That Svātantrika holds to the use of arguments merely suggests that a connection between Madhyamaka commitments and choice of dialectical tools is unlikely. It is by no means a proof, for even Svātantrikas recognize the deconstructive nature of Madhyamaka. In their view, reasonings are valid only provisionally. Ultimately, any statement radically fails to capture reality. Moreover, this discussion assumes the Tibetan style of debate originated with Cha-ba, a point that is far from being established. For a view of Cha-ba's Madhyamaka, see H. Tauscher, ed., *Phya pa Chos kyi Senge ge: dBu ma Shar gSum gyi stong thun* (Vienna: Arbeitskreis für Tibetische und Buddhistische Studien, Universität Wien, 1999).

35. Here again interesting parallels exist with contemporary higher education—particularly in the United States, where students often have little knowledge of cultural traditions. As a result, they develop sharp critical skills, but find it difficult to develop a deeper understanding of the great texts set before them.

36. Lob-zang Gya-tso gives the following yearly schedule (in Tibetan dates) for Lo-se-ling (Gyatso, *Memoirs of a Tibetan Lama*, trans. and ed. G. Sparham [Ithaca: Snow Lion, 1998], 84):

1.1–1.4	New Year
1.5–1.25	Great Prayer
1.26–1.30	Break
2.1–2.15	Debate
2.16–2.20	Break
2.21–2.30	Small Prayer *(tshogs chos)*
3.1–3.30	Break and Great Spring Debate Session *(dpyid chos chen mo)*
4.1–4.10	Break
4.11–4.30	Debate
5.1–5.15	Break
5.16–6.15	Great Summer Debate Session *(dpyaz chos chen mo)*
6.16–8.1	Summer Retreat
8.2–9.1	Fall Debate Session *(ston chos)*
9.2–9.15	Break
9.16–9.30	Debate
10.1–10.15	Break

10.16–10.30	Debate
11.1–11.15	Break
11.16–12.15	Winter Debate at Jang (*'jang dgun chos*)
12.22–12.30	Maitreya Prayer (*'byams mchod*))

This is only, however, the skeleton in which many other events were integrated. For example, the Great Summer Session at Se-ra Jay would last from 5.16 to 6.15. During this time, many events took place:

5.16–17	Formal debates during the period of wood begging (*shing slong;* i.e., the period during which monks would have been allowed to leave the monastery to beg for wood and other necessities)
5.20–21	Examination for Geshe Ling-se
5.22–23	Examination for Geshe Rig-ram
5.24	Recitation of the Constitution (*tshogs gtam chen mo*)
5.25	Reading of the Canon in the morning
5.30	Special Ritual Day
6.2–3	Ceremonial Recitation
6.15	Special Ritual Day
6.16	End of Summer Session and Beginning of Break.

As one can see, monks kept quite busy! See *Byang chub lam rim chen mo dang 'brel ba'i ser byes mkhas snyan grwa tshang bca' khrims chen mo* (Bylakuppe: Sera Jhe Printing Press, 1991), 112.

37. For example, Pal-mang Kon-chok Gyel-tsen *(dbal mang dkon mchog rgyal mtshan)* explains the schedule of his monastery, Am-chok Ga-den Chö-khor Ling *(a mchog dga' ldan chos 'khor gling),* in *Ga' ldan chos 'khor gling gi mtshan nyid grwa tshad (tshang?) thos bsam gling gi rtsod pa byed tshul legs par bshad pa* in *Collected Works* (Delhi: Gyaltan Gelek Namgyal, 1974), 7:586: "At first, one studies the *Prajñā pāramitā* literature in this way: During the winter session of the first year one achieves the Homage [of the *Ornament*] and begins [the chapter on] the Charioteers. During the first spring session one finishes [the chapter on] the Charioteers. During the second spring session one finishes [the presentation of] of the inferior and middling persons."

> thog mar phar phyin la slob gnyer byed tshul ni
> lo dang po'i dgun chos la mchod brjod rdzogs nas shing rta'i srol byed tshugs
> dpyid chos dang po la shing rta'i srol byed rdzogs
> dpyid chos gnyis pa la skyes bu chung 'bring rdzogs

38. Rabten, *The Life and Teaching,* 50.

39. Buddhist monks are not supposed to eat in the evening, but most Tibetan monks ignore this rule.

40. Gen Lob-zang Gya-tso suggests this schedule for Lo-se-ling (*Memoirs of a Tibetan Lama,* 70–72):

| 6:00–8:00 | General assembly |
| 8:00–8:45 | Morning monastery assembly |

9:00–11:00	Regional house assembly where at least tea would be provided
11:00–13:00	Pause for study in one's room or with teacher
13:00–16:00	Afternoon debate
16:00–17:00	Evening assembly
17:00–18:00	Break for study.in one's room or with teacher
18:00–20:00	Evening prayer
20:00–23:00	Night debate or recitation for younger monks not yet allowed to debate.

41. For a list of all the rituals performed daily at Lo-se-ling during the debate session, see Geshe G. Lodrö, *'Bras spungs chos 'byung*, in *Geschichte der Kloster-Universität Drepung* (Wiesbaden: Steiner, 1974), 205–8.

42. For an excellent anthropological study of Hindu *pūjā*, see C. J. Fuller, *The Camphor Flame: Popular Hinduism and Society in India* (Princeton: Princeton University Press, 1992), 57–82. For an introduction to Buddhist worship, see J. Makransky, "Offering *(mChod pa)* in Tibetan Ritual Literature," in *Tibetan Literature: Studies in Genre*, ed. J. Cabezón and R. Jackson (Ithaca: Snow Lion, 1996), 312–30. For an extensive study of tantric worship, see S. Beyer, *Magic and Ritual in Tibet: The Cult of Tārā* (1973; reprint, Delhi: Motilal Banarsidass, 1988).

43. At Lo-se-ling at the start of the debate period (which often coincided with the lunar month), the session would include thirty-three recitations of the invocation to Tārā. Three recitations were added daily until the fifteenth of the month, when the ritual reached its maximum length of seventy-five recitations. In addition to this invocation, the ritual can contain more than thirty prayers of various length (Lodrö, *'Bras spungs chos 'byung*, 207).

44. The central element of the worship of Tārā is the Homage to the Twenty-One Tārās. See Beyer, *Magic and Ritual in Tibet*, 211–14.

45. For an elaborate version of this practice, see D. Lopez, *The Heart Sūtra Explained: Indian and Tibetan Commentaries* (Albany: State University of New York Press, 1988), 216–38.

46. Rabten, *The Life and Teachings*, 51.

47. Lopez, *Elaborations on Emptiness*, 216–38.

48. Gyatso, *Memoirs of a Tibetan Lama*, 80, 120.

49. The four classes on the *Ornament* are beginning and advanced treatises *(gzhuung gsar snying)*, and beginning and advanced separate topics *(zur bkod gsar snying)*. See Rabten, *The Life and Teaching*, 38, and *bCa' khrims chen mo*, 83–84.

50. The name "reciting leader" comes from the function of this class leader during the recitations *(rtsib bzhag)*: the abbot recites by heart the appropriate passages from the monastery's manuals, and the reciting leader must then repeat each passage. This recitation is nowadays purely ceremonial, a reminder of the times when the manuals were not codified and the abbot would give his

own commentary. Then, the reciting leader would have received this teaching and shared it with his classmates.

51. According to Dharmakīrti, "Since statements do not have any concomitance with real things, one [cannot] establish the [taught] object on their [basis]. They merely express the speaker's intention" (Miyasaka, Pramāṇa, I:213).

nāntarīyakatā 'bhāvāc chabdānāṃ vastubhiḥ saha
nārthasiddhis tatas te hi vaktrabhiprāyasūcakāḥ
(sgra dngos rnams dang lhan cig tu
med na mi byung nyid med phyir
de las don grub min de dag
smra ba po'i bsam pa ston par byed)

52. Gyatso, *Memoirs of a Tibetan Lama*, 88.

53. The second class devoted to the *Ornament* is called Advanced Texts, *gzhung rnying* (lit., "Old Treatise)."

54. Lodrö, *'Bras spungs chos 'byung*, 245.

55. The state of monasticism in contemporary Tibet clearly demonstrates the importance of cross-generational transmission. After 1959, monasteries were closed down, and monks were shipped to concentration camps where most died. When the monasteries reopened in the early 1980s, a few older monks came back to train students once again. However, there was a large gap between them and this new generation. As a result, the young monks have found it difficult to find their bearings and to become socialized in ways that make possible the renewal of their institution.

56. L. Lhalungpa, trans., *The Life of Milarepa* (1977; reprint, Boston: Shambhala, 1985), 150.

57. T. Tarab, *A Brief History of Tibetan Academic Degrees in Buddhist Philosophy* (Copenhagen: Nordic Institute of Asian Studies, 2000), 18. At Se-ra Jay, the four degrees of Geshe are the Rig-ram *(rigs ram)*, Ling-se, Tsok-ram, and Lha-ram (Geshe Sopa, *Lectures on Tibetan Religious Culture* [Dharamsala: Library of Tibetan Works and Archives, 1983], 43).

58. The name Geshe Ling-se—i.e., "the [scholar examined by] mixing of communities"—may suggest that he is examined by more than one monastery. But this name seems to reflect more the past practices of Sang-pu, where the candidate was examined by both monasteries (i.e., the Upper Community and the Lower Community), than the present practices of the three monastic seats. An old title thus appears to have been integrated into a new system.

59. Following my preference for logic and epistemology, I chose Ge-dün-drup *(dge 'dun grub), tshad ma'i bstan bcos chen po rigs pa'i rgyan* (Ornament of reasoning: A great treatise on valid cognition) (Mundgod: Loling Press, 1985).

60. In Jay, as in Se-ra May, Dre-pung Go-mang, and Ga-den Jang-tse, Abhidharma is the final subject. In the other three monasteries, Vinaya is last.

61. Rato Khyongla, *My Life and Lives*, 151.

62. Geshe Rab-ten spent only two years in this class because of the events

in Tibet and the subsequent exile. Normally, he would have had to spend nine years (Rabten, *The Life and Teachings,* 103).

63. Lodrö, *'Bras spungs chos 'byung,* 278–86.

64. For a description of these difficult and tense exams, see Rato Khyongla, *My Life and Lives,* 111.

65. Ge-dün Chö-pel was famous for his sharp repartee. In one famous encounter he was answering when a Mongolian Geshe tried to make fun of him by saying, "It appears that you think that all knowables are flat." Ge-dün Chö-pel instantly replied, "The only things I hold to be always flat are the heads of Mongols" (Dor-jay Gyel, *'Dzam gling rig pa'i dpa' bo dge 'dun chos phel gyi byung ba brjod pa bden gtam 'na ba'i bcud len* [Kansu: Kansu People's Press, 1997], 27).

66. See H. Richardson, *Ceremonies of the Lhasa Year,* ed. M. Aris (London: Serindia, 1993).

67. For an example of such a "stirred-up" debate, see Lodrö, *'Bras spungs chos 'byung,* 254.

68. Ga-den and Dre-pung usually hold the festival in Mundgod, while Se-ra holds it in Bylakuppe.

69. See P. Bourdieu, *Le sens pratique* (Paris: Éditions de Minuit, 1980), 191–208.

70. The trick is to shift the subject of the consequences used in debate. For example, if one answers that the Arhat is abandoning his own negative emotions, the questioner will then say (1) "It follows that the subject, the Arhat, abandons his own negative emotions." If one accepts, the questioner is likely to say (2) "It follows that the subject, the negative emotions of the Arhat, are being abandoned by the Arhat." If one accepts, then the next consequence is likely to be (3) "It follows that the subject, the negative emotions of the Arhat, exist since they need to be abandoned." The trick is to refuse consequence (2), even though its meaning seems identical with (1). But although (2) is identical to (1) in meaning, it has a different subject, and the skilled debater will prevent his adversary from choosing a subject that would lead him into difficulty.

71. One is reminded here of H. G. Gadamer's phenomenology of play: "[A]ll play is a being-played. The attraction of a game, the fascination it exerts, consists precisely in the fact that the game masters the players" (*Truth and Method,* trans. and ed. G. Barden and J. Cumming [1975; reprint, New York: Crossroad, 1989], 106).

72. I was myself quite privileged, and hence my position was similar to that of monk-sponsor. Because I was supported by my father, I had no financial problems and was free of most institutional constraints. I did not have to attend the long ritual sessions commanded by patrons. I also did not have to work in the fields, as monks do at certain periods in the monasteries resettled in South India. Friends would tease me by saying that I had the best of both worlds.

73. There is some evidence that Dharmakīrti may have been more skeptical of this solution. For him, instructions only approximate knowledge and hence provide guidance but not full-fledged knowledge. See Dreyfus, *Recognizing*

Reality, 296, and T. Tillemans, "How Much of a Proof Is Scripturally Based Inference?" in *Dharmakīrti's Thought and Its Impact on Indian and Tibetan Philosophy,* ed. S. Katsura (Vienna: Österreichische Akademie der Wissenschaften, 1999), 395–404.

CHAPTER 12. IS DEBATE A MODE OF INQUIRY?

1. S. Batchelor, *The Faith to Doubt: Glimpses of Buddhist Uncertainty* (Berkeley: Parallax, 1990), 12–13; emphasis his.

2. H. G. Gadamer, *Truth and Method,* trans. and ed. G. Barden and J. Cumming, rev. J. Weinsheimer and D. G. Marshall, 2nd rev. ed. (New York: Crossroad, 1989), 365.

3. Gadamer, *Truth and Method,* 374.

4. Gadamer, *Truth and Method,* 367. Derrida's critique of the logic of commentary as a hermeneutical supplementation, discussed in chapter 9, also underscores the need for another kind of questioning.

5. J. B. Thompson, introduction to *Hermeneutics and the Human Sciences: Essays on Language, Action, and Interpretation,* by P. Ricoeur, trans. and ed. J. B. Thompson (Cambridge: Cambridge University Press, 1981), 6.

6. I do not make the goal here "full understanding," for such a notion is highly questionable. But we can usefully distinguish between a superficial understanding, which is bound by the authority of the text, and a more personal appropriation in which one sees what is questionable in the text.

7. I am alluding here to P. Ricoeur's distinction between the hermeneutics of retrieval and of suspicion in *Freud and Philosophy: An Essay on Interpretation,* trans. Denis Savage (New Haven: Yale University Press, 1970). Ricoeur there uses the concept of the hermeneutics of suspicion less to describe a moment in the interpretive process than to refer to the interpretive strategies of such thinkers as Marx, Nietzsche, and Freud, who seek to demystify texts rather than to listen to them. In a later work, however, Ricoeur presents suspicion as a moment of the interpretive process, which is then seen as requiring both distanciation (i.e., critical distancing) and appropriation (*Hermeneutics and the Human Sciences,* 116–19). My use of the term is closer to that in the latter text.

8. A. Hyman and J. J. Walsh, eds., *Philosophy in the Middle Ages: The Christian, Islamic, and Jewish Traditions* (New York: Harper and Row, 1967), 542. See also J. Le Goff, *Les intellectuels au Moyen Age* (1957; reprint, Paris: Seuil, 1985), 126.

9. J. Verger, *Culture, enseignement et société en Occident aux XIIe et XIIIe siècles* (Rennes: Presses Universitaires de Rennes, 1999), 159, 172–78. See also A. de Libera, *Penser au Moyen Age* (Paris: Seuil, 1991), 98–142.

10. Verger, *Culture, enseignement et société en Occident,* 179.

11. People who have gone through this training, myself included, can vouch for the effectiveness of debate as a teaching method. After more than twenty years, I can still remember clearly the topics that I debated at length. I may not

remember the exact answers that I gave, but I do remember the meaning of the main concepts, the typologies, and some of the interesting quibbles relevant to the topic.

12. Geshe Rabten, *The Life and Teaching of Geshé Rabten: A Tibetan Lama's Search for Truth*, trans. and ed. B. A. Wallace (London: Allen and Unwin, 1980), 95.

13. Rabten, *The Life and Teaching*, 36.

14. See, for example, J. Dewey, *Logic: The Theory of Inquiry* (New York: Holt, 1938).

15. There is famous historical precedent for a student debating his teacher: Tu-gen Lob-zang Chö-gyi-nyi-ma (*thu'u bkwan blo bzang chos kyi nyi ma*, 1737–1802) refuted his teacher Sum-pa Ken-po Ye-shay-bel-jor (*sum pa mkhan-po ye shes dpal 'byor*, 1702–1788). See M. Kapstein, *The Tibetan Assimilation of Buddhism: Conversion, Contestation, and Memory* (Oxford: Oxford University Press, 2000), 129.

16. Se-ra monks often named an ex-abbot of the Jay College, Ken-sur Lob-zang Wang-chuk *(blo bzang dbang phyug)*, but unfortunately he died before I could benefit from his enormous learning.

17. This origin may have had a formative influence, for certain areas of Eastern Tibet—penetrated by missionary schools and influenced strongly by China—were less insular than Central Tibet.

18. Gen Pe-ma Gyel-tsen and Gen Nyi-ma passed their exams a couple of years apart. The former created a sensation when he won the first prize; Gen Nyi-ma placed second.

19. Tibetans look at their teachers but do not look them in the eye, for such a direct gaze is considered highly inappropriate.

20. L. Gyatso, *Memoirs of a Tibetan Lama*, trans. and ed. G. Sparham (Ithaca: Snow Lion, 1998), 125. For a discussion of cutting, see J. Edou, *Machig Lab-drön and the Foundations of Chöd* (Ithaca: Snow Lion, 1996). Tom-pön wrote a short work on this topic: *dBu ma chos kyi dbyings rnam par 'byed pa'i 'grel pa smra ba ngan pa'i tshang tshing 'joms par byed pa'i bstan bcos gnam lcags me char* (Mundgod: Lo-se-ling, 1989).

21. The extent of Gen Tom-pön's hostility to cutting is hard to gauge. His main ground for opposition was that the practice took monks away from their studies, which should be their first commitment. He also seemed to view it as a marginal practice devised by yogis: it could be useful to some people but did not contain all the elements necessary to the completion of the path.

22. The term *dialectic* seems particularly appropriate here. The tension between belief and doubt is dialectical for the tradition in that it has a determined end, the development of faith. It should also be clear that in discussing faith here, I am referring to the faith of the trainees whom Haribadhra described as followers of reasoning.

23. In his *Memoirs*, Lob-zang Gya-tso, who was Gen Nyi-ma's student, expresses this view quite well: "[E]ven if a debater was off a bit from what a sacred text said, still, if his debate was based on some contact with a reality which

was authentic, then he would be admired, even praised for his honest attempt to find meaning. Even if he was in opposition to an accepted position of the monastic textbook, his straightforward and honest intellect would be praised. Who cared if a person was not following the party line if his position was one which opened up a view of reality?" (87).

24. Gen Nyi-ma himself meditated every morning but never spoke about it or encouraged his students to do the same.

25. Candrakīrti rejected not arguments per se in the context of emptiness but their classic conception, which implies that all the terms of the argument are similarly established for both parties in the debate. See K. Yotsuya, *The Critique of Svatantra Reasoning by Candrakīrti and Tsong-kha-pa: A Study of Philosophical Proof according to Two Prāsaṅgika Madhyamaka Traditions of India and Tibet* (Stuttgart: Steiner, 1999).

26. *Legitimate Insight or Specious Divide? The Svātantrika-Prāsaṅgika Distinction in Indian and Tibetan Madhyamaka Thought* (edited volume, in collaboration with Sara McClintock, in preparation).

27. By *realist*, I mean characterized by the view that language and thought can capture features of reality. Ge-luk realism, which I have elsewhere described at length in the context of Dharmakīrti's logico-epistemological tradition, is moderate. It holds that though thought captures reality, it cannot do so with complete adequacy. Thought is only a partial reflection of reality, which needs to be perceived experientially to be understood fully. See G. Dreyfus, *Recognizing Reality: Dharmakīrti's Philosophy and Its Tibetan Interpreters* (Albany: State University of New York Press, 1997).

28. See D. S. Ruegg, "The Uses of the Four Points of the *Catuṣkoti* and the Problem of the Description of Reality in Mahāyāna Buddhism," *Journal of Indian Philosophy* 5 (1977): 1–71. See also C. W. Huntington, *The Emptiness of Emptiness: An Introduction to Early Indian Madhyamika* (Honolulu: University of Hawaii Press, 1989).

29. See, for example, Śākya Chok-den, *Theg pa chen po dbu ma rnam par nges pa'i mdzod lung dang rigs pa'i rgya mtsho*, in *The Complete Works* (Thimphu, Bhutan: Kunzang Tobgey, 1975), 593–94.

30. I am here again following D. S. Ruegg's insightful distinction among negations that bear on the propositional content, on the tropic or modal element, and on the performative dimension ("Does the Mādhyamika Have a Thesis and Philosophical Position?" in *Buddhist Logic and Epistemology*, ed. B. K. Matilal and R. Devans [Dordrecht: Reidel, 1969], 235).

31. Dzong-ka-ba, *Byang chub Lam rim chen mo* (Dharamsala: Shes rig par khang, n.d.), 579–91.

32. Pa-bong-ka, *Liberation in the Palm of Y___ H___ ___ __*

33. The risk of creating a graspable but irrelevant notion of emptiness has been remarked by several teachers. See, for example, Jang-gya, *lTa mgur a ma ___ ____* (New Delhi: n.p., 1972); E. Napper, *Dependent-Arising and Empti-*

ness: A Tibetan Buddhist Interpretation of Madhyamika Philosophy Emphasizing the Compatibility of Emptiness and Conventional Phenomena (Boston: Wisdom, 1989), 147; and G. Newland, *The Two Truths in the Madhyamika Philosophy of the Ge-luk-ba Order of Tibetan Buddhism* (Ithaca: Snow Lion, 1992), 18.

34. For a very different view of the relation between philosophy and wisdom, see F. Julien, *Un sage est sans idée* (Paris: Seuil, 1998). Taking Confucius as his model, Julien argues that the wise man does not put forth any idea, for doing so would involve him in an endless quagmire from which exit is impossible.

35. I had already noticed this similarity in India when I started to read Wittgenstein. This impression was only reinforced when I had the privilege to study at the University of Virginia with Cora Diamond, one of the few minds I have encountered that could compare with Gen-la's. See her brilliant *The Realistic Spirit: Wittgenstein, Philosophy, and the Mind* (Cambridge, Mass.: MIT Press, 1991).

36. A. Klein, *Meeting the Great Bliss Queen: Buddhists, Feminists, and the Art of the Self* (Boston: Beacon, 1995), 44.

37. According to the Abhidharma, we live on the trapezoidal southern continent in one of the many world systems that exist. Our system consists of four islands surrounding a central axis, Mount Meru. See Kongtrul Lodrö Kayé, *Myriad Worlds: Buddhist Cosmology in Abhidharma, Kālacakra, and Dzogchen*, trans. and ed. the International Translation Committee (Ithaca: Snow Lion, 1995), 111.

38. A. Klein, "Mental Concentration and the Unconditioned," in *Paths to Liberation: The Mārga and Its Transformations in Buddhist Thought*, ed. R. E. Buswell and R. M. Gimello (Honolulu: University of Hawaii Press, 1992), 277.

CHAPTER 13. RATIONALITY AND SPIRIT CULT

1. Among those who attribute rationality to actions is Weber, whose view R. Brubaker explains as follows: "In so far as the individual is not the self-conscious and deliberate author of his action, in so far as he is carried along by habit . . . or carried away by feelings . . . , to this extent his conduct is non-rational. In so far as the individual acts deliberately and is consciously aware of what he is doing, on the other hand, his action is rational" (*The Limits of Rationality: An Essay on the Social and Moral Thought of Max Weber* [1984; reprint, London: Routledge, 1991], 50).

2. M. Weber, *Sociology of Religion*, trans. E. Fischoff (Boston: Beacon, 1963), 117.

3. "And do you not also give the name of dialectician to the man who is able to exact an account of the essence of each thing? And will you not say that the one who is unable to do this, insofar as he is unable to give an account of himself and others, does not possess full reason and intelligence about the matter?" Plato, *Republic* 7.534B; trans. Paul Shorey in *The Collected Dialogues of Plato*,

including the Letters, ed. E. Hamilton and H. Cairns (Princeton: Princeton University Press, 1961), 766.

4. The stark opposition between the great tradition of the literate virtuosi and the little tradition of the village practitioner is misleading. Popular and elite cultures do not exist apart from each other. Nevertheless, such a distinction is important; as B. Faure has argued in *The Rhetoric of Immediacy: A Cultural Critique of Chan/Zen Buddhism* (Princeton: Princeton University Press, 1991), 79–95, it cannot be eliminated altogether. In his study of Thai Buddhism, S. J. Tambiah makes a similar point. For him, the great tradition of monasticism and the little tradition of village practices form a single religious system (*Buddhism and the Spirit Cults in North-East Thailand* [1970; reprint, Cambridge: Cambridge University Press, 1987], 367–77). In Tibet, the interactions between these two layers of religious culture are favored by tantra and hence it is often difficult to distinguish them. Local and monastic practitioners routinely draw on each other's traditions.

5. In describing his childhood, Gen Lob-zang Gya-tso mentioned a tree belonging to his family that seemed to have a particular relation to him. It would bloom and prosper when he was at home, but declined when he was away. This was his spirit force tree *(bla shing)* (interview with author, Dharamsala, fall 1995). The idea of spirit force is quite similar to the Thai notion of *khwan* (Tambiah, *Buddhism and the Spirit Cults,* 58).

6. S. Karmay, "The Soul and the Turquoise: A Ritual for Recalling the *bla,*" in *The Arrow and the Spindle: Studies in History, Myths, Rituals, and Beliefs in Tibet* (Kathmandu: Mandala Book Point, 1998), 310–38. Besides spirit force, people also have life force *(srog)*, personal power *(dbang thang)*, and personal energy *(glung rta)*, which is connected to the good or bad fortune that they encounter (P. Cornu, *Tibetan Astrology,* trans. H. Gregor [Boston: Shambhala, 1997], 85–88).

7. Lochö Rim-bo-che, in A. Klein, comp., trans., and ed., *Path to the Middle: Oral Mādhyamika Philosophy in Tibet* (Albany: State University of New York Press, 1994), 218 n. 15.

8. The belief in such a universe is often labeled *animism* in the classical anthropological literature, where it is viewed as an irrational and primitive superstition. Such airs of superiority are misplaced, for our modern way of seeing the world is no more natural than animism. P. Descola quite helpfully distinguishes three ways of conceptualizing the human-nature relationship: animism, totemism, and naturalism ("Constructing Natures," in *Nature and Society: Anthropological Perspectives,* ed. P. Descola and G. Pálsson [London: Routledge, 1996], 87–88). All three modes are constructed, not given: they are mental templates for the ordering of the ...

... ... and belongs to a separate ontological domain (ruled by the laws of nature or God's omnipotent will). By contrast, animism and totemism are predicated on the sociocentric assumptions that humans and nature are related. Totemic systems use observable discontinuities to conceptualize social organization. Animistic systems do the opposite, endowing natural beings with human dispositions and understanding our relation with them in terms of social attributes. These three conceptualizations are culturally acquired as individuals refer natural systems to the human domain. Once taken in, presumably early in life, they become deeply ingrained and do not seem to change significantly later.

9. This belief among Tibetans that their gods had the power to crush the Chinese army does not contradict another deeply held belief: that their fate is a result of their karma and hence of their lack of detachment. Tru-shi Rin-po-che reflects on the Chinese invasion of Tibet, "When you tame the enemy within your own mind . . . the demonic armies of the ten directions will just fall in defeat by themselves" (quoted in S. Ortner, *Life and Death on Mt. Everest: Sherpas and Himalayan Mountaineering* [Princeton: Princeton University Press, 1999], 103).

10. The monastic order is the Sangha only inasmuch as it is a symbolic representation of the true Sangha. For a discussion of taking refuge, see Dzong-ka-ba, *The Great Treatise on the Stages of the Path to Enlightenment*, trans. Lamrim Chenmo Translation Committee (Ithaca: Snow Lion, 2000), 177–90.

11. In describing these gods as similar to humans in having emotions and so on, I am reflecting the Tibetan cultural perspective.

12. L. Gyatso, *Memoirs of a Tibetan Lama*, trans. and ed. G. Sparham (Ithaca: Snow Lion, 1998), 60, 204.

13. Geshe G. Lodrö, *'Bras spungs chos 'byung*, in *Geschichte der Kloster-Universität Drepung* (Wiesbaden: Steiner, 1974), 332–35.

14. Lodrö, *'Bras spungs chos 'byung*, 205.

15. G. Dreyfus, "The Shuk-den Affair: History and Nature of a Quarrel," *Journal of the International Association of Buddhist Studies* 21 (1999): 227–70.

16. Dze-may Rin-po-che, *mThu dan stobs kyis che ba'i bstan bsrung chen po rdo rje shugs ldan rtsal gyi byung ba brjod pa pha rgod bla ma'i zhal gyi bdud rtsi'i chu khur brtsegs zhing 'jigs rung glog zhags 'gyu ba'i sprin nag 'khrugs pa'i nga ro* (Delhi: n.p., 1973), 6–9. (I refer to this work as the *Yellow Book.*)

17. Dze-may, the *Yellow Book*, 4. Particularly surprising is Dze-may's inclusion of Re-treng Rin-po-che in the list of lamas punished by Shuk-den. For a rather different view of the fate of this lama, see M. Goldstein, *A History of Modern Tibet, 1913–1951: The Demise of the Lamaist State* (Berkeley: University of California Press, 1989), 310–63.

18. The Dalai Lama institution is not just political but rests on an elaborate ritual system; it is briefly described in Dreyfus, "The Shuk-den Affair," 259–64.

19. It is difficult to determine which among the popular practices monks are supposed to engage in. The Vinaya prohibits monks from taking part in popular rituals, but monks have engaged in these practices in all historically known Buddhist societies. In Tibet they do so not as a concession to custom (as in Theravada countries, where such engagement exists but is frowned on) but as part of their expected activities. Nevertheless, local custom bars certain practices as improper for monks, particularly those that involve violence.w See N. Silhé,

"Lhachö [lha-mchod] and hrinän [sri-gnon]: The Structure and Diachrony of a Pair of Rituals (Baragaon, northern Nepal)" (paper presented at the Seminar of the International Association for Tibetan Studies, Leiden, July 2000), and "Les tantristes tibétains (ngakpa), religieux dans le monde, religieux du rituel terrible: Étude de Ch'ongkor, communauté villageoise de tantristes du Baragaon (nord du Népal)" (Ph.D. thesis, Paris-X-Nanterre University, forthcoming).

20. The term *Buddhist modernism* was coined by H. Bechert; see "Buddhist Revival in East and West," in *The World of Buddhism: Buddhist Monks and Nuns in Society and Culture*, ed. H. Bechert and R. Gombrich (London: Thames and Hudson, 1984), 275–76.

21. For a discussion of the difference between traditional embedded and modern disembedded notions of rationality, see C. Taylor's masterful but difficult *Sources of the Self: The Making of the Modern Identity* (Cambridge, Mass.: Harvard University Press, 1989).

22. T. Kuhn, *The Structure of Scientific Revolutions*, 2nd ed. (Chicago: University of Chicago Press, 1970).

23. For an interesting debate on the nature of rationality in talmudic studies, see M. Fisch, *Rational Rabbis: Science and Talmudic Culture* (Bloomington: Indiana University Press, 1997), and M. Halbertal, *People of the Book: Canon, Meaning, and Authority* (Cambridge, Mass.: Harvard University Press, 1997). Whereas the former argues that the study of the Talmud relies on a logic not essentially different from that of the natural sciences as explained by Karl Popper, the latter sees a different procedure that aims at maximizing the variety and richness of textual interpretations. While rabbinic education is not my concern here, I find Halbertal's characterization more attuned to the specificities of scholasticism. I have also benefited greatly from Fisch's discussion, which frames the issue very well.

CHAPTER 14. THE LIMITS OF THE INQUIRY

1. Pur-bu-jok Jam-ba-gya-tso, *Tshad ma'i gzhung don 'byed pa'i bsdus grwa rnam par bshad pa rigs lam 'phrul gyi lde mig las rigs lam chung ba rtags rigs kyi skor* (Palampur, India: Library of Bkra Bshis Rjongs, n.d.), 6.b.

2. Aristotle explains that "definition is a phrase which signifies the what it-is-to-be" (*Topics* 1.5; trans. R. Smith [Oxford: Clarendon Press, 1997], 4).

3. For more information on the treatment of definition in Western philosophy, see H. Leonard, "The Theory of Definition," part 4 of *An Introduction to Principles of Right Reason* (New York: Holt, 1957), and K. Ajdukieewicz, "Three Conceptions of Definition," in *Problems in the Philosophy of Language*, ~~T. M. Olshewsky (New York: H~~

~~...., 1301), 091.~~

5. L. Renou, *Terminologie grammaticale du Sanskrit* (Paris: Librairie Ancienne Honoré Champion, 1957), 200–01, see F. Kielhorn, ed., *Mahābhaṣya* (1892–1909; reprint, Poona: Bhordakan Oriental Research Institute, 1962).

6. See M. Biardeau, "La définition dans la pensée Indienne," *Journal Asiatique* 245 (1957): 371–84, esp. 371.

7. See R. R. Dravid, *The Problem of Universals in Indian Philosophy* (Delhi: Motilal Banarsidass, 1972).

8. Sources for the Indian Buddhist view of definition can be found in Dharmakīrti, *Pramāṇavārttika* Y. Miyasoka, ed. (Sanskrit-Tibetan) *Acta Indologica* 2 (1971–72). III:85, III:301, and III:306. For analysis of these passages, see G. Dreyfus, "Some Considerations on Definition in Buddhism: An Essay on the Use of Definition in the Indo-Tibetan Epistemological Tradition" (M.A. thesis, University of Virginia, 1987), 80–86.

9. C. W. Huntington, *Emptiness of Emptiness: An Introduction to Early Indian Madhyamika* (Honolulu: University of Hawaii Press, 1989), 180–83.

10. "deng sang kyi rtog ge ba gang dag gzhung lugs chen mo rnams la gtsigs su mi byed par gzhan dang gshags 'gyed pa'i tshe tshig 'khri'i mtho yor kho na la skyabs su 'dzin pa dang / don gyi gnad 'gag bor ba'i thal 'gyur skam po'i lbu ba'i 'phrel ba la snying po'i mchog tu 'dzin pa la ni phyogs mthong tsam las dgongs pa ji bzhin pa don du song bas sung rab de dag kyang rdo rje tshig lta bur gyur to": Jang-gya Röl-bay-dor-jay, *Grub mtha'i rnam par bzhag pa gsal bar bshad pa thub bstan lhun po'i mrzes rgyan* (Varanasi: Pleasure of Elegant Sayings Press, 1970), 104; quoted in A. Klein, trans. and annot., *Knowing, Naming, and Negation: A Sourcebook on Tibetan Sautrantika* (Ithaca: Snow Lion, 1991), 140.

11. For an example of winning through dialectical tricks, see the debate in chapter 11 concerning the negative emotions of an Arhat; as explained in n. 70, the way out is to prevent a shifting of the terms of the debate, thereby blocking statements that seemed at first to derive necessarily from earlier statements.

12. The parable of the goldsmith is quoted in R. A. F. Thurman, trans., *Tsong Khapa's Speech of Gold in the Essence of True Eloquence: Reason and Enlightenment in the Central Philosophy of Tibet* (Princeton: Princeton University Press, 1984), 190.

13. For a view of Buddhism as a dogmatic tradition, see E. Mikogami, "The Problem of Verbal Testimony in Yogācāra Buddhism," in *Bukkyogaku kenkyu*, nos. 33–34 (1977), and R. Hayes, "The Question of Doctrinalism in the Buddhist Epistemologists," *Journal of the American Academy of Religion* 52 (1984): 645–70. For a different position on the same issue, see T. Tillemans, "On Scriptural Authority," in *Felicitation Volume for Professor A. Uno* (Hiroshima: Tetsugaku, 1986), 31–47.

14. *Mahā-Parinibbāna-Sutta*, in *Buddhism in Translations: Passages Selected from the Buddhist Sacred Books and Translated from the Original Pali into English*, ed. and trans. H. Warren (1896; reprint, Delhi: Motilal, 1987), 107.

15. H. Stoddard, *Le mendiant de l'Amdo* (Paris: Société d'Ethnographie, 1985), 144.

16. On receiving Ge-dün Chö-pel as a student, Geshe Shay-rab is reported to have said, "I, a Manjushri teacher, finally get you, a Manjushri-like student"

(Dor-jay Gyel, *'Dzam gling rig pa'i dpa' bo dge 'dun chos phel gyi byung ba brjod pa bden gtam 'na ba'i bcud len* [Kansu: Kansu People's Press, 1997], 26).

17. Stoddard, *Le mediant de l'Amdo,* 152. On formal occasions, monks in Tibet wore a water bottle *(chabs slug)* wrapped in decorative cloth. This practice has been discontinued in India, where monastic dress has tended to become simpler and lighter. Similarly, shirts made of brocade are no longer worn.

18. Gen Nyi-ma was then still a young scholar and had little to say about Ge-dün Chö-pel.

19. Later Ge-dün Chö-pel published his objections in a short work, *dBu ma'i zab gnad snying por dril ba'i legs bshad klu sgrub dgongs rgyan* (Rumteck, Sikkhim: Dharma Cakra Center, 1983). But reportedly he expressed similar ideas earlier and had gotten into a shouting match on Madhyamaka with his teacher Geshe Shay-rab on his arrival in Dre-pung.

20. rDo-rje rGyal, *dGe-'dun Chos-phel gyi byung-ba,* 28. This kind of "informal" vigilantism, which has not received much attention in the secondary literature, is fairly common in Tibetan society; people who express unpopular views are sometimes abused physically.

21. J. Cabezón, "The Regulations of a Monastery," in *Religions of Tibet in Practice,* ed. D. Lopez (Princeton: Princeton University Press, 1997), 342.

22. Rato Khyongla Nawang Losang, *My Life and Lives: The Story of a Tibetan Incarnation,* ed. J. Campbell (New York: Dutton, 1977), 142.

23. The relation between the Tibetan government and the different groups of the Ge-luk tradition is a complex matter that remains unexplored. The usual claim that the government largely represents the Ge-luk tradition has some truth in it: members of the Ge-luk school figured prominently in the coalition that brought to power the Fifth Dalai Lama and still occupy an important role. However, not all Ge-luk groups are equally supportive of the Dalai Lama's power. See G. Dreyfus, "The Shuk-den Affair: History and Nature of a Quarrel," *Journal of the International Association of Buddhist Studies* 21 (1999): 227–70.

24. The Assembly of Notables is often called the National Assembly. See M. Goldstein, *A History of Modern Tibet, 1913–1951: The Demise of the Lamaist State* (Berkeley: University of California Press, 1989), 19–20.

25. My guess is that Gen Nyi-ma was referring to Tri-jang Rin-po-che, but he could have meant somebody else. The meditational deity was the Single Yamantaka *(rdo rje 'jigs rje dpa' bo cig pa)* and the doubt related to the number of deities that a mandala must have in the anuttara yoga tantras in order to be valid.

26. Ge-dün Chö-pel, *dBu ma'i zab gnad snying por dril ba'i legs bshad klu sgrub dgongs rgyan* (Rumtek, Sikkhim: Dharma Cakra Center, 1983).

27. The other

... Theravada context, see Vajirañāṇavarorasa, *Entrance to the Vinaya* (Bangkok: King Maha Makuta Academy, 1969).

... kyon cung zad kyang med pa dge ldan pa dang mtshungs pa gangs can gyi grub mtha' gzhan gang la yang ma mchis pas / de gsum gyi sgo nas grub mtha' gzhan thams cad las dge lugs pa khyad par du 'phags pa yin te"; Tu-gen, *Grub mtha' tham cad kyi khungs dang 'dod tshul ston pa legs bshad shel gyi me long* (Varanasi: Chos rJe Lama, 1963), 238.

29. See M. Kapstein, "The Purificatory Gem and Its Cleansing," *History of Religions* 28, no. 3 (1989): 217–44.

30. Gyel-tsap, *Tshad ma rigs pa'i gter gyi rnam bshad legs par bshad pa'i snying po*, in *A Recent Rediscovery: rGyal tshap's Rigs gter rnam bshad*, ed. G. Dreyfus and S. Onoda (Kyoto: Biblia Tibetica, 1994). The views expressed by this text are similar to those of Kay-drup. See G. Dreyfus, "Introduction to rGyal tshap's *Rigs gter rnam bshad*," in Dreyfus and Onoda, 1–17.

31. See T. Kuhn, *The Structure of Scientific Revolutions*, 2nd ed. (Chicago: University of Chicago Press, 1970).

32. S. Batchelor, *The Faith to Doubt: Glimpses of Buddhist Uncertainty* (Berkeley: Parallax, 1990), 13; emphasis his. See chapter 12, above.

CONCLUSION: PAST AND FUTURE UNCERTAINTIES

1. For a study of this dynamic, see A. Ström, "The Dynamics and Politics of Institutional Continuity: Tibetan Monastic 'Colleges' in India" (Ph.D. diss., Oslo University, 2000).

2. Self-aggrandizement is not an infrequent problem among Tibetan scholars, the most famous example being Sa-paṇ's *Eight Ego Poem:*

> I am the grammarian. I am the dialectician.
> Among vanquishers of sophists, peerless am I.
> I am learned in metrics.
> I stand alone in poetics.
> In explaining synonymics, unrivalled am I.
> I know celestial calculations. In exo- and esoteric science
> I have a discerning intellect equalled by none.
> Who can this be? Sakya alone!
> Other scholars are my reflected forms.

The poem is quoted in M. Kapstein, "The Indian Literary Identity in Tibet," in *Literary Cultures in History: Reconstructions from South Asia*, ed. S. Pollock (Berkeley: University of California Press, forthcoming).

3. I have tried to communicate some sense of this enrichment as it relates to Dharmakīrti's epistemology in my *Recognizing Reality: Dharmakīrti's Philosophy and Its Tibetan Interpreters* (Albany: State University of New York Press, 1997).

4. My teachers also failed to make me a good monk. Shortly after joining the university, I ceased to be a monk. I did not see how I could be a monk in an academic setting and decided to give back my ordination. Some of my teachers were intensely disappointed. Others understood that my new circumstances made being a monk too difficult.

Select Bibliography

TIBETAN LITERATURE FOR THE
STUDY OF SCHOLASTICISM

*Byang chub lam rim chen mo dang 'brel ba'i ser byes mkhas snyan grwa
tshang bca' khrims chen mo.* Bylakuppe: Sera Jhe Printing Press, 1991.

Cha-har dGe-bshes bLo-bzang Tshul-khrims. *rJe thams cad mkhyen pa tsong
kha pa chen po'i rnam thar go sla bar brjod pa bde legs kun kyi byung gnas.*
In *The Collected Works (gsung 'bum) of Cha-har Dge-bshes Blo-bzang-
tshul-khrims,* vol. 2 (Kha), 7–791. New Delhi: Chatring Jansar Tenzin,
1971.

Dor-jay Gyel. *'Dzam gling rig pa'i dpa' bo dge 'dun chos phel gyi byung ba brjod pa bden gtam 'na ba'i bcud len.* Kansu: Kansu People's Press, 1997.

Dzong-ka-ba. *Rang gi rtogs pa mdo tsam du bshad pa* (also called *rTogs brjod
mdun legs ma*). In *The Collected Works (gsung 'bum) of Rje Tsong-kha-pa
Blo-bzang-grags-pa,* 2:302–8 (Kha bka' 'bum thor bu, fols. 52b–55b).
Delhi: Guru Deva, 1975.

Jam-yang-chok-hla-ö-ser. *Tshad ma rnam 'grel gyi bsdus gzhung zhes bya'i
sgo 'byed rgol ngan glang po 'joms pa gdong nga'i gad rgyangs rgyu rig lde
mig.* Dharamsala: Library of Tibetan Works and Archives, 1980.

Jik-may Wang-po. *Bo dong paṇ chen kyi rnam thar.* Shinhua: Old Tibetan
Texts Press, 1991.

Kay-drup. *rJe btsun tsong kha pa chen po'i ngo mtshar rmad du byung ba'i
rnam par thar pa'i 'jug ngogs.* In Dzong-ka-ba, *Collected Works (gsung
'bum) of Rje Tsong-kha-pa Blo-bzang-grags-pa,* vol. 1 (Ka), fols. 1.a–71.b.
Dharamsala: Tibetan Cultural Printing n d

⸻ ⸺

ᴠᴜ ʀɪgs ɑʀe sᴋʀun Khang, 1985.

Lo Ken-chen. sDe hd·· ─── ┈ ┈

──── ··gᴏ ʟɑᴍ gᴏᴜɪ ᴏᴜ ɪ nyi ma. Reprint of Derge edition.
Manduwalla, India: Ngorpa Center, 1985.

Lob-zang Trin-ley. *'Jam mgon chos kyi rgyal po tsong kha pa chen po'i rnam thar*. Kokonor: Kokonor People's Press, 1996.

Lodrö, Geshe G. *'Bras spungs chos 'byung*. In *Geschichte der Kloster-Universität Drepung*, 1–410. Wiesbaden: Steiner, 1974.

Long-döl. *bKa' gdams pa dang dge lugs bla ma rags rim gyi gsung 'bum mtshan tho*. In *Materials for a History of Tibetan Literature*, edited by L. Chandra, 737–830. Kyoto: Rinsen, 1981

Nga-wang-chö-drak. *Bod kyi mkhas pa snag phyi dag gi grub mtha' shan 'byed mtha' dpyod dang bcas pa'i 'bel ba'i gtam*. Thimphu, Bhutan: Kunzang Tobgey, 1979.

Ngak-wang-chö-drak. *Mkhan chen ngag dbang chos grags kyi pod chen drug gi 'grel pa phyogs sgrigs*. Rimbick Bazar, Dist. Darjeeling: Sakya Choepheling Monastery, 2000.

Paṇ-chen Sö-nam-drak-ba. *bKa' gdams gsar snying gi chos 'byung yid kyi mdzes rgyan*. Delhi: Gonpo Tseten, 1977.

Pur-bu-jok Jam-ba-gya-tso. *Tshad ma'i gzhung don 'byed pa'i bsdus grwa rnam par bshad pa rigs lam 'phrul gyi lde mig las rigs lam chung ba rtags rigs kyi skor*. Palampur, India: Library of Bkra Bshis Rjongs, n.d. Blockprint.

Sa-gya Paṇḍita. *lDom gsum rab byed*. In *Complete Works of Sa-skya Masters*, vol. 5, 297.1.1–323.2.6. Tokyo: Tokyo Bunko, 1968–69.

Sa-gya Paṇḍita. *mKhas pa la 'jug pa'i sgo*. In *The Complete Works of the Great Masters of the Sa sKya Sect*, vol. 5, 81.1.1–111.3.6. Tokyo: Tokyo Bunko, 1968.

Sa-gya Paṇḍita. *Tshad ma rigs gter*. In *The Complete Works of the Great Masters of the Sa sKya Sect*, vol. 5, 155.1.1–167.1.6. Tokyo: Tokyo Bunko, 1968.

Śākya Chok-den. *Tshad ma rigs gter gyi dgongs rgyan rigs pa'i 'khor los lugs ngan pham byed*. In *The Complete Works (gsung 'bum) of Gser mdog Paṇ chen Śākya mchog ldan*, 9:1–718. Thimphu, Bhutan: Kunzang Tobgey, 1975.

Ye-shay Wang-chuk. *Sera smad thos bsam nor gling grwa tshang gi chos 'byung lo rgyus nor bu'i phreng ba*. Bylakuppe, India: Se-ra May Printing Press, 1985.

Zongtse, C. T. *mKhas mang rgya mtsho'i bsti gnas dbus 'gyur gdan sa chen po gsum gyi ya gyal se ra theg chen gling gi chos 'byung rab gsal nor bu'i me long*. Delhi: International Academy of Indian Culture, 1995.

INDIAN AND TIBETAN SCHOLASTIC TEXTS

Āryadeva. *Catuḥśataka-śāstra* (*bstan bcos bzhi brgya pa*, D: 3846, P: 5346).

Asaṅga. *Abhidharmasamuccaya* (*chos mngon pa kun las bstus pa*, D: 4049, P: 5550).

Atiśa. *Byang chub lam gyi sgron me dang de'i bka' 'grel* (D:3947, 3948; P: 5343, 5344). Dharamsala: Council of Religious Affairs, 1969.

Bhavya. *Prajñāpradīpamūlamadhyamakavṛtti* (*dbu ma'i rtsa ba'i 'grel pa shes rab sgron ma*, D: 3853).

Buddhapālita. *Buddhapālitamūlamadhyamakavṛtti (dbu ma'i rtsa ba'i 'grel pa shes rab buddha pā li ta*, D: 3842).

Candrakīrti. *Madhyamakāvatāra (dbu ma la 'jug pa*, D: 3861, P: 5262).

Candrakīrti. *Mūlamadhyamakavṛttiprasannapadā (dbu ma'i rtsa ba'i 'grel pa tshig gsal ba*, D: 3860).

Chim Jam-pel-yang. *Chos mngon pa'i mdzod kyi tshig le'ur byas pa'i 'grel pa mngon pa'i rgyan.* Mundgod: Loling Press, 1986.

Dharmakīrti. *Pramāṇavārttikakārikā (tshad ma rnam 'grel gyi tshig le'ur byas pa*, D: 4210, P: 5709).

Dharmakīrti. *Pramāṇaviniścaya (tshad ma rnam par nges pa*, D: 4211, P: 5710).

Dignāga. *Pramāṇasamuccaya (tshad ma kun btus*, D: 4203, P: 5700).

Do Grub-chen. *dPal gsang ba'i snying po'i rgyud kyi spyi don nyung ngu'i ngag gis rnam par 'byed pa rin chen mdzod kyi lde mig.* In *The Collected Works (gsung 'bum) of Rdo Grub-chen Jigs-med-bstan-pa'i-nyi-ma*, 3:1–237. Gantok, Sikkim: Dodrub Chen Rimpoche, 1974.

Dzong-ka-ba. *bsTan bcos mngon rtogs rgyan 'grel pa dang bcas pa'i rgya cher bshad pa legs bshad gser gyi phreng ba.* Kokonor: Tsho sngon mi rigs dpe skrun khang, 1986.

Dzong-ka-ba. *Byang chub lam rim chen mo.* Dharamsala: Shes rig par khang, n.d. Blockprint.

Dzong-ka-ba. *dBu ma la 'jug pa'i rgya cher bshad pa dgongs pa rab gsal.* Varanasi: Pleasure of Elegant Sayings Press, 1973.

Dzong-ka-ba. *dBu ma rtsa ba'i tshig le'ur byas pa shes rab ces bya ba'i rnam bshad rigs pa'i rgya mtsho.* Varanasi: Pleasure of Elegant Sayings Press, 1973.

Dzong-ka-ba. *Drang ba dang nges pa'i don rnam par phye ba'i bstan bcos legs bshad snying po.* Varanasi: Pleasure of Elegant Sayings Press, 1973.

Ge-dün Chö-pel. *dBu ma'i zab gnad snying por dril ba'i legs bshad klu sgrub dgongs rgyan.* Rumtek, Sikkhim: Dharma Cakra Center, 1983.

Ge-dün-drub. *Dam pa'i chos 'dul ba mtha' dag gi snying po'i don legs par bshad rin po che'i phreng ba.* In *Collected Works*, vol. 2 (Kha).

Ge-dün-drub. *mDzod tik thar lam gsal byed.* Varanasi: Ge-luk Press, 1973.

Ge-dün-drub. *Tshad ma'i bstan bcos chen po rigs pa'i rgyan.* Mundgod: Loling Press, 1985.

Go-ram-ba. *rGyal ba thams cad kyi thugs kyi dgongs pa zab mo'i de kho na nyid spyi'i ngag gis ston pa nges don rab gsal.* In *Complete Works of the Great Masters of the Sa sKya Sect*, vol. 14, 1.1.1–167.3.3 (*Ca*, 1.a–209.a). Tokyo: Tokyo Bunko, 1968.

Guṇaprabha. *Vinayasūtra ('dul ba'i mdo tsa ba*, D: 4117, P: 5619).

Gyel-tsap. *rNam bshad snying po rgyan.* Varanasi: Pleasure of Elegant Sayings Press, 1980.

Gyel-tsap. *Tshad ma rnam 'grel gyi tshig le'ur byas pa'i rnam bshad thar lam phyin ci ma log par gsal bar byed pa.* Varanasi: Pleasure of Elegant Sayings Press, 1974.

Haribhadra. *Abhisamayālaṃkāranāmaprajñāpāramitopadeśaśāstravṛtti* (*shes rab kyi pha rol tu phyin pa'i man ngag gi bstan bcos mngon par rtogs pa'i rgyan zhes bya ba'i 'grel pa,* D: 3793, P: 5191).

Jang-gya Röl-bay-dor-jay. *Grub mtha'i rnam par bzhag pa gsal bar bshad pa thub bstan lhun po'i mrzes rgyan.* Varanasi: Pleasure of Elegant Sayings Press, 1970.

Kay-drup. *rGyas pa'i bstan bcos tshad ma rnam 'rel gyi rgya cher bshad pa rigs pa'i rgya mtsho.* In *Collected Works,* vols. 8 and 10. 1897. Reprint, New Delhi: Guru Deva, 1982.

Kay-drup. *Tshad ma sde bdun gyi rgran yid kyi mun sel.* In *Collected Works,* vol. 10. 1897. Reprint, New Delhi: Guru Deva, 1982.

Long-chen-rab-jam-ba. *Ngal gso skor gsum.* Gangtok: Dodrup Chen Rinpoche, 1973.

Long-chen-rab-jam-ba. *Rang grol skor gsum.* Gangtok: Sonam Kazi, 1969.

Maitreya. *Abhisamayālaṃkāranāmaprajñāpāramitopadeśaśāstrakrikā* (*shes rab pha rol tu phyin pa'i man ngag gi bstan bcos mgnon par rtogs pa'i rgyan zhes bya ba tshig le'ur byas pa,* D: 3786, P: 5184).

Maitreya. *Dharmadharmatāvibhaṅga* (*chos dang chos nyid rnam par 'byed pa,* D: 4023, P: 5523).

Maitreya. *Madhyāntavibhaṅga* (*dbus dang mtha' rnam par 'yed pa,* D: 4021, P: 5522).

Maitreya. *Mahāyānasūtrālaṃkārakārikā* (*theg pa chen po'i mdo sde'i rgyan gyi tshig le'ur byas pa,* D: 4020, P: 5521).

Maitreya. *Mahāyānottaratantraśāstra* (*theg pa chen po'i rgyd bla ma bstan bcos,* D: 4024, P: 5525).

Mi-pam. *dBu ma rgyan gyi rnam bshad 'jam dbyangs bla ma bgyes pa'i zhal lung.* New Delhi: Karmapa Chodhey, 1976.

Mi-pam. *Shes rab le'u'i tshig don ga sla bar rnam par bshad pa nor bu ke ta ka.* Varanasi: n.p., n.d.

Nāgārjuna. *Prajñānāmamūlamadhyamakakārikā* (*dbu ma rtsa ba'i tshig le'ur byas pa shes rab,* D: 3824, P: 5224).

Ngak-wang-bel-den. *Grub mtha' chen mo'i mchan 'grel dka' gnas mdud grol blo gsal gces nor.* Varanasi: Pleasure of Elegant Sayings Press, 1964.

Pal-den Drak-ba, Ge-she. *Legs bshad 'dad pa'i mdzes rgyan.* Mundgod: Loling Library, 1979.

Pal-mang Kon-chok Gyel-tsen. *Ga' ldan chos 'khor gling gi mtshan nyid grwa tsahd (tshang?) thos bsam gling gi rtsod pa byed tshul legs par bshad pa.* In *Collected Works,* vol. 7:586–600. Delhi: Gyaltan Gelek Namgyal, 1974.

Paṇ-chen Sö-nam-drak-ba. *dBu ma spyi don zab don gsal ba'i sgron me.* In *The Collected Works (gsung 'bum) of Paṇ-chen Bsod-nams-grags-pa,* vol. 9 (Jha). Mundgod: Drepung Loseling Library, 1985.

Pe-ma-wang-gyel. *Rang bzhin rdzogs pa chen po'i lam gyi cha lag sdoms pa gsum rnam par nges pa zhes bya ba'i bstan bcos.* Delhi: n.p., 1969.

Rang-jung Dor-je. *Zab mo nang don.* Zi-ling: Kokonor Tibetan Medical School, 1999.

Śākya Chok-den. *Theg pa chen po dbu ma rnam par nges pa'i mdzod lung dang rigs pa'i rgya mtsho.* In *The Complete Works (gsung 'bum) of Gser mdog Paṇ chen Śākya mchog ldan,* vols. 14 and 15. Thimphu, Bhutan: Kunzang Tobgey, 1975.

Śāntarakṣita. *Madhayamakālaṃkārakārikā (dbu ma'i rgyan gyi tshig le'ur byas pa,* D: 3884).

Śāntarakṣita. *Madhyamakālaṃkāravṛtti (dbu ma'i rgyan gyi 'grel pa,* D: 3885, P: 5286).

Śāntarakṣita. *Tattvasaṃgraha (de kho na nyid bsdus pa,* D: 4266, P: 5764).

Śāntideva. *Bodhisattvacaryāvatāra (byang chub sems dpa'i spyod pa la 'jug pa,* D: 3871, P: 5272).

Tsho-na-pa-shes-rab-bzang-po *(mtsho sna ba shes rab bzang po), 'Dul ba mdo rtsa ba'i rnam bshad nyi ma 'od zer legs bshad lung gi rgya mtsho.* Block, n.d.

Tsho-na-pa-shes-rab-bzang-po *(mtsho sna ba shes rab bzang po), 'Dul dhi ka nyi ma'i 'od zer legs bshad lung gi rgya mtsho.* Beijing: Tibetan Culture Institute, 1993.

Tu-gen. *Grub mtha' tham cad kyi khungs dang 'dod tshul ston pa legs bshad shel gyi me long.* Varanasi: Chos rJe Lama, 1963.

Vasubandhu. *Abhidharma-kośa-kārikā (chos mngon pa'i mdzod,* D: 4089, P: 5590). Sanskrit edition: P. Pradhan, ed. *Abhidharmakoṣabhāṣyam of Vasubandhu.* Patna: Jayaswal Institute, 1975.

Yon-den-gya-tso. *Yon tan rin po che'i mdzod kyi 'grel pa zab don snang byed nyi ma'i 'od zer.* Gangtok, Sikkim: n.p., 1969.

Zhan-pan Chö-kyi-nang-ba. *gZhung chen bcu gsum gyi mchan 'grel.* Dehra Dun: Kocchen Tulku, 1978.

MODERN SCHOLARSHIP ON TIBETAN SCHOLASTICISM AND MONASTICISM

An-che, Li. *Labrang: A Study in the Field.* Tokyo: University of Tokyo Press, 1982.

Bärlocher, D. *Testimonies of Tibetan Tulkus: A Research among Reincarnate Buddhist Masters in Exile.* 2 vols. Rikon/Zurich: Tibet-Institute, 1982.

Beckwith, C. "The Medieval Scholastic Method in Tibet and in the West." In *Reflections on Tibetan Culture: Essays in Memory of Turrell V. Wylie,* edited by L. Epstein and R. Sherburne, 307–13. Lewiston, N.Y.: Mellen Press, 1990.

Cabezón, J. *Buddhism and Language: A Study of Indo-Tibetan Scholasticism.* Albany: State University of New York Press, 1994.

Cabezón, J. "Firm Feet and Long Lives: The *Zhabs brtan* Literature of Tibet." In *Tibetan Literature: Studies in Genre,* edited by J. Cabezón and R. Jackson, 344–57. Ithaca: Snow Lion, 1996.

Cabezón, J. "The Regulations of a Monastery." In *Religions of Tibet in Practice,* edited by D. Lopez, 335–51. Princeton: Princeton University Press, 1997.

Cabezón, J., and R. Jackson, eds. *Tibetan Literature: Studies in Genre*. Ithaca: Snow Lion, 1996.

Dagpo Rimpotché. *Le lama venu du Tibet*. Paris: Grasset, 1998.

Dudjom Rinpoche. *The Nyingma School of Tibetan Buddhism: Its Fundamentals and History*. Translated by Gyurme Dorje; edited by Matthew Kapstein. London: Wisdom, 1991.

Dungkar Lobsang Thinley. "Development of the Monastic Education in Tibet." *Tibet Journal* 18, no. 4 (1993): 3–48.

Ellingson, T. "Tibetan Monastic Constitutions: The *bCa Yig*." In *Reflections on Tibetan Culture: Essays in Memory of Turrell V. Wylie*, edited by L. Epstein and R. Sherburne, 204–30. Lewiston, N.Y.: Mellen Press, 1990.

Goldberg, M. "Entity and Antinomy in Tibetan Logic." Parts 1 and 2. *Journal of Indian Philosophy* 13 (1985): 153–99, 273–304.

Goldstein, M. "A Study of the *ldab ldob*." *Central Asiatic Journal* 9 (1964): 123–41.

Goldstein, M., and M. Kapstein, eds. *Buddhism in Contemporary Tibet: Religious Revival and Cultural Identity*. Berkeley: University of California Press, 1998.

Goldstein, M., and P. Tsarong. "Tibetan Buddhist Monasticism: Social, Psychological and Cultural Implications." *Tibet Journal* 10, no. 1 (1985): 14–31.

Gyatso, L. *Memoirs of a Tibetan Lama*. Translated and edited by G. Sparham. Ithaca: Snow Lion, 1998.

Hopkins, J. "Tibetan Monastic Colleges: Rationality versus the Demands of Allegiance." In *Mythos Tibet: Wahrnehmungen, Projektionen, Phantasien*, edited by T. Dodin. Cologne: DuMont, 1997.

Jackson, D. *The Early Abbots of 'Phan po Na-lendra: The Vicissitudes of a Great Tibetan Monastery in the Fifteenth Century*. Vienna: Arbeitskreis für Tibetische und Buddhistische Studien, Universität Wien, 1989.

Jackson, D. *The Entrance Gate for the Wise*. Vienna: Arbeitskreis für Tibetische und Buddhistische Studien, Universität Wien, 1987.

Kvaerne, P. "Continuity and Change in Tibetan Monasticism." In *Korean and Asian Religious Tradition*, edited by Chai-Shin Yu, 83–98. Toronto: Korean and Related Studies Press, 1977.

Newland, G. "Debate Manuals (*yig cha*) in dGe-lugs Colleges." In *Tibetan Literature: Studies in Genre*, edited by J. Cabezón and R. Jackson, 202–16. Ithaca: Snow Lion, 1996.

Ngagyur Nyingma Institute. Bylakuppe: Ngagyur Nyingma Institute, 1995.

Onoda, S. "The Chronology of the Abbatial Successions of the Gsang Phu Sne'u Thog Monastery." *Wiener Zeitschrift für die Kunde Südasiens* 33 (1989): 203–13.

Onoda, S. *Monastic Debate in Tibet: A Study on the History and Structures of Bsdus grwa Logic*. Vienna: Arbeitskreis für Tibetische und Buddhistische Studien, Universität Wien, 1992.

Pema Wangdak. "The Sakya College—Preserving the Sakya Lineage of Tibetan Buddhism." http://www.geocities.com/Tokyo/Pagoda/4595/COLLEGE.html (accessed February 2002).

Perdue, D. *Debate in Tibetan Buddhism.* Ithaca: Snow Lion, 1993.

Rabten, Geshe. *The Life and Teaching of Geshé Rabten: A Tibetan Lama's Search for Truth.* Translated and edited by B. A. Wallace. London: Allen and Unwin, 1980.

Rato Khyongla Nawang Losang. *My Life and Lives: The Story of a Tibetan Incarnation.* Edited by J. Campbell. New York: Dutton, 1977.

Sierskma, F. "*rTsod pa:* The Monachal Disputation in Tibet." *Indo-Iranian Journal* 8 (1964): 130–52.

Solomon, E. A. *Indian Dialectics: Methods of Philosophical Discussion.* Ahmedabad: B.J. Institute of Learning and Research, 1976.

Sopa, Geshe. *Lectures on Tibetan Religious Culture.* Dharamsala: Library of Tibetan Works and Archives, 1983.

Ström, A. "The Dynamics and Politics of Institutional Continuity: Tibetan Monastic 'Colleges' in India." Ph.D. diss., Oslo University, 2000.

Tarab, T. *A Brief History of Tibetan Academic Degrees in Buddhist Philosophy.* Copenhagen: Nordic Institute of Asian Studies, 2000.

Tillemans, T. "Formal and Semantic Aspects of Tibetan Buddhist Debate Logic." In *Scripture, Logic, Language: Essays on Dharmakirti and His Tibetan Successors,* edited by T. Tillemans, 117–49. Boston: Wisdom, 1999.

Tillemans, T. "Sur le Pararthanumana en Logique Bouddhique." *Asiatiche Studien* 28, no. 2 (1984): 73–99.

Vidyabhusana, S. C. *A History of Indian Logic: Ancient, Mediaeval, and Modern Schools.* 1921. Reprint, Delhi: Motilal Banarsidass, 1978.

Wilson, J. "Tibetan Commentaries on Indian Śastras." In *Tibetan Literature: Studies in Genre,* edited by J. Cabezón and R. Jackson, 125–37. Ithaca: Snow Lion, 1996.

GENERAL SCHOLARSHIP ON SCHOLASTICISM

Baldwin, J. *The Scholastic Culture of the Middle Ages, 1000–1300.* Lexington, Mass.: Heath, 1971.

Bochenski, J. M. *History of Formal Logic.* Translated and edited by I. Thomas. Notre Dame, Ind.: University of Notre Dame Press, 1961.

Cabezón, J., ed. *Scholasticism: Cross-Cultural and Comparative Perspectives.* Albany: State University of New York Press, 1998.

Carruthers, M. *The Book of Memory: A Study of Memory in Medieval Culture.* Cambridge: Cambridge University Press, 1990.

Clarke, M. L. *Higher Education in the Ancient World.* London: Routledge, 1971.

Ehninger, D., ed. *Contemporary Rhetoric: A Reader's Coursebook.* Glenview, Ill.: Scott, Foresman, 1972.

Eickelman, D. F. *Knowledge and Power in Morocco: The Education of a Twentieth-Century Notable.* Princeton: Princeton University Press, 1985.

Fisch, M. *Rational Rabbis: Science and Talmudic Culture.* Bloomington: Indiana University Press, 1997.

Fischer, M. *Iran: From Religious Disputation to Revolution.* Cambridge, Mass.: Harvard University Press, 1980.

Fraade, S. *From Tradition to Commentary: Torah and Its Interpretation in the Midrash Sifre to Deuteronomy.* Albany: State University of New York Press, 1991.

Glorieux, P. "L'enseignement au Moyen Age; Techniques et méthodes en usage à la faculté de Paris au XIIIe siècle." *Archives d'histoire doctrinale et littéraire du Moyen Age* 35 (1968): 65–186.

Goody, J. *The Logic of Writing and the Organization of Society.* Cambridge: Cambridge University Press, 1986.

Goody, J., ed. *Literacy in Traditional Societies.* 1968. Reprint, Cambridge: Cambridge University Press, 1975.

Graham, W. A. *Beyond the Written Word: Oral Aspects of Scripture in the History of Religion.* Cambridge: Cambridge University Press, 1987.

Griffiths, P. *Religious Reading: The Place of Reading in the Practice of Religion.* New York: Oxford University Press, 1999.

Griffiths, P. "Scholasticism: The Possible Recovery of an Intellectual Tradition." In *Scholasticism: Cross-Cultural and Comparative Perspectives,* edited by J. Cabezón, 201–36. Albany: State University of New York Press, 1998.

Halbertal, M. *People of the Book: Canon, Meaning, and Authority.* Cambridge, Mass.: Harvard University Press, 1997.

Halbertal, M., and T. H. Halbertal. "The Yeshiva." In *Philosophers on Education,* edited by A. Rorty, 458–69. London: Routledge, 1998.

Hamesse, J. "Le Modèle Scholastique de la lecture." In *Histoire de la lecture dans le monde occidental,* supervised by G. Cavallo and R. Chartier, 125–46. Paris: Seuil, 1997.

Hartman, G. "Midrash as Law and Literature." *Journal of Religion* 74 (1994): 338–55.

Huntington, C. W. *The Emptiness of Emptiness: An Introduction to Early Indian Madhyamika.* Honolulu: University of Hawaii Press, 1989.

Huntington, C. W. "The System of the Two Truths in the *Prasannapadā* and the *Madhyamakāvatāra.*" *Journal of Indian Philosophy* 11 (1983): 77–107.

Hyman A., and J. J. Walsh, eds. *Philosophy in the Middle Ages: The Christian, Islamic, and Jewish Traditions.* New York: Harper and Row, 1967.

Kimball, B. A. *Orators and Philosophers: A History of the Idea of Liberal Education.* New York: Teachers College, Columbia University, 1986.

Leff, G. "The *Trivium* and the Three Philosophies." In *A History of the University in Europe, Universities in the Middle Ages,* edited by H. de Ridder-Symoens, 307–408. Vol. 1 of *A History of the University in Europe.* Cambridge: Cambridge University Press, 1992.

Le Goff, J. *Les intellectuels au Moyen Age.* 1957. Reprint, Paris: Seuil, 1985.

Libera, A. de. *Penser au Moyen Age.* Paris: Seuil, 1991.

Makdisi, G. "The Scholastic Method in Medieval Education." *Speculum* 49 (1974): 640–61.

Marrou, H. I. *A History of Education in Antiquity.* Translated by G. Lamb. New York: Sheed and Ward, 1956.

Mottahedeh, R. "Traditional Shi'ite Education in Qom." In *Philosophers on Education*, edited by A. Rorty, 451–57. London: Routledge, 1998.

Oakley, F. *Community of Learning: The American College and the Liberal Arts Tradition.* New York: Oxford University Press, 1992.

Panikkar, R. "Common Patterns of Eastern and Western Scholasticism." *Diogenes* 83 (1973): 103–13.

Perelman, C., and L. Olbrechts-Tyteca. *Traité de l'argumentation: La nouvelle rhétorique.* 2nd ed. 1970. Reprint, Brussels: Université de Bruxelles, 1983.

Petruci, A. "Lire au Moyen Age." *Mélanges de l'École Française de Rome* 96 (1984): 604–16.

Reboul, O. *Introduction à la rhétorique: Theorie et pratique.* Paris: Presses Universitaires de France, 1991.

Ridder-Symoens, H. de, ed. *Universities in the Middle Ages.* Vol. 1 of *A History of the University in Europe.* Cambridge: Cambridge University Press, 1992.

Rorty, A., ed. *Essays on Aristotle's Rhetoric.* Berkeley: University of California Press, 1996.

Saenger, P. "Silent Reading: Its Impact on Late Medieval Script and Society." *Viator* 13 (1982): 367–414.

Scholem, G. "Tradition and Commentary as Religious Categories in Judaism." In *Arguments and Doctrines: A Reader of Jewish Thinking in the Aftermath of the Holocaust*, compiled by A. Cohen, 303–22. New York: Harper and Row, 1970.

Stern, D. "Midrash and Indeterminacy." *Critical Inquiry* 15 (1988): 132–61.

Verger, J. *Culture, enseignement et société en Occident aux XIIe et XIIIe siècles.* Rennes: Presses Universitaires de Rennes, 1999.

Verger, J. *Les gens de savoir dans l'Europe de la fin du Moyen Age.* Paris: Presses Universitaires de France, 1997.

Verger, J. "Patterns." In *Universities in the Middle Ages*, edited by H. de Ridder-Symoens, 35–55. Vol. 1 of *A History of the University in Europe.* Cambridge: Cambridge University Press, 1992.

GENERAL THEORETICAL APPROACHES

Aristotle. *Topics.* Translated by R. Smith. Oxford: Clarendon Press, 1997.

Baddeley, A. D. *Human Memory: Theory and Practice.* Boston: Allyn and Bacon, 1990.

Bahrick, H. P. "Semantic Memory Content in Permastore: Fifty Years of Memory for Spanish Learned in School." *Journal of Experimental Psychology* 113 (1984): 1–29.

Bakhtin, M. M. *Speech Genres and Other Late Essays.* Edited by C. Emerson and M. Holquist. Translated by V. W. McGee. Austin: University of Texas Press, 1986.

Bourdieu, P. *Le sens pratique.* Paris: Éditions de Minuit, 1980.

Brubaker, R. *The Limits of Rationality: An Essay on the Social and Moral Thought of Max Weber.* 1984. Reprint, London: Routledge, 1991.

Brunschwig, J. "Aristotle's Rhetoric as a 'Counter-part' to Dialectic." In *Essays on Aristotle's Rhetoric*, edited by A. Rorty, 34–55. Berkeley: University of California Press, 1996.

Burke, K. *A Rhetoric of Motives*. New York: Prentice-Hall, 1950.

Burneyat, M. F. "Enthymeme: Aristotle on the Rationality of Rhetoric." In *Essays on Aristotle's Rhetoric*, edited by A. Rorty, 86–115. Berkeley: University of California Press, 1996.

Crowder, R. G. *Principles of Learning and Memory*. Hillsdale, N.J.: Erlbaum, 1976.

Derrida, J. *Limited Inc*. Evanston, Ill.: Northwestern University Press, 1988.

Derrida, J. *Of Grammatology*. Translated by G. C. Spivak. Baltimore: Johns Hopkins University Press, 1976.

Derrida, J. *Positions: Entretiens avec Henri Ronse, Julia Kristeva, Jean-Louis Houdebine, Guy Scarpetta*. Paris: Éditions de Minuit, 1972.

Descola, P. "Constructing Natures." In *Nature and Society: Anthropological Perspectives*, edited by P. Descola and G. Pálsson, 82–102. London: Routledge, 1996.

Dewey, J. *Logic: The Theory of Inquiry*. New York: Holt, 1938.

Dumont, L. *Homo Hierarchicus: The Caste System and Its Implications*. Translated by M. Sainsbury, L. Dumont, and B. Gulati. Rev. ed. Chicago: University of Chicago Press, 1980.

Durkheim, E. *Moral Education: A Study in the Theory and Application of the Sociology of Education*. Edited by E. K. Wilson. Translated by E. K. Wilson and H. Schnurer. New York: Free Press, 1961.

Eco, U. *The Role of the Reader: Explorations in the Semiotics of Texts*. 1979. Reprint, Bloomington: Indiana University Press, 1984.

Fabian, J. *Time and the Other: How Anthropology Makes Its Object*. New York: Columbia University Press, 1983.

Finnegan, R. *Literacy and Orality: Studies in the Technology of Communication*. Oxford: Blackwell, 1988.

Foucault, M. *Discipline and Punish: The Birth of the Prison*. Translated by A. Sheridan. 1977. Reprint, New York: Vintage, 1979.

Foucault, M. "The Discourse on Language." In *The Archaeology of Knowledge*, 215–37. Translated by A. M. Sheridan Smith. 1972. Reprint, New York: Harper and Row, 1976.

Friedrich-Silber, I. *Virtuosity, Charisma, and Social Order: A Comparative Sociological Study of Monasticism in Theravada Buddhism and Medieval Catholicism*. Cambridge: Cambridge University Press, 1995.

Gadamer, H. G. *Truth and Method*. Translation edited by G. Barden and J. Cumming, revised by J. Weinsheimer and D. G. Marshall. 2nd rev. ed. New York: Crossroad, 1989.

Goody, J. Introduction to *Literacy in Traditional Societies*, edited by J. Goody, 1–26. 1968. Reprint, Cambridge: Cambridge University Press, 1975.

Gough, K. "Implications of Literacy in Traditional China and India." In *Liter-*

acy in Traditional Societies, edited by J. Goody, 70–84. 1968. Reprint, Cambridge: Cambridge University Press, 1975.

Gramsci, A. *Selections from the Prison Notebooks*. Translated and edited by Q. Hoare and G. N. Smith. New York: International, 1971.

Habermas, J. *Moral Consciousness and Communicative Action*. Translated by C. Lenhardt and S. W. Nicholsen. Cambridge, Mass.: MIT Press, 1990.

Hall, R. "Dialectic." In *The Encyclopedia of Philosophy*, volumes 1–2:385–89. New York: Macmillan, 1967.

Hartman, G. *Criticism in the Wilderness: The Study of Literature Today*. New Haven: Yale University Press, 1980.

Julien, F. *Un sage est sans idée*. Paris: Seuil, 1998.

Kuhn, T. *The Structure of Scientific Revolutions*. 2nd ed. Chicago: University of Chicago Press, 1970.

Lord, A. *The Singer of Tales*. Cambridge, Mass.: Harvard University Press, 1960.

Lyotard, J. F. *La condition postmoderne: Rapport sur le savoir*. Paris: Éditions de Minuit, 1979.

MacIntyre, A. "The Recovery of Moral Agency." In *The Best Christian Writing, 2000*, edited by J. Wilson, 111–36. San Francisco: HarperCollins, 2000.

McLuhan, M. *Counter Blast*. London: Rapp and Whiting, 1970.

Mitchell, T. *Colonising Egypt*. 1988. Reprint, Berkeley: University of California Press, 1991.

Neisser, U. "Interpreting Harry Bahrick's Discovery: What Confers Immunity against Forgetting?" *Journal of Experimental Psychology: General* 113 (1984): 32–35.

Ong, W. J. *Orality and Literacy: The Technologizing of the Word*. 1982. Reprint, London: Routledge, 1988.

Parry, M. *The Making of Homeric Verse: The Collected Papers of Milman Parry*. Edited by A. Parry. Oxford: Clarendon Press, 1971.

Ricoeur, P. *Hermeneutics and the Human Sciences: Essays on Language, Action, and Interpretation*. Translated and edited by J. B. Thompson. Cambridge: Cambridge University Press, 1981.

Ricoeur, P. *Interpretation Theory: Discourse and the Surplus of Meaning*. Fort Worth: Texas Christian University Press, 1976.

Said, E. *Orientalism*. New York: Pantheon, 1978.

Schmitt, J.-C. "Religion populaire et culture folklorique." *Annales: Economies, sociétés, civilisations* 31 (1976): 941–53.

Schofield, R. S. "The Measurement of Literacy in Pre-Industrial England." In *Literacy in Traditional Societies*, edited by J. Goody, 311–25. 1968. Reprint, Cambridge: Cambridge University Press, 1975.

Schwartz, M. "Scholasticism as a Comparative Category and the Study of Judaism." In *Scholasticism: Cross-Cultural and Comparative Perspectives*, edited by J. Cabezón, 91–114. Albany: State University of New York Press, 1998.

Shils, E. *The Intellectuals and the Powers*. Chicago: University of Chicago Press, 1972.

Smith, J. Z. *Map Is Not Territory: Studies in the History of Religion*. 1978. Reprint, Chicago: University of Chicago Press, 1993.

Sperber, D. *On Anthropological Knowledge*. Cambridge: Cambridge University Press, 1985.

Stock, B. *Listening for the Text: On the Uses of the Past*. Baltimore: Johns Hopkins University Press, 1990.

Street, B. V. *Literacy in Theory and Practice*. Cambridge: Cambridge University Press, 1984.

Tambiah, S. J. "Literacy in a Buddhist Village in North-East Thailand." In *Literacy in Traditional Societies*, edited by J. Goody, 85–131. 1968. Reprint, Cambridge: Cambridge University Press, 1975.

Taylor, C. *Sources of the Self: The Making of the Modern Identity*. Cambridge, Mass.: Harvard University Press, 1989.

Tulvey, E., and W. Donaldson, eds. *Organization of Memory*. New York: Academic Press, 1972.

Wardy, R. "Mighty Is the Truth, and It Shall Prevail?" In *Essays on Aristotle's Rhetoric*, edited by A. Rorty, 56–87. Berkeley: University of California Press, 1996.

Weber, M. *Economy and Society: An Outline of Interpretive Sociology*. Translated by Ephraim Fischoff et al. Edited by G. Roth and C. Wittich. Berkeley: University of California Press, 1978.

Weber, M. "The Meaning of Discipline." In *From Max Weber: Essays in Sociology*, edited by H. H. Gerth and C. W. Wright, 253–64. Oxford: Oxford University Press, 1954.

Weber, M. *Sociology of Religion*. Translated by E. Fischoff. Boston: Beacon, 1963.

GENERAL SCHOLARSHIP ON TIBETAN BUDDHISM

Beyer, S. *Magic and Ritual in Tibet: The Cult of Tārā*. 1973. Reprint, Delhi: Motilal Banarsidass, 1988.

Cabezón, J. "The Canonization of Philosophy and the Rhetoric of Siddhānta." In *Buddha Nature: A Festschrift in Honor of Minoru Kiyota*, edited by P. J. Griffiths and J. P. Keenan, 7–26. San Francisco: Buddhist Books International, 1991.

Chandra, L., ed. *Materials for a History of Tibetan Literature*. 3 vols. 1963. Reprint, Kyoto: Rinsen, 1981.

Chogay Trichen. *The History of the Sakya Tradition A Feast for the Minds of the Fortunate*. Translated by Ven. Phende Rinpoche, Jamyang Khandro, and J. Stott. Bristol: Ganesha Press, 1983.

Cornu, P. *Tibetan Astrology*. Translated by H. Gregor. Boston: Shambhala, 1997.

Cozort, D. *Highest Yoga Tantra: An Introduction to the Esoteric Buddhism of Tibet*. Ithaca: Snow Lion, 1986.

Dreyfus, G. *Recognizing Reality: Dharmakīrti's Philosophy and Its Tibetan Interpreters.* Albany: State University of New York Press, 1997.

Dreyfus, G. "The Shuk-den Affair: History and Nature of a Quarrel." *Journal of the International Association of Buddhist Studies* 21 (1999): 227–70.

Dzong-ka-ba. *The Great Treatise on the Stages of the Path to Enlightenment.* Translated by the Lamrim Chenmo Translation Committee. Ithaca: Snow Lion, 2000.

Ekvall, R. B. *Religious Observances in Tibet: Patterns and Function.* Chicago: University of Chicago Press, 1964.

Germano, D. "Re-membering the Dismembered Body of Tibet." In *Buddhism in Contemporary Tibet: Religious Revival and Cultural Identity,* edited by M. Goldstein and M. Kapstein, 53–94. Berkeley: University of California Press, 1998.

Goldstein, M. *A History of Modern Tibet, 1913–1951: The Demise of the Lamaist State.* Berkeley: University of California Press, 1989.

Goldstein, M. "The Revival of Monastic Life." In *Buddhism in Contemporary Tibet: Religious Revival and Cultural Identity,* edited by M. Goldstein and M. Kapstein, 15–52. Berkeley: University of California Press, 1998.

Gyatso, J. "Healing Burns with Fire: The Facilitations of Experience in Tibetan Buddhism." *Journal of the American Academy of Religion* 67 (1998): 113–47.

Hookham, S. *The Buddha Within: Tathagatagarbha Doctrine according to the Shentong Interpretation of the Ratnagotravibhaga.* Albany: State University of New York Press, 1991.

Hopkins, J. *Emptiness in the Mind-Only School of Buddhism: Dynamic Responses to Dzong-Ka-Ba's "The Essence of Eloquence."* Vol. 1. Berkeley: University of California Press, 1999.

Hopkins, J. *Meditation on Emptiness.* London: Wisdom, 1983.

Jackson, D. "The Earliest Printings of Tsong Khapa's Works: The Old dGa'-ldan Editions." In *Reflections on Tibetan Culture: Essays in Memory of Turrell V. Wylie,* edited by L. Epstein and R. Sherburne, 107–16. Lewiston, N.Y.: Mellen Press, 1990.

Kapstein, M. "From Kun-mKhyen Dol-po-pa to 'Ba'-mda' dGe-legs." In *Tibetan Studies,* edited by H. Krasser, M. Much, E. Steinkellner, and H. Tauscher, vol. 1:457–76. Vienna: Österreichische Akademie der Wissenschaften, 1997.

Kapstein, M. "The Indian Literary Identity in Tibet." In *Literary Cultures in History: Reconstructions from South Asia,* edited by S. Pollock. Berkeley: University of California Press, forthcoming.

Kapstein, M. "The Purificatory Gem and Its Cleansing." *History of Religions* 28, no. 3 (1989): 217–44.

Kapstein, M. *The Tibetan Assimilation of Buddhism: Conversion, Contestation, and Memory.* Oxford: Oxford University Press, 2000.

Klein, A., comp., trans., and ed. *Path to the Middle: Oral Mādhyamika Philosophy in Tibet.* Albany: State University of New York Press, 1994.

Kongtrul Lodrö Kayé. *Myriad Worlds: Buddhist Cosmology in Abhidharma, Kālacakra, and Dzog-chen.* Translated and edited by the International Translation Committee. Ithaca: Snow Lion, 1995.

Kuijp, L. van der. "Phya-pa Chos-kyi-seng-ge's Impact on Tibetan Epistemology." *Journal of Indian Philosophy* 5 (1978): 355–69.

Lopez, D. *Prisoners of Shangri-La: Tibetan Buddhism and the West.* Chicago: University of Chicago Press, 1997.

Makransky, J. "Offering (*mChod pa*) in Tibetan Ritual Literature." In *Tibetan Literature: Studies in Genre,* edited by J. Cabezón and R. Jackson, 312–30. Ithaca: Snow Lion, 1996.

Mumford, S. *Himalayan Dialogue: Tibetan Lamas and Gurung Shamans in Nepal.* Madison: University of Wisconsin Press, 1989.

Napper, E. *Dependent-Arising and Emptiness: A Tibetan Buddhist Interpretation of Madhyamika Philosophy Emphasizing the Compatibility of Emptiness and Conventional Phenomena.* Boston: Wisdom, 1989.

Newland, G. *The Two Truths in the Madhyamika Philosophy of the Ge-luk-ba Order of Tibetan Buddhism.* Ithaca: Snow Lion, 1992.

Ngari Panchen Pema Wangyi Gyalpo. *Perfect Conduct: Ascertaining the Three Vows.* Translated by Khenpo Gyurme Samdrub and Sangye Khandro. Boston: Wisdom, 1996.

Ortner, S. *Life and Death on Mt. Everest: Sherpas and Himalayan Mountaineering.* Princeton: Princeton University Press, 1999.

Pa-bong-ka. *Liberation in the Palm of Your Hand: A Concise Discourse on the Path to Enlightenment.* Edited by Trijang Rinpoche. Translated by M. Richards. Boston: Wisdom, 1997.

Pettit, J. W. *Mipham's Beacon of Certainty: Illuminating the View of Dzogehen, the Great Perfection.* Boston: Wisdom, 1999.

Richardson, H. *Ceremonies of the Lhasa Year.* Edited by M. Aris. London: Serindia, 1993.

Rinchen, Geshe, and R. Sonam. *Atisha's Lamp for the Path to Enlightenment.* Ithaca: Snow Lion, 1997.

Ruegg, D. S. *Buddha-nature, Mind, and the Problem of Gradualism in a Comparative Perspective: On the Transmission and Reception of Buddhism in India and Tibet.* London: School of Oriental and African Studies, University of London, 1989.

Ruegg, D. S. *Ordre spirituel et ordre temporel dans la pensée bouddhique de l'Inde et du Tibet.* Paris: Collège de France, 1995.

Ruegg, D. S. *Three Studies in the History of Indian and Tibetan Madhyamakam Philosophy.* Vienna: Arbeitskreis für Tibetische und Buddhistische Studien, Universität Wien, 2000.

Samuel, G. *Civilized Shamans: Buddhism in Tibetan Societies.* Washington, D.C.: Smithsonian Institution Press, 1993.

Shakabpa, T. *Tibet, a Political History.* 1967. Reprint, New York: Potala, 1984.

Shantideva, A. *A Guide to the Bodhisattva's Way of Life.* Translated by S. Batchelor. Dharamsala: Library of Tibetan Works and Archives, 1979.

Smith, E. Gene. *Among Tibetan Texts: History and Literature of the Himalayan Plateau*. Boston: Wisdom, 2001.

Snellgrove, D. *Indo-Tibetan Buddhism: Indian Buddhists and Their Tibetan Successors*. 2 vols. Boston: Shambhala, 1987.

Snellgrove, D., and H. Richardson. *A Cultural History of Tibet*. Boston: Shambhala, 1987.

Sopa, Geshe L., and J. Hopkins, trans. *Cutting through Appearances: The Practice and Theory of Tibetan Buddhism*. Ithaca: Snow Lion, 1989.

Stcherbatsky, T. *Buddhist Logic*. 2 vols. 1930. Reprint, New York: Dover, 1962.

Stearns, C. *The Buddha from Dolpo: A Study of the Life and Thought of the Tibetan Master Dolpopa Sherab Gyaltsen*. Albany: State University of New York Press, 1999.

Stein, R. A. *Tibetan Civilization*. Translated by J. E. Stapleton Driver. Stanford: Stanford University Press, 1972.

Stoddard, H. *Le mendiant de l'Amdo*. Paris: Société d'Ethnographie, 1985.

Tauscher, H., ed. *Phya pa Chos kyi Senge ge: dBu ma Shar gSum gyi stong thun*. Vienna: Arbeitskreis für Tibetische und Buddhistische Studien, Universität Wien, 1999.

Thondup, T. *Buddha Mind: An Anthology of Longchen Rabjam's Writings on Dzogpa Chenpo*. Edited by H. Talbott. Ithaca: Snow Lion, 1989.

Thondup, T. *Buddhist Civilization in Tibet*. Cambridge, Mass.: Maha Siddha Nyingmapa Center, 1982.

Thurman, R. A. F., ed. *Life and Teachings of Tsong-khapa*. Translated by Sherpa Tulku et al. Dharamsala: Library of Tibetan Works and Archives, 1982.

Thurman, R. A. F., trans. *Tsong Khapa's Speech of Gold in the Essence of True Eloquence: Reason and Enlightenment in the Central Philosophy of Tibet*. Princeton: Princeton University Press, 1984.

Tucci, G. *The Religions of Tibet*. Translated by G. Samuel. London: Routledge and Kegan Paul, 1980.

GENERAL SCHOLARSHIP ON BUDDHISM

Bond, G. *The Buddhist Revival in Sri Lanka: Religious Tradition, Reinterpretation, and Response*. Columbia: University of South Carolina Press, 1988.

Buswell, R. E., and R. M. Gimello. Introduction to *Paths to Liberation: The Mārga and Its Transformations in Buddhist Thought*, edited by R. E. Buswell and R. M. Gimello, 1–36. Honolulu: University of Hawaii Press, 1992.

Collins, S. *Nirvana and Other Buddhist Felicities: Utopias of the Pali Imaginaire*. Cambridge: Cambridge University Press, 1998.

Collins, S. *Selfless Persons: Imagery and Thought in Theravada Buddhism*. Cambridge: Cambridge University Press, 1982.

Conze, E., trans. *Abhisamayālaṃkāra*. Rome: Ismeo, 1954.

Faure, B. *The Rhetoric of Immediacy: A Cultural Critique of Chan/Zen Buddhism*. Princeton: Princeton University Press, 1991.

Garfield, J., trans. *The Fundamental Wisdom of the Middle Way: Nāgārjuna's Mūlamadhyamakakārikā*. New York: Oxford University Press, 1995.

Gombrich, R. *Precept and Practice: Traditional Buddhism in the Rural Highlands of Ceylon*. Oxford: Clarendon Press, 1971.

Horner, I. B.trans. *The Book of Discipline*. Vols. 1, 2, and 5. London: Pali Text Society, 1938–52.

Jackson, R. "Matching Concepts: Deconstructive and Foundationalist Tendencies in Buddhist Thought." *Journal of the American Academy of Religion* 57 (1989): 561–89.

Kajiyama, Y. *Introduction to Buddhist Philosophy*. Kyoto: Kyoto University Press, 1966.

Lopez, D. "Authority and Orality in the Mahayana." *Numen* 42 (1995): 21–47.

Lopez, D. *Elaborations on Emptiness: Uses of the Heart Sūtra*. Princeton: Princeton University Press, 1996.

Lopez, D., ed. *Buddhist Hermeneutics*. Honolulu: University of Hawaii Press, 1988.

Lopez, D., ed. *Curators of the Buddha: The Study of Buddhism under Colonialism*. Chicago: University of Chicago Press, 1995.

Mohanty, J. N. *Reason and Tradition in Indian Thought*. Oxford: Clarendon Press, 1992.

Nattier, J. *Once Upon a Future Time: Studies in a Buddhist Prophecy of Decline*. Berkeley: Asian Humanities Press, 1991.

Obermiller, E. "The Doctrine of the *prajñāpāramitā* as Exposed in the *Abhisamayālaṃkāra* de Maitreya." *Acta Orientalia* 11 (1933): 1–100.

Obermiller, E., and T. Stcherbatsky. *Abhisamayālaṃkāra-nāma-prajñāpāramitopadeśa-śāstra: The Work of Bodhisattva Maitreya*. New ed. Osnabrück: Biblio, 1970.

Prebish, C. *A Survey of Vinaya Literature*. Taipei: Jin Luen, 1994

Ruegg, D. S. "Does the Mādhyamika Have a Thesis and Philosophical Position?" In *Buddhist Logic and Epistemology*, edited by B. K. Matilal and R. Devans, 229–37. Dordrecht: Reidel, 1969.

Ruegg, D. S. "The Uses of the Four Points of the *Catuṣkoti* and the Problem of the Description of Reality in Mahāyāna Buddhism." *Journal of Indian Philosophy* 5 (1977): 1–71.

Samaṇa, P. M. *The Entrance to the Vinaya*. 3 vols. Bangkok: King Mahā Makuta Academy, 1969–83.

Schopen, G. *Bones, Stones, and Buddhist Monks: Collected Papers on the Archaeology, Epigraphy, and Texts of Monastic Buddhism in India*. Honolulu: University of Hawaii Press, 1997.

Sharf, R. "Buddhist Modernism and the Rhetoric of Meditative Experience." *Numen* 42 (1995): 228–83.

Spiro, M. *Buddhism and Society: A Great Tradition and Its Burmese Vicissitudes*. New York: Harper and Row, 1970.

Tambiah, S. J. *Buddhism and the Spirit Cults in North-East Thailand*. 1970. Reprint, Cambridge: Cambridge University Press, 1987.

Tillemans, T. "How Much of a Proof Is Scripturally Based Inference?" In *Dharmakīrti's Thought and Its Impact on Indian and Tibetan Philosophy,* edited by S. Katsura, 395–404. Vienna: Österreichische Akademie der Wissenschaften, 1999.

Tillemans, T. "On Scriptural Authority." In *Felicitation Volume for Professor A. Uno,* 31–47. Hiroshima: Tetsugaku, 1986.

Tiyavanich, K. *Forest Recollections: Wandering Monks in Twentieth-Century Thailand.* Honolulu: University of Hawaii Press, 1997.

Vajirañāṇavarorasa. *Entrance to the Vinaya.* Bangkok: King Maha Makuta Academy, 1969.

Warder, A. K. *Buddhism.* Delhi: Motilal Banarsidass, 1970.

Wijayaratna, M. *Buddhist Monastic Life: According to the Texts of the Theravada Tradition.* Cambridge: Cambridge University Press, 1990.

Yotsuya, K. *The Critique of Svatantra Reasoning by Candrakīrti and Tsongkha-pa: A Study of Philosophical Proof according to Two Prasangika Madhyamaka Traditions of India and Tibet.* Stuttgart: Steiner, 1999.

Index

abbots, 43, 49, 50, 275, 277; admission of monks by, 58–59; Ge-luk and Sang-pu links, 145; government appointing, 317; respect for, 256–57; titles, 136, 351n18

Abelard, Peter (1079–1142), 202–3

Abhidharma, 117–18, 155, 173, 254; and acumens, 166–67; categories, 224, 259; commentaries, 114–15, 117–18, 127, 130, 133, 172–73, 277; cosmology, 290, 394n37; degrees, 144; examinations and, 254, 256, 259

Abhidharmakośa/Treasury of Abhidharma (Vasubandhu), 114–15, 117–18, 127, 130, 133, 172–73

Abhidharma-samuccaya (Asaṅga), 117, 130, 133

Abhisamayālaṃkara. See Ornament of Realization/Abhisamayā-laṃkara

acumens, 165–68, 172, 177–78, 332; critical, 23, 156, 165, 200; from listening, 165, 166, 332, 370–71n2; from meditation, 166, 167, 172; from thinking, 165–66, 167, 289. See also understanding; wisdom

administration, monastic, 43, 49–53, 318, 348n53, 349n58

admission, to monastery, 42, 44, 55–59, 90

advisory speeches, 151

advisory texts, 106

aesthetics, in curriculum, 103

agreement, debate, 211–12, 214–15

Amdo: Dzong-ka-ba birthplace, 140; Ga-den Chö-khor Ling monastery, 47; Ge-dün Chöpel from, 313; Ge-luk hegemony, 30; influx of monks to India from (1980s–1990s), 328; literacy, 81; nonsectarian movement, 148. See also La-brang monasteries

animism, 395–96n8

Annotations (Zhan-pan), 184

Aquinas, Thomas, 10, 203

argumentation pro and contra, 10, 149

arguments, 206–11, 252, 379n27, 386n34, 393n25

aristocracy, monks from, 51–52

Aristotle: curriculum influenced by, 104, 105; and definition, 308; and dialectic, 200–201, 245; enthymeme, 378–79n24; forbidden debate topic, 270; logic, 104, 199, 204–5, 206, 207; recovered texts, 104, 153; rhetoric, 104, 378n10

arts and crafts, in curriculum, 101

Āryadeva, 129

Asaṅga, 117, 130, 133, 174

asceticism, 34–35, 343n4

assembly hall, monastery, 44–45, 49

astrology and astronomy: in curriculum, 102, 104; traditional schools devoted to, 82

Compositor: G & S Typesetters, Inc.
Text: 10/13 Aldus
Display: Aldus